Osage Grammar

STUDIES
IN THE ANTHROPOLOGY OF
NORTH AMERICAN INDIANS

OSAGE GRAMMAR

Carolyn Quintero

Published by the University of Nebraska Press
Lincoln and London

In cooperation with the American Indian Studies Research
Institute, Indiana University, Bloomington

Manufactured in the United States of America

∞

Library of Congress Control Number: 2004117475
ISBN: 0-8032-3803-7 (cloth)

Dedication

Frances Oberly Holding (Osage name *Letǫ́wį*, of the *Hcížo* Clan), respected Osage elder, worked with me more steadfastly than anyone during the years of arduous labor it has taken to gather the knowledge of Osage set forth in this volume. Without her many hours of help and her insight into and love of the language, this first grammar of Osage would not have been possible. I, along with Siouan linguists and the Osage tribe, present and future, owe *Letǫ́wį* a debt of gratitude. This volume is dedicated to her, with esteem and appreciation.

Wažáže íe šǫǫšǫ́we mą̨ðį ðée hkǫ́bra.
'I want this Osage language to go on.'
Frances Oberly Holding, January 1994, Hominy, Oklahoma

Contents

List of tables

Acknowledgments

A native of Osage County, Oklahoma, I grew up in Hominy and left there to study modern languages (French, Russian, Spanish) at the University of Oklahoma in Norman. Fifteen years of residence in Venezuela gave me ample time to polish my Spanish, raise two children, and earn a master's degree in linguistics at the Universidad Central de Venezuela. Then I went to the University of Massachusetts at Amherst to study for a Ph.D. in linguistics. My work on Osage began in the early 1980s when I began to wonder about the language that was spoken by my Osage friends' grandparents when I was growing up in Hominy. I met Robert Bristow, who had been collecting words and sentences in Osage for many years, and he and I began work on the language together. One of my earlier efforts, refined in 1999, resulted in a textbook of forty lessons in beginning Osage, edited by Priscilla Hokiahse Iba.

I had begun translating in Tulsa, Oklahoma, in 1984, and became accredited by the American Translators Association for translation into and from Spanish. Taking a few years off from Osage, I founded Inter Lingua, Inc., a company in Tulsa, Oklahoma, where business translations to and from over twenty languages are accomplished on a daily basis. But unfinished work on Osage called me, and I have returned to it again and again.

A thirty-month-long grant from the National Endowment for Humanities, through the Center for the Study of Native Languages of the Plains and Southwest at the University of Colorado, Boulder, under the guidance of Dr. David Rood, has made this volume possible. The crucial input provided by Dr. Robert Rankin (University of Kansas) has been deeply appreciated and has improved this volume in considerable measure. John Koontz (University of Colorado and National Institute of Standards and Technology) also contributed to this effort through both help with software and his extensive knowledge of Omaha-Ponca.

During the first several years of my interest in Osage, Robert Bristow of Tulsa, Oklahoma, was a major source of inspiration, insight and encouragement. The dictionary which is a planned companion volume to this grammar will be dedicated to his memory. Early encouragement of Robert and me as a team working on the Osage language came from Dr. Kenneth Hale at MIT. Two other linguists who were important in helping and inspiring me to do serious work on Osage are Drs. Francesco D'Introno and Emmon Bach, both at the University of Massachusetts at Amherst.

Robert Bristow's mother, Annette Oswald of Huntsville, Alabama, has been constant in her loving support. Many other persons and institutions have contributed indirectly to the accomplishment of this project in a variety of ways: Robert Hart of Chicago; Dr. Dan Swan at the Gilcrease Museum in Tulsa; Priscilla Hokiahse Iba (*Wažáže Mihcéxi*) of Tulsa; E. Sean StandingBear (*Letǫ́ Xóe* 'Gray Hawk') formerly of the Osage Tribal Museum in Pawhuska, Oklahoma; Geoffrey Mongrain Standing Bear, (*Žį̌ka Kahíke* 'Child Chief") attorney in Pawhuska; Billie Ponca (Osage) at Whitehair Memorial in Fairfax, Oklahoma; David Nagle (*Mą́ze Wanǫ́pˀį*) at the Friends Meeting House in Hominy, Oklahoma; Kathryn Ramsey at the Hominy Public Library; Mongrain Lookout (Osage) from Hominy, Oklahoma; Thomas Libby (Osage) from Pawhuska; the Jesuit Archives in St. Louis, Missouri; the President's Office at the University of Tulsa; Douglas Parks at Indiana University; and most recently Talee Redcorn (*Hpá Paaxǫ́* 'Broken Nose') and Justin McBride, linguist.

On a more personal level, Julie Ahrend deserves special thanks for managing Inter Lingua, Inc., almost singlehandedly for the first two years of my work on the dictionary and grammar, a task she accomplished with grace and proficiency. Thereafter, Pat Dent did the same, with great patience and support, for the time it took to return to this project and prepare it for publication. I especially thank Gordon J. Leaman, Jr., for his generosity of spirit and encouragement during the final stretch of preparation of this manuscript.

The most important contributors are the many Osage speakers who shared their time and their knowledge with me during the 1980s and 1990s, all of whom are now deceased: Frances Oberly Holding, Laura Shannon, Jo Ann Shunkamolah Alred, Gladys Shunkamolah, Margaret Red Eagle Iron, Preston Morrell, Hazel Harper, Edward Red Eagle, Sr., Leroy Logan, Mary Lookout Standing Bear, and Robert Bristow. They were all unfailingly patient with my questions and repetitions, maintaining a positive attitude at a time when the Osage language was endangered. Theirs are the words on these pages. One speaker deserves special mention for her dedication to this effort: Frances Holding.

Abbreviations and symbols

Abbreviations

1	first person
1D	first person dual
1P	first person plural
1S	first person singular
2	second person
2P	second person plural
2S	second person singular
3	third person
3P	third person plural
3S	third person singular
A	agent (as first element of a pronominal gloss such as A2S 'second person singular agent', A1P 'first person plural agent')
AG	position of agent prefixes in the verb
C	consonant
CAU	causative
CONT	continuative
DAT	dative
DECL	declarative
DISP	dispersed
EMPH	emphatic
EP	epenthetic
EVID	evidential
FUT	future
IMPER	imperative
IMPER.CONT	continuing imperative
INDEF	indefinite
INCEP	inceptive
INJ	injunctive
ITER	iterative
KI	position of object reference prefixes in the verb
LIE	lying, reclining

LOC	locative
LF	Francis La Flesche
MOV	moving
NEG	negative
NOM	nominalizer
NP	noun phrase
P	patient (as first element of a pronominal gloss such as P1S 'first person singular patient', P2P 'second person plural patient')
PAT	position of patient prefixes in the verb
PL	plural
PLU	plural article
POSS	possessive
PREV	preverb
PRON	pronoun
QUES	question marker
RECIP	reciprocal
REFL	reflexive
SIT	sitting
SOV	subject-object-verb word order in a sentence
STA	standing
SUBJ	subject marker
SUPP	suppositional
SUU	suus (possession by subject)
V	vowel
VAL	valence reducer
VERT	vertitive
VP	verb phrase

Symbols

*	(marks forms reconstructed for an earlier, unattested stage of the language)
**	(marks ungrammatical forms)
~	varies with
→	becomes (in synchronic derivations)
>	changed to (in historical derivations)
<	derives from
<>	(angle brackets; enclose original orthography of earlier sources)

Presentation of Osage examples

Most Osage examples in this volume are presented in four lines. The first line is the Osage form as spoken; the second analyzes the Osage form into morphemes (i.e., its smallest meaningful units); the third provides English glosses of those morphemes; and the fourth is a free (not word-by-word or morpheme-by-morpheme) English translation of the example.

All words and sentences used here are taken from Osage speakers and have been reelicited and confirmed. In almost all cases, I have taken the colloquial English form used by the Osage speaker as the free translation, in the belief that by changing the English I would risk adding or subtracting some part of the meaning of the expression. Comments by the speaker are often included. (I have sometimes added clarifying expressions in brackets, or alternative translations marked "lit." for "literal.")

Osage verb inflection does not distinguish gender ('he' vs. 'she'). In the translation of most examples where a third person pronoun is required and there is no noun in the context to narrow the interpretation to a feminine one, 'he' or 'him' is used, although in all such cases the participant could equally well be feminine ('she', 'her'). And, in general, not every possible translation for each Osage sentence is given, as this could quickly become cumbersome. For example, a single third person sentence would have to be glossed as 'he/she/they' and as past and present ('was doing, were doing, did, is doing, are doing, does, used to do, have been doing') in a long gloss that would be nearly unreadable. By the time the principles governing certain parts of the grammar were worked out, speakers were not available who could produce the exact examples needed to succinctly illustrate each principle. Thus, the principles given here are illustrated with Osage examples that were available from the corpus of collected data. The cumulative effect of the various examples, however, will quite adequately illustrate the point in each instance if examined carefully.

The third person form of verbs is used here as the equivalent of an uninflected form, since it lacks inflectional affixes. Thus *ðuwį́* is 'he, she, it buys, they buy' and is also used for the equivalent of 'buy'. I have retained the accent of the third person form on the uninflected form as well, and it is this form that is used in the morpheme analysis in the second line of each example. Where certain details of the underlying form are irrelevant, they are not represented in the morpheme analysis line of the example, which may then be almost identical to the surface form; in other words, the morpheme analysis line may vary in abstractness, depending on the discussion at hand. The morpheme analysis line may also include elements that are not strictly speaking morphemes; for example, epenthetic consonants that appear in the surface form, such as *w* between *o* and *a*. Thus the Osage morpheme line and the line giving English glosses of those morphemes are best thought of as explanatory rather than asstrictly morphological representations. Osage is characterized by null pronominal markers in the verb signaling third person subjects and third singular object. Such subjects and objects, while undectable auditorily, are, for the most part, symbolized in the examples here by Ø in the Osage morphemic line. Where such null subjects and objects have not been included in the morpheme line, which happens in a few places especially where the subject and object nouns themselves are included in the Osage example, they should nevertheless be thought of as appearing in the underlying representation of the verb.

Many pronominal markers are shared by singular and plural verb forms, or by both dual and plural forms (see chapter 3). The morpheme gloss for such markers show the number that is understood in the context of the example. Thus the second person agent marker (*Ya* in underlying form) is glossed A2P for 'second person plural agent' when its verb is followed by *api* 'pluralizer' or a plural continuative marker, but as A2S 'second person singular' when no such pluralizer follows. Likewise, the prefix *ąk*, is sometimes glossed A1P 'first person plural agent' and sometimes A1D 'first person dual agent'.

For convenience, the postverbal element *api* is consistently glossed PL 'pluralizer', even when it is used in a third person singular sentence where its role is clearly not as a pluralizer (see chapter 5).

The nature of the Osage morpheme analysis line and the morpheme gloss line as explanatory rather than as underlying representations may also be seen in the treatment of morphemes such as *wa* 'third person plural patient' and *a* 'first person singular agent'. These are analyzed here as occurring underlyingly in the order *wa* + *a* but subsequently metathesized, resulting in the reverse order, *a* + *wa*, on the surface. Often, the morpheme analysis line shows this metathesized order rather than the underlying order of morphemes.

In the English morpheme gloss line, periods connect words that gloss a single Osage morpheme. Thus, for example, 'do.one's.best' glosses the single Osage item *waašką́*.

Throughout this work, I have for the most part written many postverbal elements separately from the verb and from each other. This is done merely for readability, since I find that writing, for example, *wéeðinąpi akxái* 'she's grateful to you [plural]' as *wéeðinąpiakxái,* or writing *wacˀéąðapaži nai* 'we don't kill' as *wacˀéąðapažinai* slows down interpretation of the word or phrase by making its visual form harder to parse. In these phrases, for instance, *akxái* and *nai* set off by spaces will be easily recognizable to anyone who is somewhat familiar with Osage. No doubt some linguists would propose writing all the postverbal elements as a one-word auxiliary. Thus, what I write as *šcée hta ðatxą́še nai* 'you will always be going' ('you go' [verb] + 'future' + 'standing' + 'iterative' + 'declarative') would be written as *šcée htaðatxą́šenai* (with the auxiliary elements all together but separated from the verb), or even as *šcéehtaðatxą́šenai* (with the auxiliary attached to the verb), which I find too difficult to sort out. Nothing crucial rests on the decision to write the morphemes separately here; spaces are not meant to have any theoretical status.

A note on continuative auxiliaries (see chapter 5) in examples is also in order. The use of the first and second person continuative auxiliaries is rather clear and is also more optional than in third person, possibly because pragmatic control is naturally closer in a first and second person conversational exchange. The verb forms offered throughout this volume to illustrate inflectional patterns and other facets of the language for the most part do not include any first and second person auxiliaries. However, third person continuative auxiliaries have sometimes been included, although this does not signify that they are considered to be part of the verb stem. Speakers will often offer the first and second person forms without position markers, but will insist on adding the markers to third person forms, even in isolation. While first and second person inflection is usually overtly marked on the verb (by prefixes), agent inflection for third person is phonologically null, so that the third person singular and plural inflected forms are often identical to the citation form and need the suffixes *akxa* or *apa* to support their identity as sentences rather than merely citation forms. The paradigms offered here are thought to be more natural for Osage than the isolated verb forms for all persons would be.

1 Introduction

This chapter presents a sketch of selected aspects of the cultural background of the Osage language, such as history, regional variations, and the state of language decay, followed by some highlights of the content of this work, with an outline of phonology, morphology, and syntax, and a sketch of the verb complex.

1.1 Background

Rankin (in press) summarizes the position of Osage and other Dhegiha languages within the Siouan family as follows:

> At the time of contact by the earliest French explorers of the Mississippi Valley, Siouan languages were spoken in a broad belt stretching from the mouth of the Arkansas River north and westward across the western prairies and the great plains to the Black Hills. In addition there were Siouan languages scattered in the East in what are now Virginia, Alabama and Mississippi. The Siouan language family is distantly related to the extinct Catawban languages of the Carolinas.
>
> . . . . The more than fifteen separate Siouan languages fall into several well-defined subgroups. Individual language names are italicized.
>
> Missouri River Siouan
>   *Crow*
>   *Hidatsa*
>
> *Mandan*
>
> Mississippi Valley Siouan
>   *Dakotan*
>   Chiwere-Winnebago
>   *Ioway, Otoe, Missouria*
>   *Winnebago*
>   Dhegiha
>   *Omaha-Ponca*
>   *Kansa, Osage*
>   *Quapaw*

Ohio Valley Siouan
Tutelo, Saponi, Moniton
Biloxi
Ofo

Rankin goes on to note that the five tribes that speak (or spoke) the languages that make up the Dhegiha subgroup of Siouan—the Osages, Omahas, Poncas, Kansas (Kaws) and Quapaws—had already existed as separate tribal groups when they first came into contact with the French in the late seventeenth and early eighteenth centuries.

From its earlier environs in what are now Missouri, Arkansas and Kansas, the Osage tribe moved in the early 1800s to what is now northeastern Oklahoma and southeastern Kansas. Their dominion further diminished in the 1870s to the 1.7 million acre tract of land that is now Osage County, Oklahoma.

Early references give the number of Osages from ca. 1700 to ca. 1775 as 4500 to 6000, including women and children. Bailey (1973) reports that there were approximately 3700 full-bloods in 1872 at the time of removal to Oklahoma, and only 1000 full-bloods twenty years later.

The 1906 roll shows 2229 Osages. Their descendants in December of 1995 numbered approximately 14,750, with the great majority of these much less than half Osage and only a few full-bloods remaining.

Regional variation within Osage is limited. Some slight differences in lexical items are seen among speakers of the different districts (Hominy, Grayhorse-Fairfax, Pawhuska), but the number of these items is so small as not to constitute reason for positing a separate dialect. The most notable difference detected is that a number of speakers, including many of those in the Hominy district, palatalize *c* when preceded by *š*. (That is, *šc* becomes *šč* for these speakers.) No other major differences have been noted.

Fluent native speakers, all of whom were bilingual, numbered only a handful by the close of the twentieth century, all over the age of seventy-five, none of whom used Osage in daily life.[1] Many other Osages have some knowledge of the language and are fond of interjecting Osage into their conversations with each other. Until recently, tribal ceremonies usually featured one or two short talks in Osage by an elder. Status accrues to those semispeakers or learners who can say a few words to address a gathering or say a prayer in public. There is a great deal of interest among the adult members of the tribe in preserving the language by learning more

[1] By nearly everyone's estimates, there were approximately five to ten speakers of Osage alive in 1996, and these numbers had been reduced by half by the close of the century. Without extensive exploration, it is difficult to decide who is a speaker and who is a semispeaker, as the language has lapsed into disuse. Some elders profess to understand Osage, but few claim to be able to speak it.

of it themselves and by teaching it to their children, but this has been impossible as no comprehensive grammatical description was available. Recovery of the language is unfortunately highly politicized among the Osages, and one can only hope that the different factions, most of which are involved only superficially in any kind of preservation effort, will decide to pool their efforts in a common concern over their language. The dedication of the speakers who cooperated in this work should be strongly commended. They were experiencing the demise of their language and for them, engaging in such a task was oftentimes painful, and certainly qualifies as an act of faith by those who wanted to see their language go on.

An Osage dictionary published in 1932 was compiled by an Omaha, Francis La Flesche. La Flesche also published some texts in Osage and English (1921, 1939). Since then, no other substantial work in linguistics has been carried out on the language. Robert Bristow's collection of Osage words and sentences (1988), collected from about 1965 to 1985, was an important contribution. James O. Dorsey worked with some Osages in Washington around 1882 and left some texts (1883a, 1888) and a slip file (1883b) as a record. Robert Rankin did brief fieldwork on Osage in 1978, and in 1979 did some consulting with the tribe with a view to developing an orthography and some lessons for language learning. Three brief articles on Osage were published in the 1950s by Hans Wolff (1952a, 1952b, 1958). (See section 2.5 for some discussion of both La Flesche and Wolff.) Dorsey's work was used in this study only minimally, principally in reference to the *x/ɣ* distinction. For nearly all of this work, I have relied completely on my own fieldwork, supplemented by materials gathered by Bristow and subsequently entirely reelicited by me, and discussions with the Siouanist scholars David Rood, Robert Rankin, and John Koontz.

All examples cited here were gathered either during the early 1980s in sporadic fieldwork which Robert Bristow and I carried out, or during the period from 1993 to 1996 and in 1999 when I worked more intensively with native speakers.[2] The earlier work has been refined for inclusion here, as important phonetic and phonological detail had been overlooked.

The task of gathering or checking language data for the Osage language was an arduous one for both speaker and researcher, requiring hundreds of hours to confirm even a relatively moderate corpus. The few remaining speakers during data collection for this volume were elderly, some were in ill health, and none used the language in day-to-day life. When two speakers met, English was used; this had been the case for a number of years. Since the language was no longer actively used, it was understandable that no one could readily remember it without pondering

[2] This work was partially funded by the National Endowment for the Humanities.

words and phrases that were elicited. Even with patience and time to think things over, the exact phrase often could not be recalled. Of course, depending on the nature of the words or phrases, ease of recall varied widely, from immediate and certain to tentative or impossible. Recording sessions with any speaker necessarily proceeded rather painstakingly, with speaker and linguist eking out what could be recalled with difficulty, a task that could be accomplished only by the most dedicated of speakers and fieldworkers. Work proceeded in a fashion remarkably different from what might be expected by linguists who have worked with a language that is in use by even a few active speakers. The speakers themselves often struggled against frustration and a sense of tragedy that the language was nearly gone.

A study of language at this stage of obsolescence requires a combination of relentless pursuit plus a great deal of delicate handling and patience to sort through data whose form at utterance level can be distorted by disuse, or quite often not available at all in the speakers' memory. Fortunately for this study, one speaker was quite interested in the effort and would not allow her impatience with her own memory gaps to stop our joint attempt to sort out this fascinating language to the extent still possible.

All audio tapes and materials will be available for study in the archives of the Tribal Museum in Pawhuska, Oklahoma.

1.2 General characteristics of Osage

1.2.1 Phonology

Osage has a typical Siouan system of five oral vowels (*a e i o u*) and three nasal vowels (*ą į ǫ*). There are normal and long vowels (for example, *ą* and *ąą*), but spontaneous lengthening or shortening at utterance level also occurs.

The consonantal system shows five stop series (voiceless preaspirated or fortis, voiceless plain or lenis, postaspirated, glottal, and voiced). There is also an interesting affrication of *t* and *ht* before *i į e u*. The phonetic realization of postaspirated stops is linked to the same context.

Osage has a simple expanded *CV* syllabic template: *(C(C))V(V)*. General second syllable accent rounds out the picture.

1.2.2 Morphology

An agglutinative language, Osage combines morphemes to create larger words. Most of the interesting morphology is in the verbal complex. Osage shows inalienable possession in its kinship system and alienable possession elsewhere, and has an extensive deictic-positional system which assigns position or shape to nouns and pronouns.

First person singular, first person plural, and second person are distinguished by inflectional morphemes, but third person inflectional markers are phonologically null except for third person plural in some configurations. A distinction is made between first person dual and plural by choice of continuative aspect marker or by a pluralizer in post-root position. The same pluralizer distinguishes second person plural from second person singular, and also appears plentifully elsewhere in the morphology.

The language exhibits two classes of verb agreement, the so-called active and stative morphology, as is typical of Siouan. These two classes of agreement are marked by agent and patient pronominal affixes on verbs, respectively. The subject of some intransitives is marked with the agentive pronominal. For other intransitives, the patient pronominal appears marking the subject. The patient pronominals also mark the objects of transitive verbs and the agent pronominals mark the subjects of most transitive verbs. (There are even a few transitive stative verbs where patient pronominal inflection marks both the subject and the object of the stative verb; these are called doubly stative verbs here.) The terms "active" and "stative" are not semantically valid in all instances for Osage, but this terminology is used here since it is customary in Siouan studies.

1.2.3 Syntax

Osage is a verb-final (subject-object-verb, "SOV") language, and in the classification of Greenberg (1966) belongs to the rigid subtype of III, having both adverbial modifiers preceding the verb and postpositions. Sentence adverbial markers typically precede the SOV string. Qualifying adjectives follow the noun. The genitive precedes the noun but is accompanied by a possessive pronoun following the noun ('John house his'). Yes-no questions are signalled prosodically, by added length and higher pitch in the last accented syllable of the verb root, although there is an occasional sentence-final particle which may appear on questions. Question words are most often at the beginning of the sentence, but may appear in situ.

The subordinate verb precedes the main verb, and the condition clause precedes the consequent in conditional sentences. As expected in the rigid subtype of III, the subordinate adverbial clause precedes the main verb in constructions of volition and purpose. Adverbs usually precede adjectives, and relative clauses precede their main clause, with the head inside the relative appearing as an indefinite. Pronominal enclitics or affixes precede the verb root, with the object pronominal coming before the subject pronominal (usually contiguous, but not always), although this order is reversed for first person plural agents, and third person pronominal markers are phonologically null except for the plural object marker with certain verbs.

Derivational and inflectional material precedes the root, and may occur among parts of the root or parts of the stem, that is, either between semantically opaque syllables of the root (for example, in the verb *mą̨ðǫ́* 'steal' where subject inflection occurs between the two syllables *mą* and *ðǫ*) or between semantically transparent morphemes of the stem (for example, *cˀéðe* 'kill', where inflection appears between *cˀé* 'die' and *ðe* 'cause'). For the most part, derivational affixes precede inflectional items (cf. Baker 1985). Affixes of tense, aspect, and mode follow the root.

Number is not expressed directly on nouns, and there is a limited gender system contained in the positional (or postural or configurational) articles that may appear following the noun or pronoun. These articles indicate number in an interesting and indirect fashion. Plurality is communicated by using, for example, the 'singular, vertical, inanimate' article on a noun of 'singular, round/sitting, inanimate' gender, thus signalling a collocation of the latter which is now to be interpreted as a member of the 'vertical' class.

In post-root position, continuative aspect markers (also called "auxiliaries" by some Siouanists) indicate position or posture of the subject of the sentence: 'standing', 'sitting', 'lying', or 'moving'. This is especially clear in first and second person. In third person, different semantic information is signaled by the continuative aspect markers, including motion vs. lack of motion (or more precisely, travel through space). If a continuative marker is not used, a completed action (declarative) marker, or an evidential, suppositional, injunctive or reportative element may appear.

First person distinguishes singular, plural, and dual number; no inclusive/exclusive distinction is present. The same pluralizer that marks nondual plural in first person is used with second person to indicate simple plurality (i.e., two or more individuals). Where morphemes indicating both number and subject status are present, the order is noun + number + subject marker. If an adjective follows the noun, it groups with the noun and is followed by the subject marker: noun + adjective + subject marker. Homophonous with third person continuatives *akxa* and *apa*, the subject markers on subject NPs (called "definite articles" by some Siouanists, through restricted subjects), carry information about presence and movement of subject when the sentence is uttered. A set of positional articles may appear optionally on patient subjects of intransitives and on patient objects of transitive verbs which are demonstratives that are also used elsewhere and are not considered inflectional markers.

1.2.4 Sketch of the verbal complex

The verbal complex is made up of the verb root, including compound verb root, and an extensive set of affixes, plus a set of enclitics or suffixes. The affixes include both inflectional and derivational elements. Derivational affixation generally alters the meaning of the verb root (usually, the root can occur independently with a related meaning); the semantics of the derived form sometimes shows clear compositionality, sometimes not.

In preverbal or pre-root position (that is, to the left of derivational morphemes and root, or to the right of derivational morphemes and preceding the root) we find the formants that convey mostly inflectional information regarding person, number, status as subject, or derivational information on instrument, valence, and role. In post-root position, we find elements that encode mostly tense, aspect (iteration and duration), mode, negation, plurality, and position or motion. Included among the post-root elements are what are here called continuatives, and elsewhere among Siouanists "positional auxiliaries," which indicate position (that is, posture) of the subject and carry aspectual information. First person dual and plural and second person singular and plural are distinguished postverbally by the continuatives or by a nondual plural morpheme *api*.

Tables 1.1 and 1.2 display a simplified representation of the Osage verbal complex, divided into two main parts: pre-root (table 1.1) and post-root (table 1.2). In both these tables, I have separated the several components of the verbal complex into tiers (rows in the table), in order to group functionally similar morphemes together in a tier. In table 1.1, the first of the three tiers contains derivational material—preverbs, locatives, and the outer instrumentals. Preverbs are those morphemes which form part of the verb stem and precede the point of inflection. (When such morphemes can be identified as locatives or instrumentals, or morphemes of object reference, or the base of a morphological causative, they are usually labeled more specifically.) The derivational group also includes the vertitive *kik* and inceptive *ki* (homophonous with dative *ki*) and the inner instrumentals. Two or more locatives may be found "stacked" within one verb in some instances, a complication not directly represented in the simplified arrangement of this table. The second tier, object reference, includes the valence reducer *wa* (which usually intransitivizes), plus, in other slots, the dative, reciprocal-reflexive, and suus forms, which refer in some fashion to the subject-object relationship. These elements may be considered an intermediate group between strictly derivational elements in the first tier and strictly inflectional elements in the third tier. The lowest tier consists of person and number inflection.

TABLE 1.1. OSAGE VERBAL COMPLEX: PRE-ROOT

	1	2	3	4	5	6	7	8	9	10
	VAL		LOC	A1P	LOC	INSTR (outer)	PATIENT	AGENT		INSTR (inner)
DERIV		preverb primary root in causative	*i*		*á* *o*	*po* *pa* *taa*			*ki* (inceptive, *kik* vertitive)	*ðaa* *ðii* *ðuu* *nąą* *paa* *kaa*
OBJ REF	*wa*								*ki* (dative) *hkik* (reflexive, reciprocal) *kik* (suus)	
INFL				*ąk*			*ą* *ði* *Ø* *wa* *wa* ~ *Ø*	*a* *ða* *Ø*		

NOTE: A1P = first person plural agent; DERIV = derivation; INFL = person and number inflection; INSTR = instrumental; LOC = locative; OBJ REF = object reference; VAL = valence reducer; the term "vertitive" 'going back; returning' was coined by Terrence Kaufman (p.c. 1 September 2004).

TABLE 1.2. OSAGE VERBAL COMPLEX: POST-ROOT

	11	12	13	14	15	16	17
	VERB ROOT	PLURAL	NEGATION	ITERATIVE, DURATIVE	FUTURE-POTENTIAL	CONTINUATIVE	DECLARATIVE
ROOT	**root**						
PERSON, NUMBER		*api*				*mįkšé* (etc.)	
ASPECT, MODE, ETC.			*aži* *ðįké*	*ną* *štą* *šǫ*	*hta*	*mįkšé* (etc.)	*ðe*

In table 1.2, the morphemes which follow the verb root appear. The root itself occupies the uppermost tier in this chart. The second tier groups together the indicators of person and number for both patient and agent pronominal inflection, which are often (but not always) redundant with inflectional elements in pre-root position. The final tier groups morphemes of aspect, mode, negation and so forth. The continuatives (e.g., *mįkšé*, and the many others too numerous to list here; they are discussed in sections 5.5–5.6) in a sense belong on two tiers.

I now review the types of morpheme that are displayed in these tables, beginning with table 1.1 and following the numerical order of the columns.

1. Valence reducer *wa*. The only affix in this position is the valence reducer *wa* whose addition changes a transitive verb to an intransitive verb: *ðaawá* 'count' (transitive); *waðáawa* 'count' (intransitive).

2. Preverb or primary root (in causatives).

3. Locative *i*. (See discussion under 5 below.)

4. First person plural agent (A1P) inflection *ąk*.

5. Locative. The prefixes *o*, *á* (and *i* in column 3) are called locatives only because they group together morphologically and *á* is a locative. In many cases the original locative meanings of *o* and *i* have become opaque. There is no obvious semantic uniformity among these affixes. The phonological processes affecting them will be linked to the specific affix in a specific phonological context. Also, the opaque primary root or preverb *mą* groups with these affixes owing to its morphological behavior. Locatives precede instrumentals, as in, for example, *oðíbrą* 'cause to emanate an odor' (used in expressions about burning cedar), in which *o* 'in' is followed by the instrumental *ði*~*ðii* 'by hand; cause'. Another example of locative preceding instrumental is *ákaaɣace* [LOC-by striking-

spread] ‘cover, overspread’. The locatives are split into two columns in the chart (3 and 5), based on whether they occur before or after the A1P pronominal inflection *ąk* (see chapter 3 for more discussion).

6. Instrumental. These are the outer instrumentals, those occurring before (leftward of) the inflectional markers. One of these is *taą* ‘by extreme of temperature’.

7. Patient pronominals; 8. Agent pronominals. A verb that does not have any of the optional derivational affixes will have one of these pronominals as its initial element. A rather complex set of phonological rules serves to adjust the surface form of the underlying pronominal. Certain rules which change the order of elements in the verbal complex affect inflection, as we will see in chapter 3. Slot 7, patient inflection, conveys information as to the object of active transitive verbs, or the patient subject of stative verbs. Patient inflection, used for both theme and recipient on active verbs, is as in table 1.3. Also included in these slots is the portmanteau *wi* ‘first person singular agent with second person patient’ (P2<A1S). Agent inflection in slot 8 takes many different shapes on the surface. This is addressed in chapter 3.

TABLE 1.3. PATIENT INFLECTIONAL PREFIXES

1S	*ą*	1P/1D	*wa...(api)*
2S	*ði*	2P	*ði...(api)*
3S	*Ø*	3P	*wa*

9. Object reference, inception, and vertitivity. These are derivational slots where other material (in addition to the valence reducer of slot 1) affecting reiteration of action or object reference is inserted. Slot 9 contains the dative (action with respect to another person), the (derivational) inceptive referring to initiation or reinitiation of action, and the vertitive (returning to source) elements. Dative and inceptive are phonologically and phonetically identical on the surface: *ki*. An example of dative is:

> *ðuwį* ‘buy’ → *kiðuwį* ‘buy for someone else’ (dative)

In the same slot, the affixes *hkik* ‘reciprocal/reflexive’ or *kik* ‘suus’ (‘subject’s own’; also called “reflexive possessive”) may appear. Certain phonological rules changing *kik* + *ð* to *l* and *hkik* + *ð* to *hkil* apply.

10. Inner instrumentals. In this slot appear the instrumental prefixes that occur to the right of inflection. These instrumental prefixes generally have a clear semantic interpretation (*ðuu* ‘by hand’, *kaa* ‘by striking’, *ðaa*

'by mouth', and so forth) and, as might be expected, are quite productive with roots of the type 'break', 'cut', and similar verbs. These instrumentals often transitivize the root, and often add a causative sense, especially in the case of *ðuu* 'by hand' and others. For example, to intransitive *xǫ* 'break' may be added the instrumental *ðuu*, giving transitive *ðuuxǫ* 'break by hand'. Adding the instrumental *nąą* 'by foot', we get *nąąxǫ́* 'break by foot'; *ðaa* 'by mouth' gives *ðaaxǫ́* 'break by biting or with the mouth'.

The elements from table 1.2 appear rightward of the verb root, and are covered in chapter 5. They convey number of the subject or object, negation, iteration or duration of the activity described by the verb, irrealis/potential/future of the verb, whether the action is continuative or not, and other information.

1.2.5 Compound verbs and doubly inflected verbs

In the compounding of two verbs, the first verb of the compound hosts object inflection (if its argument structure demands it) and subject inflection; the second verb inflects only for subject and not for object. In the motion verbs, the portatives show compounding; for example, *aðį* 'have' + *ali* 'return' = *aðįali* 'bring back'. 'I brought them back' would be *waabrįali* (*waabrį* 'them-I-have' + *alí* 'I-return'). Compounded verbs will always have identical subjects.

In contrast to portatives, other doubly inflected verbs cannot be analyzed in semantically compositional terms.[3] In *_kǫ́_ða* 'want', for example, neither of the parts is transparent semantically. Each part, *kǫ́* and *ða*, inflects for subject. The underscores in *_kǫ́_ða*, as elsewhere, indicate the points of inflection.

(1) *hkǫ́bra*
Wa-kǫ́-Wa-ða
A1S-PREV-A1S-want
'I want'

(2) *škǫ́šta*
Ya-kǫ́-Ya-ða
A2S-PREV-A2S-want
'you want'

[3] In those cases where a semantically opaque syllable precedes the inflected root, both in a doubly inflected verb such as *kǫ́ða* 'want', where *kǫ* is itself inflected, or in others where the first part does not inflect (e.g. *mą* in *mąðǫ́* 'steal'), the syllable in question is often glossed here as 'preverb' (abbreviated PREV in the interlinear gloss). Where the preverb is an identifiable morpheme (such as a locative *á*, *o*, or *i*), it is usually given an appropriate gloss (such as LOC for 'locative').

(3) *kǫ́ða*
Ø-kǫ́-Ø-ða
A3S-PREV-A3S-want
'he, she, it wants'

(4) *ąkǫ́ða*
ąk-kǫ́-ða
A1P-PREV-want
'we want'

(5) *kǫ́ða*
Ø-kǫ́-Ø-ða
A3P-PREV-A3P-want
'they want'

No phonological rules have been found to operate between the members of the compound.

When certain suffixes with initial *a* occur immediately following the root, vowel contraction takes effect. The effect is to replace final *e* of the root with *a* (see section 2.3.3). This process has been called "ablaut" by Siouanists, but will be explained here under a different rubric.

No phonological rules alter the post-root elements specifically, and there is no evidence for hierarchy among them. Note that each of them is optional. The features of person and number on the continuatives are usually redundant with the same features characterizing the subject inflection in the verb.

1.3 Male and female speech

Among Osages there is a widely held opinion that men speak differently from women, although no characterization of the difference can be expressed by those who comment. There are a handful of isolated lexical items which are specific to the sex of the speaker, but these are only the word for 'yes' (*hówe* for men, *ąhą́* for women) and certain kinship nouns.

No systematic differences in speech are easily detectable, except for the following. A limited number of sentences available from the two or three remaining male speakers (including one who could speak uninterruptedly for long periods of time in the early 1980s) seem to suggest that male speech completely omits declarative *ðe* after continuatives, producing surface sentence-final forms such as *akxá*, *apá*, instead of *akxái*, *apái*, and the second person emphatic pronoun is *ðí* instead of *ðíe*.[4] However, these same male speakers cannot directly identify *akxái*, *apái*

[4] Males do, however, use the ending *pe*, from *api* 'plural' plus *ðe* 'declarative'.

and so forth as a characteristic of female speech. In fact, the two male speakers interviewed on this topic denied that it is female speech, and asserted that men say *akxai*, *apai*, not just females. Still, this is the best candidate at hand for a difference between male and female speech at the present stage of the language. Undoubtedly such a contrast did exist in the past but has largely been lost, while the idea of such differences remains a popular one, even though little or no modern language data remains to support it. (For a more complete discussion of the continuative auxiliaries, see sections 5.5–5.6.)

It is hardly certain that forms like *akxai* are characteristic of female speech. Apart from the fact just noted, that male speakers do not report such forms as female, the form *akxai* occurs in example (6). This example is from a dialog written for a man to speak, or at least, was assigned to and rehearsed by a man in an Osage language class taught by a (female) native speaker in the 1970s. This fact seems to contradict the hypothesis that *i* in *akxái* (and in many other similar contexts) is characteristic of females only.

(6) *hǫpái mą́ąɣe akxa ðáalį ąkxái*
hąpa-ðe mą́ąɣe akxa ðáalį akxa-ðe
day-this weather SUBJ good 3.CONT-DECL
'today the weather is good'

In many of the Osage language classes taught in the 1960s and 1970s, as far as can be determined, little or no attention was paid to the differences in male and female speech, if any such differences still existed by that stage. Even in a classroom situation where men were rehearsing parts in a skit, no effort was made to steer the classroom males toward "male speech" and they were allowed to read their parts with "female" declarative endings. Indeed, I have never found any speaker who can point to even a single difference between male and female speech, other than the handful of differing lexical items mentioned above. It may be that identification of such differences is part of speakers' unconscious knowledge and impossible for them to articulate, as is much of any speaker's linguistic knowledge. But we should not dismiss the possibility that the *ðe* ending here could be some other phenomenon than an expression of speaker gender.

Another possible candidate for a characteristic of male speech vs. female speech seems to be a higher occurrence of double inflection in male speech, especially perhaps on motion verbs: *amąbrį* 'I walk', *ðamąšcį* 'you walk', and so forth, where the expected forms are *mąbrį́* and *mąšcį́*. (For agent inflection, see chapter 3.) Examples (7)–(10), all from one male speaker, show double inflection; the expected forms of the verbs in question are *bráanį̨* 'I consumed', *bráache* 'I ate', and *brée* 'I am going'.

(7) *súhka záani abráanį̨*
súhka záani Wa-Wa-ðaanį̨
chicken all A1S-A1S-consume
'I ate all the chicken'

(8) *súhka hépe abráache*
súhka hépe Wa-Wa-ðaaché
chicken portion A1S-A1S-eat
'I ate some of the chicken'

(9) *waachí abrée*
waachí a-Wa-Wa-ðée
dance PREV-A1S-A1S-go
'I'm going to dance'

(10) *ówehci abrée*
ówe-hci a-Wa-Wa-ðée
food-house PREV-A1S-A1S-go
'I'm going to the grocery store'

Single inflection of these same verbs, as in example (11), is also regarded as correct by the speaker who doubly inflects, and is considered by him to be merely less emphatic.

(11) *ówehci brée*
ówe-hci a-Wa-ðée
food-house PREV-A1S-go
'I'm going to the grocery store'

Siouanists have commented that double inflection may be a characteristic of a language whose use is declining. (For instance, the double inflection that is reportedly characteristic of Chiwere *r*-stems is said to be getting more common as time goes on [Robert Rankin, p.c. 1995].) If this is the case, then this phenomenon is most likely not one that has historically differentiated male from female speech.

Another male speaker suggested that women inflected verbs where men did not, but it was not clear that his speech substantiated this observation.

1.4 Organization of the grammar

The chapters of this description of Osage discuss successively phonology, verbal inflection, verbal derivation, verb suffixes, nominal and other nonverbal categories, and phrasal phenomena. All examples came from native speakers of the language and the free translation in English is often given verbatim from the speaker.[5]

An attempt is being made to include all words mentioned here in the companion dictionary (nearing completion). The two volumes should complement each other; it will be possible to find information lacking in one by consulting the other.

In some of the discussion in this grammar, many more examples are given than are needed to support the discussion. These "excess" examples have been retained since Osage has essentially no active speakers left, and lacks modern texts. Tribal members wishing to teach or learn Osage may find the examples useful, and I bow here to the tribe's needs. Linguists reading this grammar may skip over examples once they have grasped the point being illustrated.

[5] A note on names is in order here. It has been suggested that Osage names should replace English names such as *John* in the example sentences. The problem with using, for example, *Wižįke* 'Sonny' (really a kinship term) as an imaginary person in an example is that *Wižįke* refers to someone real and very specific for virtually every speaker. *John* is more vague (the speaker may not know a person named John or may know several people with this name). Even though the speaker may know several people by this name, still it can be used comfortably to label an imaginary person. An imaginary person must be used in sentences describing the imaginary situation of that person being present while the sentence is being spoken. This is all too often necessary since most of the material at this stage of language disuse must be elicited. It is too confusing to try to pretend that a real person (e.g., *Wižįke*) is present right now while you and I are talking, when that real person is likely known to be elsewhere (e.g., at work in Tulsa today). Imaginary John, however, can be imagined to be here with us as we speak, a quite useful construct.

Also relevant is that Osages have not used the Osage language in daily life for many years now. Imposing an Osage name might seem somewhat unnatural for the speakers. Additionally, Osage names are held with a degree of reserve and are not used freely outside of close tribal contexts.

2 Phonology

This chapter presents the consonantal system (including an extensive discussion of the complex stop system), the vocalic system, and a partial account of accent in Osage. Some phonological rules are discussed in this chapter, but most appear in chapter 3, and additional discussion of morphophonology is scattered throughout subsequent chapters as well. A brief review of earlier accounts of Osage phonology is presented in section 2.5.

Although this study is meant to be couched in terms that are, to the extent possible, independent of any particular phonological theory, the discussion of rules embodies an attempt to make a sort of synchronic sense of the data encountered. Any device chosen, whether lexical compart mentalization, a hierarchy of constraints, naturalness conditions, or some other, will have to deal with the ravages of time on the language in a semiarbitrary manner. Since the model used here for the discussion of the phonology of Osage does not include the dimension of time, synchronic mechanical devices are employed to portray the effects in the phonology of changes that have taken place historically. The competing rules and changes introduced over time defy a completely elegant rendering of the phonological processes at work.

2.1 Consonantal system

2.1.1 Consonant inventory

The phonemic inventory for consonants is presented in table 2.1. The underlying segments *ph*, *th*, and *kh* never emerge on the surface (see section 2.1.3.5), and so are given in bold in the table.

Below, I discuss first the segments that are not members of the stop system (section 2.1.2), then the stop system and related matters (section 2.1.3). In the lists of examples offered in this chapter, a double asterisk (**) preceding a sequence indicates that the sequence is ungrammatical, that is, not permitted. A few other sequences are possible Osage sequences but are unattested (or at least not found by this researcher), and these are

TABLE 2.1. CONSONANTS

	LABIAL	DENTAL	PALATO-ALVEOLAR	VELAR	GLOTTAL
STOPS					
glottalized	*p*ʔ	*c*ʔ		*k*ʔ	
lax	*p*	*t* *c*	*č*	*k*	
preaspirated	*hp*	*ht* *hc*	*hč*	*hk*	
aspirated	***ph***	***th*** *ch*		***kh***	
voiced	*b*				
FRICATIVES					
voiceless		*s*	*š*	*x*	*h*
voiced		*z*	*ž*	*ɣ*	
NASALS	*m*	*n*			
APPROXIMANTS	*w*	*l*, *ð*, *r*			

labeled "unattested." The initials LF stand for La Flesche; forms so marked are entries from his dictionary that were not confirmed by modern speakers.

2.1.2 Comments on fricatives, nasals, and approximants

2.1.2.1 *s*, *z*, *š*, *ž*, *x*, *ɣ*

With regard to the sibilants, variations both synchronic and diachronic suggest that perhaps voicing may not have been the distinctive feature differentiating *z* and *ž* from *s* and *š*, although undoubtedly they were always distinct as evidenced by numerous minimal pairs, such as *si* 'foot' vs. *zi* 'yellow' and *áši* 'outside' vs. *aži* 'negative'.

The voicing of *z* and *ž* is quite faint, and this fact explains why one finds words such as *wažáže* 'Osage' rendered in English orthography historically as *washáshe*, in the few instances where people tried to write Osage words in an English context. The feature distinguishing *s* and *š* from *z* and *ž* is probably tenseness vs. laxness more than voicelessness vs. voicing.

Tenseness of *s* and *š* is so pronounced that it can easily be mistaken for length, especially following an accented syllable. For example, in *ðuušápe* 'darken' the tenseness of *š* is somewhat less than in, e.g., *ą́šupe* 'pay for it for me' (from *ą* 'to me' + *kaašúpe* 'pay for'; the underlying morpheme *kaa* is suppressed in the surface form *ą́šupe*), where we find a very tense *š*. Likewise we find that the tenseness of the *s* in *ðuusé* 'cut one's hair' is especially noticeable in the 1S form, as in *hpáxį brúuse hta mįkše* 'I am going to cut my hair', where *s* follows an accented syllable. The same is true of *ðaasé* 'bite through a cordlike object', with especially tense *s* after the *áa* in *bráase hta mįkšé* 'I'm going to bite through it'.

This same tense/lax distinction may be operative as well in the contrast of *x* with *ɣ*.

For all six segments (*s z š ž x ɣ*), no restrictions exist with respect to the following vowel:

sápe 'black'; *hkilísą* 'turn around'; *si* 'foot'; *sįce* 'tail'; *wacúe sóso* 'dumplings'

záani 'all'; *kaazą́* 'scold'; *ząącéolįį* 'dwelling on the prairie' (name used for Hominy district); *hpazé* 'evening'; *pázo* 'finger'; *zi* 'yellow'; *ízizike* 'dirty'; *házu* 'grape'; (*zǫ, zį* unattested)

šáhpe 'six'; *íðišąha* 'avoid'; *še* 'there near hearer'; *ši* 'again'; *wašį́* 'bacon'; *šo ðée* 'go where you are'; *šǫ* 'while'; *šúpe* 'entrails'

ažamį́ 'I think'; *žą́ą* 'tree'; *žéka* 'leg'; *aži* 'negative marker'; *žį* 'small'; *žóle* 'accompany'; *ékižǫ* 'you do'; *žúoka* 'body'

In the *x/ɣ* pair, *x* is voiceless and has quite strong fricative noise (or "stridency" in the Jakobson tradition), and is the fortis member; *ɣ* is the more voiced and is the lenis member. Both *ɣ* and *x* are articulated far back in the buccal cavity and with considerable turbulence. Initial *x* sounds as if it were executed farther back than *ɣ*, its less strident counterpart, and with much more turbulence than the simple *h*. If a consonant series voices historically, the voicing typically begins with the labial members of the series, and ends with the velar members. Anterior members, like *s/z*, get voiced first. It may be the case in Osage that the velars *ɣ* and *x* are both still mostly voiceless. If this is the case, then the real distinction is lenis/fortis for *ɣ/x*, with voicing being concomitant. Moreover, the two sounds, once distinct, are merging in modern, obsolescing Osage. Auditorily, *ɣ* and *x* are so similar that even with the few minimal pairs which exist, speakers sometimes cannot consistently distinguish or reliably compare the sounds they themselves make. One of the few minimal pairs is *ɣǫ́ǫce* 'sloppy' vs. *xǫ́ǫce* 'cedar'. A near-minimal pair is *káaɣa* 'make it' (imperative) vs. *káxa* 'creek'. The *x* also occurs in such syllable onsets as *x* + stop and stop + *x*, and examples of these appear in the lists with the pertinent stops.

Neither *ɣ* nor *x* seems to be restricted as to quality of the following vowel. (Normal and long vowels are grouped together here.)

káaɣa 'make it!'; *ɣoį́* 'whew, it stinks'; *ɣǫ́ǫce* 'sloppy'; *nąɣúuce* 'ear'; *kšíɣe* 'make/do for another'; *nąą́ɣe* 'spirit'; *ną́ɣe* 'ice'; *hkáɣe* 'crow'; *ðóɣe kahíka*

'Buffalo Chief'; *ɣaaké* 'cry'; *káaɣi akxa* 'he's making' (variant of *káaɣe*); (*ɣą*, *ɣį* unattested)

káxa 'creek'; *íxa* 'laugh'; *xóce* 'gray'; *xǫ́ǫce* 'cedar'; *xúða* 'eagle'; *xúuða* 'wrinkled'; *kaaxúɣe* 'crack' (verb); *xémąke* 'frost [on the ground]'; *mį́įhcexi* 'difficult or precious female; first daughter name in Bear Clan'; *xíða* 'fall stumbling, die'; *haxį́* 'blanket'; (*xą* unattested)

2.1.2.2 *r*

The approximant *r* occurs only in the cluster *br*. In the 1S verb, where *br* occurs quite frequently, surface *r* can be shown to be derived from the inflectable initial of the verb, which is *ð*. Examples of these morphologically complex forms are: *bríištą* 'I'm finished'; *abrį́* 'I have'; *waabrǫ́* 'I sing'; *brúucˀake* 'I am unable'. In such examples, *r* is merely an allophone of *ð*. But aside from these 1S bimorphemic occurrences of *br*, there are instances of a morphologically opaque *br* such as the following: *oðíibrą* 'make to smell'; *brą* 'smell, emanate an odor'; *íbrą* 'have/get enough of'; *bráaska* 'flat'; *bréhka* 'thin'; *bróka* 'dollar, whole'. No restrictions exist with respect to the following vowel, or to initial or medial position.

2.1.2.3 *n*, *ð*, *l*

The segments *n*, *ð*, and *l* are historically related, although there are many clear minimal or near-minimal pairs: *níi* 'water, fluid'; *ði* 'you'; *ðaanį* 'consume'; *ðáalį* 'good'; *nǫ́ǫ* 'old folks'; *lǫǫhú* 'thunder'. There are no distributional restrictions with regard to initial or medial position in the word for *n*, *ð*, or *l*. Neither are there any restrictions with regard to the following vowel:

ną ~ *na* (iterative); *ną́ąke* 'run'; *níni* 'cold'; *nį* 'you wear'; *mǫ́noi* 'prairie chicken' (variant); *nǫ́ǫ* 'old folks'; *núhkiacˀį* (variant of *níhkiacˀį*) 'mirror' (*ne* unattested)

ðaaché 'eat'; *ðą́ące* 'heart'; *ðée* 'this, that'; *ðįké* 'nothing'; *ðóha* 'almost' (variant of *ðǫ́ha*); *waaðǫ́* 'sing'; *ðuu* 'by hand' (prefix)

laacé 'name one's own'; *lą́ðe* 'large'; *žóle* 'accompany; with'; *alí* 'return here'; *lį́ka* 'sit down'; *palóhkie* 'make to be low'; *lǫ́ǫ* 'thunder'; *lúwį* 'buy for one's own'

In certain contexts, such as between nasal vowels, *n* may appear as a variant of intervocalic *ð*. Some speakers show a greater tendency than others to this variation. It is attested also in tapes of speakers from fifty years ago. This variation *n* ~ *ð* seems to trace historically to epenthetic (intervocalic) **r*. (A preceding * signals a reconstructed form.) In the data I have recorded, Osage *r* is restricted to the cluster *br*, and never undergoes nasalization to *n*. Variation of *n* with *ð* is very common in the frequently occurring 1D position marker *ąðįkše* and in *ðą́ące* ~ *ną́ące* 'heart'.

(1) *ątíðe šǫ́ ąnįkše* ~ *ąðįkše*
ą-tíðe šǫ́ ąðįkše
A1D-gossip still 1D.CONT
'we were still gossiping'

This intervocalic *ð* may be rendered occasionally with extreme palatalization. In the following, *áðįįkxa* is the expected form; I use *y* to represent a *ð* with extreme palatalization.

(2) *áyįkxa žįhe brée*
á-ðįįkxa žįhe Wa-ðee
LOC-lie sleep A1S-go
'I'm going to lie down'

(3) *áyįkxa žįhe mąðį́*
á-ðįįkxa žįhe mą-ðį́
LOC-lie sleep PREV-go
'you better go lie down'

In (4) (from the same speaker), *ð* did not become *y*, as it did in (2) and (3):

(4) *záani áðįįkxa ážį[h]apé*
záani á-ðįįkxa ą-žįhe-api-ðe
all LOC-lie A1P-sleep-PL-DECL
'we all lay down'

This phenomenon was noted also by Bristow (p.c. 1985), and Rankin (p.c. 1986) confirms that in Kansa all instances of *ð* became *y*. In Dakotan dialects, too, **r* > *y* in the environment *(#V)__V*. The related segment *l* is derived from Proto-Siouan **kr* and **xr*. According to Rankin (p.c. 1995), Osage *l*, *r*, and *ð* are all reflexes of earlier **r*. Furthermore, *r* and *ð* are still not clearly phonemically distinct in a formal sense (see comments under *b* and *r* in section 2.1.2.2). Phonemicized by cluster simplification, *l* contrasts synchronically with *ð* and *r*, the other two reflexes of Proto-Siouan **r*. The various *l*-sounds, historically, were derived as follows (where ~ represents 'varies with'):

kð > *gð* > *gl* > *dl* > *hl* ~ *l*

xð > *xl* > *hl* ~ *l*

ð > *l* (variably), but *ð* > *n* (preceding a nasal vowel)

Modern Osage *l* is found in many places where La Flesche (1932) writes *xth* or *gth*.

Rankin (p.c. 1995) notes that the following historical changes occurred in other Siouan languages. In Kansa, *r* > *y*; *kr* > *l*; *br* > *bl*; *gr* >

gl; *r* > *n* before nasal vowel. In Lakota, after *b* and *g*, *r* > *l*; otherwise, *r* > *n*, *r* > *y*. In Quapaw, *r* > *d* except before nasal vowel; *r* > *n* (frequently) preceding nasal vowel; *r* remains after *b*; and *r* > *ð* in most other environments.

Osage *l* has occasional variant surface forms [*hl*], [*dl*], but more commonly appears as plain *l*. Where *hl* does occur it is considered a cluster here; it arises historically from *xl*, which in turn derived from earlier **xr* or Osage *xð* (La Flesche's <xth>). Historic *hl* appears to be merging with *l* in Osage and today no *xl* is heard at all. Examples with *hl* ~ *l* are: *hlaaská* 'flower' < **xðaska*; *hlį* 'flint' < **xðį*; *wahléhle* 'flag [blowing], banner, streamer; staff with streamers' < **waxðexðe*; *hpahlį́* 'mucus' < **hpaxðį*. In this study I note all occurrences of *hl* as such in the first line of the example, but write underlying *l* in the morpheme analysis line.

At times a light *d* can be heard preceding an *l*, especially medially. As Robert Rankin points out (p.c. 2000), while many of the occurrences of *hl* today are from **xl*, present-day *dl* is historically from **kð* and **gð*; thus, for example, *wálį* or *wádlį* 'very, really' is from earlier **wagðį*.

In a similar manner, *dn* (also heard, but rarely) is from Proto-Siouan **kr* before a nasal vowel. For example, for *éna* 'so, therefore'; one may hear *éedna*.

While the above are historical processes, it is worth noting that *kð* → *l* also occurs synchronically in reflexive and suus forms in Osage. There are many verbs in which the suus ('subject's own') prefix *kik* combines with a following *ð* to produce *l*. (The *l* stemming from *kik-ð* will appear as *kik-ð* on the morpheme analysis line in such examples.) Such a suus form is *lúwį* 'buy subject's own', derived from *ðuwį́* 'buy'. (See sections 4.6.2 and 4.6.4 for more detail.)

2.1.2.4 *m*, *w*

Both *m* and *w* can occur in all positions and with no restrictions on what vowel may follow.

mážį '1s negative'; *mąxíðe* 'deceive'; *háamą* 'whatever I do'; *míi* 'sun'; *mį* 'I wear'; *mǫ́hka* ~ *mą́hka* 'medicine'; *méį* (variant of *mąðį́*) 'walk, go'; *muskóke* 'Muskogee tribe' (probably a borrowing from English or Muskogee) (*mo* unattested)

wa 'third person indefinite object'; *ąwą́hką* 'help me' (epenthetic *w*); *wéeli* 'head'; *wihcími* 'my aunt'; *wi* 'first person subject with second person object'; *wį* 'one, a'; *sakíwo* 'Sac and Fox [tribe]' ; *éwǫ* 'he did' (epenthetic *w*); (*wu* unattested)

2.1.2.5 *h*

The voiceless fricative *h* is classed as glottal in table 2.1, but varies in point of approximation forward to the soft palate area when preceding a high front vowel. It occurs freely with any following vowel: *haxį* 'blanket'; *hą́ą* 'evening'; *wahéhe* 'weak'; *híi* 'tooth'; *hį́į* 'whisker; hair'; *hówe* 'yes' (males); *wahǫ́į* 'address as friends and family'; *huu* 'large amount'. There are no restrictions with respect to initial or medial position.

2.1.3 General comments on the stop series

In this section we offer first a few general comments on the stop series, then treat each series in its own subsection. As seen in table 2.1, it is plausible to claim that five sets of stops exist in Osage, at least historically: (i) the voiceless preaspirated stops, which are also termed fortis or tense and which may also surface as phonetically geminate; (ii) the plain stops, which are voiceless and unaspirated, and are also called lenis or lax; (iii) the ejective (glottalized) stops; (iv) the postaspirate stops (which, however, mostly do not surface as such); and (v) a partial set of voiced stops consisting of one member only, *b*.

Affricates are classified here with the stops. Most important in Osage are the dental affricates *c hc cˀ ch*, which have developed from earlier Common Dhegiha dental stops *t ht tˀ th* preceding nonback vowels *i u e* (*u* is a central to front vowel in Osage). Each of these will be discussed below. Additionally, palatal affricates *č* and *hč* occur in just a few forms (see section 2.1.3.7).

All preaspirated stops, all reflexes of postaspirated stops, all plain stops, and the voiced stop can occur in initial and medial positions. No distributional limitations exist, except with respect to the appearance of stops within consonant clusters. Only the lenis versions (*p t c k*) occur as a member of a consonant cluster (and always in second position within the cluster, but see comments below in 2.1.3.5 on *px*, etc.). Neither the glottalized stops nor the preaspirated stops nor the postaspirated stops can appear as a member of a consonant cluster.

In the remainder of this section, I list the stops in combination with following vowels and also in all possible consonant clusters in combination with following vowels. (The syllable is discussed later, in section 2.1.4.) The distribution of the stops with respect to the following vowel is complex, and the same complex distribution holds whether the stop appears alone or as one of the members of a cluster. Therefore, it seems less confusing to discuss clusters together with single stops. A further reason to do so is that it is somewhat debatable whether certain surface reflexes of stops themselves represent single phonemes or clusters.

Throughout this discussion, when the term "stem" is used, as in "*ð*-stem", it refers to the part of the stem that occurs to the right of the point of inflection; thus, e.g., "*ð*" in "*ð*-stem" refers to the inflectable initial segment that follows the patient and agent pronominals of verbal inflection.

2.1.3.1 Voiced stop: *b*

The voiced stop set consists of *b* only, which appears only in the cluster *br*, never on its own. It is common in the 1S verb form, and somewhat infrequent otherwise. In the 1S verbs, *b* can be shown to derive from the underlying 1S agent prefix *W*(*a*), while the *r* derives from the inflectable initial *ð* of the verb stem. In La Flesche (1932), these clusters appear as <bth>, corresponding to *bð* in our notation. At least some instances of *b*, then, are from *w*, and it would be possible to consider *b* as an allophone of *w* in 1S verbs. But, as discussed above in section 2.1.2.2, the cluster *br* also occurs within single morphemes: for example, *oðíibrą* 'make to smell'; *brą* 'smell, emanate an odor'; *íbrą* 'have/get enough of'; *bráaska* 'flat'; *bréhka* 'thin'; *bróka* 'dollar, whole'. The *b* in these lexical items does not alternate with *w* (nor the *r* with *ð*). An appeal to speaker intuition would most certainly rule out positing, say, *wðą* for *brą* 'smell, emanate an odor', although the simplicity metric would favor such a representation. Throughout this work, *br* will appear in the underlying representation for the purposes of glossing wherever it does not obviously derive from agent *Wa* + *ð*-stem verb.

2.1.3.2 Glottalized stops: *pˀ cˀ kˀ*

The segments *pˀ*, *cˀ*, and *kˀ* make up the glottalized set of stops.[1] The segment *tˀ* does not occur in Osage, where **tˀ* has become *cˀ*. Although historically many of the occurrences of present-day *cˀ* can be traced to **tˀ*, in a few instances glottalized *cˀ* is from earlier **sˀ* or **šˀ*. A nonproblematic set, *pˀ*, *cˀ* and *kˀ* are units. They cannot appear as second member of a cluster.[2]

[1] There is a bit of variation in the pronunciation of *pˀ*. It has been heard from one of the most competent native speakers as [px]: for example, *nǫpxį́* for *nǫpˀį́*; also in *žą́ąnǫpxí* 'wooden collar' instead of the expected *žą́ąnǫpˀį*. Such occasional aspiration and obstruentization deriving from ˀ may reflect language obsolescence.

[2] One piece of evidence that plain *k* and the *k* portion of *kˀ* are not the same segment is the fact that in a sequence of *hkik* + *kˀ* , the final *k* of *hkik* vanishes and has no effect on *kˀ*, even though this same *hkik* will cause preaspiration or gemination of a following plain *k*.

haxį́ hkikˀúpe
haxį́ *Ø-hkik-kˀu-api-ðe*
blanket A3P-RECIP-give-PL-DECL
'they gave each other blankets'

pˀ

pˀa	unattested
pˀą	*opˀą́ða* 'steam; fog on water'
pˀe	unattested
pˀi	unattested
pˀį	*wanǫ́pˀį* 'necklace'; *Mą́ze Nǫpˀį́* 'Metal Necklace'; *ðuupˀį́pˀįze* 'blink repeatedly'
pˀo	*pˀóðǫ* (LF) 'steam'
pˀǫ	*pˀǫ* 'swollen, swelling?'
pˀu	unattested

cˀ

cˀa	*ðuucˀáke* 'unable'; *cˀáðe* 'sour' (<**sˀ*)
cˀe	*cˀé* 'die, death' (<**tˀe*)
cˀi	unattested
cˀį	*cˀį́že* 'crooked'; *núhkiacˀį* (~ *níhkiacˀį*) 'mirror'; *hpa ocˀį́ze* 'stuffed-up nose'
cˀo	*cˀóxe* 'hunchback'
cˀu	unattested

kˀ

kˀa	*hcéokˀa* 'frog'
kˀą	*kˀą́saaki* 'fast, rapid'
kˀe	*kˀé* 'dig'; *mihkákˀe* 'star'
kˀi	*ðiikˀíðe* 'scratch, tickle'
kˀį	*ðaakˀį* 'spit'
kˀo	*kˀó* 'hole'; *wakˀó* 'woman'
kˀǫ	*kˀǫ́* 'game'
kˀu	*kˀú* 'give'; *íkˀuce* 'try'

2.1.3.3 Lenis stops: *p t c k*

Plain unaspirated lenis *p*, *t*, *c*, and *k* are lax stops, and sometimes sound almost voiced to English speakers, owing to their being unaspirated. There are many clear minimal or near-minimal pairs for the contrast between lenis and fortis (preaspirated): for example, lenis *t* in *sáta* 'stiff' vs. fortis *ht* in *sáhtą* 'five'; likewise *ąkóota* 'we borrow' vs. *ąkóhta* 'ours'; *hkée* 'turtle' vs. *ke* 'scattered, dispersed'.[3]

The segment *t* has today a strong tendency toward limited distribution, not occurring before nonback vowels *u*, *i*, *e* or *į* except for a handful of

[3] The contrast between the preaspirated stops and the plain stops has been ignored by the orthographies devised by English-speaking persons trying to teach or learn Osage, but is obviously a contrast of central importance in the language, without which no learner can master correct pronunciation.

cases listed here: *wahtį* 'be showing, be visible'; *tíðe* 'gossip' (possibly from *ta* + *iðe*), and *teðáalįži* 'mischievous' (underlyingly *taiðáalįži*). Within the kinship system, *te* appears in some forms by contraction of *a* + *i* to *e*. Thus, *wihtáižį* commonly becomes *wihtéžį* 'my younger sister'. Actually, the quality of this [e] segment is often different from the standard Osage *e*; in speech it may be a very rapid *ai* sequence.

Similarly, the segment *c* does not generally occur preceding back vowels *a ą o ǫ*. A systematic exception is that *c* may be followed by a back vowel *a* when the *a* is a product of the rule deleting the first member of a two-vowel sequence across a compound boundary. For example, *co* occurs across such a boundary in the compound *hkɋ́ące* 'fruit' + *oolą́* 'put in' → *hkąącólą* 'pie'.

Arguably, then, if *t* and *c* are in complementary distribution (with the exceptions just discussed) and never contrast preceding identical vowels, *c* could be considered not a phoneme at all, with all instances of surface *c* being written as underlying *t*. Whether this is the correct approach depends on how much importance we attribute to the exceptions. It could be argued that they are not significant, given that they are few in number, and that the contractions responsible for many of them are near-surface phenomena; in many cases the unreduced form (e.g., *hkąące-óolą* 'pie' and *wihtáižį* 'my younger sister') is also acceptable, especially when spoken rapidly. The same issue arises with *hc* (see examples under *hc* in section 2.1.3.4 below).

In this work, the underlying forms of words with surface *ce, ci, cį, cu* are written with *c*, a concession to synchronic competency of speakers for whom the more abstract sequences *te, ti, tį, tu* do not exist consciously and would be confusing. The same is true of *hce, hci, hcį, hcu*.

In this subsection, examples of initial stop appear first, then examples of that stop following other segments in onset clusters. Absent from the list is *xk*, since it does not exist. Double asterisks ** before a form again indicate its ungrammaticality, signalling that such a sequence is "not Osage." Mere nonoccurrence (i.e., absent in our data) is marked "unattested." Proto-Siouan forms (or earlier, prehistoric, forms of Osage) are marked with a single asterisk to the left of the form, as is customary.

p

pa	*pažáža* 'zigzag cut'; *paašpú* 'cut corn'
pą	*wapą́* 'call folks'
po	*pobraska* 'flatten by shooting' (LF)
pǫ	*pǫšcéka* 'strawberry'[4]

[4] There is a great deal of variation between *ą* and *ǫ* which is reflected in the lists here. Several gaps for *ǫ* and *ą* could be filled with the form given in the other slot. The same is true for many cases of *i* and *u*.

pu *púuspe* 'hide something'
pi *opíxa* 'blow into'
pį unattested
pe *petxą́* 'around, surrounding'

sp

spa *wáaspa ðį* 'stay!' (from *wáaspe* 'stay')
spą *paaspą́* 'nudge' (<ba-çpo^{n}′> LF)
spo unattested
spǫ unattested
spu unattested
spi *wáaspi akxa* 'he's staying' (variant of *wáaspe*)
spį unattested
spe *wáaspe* 'stay'

šp

špa *kaaðéšpa* 'push away; give away'; *íšpaðǫ* 'Spanish'
špą (see *špǫ*)
špo unattested
špǫ <shpo^{n}> 'sodden' (LF)
špu *paašpú* 'cut corn'
špi *špížǫ* 'you know'
špį unattested
špe *kaašpé* 'bit, chip'; *ákaašpe* 'cover completely'

xp

xpa *oxpáðe* 'fall'; *héxpa* 'disheveled'; *waxpáðį* 'pitiful'
xpą (see *xpǫ*)
xpo unattested
xpǫ *xpǫ* 'thaw out' (LF)
xpu *mǫ́xpu* 'cloud'
xpi *xpi* 'flatulence'
xpį unattested
xpe *xpéka* 'dull, not shiny; faded'

t

ta *taa-* 'by extreme of temperature'
tą *tą* 'when, if'
to *tóe* 'some'
tǫ *tǫ́pe* 'look, see'
ti *tíðe* 'gossip' (from *ta iiðe*?)
te *teðáalįži* 'mischievous' (from *ta-i-ðáalį-aži*?)
Not permitted: ***tu* ***tį*

st

sta	*ostá* 'slip, slide'; *kaastá* 'hammer, pound'; *stáðe* 'paint, apply ointment'
stą	*wastą́įke* 'persimmon'
sto	*ostówe* 'in a row, in a line'; *hkiistó* 'council'; *watástoe* 'pecan'
stǫ	*wastǫ́įke* (variant) 'persimmon'
	Not permitted: ***stu* ***ste* ***sti* ***stį*

št

šta	*įįštá* 'eyes'; *hpeeštá* 'bald'; *puštá* 'iron' (verb)
štą	*štą* 'repetitively; incessantly'
što	*ðiištówe* 'take off, as a garment'
štǫ	*štǫ́pe* 'you look'; *štǫ́ke* 'soft'
	Not permitted: ***štu* ***šte* ***šti* ***štį*

xt

xta	*ðaaxtáke* 'bite'; *okáxta* 'pour, dump out'; *óxta* 'cherished, loved, honored'; *wáxta* 'worm, caterpillar'; *žą́xta* 'stink; body odor'
xtą	variant of *xtǫ* 'spill' (LF)
xto	*ðíxtoe* 'snotty'; *hpahlį́xtoe* 'runny nose'
xtǫ	*xtǫ* 'spill' (LF) (variant of *xtą*)
	Not permitted: ***xtu* ***xte* ***xti* ***xtį*

c

ca	*ðaacápe* 'they named' (from *ðaacé-api-ðe*)
co	*hkǫǫcólą* 'pie' (from *hkǫ́ǫce-oolą́*)
cu	*cúða* 'ragged'; *cúuce* 'cooked, done, ripe'; *wacúe* 'bread'
ci	*wacípxą* 'town crier'
cį	*íhkiacį* 'fan'
ce	*hpéece* 'fire'; *hį́įce* 'plate; tree-bark'
	Not permitted: ***cą* ***cǫ*

sc

scu	*wascúce* 'be slow'
sci	unattested
scį	unattested[5]

[5] La Flesche (1932) has several 2S verbs with *sci* and *scį*, such as *saki ascimą* 'you fastened it'; *scíxǫ* 'you break it'; *scíttą* 'you touched it'; *oscį́ke* 'you grasp'; and *scį́wi* and *sciwįa* 'you buy it'. (LF writes *sc* as <sts>.) However, these are most likely typographical errors and should all be *šc*, following the usual pattern for *ð*-verbs in second person.

sce	*scéce* 'long, tall'; *okísce* 'half'
	Not permitted: ***sca* ***scą* ***sco* ***scǫ*
šc	
šcu	*ðaašcúe* 'swallow'; *mąšcúce* 'slide [e.g., on ice]'
šce	*šcée* 'you go'; *pǫšcéka* 'strawberry'; *mą́ąšcé* 'hot weather'
šci	*šcíxǫ* 'you broke'
šcį	*íšcįka* 'caress, kiss' (verb); *mąšcį́ka* 'rabbit'
	Not permitted: ***šca* ***šcą* ***šco* ***šcǫ*
xc	
xce	*wį́xce* 'number one'; *paaxcé* 'tie down [e.g., a drum]'; *xce* 'tie down'
xci	*exci* 'verily' (LF) ; *hǫ́ǫxci* 'what kind'
xcį	*xcį́* 'exactly' (variant of *xci*); *éžixcį* 'funny-looking'
xcu	unattested
	Not permitted: ***xca* ***xcą* ***xco* ***xcǫ́* ***xcu*
k	
ka	*káa* 'here!'
ką	*ką́ąze* 'Kaw, Kansa'
ko	*kootáha* 'further'
kǫ	*kǫ́ða* 'want'
ki	*kípą* 'call him'; *htaacé saakí* 'strong wind'
kį	*kį́į* 'fly' (verb)
ke	*kahíke* 'chief'; *kootą́įke* 'far away distance or time'
ku	*kúpi* 'come here'
sk	
ska	*ska* 'white'
ską	*táaską* 'melt'
sko	*muskóke* 'Muskogee'; *mą́zeskožu* (< *mą́zeska ožú*) 'purse, money bag'
skǫ	unattested
sku	*skúðe* 'sweet'
ski	*kaskíke* 'tired'
skį	unattested
ske	*wapóske* 'wheat; grain; harvest' ; *íkaske* 'hearty laugh or choking that leaves one breathless' (variant of *íkaski*)
šk	
ška	*škáce* 'play'; *ška* 'quiet'; *áška* 'nearby, close'
šką	*šką́* 'move; function; be active, be activated'
ško	*škópe* 'deep' (LF)

šką	*šką* 'be active' (LF) (variant of *šką́* 'move')
šku	*škúpe* 'deep' (LF)
ški	*škíke* 'heavy'; *ški* 'also'
škį	unattested
ške	*kaašké* 'tie [e.g., shoes]'

2.1.3.4 Preaspirated (fortis) stops: *hp ht hc hk*

The tense or fortis stops *hp ht hc hk* occur initially or medially as lightly preaspirated stops, or as geminates *pp tt cc kk*. The realization of fortis consonants as alternately preaspirated and geminate is somewhat reminiscent of Icelandic, where geminates have become preaspirated. A complete study of the exact conditions for this variation or alternation has not been undertaken. Impressionistically, I believe that there is a tendency for the geminate version to precede nasal vowels more frequently than oral vowels: e.g., *ttąą*. Especially the dental preaspirate *ht* seems to occur more commonly as geminate *tt* when preceding a nasal vowel, whether in medial position or initial position, accented or unaccented.[6]

Distributional patterns for *hc* vs. *ht* are similar to those of *c* vs. *t* described above in the section on lenis stops. We find *hc* followed by a back vowel only in the sequence *hco*, and this only in a few kinship terms such as *wihcóšpa* 'grandchild' (possibly from *wihci* + *ošpa*) and across morpheme boundaries in a few compounds, those listed below being the only ones encountered so far.

The question of whether to analyze the preaspirated stops as monosegmental or bisegmental is a question that plagues Siouanists.[7] If we were to approach this phenomenon from the perspective of underlying phonology, then sometimes the surface preaspirates would be clusters, deriving from two demonstrably distinct underlying segments, and sometimes they

[6] Occasionally as a surface phenomenon, the reflex *h* of the preaspirate portion of the fortis obstruent can be heard as nasalized and semivoiced, especially when preceded by a nasal vowel. Thus *h* in the following example is phonetically [h̃]:

táatą lą́ðe wį hpáaɣe
táatą lą́ðe wį Wa-káaɣe
thing big a A1s-do
'I did a big thing'

[7] This question depends on (a) the model of phonology one chooses, (b) the role of speaker intuitions, where *p*, *hp*, *ph*, and *pʔ* are four distinct phonemes, (c) whether underlying morphological structure is taken into consideration, and (d) how the notion of parsimony is interpreted. Boas and Deloria (1941:5) treat aspirated and glottalized stops as double consonants, but Boas eschewed phonemic theory as such. Both Dorsey (1890) and La Flesche (1932) do the same, but did not have any phonological theory in this respect. Rood and Taylor's Lakota sketch (1996) considers the Lakota ejective stops and aspirated stops as units, rather than clusters of *p* + *ʔ*, *p* + *h*, etc. Rankin, like the speakers he works with, treats them as single units on the surface.

would be single phonemes, when there was no alternation to support a bimorphemic, cluster analysis. On the other hand, a surface phonology approach will treat preaspirates as single segments both initially and medially, even when morphemically they are underlyingly two single segments.

Morphemically complex postaspirates also exist, and many of the same issues arise. These are discussed in section 2.1.3.5.[8]

hp

hpa	*čáahpa* 'round, squat'; *hpahlį* 'mucus'
hpą	*kíhpą* 'invite one's own'; *ahpą́ha* 'I get up'
hpo	*ppoé* 'ignite' (LF)
hpǫ	*hpǫ́hka* 'Ponca tribe'
hpu	*hpuzá* 'sand' (noun); *okúhpu* 'full'
hpi	*hpíǫ* 'know'; *hpíiži* 'bad'
hpį	unattested
hpe	*hpéece* 'fire'

ht

hta	*htáa* 'meat, deer'; *hta* 'future'
htą	*htą́ą* 'big'; *htą́wą* 'town'
hto	*htóho* 'blue/green'
htǫ́	*htǫ́pe* 'I see'
hte	*wihtéžį* 'my younger sister' (from *wihtáižį*)
htį	*wahtį́* 'be showing; be visible'
	Not permitted: ***htu* ***hti*

hc

hco	*ihcóška* 'nephew'; *wihcóšpa* 'grandchild'; *nixócožu* 'ashtray'[9]
hcu	*hcúhapa* 'ladle'; *hcúke* 'spoon'; *hcúxe* 'mangy'
hci	*hci* 'house'
hcį	*ccį* 'moist' (LF)
hce	*hce* (injunctive); *híce* 'hurry' (intransitive verb)
	Not permitted: ***hca* ***hcą* ***hcǫ*

[8] The question of the relationship between underlying morphemic complexity and monosegmental vs. bisegmental analysis also arises in the case of *l*, which can derive from *kð* underlyingly, in a productive process whereby bimorphemic *k* + *ð* becomes the single segment *l*. The *k* segment in this process is the same underlying final *k* of reflexive ***hkik*** or suus *kik* that converts a following *p*, *t*, or *k* to preaspirated *hp*, *ht*, or *hk* (see section 4.6).

[9] From *níi* 'fluid' + *xóce* 'gray; ashes'+ *ožu* 'put in'.

hk

hka	*tóohka* 'wet'
hką	*hkáące* 'apple; fruit'; *óhką* 'help folks'
hko	*hkoohkósa* 'pig'
hkǫ	*hkǫ́bra* 'I want'
hku	*sáhku* 'watermelon'
hke	*hkée* 'turtle'
hki	*hkik* 'reflexive'; *hkiistó* 'council'
hkį	*hkį́hkįnį* 'curly; kinky'

It is predictably difficult for the learner of the language to distinguish auditorially between preaspirated (fortis) *hc*, nonpreaspirated (lenis) *c*, and postaspirated *ch*. Some examples of contrast are:

žúuce 'red'; *hce* 'buffalo'; *níhce* 'cold'; *che* 'standing inanimate'

ci 'in, at, to'; *waachí* 'dance'; *achí* 'arrive here'; *hci* 'house'; *ochį́* 'hit'

wacúe 'bread'; *wachúu*, *chúu* 'copulate, engage in sexual intercourse'; *hcúuke* 'spoon'

2.1.3.5 Postaspirated stops *ph th ch kh*: obstruentization and affrication

All Dhegiha languages except Osage have a set of postaspirated (or "aspirate" or "aspirated") stops *ph th kh*. Historically, Osage did as well, but in Osage the aspiration feature (the *h* portion) has obstruentized, and has done so in two different directions. The historically postaspirated stops present interesting and complex problems for rule interpretation and ordering, problems of a segmental nature and others. I assume here that Osage has underlying postaspirated stop phonemes (*ph*, *th*, *kh*), but that they undergo certain changes owing to two rules. (Because *ph th kh* never emerge on the surface, they are distinguished by boldface type in table 2.1 above.)

The general distribution of the surface manifestations of these stops is quite clear: *ph*, *th*, and *kh* become *px*, *tx*, and *kx* respectively before back vowels (*o*, *ǫ*, *a*, *ą*), and *pš*, *ch*, and *kš* before nonback vowels (including *u*, which is a rounded front or central vowel in Osage). Of the underlying postaspirated stops, *th* alone preserves aspiration, becoming *ch* before nonback vowels by a rule of Early Affrication (section 2.3.3.4). Otherwise, obstruentization of the underlying *h* component of postaspirate stops occurs everywhere, resulting phonetically in a set of two-consonant clusters: *px*, *tx*, *kx*, *pš*, and *kš*.

The answer to the question whether to interpret these surface reflexes as underlyingly clusters or as single segments will differ from phonologist to phonologist, and possibly also from word to word depending on underlying morphemic complexity and how one views its relationship to segmental analysis. Thus we could say that the postaspirates are both units and clusters at different points in derivation. Some postaspirates begin as clusters split between two morphemes, as in the case of *pšu* (from *p* + *hu* 'I'm coming'), where the *p* derives from underlying *Wa* '1S agent' and the *š* from the inflectable initial *h* of the verb. In the morpheme analysis line of examples, the surface forms of postaspirated stops are used (*pš* or *px*, *ch* or *tx*, and *kš* or *kx*).[10]

Below are examples of the surface distribution of segments. A double asterisk (**) before a sequence indicates that the sequence is ungrammatical. Other sequences (labeled "unattested") are possible Osage sequences but accidentally do not occur or have not been found in the data.

px

pxa	*opxá* 'down the middle'; *opxáži* 'ignorant'; *pxáðaži* 'unable to understand'
pxą	*ópxą* 'elk'; *lapxą́ąke* 'mosquito'
pxo	*kaapxóke* 'pop, burst, explode'
pxǫ	unattested
	Not permitted: ***pxu* ***pxe* ***pxi* ***pxį*

tx

txa	*háatxa* 'how far'; *katxá* 'a little while'
txą	*txą* 'standing'; *otxą́* 'put on, e.g., leggings, pants, shoes'; *ópetxą* 'tie in a bundle'; *watxą́* 'squash'
txo	unattested
txǫ	unattested
	Not permitted: ***txu* ***txe* ***txi* ***txį*

kx

kxa	*akxa* subject marker; *ípukxa* 'wipe it [with]'; *kxážį* 'third son and successive sons'
kxą	*šíkxą* 'sister-in-law, woman speaking'
kxo	*kíkxo* 'feast'
kxǫ	unattested
	Not permitted: ***kxu* ***kxe* ***kxi* ***kxį*

[10] In trying to classify postaspirates as single segments or clusters along the lines of morphemic complexity, some might appeal to the intuitions of native speakers. However, that will not aid in classification. Even in clearly bimorphemic examples, such as *ékipše* 'I say', where *p* is a reflex of underlying 1S subject pronominal *Wa* and *š* is a reflex of root-initial *h*, speakers will never split *p* from *š*. Speaker intuition is an unreliable means of determining bimorphemic status; whether the example is underlyingly mono- or bimorphemic, and despite the influence of English, speakers will not split the postaspirates into two segments.

For some speakers from the Hominy area, *tx* becomes *tkx* or *kx*. Thus three variants exist for 'when?': *hatxą́ta, hatkxą́ta*, and *hakxą́ta*. It seems that any given speaker produces just *tx*, just *tkx*, or just *kx*, but all speakers accept all variants. Other examples are *otkxą́* 'next' and *watkxą́* 'squash', for *otxą́* and *watxą́* respectively. I have taken the *tx* form as basic in the present work in those words showing such variants.

Robert Rankin (p.c. 2000) advises that in Kansa all *tx* before a non-front vowel became *kx*. Rood (p.c. 2000) reports that also in some Lakota dialects, *t* assimilates to a following *x* and becomes *k*, citing Dakota *txate* ~ *kxate* 'wind'.

pš

pša	*pša* 'pound it!' (from *pše-a*)
pšu	*pšu* 'I come here' (from *p-hu*)
pše	*pše* 'pound'
pši	*pši* 'I arrived there' (from *p-hi*)
pšį	unattested
	Not permitted: ***pšą* ***pšo* ***pšǫ*

ch

cha	*ðaachápe* 'he ate it' (from *ðaaché-api-ðe*)
chi	*waachí* 'dance' (noun or verb)
chį	*ochį́* 'hit'
chu	*wachúu* 'copulate'
che	*ðaaché* 'eat'
	Not permitted: ***chą* ***cho* ***chǫ*

kš

kšu	*wakšúįze* 'teach, instruct' (variant of *wakšíǫze*)
kše	*wį́kše* 'truth'
kši	*ąkšíǫza* 'teach me!'; *kšíye* 'make/do for another'
kšį	*ðuukšį́įce* ~ *ðiikšį́įce* 'miss [as when throwing or catching a ball]'
kšǫ	*kšǫ́ka* 'second son'
kšą	*kšą́ka* 'second son' (variant)
kša	*wįkšáži* 'untruthful' (from *wį́kše* 'truthful' + *aži* 'negative')
	Not permitted: ***kšo*

2.1.3.6 Distribution of affricates *c ch hc*

We have seen that *c*, *ch*, and *hc* are in nearly perfect complementary distribution with *t*, *tx*, and *ht*. Whereas the latter nearly always occur preceding back vowels, *c ch hc* cannot generally occur there, but are found almost exclusively in other environments (namely, before nonback vowels). Only a handful of exceptions occur at surface level, nearly all of them clearly owing to late phonological processes: (i) *c*, *ch*, and *hc* appear before *a* that has been produced by vowel contraction between a verb and a following negative marker, pluralizer, or imperative marker; (ii) *hco* appears in two older kinship terms; (iii) vowel truncation taking place across morpheme boundaries in a compound may result in surface sequences of *c*, *ch*, or *hc* plus back vowel, as in *niixócožu* 'ashtray' (from *niixóce* 'ashes' + *ožu* 'put in'); (iv) *t* and *ht* exceptionally occur before nonback vowels in *tíðe* 'gossip', *teðáalįži* 'misbehave', and *wahtį* 'be visible'.[11] Synchronically, these several exceptions can be said to have phonologized the opposition between *t th ht* and *c ch hc*.

It should be noted that *t* and *c* as the second member of consonant clusters are in the same distribution. Clusters ending in *t* (*st št xt*) occur only before back vowels, while clusters ending in *c* (*sc šc xc*) occur only before nonback vowels (including *u*). The possible first member of a cluster with *t* or *c* is *s*, *š*, or *x*.

2.1.3.7 *č* and *hč*

The affricates *č* and *hč* are quite rare. Both usually indicate diminutive, in most cases diminutive of a form in *t* (c) or *ht* (*hc*) respectively, and thus represent sound symbolism. (See section 2.6.) It is convenient to distinguish three subcases, as follows:

(i) *č* is attested in only two words found so far, both diminutives, *čóopa* 'a little, a little bit, a few' (possibly from *tóe* 'some, a few', or perhaps from *tóopa* 'four') and *čáahpa* 'short and round, squat' (from *táahpa* 'round').

(ii) *hč* is found in some kinship terms, where diminutivization from a base *hc* optionally occurs. Thus, as an endearment or diminutive, *wihčóšpa* can replace *wihcóšpa* 'my grandchild'.

(iii) Non-sound-symbolic *č* is found allophonically in the Hominy district pronunciation pattern in the cluster *šč*, which corresponds to *šc* in the speech of other speakers. This includes both underlying monomorphemic *šc* and *šc* that derives from underlying abstract second person agent *Ya* + *ð* inflectable initial of the verb where *ð* is followed by *i*, *į*, *e*, or *u*. Thus *šcée* 'you go' is *ščée* in Hominy pronunciation. This is the only difference in pronunciation among the three districts where Osage was historically spoken that I detected during my research. In the related language Kansa, *c* has become *č* everywhere, except for glottalized *c*ˀ.

[11] Affrication processes that convert *t th ht* to *c ch hc* interact with the V1-V2 Rule, which contracts vowels, and for this purpose must be divided into "early" affrication (before the V1-V2 Rule) and "late" affrication (after the V1-V2 Rule); see section 2.3.3.4.

2.1.3.8 The glottal stop

The glottal stop is a special case. It occurs as part of the stop series (*pʔ*, *cʔ*, and *kʔ*) discussed in section 2.1.3.2. It is also heard in initial and final position in citation of isolated words. In addition, underlying glottal stop appears to be distinctive in a few verb roots where it affects the choice of first and second person pronominal markers, notably historical *ʔį* 'wear' and *ažáʔį* 'think', but of these two, only in *ʔį* 'wear', when preceded by the final vowel of a preceding word, can its presence occasionally be directly detected. In citation forms, the glottal stop is nonorganic and predictable (that is, inserted) at the beginning and end of an isolated word when citing words in a list, but organic and nonpredictable (that is, underlying) in the verbs mentioned here.[12]

2.1.4 The Osage syllable

The syllabic template for Osage is quite simple: *((C) C) V (V)*. There does not seem to be any reason for positing postnuclear consonants. No phonological rules have been found that act on syllable structure that would indicate the syllabification of medial consonants as coda instead of onset. Moreover, all clusters occur as initial on roots and morphemes; this, coupled with the principle of onset maximalization, lends support to the claim that there are no coda consonants. Also pertinent is the fact that there are no word-final consonants. (But see below at the end of this section and in section 7.3.1 for the two truncated forms *aap* and *aakx*.) Speakers consistently add [a] (sometimes [ə]) to all English names ending in consonants when used in Osage sentences; for example, *Carolyn* becomes *Carolyna*. (This *a* is glossed in the morpheme analysis line in examples as SYL, as it is a device for syllabifying the final consonant as the onset of a new syllable, thus adhering to the syllabic template for Osage.) Native speakers consistently syllabify all consonants as onsets.

Independently of the issue of classification as clusters or single segments, we find the following syllable onsets in Osage (classed by place of articulation of the first segment).

Labial: *pš px pʔ p hp*; *br m w*

Dental: *c tx cʔ ch hc ht*; *s z*; *sp st sc sk*; *ð l (hl) n*

Alveopalatal: *š č ž*; *šp št šc šk*; *šč*

Velar: *k kš kx kʔ hk*; *x ɣ xp xt xc*

Glottal: *h*

[12] Boas and Deloria (1941:5) treat glottalized stops as consonant sequences in Dakota.

Obviously, Osage onsets will not all be accounted for by a sonority theory of the syllable. There are, for example, *pxa* and *xpa*, which will have quite different sonority contours. I will not address this issue here.

All onsets occur within single morphemes, and all occur in both initial and medial position within the word. Some clusters are also found across a morpheme boundary, in forms containing reflexes of the 1S or 2S agent inflectional marker, or of the reflexive, reciprocal, suus, or dative prefix. (But see also discussions of two-consonant sequences in section 2.1.3.)

First person singular agent + root: *hp, pš, br, ht, hk* (*hpáaɣe* 'I make'; *pši* 'I arrive there'; *bráache* 'I eat'; *htǫ́pe* 'I watch'; *hkǫ́bra* 'I want')

Second person agent + root: *šp, št, šc* ~ *šč, šk* (*íšpahǫ* 'you know'; *štáape* 'you went'; *ščée* 'you go' [Hominy version]; *šcée* 'you go'; *škáaɣe* 'you make')

Dative + root (historically): *kš* (*kšíɣe* 'make')

On the whole, morpheme boundaries otherwise correspond to syllable boundaries. But when the first person plural agent prefix *ąk* is followed by a vowel, its *k* syllabifies with the following vowel (*a-kV*) creating a bimorphemic sequence *kV* (see section 3.1.3). Bimorphemic *CV* syllables also occur in the nasal vowel stems (historically the ʔ-stems), in 1S *mV* and 2S *žV*; *m* and *ž* in these forms represent the pronominal prefixes, while *V* is the initial vowel of the verb (see section 2.3.1 for examples)

For the most part, postnuclear consonants in surface forms occur only in very limited contexts, such as ceremonial speech. The truncated form of *áape* 'they said', *aap*, is quite common in speeches made by males, especially, and is the only occurrence of a postnuclear consonant except for the extremely rare truncated forms *eep* from *éepe* 'they said', and *áakx* from *áakxa* 'he is saying'.

2.2 Vocalic system

2.2.1 Vowels

Osage has five oral vowels *i e a o u* and three nasal vowels *į ą ǫ*.

i	high front unrounded vowel
e	mid front unrounded vowel
a	low back unrounded vowel
o	mid back rounded vowel
u	high front or central rounded vowel [ü] (IPA [y]); frequently unrounded to [i]

į	high front nasal vowel
ą	low back nasal vowel
ǫ	mid back nasal vowel

2.2.1.1 Variation between *ǫ* and *ą*

Minimal pairs for *ǫ* and *ą* are hard to come by, but a few exist, such as *nǫ́hį* 'old age' vs. *ną́hį* 'baby board; board', and *lǫ́ðe* 'drunk' vs. *lą́ðe* 'big, great'.[13]

In many forms, *ǫ* and *ą* are interchangeable: *štǫ́ke* ~ *štą́ke* 'soft'; *ąk* ~ *ǫk* 'A1P pronominal'; *nąpé* ~ *nǫpé* 'recurring action [iterative]; enduring state' (verb suffix).

In a few other forms, only *ǫ* or only *ą* is acceptable, and the word made by substituting one vowel of the pair for the other vowel has no meaning: *ðuušką́* 'start' (but not ***ðuuškǫ́*); *ną́ąke* 'run' (but not ***nǫ́ǫke*); *nǫhpewái* 'scary' (but not ***nąhpewái*); *waaðǫ́* 'sing' (but not ***waaðą́*) and *ékǫ* 'in this/that manner' (but not ***éką*).

Wherever *ǫ* and *ą* occur, they are often replaced by [ɔ̨] in speech. Either *ǫ* or *ą* may be used for both of the vowels in such common nouns as *mą́žą* 'land' and in *mǫ́šǫ* 'feather', and for the nasal vowel in *hą́pa* 'day'. Where back nasal vowels are interchangeable, the variant most generally used nowadays seems to be [ą] (or [ɔ̨]) rather than [ǫ].

2.2.1.2 Length

One fairly intractable issue in the data is long vowels. These are written in the present work as double vowels (e.g., *aa*); no rearticulation is implied by this orthographic device. Vowels written as long vowels in the morpheme analysis line in examples are considered to be underlyingly long. The other Dhegiha languages—certainly Kansa and Quapaw, and probably also Omaha-Ponca—also have long vowels (as do some other Siouan languages), although they most often were not recorded as such. It is difficult to sort out length from accent in many Osage forms (see section 2.4 for accent).

In many instances the long vowel is absolutely clear in a word, and in some cases minimal pairs can even be found; these include *wéeli* 'head' vs. *wéli* 'oil';[14] *ną́ye* 'ice' vs. *ną́ąye* 'spirit'.

At other times, the otherwise indisputably long vowel seems to be short, or at least shorter, especially when the long vowel is not accented due to its new position in a word. As Robert Rankin suggests (p.c. 2004), there may be several grades of length: long vowel, long vowel shortened,

[13] But *lą́ðe* is most likely a borrowing from Spanish *grande*.

[14] Variants are *wéedli* 'head' and *wédli* 'oil', both of these with *dl* (not *hl*).

normal vowel, normal vowel shortened. In most instances, the long vowel, once detected, has been written in unaccented syllables here, but some shortening will be expected to occur naturally in unaccented syllables in speech.

Many monosyllabic words that are major-class roots, especially nouns, seem to have inherently long vowels, such as *hkée* 'turtle', *htáa* 'deer; meat'. Polymorphemic syllables have a tendency to exhibit long vowels. Many instances of unaccented but inherently long *waa* occur in verbs such as *waachí* 'dance'.

In addition to changes in position of long-voweled syllables, other influences may be at work, not the least of which may be the alterations in normal patterns brought about by language disuse. I have done my best to portray long vowels in those words where they are heard in the majority of the instances recorded. At times I have looked to Miner's (1992) lexicon of Winnebago (as the only published record of vowel length distinctions in a related language) and to colleagues in the field working on closely related languages for confirmation.

No distinctions in distribution or in applicability of phonological rules have been found between long and short vowels. Any statements in this volume about cooccurrence or about phonological rules should be presumed to apply to long and short vowels equally.

2.2.1.3 Variation between *i* and *u*

The high vowels *i* and *u* present overlaps in pronunciation. Phonetically, *u* is routinely rendered [ü],[15] with greater or lesser degrees of fronting and unrounding, so that sometimes [ü] is nearer to [i] and sometimes nearer [u].

Fronting is most pronounced following *ki*, *hk*, or *k*, and elsewhere when a neighboring vowel is high and no intervening obstruent is present to block assimilation. Thus, the *u* occurring after *k* or *hk* is extremely fronted, as for example in *ohkúla* 'clothes', *skúðe* 'sweet', *okúce* 'quilt', *sáhku* 'watermelon', *wahkúcˀa* 'lame', *íkˀuce* 'try'. In the motion verb set, the forms *ahú* 'come here' and *akú* 'return here' have extremely fronted *u*.

In Quapaw and in Omaha-Ponca, Proto-Siouan **u* became [ü] and then *i*. The [ü] stage is preserved in Kansa and Osage, although some instances of [ü] have unrounded in both, becoming *i*.

Minimal pairs do exist for the contrast between *u* and *i*. For example, *xúða* 'eagle' is pronounced [xǘða], but never [xíða], perhaps because of the existence of *xíða* 'stumble, fall'.

[15] IPA [y].

Variation between [ü] and [i] is especially common following *ð* and *n* (which also are quite transparent to nasalization). This variation is frequent in the instrumental prefix *ðuu* 'by hand', which becomes *ðii* in many derivations (sometimes shortened to *ði*). The verb *ðuwį́* 'buy' varies with *ðiwį́*. In such words, *u* has become so fronted that it is auditorily difficult to distinguish from *i*. Speakers hear this *u* as identical to *i*.

Underlying *i*, however, cannot usually become [ü], except in some cases where [ü] occurs in the next syllable (e.g., *nǘžü* for *nížu* 'rain'). Even with a following [ü], *i* in prefixes such as *hkik* 'reflexive' and *ki* 'dative' consistently remains [i]. In other contexts, underlying *i* remains [i]: thus, in *waachí* 'dance' and *ichį́* 'hit with', *i* does not alternate with [ü] at all; *ðiihíce* 'tease' likewise never has [ü] and clearly contrasts with *ðuuhúce* 'pull down'.

Fronting occurs along a continuum and in some words, several degrees of it occur. For example, *kisúðe* 'remember' may have an extremely fronted [ü], and *kisíðe, kisüe, kisúe* (with less fronted *u*), *küsúe* (with rounding of *i*) are all possible, although ***kusúe* (with both *u*'s somewhat less fronted) does not occur. (Elision of *ð*, as in several of these forms, is common; see section 2.3.2.1.)

2.2.2 Nasal vowels and associated phenomena

Nasal vowels clearly contrast with oral ones; minimal pairs are easily found: for example, *hápa* 'corn' vs. *hą́pa* 'day'; *híi* 'tooth' vs. *hį́į* 'hair, fur' (although there is some variation in speech: *híi* ~ *hį́į*); *óhoo* 'bark' vs. *óohǫ* 'cook'; *óhka* 'space' vs. *óhką* 'help folks'; *oðáha* 'follow' vs. *ooðáhą* 'you cook'. The nasal vowels occur in both accented and unaccented (and deaccented) syllables; they may be long as well (*ąą, ǫǫ, įį*). Some minimal pairs for the length contrast can be found: for example, *ną́ɣe* 'ice' vs. *ną́ąɣe* 'spirit'.

Nasal and oral vowels also contrast after nasal consonant: for instance, *míi* 'sun' vs. *mį* 'blanket; something one wears';[16] *ną* 'iterative' (often *nǫ* in speech of Osages recorded several years ago) vs. *na* ~ *ną* 'only' (never ***no*).

In speech, however, nasality often spreads from a nasal consonant to the following vowel (so that, e.g., 'sun' is sometimes *mį́į* instead of the expected *míi*). Moreover, a nasal vowel may nasalize an oral vowel in the preceding or following syllable. When a nasal vowel remains nasal after nasalizing the vowel of an adjacent syllable, we speak of "spread" of nasality; when a basically nasal vowel loses its nasality after nasalizing the vowel of an adjacent syllable, we speak of "transfer" of nasality. Spread

[16] The word for 'sun' in related languages is *wi* or *bi*.

and transfer may operate either rightward (progressive) or leftward (regressive), and may cross morpheme boundaries. Nasality spread and transfer occur most readily when the consonant separating the vowels in question is not an obstruent. This is consistent with what has been observed in Kansa, where only obstruents block transfer of nasalization, according to Rankin (p.c. 2000).

In addition, nasality may disappear entirely.

These processes that change the nasality specification of vowels are sporadic and optional in all contexts. It is quite unpredictable when they will occur in the speech of any Osage speaker so far consulted; during a single session with a given speaker, variation in nasality takes place sporadically. Consequently, processes of nasalization and denasalization do not have the same status as Affrication, Obstruentization, and similar processes described in this chapter. Nasality-affecting processes, though sporadic and optional, are nonetheless quite productive and do not seem at all like slips of the tongue by one or two individuals. This phenomenon complicates considerably the task of the linguist or learner when trying to determine precisely which are the true underlying vowels in certain forms. The best available tool for these cases is comparison with related languages where the data is clearer than it is in Osage at this time.

2.2.2.1 Denasalization

Denasalization in a final unaccented syllable is common. Of many available examples, I will offer the following, whose final vowels I consider underlyingly nasal, but are frequently nonnasal in speech: *íhpahǫ* ~ *íhpaho* 'I know'; *sáhtą* ~ *sáhta* 'five'; *táatą* ~ *táata* 'what, something, a thing'.

2.2.2.2 Leftward transfer of nasality

This process involves regressive assimilation of nasality followed by progressive dissimilation, resulting in a metathesis of nasality. That is, in a sequence of two syllables of which the first has a basically oral vowel while the second has a basically nasal one, the first vowel may become nasal while the second becomes oral. This may be somewhat informally represented as follows:

$$V1[-\text{nas}] + V2[+\text{nas}] \rightarrow V1[+\text{nas}] + V2[-\text{nas}]$$

For example, in *o* + *wi* + *hką* below, the syllable *wi* has acquired nasality from the following syllable *hką*, which has lost nasality.

(5) *owį̨hka*
ó-wi-hką
PREV-P2S<A1S-help
'I helped you'

2.2.2.3 Rightward transfer of nasality

This process involves progressive assimilation of nasality, followed by regressive dissimilation. The effect is, again, a metathesis of nasality, rather than a global denasalization, since nasality is not merely lost, but shifts rightward to a vowel which was previously nonnasal. This is represented schematically as follows:

V1[+nas] + *V2*[–nas] → *V1*[–nas] + *V2*[+nas]

In (6), nasalization has wandered off *wį* onto *a*.

(6) *wíąkše hta mįkše*
wį́-Wa-kše *hta* *mįkše*
PREV-P1S-be.truthful FUT 1S.CONT
'I'm telling the truth'

2.2.2.4 Leftward spread of nasality

Leftward spread of nasality (regressive assimilation) can occur sporadically in speech; it can be schematized as:

V1[–nas] + *V1*[+nas] → *V1*[+nas] + *V2*[+nas]

(That is, a vowel acquires nasalization from the vowel of the following syllable, but the latter does not lose its nasality.) In (7), vowel harmony (assimilation) has occurred, changing preverb[17] *o* to *a* (see section 3.4.2.1); nasality then spreads from *ą* leftward to the preverb, producing *ąwą́*:

(7) *ąwą́hkia*
o-ą́-hkik-íe-a
PREV-P1S-REFL-talk-IMPER
'talk to me'

Example (8) shows the same word undergoing leftward transfer of nasality rather than spread: *o* becomes *a* and assimilates nasality from the following *ą*, but then that following *ą* denasalizes:

[17] "Preverb" is used here to refer to earlier parts of a verb which are separated from the verb root by inflection or some other intervening element such as a reflexive, reciprocal, suus, dative, vertitive, or inceptive. One example is the *a* of *a_ðée* 'go'. In compounds such as *_kǫ́_ða* 'want', the initial syllable is also glossed in the interlinear morpheme gloss as preverb (abbreviated PREV). Even the locatives *o*, *á*, and *i* are sometimes glossed as PREV, as they pattern with other preverbs.

(8) *ąwáðahkie*
o-ą-Ya-hkík-e
PREV-P1S-A2S-REFL-talk
'you talk to me'

2.2.2.5 Rightward spread of nasality

In rightward spread of nasality, a nasal vowel may cause nasalization of the vowel of the following syllable; the first vowel remains nasal. Schematically, this is:

V1[+nas] + *V2*[–nas] → *V1*[+nas] + *V2*[+nas]

In (9), for instance, nasality of the final *ǫ* of the verb spreads across the word boundary, passing to the following *ði* 'you (emphatic)' (which has nonnasal [i] under normal circumstances).

(9) *ánąąkˀǫ ðį*
á-ą-nąkˀǫ́ ði
LOC-P1S-hear 2S.PRON
'listen to me'

2.2.2.6 Loss of nasality: regressive dissimilation

A process of regressive dissimilation takes places in scores of examples where an underlying nasal vowel denasalizes before a nasal vowel in the next syllable; it may be schematically represented as:

V1[+nas] + *V2*[+nas] → *V1*[–nas] + *V2*[+nas]

In (10) the final *ą* of *hóolą* 'fish' (verb) denasalizes in anticipation of the upcoming initial *ą* of *ąkái* '1P moving':

(10) *mą́ąɣe ðáalį tą́, hóola ąkái hta ąkái*
mą́ąɣe ðáalį tą́ hó-oolą́ ąk-aðé hta ąkáðe
weather good if fish-put.on P1P-go FUT 1P.CONT
'if the weather is good, we are going fishing'

Both this kind of anticipatory loss of nasality and rightward transfer of nasality (section 2.2.2.3), as suggested by Koontz (p.c. 1994), may be subcases of a single phenomenon, concentration of nasality on the last segments of certain sequences, whatever their underlying specification for nasality.

2.3 Phonological rules

A few phonological rules have already been mentioned above, such as Affrication and Obstruentization. Below, I discuss the important assimilation processes in 1S and 2S verb forms (section 2.3.1), deletion and epenthesis of *ð*, and sometimes of other consonants (section 2.3.2), and processes of vowel contraction, especially the V1-V2 Rule (section 2.3.3). An alternative account of the process commonly called "ablaut" among Siouanists is offered (sections 2.3.3.5–2.3.3.7). The V1-V2 Rule is shown to interact with the important processes of Affrication and Obstruentization in 2.3.3.4.

2.3.1 Agent prefix adjustment rules

This subsection describes synchronic processes of contraction of agent pronominals with the inflectable initial segment of verb stems in Osage. ("Stem" in this section will be used to mean "the part of the verb that follows pronominal prefixes, up through the end of the root." As will be discussed in chapter 3, many Osage verbs have those prefixes inserted into them rather than prefixed to them.)

There is a group of verbs in Osage for which inflection is highly productive, here called the regular verbs (informally also called the *a-ða* verbs, after the A1S prefix *a* and A2S prefix *ða*). For the regular stems, the *W* of the 1S marker *Wa* (still found in the corresponding Dakota prefix *wa*) has been lost in Osage, leaving *a* as the most productive 1S allomorph. A rule eliding *W* produces the regular 1S agent allomorph *a*.

There are a number of other groups ranging from productive to nonproductive that show irregularities. These irregularities are generated by two major synchronic processes, the first being vowel syncope in the agent pronominal, and the second process being assimilation of the remaining consonant of the pronominal prefix to the inflectable initial consonant of the verb stem. These irregular verbs, referred to here as syncopating stems, are classified according to the inflectable initial segment (the segment that follows pronominal prefixes), which is the primary environment for conditioning prefix allomorphs. Thus, within the class of syncopating stems, *ð*-stems are stems whose inflectable initial segment (visible in 3rd person forms) is *ð*; *h*-stems have *h* as their inflectable initial segment; ʔ-stems historically had ʔ as their inflectable initial segment, though now they are more accurately characterized as having a nasal vowel as inflectable initial; and stop-stems have a stop *p*, *t*, or *k* as their inflectable initial segment. Stop-stems may be further divided into "mutating" (where the inflectable initial *k* becomes *hp* in 1S agent forms) and "fortisizing" (where the inflectable stop becomes fortis [preaspirated]); see section 3.2.4.2. Table 2.2 compares the agent forms of typical syncopating stems with those of regular *a-ða* stems.

TABLE 2.2. AGENT INFLECTION OF REGULAR AND SYNCOPATING STEMS

		AGENT FORM	EXAMPLE
REGULAR (NONSYNCOPATING) STEMS			
without *ð*-insertion	1S	*a*	*aɣáake*
	2S	*ða*	*ðaɣáake*
	3S		*ɣaaké*
	1P		*ą̨ɣáake*
			'cry'
with *ð*-insertion (*i*-initial verbs)	1S	*ðá*	*iiðáðe*
	2S	*ða*	*íiðaðe*
	3S		*íiðe*
	1P		*ąnǫ́ðe*
			'see'
SYNCOPATING STEMS			
ð-stems	1S	*b*	*bráache*
	2S	*š*	*štáache*
	3S		*ðaaché*
	1P		*ąðáache*
			'eat'
h-stems	1S	*p*	*épše*
	2S	*š*	*éše*
	3S		*ée*
	1P		*éąkíe*[a]
			'say'
nasal vowel stems (ʔ-stems)	1S	*m*	*ékimǫ* ~ *ékimą*
	2S	*ž*	*ékižǫ*
	3S		*ékiǫ*
	1P		*eą́kiǫ* (rare)
			'do'
mutating *k*-stems	1S	*hp*	*hpáaɣe*
	2S	*šk*	*škáaɣe*
	3S		*káaɣe*
	1P		*ąkáaɣe*
			'make; do'
fortisizing stop-stems	1S	*hC*	*htǫ́pe*[b]
	2S	*šC*	*štǫ́pe*[b]
	3S		*tǫ́pe*
	1P		*ątǫ́pe*
			'look'

[a] The nondative form of this stem is not available.
[b] *C* = *p/t/k* inflectable initial of verb.

For many syncopating stems, the first person singular form contains a bilabial consonant such as *b* or *m*. Clearly, then, there is evidence for an underlying form of the 1S agent prefix incorporating a bilabial consonant of some type which is unmarked for voice. An abstract bilabial *W*, then, is posited in these cases, from which surface *w*, *p*, *b*, and *m* are derived (as the *a* of *Wa* drops out, leaving the *W* to adjust to following segments).[18] A surface *w* is well attested in many 1S pronominal forms other than the agentive prefixes (possessives, such as *wíhta* 'mine', emphatic pronominals, and so on; there are also 1S prefixes with *w* in the inalienably possessed kinship terms).

For the syncopating verbs, the surface forms of 1S *Wa* can be schematized as follows:

ð-stems:	*Wa* → *b* / __ *ð* (subsequently, *ð* → *r*)
nasal vowel stems:	*Wa* → *m* / __ nasal vowel
h-stems:	*Wa* → *p* / __ *h* (subsequently *h* → *š*)
fortisizing stop-stems:	*Wa* → *W* (contracts with following lenis stop *p t k* to produce fortis *hp ht hk* or geminate *pp tt kk*)
mutating *k*-stems:	*Wa* → *W* (contracts with the following lenis *k* to produce fortis *hp* or geminate *pp*)

The surface forms corresponding to the 2S agent prefix are *ða* (for regular verbs), *š* (for most syncopating stems), and *ž* (for nasal vowel stems). I posit *Ya* as the underlying form of the second person agent prefix; the symbol *Y* represents the commonality among *ð*, *š*, and *ž*. (Other Siouan languages have *y* in this prefix.) Before a consonant, *Y* becomes *š*, resulting in forms such as *škáaɣe* 'you make'; on the other hand, when *Y* precedes nasal vowels (that is, in the historical ʔ-stems called here the nasal vowel stems) it will become *ž*. Otherwise, *Y* becomes *ð*, producing the A2S subject prefix *ða*. The processes involving *Ya* in syncopating verbs can be summarized as follows:

[18] The symbol *W* stands for an underlying [-vocalic, +anterior, −coronal] segment and nothing more; this notation has no real theoretical status in the phonology, but is merely a practical way of dealing with the alternating surface forms. The same is true for the *Y* segment posited for the 2S prefix (*Ya*). The surface segment *w* also occurs in many other contexts in Osage that are not associated with 1S pronominals and hence are not derived from *W*.

ð-stems:	*Ya* → *š* / __ *ð* (subsequently *ð* → *t*; *c* before *i*, *e*, *u*)
nasal vowel stems:	*Ya* → *ž* / __ nasal vowel
h-stems:	*Ya* → *š* / __ *h* (subsequently *h* → *Ø*)
stop stems:	*Ya* → *š* / __ *p*, *t*, *k* (subsequently *t* → *c* before *i*, *e*, *u*)

It should be noted that stems are classified for inflectional purposes (as *ð*-stems, stop-stems, etc.) by the consonant or vowel that immediately follows the pronominal prefix. That consonant or vowel will not necessarily be the initial segement of the verb root, since another prefix, such as dative or inceptive *ki*, reflexive *hkik*, suus *kik*, or an instrumental prefix, may intervene between the agent prefix and the root, and will then determine the inflectional type of the verb.

I now present in detail the rules operative in syncopating verbs.

2.3.1.1 Agent Simplification via syncope

Syncope of the vowel in agent inflection is accomplished via a morphologically conditioned rule (Agent Simplification). In these rules, *Wa* is 1S agent and *Ya* is 2S agent; recall that *W* behaves differently from *w*.

Agent Simplification:	*Wa* → *W* / __ *p*, *t*, *k*, *ð*, nasal *V*, *h*
	Ya → *Y* / __ *p*, *t*, *k*, *ð*, nasal *V*, *h*

The various subclasses of inflection of syncopating stems are produced by rules adjusting the sequences that result from Agent Simplification, as was summarized just above; the rules involved are presented in more detail in sections 2.3.1.2–2.3.1.6.

Admittedly, Agent Simplification is not a very natural-looking phonological rule (although it is a very old one).[19] Its inelegance is compensated for, however, by the relative naturalness of the subsequent rules that adjust the consonant clusters (and consonant + nasal vowel sequences) it creates. Moreover, Agent Simplification can be easily extended to the many inflected kinship terms and pronominal forms in Osage which have *w* and *ð* initials (see the Appendix for kinship terms, and section 6.10 for pronominal forms).

[19] According to Rankin (p.c. 1994), this rule is quite old, affecting all Mississippi Valley Siouan languages at one time probably, but now it is morphologically conditioned. For *h*-initial verbs of more recent vintage, for example, this syncope *Wa* → *W* would not apply. Instead, the 1S form would be *a*, and 2S would be *ða*, in the regular pattern.

The number of forms accounted for by Agent Simplification and the subsequent adjustments is enormous; there are very few exceptions. Apart from the *h*-initial stems of more recent vintage (cf. n. 19), the only important exception, where Agent Simplification's context is met but where the rule does not apply, is in verbs of the form *X* + *ðe*, where *ðe* is the causative morpheme (e.g., *cˀéðe* 'cause to die, kill'); these do not undergo Agent Simplification, and legitimately so, as the *ð* of the causative morpheme is epenthetic historically.[20] Thus, for example, the 1S form of *cˀéðe* is *cˀéaðe* 'I killed'; 2S is *cˀéðaðe* 'you killed', with regular inflection.

The term "historical ˀ-stem" is used in a few places in this study to facilitate comparison with verbs in other Siouan languages where ˀ has been retained. In the Osage form of these verbs, ˀ is no longer present in speech. These historically ˀ-initial stems have a nasal vowel initially in modern Osage, and are more properly called the nasal-vowel-initial stems.[21] The rule of Agent Simplification above is stated in terms of nasal vowels rather than ˀ.

It should also be noted that Agent Simplification applies to the fortisizing stop stems and mutating *k*-stems, but not to other stems which may begin with *k*, for example, the suus prefix *kik* (section 4.6.4) or the dative prefix *ki* (section 4.6.5).

The following subsections detail other rules that affect the agent prefixes. The verb *_kǫ́_ða* 'want' will be used in many of the sample derivations here, since it is doubly inflected, that is, has two roots compounded together, each of which takes agent inflection. Thus, its 1S form is underlyingly *Wa* + *kǫ́* + *Wa* + *ða*, to which Agent Simplification (syncope) applies to give *Wkǫ́Wða*; its 2S form is underlyingly *Ya* + *kǫ́* + *Ya* + *ða*, to which Agent Simplification applies to give *Ykǫ́Yða*.

2.3.1.2 Rhotacization

The inflectable initial *ð* following the simplified 1S agent marker *W* becomes *r*; that is, *ð* has the variant *r* after *W*.

Rhotacization: *ð* → *r* / *W*__

ð is a weak member of the onset. *ð* and *r* are related historically. Osage *r* may have been a tap in the past, but is not so today; the *r* in Osage today is identical to the American English *r*. The effect of the Rhotacization rule is to change *ð* to *r* when *ð* appears immediately to the right of the subject inflection; thus, with the verb *_kǫ́_ða*, in 'I want':

[20] *ð* is the epenthetic glide in Osage in several contexts. In Siouan generally, the epenthetic glide was **r*.

[21] Osage *nǫpˀį* 'wear around the neck' exhibits a relic of the glottal stop in the nasal vowel stem verb *(ˀ)į* 'wear'.

Wkǫ Wða → *Wkǫ Wra*

Similarly, the 1S form of *ðaaché* 'eat' is *bráache* 'I eat'.

2.3.1.3 Assimilation of *W*

W, the abstract segment comprised of features common to *p*, *b*, *m*, and *w*, contracts with a following lenis stop (*p t k*) to becomes a fortis (pre-aspirated or geminate) stop; that is, *Wk* becomes *hk* ~ *kk*, *Wt* becomes *ht* ~ *tt*, and *Wp* becomes *hp* ~ *pp*.

Assimilation A: *W* → *h* / __ *p*, *t*, *k*

Thus, the 1S of *tǫ́pe* 'see' (a fortisizing stop-stem) is *htǫ́pe*, that is, underlying *Wa* + *tǫ́pe* becomes *Wtǫ́pe* by Agent Simplification, as is expected when the stem-initial segment is *t*; to this, Assimilation A applies to give *htǫ́pe*. The 1S form of *pą* 'yell' is *hpą* 'I yell'. Similarly, Assimilation A applies to *Wkǫ́Wra* (the 1S form of 'want', after Agent Simplification and Rhotacization), giving *hkǫ́Wra*.

A second sort of assimilation affecting *W* is that it takes on nasality of the following vowel.

Assimilation B: *W* → *m* / __ nasal vowel

In a verb such as *į* 'wear' (from **ˀį*), application of Agent Simplification and Assimilation B results in *Wį* → *mį* 'I wear'.

For mutating *k*-stems, of which only two have been found, *káaɣe* 'make, do' and *kǫ́žįka* 'not know, be ignorant of', the stem-initial stop first becomes *p* before Assimilation A applies. For more examples, see section 3.2.4.3.

(11a) *hpǫ́žįka*
Wa-kǫ́žįka
A1S-know.not
'I don't know it, I'm ignorant of it'

(11b) *hpáaɣe*
Wa-káaɣe
A1S-make
'I make'

2.3.1.4 Stop Formation

The sequences *Wr* and *Wh*, resulting from Agent Simplification and Rhotacization, are subject to a rule converting *W* to a bilabial stop.

Stop Formation: *W* → *b* / __ *r*
W → *p* / __ *h*

Thus, *hkǫ́Wra* 'I want' becomes *hkǫ́bra* (the surface form of the word).

For the *h*-stem verb *(a)hi* 'arrive there', we apply Agent Simplification, then Stop Formation:

(Agent Simplification) *Wa hi → Whi*

(Stop Formation) *Whi → phi*

Then *phi* will later become *pši* 'I arrive there' by Obstruentization (see section 2.1.3.5).

2.3.1.5 Assibilation in 2S forms

The simplified 2S agent prefix *Y* becomes *š* before consonants and *ž* before nasal vowels.

Assibilation: *Y → š / ___ p, t, k, ð*

Y → ž / __ nasal vowel

Thus, the 2S form of *tǫ́pe* 'see' begins as *Ya + tǫ́pe*; Agent Simplification converts this to *Ytǫ́pe*, and Assibilation then produces the surface form *štǫ́pe* 'you see'. For *į* 'wear', *Ya + į* becomes *Yį* by Agent Simplification, and this becomes the surface form *žį* 'you wear' by Assibilation.

2.3.1.6 Manner Dissimilation

Stem-initial *ð* changes manner of articulation and devoices to *t* after the form *š* (result of Agent Simplification and Assibilation of the 2S agent prefix).[22]

Manner Dissimilation: *ð → t / š* __

Thus, the 2S form of *_kǫ́_ða* 'want' is derived as follows:

(Agent Simplification) *Ya + kǫ́ + Ya + ða → Ykǫ́Yða*

(Assibilation) *Ykǫ́Yða → škǫ́šða*

(Manner Dissimilation) *škǫ́šða → škǫ́šta* 'you want' (surface form)

2.3.1.7 Regular Verb Simplification

Given the relative complexity of the adjustment of the form of the agent prefixes, it is understandable why in the past some students of related languages with similar processes have chosen to posit underlying distinct sets of markers for the *ð*-stems, regular stems, and nasal vowel-stems. But under the analysis offered here, the rest is easy once we have recognized

[22] *ð* is rhotacized to *r* in some related languages.

Manner Dissimilation: no other verbs will meet the structural description of Agent Simplification and for these, a rule of Regular Verb Simplification applies. These are the nonsyncopating (that is, regular) verbs, formed with regular verb simplification of subject pronominals.

Regular Verb Simplification: *Wa* → *a*
(alternatively, *W* → *Ø* / __ *V*)
Ya → *ða*

The rules above, from Agent Simplification through Regular Verb Simplification, will in combination give the verb classes discussed further in chapter 3.

2.3.2 Elision and insertion of consonants

2.3.2.1 Elision of *ð*

The consonant *ð* is often (though never obligatorily) elided between vowels, as in (12)–(13). This may drastically affect the appearance of surface forms.

(12) *ąkáðe*
ąk-a-ðée
A1P-PREV-go
'we go'

(13) *ąkáe* ~ *ąkai*
ąk-a-ðée
A1P-PREV-go
'we go'

There are contexts where homonyms or near homonyms are created by elision of *ð*. The verb *íe* 'speak' has as its 2S form *íðae*, as in (14). This is extremely similar to *íiða[ð]e*, the 2S of 'see' (with elision of its second *ð*), as seen in (15); even native speakers cannot reliably distinguish between these two.

(14) *pée íðai ðaašé?*
pée í-Ya-e ðaįšé
who PREV-A2S-speak 2S.CONT
'who are you talking about?'

(15) *pée íiðai ðaašé?*
pée íi-Ya-ðe ðaįšé
who PREV-A2S-see 2S.CONT
'who do you see?'

Elision of *ð* occurs within enclitics as well as within roots and prefixes. Notably, the *ð* of the declarative enclitic *ðe* is usually elided after the plural enclitic *api*, with the resulting vowel sequence *ie* contracted to *e* (cf. section 2.3.3.7).[23]

When *ð* is elided between *o* or *ǫ* and another vowel, an epenthetic *w* may appear. Thus, *oðíhtą* 'car; wagon' may also appear as *oíhta* or *owíhtą*, as in (16).

(16) *owíhta žúuce žį wíht[a] olįį hu*[24]
o-ðiihtą žúuce žį wíhta o-lįį hu
LOC-pull red small 1S.POSS LOC-sit come.here
'come ride in my little red wagon'

Insertion of *w* between *o* or *ǫ* and a following vowel is a natural enough fast-speech process; it may happen as well when the vowel sequence does not arise by elision of *ð*. An example of a word containing such a vowel sequence is *ooálą* in (17); this may alternatively be pronounced *oowálą* or even *wálą*.

(17) *oálą mįkšé*
oo-Wa-lą́ mįkšé
PREV-A1S-pout 1S.CONT
'I'm pouting'

2.3.2.2 Elision of other consonants

We have seen that *ð* elides quite generally. In a few cases, *ž* also elides. For example, *wažáže* 'Osage' is optionally reduced to *wažái*. The frequency of *ž*-elision is much lower than that of *ð*-elision.

(18) *wažái hcí*
wažáže hcí
Osage house
'Osage house'

Other consonants may also elide. For example, from *hkáwa-xóce* 'horse-gray' we have the personal name *hkáwaxoe* 'grayhorse', with elision of *c*. Names seem to preserve evidence of many older processes no longer visible in modern Osage. Elision of *c* apparently is not a common process nowadays, although a few additional examples can be found; for instance, *žúuce* 'red' is shortened to *žúe* in (19). Interestingly, although *c* is

[23] At least one speaker has been found to use *pie* where others use *pe* (from *api-ðe*), but this same speaker says that *pie* is exactly equivalent to *pe*. For this speaker, although the *ð* of *api* + *ðe* has elided, contraction of *ie* to *e* does not occur.

[24] The final *a* of *wíhta* in the example may be dropped in fast speech, followed by liaison of *t* to *o*. Thus, *wíhta* + *olįį* → *wíhtolįį*.

occasionally elided, *t* is never elided, although it is the historical source of surface *c* (cf. section 2.1.3.3).

(19) *hkǫ́ące žúe tóe ąkʔú*
hkǫ́ące žúuce tóe ą-kʔú
apple red some P1S-give
'give me some tomatoes'

We also find optional elision of *p* in several words, such as *tǫ́pe* ~ *tǫ́e* 'watch, see' and *wasápe* ~ *wasáe* 'bear'.

2.3.2.3 *ð*-Epenthesis in A1S

ð is inserted (epenthesized) between certain sequences of vowels. In verbs in which *i* or *ii* precedes the 1S agent prefix *a*, *ð* is inserted before the *a*. (See also section 3.2.2.1.)

ð-Epenthesis A: *Ø → ð / i __ á*

Thus, the 1S form of *íiðe* 'see' is derived as follows:

(underlying form)	*íi + Wa + ðe*
(Regular Verb Simplification, Accent Adjustment)	→ *iiáðe*
(*ð*-Epenthesis)	→ *iiðáðe* 'I see [it]' (surface form)

2.3.2.4 *ð*-Epenthesis in other contexts

This epenthesis of *ð* has also occurred historically in verbs where locative *i* followed by locative *o* has become *oðo* (as pointed out by Robert Rankin and John Koontz, p.c. 2000). See section 4.1.6 for more examples of *oðo*.

ð-Epenthesis B: *Ø → ð / i __ ó*

This is presumably why *oðo* verbs are not syncopating verbs; that is, they are not true *ð*-stems, since their *ð* is merely epenthetic. True *ð*-stem verbs, that is, verbs with inflectable initial *ð*, have historically nonepenthetic *ð*.

ð-Epenthesis also occurs where *wa* is followed by the locative prefix *á*. The locative prefix *á* does not metathesize with *wa* (although other sequences of *wa* + *a* sequences do metathesize, becoming *a-wa*). Instead, epenthetic *ð* is inserted between *wa* and *á*, as in (20) (with *ð* epenthesized between the patient prefix *wa* 'us' and the locative *á* of the verb stem *átǫpe* 'watch over, look on'.)

(20) *waaðáhkittǫpapi*
wa-ð-á-hkik-tǫ́pe-a-api
P1P-EPð-LOC-REFL-look-IMPER-PL
'look down upon us'[25]

It is not clear whether epenthesis of *ð* in these forms is purely phonologically conditioned, or whether the morphological status of inherently accented *á* as locative may be the determining factor; the fact that the *i* + *o* > *oðo* phenomenon above involves only locatives favors the latter hypothesis. But see section 3.2.2.2 for discussion of *i_áahpe* 'wait for'.

Historically speaking, *ð*-Epenthesis also occurred in other contexts, such as the causatives ending in *ðe* (with pronominal prefixes inserted before *ð*). These are not true *ð*-stems, as they do not follow the syncopating pattern of inflection (cf. section 2.3.1.1); presumably this is because the *ð* of causative *ðe* was originally epenthetic. There are other minor forms such as *ðįkšé* (demonstrative for third person, sitting) where the *ð* may be epenthetic.

2.3.3 Contraction of vowel sequences, Affrication, Obstruentization

2.3.3.1 Vowel sequences preceding the root: contraction of *a* + *i*

In contrast with epenthesis of *ð*, which makes two contiguous vowels more independent by coming between them, two vowels may contract when they are brought together by derivation or inflection. This is commonly seen in the preverb (the part of the verb that precedes pronominal prefixes), especially in forms with an underlying sequence *wa* + *i*. This sequence regularly becomes *we*. Consider the following examples, where *wa* + *i* in the morpheme line can be approximately and informally translated 'with which; tool; means':

(21) *wéhkile*
wa-i-hkik-ðe
VAL-PREV-RECIP-see
'a visit' (lit., 'a means to see each other')

[25] The verb incorporates *hkik* 'reflexive' with the sense of 'one's own': 'look down upon us, your own'. A closely similar form exists with the nonpreaspirated dative prefix *ki*, meaning 'another', as in the following example:

waaðákitǫpapi
wa-ð-á-ki-tǫpe-a-api
P1P-EPð-LOC-DAT-look-IMPER-PL
'look down upon us'

The same verb *átǫpe* may take the suus prefix *kik* as well.

(22) *wékaacuɣe*
wa-i-kaa-cuɣe
VAL-with-strike-brush
'broom' (lit., 'a means for brushing with sudden force')

In these examples, *a* + *i* is always fully contracted to *e*. But in the kinship system, we find both surface sequences: uncontracted *ai* and fully contracted *e*. Thus, for 'my younger sister', both *wihtáiži* and *wihtéži* are common in speech. The sequence *wa* + *i* in verbs is discussed in section 3.4.1.

2.3.3.2 Root and post-root vowel sequences: the V1-V2 Rule

The remainder of section 2.3.3 deals in large part with the phenomenon known to Siouanists as "ablaut," which is usually characterized as a change in verb root-final *e* to *a* in certain contexts.[26] However, I present an alternative explanation of this synchronic and quite productive process, confirming an interpretation originally suggested by Rankin (1995). I reformulate "ablaut" as vowel contraction, or more precisely, regressive assimilation and optional shortening, as a result of which root-final *e* is deleted before the initial *a* of an enclitic. Vowels other than *e* in diverse contexts also tend to undergo this general rule of vowel contraction or collapse, called here for short the V1-V2 Rule:

V1-V2 Rule: *V1 + V2 → V2(V2)*

(The notation *V2(V2)* in the rule represents an optionally long vowel, rather than a rearticulation of the vowel.) This rule may be thought of as truncation of weak *e*.[27] This truncation of the root-final vowel occurs before the three enclitics *aži* 'negative', *a* 'imperative', and *api* 'pluralizer'. The V1-V2 Rule affects every verb-root-final *e*, implying that *e* is the weakest vowel in Osage.

The effect of the contraction rule is to remove the root-final *e*, with the *a* of the following enclitic remaining. Root-final vowels other than *e*—that is, root-final *a ą o ǫ i į*—are not deleted by the vowel contraction rule, but remain before all three enclitics.[28]

[26] In Dakota and Lakota, change of *a* or *ą* to *e*.

[27] Final nonaccented *e* is often relaxed in Osage and is often perceived auditorily as [ɔ]. This can easily be misinterpreted as a relaxed version of *a*, and occasionally, too, final *a* (e.g., in imperatives) will be [ɔ], so that some confusion on the part of learners of the language is to be expected.

[28] In the many applications of the contraction rule in other contexts, for the most part *e* is deleted before another vowel (sometimes with lengthening of the second vowel). It would be interesting to see if there is a hierarchy among vowels with regard to which delete, taking into account accent, nasality, elision of *ð*, and other elision. The

When the root-final vowel fails to delete before an enclitic, the initial *a* of the enclitic is itself deleted, as in the case of *waaðǫ́* 'sing': *waaðǫ́pe* 'they sang' from *waaðǫ́-api-ðe*; *waaðǫ́ǫži* 'not to sing' from *waaðǫ́-aži*; *waaðǫ́!* 'sing!' (imperative) from *waaðǫ́-a*.

This fact, which partially obscures the underlying phonological form of these enclitics, is probably what has led some to view the deletion of *e* before them as replacement of *e* by *a* ("ablaut"). In support of the claim that the underlying form of the negative enclitic is *aži* rather than *ži*, note that the plural negative form is *apaži*, from underlying *api* + *aži*; also note that the negative has a first person singular form *maži*, from *m* + *aži*. (For further discussion of the form of the negative and plural enclitics, see chapter 5.)

2.3.3.3 Alternation between *e* and *a*

Possible relics of an alternation between *e* and *a* are found in two contexts. First, the enclitic *hce* 'polite injunctive' has *htai* as its plural form (more exactly, the form used for three or more total persons), perhaps from earlier *hte* + *api*. One might also speculate that the enclitic *hta* 'future' is derived from injunctive *hce*, but there is no obvious advantage to that; in fact, examples of future *hta* at the end of a phrase—that is, with no enclitics, let alone *a*-initial ones, following it—have been found. Second, the forms *haatxą́ce* 'when (interrogative, past)' and *haatxą́ta* 'when (interrogative, future)' are perhaps related to the enclitic *hta* 'future'. But these minor *e* ~ *a* alternations will not be discussed further here, since there seem to be no data suggesting a productive connection between them and the active vowel contraction process involving the plural, negative, and imperative enclitics.

2.3.3.4 Interaction of the V1-V2 Rule with Affrication and Obstruentization

The effect of the V1-V2 contraction rule is removal of the verb-final *e*, with *a* of the following enclitic remaining.

The interaction of the V1-V2 Rule with other phonological processes is somewhat complex. Briefly, the major phonological processes discussed so far apply in the following order:

th → *ch*	(Early Affrication)
Ch → *Cš* or *Cx*	(Obstruentization)

cases most frequently attested are: *a* + *ǫ́* → *ǫ́(ǫ)*; *a* + *o* → *o(o)*; *a* + *i* → *í(i)*; and *a* + *e* → *e(e)*.

ea → *aa* (V1-V2 Rule)

t → *c* and *ht* → *hc* (Late Affrication)

Early Affrication and Obstruentization apply before *e* is deleted by the V1-V2 Rule. This means that *ch* and *Cš* will unexpectedly precede *a* in some surface forms. On the other hand, Late Affrication only gets its chance to apply after the V1-V2 Rule; this means that when a verb root ends in *e* and this *e* is deleted by the V1-V2 Rule, Late Affrication will not be able to affect *t* or *ht* preceding the root-final vowel.

We may now exemplify these claims in more detail.

Early Affrication (change of *th* to *ch* before nonback vowels) converts, for example, *ðaathé* to *ðaaché* 'eat'. An *e* that induces Early Affrication of *th* to *ch* may be subsequently removed by the V1-V2 Rule. In such cases, *ch* remains, even though on the surface it is followed by the back vowel *a*, as in (23) (and many other examples in this work).

(23) *súhka ðaachápe*
súhka Ø-ðaaché-api-ðe
chicken A3P-eat-PL-DECL
'they ate the chicken'

Obstruentization of the *h* portion of the postaspirate stops *ph th kh* causes these to become *pš kš* before front vowels (in this context, *th* becomes *ch* by Early Affrication) and *px tx kx* before back vowels. (Obstruentization does not apply across the boundaries between the stem and a following compounded stem.) Thus, underlying *ophe* becomes *opšé* 'obey'; *óphą* becomes *ópxą* 'elk'; *thą* becomes *txą* 'standing'; *khe* becomes *kše* 'lying'; *kháží* becomes *kxáží* 'third son; any successive son'; and so on. Since Obstruentization precedes the V1-V2 Rule, when a clitic beginning with *a* follows a root that underlyingly ends in *phe* or *khe*, deletion of the *e* by the V1-V2 Rule results in surface instances of *pš* or *kš* before the back vowel *a*. Thus, underlying *ophé* + *aži* ('obey' + 'negative') becomes *opšé* + *aži* by Obstruentization; the V1-V2 Rule then deletes *e* to produce the surface form *opšáži* 'not obey'. Similarly, underlying *wįkhé* + *aži* ('truthful' + 'negative') becomes *wįkšáži* 'not truthful'. Additional examples are:

(24) *ąpšápe*
ą-Ø-pšé-api-ðe
A1P-P3S-pound-PL-DECL
'we pounded it'

(25) *pšá!*
Ø-pše-a
P3S-pound-IMPER
'pound it!'

Affrication processes that convert *t th ht* to *c ch hc* interact with the V1-V2 Rule (section 2.3.3.2), which contracts vowels, and for this purpose must be divided into Early Affrication (before the V1-V2 Rule) and Late Affrication (after the V1-V2 Rule). Early Affrication, as noted above, changes *th* before a nonback vowel to *ch*, as in *ðaaché* 'eat'.

The affrication process whereby *t* becomes *c* and *ht* becomes *hc* before a nonback vowel is termed Late Affrication since it must follow the V1-V2 Rule. Because of this ordering, when a root-final *e* is deleted before the *a* of an enclitic by the V1-V2 Rule, a preceding *t* or *ht* will not be affricated. For example, underlying *ðaaté* 'to name' normally appears as surface *ðaacé*; but the underlying *t* remains when *ðaaté* is followed by the enclitics *aži* 'negative', *a* 'imperative', or *api* 'plural'. In these cases, the V1-V2 Rule removes *e* before Late Affrication has a chance to apply. Thus we have the surface forms *ðaatáaži* 'he didn't name it', *ðaatá* 'name it!' (imperative), and *ðaatápe* 'they named it' (*ðaaté* + *api* 'plural' + *ðe* 'declarative'). Further examples can be seen in (26a)–(33).

(26a) *océ mąðį!*
o-té mąðį!
PREV-look go
'go look for it!'

(26b) *otá!*
Ø-ote-a
P3S-look.for-IMPER
'look for it!'

(26c) *ąwátape*
o-ą-Ø-te-api-ðe
PREV-me-A3P-look.for-PL-DECL
'they're looking for me'

(26d) *otáži*
Ø-océ-aži
P3S-look-NEG
'not to look for it'

(27a) *kakšįįce*
kaa-khįįte
by.striking-miss
'shoot at and miss'

(27b) *kakšį̨tape*
Ø-Ø-kaa-khį̨te-api-ðe
P3S-A3S-by.striking-miss-PL-DECL
'he shot at it and missed'

(28a) *ðiihíce*
ðiihíte
'play with, tease'

(28b) *ðiihítaži apai*
Ø-Ø-ðiihíte-aži apa-ðe
P3S-A3P-play-NEG 3.CONT-DECL
'they won't play with it'

(29a) *paaxcé*
paaxté
'gather and tie'

(29b) *paaxtáži apai*
Ø-Ø-paaxté-aži apa-ðe
P3S-A3S-gather.and.tie-NEG 3.CONT-DECL
'they're not gathering it up and tying it into a bundle'

(30a) *šcée*
Ya-ðee
A2S-go
'you go'

(30b) *štáaži*
Ya-ðee-aži
A2S-go-NEG
'you [singular] do not go'

(31a) *mąąšcé*
mąąšté
hot.weather
'it's hot [weather only]'

(31b) *mąąštáži əkxai*
mąąšté-aži akxa-ðe
hot.weather-NEG 3.CONT-DECL
'it's not hot'

(32a) *táahkace*
táa-hkate
by.temperature-be.hot(?)
'hot [to the touch]'

(32b) *táahkataži akxa*
táa-Ø-hkate-aži *akxa*
by.temperature-P3S-be.hot(?)-NEG 3.CONT
'it's not hot'

(33) *ékištaži nįkšé*
é-ki-Ya-ðe-aži *nįkšé*
PREV-PREV-A2S-think-NEG 2S.CONT
'you don't think so'

For examples of underlying *ht*, see (34)–(37). Example (34) shows *ht* in a context in which it affricates to *hc*, while (35)–(37) show the same root in contexts where the V1-V2 Rule removes root-final *e* before Late Affrication has had a chance to apply.

(34) *níhce*
níhte
'cold'

(35) *nihtaži*
nihte-aži
cold-NEG
'not cold'

(36) *níhtape*
níhte-api-ðe
cold-PL-DECL
'they were cold'

(37) *nįąhtamažíe*
ní-ą-hte-maží-ðe
PREV-P1S-cold-1S.NEG-DECL
'I'm not cold'

As a consequence of these rules and their ordering, *t* will alternate with *c*, and *hc* with *ht*, in the surface forms of roots whose underlying forms end in *te* or *hte*, depending on whether *e* is deleted by the V1-V2 Rule. However, *ch* does not alternate with *th*, as we have seen. The glottal *cʔ* is not at all affected by the rules discussed here. As it is not created by either Early or Late Affrication, it never alternates with *tʔ*. When a root-final *e* contracts with *a* by the V1-V2 Rule, preceding *cʔ* remains unaffected: for example, *cʔáži* 'doesn't die', from *cʔé* + *aži* ('die' + 'negative'). Historically, all **tʔ* became *cʔ* in Osage; there is now no *tʔ* in underlying or surface forms.

2.3.3.5 Vowel changes with *aži* 'negative'

The negative enclitic has a special 1S form *maží*. On the one hand, this form supports the claim that the underlying shape of the negative enclitic is *aži* rather than simply *ži*. On the other hand, it poses problems for my claim that the phenomenon called "ablaut" is really deletion of *e*, or assimilation of *e* to *a*, before the initial *a* of an enclitic by the V1-V2 Rule. Given a verb form ending in *ee*, such as *brée* 'I go', one would expect it to maintain the *ee* before the 1S negative *maži*, giving a surface form *bréemaži* for 'I'm not going'. Since the *ee* is not immediately followed by *a*, it should not be affected by the V1-V2 Rule. However, a reanalysis has occurred for some speakers: root-final *ee* becomes *aa* before the 1S negative *maží*.

(38) *bráamąží*
Wa-ðee-maži
A1S-go-1S.NEG
'I'm not going'

Historically, such forms are easy to explain, in either of at least two ways. According to Rankin (p.c. 1994), the creation of an auxiliarylike negative that is inflected for 1S (only) took place in the very recent past, long after the V1-V2 Rule was general in Osage and other Mississippi Valley Siouan languages. The earlier form of the 1S negative of 'go', then, was **braa aži* (with root-final *ee* assimilated to the *a* of *aži* by regular application of the V1-V2 Rule). Subsequently, the 1S prefix *m-* was preposed to *aži*. (These data, then, would imply that stem-final *aa* [from *ee*] and negative-initial *a* constitute a sequence of vowels rather than a single long vowel.)

An alternative account would be that the 1S negative *maži* is particularly old and a member of what was once a fully inflected paradigm for 'negative', which has now lost its other inflected forms. Supporting this analysis is the fact that on one occasion, a speaker gave a 2S negative as *nąží*.

Verbs ending in a vowel other than *e* retain that vowel before the negative and other *a*-initial enclitics. After such verbs, the negative enclitic sometimes retains its *a*, and sometimes deletes it with lengthening of the verb-final vowel. Thus, the negative of *waaðǫ́* 'sing' is either *waaðǫ́aži* or *waaðǫ́ǫži* 'not sing'.

In the negative examples (39)–(41), *ízizike* 'dirty' + negative has been lexicalized as a new verb, 'not to be dirty'. This can be seen from the fact that the first person singular form of this verb, seen in (41), has the negator *aži*, rather than *maži* as we might expect. In these forms too, the final *e* of 'dirty' and the initial *a* of the negative have collapsed to *a* by application of the V1-V2 Rule.

(39) *ízizike*
'dirty'

(40) *ízizikaži ekxai*
ízizike-aži akxa-ðe
dirty-NEG 3.CONT-DECL
'they're not dirty'

(41) *ízizikaži mįkšé*
ízizike-aži mįkšé
dirty-NEG 1S.CONT
'I'm not dirty'

Replacement (or apparent replacement) of verb-final *e* by *a* before *a* of the negative marker applies only when the negative marker is *aži/mažį́*. No such process applies when the negative marker is the emphatic negative *ðįké*. Thus, the verb *aðée* 'go' retains *ée* in the example below. (However, *ðįké* itself in this example undergoes the V1-V2 Rule, being followed by the plural enclitic *api*.)

(42) *aðée įkápe*
a-Ø-ðée ðįké-api-ðe
PREV-A3S-go-NEG-PL-DECL
'he/they didn't go'

2.3.3.6 Vowel changes with imperative

As we have seen, root-final *e* disappears before the imperative enclitic *a*, by the V1-V2 Rule. Many Osage verbs do end in *e* (perhaps even the majority do). Below are two further examples of imperatives, contrasted with nonimperative stems.

(43a) *paaxcé*
paaxté
'gather up and tie into a bundle'

(43b) *paaxtá!*
Ø-paaxté-a
P3S-gather.and.tie-IMPER
'gather it up and tie it into a bundle!'

(44a) *káaɣe*
'make, do'

(44b) *káaɣa*
Ø-káaɣe-a
P3S-make-IMPER
'make it; do it'

Differing patterns of accent may be found with some verbs in the imperative form. In particularly emphatic contexts, accent on the final syllable is likely, as in (45):

(45) *kakonáa kaaɣá*
kakoná káaɣe-a
end make-IMPER
'don't do that any more'[29]

Further examples of imperatives of stems with final *e* may be seen below. (In the first of these examples, the imperative is followed by *mąði* 'go', which is often used appositively as a sort of general purpose imperative similar to 'now get going!')

(46) *íkˀuca mąði*
ikˀuce-a mąði
try-IMPER go
'go try!'

(47) *oðáaka*
o-ðáake-a
LOC-tell-IMPER
'tell!'

(48) *kisúða!*
kisúðe-a
remember-IMPER
'remember!'

(49) *ąwą́ðaaka*
o-Ø-ą-ðáake-a
PREV-P3S-P1S-tell-IMPER
'tell it to me'

(50) *ąwą́hkia*
o-ą-hkik-ie-a
PREV-P1S-RECIP-talk-IMPER
'talk to me'

[29] More literally, 'make that the end', somewhat equivalent to the English admonition "That'll be enough of that now."

The emphatic negative *ðįké* undergoes the V1-V2 Rule, changing to *ðįká*, as seen in (51), and in (42) above. (The sentence-final *ði* in this example is the emphatic 'you' sometimes added to 2S imperatives.)

(51) *aalǫ́ðį įká ði!*
áa-lǫ-ðį *ðįké-a* *ði*
PREV-PREV-remember NEG-IMPER 2S.PRON
'don't forget!'

When the final vowel of the verb stem is something other than *e*, imperative *a* does not appear on the surface. The imperative form of the verb in such cases is identical to the citation form, sometimes with a lengthened final vowel (*mąðįį́*) and sometimes without length.

(52) *mąðį́*
mąðį́-a
get.moving-IMPER
'go!; get moving!'

Similarly, imperative *a* is deleted after the negative enclitic *aži*, since the latter ends in a vowel other than *e*.

(53) *oðáakaži*
o-ðáake-aži-a
LOC-tell-NEG-IMPER
'don't tell!'

2.3.3.7 Vowel changes with *api* 'plural'

It has already been noted (section 2.3.2.1) that the normal surface reflex of *api* 'plural' + *ðe* 'declarative' is *(a)pe*, by elision of intervocalic *ð* followed by contraction of the resulting vowel sequence *ie* to *e*.[30] Below are some examples of plural declarative *(a)pe* after *e*-final roots.

[30] As the use of English has increased among Osage speakers over the years, the application of some of these processes has begun to diminish. Occasionally in the 1990s one could hear *pie* for plural declarative, with no contraction of vowels between the pluralizer *api* and the declarative *(ð)e*. (The full sequence *api* + *ðe* is never heard in speech.) Occasionally, too, a speaker will not apply the V1-V2 Rule before any of the enclitics *api*, *aži*, or *a*, although this is quite rare. It is conceivable that this omission could be characteristic of an earlier form of Osage, rather than symptomatic of language obsolescence; "ablaut" (here reformulated as application of the V1-V2 Rule) has exceptions in other Siouan languages as well. The following is an example where root-final *e* has failed to be deleted by the V1-V2 Rule:

sitǫ́į suhka ąðáachipe
sitǫ́į *suhka* *ą-ðaaché-api-ðe*
yesterday chicken A1P-PL-DECL
'yesterday we ate chicken'

(54) *záani wanǫ́brape*
záani wanǫ́bre-api-ðe
all dine-PL-DECL
'we all ate together' (lit., 'everyone ate together')

(55) *ée hóxpape*
ée hóxpe-api-ðe
3.PRON cough-PL-DECL
'they coughed'

(56) *hlékape*
Ø-léke-api-ðe
A3S-shatter-PL-DECL
'it broke'[31]

2.3.4 Minor processes

There are several minor phenomena occurring at surface level which are interesting for synchronic comparative as well as historical purposes. We will look at some of them in this section.

2.3.4.1 More vowel contraction

The rule *V1 + V2 → V2 (V2)* discussed above is obligatory in vowel sequences involving *e* followed by initial *a* of the enclitics *api*, *a*, and *aži* (with only sporadic exceptions, possibly owing to language obsolescence) and is responsible for an important process in Osage. The same rule applies in several other minor contexts, where it has varying degrees of optionality. In some cases both the version with contracted vowels and the version with full, unaffected vowels are correct, and speakers will regard the two as equivalent. (The application of the V1-V2 rule in these cases does not seem to depend on fast speech.) In other instances, the rule is obligatory. A full study of all applications of the V1-V2 Rule would have to be carried out to determine the degrees of optionality in all these cases. A continuum emerges, with cases ranging from those where contraction by the V1-V2 Rule is obligatory to cases where the form with contraction and the form without it are equally acceptable. The relative strength of the vowels involved would likely prove to be a decisive factor in determining rule optionality, along with morphological context. Such a study may be impossible to carry out at this late date. The data presented here portray a wide-ranging tendency in the language, but a tendency whose exact outlines must remain somewhat obscure.

[31] The pluralizer is often used in verbs with 3S subject; see section 5.1.5.

As examples below will show, the V1-V2 Rule may apply in the verb stem itself, between inflectional material and the causative root *ðe*, across word boundaries, and across other internal boundaries.

***aðǫ* → *aǫ* → *ǫǫ*.** After elision of *ð*, the two syllables of the verb stem *maðǫ́* 'steal' optionally can merge, becoming *mǫǫ*.

(57) *waðímǫǫ akxai*
wa-ðí-ma-ðǫ́ *akxa-ðe*
VAL-P2S-PREV-steal 3.CONT-DECL
'he stole from you'

***wa* + *ǫ́* → *wǫ́*.** When *wa* 'them' is prefixed to *ǫ́ðe* 'discard', *a-ǫ́* obligatorily becomes *ǫ́* (or *ǫ́ǫ*):

(58) *wǫ́ǫbre*
wa-ǫ́-Wa-ðe
P3P-PREV-A1S-discard
'I left them, quit them'

***a* + *ðe* → *e*.** The semantically opaque but morphologically causative verb *mąxíðe* 'deceive' takes regular inflection, such as valence reducer *wa* and A1S *Wa*, immediately to the left of *ðe*, and the *ð* tends to elide, leaving *mąxíwae* 'deceive folks', whereupon the resulting vowel sequence *ae* optionally contracts to *e*:

(59) *mąxíawe*
mąxi-Wa-wa-ðe
deceive-A1S-VAL-CAU
'I'm lying; I'm deceiving someone'

The same thing frequently happens in other *ðe* causatives. Another is *toníðe* 'scold within an inch of one's life' (more literally, 'barely allow to live'; even more literally, 'cause to be barely alive').

(60) *toníðape*
to-ní-Ø-Ø-ðe-api-ðe
barely-be.alive-P3S-A3P-CAU-PL-DECL
'they bawled him out'

Here, too, we may see vowel contraction reducing a vowel cluster that results from deletion of *ð* (in this case, *aa* from *aða* in *toníwaðape*).

(61) *toníwaape*
to-ní-wa-Ø-ðe-api-ðe
barely-be.alive-P1P-A3P-CAU-PL-DECL
'she bawled us out'

a + o → o. The V1-V2 Rule optionally applies even across word boundaries. Thus, in the example below, the final vowel of the subject marker *akxa* (last element of the noun phrase *níi akxa* 'water [subject]') is deleted before initial *o* of the following verb.

(62) *mąąšcé tą níi əkx opˀą́į nąpée*
mąąšcé tą níi akxa opˀą́ðe ną-api-ðe
hot.weather when water SUBJ steam ITER-PL-DECL
'in hot weather that water steams'

A similar contraction occurs between members of a compound in the next example: the final *a* of *sį́ka* 'squirrel' is deleted before the initial vowel of *océ* 'look', leaving *o* only, in 'squirrel-hunting'. (It is not unusual to find accent shifting to the morphologically complex syllable.)

(63) *sįkóce ąkái hce*
sįka-océ ąk-aðe hce
squirrel-look.for A1P-go INJ
'let's go squirrel hunting'

Likewise, the *a* of *htáa* 'meat' disappears before the *o* of *oolą́* 'put on' in the following compound.

(64) *htóolą*
htáa-oolą́
meat-put.on
'sandwich'

Contraction is optional in this compound, however; the alternative form *htáaoolą* is equally correct.

a + į → į. Contraction of *aį* to *į* may be seen in the 3rd person form *ažį́* 'he thinks', and in the first person dual-plural form *ąkážį* 'we think'. (The underlying form of the stem 'think' is *aža_į*, as other forms in the paradigm below make clear. See, however, the discussion of *ažį́* as optionally inflecting in section 3.2.4.4.) Contraction is obligatory in this verb.

(65) *ažámį*
aža-m-į
PREV-A1S-think
'I think'

(66) *ažážį*
aža-ž-į
PREV-A2S-think
'you think'

(67) *ažį*
aža-Ø-į
PREV-A3S-think
'he thinks'

(68) *ąkážį*
ąk-aža-į
A1P-PREV-think
'we think'

***a* + *a* → *a*.** Contraction of identical vowels between members of a compound is seen in the example below. (The final long vowel *įį* has secondary stress.)

(69) *hkáwalįį*
hkáwa-á-lįį
horse-upon-sit
'horseback'

2.3.4.2 Raising of *e* to *i*

There is a general rule in Osage at the utterance level that optionally raises *e* to *i* in word-final position, especially when accented, but also when unaccented, as is the case with *níhce* in the example below.

(70) *níhci akxái*
ní-Ø-hce akxá-ðe
PREV-P3S-cold 3.CONT-DECL
'he's cold'

This raising seems to be especially prevalent with frequently used expressions, indicating perhaps a less formal pronunciation. The common expression for 'it's cold' (speaking of the weather) varies between *níwahce* and *níwahci*.

Raising of *e* to *i* may prevent *e* from being deleted by the V1-V2 Rule. Thus, the final *e* of the stem *ðaaché* 'eat' in (71) is raised to *i* instead of being lost before *api* 'plural'.

(71) *sitóį súhka ąðáachipe*
sitóį súhka ą-ðaaché-api-ðe
yesterday chicken A1P-eat-PL-DECL
'yesterday we ate chicken'

2.4 Accent

A complete study of accent in Osage has not been undertaken. This section contains observations and a rough approach to an analysis for accent, based on a general review of data. As most Siouanists would agree, exact rules for accent are difficult in these languages, whose history has obscured many of the processes that affect surface accent patterns.

It may prove ultimately to be the case that Osage has a pitch accent system, rather than an accent system. Investigators in related languages are beginning to analyze their accent systems in this light (so reported by Koontz [p.c. 1994] for Omaha-Ponca; see also Rankin [1996]).

Generally speaking, accent is found on the first or second syllable of the Osage word. Secondary accent usually occurs on every second syllable thereafter, but is not marked here.

Recall that the form of the verb root used on the morpheme analysis line of examples (the second line) is the citation form, which is, in fact, the same as the third person form.[32] Speakers very commonly refer to a citation form of an Osage verb and give its English gloss as, e.g., 'to eat', or 'to hit someone with something'. Hence, an accent has been included on the syllable on which it falls in third person. (Thus in the morpheme analysis line, 'eat' is given as *ðaaché*, the same as the form meaning 'he/she eats'.)

With the multiple derivational elements found in many Osage verbs, and their interaction with inflectional material, as well as what often seems to be arbitrary lengthening and shortening of vowels, it is difficult to sort out accent in Osage. The simple guidelines offered in this section will shed light on many forms but will not explain all of those found. A thorough study of the underlying forms of roots and stems under a diachronic focus, and correlation of these factors with the classes of inflectional and derivational morphemes which are added synchronically to the basic forms would be needed in order to produce a more coherent account of the behavior of accent in this language.

2.4.1 Accent in nouns, modifiers, and other nonverbal elements

In nouns, modifiers, and other nonverb elements, it is common to find accent on the first syllable.

Rankin (p.c. 1994) adds support to this impressionistic evaluation, with the historical insight that, for many such noun stems, the stressed syllable was formerly preceded by an unstressed syllable such as **wi* that was then deleted. That is, the present-day first syllable of such stems was the second syllable historically. Thus the more regular rule operating in most verbs, that is, accent on the second syllable, likely was quite general earlier in the evolution of Osage.

[32] Only one exception comes to mind: *aža_į* 'think, believe' has a third person form *ažį́* 'he thinks' via vowel contraction.

Examples of nouns and other forms with first syllable accent include: *htóho* 'green, blue'; *šáhpe* 'six'; *šáake* 'hand'; *níhka* 'man' ; *hcéska* 'cow'; *mą́ze* 'metal'; *hcéka* 'new'; *mǫ́šǫ* 'feather'.

There are many counterexamples to the general rule of first syllable accent in nonverbal elements. Some of these have obvious explanations. Two such are *wakʔó* 'woman' and *wažį́ka* 'bird', both of which have the derivational *wa* as first syllable.

It is not surprising that a few verbs, such as the active *wį́kše* 'tell the truth; be true' and the stative *níhce* 'be cold', that are identical to nouns (*wį́kše* 'truth' and *níhce* 'cold'), retain accent on the first syllable and thus are exceptions to the general second-syllable accent pattern of verbs.

(72) *wį́ðakše?*
wį́-Ya-kše
PREV-A2S-be.truthful
'are you telling the truth?'

(73) *wį́ąðakše hta ðąąšé*
wį́-ą-Ya-kše *hta* *Ya-ðaįšé*
PREV-P1S-be.truthful FUT 2S.CONT
'will you be true to me?'

(74) *wį́kše akxa*
wį́-Ø-kše *akxa*
PREV-A3S-be.truthful 3.CONT
'he's telling the truth'

2.4.2 Accent in verbs

Broadly speaking, accent falls on the second syllable of the Osage verb, including any prefixes, and rarely if ever later than that syllable. In general, that is, if a prefixed syllable (inflectional or derivational material) is added to the left of the verb root or stem, counting of syllables begins anew from the left to retain second-syllable accent; the effect is that accent will then fall one syllable leftward of where it would have fallen without the added syllable.

Thus, for instance, when the locative prefix *o* is added to *ðuucʔáke* 'be unable', accent shifts to the syllable *ðuu* to give *oðúucʔake* 'be tired of'; when the valence reducer *wa* 'stuff, folks' is prefixed to *ðaawá* 'count', accent shifts to the syllable *ðaa*, giving *waðáawa* 'count stuff'.

Similarly, 'cry' without prefixes is *ɣaaké*, but accent shifts to the syllable *ɣaa* when an agent pronominal prefix is added: *aɣáake* 'I cry', *ðaɣáake* 'you cry', *ąɣáake* 'we cry'. 'Help' is *ohká*, but 'he helps me' (with 1S patient prefix *ą*) is *ową́hką* (or harmonized *ąwą́hką*). Further examples of accent shift owing to inflectional prefixation can be seen with *ootá* 'borrow' in the following set of examples:

(75) *mą́zeska oowáta hkǫ́brai*
mą́ze-ska oo-Wa-tá Wa-kǫ́-Wa-ða-ðe
metal-white PREV-A1S-borrow A1S-PREV-A1S-want-DECL
'I want to borrow money'

(76) *ooðátaai*
oo-Ya-tá-ðe
PREV-A2S-borrow-DECL
'you borrow'

(77) *ąkóotape*
ąk-ootá-api-ðe
A1P-borrow-PL-DECL
'we borrow'

(78) *ée ootápe*
ée oo-Ø-Ø-tá-api-ðe
3.PRON PREV-P3S-A3S-borrow-PL-DECL
'he borrowed it'

(79) *ootá!*
Ø-ootá-a
it-borrow-IMPER
'borrow it!'

Similarly, accent predictably shifts to the initial syllable *ðaa* 'by mouth' of the verb stem *ðaak*ˀ*į́* 'spit' when it ends up as the second syllable in the word, after *ą(k)* '1P agent' is added to the left of the verb stem.

(80) *ąðáak*ˀ*įpe*
*ąk-ðak*ˀ*į́-api-ðe*
A1P-spit-PL-DECL
'we spit'

In the following example, accent is removed even from the root (which is *ðaahtą́* 'drink' in unprefixed form), and falls instead on the derivational prefix *wa* 'stuff' (valence reducer), since *wa* is the second syllable of the word once the inflectional prefix *ąk* is added.

(81) *ąwáðaahtą na*
ąk-wa-ðaahtą́ na
A1P-VAL-drink ITER
'we drink'

2.4.2.1 Accent placement precedes Agent Simplification

Determining which is the second syllable of the verb for purposes of second-syllable accent generally takes account of the underlying forms of inflectional and derivational morphemes; it ignores the contraction of syllables by the V1-V2 Rule and syncopation of agent prefixes (i.e., Agent Simplification). This means that accent falls on the (surface) first syllable of a verb if Agent Simplification or the V1-V2 Rule has removed the vowel of the underlying first syllable of the verb.

For example, consider *ðaaché* 'eat'. Addition of *Wa* '1S agent' produces *Wa* + *ðaaché*, in which *ðaa* is the new second syllable. Accent now falls on that syllable, giving *Waðáache*. Then *Wa* becomes *b* by Agent Simplification plus Stop Formation, while *ð* changes to *r* (by Rhotacization), giving *bráache* (not ***braaché*). In a rule-ordering model, we would have to say that accent is assigned before vowel syncope (Agent Simplification and the V1-V2 Rule) occurs.

Similar accentual behavior can be seen in the 1S forms of *ðaahtą́* 'drink', *ðuucʔáke* 'be unable', and *ðuwį́* 'buy', which are respectively *bráahtą* 'I drink', *brúucʔake* 'I am unable', and *brúwį* 'I buy'.

The agent prefix is not always the first syllable of the underlying form of the verb. For example, the stem *waaðǫ́* 'sing' places pronominal prefixes before the syllable *ðǫ* and after *waa*, so that the 1S form is underlyingly *waa-Wa-ðǫ* (with prefix *Wa* '1S agent'). To this, second-syllable accent placement applies, giving *waa-Wá-ðǫ*. When Agent Simplification then deletes the vowel of the pronominal prefix (with adjustment of *W* to *b* and *ð* to *r*), accent moves onto the following syllable, giving the surface form *waabrǫ́* 'I sing'.

2.4.2.2 Accent placement follows *wa*-Metathesis

Second syllable accent placement follows the rule of *wa* (or *waa*) Metathesis (for which, see section 3.4.1.1; metathesis of *wa(a)* occurs regardless of whether that element is the valence reducer or simply an opaque part of the stem). This can be seen in verbs like *waachí* 'dance', *waašká* 'do one's best', and *wanǫ́bre* 'dine', all of which have second syllable accent in citation form and take regular inflection after the preverb *wa* or *waa*. The 1S form has a regular agent pronominal *a*. Then *wa-a* metathesis switches the positions of *wa* or *waa* and the agent prefix *a*, and accent is placed on the second syllable of the resulting form, as seen in (82)–(84).

(82) *awáachi hta mįkšé*
 waa-Wa-chí hta mįkšé
 PREV-A1S-dance FUT 1S.CONT
 'I'll dance'

(83) *awáaškǫ*
waa-Wa-šką́
PREV-A1S-do.one's.best
'I'm doing my best'

(84) *awánǫbre*
wa-Wa-nǫ́bre
PREV-A1S-dine
'I dined'

The same thing happens when the pronominal prefix is *ą* (from *ąk* '1P agent'), as in (85).

(85) *ąwáachipe*
ąk-waa-chí-api-ðe
A1P-PREV-dance-PL-DECL
'we danced'

2.4.2.3 Locative prefixes and accent placement

The locative prefixes *á*, *i* (or *ii*), and *o* affect accent placement in different ways.

In verbs with prefix *o*, accent follows the normal second syllable rule, as in *oðúucˀake* 'be tired of' (compare *ðuucˀáke* 'be unable'), *oðáake* 'tell [as a story]', *ochį́* 'hit'. (For accented prefix *ó* from *wa* + *o*, see section 2.4.2.4.)

In verbs with the prefix *á*, the *á* remains accented throughout the inflected paradigms, even when it is the first syllable of the word. Witness the inherently accented locative-benefactive *á* retaining accent in 'crying on/over you' (86), preempting the second-syllable accent rule.

(86) *áðiɣaaki apai*
á-ði-ɣaaké apa-ðe
LOC-P2S-cry 3.CONT-DECL
'they're crying for you'

The locative-benefactive *á* contracts with *ą* '1S patient' in (87) and with *ą* '1P agent' in (88) to give accented *ą́* (or possibly *ą́ą*).

(87) *ą́ðuuwį*
á-ą-ðuuuwį́
LOC-P1S-buy
'buy for me'

(88) *ą́ðaakˀįpe*
á-ą-ðaakˀį́-api-ðe
LOC-P1S-spit-PL-DECL
'they spit me out; they spit on me'

Inherently accented locative *á* likewise remains accented in the doubly inflected compound *áa_lǫ_ðį* 'forget':

(89) *áalǫbrį*
áa-Wa-lǫ-Wa-ðį
LOC-A1S-PREV-A1S-forget
'I forget'

(90) *áðalǫšcį*
áa-Ya-lǫ-Ya-ðį
LOC-A2-PREV-A2-forget
'you forget'

(91) *áalǫðį apái*
áa-Ø-lǫ-Ø-ðį *apa-ðe*
LOC-A3-PREV-A3-forge 3.CONT-DECL
'he forgets; they're forgetting; he's forgotten'

In *i*- or *ii*-initial regular verbs with *ð*-Epenthesis, accent is on the *i*- or *ii*- throughout the paradigm, except that accent shifts to the second syllable in the 1S agent form. This accent shift is the sole distinguishing feature separating 1S agent forms from 2S agent forms for these verbs. The first *ð* in the 1S form is epenthetic.

(92) *íiðe*
íi-Ø-ðe
PREV-A3S-see
'he/she sees'

(93) *iiðáðe*
ii-ð-Wa-ðe
PREV-EPð-A1S-see
'I see'

(94) *íiðaðe*
ii-Ya-ðe
PREV-A2-see
'you see'

Hundreds of other *ii*- or *i*- verbs exist exhibiting this same accent pattern.

2.4.2.4 Coalescence

A syllable resulting from the coalescence of two morphemes is usually accented when it is the first or second syllable in the word. This generalization accounts for many cases of first-syllable accent.

One common situation in which coalescence occurs is when a prefix of the shape *wa* (the valence reducer, or the 3P patient prefix) is followed by one of the locative prefixes *á*, *i*, or *o*. The prefixes contract as follows:

wa + *á* becomes *wá*; *wa* + *i* becomes *wé*; and *wa* + *o* becomes *ó* (with deletion of *w* before the rounded vowel *o*). Thus, for instance, when the valence reducer *wa* is prefixed to *oxpáðe* 'lose (transitive)', the result is *óxpaðe* 'lose stuff (intransitive)'. The following examples illustrate the same process with the transitive verb *o_ðáake* 'tell; recount'.

(95) *oðáaka*
o-Ø-ðáake-a
PREV-P3S-tell-IMPER
'tell it' (imperative)

(96) *óðaake*
wa-o-ðáake
VAL-PREV-tell
'tell things' (citation form)

(See also sections 4.1.4–4.1.5 for further discussion of derivation and accent with respect to *o*.)

When *wa* is prefixed to an *i*-initial stem, the effect of coalescence is to erase the stress difference that distinguishes 1S agent from 2 agent forms with such stems (see section 2.4.2.3). This happens as follows: The addition of *wa* causes the *i* to be the second syllable; the second-syllable accent rule then applies before the coalescence of *wa-i* to *we*. Thus, *wéðaðe* means both 'I see them' (from the stem *íiðe* 'see', with prefixes *wa* '3P patient' and *a* '1S agent') and 'you [singular] see them' (with prefix *ða* '2S agent').

Another sort of coalescence involves the dative prefix *ki* and the instrumental prefix *kaa*. These prefixes are typically obscured by presence of inflectional prefixes, but the inflectional prefix then bears accent. (See section 4.4.3 for discussion and examples of *kaa* 'by striking, by sudden application of force', and section 4.6.5 for *ki*.)

In some verbs, an otherwise unexplained first-syllable accent can be traced to the historical coalescence of the initial syllable of the stem with a prefix that is now opaque. It is quite likely, for example, that the accented initial locative prefix *á* and the accented initial *í* found in many verbs come from morphemically complex forms historically where second syllable accent applied before coalescence, leaving an initial accented syllable. The inflectional prefix *wi* '1S agent with 2 patient' often retains accent as well when it is the initial syllable of a verb form (see section 3.1.5); this may be because *wi* is historically complex, derived by coalescence from *Wa* '1S agent' + *ði* '2S patient'. The prefix *hkik* 'reflexive' also seems to retain accent when it is initial, and may derive from a complex older form comprised of two syllables, now opaque.

2.4.2.5 Accented *wá*

Some instances of initial-syllable accent cannot be explained by underlying morphemic complexity. I account for these by specifying that certain derivational or inflectional morphemes carry inherent accent under certain conditions, and as such will preempt the second-syllable accent rule. For example, 3P patient with *ð*-stems is accented *wá*, rather than the accentless *wa* found with other verbs. Why this should be so is unclear; we simply stipulate that with *ð*-stems, *wá* P3P has inherent accent. Thus *wá* '3P patient' + *ðaawá* 'count' becomes *wáðaawa* 'count them', wherein the general rule of second syllable accent has been overridden by inherent accent on *wá*; that is to say, *wá* retains its accent even when it is in first syllable position. The 3P patient prefix contrasts with the valence reducer, which is unaccented *wa* even with *ð*-stems; the valence reducer added to *ðaawá* gives *waðáawa* 'count things, stuff'.

In (97), a form of *mąðǫ́* 'steal' appears, where again there is a 3P patient *wa* taking inherent stress before a *ð*-stem, thus overriding the second syllable accent rule. And in (98) we see that the valence reducer *wa* does not override the second syllable accent rule (that is, is not inherently accented); accent in this form has shifted to the second syllable. (See section 4.1.2 for more discussion of this verb.)

(97) *wámąbrǫðe*
wá-mą-Wa-ðǫ́-ðe
P3P-steal-A1S-CAU-DECL
'I stole them'

(98) *wamą́brǫ̀[ð]e*
wa-mą-Wa-ðǫ-ðe
VAL-steal-A1S-CAU-DECL
'I stole [things]'

In (98) and (99), the newly assigned accent on *mą́* is followed by a syllable that retains some of the original accent for this verb (*mąðǫ́*), so that both *mą́* and the following syllable are heard as rather forcefully accented; although the accent on third-syllable *ǫ* is secondary, it is especially noticeable owing to its unusual occurrence contiguous to the primary accent. (In (97), secondary accent occurs on the third syllable, *brǫ*, as well, but this represents the normal pattern whereby every second syllable after a primary accent receives secondary accent.)

(99) *wamą́ðǫ̀e*
wa-mąðǫ́-ðe
VAL-steal-CAU
'steal [things, stuff]'

2.4.2.6 Compounds and causatives

In compounds of two roots, the first of the two roots is accented and retains this accent. Thus, the verb *_kǫ́_ða* 'want', a doubly-inflecting compound, with two syncopating members, retains accent in the first syllable. (As evidence that *kǫ́ða* is a compound, note the double inflection in, e.g., *hkǫ́bra* 'I want', from underlying *Wa + kǫ́ + Wa + ða*.)

A common sort of compound is that in which a root is followed by the causative root *ðe*. In such compounds, too, the first, or primary, root bears the accent, as in *cˀéðe* 'make to die, kill'. Another causative compound, *ščéðe* 'doctor', can be seen in (100)–(103).

(100) *ščéą̨ða!*
ščé-ą̨-ðe-a
doctor-P1S-CAU-IMPER
'doctor me!'

(101) *ščéwiemą̨ži*
ščé-wi-ðe-maži
doctor-A1S.P2S-CAU-1S.NEG
'I won't doctor you'[33]

(102) *ščéwai hta mį̨kšé*
ščé-wa-ðe hta mį̨kšé
doctor-P3P-CAU FUT 1S.CONT
'I'll doctor them'

(103) *tówa kše ščéða!*
tówa kše ščé-ðe-a
3.PRON LIE doctor-CAU-IMPER
'doctor him!' (more precisely, 'doctor that one lying there!')

Inflectional elements which follow the first member of the compound belong to the second member of the compound, and these thus will not affect the accent on the primary root in these compounds. Thus, in (100) the accent has not shifted to the 1S patient inflection *ą̨*, and in (101) it has not shifted to *wi*.

2.4.2.7 Accent deflection

Surprisingly, in some contexts, 1P patient *wa* 'us' is an accent deflector, deflecting accent one syllable to the left of itself. This is possibly a corollary to the inherent accent on 3P patient *wá* before *ð*-stems mentioned above. Contrast (104) with (105). In the first of these, the accent falls predictably on the second syllable (1S patient *ą̨*). In (105), 1P patient *wa* is

[33] In this example, verb-final *e* has not been replaced by *a* before the negative as one might expect (see section 2.3.3.5). The same speaker does, however, also accept the contracted form *ščéwiamaží*.

in second syllable position, and would be expected to bear accent. However, here as in numerous other similar cases, 1P patient *wa* seems to be accent-shy; that is, it rarely receives accent and seems to deflect the point of accent one syllable leftward. It should be mentioned, however, that this particular verb is principally stative except for the instance with two animate arguments such as the one mentioned here, so that other factors may be at play.

(104) *ǫwą́ðaxpai*
o-w-ą-Ya-xpáðe
PREV-EP*w*-P1S-A2S-lose
'you lost me'

(105) *ówaðaxpai*
o-wa-Ya-xpáðe
PREV-P1P-A2S-lose
'you lost us'

2.4.2.8 Vowel length

Vowel length can give rise to apparent accent. One of the difficulties of Osage is its long vowels, unrecorded in all previous work on the language. Length can easily be perceptually mistaken as accent by the linguist or learner. Thus, the verb *hiiðá* 'bathe' is easily mistakenly transcribed as *hiiðaa* or as *híðá*. Long vowels that can be mistaken for accented ones can also be created by the addition of the declarative ending *ðe* to a verb with final *e*, followed by elision of *ð*, creating a double vowel sequence *ee*. For example, *škáaɣee* 'you've done it, made it' in (106) below can readily be misheard as *škáaɣée*. The verb form would be *škáaɣe* under normal circumstances. The final long *ee* emerges from *škáaɣe ðe*, with *ðe* being the declarative ending, the appropriateness of such an ending being enhanced by the semantic context.

(106) *ðáalį škáaɣee*
ðáalį Ya-kaaɣe ðe
good A2S-make DECL
'you've done well; you've made that well'

2.5 Osage phonology in the work of previous scholars

2.5.1 La Flesche

Francis La Flesche accomplished much valuable work in gathering words for inclusion in a lexicon (1932).[34] La Flesche's efforts are quite remarkable for the time, and also include several different works recording various rites and ceremonies of the tribe. La Flesche was a scholar, but not strictly speaking a linguist, and unfortunately his knowledge of his native language, Omaha-Ponca, influenced his transcription of Osage. For example, he writes <b> for the lenis voiceless labial stop rather than <p>. (When it appears in clusters, however, he writes it as <p>, as in <psh> for *pš*.) He writes the fortis voiceless labial stop *hp* or *pp* as <p̣> (with an underdot), but describes it as "a medial p (between p and b)" (La Flesche 1932:3), which is more appropriately a description for the lenis *p* which he wrote as <b>. Such confusion is pervasive in his lexicon; thus it is easy to understand why many people have had difficulty in trying to use this otherwise valuable work.

Other phonetic problems exist; for example, for *tx*, La Flesche writes <t> alone (sometimes with an underdot: <ṭ>) and sometimes <d>. Also, he is an unreliable source for the distinction between *x* and *ɣ*, as well as for that between regular and long vowels. He also uses <ç> to represent both *s* and *z*, which are certainly distinct in present-day Osage.

La Flesche's Osage dictionary includes many incorrect forms which are likely from his own Omaha language, especially in inflectional paradigms. The following is not an exhaustive list, but is offered to elucidate some parts of table 2.3.

(a) Erroneous *šn-* for *št-/ šc-*. La Flesche very frequently gives *šn-* forms for the 2s of verbs with inflectable initial *ð*, instead of the correct Osage form *št-* or *šc-* (depending on the following vowel). The erroneous *šn-* forms sound completely un-Osage and even comical to Osage ears, usually eliciting a laugh. Thus, for example, from *áðiitą* 'pull to, pull over', we find La Flesche <a´-shni-do^{n}> 'you pulled it over' (La Flesche 1932:15), which should be *áščitą*. This error occurs as well in his recordings of the (uninflected) Osage iterative *štą*, giving erroneous <shna> 'habitually' as in the example given under <ça´-ḳiu> 'watermelon' (La Flesche32:29) and in other places; but curiously *štą* is given correctly as <shto^{n}> 'in the habit of; habitually; constantly' in its own entry (La

[34] I have reworked a good portion of this for incorporation in a dictionary of Osage now in progress and nearing completion, and plan as well to process the remaining portions of the La Flesche dictionary in the future.

Flesche 1932:134). The user should be aware that such inconsistencies are common in La Flesche's dictionary.

(b) Erroneous *sn-* for *st-, sc-*. La Flesche erroneously lists Omaha-Ponca *sn-* (written by him as <çn->) instead of the correct Osage *st-/sc-* in, e.g., <çna′-the> 'to grease a wagon or oil machinery' (La Flesche 1932:31), which should be *stáðe* (*sta_ðe*) 'apply a smooth coating such as paint, grease, oil, ointment; anoint; paint' (transitive verb).

(c) Erroneous *n-* for *št-/šc-*. Another problem is La Flesche's use of *n* in lieu of the correct *šc* or *št*, as in the verb <tha-shtoⁿ′> (La Flesche 1932:141) 'stop' (*ðaaštą́* 'finish, stop, by mouth or with the mouth'), where La Flesche's 2s form <na-shtoⁿ> 'you stop crying' should be *štáaštą*. Similarly, his 2s form <u-ni ge> 'you hold' (La Flesche 1932:181, under the entry <u′-xta>) which should be *oščįįke*. (Elsewhere, however, La Flesche gives this form more properly as <u-stsiⁿ′-ge> [La Flesche 1932:177] 'you seized him', corresponding to modern *oščįįke*.) Likewise, the verb *ðiištą́* (his <thi-shtoⁿ′> [La Flesche 1932:149]) 'finish, stop' should have *šcíištą* as its 2s form and not La Flesche's <ni′-shtoⁿ>.

(d) Erroneous <t> or <ṭ> for *ch* or *hc*. These usages by La Flesche reflect forms that were possibly undergoing change in the late nineteenth and early twentieth century rather than unabashed use of Omaha-Ponca in lieu of Osage forms as in the *šn*, *sn*, and *n* errors discussed just above. In nearly every instance where La Flesche has <te ti tu> we will find in modern Osage *che chi chu*. (In some places La Flesche uses <d> or <t> where *tx* should appear, or <k, ḳ> for *kx* and <p> for *px*, but we will not illustrate this additional problem here.)

La Flesche's under-dot series <ṭe ṭi ṭu> corresponds to modern Osage *hce hci hcu*, and even occasionally *che chi chu*. For example, four forms in <ṭe> appear on page 139 of La Flesche (1932), one of which suffices to illustrate: <ṭe-zhe-be te oⁿ-gu-ga′-ts'iⁿ> 'we peeped in the door'. The correct version would be *hcižépe che ąkókaacʔį́* (this retranscription also includes the correction of several other errors not under discussion here). La Flesche lists only two forms in initial <ṭi> (1932:155), both of which should have initial *hci*: <ṭi-dse> 'the sound of a drum or the thud of many feet' (*hcíce*) and <ṭi-thu'-zha> 'to scrub the house' (*hcí ðuužá* or *hciðúuža*). As for La Flesche's <ṭu>, it is usually *hto* in modern Osage.

In a different vein, La Flesche represents Osage *br* as <bth>, which may be historically valid, but is suspiciously similar to Omaha. Likewise, most words that now have *l* in Osage appear in the La Flesche dictionary with <gth>. He writes <u> in many Osage words that now have *o* or *i*. Several of these problems are probably the result of rapid language evolution, rather than errors by La Flesche. He transcribes *ą* as <ǫ>; in this regard, one should note that there is quite a bit of variation between *ǫ* and *ą* in Osage speech today.

There are a number of other problems with using La Flesche's work, including simple typographical errors and transcriptional errors, perhaps introduced by his assistants. For a reliable review of these considerations, see Koontz (1993).

Table 2.3 compares La Flesche's transcription of Osage with mine. It includes not only the correspondences that are regular and purely orthographic, but also many which are merely corrective, encompassing most of the errors that characterize his lexicon.

TABLE 2.3. COMPARISON WITH LA FLESCHE'S TRANSCRIPTION

LA FLESCHE	QUINTERO
'	ʔ
a	*a*
b	*p*
b	*b*
ç	*s, z*
çd	*st*
çk	*sk*
çp	*sp*
çts	*sc*
d	*t, tx*
ds	*c, č*
e	*e*
g	*k*
gth	*l*
h	*h*
i	*i, u*
iu	*i, u*
*i*ⁿ	*į*
k	*kx, kš*
ksh	*kš*
kch	*kš, kx*
ḳ	*hk, kx*
ḳ'	*kʔ*
m	*m*
n	*n*
n (in second person of *ð*-stems)	*št, šc*
o	*o*

LA FLESCHE	QUINTERO
*o*ⁿ	*ą, ǫ*
p	*px, pš*
psh	*pš*
p̣	*hp, p, px*
p̣'	*pʔ*
sh	*š*
shk	*šk*
shn	*št, šc*
shp	*šp*
sht	*št*
sn	*št, šc*
sts	*šc*
t	*tx, ch*
th	*ð, r*
ts	*ch, hc*
ṭ	*ht*
ṭs	*hc, ch*
ṭ'	*cʔ*
ṭs'	*cʔ*
u	*i, o, u*
w	*w*
x	*ɣ, x*
xth	*l*
xp	*xp*
xt	*xt*
xts	*xc*
zh	*ž*

2.5.2 Wolff

Hans Wolff's description of Osage phonology (Wolff 1952a, 1952b) suffers from many defects. One source of problems is that, like many of his contemporaries, Wolff thought Osage would be just like Dakota with a few minor adjustments. This is not the case. Even apart from this erroneous assumption, though, there is a great deal wrong with Wolff's analysis of Osage. No claim can plausibly be made that he was describing an earlier dialect or more conservative phonology.[35]

[35] In fact, the most reliable transcription of Osage from early days comes from Dorsey (1883a, 1883b, 1888), who recorded forms match those I have collected from speakers in the late twentieth century and which appear throughout this volume. After a

Wolff claims that there are two dialects of Osage, a *br* dialect and a *bl* dialect. In reality, only *br* appears in Osage, any words pronounced with [bl] sounding to speakers as if they are Ponca words. Thus Wolff's description of dialects in Osage is false; no such *bl* dialect exists or was described by any earlier record.

Wolff mistakenly regards preaspirated or "long" (that is, geminate) stops and long vowels as a stylistic device. He states that they characterize "Style II," which he describes as having a slow, deliberate tempo, frequent pauses and emphatic syllable division; but, he says, "long" stops and long vowels do not appear in "Style I" ("normal conversational discourse") (1952a:63). The truth is that these geminate or preaspirated stops and long vowels are lexically distinctive and certainly not merely a matter of style. Unfortunately, Wolff chooses to regard Style I (the one he says is lacking these important geminate stops and long vowels) as the norm in his discussion of Osage phonemics, and predicates his entire analysis on this error.

Wolff considers nasality a separate phoneme, rather than a feature of nasal vowels. There is no obvious advantage to this, but it is quite a minor point and stems merely from the differing historical background of Wolff's work. But Wolff also states that "nasal vowels are short, regardless of their position" (1952a:65), which is patently misleading; there are many examples of long nasal vowels in the language, and several minimal pairs contrasting short vs. long nasal vowels.

Wolff asserts that "oral vowels are always long before nonstop consonants and in final accented position" (1952a:65). In support of this, he cites [wéeli] 'head'. His transcription of this example is phonetically accurate, but the distributional claim is wrong. A contrasting form, *wéli* 'oil, grease, fat', also exists, with a short vowel before the same consonant. Indeed, within Wolff's article there are many examples given by the author which contradict his own claims about where long vowels appear. In *brakˀá* 'flat' (1952a:64, 67), for instance, we have a word (correctly transcribed) with a final short accented *á* contradicting his claim that oral vowels are always long in final accented position; Wolff's transcription *iðá mą̨žì* 'I did not see' (1952a:65) presents a short vowel before a nonstop consonant, unless we assume that this is merely a typographical error. (In fact, Wolff's transcription of the latter example is wrong; the correct form is *iiðámaži,* which does have a long vowel before the nonstop consonant.) Such internal contradictions in Wolff's work should be worrisome to the serious reader.

---

certain amount of decoding of Dorsey's orthography, his work is completely readable and agrees with the analysis I have presented here, based on data I gathered from speakers before ever examining Dorsey's work.

Vowels preceding a preaspirated stop, such as in *ðaahtą́* 'drink' are not always, as Wolff claims "very short and clipped" (1952a:66), although very short vowels may be found in this position. One supposes that what he describes as "clipped" was his interpretation of the preaspiration [h].

Wolff represents fortis (preaspirated or geminate) stops as combinations of a phoneme of syllabic juncture # with a following stop: *#p #t #k*. He claims that this juncture phoneme "may occur immediately following the stressed syllable and at the end of any subsequent syllable" (1952a:65) and "does not occur after nasal vowels, vowel clusters, nor before CC" (1952a:66). In other words, he claims that fortis stops do not occur initially in accented syllables nor in syllables before the accent, and also do not occur after nasal vowels. These claims about the distribution of fortis stops are incorrect. Fortis stops do occur in positions before the accent (as, for example, in *wahką́ta* 'God', mistranscribed by Wolff as *waką́ta* [1952a:65], and in many other examples in the present work). Even word-initially, they can be quite clearly heard (perhaps after some practice), especially if another word precedes the word whose initial consonant is a fortis stop; an example of such a word is *hką́ące* 'apple, fruit', transcribed by Wolff as *ką́tse* (and glossed by him as 'plum, peach' [1952a:66]). Fortis stops occur after nasal vowels, too, as in *šómįhkasi* 'coyote', *mą́įhka* ~ *mǫ́įhka* 'earth, soil', *mąhkása* 'coffee', *mąhká* 'medicine'.

Wolff failed to perceive the distinction between lenis *c* and fortis *hc*; thus, he incorrectly writes *tsí* or *tší* (in his orthography, corresponding to *ci*, *či* in mine) for *hci* 'house', and *tséska* for the correct *hceská* 'cow' (1952a:65).

In addition, there are numerous words where Wolff failed to hear fortis stops even in postaccentual positions. For example, he writes *štátą* for *štáahtą* 'you drank it', *pšiita* (erroneously glossed 'I'll come') for *pší hta* 'I'll arrive there' (where *hta* is the future marker, not specifically identified as such by Wolff), and *súka* for *súhka* 'chicken' (Wolff 1952a:65).

Wolff has problems with postaspirates too. His *ðacpé* 'eat' should be *ðaaché*, and may be a typographical error. He does not specifically mention postaspirated *ch*, nor the related sequences *px tx kx* before back vowels and *pš kš* which occur before nonback vowels.

Wolff fails to distinguish between *x* and *ɣ*, writing only *x* and mentioning "variants": "[ɣ] intervocalically and [x] in other positions" (1952a:64). In reality, both *x* and *ɣ* occur initially and intervocalically, and contrast with each other (although only *x* occurs in clusters). Admittedly, the distinction between *x* and *ɣ* is difficult to hear without some experience or help.

Wolff reports *ð* as [d] initially, of which there is no evidence in modern Osage. His account of *ð* as *y*, however, is reflected in an early tape of an Osage event recorded by others.

Wolff also transcribes *ðáabrį* 'three' as [ðabǫðį]; this pronunciation is confirmed as well by an early sound recording, but the modern word is *ðáabrį*.

He considers *br* a single phoneme, presumably so as not to contradict his generalization that "only voiceless consonants form clusters" (1952a:64). In fact, most instances of *br* can be shown to derive from underlying *Wa* '1S agent' plus initial *ð* of the verb stem; it is surely most reasonable to treat *br* as a cluster.

Wolff's list of first consonants in clusters, given as *s*, *š*, *x*, and *h*, in effect splits off the *h* of the preaspirated "variants" [ʰp ʰt ʰk] as a separate member of a cluster, which seems contradictory to his treatment of fortis consonants elsewhere. He reports the sequence *xk* as a cluster, giving *mǫįxka* 'soil' as an example. In fact, *xk* does not exist in Osage, and 'soil' is *mą́įhka* or *mǫ́įhka*, itself a counterexample to Wolff's claim that fortis stops do not occur after nasal vowels.

Wolff treats the glottal stop (ˀ) as an allophone of *h*, giving *cˀe* 'die, he died' an underlying form *che*. This is patently false. The form *che* in Osage is a demonstrative and a subordinating conjunction, clearly contrasting with *cˀe* 'die'. As for *h*, he only states "Phoneme h is always voiceless" (1952a:64), and he does not discuss its distribution as a single segment or in clusters (except for proposing *hC* clusters, as noted above).

Various other mistaken assumptions and incorrect forms occur here and there throughout Wolff's articles.

2.6 Sound symbolism

Certain occurrences of sound symbolism are found in Osage, conveying degree or intensity by means of a phonetic progression.

Vowel and consonant changes are seen in the series *paakˀǫ́* 'stoop over a little'; *paacˀó* 'stoop over'; *paacˀį́* 'stoop over as to touch toes'.

Consonant gradation often reflects degree of intensity in forms that are semantically related, as in *skike* 'tired', *škike* 'heavy'. The articulatory gradation from *s* to *š* in 'tired' to 'heavy' matches a semantic progression to greater degree; voicing remains constant. In modern speakers, this distinction appears to be fading.

A few other such series can be found, such as the case of *z ž ɣ* contrasts, although examples are hard to come by. For instance, Osage has *bráze* 'torn' and *bráɣe* 'edge' (compare Kansa *blaze* ~ *blaže* 'torn' and *blaɣe* 'edge').

The color names also illustrate a regular and reasonably productive process. While voicing remains constant (specifically, the affected segment is voiceless), there is a clear progression toward the back of the articulatory cavity *s* → *š* → *x*, reflecting increasing intensity semantically. Compare (107a) with (107b), and (108a)–(108c) with (108d)–(108f).

(107a) *sápe*
'black'

(107b) *šápe*
'dark'

(108a) *šóce*
'smoke'

(108b) *níišoce*
nii-šoce
fluid-smoke
'smoke, fog, haze'

(108c) *níišoce akxai*
nii-šoce
fluid-smoke 3.CONT
'it's smoky, there's a fog'

(108d) *xóce*
'gray'

(108e) *níixoce*
nii-xoce
fluid-gray
'ashes'

(108f) *niixócožu*
nii-xóce-o-žu
fluid-gray-PREV-put.in
'ashtray'

The next set of examples, involving the yellow to brown range, obviously shows one and perhaps two progressions or gradations, although this is an area where speakers are hesitant to give categorical glosses, and thus the exact progression is not clear.

(109a) *zi*
'yellow'

(109b) *zíhi*
'yellow, yellow-orange'

(109c) *ži*
'yellow, brown'

(109d) *žíhi*
'brown'

(109e) *zizíhe*
'dark brown'

(109f) *zíži*
'gray(?)'

Palatalization of *t* to *č* and *c* to *č* is used as a diminutive. This type of sound symbolism is pan-Siouan. Related to *wahošta* 'little, narrow, slim; little one, small one, young one', we find:

(110) *wahóščažį*
wa-hóšta-žį
VAL-little-small
'a little bit'

Kinship terms show palatalization for endearment or baby talk; e.g., *wihčóšpa* 'my grandchild' rather than plain *wihcóšpa*. Palatalization of *t* to *č* appears in a very limited number of forms outside the kinship system: *táahpa* 'round' is fairly clearly related to *čáahpa* 'round and short, squat'; more questionably, *tóopa* 'four' may be related to *čóopa* 'a little bit'.

As pointed out by Rankin (p.c. 1994), a similar affrication of dentals before back vowels (but without any sound symbolism) is seen in the kinship terms where historically *ht* has affricated to *hc*:

(111) *ihcóšpa*
'his/her/their grandchild'

(112) *ihcóška*
'nephew' (man's sister's son or woman's brother's son; that is, male offspring of sibling of opposite sex)

(113) *ihcóžąke*
'niece; her brother's daughter' (variant of *ihcióžąke*)

(114) *ihcížo*
'niece; his sister's daughter'

2.7 Reduplication

Root reduplication (more exactly, reduplication of what diachronically was the root, which now may be only part of the root) is evident in Osage, and is fairly productive. Two cases (only) have been found of reduplicated forms based on roots with final *e* that have the vowel *a*, not *e*, a fact unexplained by the V1-V2 Rule (section 2.3.3.2), namely *heháha* 'breathing hard, panting' and *paasása* 'dice'. Other *e*-final roots retain *e* when reduplicated: *eešéše* 'you keep saying', *wahéhe* 'weak', *wahléhle* 'banner, flag', and *šǫǫðéðe* 'forever'. Semantically, the reduplicated forms given here are pervasives, either repeated events or movements, as in set A below, or enduring states, as in set B.

Set A: Repeated events or movements

ðiižą́žą 'shake' (intransitive ***žą́žą* is not used)
ðuusą́sąwį 'twist around, like crepe streamer; shake; turn something over and over' (e.g., *weehli ðuusą́sąwį* 'shake head'; cf. *ðuusáwį* 'turn over, like a plate')
ðuuštáštai 'jerk all one's hair out; make bald'
ðuupˀį́pˀįze 'blink repeatedly'
ðibrúbruɣe 'tremble, shiver' (used for people, animals, and jello, and for 'tree quivering')
ðóðo 'be greasy'
eešéše 'you keep saying' (cf. *éeše* 'you say')[36]
heháha 'breathing hard, panting' (LF *hehé*)
íizizike 'bad things; sick' (cf. *iizíke* 'embarrassed')
kaamášiši 'bouncy, as in a rough car or wagon ride' (cf. *kaamáši* 'bounce up')
kaazą́zą 'bawl out, scold harshly' (cf. *kaazą́* 'scold')
lįįlįįe 'sleep sitting up'
leeléepe 'vomit repeatedly' (cf. *léepe* 'vomit')
nąsą́sąwa 'clap hands'
nąlǫ́lǫ 'call names repeatedly' (cf. *nąlǫ́* 'call names')
níiǫpapa 'lightning'
paasása 'dice' (cf. *paasé* 'cut up [e.g., meat and potatoes]')
pašǫ́šǫwe 'zigzag'
pažáža 'zigzag'
šką́šką́ 'trembly, moving' (e.g., *waskúðe šką́šką́* 'jello'; cf. *šką* 'move')
wáðastástá 'sticky' ('keeps sticking to stuff')
waðíðiški 'a gathering of people' (cf. *ðíški* 'gather')
wahéhe 'weak' (*wahé* is not attested)
wahléhle 'banner, flag'
xíxiða 'stumble' (cf. *xíða* 'fall; stumble')

Set B: Enduring states

šǫǫšǫ́we 'forever; always' (cf. *šǫ* 'while')
šǫǫðéðe 'forever' (cf. *šǫǫðé* 'during that time')
škaškáðe ~ *škaškáða* 'harmonious; harmony, peace' (cf. *ška* 'quiet')

[36] In *eešéše* 'you keep saying', reduplication includes inflectional morphology; this is the only such reduplicated form that I have noted in the data.

3 Agent and patient inflection

The behavior of pronominal markers of inflection on verbs is an area of grammar especially resistant to elegant analysis in Siouan languages. Topics to be covered in this chapter are the distinction between active and stative (and doubly stative) verbs; classes of verbs based on the initial segment of that part of the stem that follows the point of inflection; and the canonical order of inflectional material and its point of occurrence in the verb (as marked with an underscore: *ó_hką*), along with derivational markers of object reference (reflexive, reciprocal, suus, dative) and inceptive or vertitive.

The A1P prefix *ąk* requires special attention here, as various nonpronominal morphemes, when present, intervene between it and the other pronominals. This special position of *ąk* is merely stipulated here, and not described in terms of movement as other variations in prefix order are. In Osage and in other Siouan languages this area of the grammar tends to defy coherent description.

3.1 Overview of pronominal inflection

3.1.1 Active and stative verbs

Verbs are labeled active or stative here following the morphologically based classification customary in Siouan studies (Mithun 1991). The labels "active" and "stative" are not semantically valid in some cases and should not be confused with semantic classes. "Active" is applied to those verbs that mark subject by the agent paradigm, and "stative" is applied to those verbs that mark subject (or experiencer) by the patient paradigm. See section 3.3 below for more on the active/stative distinction in Osage.

3.1.1.1 Active verbs: subject marked by agent pronominals

Active verbs, whether transitive or intransitive, inflect for subject by means of the agent prefixes, whose forms in regular verbs are displayed in table 3.1. Underlying forms *Wa* and *Ya* for 1S and 2S never emerge as *Wa* and *Ya* on the surface (see chapter 2).

TABLE 3.1. AGENT INFLECTION OF REGULAR VERBS

TRANSLATION	GLOSS	SURFACE FORM	UNDERLYING FORM
'I'	1S	*a*	*Wa*
'you'	2S	*ða*	*Ya*
'he/she/it'	3S	*Ø*	*Ø*
'we'	1P	*ąk* ~ *ą*	*ąk*
'they'	3P	*Ø*	*Ø*

As discussed previously in section 2.3.1 and below in sections 3.2.3–3.2.4, many active verbs (the syncopating verbs) will have surface forms of the agent prefixes that differ considerably from the regular forms *a* and *ða* seen in table 3.1.

It is the morpheme following the agent prefix, and especially that morpheme's initial sound (which will be referred to as the "inflectable initial" of the verb to distinguish it from the actual initial segment of the verb), that determines which surface form (regular or syncopating) of the agent prefixes will appear. This morpheme may be a reflexive element, a suus element, a dative, an instrumental prefix, some other prefix, or a verb root. That is, the verb root itself determines which surface form will emerge from underlying *Wa* and *Ya* only when no prefix intervenes. As material is added leftward of the verb root, but rightward of the point of inflection, a new inflectable initial is created.

Certain regular (*a-ða*) verbs have an epenthetic *ð* in the A1S form; these are illustrated in section 3.2.2, and are referred to as regular *i*-verbs.

Of the various subgroups of the sycopating stems, the largest number of verbs is found in the *ð*-stem group (see section 3.2.3).

Plurality of the subject is marked by the suffixed pluralizer *api*. When the 1P agent prefix *ąk* ~ *ą* is not accompanied by *api*, it is interpreted as dual (I and one other person; glossed as 'A1D'). First person plural (I and two or more other persons; 'A1P') is represented by prefix *ąk* ~ *ą* plus suffixal pluralizer *api*. Osage 1P and 1D are indifferently inclusive ('I and you') or exclusive ('I and he/she/it/they'); see section 5.1.1 for more discussion. The first person dual will not be further treated here. For the alternation between *ąk* and *ą* in the surface form of the A1P (A1D) prefix, see section 3.1.3.

Likewise, simple plurality of second person ('A2P') is signalled by the addition of the suffixal plural marker *api* to a form with the 2S prefix *Ya*. The prefix *Ya* is interpreted as singular in the absence of *api*. Since there is no variation in the prefixal subject inflectional marker, 2P need not be discussed here.

The transitive members of the group of active verbs take object inflection from the set of patient inflectional prefixes, displayed in table 3.2.

TABLE 3.2. PATIENT INFLECTION

TRANSLATION	GLOSS	AFFIX
'me'	P1S	*ą*
'you'	P2S	*ði*
'him, her, it'	P3S	*Ø*
'us'	P1P	*wa...api*
'them'	P3P	*Ø* ~ *wa*

3.1.1.2 Stative verbs: subject marked by patient pronominals

Stative verbs are those that take patient inflection for their semantic subject. Patient prefixes, which are also used for object inflection in active transitive verbs, were presented in table 3.2. Stative is strictly a morphological classification. Although the subjects of many stative verbs are semantically nonagentive, not all are. (The grammatical function "subject" corresponds to the argument used as subject in the English gloss, but in fact could be called merely the primary argument of the verb in Osage. With that caveat, we will continue to use the term "subject" here for ease of reference.)[1]

Some typical stative verbs are the following (where the underscore marks the point where patient inflection occurs): *ní_hce* 'be cold'; *_níe* 'ache, hurt'; *_húheka* 'be sick'; *o_xpáðe* 'be lost; fall; lose [an item]'; *_ðįké* 'lack'. Some other statives freely vary between agent or patient pronominal in 2S: *_hehé* 'pant'; *í_xope* 'tell a lie'.

The following Osage verbs are listed as stative by Rankin (1999), based on La Flesche (1932), but seem to be inflected today for 1S or 2S subject only by addition of the continuative auxiliary (1S *ąhé* or *mįkšé*; 2S *ðaįšé* or *nįkšé*): *paxíce* 'perspire'; *wapį́* 'bleed'; *ðakʔíðe* 'itch'; *héchį* 'sneeze'. (For continuatives, see chapter 5.)

[1] The subject as defined here for stative verbs is usually the experiencer in the Osage sentence and in a few stative sentences appears marked by a subject marker *apa* or *akxa*. If a continuative auxiliary is present, it agrees with this argument, in sentences found so far. Data on stative verbs is much less exhaustive than on active verbs, either owing to their being much less common than active verbs or owing to their particular disuse by speakers in the 1980s and 1990s.

Some verbs listed as stative by Rankin (1999) now take active inflection: *_léepe* 'vomit'; *_kisúðe* 'remember'; *_ðipíxa* 'fart'; *_hǫ́xpe* 'cough'; *wawé_kʔǫ* 'belch'.

For a discussion of a few of the adjectivelike verbs that optionally take patient pronominals, see section 6.7.

There are a small number of stative verbs with two arguments. For such verbs, inflection representing the second argument will also come from the patient set. Only a few verbs of this kind have been found; these are labeled "doubly stative" elsewhere in this work. Some stative verbs, such as *ðįké* 'lack', have two arguments, but represent only one with patient inflection (in the case of *ðįké*, this argument is the person lacking something), and with no overt pronominal for the second argument (in the case of *ðįké*, the item that is lacked).

Combinations of pronominal inflection are shown in table 3.3.

TABLE 3.3. TYPES OF PRONOMINAL INFLECTION

		INFLECTION
ACTIVE	*intransitive*	agent
	transitive	agent + patient
STATIVE	*intransitive*	patient
	transitive (doubly stative)	patient + patient
	transitive (no inflection for second argument)	patient + Ø

3.1.2 Morpheme position and order

With Siouan languages it is difficult to say anything very straightforward about the order of inflectional elements. However, certain canonical patterns can be postulated, and rules applied to make subsequent minor changes in the canonical order. The position of the 1P agent prefix *ąk* differs from that of the other agent prefixes. According to Rankin (p.c. 1994), historically *ąk* was probably added in front of other agent pronominals; thus it should not be surprising that its placement is still different from that of the other agent pronominals in Osage today. Below, I simply stipulate the various positions where *ąk* can appear. Other pronominal inflection occurs at the "point of inflection," just left of the inflectable initial of the verb, and is unaffected by the position of *ąk*. In some cases *ąk* does occur at the same point as other pronominal inflection, notably in causatives and some compounds, but it is always leftward of the other inflection.

For all pronominal inflection except *ąk*, the basic order of inflectional elements is as follows:

PATIENT + AGENT (+ KI)

For active verbs, patient will be the theme, experiencer, or other object argument, while agent will be the subject. "KI" refers to the three forms *kik* 'suus' (reflexive possessive), *hkik* 'reflexive-reciprocal', and *ki* 'dative; inceptive'—all discussed in chapter 4.[2] These three forms can plausibly be viewed as derivational elements rather than inflectional elements (or as a hybrid of derivation and inflection). "KI" also includes vertitive *kik* and inceptive *ki* (homophonous with suus and dative, respectively), which are certainly derivational and not object reference forms. Whether the object reference, vertitive, and inceptive prefixes are derivational or inflectional, it is useful to treat their ordering properties together with the patient and agent prefixes, as is done here, since all occur at the same point in verb structure.

In a very few cases, the patient (object) marker will be separated from the agent and object reference markers by an intervening morpheme, but overall order remains constant.

The inflectional elements patient and agent (not counting 1P agent) and the object reference (and homophonous) prefixes may conveniently be referred to by the formula "PAT AG KI". In representing verb stems, it will usually be convenient to indicate where the PAT AG KI prefixes occur—the point of inflection—by an underscore, as in *ó_hką* 'help', *mą_ðǫ́* 'steal'. The site for insertion of the elements PAT AG KI varies according to the verb, and is often not word-initial. In this chapter, the term "verb base" is used for that part of the verb stem that occurs rightward of the point of inflection, minus any derivational prefixes, and the verb stem is the root plus derivational prefixes. (Derivational prefixes include inner instrumentals, preverbs such as *mą,* and the elements represented by KI—reflexive, reciprocal, dative, suus, plus inceptive and vertitive.) In stems that contain more than a root, the point of inflection may occur in the positions exemplified in table 3.4.

The term "preverb" refers to stem elements preceding the point of inflection, such as *mą* in *mą_ðǫ́* 'deceive'. Similarly, *ki* in *ékiǫ* 'do', for example, is no longer a dative marker in the same sense as the dative *ki* that appears rightward of the point of inflection, but has been lexicalized as a preverb.

[2] The term suus comes from the Latin and is used here with the meaning 'one's own', referring to subject's own things or subject's own family, clan, people.

TABLE 3.4. POINT OF INFLECTION

COMPONENTS OF STEM	OSAGE EXAMPLE	GLOSS
_ Instrumental + Root	*_kaa-xǫ*	'break by striking'
Locative _ Base	*á_kaasįįce*	'slam on'
_ Instrumental + Base	*_ðaaxǫ́ke*	'chew into pieces'
Preverb _ Root	*mą_ðǫ́*	'deceive'
Primary Root _ Causative	*ðakʔé_ðe*	'be kind to'
Valence Reducer _ Base	*wa_ðáahtą*	'drink'(intr.)
Valence Reducer + Primary Root _ Causative	*wacʔé_ðe*	'kill' (intr.)
Locative + Primary Root _ Causative	*í-ðakʔé_ðe*	'be kind with'

Instrumental prefixes that precede the point of inflection are called "outer instrumentals"; those that follow it are called "inner instrumentals". Additionally, there are quite a number of verbs with two points of inflection (signalled by two underscores); these are discussed in section 3.5.3.

If a compound verb with two points of inflection, such as *_hpí_ǫ* 'know, learn', adds a reflexive *hkik* 'oneself', this creates a new verb with three points of inflection, such as *_hki_hpí_ǫ* 'know for oneself, learn for oneself'. Subject inflection occurs at all three points: ***aahkíšpižǫ*** 'you learned for yourself'.

Table 3.5 displays the location of pronominal inflection and object reference or vertitive or inceptive with respect to other verb parts. Locations of inflectional elements are shaded. Certain complex patterns are not portrayed in this table. For example, the valence reducer *wa* may appear to the left of the causative primary root (e.g., ***wacʔéðe*** 'kill folks'), as may locative *i* 'with' (e.g., *íðakʔéðe* 'be kind to with').

3.1.3 The 1P agent prefix

3.1.3.1 Position in the verb

The most prominent deviation from the order PAT AG KI is that when the agent prefix is A1P *ąk*, it frequently appears earlier in verb structure than the point of inflection (as seen in table 3.5). Thus *ąk* occurs to the left of locative *o* (*ąkóohǫ* 'we cook'), of (some cases of) locative *á* (*ąkálįį* 'we sit upon'), and of the opaque preverb *mą* of *mą_ðó* (*ąmą́ðope* 'we steal'). No example of *ąk* to the left of an outer instrumental has been found nor could it be elicited successfully. In cases where the valence reducer *wa* has been lexicalized onto an inflected root, *ąk* will occur leftward of that *wa*: for example, *ą* + *wa_ðaahtą* 'we drink [alcohol]', *ą* + *wá_nǫbre* 'we dine'.

TABLE 3.5. ORDER OF ELEMENTS BEFORE THE ROOT

DERIVATION		DERIVATION	PAT	AG	KI	DERIVATION	ROOT
Causative primary root *i* locative (prefix *i* or *ii*-) Preverb *e* (*eą́kię* 'we do') Preverb *wį́* (*wį́ąkše* 'we tell the truth')	*ąk* (A1P)	*o* locative *á* locative Valence reducer *wa* Preverb (e.g., *mą*) *ki* as preverb Outer instrumental			object reference: reflexive reciprocal suus dative vertitive inceptive	Inner instrumental	Verb root; causative *ðe*

As shown in table 3.5, *ąk* appears leftward of a patient prefix such as *ði* P2S 'you'; the order PAT AG KI does not apply when *ąk* is involved: *ąkóðihką* (from *ó_hką)* 'we help you'.

Causatives with *ðe* consist of a primary stem followed by causative *ðe*. In such causatives, the point of inflection is always between the primary stem and *ðe*. A1P *ąk* occurs after the primary stem in such *ðe* causatives along with other pronominals, but to the left of the other pronominals. Likewise *ąk* occurs to the right of the preverb *e* in such verbs as *ékiǫ* 'do' (A1P *eąkiǫ* 'we do').[3] Additionally, the locative *i* or *ii* normally precedes *ąk*.[4]

Thus, *ąk* only occurs leftward of *o*, *á*, and *mą*, plus certain instances of *ki* (as in *ekiǫ* 'do'), lexicalized *wa*, and pronominal prefixes.

ąk follows *we*, derived from *i-wa* by metathesis and contraction (section 3.4.1.2):

(1a) *weąpaho*
wa-i-ąk-pahǫ
VAL-LOC-A1P-know
'we know it'

(1b) *wawéąkʔope*
wa-wa-i-ąk-kʔo-api-ðe
VAL-VAL-LOC-A1P-belch-PL-DECL
'we belched'

(1c) *wéąðaahpe ąkakxái*
wa-i-ąk-ð-aahpe *akatxą́-ðe*
VAL-LOC-A1P-EPð-wait 1P.CONT-DECL
'we were waiting for people'

A few examples of verbs with *ąk* follow. In some of these the form of *ąk* or of other morphemes is modified by phonological rules to be discussed later.

[3] This verb in fact contains two preverbs, *é* and *ki*. The latter is a lexicalized version of dative *ki*, which unlike normal dative *ki* precedes the point of inflection. 1S and 2S agent inflection occurs after *ki*: *ékimǫ*, *ékižǫ*; A1P *ąk* occurs after *é* but before *ki*. Also a possible A1P form is the following, where *é* has been dropped:

ąkíǫ ąkátxai
'we are doing [standing]'

[4] Actually, phonological changes make it unclear whether *ąk* precedes or follows an initial *i* (see below, section 3.4.3.2). Versions without harmony, however, suggest that *ąk* follows *i*: e.g., *įðą́xope* 'we tell lies' instead of the expected *ąnáxope*; *weąpahǫ* (<*wa-i-ąk-pahǫ*) 'we know'.

Examples with *á*. In the case of the prefix *á*, there is some variation. Most verbs with *á* have *ąk* + *á*... for 1P. Other verbs with *á* have optionally a form where *ąk* occurs as *ą* at the point of inflection. For example, either *ąkálį* 'we sit upon' or *ą́ąlį* 'we sit upon' is correct.

Examples with *o*. Taking a sentence with the verb *o_hką́* 'help' as an example, we see that *ąk* precedes the *o*, as in (2). The same example shows that the object inflection *ði* 'you' occurs at the point of inflection between the preverb *o* and the verb base *hką*.

(2) *ąkóðihkąpe*
ąk-o-ði-hką-api-ðe
A1P-PREV-P2S-help-PL-DECL
'we helped you'

Observe also the regularly inflected verb *o_hí* 'beat' in (3). Again, *ąk* occurs in initial position, rather than at the inflection site marked with an underscore as stipulated here; however, the object inflection P3P *wa* occurs at the inflection site.

(3) *ąkówahie*
ąk-o-wa-hi-ðe
A1P-PREV-P3P-beat-DECL
'we beat them [at a game, not a race]'

Examples with *i*. Note that in the case of locative *i*, for example in (4), vowel harmony (changing *i* to *ą*) obscures the order of *ak* and *i* (though I assume that *i* precedes *ąk*). The *k* of *ąk* has been deleted (see section 3.1.3.2). See section 3.2.4 for other rules relevant to examples such as (4).

(4) *ąną́ðiðaahpe*
i-ąk-ði-ð-áahpe
PREV-A1P-P2S-EPð-wait
'we wait for you'

3.1.3.2 *k*-Deletion

The A1P prefix *ąk* sometimes surfaces as *ą*. This alternation is easily described: *ąk* appears only before a back vowel, and *ą* alone is found elsewhere. There are no processes of *k*-insertion or *k*-deletion elsewhere in the language; I arbitrarily assume *k*-deletion, though a case could also be made for *k*-insertion.[5]

k-Deletion: *ąk* → *ą* / __ {nonback vowels, C}

[5] One gets a simpler rule by assuming that the *k* is absent in the underlying form and epenthesized before back vowels (even though that is historically wrong); this is a good example of how an historical process can gradually change into a seemingly opposite synchronic rule (David Rood, p.c. 2000).

This rule applies to *ąk* regardless of whether the segment that follows belongs to a bare root, a preverb, an instrumental, the reflexive, or some other element. The verb stems have not been analyzed in the following examples for the most part, since this is not necessary to illustrate the principle under discussion.

(5a) *a_ðée*
aðée
'go'

(5b) *ąkáðe*
ąk-aðée
A1P-go
'we go'

(6a) *_ðaaché*
'eat'

(6b) *ąðáache*
ąk-ðaaché
A1P-eat
'we eat'

(7a) *_lúuža*
kik-ðuužá
SUU-wash
'wash one's [face, hands, etc.]'

(7b) *šáake ąlúuža*
šáake ąk-kik-ðuužá
hand A1P-SUU-wash
'we wash our hands'

(8a) *o_chį*
'hit'

(8b) *ąkóchį*
ąk-ochį
P1P-hit
'we hit him'

After *k*-Deletion, the form of the A1P prefix is homophonous with the P1S prefix *ą* 'me', a fact which will cause ambiguities such as those in (9) and (10) below.

(9) *cˀéą̧ðape*
cˀé-ą-Ø-ðe-api-ðe
die-P1S-A3S-CAU-PL-DECL
'he/they killed me'[6]

(10) *cˀéą̧ðape*
cˀé-ąk-Ø-ðe-api-ðe
die-A1P-P3P-CAU-PL-DECL
'we killed him'

3.1.4 Position of inflection in causatives

With causatives in *ðe*, the root preceding *ðe* is the primary stem; for example, *cˀé* 'die' in *cˀé* + *ðe* 'cause to die, kill'. Inflection of such causatives is placed between the primary stem and *ðe*: *cˀé_ðe*. The convention for morpheme glossing used for semantically opaque primary stems is that the primary stem is glossed as PREV (for "preverb"), while the meaning of the entire causative verb appears as the gloss of *ðe*; thus, for instance, the transitive verb *šcé_ðe* 'to doctor' will have *šcé* glossed as PREV and *ðe* as 'doctor'. But in semantically transparent causative verbs, such as *cˀéðe* 'kill' (*cˀe* 'die' + *ðe* 'causative', the primary stem appears with its own gloss and *ðe* is glossed as "CAU," as in (11).

(11) *cˀéwaðai hta nįkšé*
cˀé-wa-Ya-ðe hta nįkšé
die-P3P-A2S-CAU FUT 2S.CONT
'you're going to kill them'

Since inflection is just left of the causative *ðe*, one sees complex forms such as:

(12) *cˀéwaðai hta nįkšé*
cˀé-wa-Ya-ðe hta nįkšé
die-P3P-A2S-CAU FUT 2S.CONT
'you're going to kill them'

The A1P *ąk* does not normally occur leftward of the primary root. In contrast, the valence reducer *wa* may appear left of the primary root, as in the following example, where it is prefixed to the primary root *cˀé*, not to the causative morpheme *ðe*, as in (13).

[6] Besides marking plurals, *pe* (underlying *api-ðe*) usually marks a finite event in the past on third person singular verbs. This is in direct opposition to continuative aspect, marked with *akxa* or *apa* in approximately the same position.

(13) *wacʔé_ðe*
wa-cʔé-ðe
VAL-die-CAU
'kill folks'

Even in such forms as (13), *ąk* appears along with other inflectional material, between the heavy primary root *wacʔé* and the causative *ðe*, as in (14) and (15).[7] (In (15), the causative morpheme *ðe* becomes *ða* via the V1-V2 Rule .)

(14) *wacʔéąðe ðįįké*
wa-cʔé-ąk-ðe ðįįké
VAL-die-A1P-CAU NEG.EMPH
'we don't kill at all'

(15) *wacʔéąðapaži nąi*
wa-cʔé-ąk-ðe-api-aži ną-ðe
VAL-die-A1P-CAU-PL-NEG ITER-DECL
'we don't kill'

3.1.5 Portmanteau *wi*

The portmanteau *wi* represents the combination of 1S agent with 2S patient inflection (as shorthand, *wi* 'I-to-you', and glossed interlinearly as P2<A1S).[8] It replaces the customary 1s agent inflection *a* in regular verbs, as in *íwixa* 'I laugh at you' and (16a)–(17c).

(16a) *o_hi*
'beat, best someone in a contest'

[7] At least one speaker treats *cʔé* + *ðe* 'kill' differently, placing *ąk* before the primary root, although object inflection and other subject inflection stays between the primary root and *ðe*. This means that for this speaker, the primary root of this causative is treated as if it were not a causative at all as regards placement of *ąk*. Sentences (i) and (ii) are from the same speaker. In (i), *wi* appears at the normal point of inflection for causatives. In (ii), A1P *ą* appears left of the primary root *cʔé*.

(i) *wáli tae ðáalįži ðąįše cʔéwie hta mįkše*
wáli tae ðáalį-aži ðąįše cʔé-wi-ðe hta mįkše
very behavior good-not 2S.CONT die-A1S>P2S-CAU FUT 1S.CONT
'you're really behaving bad, I'm gonna kill you'

(ii) *wáli tae ðáalįži ðąįše ącʔéðie hta ąkatxai*
wáli tae ðáalį-aži ðąįše ąk-cʔe-ði-ðe hta ąkatxa-ðe
very behavior good-not 2S.CONT A1P-die-P2S-CAU FUT 1P.CONT-DECL
'you're really behaving bad, we're gonna kill you'

[8] *wi* is possibly a contraction of A1S *Wa* + P2 *ði*, via *ð*-elision and V1-V2 contraction.

(16b) *oáhie*
o-Ø-Wa-hi-ðe
PREV-P3S-A1S-beat-DECL
'I beat him'

(16c) *owíhie*
o-wi-hi-ðe
PREV-P2S<A1S-beat-DECL
'I beat you'

(17a) *ó_hkǫ*
'help'

(17b) *Mary owáhkǫ*
Mary o-w-Ø-Wa-hkǫ
Mary PREV-EP*w*-P3S-A1S-help
'I help Mary'

(17c) *owíhkǫ*
o-wi-hka
PREV-P2S<A1S-help
'I help you'

In *ð*-stems and other syncopating stems, *wi* cooccurs with (redundant) agent inflection. This is seen in the following three examples with syncopating verbs, where *wi* is followed by A1S *b* (from underlying *Wa*).

(18) *wíbruwį*
wi-Wa-ðuwį́
P2S<A1S-A1S-buy
'I buy for you'

(19) *wíbrihice*
wi-Wa-ðihice
P2S<A1S-A1S-tease
'I tease you'

(20) *wíbraace*
wi-Wa-ðaacé
P2S<A1S-A1S-name
'I name you'

See also section 3.2.2.2 for *wi* with *i*-verbs.

The form *wi* can occur with all transitive verbs, both actives and statives. It replaces both P1 and P2 in doubly stative verbs: *wióxta* 'I love you' (see section 3.3.2).

3.2 Active verbs

Agent adjustment rules were given in section 2.3.1 as part of the phonology. Since inflection interacts with derivational elements in the verbal complex, it is reviewed briefly here and additional examples are listed. Table 3.6 gives a quick overview of the fate of the 1S and 2S agent prefixes (underlying *Wa* and *Ya*, respectively) with the various types of verb stem.

In regular verbs, 1S *Wa* → *a*; that is *W* → *Ø*, resulting in the regular 1S agent inflection *a*. Such regular verbs are discussed in sections 3.2.1 and 3.2.2. In nonregular, or syncopating, verbs, the agent prefix vowel is dropped, and the surface form of *W* or *Y* is shaped by the following segment of the verb. These syncopating verbs are treated in sections 3.2.3 and 3.2.4. Table 3.6 shows agent inflection for regular verbs and syncopating verbs. Reflexes of the agent pronominals are in bold. In the category "Fortisizing stop-stems," *C* stands for the inflectable initial consonant of the stem, such as *t* in *tǫ́pe* 'look', *k* in *kǫ́ða* 'want', and *p* in *ípahǫ* 'know'.

TABLE 3.6. AGENT INFLECTION OF REGULAR AND SYNCOPATING STEMS

	A1S	A2S
REGULAR STEMS		
Normal	***a***	***ða***
With *ð*-Epenthesis after *i*	***iðá***	***íða***
SYNCOPATING STEMS		
ð-stems	***br***	*št, šc*
h-stems	***pš***	*š*
ʔ-stems (i.e., nasal-vowel stems)	***m***	*ž*
Mutating *k*-stems	***hp ~ pp***	*šk*
Fortisizing stop-stems	***hC ~ CC***	*šk*

3.2.1 Regular (*a-ða*) verbs

One of the two principal types of active inflection in Osage is the *a-ða* pattern, which is the regular pattern for active verbs. 1S agent inflection is surface *a*; 2S is *ða*; 3S and 3P are *Ø*, and 1P is *ą* or *ąk*.

A typical regular verb is *kʔu* 'give', with 1S *akʔú,* 2S *ðakʔú,* 3S *kʔú,* 1P *ąkʔú*. Nothing precedes the point of inflection in this verb. Many verbs, however, will have other elements leftward of the point of inflection. These regular verbs are illustrated by examples thoughout the various chapters of this volume.

Two peculiarities within the regular verbs are worth mentioning here. One is the behavior of the simplified A1S *a* in verbs with *wa* or *waa* preverb. A second oddity within the group of regular verbs is the location of A1P *ąk* in certain verbs rightward of the preverb.

3.2.1.1 Metathesis of *wa* and *a* in regular verbs

One peculiarity in otherwise regular forms is that when the verb begins with a preverb *wa(a)*, the 1S agent inflection *a* metathesizes with the *wa(a)* (see the detailed discussion of *wa* metathesis in section 3.4.1.1). The verbs *waa_chí* 'dance', *wa_nǫ́bre* 'dine', and dozens of others follow this pattern for 1S. By this rule, first-person-inflected *waa-a-chi* becomes *a-waa-chi* 'I dance' as the first two morphemes exchange places. The examples below show the inflection of the verb *waa_šką́* 'do one's best'; *wa* metathesis has occurred in the 1S form (21).

(21) *awáašką hta mįkšé*
a-wáa-šką *hta* *mįkšé*
A1S-PREV-do.one's.best FUT 1S.CONT
'I'll do my best'

(22) *waaðášką hta nįkšé*
waa-Ya-šką *hta* *nįkšé*
PREV-A2S-do.one's.best FUT 2S.CONT
'you'll do your best'

(23) *waašką́ akxái*
waa-Ø-šką́ *akxá-ðe*
PREV-A3S-do.one's.best 3.CONT-DECL
'he is doing his best'

(24) *ąwáašką hta ąkáðe*
ą-waa-šką́ *hta* *ąkáðe*
A1P-PREV-do.one's.best FUT 1P.CONT
'we'll do our best'

3.2.1.2 Location of *ąk* rightward of "heavy" preverbs

Whereas A1P subject pronominals occur leftward of preverbs such as *waa* in *waa_šką́* 'do one's best', with a few verbs such as *wį́_kše* 'tell the truth, be truthful; be true to', *ąk* cannot occur leftward of the preverb. We have termed such preverbs "heavy," as they prevent *ąk* from occurring in its customary position left of the preverb. The verb *wį́_kše* is regular in its inflection otherwise. Thus this verb groups with causatives with regard to behavior of *ąk*. Another verb with a heavy preverb is *ékiǫ* 'do', which is treated elsewhere (sections 3.1.2, 3.2.4.4, 4.6.5.6).

(25) *wįakše hta mįkše*
wį-Wa-kše *hta* *mįkše*
PREV-A1S-be.truthful FUT 1S.CONT
'I'm telling the truth'

(26) *wįðakše?*
wį-Ya-kše
PREV-A2S-be.truthful
'are you telling the truth?'

(27) *wįąðakše hta ðąąšé?*
wį-ą-Ya-kše *hta* *ðaįšé*
PREV-P1S-A2S-be.true FUT 2S.CONT
'will you be true to me?'

(28) *wįkše akxa*
wį-Ø-kše *akxa*
PREV-A3S-be.truthful 3.CONT
'he's telling the truth'

(29) *wįąkše*
wį-ąk-kše
PREV-A1P-be.truthful
'we are telling the truth'

3.2.2 Epenthetic *ð* in regular *i*-stems

There is a large group of regular verbs with initial *i* (or *ii*, as the two are treated identically here), which show the "*íða, iðá*" pattern exhibited in the verb 'see' (table 3.7). In this group, an epenthetic *ð* is inserted between *i(i)* and 1S agent *a*, causing the 1S form to be identical with 2S (which has the expected pronominal *ða*); only accent distinguishes 1S (accent on agent prefix) from 2S (accent on *i(i)*). Some of the dozens of other verbs of this type appear in examples below. This epenthesis rule was also described briefly in section 2.3.2.3.

TABLE 3.7. REGULAR *i*-VERB (*iiðe* 'TO SEE')

1S	*iiðáðe*	'I see'
2S	*íiðaðe*	'you see'
3S	*íiðe*	'he sees'
1P	*ąnáðape*	'we see'

3.2.2.1 *ð*-Epenthesis in A1S of *i*-verbs

Part A of the epenthesis rule, as formulated in section 2.3.2.3, provides for the insertion of *ð* before the first person subject.

Ø → ð / i __ á

Thus, the verb *íi_ðe* 'see' with the addition of *a* for A1S *Wa* gives *íi-a-ðe*. The accent moves, by the rule of second syllable accent adjustment, giving *iiáðe*. Then *iiðáðe* emerges as surface form after *ð*-epenthesis for 'I see [it]' (see table 3.7 above). This rule then accounts for the "*iða* subset" of the regular verbs.

Part B of the rule as formulated in section 2.3.2.4 inserts *ð* in the context *i_ó*, that is, between two locatives (specifically, *i-o* → *oðo*, with locative prefixes *i* and *o*) and between *wa* and locative *á* (i.e., *wa-á* → *waðá*). (See also section 4.5.3 for locative *á*). This *ð*-epenthesis may be a more general rule:

Ø → ð / V __ V′ (where *V′* = accented vowel)

As formulated here, *ð*-epenthesis will account for all regular *i*-verbs, as well as the 'wait' forms found in section 3.2.2.2. Further examples of *i*-verbs are shown below. Example (30) uses the verb *ii_nąhį* 'agree' (2S *íiðanahį*, 1P *ąnąnahį*); (31) exemplifies *ii_hǫ́* 'ask someone to do something' (2S *íiðahǫ*, 1P *ąnąhǫ*).

(30) *iiðánąhįmąži mįkšé ąži ą́ðanakˀǫ́ žie*
ii-ð-Wa-nąhį-maži *mįkšé* *ąži*
PREV-EPð-A1S-agree-1S.NEG 1S.CONT but
á-ą-Ya-nakˀǫ́-aži-ðe
LOC-P1S-A2S-listen-NEG-DECL
'I objected to it but you didn't listen to me'

(31) *Mary ðée che iðáhǫę*
Mary a-ðée che ii-ð-Wa-hǫ-ðe
Mary PREV-go INJ PREV-Epð-A1S-ask-DECL
'I asked Mary to go'

Additional verbs of this type include the following:

ii_lána 'make a mistake': 1S *iiðálana*, 2S *íiðalana*, 1P *ąnąlana*

ii_táðe 'give birth to': 1S *iiðátaðe* (*iiðátae*), 2S *íiðataðe* (*iiðatae*), 1P *ąnątaðe* (*ąnątae*)

í_xa 'laugh [at someone]': 1S *iðáxa*, 2S *íðaxa*, 1P *ąnąxa*

í_si 'dislike': 1S *iðási*, 2S *íðasi*, 1P *ąnąsi*

í_kišike 'be lonesome for, to miss another': 1S *iðákišike*, 2S *íðakišike*, 1P *ąnąkišįke*

í_kˀuce 'try': 1S *iðákˀuce*, 2S *íðakˀuce*, 1P *ąnąkˀuce*

í_xope 'tell a lie': 1S *iðáxope*, 2S *íðaxope*, 1P *ąnąxope*

3.2.2.2 *ð*-epenthesis before accented *á*: *i_áahpe* 'wait'

The *ð* of *iðáahpe* 'wait' is epenthetic as well. The underlying form for 'wait' is *i_áahpe*; *ð* appears when prefix *i* emerges to the left of the root-initial *á* with no intervening consonant. This verb is thus quite similar to other regular *i*-verbs, such as *i_xa* 'laugh'. In all such verbs, *ð*-epenthesis occurs between *i* and accented *á*, giving *iðá*.

The verb *iðáahpe* 'wait' is unique only in that the accented *áa* that forms the context for *ð*-epenthesis is part of the stem. The result is that the A1S and A3S forms are identical (see the examples below), while the first person singular and second person singular differ only by accent.

(32) *iðáahpe*
i-ð-Wa-áahpe
PREV-EPð-A1S-wait
'I waited'

(33) *íðaahpe*
i-Ya-áahpe
PREV-A2S-wait
'you waited'

(34) *iðáahpe*
i-ð-Ø-áahpe
PREV-EPð-A3S-wait
'he waited'

3.2.2.3 Broadened rule of *ð*-Epenthesis: A1P of *i*-verbs

In *i*-verbs (including *ii*-verbs) an additional peculiarity emerges in the 1P forms, where vowel harmony occurs between stem initial *i* and the 1P agent prefix *ąk*. In the sequence preverb + A1P, after *k* of *ąk* elides, we have a sequence *i-ą́*. This is another context for *ð*-insertion:

ð-Epenthesis, part C: Ø >ð / i __ ą́

The resulting sequence *iðą́* optionally but most frequently becomes *iną́* (which is easily explicable phonetically) and then becomes *ąną́* via vowel harmony. The *ą* appearing in the context of the rule can be the *ą* of *ąk* (1P agent inflection) or *ą* 1S patient inflection (meaning 'to me' or 'me'), or it can be some other *ą*. For present purposes, the interesting part of this rule is its application to 1P forms of *i*-verbs. This rule produces the 1P form *i_xope* 'lie' in the example below, and all the A1P forms in examples above.

(35) *ąnáxope*
i-ąk-xope
PREV-A1P-lie
'we're lying'

In the next example, note the object inflection *ði* at the point of inflection in *í_xope*, with *ąk* occurring to the left of P2S *ði*:

(36) *ąnáðixope ąkái*
i-ąk-ði-xope *ąkáðe*
PREV-A1P-P2S-lie 1P.CONT
'we've been lying to you'

A1P *ąk* precedes the other locative prefixes *o* and *a* (as in *ąk* + *óhką* 'we help', *ąkáðe* [from *ąk* + *aðée*] 'we go'). Still, there is some evidence that *ąk* follows *i(i)*, even though this is obscured by vowel harmony in examples above. One piece of evidence is provided by forms in which P3P *wa* precedes A1P, as in the underlying form *i-wa-ąk-xope*. The rule of *i-wa* Metathesis (section 3.4.1.2) changes *í-wa* to *wa-i*, producing *wa-i-ąk-xope*; then *wa-i* contracts, giving *we-ą́k-xope*; *k*-Deletion then produces the surface form *weą́xope* 'we're lying to them'. Such forms would be hard to explain on the assumption that *ąk* preceded *i(i)*. (See also section 2.3.3.1 for *a* + *i* contraction in other contexts.)

3.2.2.4 Portmanteau *wi* in regular *i*-verbs

The portmanteau *wi* 'P2S<A1S' replaces patient and agent inflection in the *i*-verbs, as it does with other regular verbs (see section 3.1.5). The context for *ð*-epenthesis does not occur when *wi* is present, and accent remains on the initial syllable.

(37) *íiwixa mįkšé*
i-wi-xa *mįkšé*
PREV-P2S<A1S-laugh 1S.CONT
'I'm laughing at you'

(38) *íiwiðe*
íi-wi-ðe
PREV-P2S<A1S-see
'I see you'

(39) *íwitae*
íi-wi-taðe
PREV-P2S<A1S-bear
'I bore you; I gave birth to you'

(40) *íiwiði áha*
íi-wi-ðe áha
PREV-P2S<A1S-see whenever
'when I see you [singular]'

(41) *íiwiðape*
íi-wi-ðe-api-ðe
PREV-P2S<A1S-see-PL-EMPH
'I see you all'

Curiously, examples have been found with *íiðe* 'see' in which patient *ði* plus agent *Wa* occurs where *wi* is expected, as in the example below. (The suffix *api* pluralizes the patient 'you' in both (41) and (42).)

(42) *íiðiðaape*
íi-ði-ð-Wa-ðe-api-ðe
PREV-P2S-EPð-A1S-see-PL-EMPH
'I saw you [pl.]; I saw you all'

3.2.3 Syncopating verbs: the *ð*-stems

The other main pattern of inflection in Osage verbs, contrasting with the regular pattern discussed in the previous section, is the nonregular pattern, which shows syncope of the vowel in 1S and 2S. Verbs with this behavior are called syncopating stems and are grouped into several subsets, illustrated in this and the following sections. (See also section 2.3.1 for agent prefix adjustment rules.) There is no semantic distinction dividing the syncopating verbs from verbs that show the regular pattern (*a, ða* in 1S and 2S, respectively), other than the semantics of some derivational prefixes that form syncopating verbs (*ðuu, ðii, ðaa*; see section 4.4).

Table 3.6 summarized the process of A1S subject adjustment for the various patterns of the syncopating verbs. The vowel of the 1S and 2S agent morphemes *Wa* and *Ya* syncopates, or falls out, leaving the remaining *W* or *Y* to adjust to the following segment.

The syncopating verbs include those exhibiting the typical *br-š* pattern of inflection in the *ð*-stem verbs. The *ð*-stems form the largest subset of the syncopating verbs. These verbs have *ð* as their inflectable initial segment (just to the right of the point of inflection). The contrast of syncopating verbs with regular verbs occurs in the first and second persons. Other persons in syncopating verbs have a pattern identical to regular verbs; that is, 1P is usually *ą* ~ *ąk*, and 3S and 3P are *Ø*. The first and second person patterns for syncopating *ð*-stems are:

1s *br* (where *b* is the reflex of *Wa,* and *r* the reflex of the *ð* inflectable initial of the verb)

2s *št* (before back vowels *a ą o ǫ*; *š* is the reflex of *Ya,* and *t* the reflex of the *ð* of the verb)

2s *šc* (before nonback vowels *i į e u*, by affrication of *t*; *šc* becomes *šč* in the Hominy dialect)

3.2.3.1 Examples and sources of *ð*-verbs

Some *ð*-stem verbs are simple *ð* inflectable initial roots such as *a_ðée* 'go'; *a_ðį́* 'have'; *mą_ðǫ́* 'steal'; *waa_ðǫ́* 'sing'. Others are made up of verbs that have acquired one of the productive inner instrumental prefixes with initial *ð*: *ðaa* 'by mouth' (with extended meaning of 'by speech, by voicing' etc.), as in *_ðaahtą́* 'drink', *_ðaaché* 'eat' (transitive), *_ðaacé* 'name'; *ðii* ~ *ðuu* 'by hand' (the meaning 'by hand' is not always transparent), as in *_ðihíce* 'tease', *_ðiištą́* 'be finished', *ðuuhkáama* 'ring, as a bell'; and the morphological causative *ðuu* (which is not clearly distinct from *ðii* ~ *ðuu* 'by hand'), as in *_ðuuwásu* 'clean' (transitive). Verbs such as *_ðuwį́* 'buy' and *_ðuucˀáke* 'be unable', although opaque, likely belong to one of the groups specified here.

The verb forms from all these sources have the point of inflection immediately preceding the *ð*. Almost all verbs with *ð* are members of this large subset (the *ð*-stems) of the syncopating verbs. An exception is the numerous *ðe* causatives, which have the regular pattern of inflection. (See section 4.2 for causatives.) Examples of *ð*-stems appear below, and throughout this volume. Below are shown the agent paradigms of *ðuwį́* 'buy' and of *o_ðáake* 'tell [e.g., a story]'.

(43a) *brúwį*
Wa-ðuwį
A1S-buy
'I buy'

(43b) *šcúwį*
Ya-ðuwį
A2S-buy
'you buy'

(43c) *ðuwį́*
Ø-ðuwį
A3S/P-buy
'he/she buys; they buy'

(43d) *ąðúwįpe*
ąk-ðuwį-api-ðe
A1P-buy-PL-DECL
'we buy'

(44a) *obráake*
o-Wa-ðáake
PREV-A1S-tell
'I tell'

(44b) *oštáake*
o-Ya-ðáake
PREV-A2S-tell
'you tell'

(44c) *oðáake*
o-Ø-ðáake
PREV-A3S/P-tell
'he/she tells; they tell'

(44d) *ąkóðaakape*
ąk-o-ðaake-api-ðe
A1P-PREV-tell-PL-DECL
'we tell'

3.2.3.2 An unusual *ð*-stem: *ðį*

There is one unusual example of a *ð*-stem used as a copula in first person and second person with certain adjectival and other words, such as *wažáže* 'Osage', *šcéce* 'tall', *wáaspe* 'remaining, staying':

1S *brį*
2S *nį*

No third person forms were found, but *ðį* occurs in the 1P form *ąðį́pe*. If the underlying form is *ðį*, as the 1S form suggests, the 2S form expected would be ***šcį*; but this form is unacceptable, at least to some speakers, as signaled by the double asterisk. This unusual paradigm has a *br* form in 1S, characteristic of 1S the *ð*-stem paradigm, but a 2S form in *n*, characteristic of 2S in the nasal vowel initial (formerly ˀ-stem) paradigm. One occurrence of *mį* for A1S was also encountered on an old recording:

(45) *nihkáši mį*
nihkáši Wa-ðį
man A1S-be
'I am a person'

3.2.3.3 Instability of 1P forms: uninflected 1P *ékiðe*

1P is the least stable of the pronominal inflection forms, both as agent and as patient in all the inflected classes; in otherwise quite predictable paradigms we find variation in 1P forms. One of these variations is absence of any A1P marker. Active verbs without inflection in 1P are termed active-*Ø*—that is, active verbs with *Ø* for 1P agent inflection, or simply without any agent inflection. One example is *éki_ðe* 'think about doing; think so'. This is a syncopating *ð*-stem with preverb *é* plus lexicalized dative *ki* as a second preverb. Its 1P form takes no agent inflection on the verb, merely using the 1P (or 1D) auxiliary in postverbal position to express person and number as in (46), or the emphatic pronoun *ąkóe* (47).

(46) *ékiðe ąkáðe*
é-ki-ðe *ąkáðe*
PREV-PREV-think 1P.CONT
'we're thinking about doing it [three or more persons]'

(47) *ąkóe ékiðapaži*
ąkóe *é-ki-ðe-api-aži*
1P.PRON PREV-PREV-think-PL-NEG
'we don't think so'

Non-A1P forms for these verbs inflect normally, as in (48)–(52).

(48) *ékibre*
é-ki-Wa-ðe
PREV-PREV-A1S-think
'I'm thinking toward that way'

(49) *ékibramažie*
é-ki-Wa-ðe-maži-ðe
PREV-PREV-A1S-think-1S.NEG-DECL
'I don't care to, I don't want to'

(50) *ékibre įké*
é-ki-Wa-ðe *ðįké*
PREV-PREV-A1S-think NEG
'I don't care to, I don't want to'

(51) *ékištaži nįkšé*
é-ki-Ya-ðe-aži *nįkšé*
PREV-PREV-A2S-think-NEG 2S.CONT
'you don't think so'

(52) *ékiðe įkí ekxai*
é-ki-Ø-ðe *ðįké* *akxa-ðe*
PREV-PREV-A3S/P-think NEG 3.CONT-DECL
'they aren't thinking about doing it'

Another example is *ékią* 'do', for which speakers are reluctant to produce the 1P form *eąkią*. For 1P, the uninflected (citation) form is usually used, with an auxiliary or other device to show person and number, as in (46) above. (Also see *ii_táðe* 'give birth' in section 3.2.5, which is not inflected in A1P.) Other than the unusual behavior of 1P forms, such verbs take the expected syncopating inflection. For unusual behavior of 1P statives, and discussion of stative-*wa*, stative-*ąk* and stative-*Ø* (statives with no inflection in 1p), see section 3.3.1.

3.2.4 Other syncopating stems

The other stems in the syncopating set inflect in patterns somewhat resembling syncopating *ð*-stem verbs, but with certain peculiarities. Four subpatterns of syncopating verbs appeared in table 3.6 (summarized in table 3.8) and are illustrated below.

TABLE 3.8. SUBGROUPS OF SYNCOPATING VERBS

	A1S	A2S
h-STEMS	*pš*	*š*
NASAL VOWEL STEMS	*m*	*ž*
MUTATING *k*-STEMS	*hp*	*šk*
FORTISIZING STOP-STEMS	*hp, ht, hk*	*šp, št (šc), šk*

3.2.4.1 *h*-stems: *ahí, ahú, ée, ékie*

The *h*-stems are verbs with *h* as their inflectable initial, and have *pš* and *š* as their 1S and 2S forms respectively. Two of the most prominent members of this group are the motion verbs *a_hí* 'arrive there' and *a_hú* 'come here'. Typically for motion verbs, both (usually) show *a* in third person forms which remains in first person plural, but is lost in 1S and 2S:

a_hí 'arrive there [motion completed]': 1S *pši*, 2S *ši*, 3S *ahí*, 1P *ąkáhi*

a_hú 'come here [motion underway]': 1S *pšu*, 2S *šu*, 3S *ahú*, 1P *ąkáhu*

Two other verbs exhibiting the pattern seen in *ahí* and *ahú* lack the *h* in surface forms, but its effect can be seen in the 1S and 2S forms. The verb *é_[h]e* 'say' and its dative form *éki_[h]e* 'say [to another; in presence of another]' have an *h*-stem pattern. Neither the form *éhe* nor its dative counterpart *ékihe* ever occurs on the surface, as the *h* is lost, but positing *é[h]e* as the underlying form seems necessary to explain forms such as 1S *épše*. The dative version, *éki*[*h*]*e*, contains the dative *ki* lexicalized as a second preverb.

é_[h]e 'say': 1S *épše*; 2S *éše*; 3S *ée* (for 1P 'we say', only dative *éąkie* seems to be used)

éki_[h]e 'say [to another, or in the presence of another]' (dative): 1S *ékipše*; 2S *ékiše*; 3S *ékie* 'he says'; 1P *éąkie*

The expected nondative form *ée* is not usually found in imperatives, but rather the *ki* form, as in the example below.

(53) *šée ékia*
šée é-ki-e-a
that PREV-PREV-say-IMPER
'say that'

3.2.4.2 Fortisizing stop-stems

Certain *p*, *t*, *k* initial verbs will inflect with the pattern *hC*, *šC*, *C* for 1S, 2S, 3S respectively (where *C* is the initial consonant of the verb, that is, *p*, *t*, or *k*). In this very small subset of the syncopating stems the stem segment rightward of the point of inflection becomes preaspirated (or occasionally geminate). In this set, we find such verbs as *pą* 'yell', *í_pahǫ* 'know', *_kǫ́_ða* 'want', and *_tǫ́pe* 'see'. Only the 1S form shows preaspiration or gemination (*hpą* 'I yell', *htǫ́pe* 'I see', *íhpahǫ* 'I know', *hkǫ́bra* 'I want'); the 2S form will show *šp, št, šc* or *šk*, depending on the initial of the stem.

In the 1S form, preaspirated initials *hp ht hc hk* are more commonly found than geminates *pp tt cc kk*, except perhaps preceding nasal vowels where geminates often are heard. (This distribution of allophones is normal for the fortis stops; see section 2.1.3.4.) For ease of presentation, we refer to this group as the fortisizing stop stems.

í_pahǫ 'know [a person, a fact]': 1S *íhpahǫ*; 2S *íšpahǫ*; 3S *ípahǫ*; 1P *ąną́pahǫpe*

_tǫ́pe 'see, watch, look': 1S *htǫ́pe*; 2S *štǫ́pe*; 3S *tǫ́pe*, 1P *ątǫ́pape*

The verb *tǫ́pe* is unique in its inflection; that is, no other verbs with *ht* in A1S are known.

The verb 'want' *_kǫ́_ða* is doubly inflected; it is the inflection before *k* that is fortisizing:

_kǫ́_ða 'want': 1S *hkǫ́bra*; 2S *škǫ́šta*; 3S *kǫ́ða*; 1P *ąkǫ́ðape*

Many verbs with the inner instrumental *_paa* (or *_pa)* 'push, with a long object such as a rod; push with a knife; push with the hands or body' follow the fortisizing pattern of *ípahǫ*:

_paasé 'cut up [e.g., meat or potatoes]': 1S *hpáase*; 2S *špáase*; 3S *páase*; 1P *ąpáase*

_paasása 'dice' 1S *hpáasasa*; 2S *špáasasa*; 3S *paasása*; 1P *ąpáasasa* *_paahí* 'pick, as flowers, pick up scattered small items': 1S *hpáahi*; 2S *špáahi*; 3S *paahí*; 1P *ąpáahi*

_paakˀó 'dig [as a grave]': 1S *hpaakˀǫ́*; 2S *špaakˀǫ́*; 3S *paakˀǫ́* (LF)

_paaɣó 'push': 1S *hpáaɣo*; 2S *špáaɣo*; 3S *paaɣó*; 1P *ąpáaɣo*

_paaná 'stop, adjourn, quit, end something': 1S *hpáana*; 2S *špáana*; 3S *páana*; 1P *ąpáana*

Some of these verbs can be seen in the following examples:

(54) *katxá ąpána htai*
ka-txą ą-paaná htai
that-time A1P-adjourn INJ
'let's stop for a while'

(55) *ą́špaɣo ðaįšé*
ą-Ya-paɣo ðaįšé
P1S-A2S-push 2S.CONT
'you're pushing me'

(56) *htáa ąpáase ąkąkxai*
htáa ąk-paasé ąkatxą́-ðe
meat A1P-cut 1P.CONT-DECL
'we're cutting up meat'

A "false" fortisizing verb is *_hpí_ǫ* 'know, understand, possess a skill'. It resembles the fortisizing set under discussion here, and is grouped with that set for convenience, but it differs in having a preaspirate *hp* not only in 1S but also in 3S. It is also unusual in that it is doubly inflected:

_hpí_ǫ 'know, understand': 1S *hpímą* ~ *hpímǫ*; 2S *špížǫ*; 3S *hpíǫ*; 1P *ąhpíǫpe*

(See mention of *hpíǫ* in section 3.2.4.4 below.)

3.2.4.3 Mutating *k*-stems: *káaɣe* and *kǫ́žika*

The unusual pattern *hp, šC, C* characterizes this subgroup, with the unexpected ("mutant") *p* in A1S on a *k*-initial verb. These verbs are otherwise similar to fortisizing stop-stems. In 2S, these mutating stems are like fortisizing stop-stems, with *šk*. There are very few members in the mutating *k*-stem class, the two shown here and perhaps two other verbs that are rare and difficult to elicit, all velar-initial.

_káaɣe 'make, do': 1S *hpáaɣe*; 2S *škáaɣe*; 3S *káaɣe*; 1P *ąkáaɣe*

_kǫ́žįka 'not to know something; not to know how to do something': 1S *hpǫ́žįka*; 2S *škǫ́žika*; 3S *kǫ́žįka*; 1P *ąkǫ́žįka pe*

3.2.4.4 Nasal vowel stems (historical ˀ-stems)

The stems in this group can most conveniently be termed nasal vowel initial stems, instead of the usual Siouanist term "ˀ-stems," since forms with ˀ do not normally occur at utterance level in Osage. Inflection in this subgroup is characterized by *m* in 1S and *ž* in 2S. Etymologically, glottal stops were present in 3S/P, but always lost in 1S and 2S forms (Robert Rankin, p.c. 1995). Their presence can still be detected only when *į* 'wear' is preceded by a word ending in *į*: *haškámį ˀį aakšíe* 'I put that shawl on him' (more literally, 'I had him wear that shawl'). The historical presence of a glottal stop is further deduced from the behavior of the cognate stems in Dakota and Winnebago.

A fairly typical verb in this subclass is *į* 'wear' (from earlier *ˀ*į*), one of several verbs with this meaning.

(57) *haaská ščúuce mį ąhé*
haaská ščúuce Wa-į ąhé
clothing thick A1S-wear 1S.CONT
'I'm wearing warm clothes'

(58) *haaská ščúuce žį ðaašé*
haaská ščúuce Ya-į ðaįšé
clothing thick A2S-wear 2S.CONT
'you're wearing warm clothes'

(59) *haaská ščúuce į apái ðe*
haaská ščúuce Ø-į apá-ðe ðe
clothing thick A3P-wear 3.CONT-DECL DECL
'they're wearing warm clothes'

Unexpectedly, the form *brį* for 1S, instead of the expected *mį,* also occurs, as in the next example. This switch from ˀ-stem to *ð*-stem is reported to be a common development in Siouan languages.

(60) *haaskámį brį ąhé*
haaskámį Wa-į ąðįhé
shawl A1S-wear 1S.CONT
'I'm wearing my shawl'

For some types of clothing, another nasal vowel initial stem verb can be used: *á_ǫ* 'wear draped or wrapped' from historical **á*ˀ*ǫ,* with the expected *m* and *ž* forms for 1S and 2S.

(61) *ážǫ ðaįšé*
á-Ya-ǫ ðaįšé
PREV-A2S-wear 2S.CONT
'you're wearing it [warm clothing]'

Two other examples are the verbs *éki_ǫ* in (62a)–(62c) and *é_ǫ* in (63a)–(63c). Both mean 'do'; the former contains two preverbs, *é* and *ki*. The difference between these two verbs for 'do' is that *éki_ǫ* has a dative sense 'do for/with/in presence of another' (its preverb *ki* is a lexicalized dative marker); *é_ǫ* does not refer to others at all.

(62a) *ékimǫ ~ ékimą*
é-ki-Wa-ǫ
PREV-PREV-A1S-do
'I do'

(62b) *ékižǫ*
é-ki-Ya-ǫ
PREV-PREV-A2S-do
'you do'

(62c) *ékiǫ*
é-ki-Ø-ǫ
PREV-PREV-A3S-do
'he does'

(63a) *émǫ ~ émą*
é-Wa-ǫ
PREV-A1S-do
'I do'

(63b) *éžǫ*
é-Ya-ǫ
PREV-A2S-do
'you do'

(63c) *éwǫ*
é-w-Ø-ǫ
PREV-EPw-A3S-do
'he does'

Another member of the group is *_hpí_ǫ* 'know how to, learn, be skilled at', from historical **hpíˀǫ*, as regards the inflection before the second syllable *ǫ* of the doubly inflecting stem:

_hpí_ǫ: 1S *hpímą ~ hpímǫ*; 2S *špížǫ*; 3S *hpíǫ*; 1P *ąhpíǫpe*

The verb *aža_į* 'think' also shows this *m, ž* pattern of inflection (64a)–(69). In the third person *ažį* (66a), (66c), contraction of underlying *ažaį* via application of the V1-V2 Rule normally (but not always, for this verb) occurs. (This rule of vowel collapse also applies in the imperative.) In 1S and 2S, the context for application of the V1-V2 Rule does not emerge, owing to the intervening *m* and *ž*, respectively (see (64a)–(65c)).

(64a) *ažámį*[9]
aža-Wa-į
PREV-A1S-think
'I think'

(64b) *ékǫ ažámį*
é-kǫ aža-Wa-į
that-manner PREV-A1S-think
'I think that's right'

(65a) *ažážį*
aža-Ya-į
PREV-A2S-think
'you think'

(65b) *ékǫ ažážį?*
é-kǫ aža-Ya-į
that-manner PREV-A2S-think
'do you think that's right?'

(65c) *haakǫ́ ažáži?*
haa-kǫ́ aža-Ya-į
INDEF-manner PREV-A2S-think
'what do you think of it/him?'

(66a) *ažį*
aža-Ø-į
PREV-A3S-think
'he thinks'

(66b) *ðáalį ąąžį ðįkí apái*
ðáalį ą-aža-Ø-į ðįké apa-ðe
good P1S-PREV-A3S-think NEG 3.CONT-DECL
'he doesn't think well of me; he doesn't like me'

(66c) *hóo ðáalį aščį ažį ąži ohláži aščįe*
hóo ðáalį a-Ya-ðį aža-Ø-į ąži ohlá-aži
voice good PREV-A3P-have PREV-A3P-think but up.to.par-NEG
a-Ø-Ya-ðį-ðe
PREV-P3S-A2S-have-DECL
'they think you have a good voice but it isn't right'

[9] The 1S form varies between *ažámį* and *áažamį*, and is optionally doubly inflected: *_aža_į*, with patient inflection and optional regular agent inflection in the left slot, and syncopating agent inflection in the right slot. The 2S form likewise varies between *ažáži* and *ðažáži*.

(67a) *ąkáži̧ ąðįkše*
ąk-aža-i̧ ąðįkše
A1P-PREV-think 1D.CONT
'we [dual] think'

(67b) *ąkáži̧ ąkatxái*
ąk-áža-i̧ ąkatxą́-ðe
A1P- PREV-think 1P.CONT-DECL
'we [plural] think'

(68) *ą́ąži*
ą-a-ža-i̧-a
P1S-PREV-think-IMPER
'think of me'

3.2.5 Patient inflection

3.2.5.1 Patient for theme and receiver

The patient pronominals are seen in table 3.9. All active transitive verbs, including regular stems and syncopating stems, use the same set of patient prefixes for theme or receiver. These patient pronominals also function as subject or experiencer in stative verbs, and indeed this is the very thing that makes such a verb "stative," rather than any semantic consideration.

TABLE 3.9. PATIENT PRONOMINALS

P1S	*ą*	P1P	*wa...api*
P2S	*ði*	P2P	*ði...api*
P3S	*Ø*	P3P	*wa, Ø, wá*

NOTE: P3P *wá* is used mainly with *ð*-stems.

In this section we observe several active verbs with patient theme or receiver, e.g. 'take', 'wake up', 'give', 'teach', 'see', and 'give birth to'.

In (69)–(72), the receiver is represented by a patient prefix; the theme (the object that is transferred, represented by 'it' in the free translations) is phonologically null.

(69) *wáaðilaa*
wa-aði̧-a-lée-a
P3P-A3S-have-PREV-go.back-IMPER
'take [it] to them'

(70) *ąkʔúpe*
ą-Ø-kʔú-api-ðe
P1S-A3S-give-PL-DECL
'he gave [it] to me'

(71) *ðikʔúpe*
ði-Ø-kʔú-api-ðe
P2S-A3S-give-PL-DECL
'he gave [it] to you'

(72) *kʔúpe*
Ø-Ø-kʔu-api-ðe
P3S-A3S-give-PL-DECL
'he gave [it] to him/her'

The verb *ðixí* 'wake up' (transitive) appears in the next two examples, with patient pronominals.

(73) *ąwáðixíe*
ąk-wa-ðixí-ðe
A1P-P3P-wake-DECL
'we [dual] woke them up'

(74) *ą́ðixi əkxai*
ą-Ø-ðixi akxa-ðe
P1S-A3S-awaken 3.CONT-DECL
'he's waking me up'

The next example has undergone the *a-wa* metathesis rule (see section 3.4.1.1).

(75) *ąwálǫpaži nai*
ą-wa-lǫ́-api-aži nąą-ðe
A1P-P3P-call.names-PL-NEG ITER-DECL
'we [dual/plural] never called them names'

(76) *awálǫmąží nai*
Wa-wa-lǫ́-maží nąą-ðe
A1S-P3P-call.names-1S.NEG ITER-DECL
'I never call them names'

In *kšúįze* 'teach' (variant of *kšíǫze*) in the next example, P3P *wa* and A1S *Wa* also undergo *a-wa* metathesis.

(77) *awákšuįze*
Wa-wa-kšuįze
A1S-P3P-teach
'I teach them [e.g., my kids]'

(78) *Johna záani wéðape*
Johna záani wa-ii-Ø-ðe-api-ðe
John all P1P-PREV-A3S-see-PL-DECL
'John saw all of us'

The 1P patient pronominal *wa* 'us' is normally accompanied by the pluralizer suffix *api*, as in the following two examples. (See section 5.1 for discussion of *api*.)

(79) *wakˀúpi*
wa-kˀú-a-api
P1P-give-IMPER-PL
'give it to us'

(80) *wakˀupe*
wa-Ø-kˀu-api-ðe
P1P-A3P-give-PL-DECL
'they gave it to us'

The verb *ii_táðe* 'give birth to' in (81)–(88) is a regular *i*-verb (this term includes *ii*-initial verbs) that is quite common in speech.[10] (The full form is *iitáðe.* It is often shortened to *iitái* by *ð* elision and raising of *e* to *i* in final position.) Since P3S subject pronominal is null, in (81) no overt 'him' is present. The P1S and P2S elements can be seen in (82) and (83) respectively, although in (82), vowel harmony and *ð*-epenthesis, followed by harmonization to *n*, have altered the verb (see section 3.4.1 for these processes).

(81) *iiðátaðe*
ii-Ø-ð-Wa-taðe
PREV-P3S-EPð-A1S-birth
'I gave birth to him'

(82) *ąną́ta[ð]ape*
ii-ą-Ø-taðe-api-ðe
PREV-P1S-A3S-birth-PL-DECL
'I was born' (lit., 'she bore me')[11]

[10] The verb *ii_táðe* does not seem to inflect for 1P subject.

[11] Note that the English intransitive meaning, 'be born', is expressed in Osage with an active verb taking an object (therefore transitive): 'I was born' is expressed as '[she] bore me'. It takes patient inflection for object, as might be expected; this object corresponds to the English subject. We have kept the intransitive 'be born' for the gloss in English as it seems most natural and was the one offered by our speakers, although it is syntactically misleading.

(83) *iiðita[ð]ape*
ii-ði-Ø-taðe-api-ðe
PREV-P2S-A3S-birth-PL-DECL
'you were born' (lit., 'she gave birth to you')

The P1P *wa*, after metathesis, contracts with the locative prefix *ii* by the vowel contraction described in section 3.4.1.2, forming *wé*, as in (84) and (87).

(84) *wétaape*
wa-ii-Ø-taðe-api-ðe[12]
P1P-PREV-A3S/P-birth-PL-DECL
'we were born'

(85) *kóoci anǫ́taape*
kóoci ii-ą-Ø-taðe-api-ðe
long.ago PREV-P1S-A3SPL-birth-PL-DECL
'I was born a long time ago'

(86) *ðíe haatxą́ci íiðitaape?*
ðíe haatxą́ci ii-ði-Ø-táðe-api-ðe
2S.PRON when PREV-P2S-A3S-birth-PL-DECL
'when were you born?'

(87) *hą́mąðį įkši wétaape*
hą́-mąðį įkši wa-ii-Ø-taðe-api-ðe
night-walk in.ROUND P1P-PREV-A3S/P-PL-DECL
'we were born in Hominy'[13]

(88) *hpáažį wį ítaape*
hpáažį wį ii-Ø-taðe-api-ðe
baby a PREV-A3S-birth-PL-DECL
'she had a baby'

3.3 Stative verbs

Stative verbs are those that do not inflect with the agent inflectional markers but instead use patient inflectional markers for experiencer or actor. Sometimes, for ease of reference, we refer to this patient marker as the subject of the stative verb, although its subject status is controversial. A much more thorough study of all the categories and relevant verbs would be needed to establish exactly what the facts were when Osage was actively spoken, but such a study is no longer feasible. In recent years it has been quite difficult to find consistency in the use of stative patterns for

[12] Special positioning of *wa-i* is dealt with in sections 2.3.3.1 (vowel contraction) and 3.4.1.2 (*i-wa* Metathesis).

[13] The name of the town of Hominy, Oklahoma, is from *hą́-mąðį* 'Nightwalker' (an ancestor of Mrs. Frances Holding).

more than a few verbs, and examination in depth has been impossible owing to speakers' hesitancy in dealing with these forms. Only examples dealt with consistently in many different conversations held over time can be taken to validate a usage in this interesting area of Osage grammar—and even these usages may have been affected by several years of inactivity in the language.

The same patient pronominals (1S *ą*, 2S *ði*, 3S Ø, 1P *wa...(api)*, 3P *wa* (or 3P *Ø*) are used for stative verbs and for objects of active transitive verbs. As with other classes of Osage verbs, the first person plural is the most unstable form; some of the inflectional peculiarities in 1P are shown below in section 3.3.1. In section 3.3.2, doubly stative verbs are given; and in section 3.3.3, alternating active/stative inflection. *KI*-verbs are treated in section 4.6.5, showing their particular pattern of stative inflection (1S *ą́*; 2S *ðí*; 3S *Ø* ~ *kí*, 1P *wá...(api)*, 3P *wá* ~ *ki*).

While variation in only the 1P form characterizes many statives, it should also be pointed out that, in fact, it is not unusual to find statives sporadically uninflected and relying on an auxiliary to communicate person and number. This phenomenon is especially prevalent in 1P, and fairly prevalent in 3P as well.

The semantics of stative verbs seems to be frequently nonvolitional and stative, but there are exceptions to this general characterization. And among active verbs we find, e.g., 'be old' and others that seem nonvolitional. Agency takes precedence over eventhood in Osage, as it does in Lakota, for determining the active or stative nature of verbs (Mithun 1991). For Mithun, agents are characterized by the combination of performance/effect/instigation with control. In Osage, several verbs that involve performance without control ('hiccup', 'sneeze', 'cough', 'smile', and so forth) take agent inflection although control is not present.

There are a few verbs with two core arguments both of which core arguments are classified as nonagents, where neither participant performs, effects, instigates or controls. Examples are *óxta* 'cherish, love' and *íbrą* 'have enough of, be sated with'. Up to here, there are many similarities to Mithun's account of Lakota.

However, agent inflection is used in 'die' and 'stumble' in Osage (*acˀé* 'I died'; *axíbra* 'I stumbled'), contrasting with Lakota in which 'die' and 'slip' take patient inflection. Osage 'lose' and 'fall', however, which would seem to be similar to 'die' and 'stumble' on a semantic basis, do take patient inflection in Osage. 'Fall' and 'lose [i.e., suffer the loss of an item]' are both stative *oxpáðe* (based on *xpáðe*, which seems to have an abstract meaning of 'sever; separate').

Moreover, those verbs that do not describe an event, and for which no performance, effect, instigation or control is involved, and which are inherent attributes, are found in Osage to pattern with Central Pomo rather than Lakota, in that they take agent inflection: for example, 'be old', 'be alive'. Other nonevents without performance, effect, instigation or control but expressing temporary states affecting the person (such as 'be sick, 'be tired', 'be cold') have patient inflection in Osage. Especially intriguing are those few verbs (such as *íxope* 'lie, tell untruths') which are fluid in 2S in that they show optionally either agent or patient inflection, with the other person forms having one type of inflection, either agent or patient, as the case may be. In these fluid verbs it is not clear that the agent-patient division patterns with involvement of the subject in the action or state of the verb, or if some other criterion is in play. Some of these verbs are given in section 3.3.3.

3.3.1 Peculiarities in 1P forms

The expected P1P form for a stative verb is discontinuous *wa...(api)*, and those that use this expected form are sometimes referred to here as stative-*wa* verbs for ease of discussion and contrast. A group that behaves differently is called the stative-*ąk* group and comprises those stative verbs that unexpectedly take *ąk* for 1P (*ąk* is from the active paradigm). A third group is the stative-*Ø* group, which are those that unexpectedly take *Ø* in 1P.

3.3.1.1 Stative-*wa*

One common stative verb is *_húheka* 'be sick', seen in the next example set. This verb shows the expected stative P1P form with *wa*, and thus is a stative-*wa* verb.

(89) *wáli ąhúhekai*
wáli ą-húheka-ðe
very P1S-sick-DECL
'I'm really sick'

(90) *wahúheka aðįkše*
wa-húheka aðįkše
P1P-sick 1D.CONT
'we're really sick [dual]'

(91) *wahúheka ąkai*
wa-húheka ąkaðe
P1P-sick 1P.CONT
'we're really sick [plural]'[14]

[14] For analysis of the continuative aspect markers, see sections 5.5–5.6.

Plausibly a combination of the regular active verb *a_ðį* 'have' plus the negative *ðįké* , the stative verb *ðįké* 'lack' appears in the next example; it too shows the expected P1P *wa*. (For this verb, P3P is *Ø* and not *wa*, for reasons which are unclear.) Its complete inflectional paradigm is as follows:

(92a) *ąðįįke*
ą-ðįįke
P1S-lack
'I don't have any'

(92b) *ðiðįįke*
ði-ðįįke
P2S-lack
'you don't have any'

(92c) *waðįįke*[15]
wa-ðįįke
P1P-lack
'we [dual or plural] don't have any'

(92d) *ðįkí akxai*
Ø-ðįké akxa-ðe
3S/P-lack 3.CONT-DECL
'he doesn't have any; they don't have any'

The stative-*wa* verb *ní_hce* 'cold' shows variation (*Ø* or *wa*) for P1P, as shown in (96a)–(96c) below.

(93a) *nią́hce*
ní-ą-hce
PREV-P1S-cold
'I'm cold'

(93b) *nią́tamąžie*
ní-ą-hce-maží-ðe
PREV-P1S-cold-1S.NEG-DECL
'I'm not cold'[16]

[15] Note that the *api* portion of the 1P patient inflection is sometimes absent, both where its pluralizing effect is accomplished by the plural auxiliary, for example *ąkáðe* '1P continuative [moving]', and *waðįįke* in this example, where there is no clear reason for absence of *api*. See also the discussion of *api* in chapter 5 and the *oxpaðe* examples in 4.1.5.

[16] See 2.1.3.3 for alternation of *c* and *t* in (110a)–(110b). In Omaha-Ponca, this form is *sni_tte*.

(94) *níðihce*
ní-ði-hce
PREV-P2S-cold
'you're cold'

(95a) *níhcipé*
ní-Ø-hce-api-ðe
PREV-P3S-cold-PL-DECL
'he was cold'

(95b) *níhci akxái*
ní-Ø-hce akxá-ðe
PREV-P3S-cold 3.CONT-DECL
'he's cold; he was cold'

(96a) *níwahce*
ní-wa-hce
PREV-P1P-cold
'we're cold'

(96b) *níwahce ąkáe*
ní-wa-hce ąkáðe
PREV-P1P-cold 1P.CONT
'we're cold'

(96c) *níhce ąkáe*
ní-hce ąkáðe
PREV-cold 1P.CONT
'we're cold'

Its 3P forms freely occur with or without the patient inflection *wa*:

(97) *níhci apai*
ní-hce apa-ðe
PREV-cold 3.CONT-DECL
'they're cold'

(98) *níwahci əpai*
ní-wá-hce apa-ðe
PREV-P3P-cold 3.CONT-DECL
'they're cold'

Some verbs are not used in 1P, for unclear reasons. The stative *í_hpiiži* 'be gravely ill or bad off; be troubled' is one such case. The tendency is to substitute *_húheka* 'sick, ill' only for the 1P form.

(99) *íhpiiži*
i-Ø-hpiiži
with-P3S-be.troubled
'he's sick; he's troubled [by an illness]'

3.3.1.2 Stative-*ąk*

A few verbs deviate from the standard patient paradigm in 1P by using A1P *ąk* from the active paradigm. One example in this small set is the (otherwise) doubly stative *óxta* 'cherish; love'. The 1P form is further deviant in that it does not retain the *k* of *ąk* before *o*. Thus the A1P inflection looks suspiciously like stative P1S *ą*; but note that an emphatic 1P pronoun *ąkóe* was added in the following example.

(100) *ąkóe ą́oxtape*
ąkóe ąk-oxta-api-ðe
1P.PRON A1P-cherish-PL-DECL
'we love him'

3.3.1.3 Stative-*Ø*

Although we saw just above that *ðįké* 'not to have, to lack' was a stative-*wa* type verb, we find that it also inflects with *Ø* as the 1P inflection marker, as seen in the examples below, where the inflectional paradigm is 1S *ą*, 2S *ði*, 3S *Ø*, 1P *Ø*.

(101) *mą́zeska ąðį́ke mįkše*
mą́zeska ą-ðįké mįkše
money P1S-lack 1S.CONT
'I don't have any money'

(102) *mą́zeska ðiðį́ke nįkšé*
mą́zeska ði-ðįké nįkše
money P2S-lack 2S.CONT
'you don't have any money'

(103) *mą́zeska ðįké ąkátxai*
mą́zeska Ø-ðįké ąkátxai
money P1P-lack 1P.CONT
'we [plural] don't have any money'

(104) *mą́zeska ðįké ąðį́kše*
mą́zeska Ø-ðįké ąðįkše
money P1D-lack 1D.CONT
'we [dual] don't have any money'

Alternatively, the prefix *wa* may be used for first person dual or plural, in the stative-*wa* pattern.

(105) *mą́zeska waðį́ke*
mą́zeska wa-ðįké
money P1P-lack
'we don't have any money'

For 3S sentences, no *wa* is expected, since the third singular patient form is phonologically null, as in the next example. Subject markers (like *apa* in this example) optionally appear on noun subjects of statives.

(106) *wižį̨ke apa mą́zeska ðįkí apai*
wižį̨ke apa mą́zeska Ø-ðįké apa-ðe
Sonny SUBJ money A3S-lack 3.CONT-DECL
'Sonny doesn't have any money'

3.3.2 Doubly stative verbs

A small set of stative verbs is doubly stative. These are transitive verbs that take patient markers for both subject (experiencer) inflection and object (theme) inflection. Only two such verbs have been found in Osage thus far: *óxta* 'cherish, love' (section 3.3.2.2; see also section 3.3.1.2) and *íbrą ~ íbra* 'have/get enough of; be sated with' (section 3.3.2.1).[17]

3.3.2.1 *íbrą* 'be sated with'

Examples in which both subject and object (experiencer and theme) are represented by overt patient pronominals are fairly rare, since only a few combinations of subject and object pronominals will produce the two. Infrequency of such forms may also be due in part to a slight reluctance to use the verb *íbrą* because of a possible sexual connotation.

When the subject and object pronominals are both *wa*, one of them optionally is dropped: compare (107), with two *wa* prefixes, to (108), with only one. (Admittedly in the latter case it is hard to tell which prefix is retained. I assume here it is the P1P prefix, since *wa...api* is normal P1P marking.)

(107) *wawébrąpe*
wa-wa-í-brą-api-ðe
P3P-P1P-PREV-have.enough-PL-DECL
'we're tired of them'

(108) *wébrąpe*
wa-í-brą-api-ðe
P1P-PREV-have.enough-PL-DECL
'we've had enough of them'

Examples (109)–(114) illustrate other inflectional forms of this verb.

(109) *ąną́ðibrą nįkše?*
i-n-ą-ði-brą nįkše
PREV-EP*n*-P1S-P2S-have.enough 2S.CONT
'have you had enough of me?'

[17] Such verbs also exist in Lakota: for example, 'resemble', 'be proud of'.

(110) *anǫ́bra*
í-n-ą-brą
PREV-EP*n*-P1S-have.enough
'I've got enough'

(111) *ąnǫ́bra įke mįkše*
í-n-ą-brą ðįké mįkšé
PREV-EP*n*-P1S-have.enough NEG 1S.CONT
'I haven't had enough'

(112) *íðibra nįkšé?*
í-ði-brą nįkšé?
PREV-P2S-have.enough 2S.CONT
'have you had enough?'

(113) *wébra ąkátxai*
wa-í-brą ąkátxa-ðe
P1P-PREV-have.enough 1P.CONT-DECL
'we've had enough'

(114) *níi wébra ąkatxái*
níi wa-í-brą ąkátxa-ðe
water P1P-PREV-have.enough 1P.CONT-DECL
'we've had enough water'

Three versions of 'they've had enough water' were recorded, apparently synonymous:

(115a) *níi wébrąpe*
níi wa-í-brą-api-ðe
water P3P-PREV-have.enough-PL-DECL
'they've had enough water'

(115b) *níi íbrą apai*
níi í-brą apa-ðe
water PREV-have.enough 3.CONT-DECL
'they've had enough water'

(115c) *níi wébrą apai*
níi wa-í-brą apa-ðe
water P3P-PREV-have.enough 3.CONT-DECL
'they've had enough water'

The P1P experiencer form of this verb varies between *wébrą* and *įðǫ́brą*; at least one speaker preferred the latter but considered both correct.

(116) *wébrą*
wa-í-brą
P1P-PREV-have.enough
'we've had enough'

3.3.2.2 *óxta* 'cherish, love'

The verb *óxta* 'love, like; cherish, honor', is a somewhat problematical verb. It does take patient pronominals for both the experiencer (the one who loves, cherishes) and the loved or cherished person. But in some cases where two markers are expected only one occurs (as mentioned for *íbrą* in section 3.3.2.1). Only two examples were found where two overt patient markers are present in the same sentence:

(117) *ą́ðioxta*
ą-ði-óxta
P1S-P2S-cherish
'you love me'

(118) *žįkážį wáð[i]oxta ðąaše*
žįkážį wa-ði-óxta ðąaše
children P3P-P2S-cherish 2S.CONT
'you are honoring the children'

The portmanteau *wi* replaces both patient pronominals in instances where theme is 2S and experiencer is 1S:

(119) *wíoxtai*
wi-óxta-ðe
P2S<A1S-cherish-DECL
'I love you'

Otherwise, P1S 'me' precedes P2S 'you' in doubly stative verbs; cf. *ą́ðioxta* 'you love me' in (117).

Other unusual features of this verb were noted in section 3.3.1.2. For one thing, it apparently takes active inflection for 1P experiencer; moreover it fails to retain the *k* of *ąk* A1P before back vowel *o*.

(120) *ąkóe ą́oxtape*
ąkóe ąk-oxta-api-ðe
1P.PRON A1P-cherish-PL-DECL
'we love him'

This gives the sequence *ąo*, which in this position is unusual for Osage. Presumably, the *k* has elided, and only *ą* remains; the alternative would be to analyze this *ą* as a peculiar use of the singular *ą* P1S. Neither explanation is entirely satisfactory; example (120) shows clearly the experiencer reading for *ą* (see also (122)–(124)). In (121), either theme 1P or experiencer P3P is marked by *wa*:

(121) *ąkóe, waóxtape*
ąkóe *wa-oxta-api-ðe*
1P.PRON P1P-cherish-PL-DECL
'they like us'

The *o* of this verb is not the locative *o* seen elsewhere. The locative *o* precedes inflection in 1S and 2S, and follows the 1P inflectional marker. In *óxta*, the nonlocative *o* follows inflectional marking in 1S and 2S.

No *wa* is present for 'them' in the next two examples, but this is not surprising, as *wa* is missing from the patient paradigm in some other stative verbs as well.

(122) *ą́oxtai*
ą́-oxta-ðe
P1S-cherish-DECL
'I cherish them; I love them, I like it/them'

(123) *ą́oxta*
Ø-ą-oxta
P3S-P1S-cherish
'I like him/her'

Example (118) above, however, has both a noun object and *wa*.

Further inflected forms of *óxta* are given in the following examples.

(124) *ą́oxta*
Ø-ą-oxta
P3P-P1S-cherish
'I like them'

(125) *ðíoxta íhpaho mįkšé*
Ø-ðí-oxta *í-Wa-pahǫ* *mįkšé*
P3S-P2S-cherish PREV-A1S-know 1S.CONT
'I know you love him/her'

(126) *ðie ðíoxtái*
ðie *Ø-ðí-óxta-ðe*
2S.PRON P3S-P2S-cherish-DECL
'you love him'

(127) *ðíoxta*
Ø-ði-óxta
P3S-P2S-cherish
'you like him'

(128) *ée ą́oxtapé*
ée ą-óxta-api-ðe
3S.PRON P1S-cherish-PL-DECL
'he/she/it loves me'

(129) *ðíoxtapé*
ði-Ø-óxta-api-ðe
P2S-P3S-cherish-PL-DECL
'he loves you'

A derived form of *óxta* has an additional *o* (the locative *o* prefix, 'culmination') and epenthetic *ð*, and is used in referring to 'something one values'. The valence reducer *wa* has collapsed into the *ó* (section 4.1).

(130) *óðoxta*
wa-o-ð-óxta
VAL-LOC-EPð-cherish
'something or someone that one loves'

(131) *óðoxta škáaɣe*
wa-o-ð-óxta Ya-káaɣe
VAL-PREV-EPð-cherish A2S-make
'you're making something that you like; you're showing how you like it; you make him a favorite, favored one'

3.3.3 Fluid active-stative paradigms

Variation between agent inflection and patient inflection for the same argument, with no discernible change in meaning, occurs in a few verbs; these paradigms are termed fluid. This variation occurs principally in the second person forms, but also occasionally in first person (singular, dual and plural) forms (see section 3.3.1). Thus, variation between 2S patient *ði* and 2S agent *ða* can be seen in a few verbs, for example, *íxope* 'lie, tell untruths' and *íšcewai* 'dress up'; though classed with the regular active verbs, both *íxope* and *íšcewai* may show patient inflection *ði* in second person, instead of the expected agent (active) *ða*. These verbs in 1S use a clear regular active form (with epenthetic *ð*; e.g., 1S *iðáxope* 'I told a lie'). Verbs with an otherwise agentive paradigm but showing the second person variation *ða* ~ *ði* may be thought of as sporadically being used statively.

3.3.3.1 *íšcewai* 'dress up'

The following examples show active *íšcewai* 'dress up'. This verb exhibits fluidity, having three different second person forms: with 2S agent *ða* (132); without any second person pronominal (neither *ði* nor *ða*) in (133), or with 2S patient *ði* as in (134) and (135). The regular 1S agent pronominal is shown in (136). Interestingly, La Flesche shows *íšcewa* 'dress up' as stative.[18]

(132) *íðašcewa apai*
í-ða-šcewa apa-ðe
PREV-A2S-dress.up 3.CONT-DECL
'you [plural] are very dressed up'

(133) *haakǫ́ta íšcewai ðą́įše?*
haakǫ́ta í-šcewa ðaįšé
why PREV-dress.up 2S.CONT
'why are you [singular] dressed up?'

(134) *íðiščewai nįkšé*
í-ði-šcewa nįkšé
PREV-P2S-dress.up 2S.CONT
'you're [singular] all dressed up'

(135) *wáli íðišcewa apai*
wáli í-ði-šcewa apa-ðe
very PREV-P2S-dress.up 3.CONT-DECL
'you [plural] are very dressed up'

(136) *íðašcewa mįkše*
í-ð-Wa-šcewa mįkše
PREV-EPð-A1S-dress.up 1S.CONT
'I'm really going to dress up'

3.3.3.2 *ibrą* 'have enough of'

The same variation is found in doubly stative *íbrą* 'have enough of' (see also section 3.3.2.1). Upon close examination with speakers, no semantic difference can be established between the *ða* and *ði* versions for 2S *íbrą*. Both apply with equal appropriateness to (getting enough of) eating, watching TV, riding horses, talking, listening, and items of food.

(137) *íðibrą nįkšé?*
í-ði-brą nįkšé
PREV-P2S-get.enough 2S.CONT
'did you get enough?'

(138) *ąwą́ðahkie íiðibrą?*
o-w-ą-Ya-hki-ie í-ði-brą
PREV-EPw-P1S-A2S-RECIP-talk PREV-P2S-get.enough
'did you get enough of talking to me?'

[18] In examples (132) and (135), third person continuative *apa* is unexpectedly used in a clause with A2P, where *paašé* is the norm.

For 1P, the active inflection *ąk* is used, rather than the expected stative P1P *wa*.

(139) *ąnąbra ąkatxái*
ąk-í-brą ąkatxá-ðe
A1P-PREV-have.enough 1P.CONT-DECL
'we got enough'

3.3.3.3 *íxope* 'lie, tell untruths'

The verb *i_xope* 'lie, tell untruths' also shows variation between *ði* and *ða*. This is the kind of verb where some languages use active vs. stative to signify control vs. lack of control. Unfortunately, it is difficult to say at this stage of disuse of the Osage language whether such a distinction ever existed.

For 1S three different forms are found: *iðáxope*, *įðąxope*, and a harmonized version *ąnąxope*. This could be a matter of dialect, regularization, or an accidental interruption in rule application, possibly owing to language disuse.

(140) *įðąxopamąži*
i-ð-ą-xope-maži
PREV-EPð-P1S-lie-1S.NEG
'I don't lie'

(141) *iðáxope mįkše*
i-ð-Wa-xope mįkše
PREV-EPð-A1S-lie 1S.CONT
'I'm telling a lie'

For the 2S form, both *ða* and *ði* occur:

(142) *íðaxope nįkšé*[19]
i-Wa-xope nįkše
PREV-A1S-lie 2S.CONT
'you're telling a lie'

(143) *íðixope ðąįšé*
i-ði-xope ðaįšé
PREV-P2S-lie 2S.CONT
'you have been lying'

[19] For 2S.CONT in these sentences, as elsewhere, either the 'sitting' 2S continuative auxiliary *nįkšé* may be used, or the 'moving' 2S continuative auxiliary *ðaįšé*. The other two options are 'standing' and 'lying' auxiliaries. All four signal continuative aspect. See section 5.5 for discussion.

(144) *íðixope nįkšé*
i-ði-xope nįkše
PREV-P1S-lie 2S.CONT
'you're telling a lie'

(145) *íðixope nąží*
í-ði-xope ną-aži
PREV-P2S-lie ITER-NEG
'you don't lie'

Note that the expected stative-*ąk* form for 1P is *ąnąxope*, via vowel lowering and *ð*-insertion, followed by the *ð* nasalizing to *n*, the normal pattern for *i*-verbs using *ąk* in 1P.

(146) *ąnąxope ąkáe*
i-ą-xope ąkáðe
PREV-A1P-lie 1P.CONT
'we've been lying'

Two alternative 1P forms appear as well. In (147) the *k* of *ąk* has elided, and epenthetic *ð* appears instead of the *n* expected from harmonization.

(147) *ąðąxope ąkáe*[20]
i-ąk-xope ąkáðe
PREV-A1P-lie 1P.CONT
'we've been lying'

The third possibility is the plain verb with no pronominal inflection in the stem at all:

(148) *íxope ąkáe*
i-xope ąkáðe
PREV-lie 1P.CONT
'we've been lying'

The 1P patient form *wa...(api)* was not encountered with this verb.

[20] In this example, vowel lowering and nasality assimilation (*i* → *ą*) have occurred, with *ð* emerging between the two nasal vowels instead of the expected *n*. It is not unusual to see *n* emerge before a nasal vowel or between nasal vowels in place of an underlying *ð*, nor is the opposite case, with an epenthetic *ð* in the surface form in lieu of *n*, as in the form here, very surprising. It is difficult to speculate whether the variant 1P forms *ąnąxope,* heard during the early 1980s from other speakers, and *ąðąxope* (or even *įðąxope*, elsewhere, from the same speaker), heard in the 1990s, which represent different stages of the two harmonization processes in this verb, are symptomatic of an emerging repeal of rules as the language is less and less used, or if this is merely a variation that has been present for some time. With few speakers remaining, none of whom is using the language actively, data are too scarce to say.

3.4 Rules that interact with inflection

I will now discuss in more detail several rules of movement and phonological processes, briefly mentioned in chapter 2, that operate on inflectional elements and locative preverbs. The rule of *k*-Deletion was fully presented in section 3.1.3.2 and does not need to be discussed further here. Rules examined in this subsection include those for metathesis of *wa* and *a*/*ą*, a second metathesis rule that affects *i-wa* sequences (closely followed by vowel contraction), epenthesis of *ð*, a rule of vowel harmony involving *o* and *ą*, and a rule of harmonization involving *n*.

3.4.1 Metathesis, contraction, epenthesis

Here two metathesis processes will be presented, followed by a discussion of *ð*-Epenthesis. The first of these processes, metathesis of *wa-a* or of *wa-ą*, is presented in 3.4.1.1 (see also discussion of *wa-a* in A1S in section 3.2.1.1). The second process affects *i-wa*, and will be covered in section 3.4.1.2 below. The epenthesis of *ð* was presented above in 3.2.2.1 and 3.2.2.3.

3.4.1.1 *wa*-Metathesis

The subject pronominal *Wa* becomes *a* in regular verbs. We continue to write *Wa* in interlinear glosses of examples elsewhere in this work, but in this subsection only, glosses show all elements after A1S *Wa* becomes *a* and after any movement rules have applied. The rule of *wa*-Metathesis switches the positions of *wa* (or *waa*) and either *a* A1S or *ą* P1S. Thus, *wa-a* becomes *awá*, as in *awánǫbre* 'I dine' from *wa_nǫ́bre*, and *awálǫ* 'I call names' from *wa_lǫ́*; and *wáa-a* becomes *a-wáa*, as in *awáachi* 'I dance' from *waa_chí*.

No such metathesis need apply to *ąk* A1P, simplified to *ą*, since we consider *ąk* to be generated where it occurs, leftward of the preverb in such forms as *ąwánǫbre* 'we dine' from *wa_nǫ́bre*, *ąwáðaahtą* ' we drink' from *wa_ðáahta,* and *ąwáata* 'we pray'from *waa_tá*.

The rule affects any *wa*, including P1P *wa* 'us; to us'; P3P *wa* 'them; to them'; the valence reducer *wa*; and preverbs *wa*, *waa* or *wá, wáa*. Locative *á* does not undergo this rule.

In second person, the context for the metathesis rule does not occur. Example (149) shows the second person form of *waa_chí* 'dance' with the A2S prefix (underlying *Ya*, surface *ða*) following the initial preverb *waa*.

(149) *waaðáchi*
waa-Ya-chi
PREV-A2S-dance
'you dance'

Similarly, for *wa_lǫ́* 'call names', we find 2S *waðálǫ* 'you call names', but in the 1S form *wa-a-lǫ́* becomes *a-wa-lǫ́* via metathesis, leaving *awálǫ* 'I call names' as surface form.

Metathesis of P3P *wa* can bee seen in the two examples below. First the patient and agent pronominals *wa* and *a* insert at the point of inflection (e.g., *mąxí-wa-a-ðe* [deceive-P3P-A1S-CAU]), then they metathesize.

(150) *mąxíawaðe*
mąxí-a-wa-ðe
deceive-A1S-P3P-CAU
'I deceived them'

(151) *cˀéawaðe*
cˀé-a-wa-ðe
die-A1S-P3P-CAU
'I killed them'

3.4.1.2 *i-wa* Metathesis and contraction of vowels

The rule of *i-wa* Metathesis involves the preverb *i* (or *ii*) in the *i-* or *ii-* initial verbs and the *wa* pronominal or the *wa* valence reducer. The result of this rule is that *wa* moves leftward, whereas in *wa*-Metathesis above, *wa* moved to the right of *a* or *ą*. In the the rule-ordered model pursued here, a P3S *wa* appears first at the point of inflection following the preverb (or locative) *i*, and the sequence will metathesize becoming *wa-i*.

Thus, *íi_ðe* 'see' with P3P *wa* and A1S *a* is *íi-wa-a-ðe*, which becomes *wa-íi-a-ðe* via *i-wa* Metathesis. The *wa-ii* sequence produced will collapse via contraction of *a* + *i*, already mentioned in section 2.3.3.1 (see also section 3.2.5.1). This rule of vowel contraction produces the final surface form *wéeaðe* 'I see them'. Likewise, when the valence reducer *wa* is added to the A1S form *i-a-chį* of the verb *i_chį́* 'hit with', producing *wa-i-á-chį*, contraction of *a* + *i* applies to produce the surface form *weáchį* 'I hit him with something'.

The rule of *i-wa* Metathesis applies regardless of accent and to all such sequences in the data. The vowel contraction rule changes all *wa-i* sequences to *we*. Another popular verb with this behavior is shown in (152)–(153).

(152) *ii_šcį̨ka*
ii-šcį̨ka
PREV-caress
'caress, kiss'

(153) *wéakiščį̨ka*
wa-ii-Wa-kik-ščį̨ka
P3P-A1S-SUU-caress
'I caressed them [my children]'[21]

3.4.2 Harmonization rules

Perhaps more properly termed assimilation of place across an intervening consonant *w* or *ð*, the phenomenon of lowering of a vowel to harmonize with an adjacent vowel occurs in Osage in two basic contexts: (i) with a combination of *o* or *ǫ* and *a* or *ą* across the intervening, perhaps epenthetic, consonant *w*, and (ii) with *i* and *ą* in adjacent syllables across the intervening epenthetic *ð*. The result in context (i) is *awá* or *ąwą́* sequences from *oa* and *oą* respectively; in context (ii) the result is *ąną* (and occasionally *iðą* or *iną* which perhaps reflect historically earlier or morphologically underlying forms).

3.4.2.1 *o*-Lowering

With nonnasal vowels, there is an optional *o-a* harmonizing rule applying in the context of 1S inflection (*a* or *ą*) in verbs like *o_chį́* 'hit'. The unharmonized form of 'I hit it' is *oáchį*, or *owáchį* with an epenthetic *w*. If the optional rule applies, *o* lowers to *a*, giving *awáchį*. A given speaker may use both a harmonized and an unharmonized form, possibly depending on speech rate, level of formality, or some other factor.

Lowering of the *o* to *a* seems to be less likely to occur if the vowels are nonnasal than if they are nasal; consider the next three examples, where *ó* fails to lower to *á*.

(154) *ówahką-api*
ó-wa-hką-a-api
LOC-P1P-help-IMPER-PL
'you [singular or plural] help us!'

(155) *oáhką ąhe*
o-Wa-hką ąhe
PREV-A1S-help 1S.CONT
'I'm helping, I've been helping'

[21] The *ki* appearing in the surface form is the suus *kik*, since the speaker insisted on adding 'my children'. The dative version, however, would be identical in surface form.

(156) *owáchį*
o-Ø-w-Wa-chį
PREV-P3S-EPw-A1S-hit
'I hit him'

With nasal vowels, the rule is still optional, but it is more likely that lowering will apply. There is some variation in application of the rule that changes preverb *o* followed by inflection *ą* (usually meaning, 'me, to me', as object) to *ąwą*. For example, unharmonized *oą́štaake* 'you are telling me' can be found occasionally, but we would normally find *ąwą́štaake*, in which lowering has applied. The following two examples show this process in inflectional forms of *ó_kˀu* 'lend'.

(157) *waléze toa ąwą́ðakˀu ną*
waléze toa o-ą-Ya-kˀu ną
book some PREV-P1S-A2S-loan ITER
'these are the books that you loaned me'

(158) *ą́wąkˀu*
ó-ą-kˀu-a
PREV-P1S-lend-IMPER
'lend it to me'

In the next example, based on the verb *o_hí* 'win', *o-ą-hí* → *owąhi* → *ąwą́hi,* and spontaneous denasalization of *wą* to *wa* occurs.

(159) *ąwáhipe*
o-ą-ą́-hi-api-ðe
LOC-P1S-A3S-conquer-PL-DECL
'he beat me'

Lowering is also seen in sentence (160), with *o_žú* 'put inside; pour' (*oąžu* → *owąžu* → *ąwą́žu*, plus spontaneous denasalization to *ąwážu*); in (161)–(162), with *ó_hką* 'help'; and in (163), with P1S inflection of *o_chį́* 'hit'.

(160) *mǫhką́sa tóa ąwážu, wihtą́ke*
mǫhką́sa tóe o-ą-žú wihtą́ke
coffee some PREV-P1S-put.in sister
'pour me some coffee, sister'

(161) *ąwą́hkąpe*
o-ą-hką-api-ðe
PREV-P1S-help-PL-DECL
'they helped me'

(162) *ą̨wą́hką!*
o-ą̨-hką-a
PREV-P1S-help-IMPER
'help me!'

(163) *ą̨wą́chį*
o-ą̨-chį́
PREV-P1S-hit
'he hit me'

The 1P subject inflection *ąk* does not provide a context for lowering of *o*, since *ąk* occurs leftward of the prefix and does not lose its *k* in that context. Thus, for example, the A1P form of *ó_kʔu* 'lend' is *ąkókʔu* 'we lend [it]'.

3.4.2.2 *ð*-Epenthesis, *i*-Lowering, and *ð*-Harmonization

In *i*-verbs, the general rule of *ð*-epenthesis applies between *i* and *ą* (P1S or A1P), producing *iðą* (see 3.2.2.1 and 3.2.2.3). Harmonization takes place, lowering and nasalizing the *i* to *ą́* (*ąðą́*) and changing the *ð* to *n* in between nasal vowels.

ð-Epenthesis:	*Ø* → *ð* / *i* __ *ą́*, *á*
i-Lowering and nasalization:	*i* → *ą* / __ *ðą*
ð-Harmonization:	*ð* → *n* / *V* [+nas]__*V* [+nas]

A sample derivation is:

(164)	(underlying)	*i-ąk-pa-hǫ*
	(*k*-Deletion)	*i-ą-pa-hǫ*
	(*ð*-Epenthesis)	*i-ðą-pa-hǫ*
	(*i*-Lowering)	*ą-ðą-pa-hǫ*
	(*ð*-Harmonization)	*ąnąpahǫ*
		'we know him'

The rules *ð*-Epenthesis and *i*-Lowering affect any *i* + *ą* sequence, regardless of whether *ą* represents A1P *ąk*, as in (164) above, or P1S *ą* 'me; to me':

(165) *i-ą-pa-hǫ* → *ąnąpahǫ* 'he knows me'

(Thus, *ąnąpahǫ* is ambiguous between 'we know him' and 'he knows me'.)

This is a widespread phenomenon in Osage, affecting virtually every verb that begins with *i* or *ii*. Further examples in which these rules apply are:

(166) *ąną́xope ąkáe*
i-ą-xope ąkáðe
PREV-A1P-lie 1P.CONT
'we've been lying'

(167) *ąną́xope ąðįkšé*
í-ąk-xope ąðįkšé
PREV-A1P-lie 1D.CONT
'we're [dual] telling a lie'

(168) *ąną́ðape*
íi-ąk-Ø-ðe-api-ðe
PREV-A1P-P3S-see-PL-DECL
'we [plural] see it'

3.5 Special cases of irregularities in verbs

Some verbs show certain stem irregularities, such as a vowel change in certain inflected forms, and are treated in 3.5.1. Other verbs seem to be preferred with no inflection at all except via continuative auxiliaries (section 3.5.2). Others are doubly inflected (section 3.5.3).

3.5.1 Stem irregularities

There are a few verb paradigms that are unlike any others, where it is not clear exactly what processes are affecting the verb patterns. One of these verbs is *óohǫ* 'cook [things]' (a valence-reduced verb; see section 4.1), which is unusual not in its inflectional markers but in the stem. This verb takes the *a-ða* subjects, but has *a* (varying with *ą*) instead of expected *ǫ́* of the stem in 1S and 2S: 1S *oowáha* ~ *oowáhą*, 2S *ooðáha* ~ *ooðáhą*, 1D *ąkóohǫ įkšé*, 1P *ąkóohǫpe*. This could be a reflex of the vowel harmony discussed in section 3.4.2.1: *oowáhǫ* becomes *oowáha*, with vowel lowering and denasalization.

In *_hpí_ǫ* 'know, know how to, learn; be skilled at' too, the 1S form *hpímą* (optionally) shows *ą* instead of the expected *ǫ* in final position. The same is true for *hpą́žįka* 'I don't know how', the A1S form of *_kǫ́žįka* 'not know; be ignorant of', but there it is the initial syllable that optionally changes: *hpǫ́žįka* → *hpážįka* ~ *hpą́žįka*. This lowering of back vowels in 1S (and 2S) is unexplained but unsurprising in Osage, as there is variation elsewhere between the low back vowels.

3.5.2 Uninflected verbs

There are a small number of verbs in Osage that do not carry inflection marked on the verb itself. These verbs are marked for person and number only by the continuative aspect marker, which carries (usually redundant) person and number information. In fact, some of these may be more appropriately classified as adverbs, but the issue of strict classification of these forms is not addressed here.

A few of the examples given below have been gathered as isolated sentences and their deviation from normal patterns may be owing to some reason not immediately apparent. Other examples are from verbs whose full paradigms consistently remained uninflected, such as 'gossip', 'worry', 'behave'.

3.5.2.1 Examples of uninflected verbs

The three verbs presented here are examples of verbs that have never been found in inflected forms in the data (with one exception, noted below).

(169a) *tíðe ąąhé*[22]
tíðe ąðįhé
gossip 1S.CONT
'I have been gossiping'

(169b) *tíðe mįkšé*
tíðe mįkšé
gossip 1S.CONT
'I'm gossiping'

(169c) *ðie tíðe nįkšé*
ðie tíðe nįkšé
2S.PRON gossip 2S.CONT
'you're gossiping; you're the one who's gossiping'

(170a) *óðąąceši*
'worry about something'[23]

(170b) *oðíhta óðąąceši akxái*
oðíhta óðąąceši akxá-ðe
car worry 3.CONT-DECL
'he's worried about the car'

(170c) *óðąąceši mįkšé*
worry 1S.CONT
'I'm worried'

[22] The sequence *ti* is highly unusual for Osage. Only a couple of such forms exist. 'Gossip' may be derived from *ta-iðe* 'speak', where *ta* may be a shortened version of *táatą* 'what, something', giving 'say something' (cf. Omaha-Ponca *edaphe* 'I say something', *edaše* 'you say something', *ede* 'he said something'). No instances of inflected *tíðe* have been found.

[23] The word *ðą́ące* is 'heart' and *ši* denotes 'vigor' or 'activity, energy'. Worry then seems to be approximately a 'state where the heart flutters'.

(171a) *óðohta ąąhé*
straight 1S.CONT
'I'm behaving'

(171b) *óðohta ðaįšé*
straight 2S.CONT
'you're behaving'

The exception is the example below, in which *óðohta* 'behave' has 1S agent inflection.

(172) *oáðohta ąmąbrį ąškáaɣe ikʔúca*
o-Wa-ðohta Wa-mą-Wa-ðį ą-Ya-káaɣe ikʔúce-a
PREV-A1S-straight A1S-PREV-A1S-walk P1S-A2S-make try-IMPER
'try to make me behave'

3.5.2.2 Examples of optionally inflected verbs

Some verbs in Osage are used without inflectional markers optionally and frequently, but also may take full inflection: e.g., *wáaspe* 'stay' (173a)–(173c), *olį́į* 'ride' (174a)–(174b), and stative *nǫhpéhi* 'be hungry' (175a)–(175c).

(173a) *wáaspe hta apai*
wáa-spe hta apa-ðe
PREV-stay FUT 3.CONT-DECL
'they're going to stay'

(173b) *wáaspe hta nįkšé?*
wáa-spe hta nįkšé
PREV-stay FUT 2S.CONT
'are you going to stay?'

(173c) *waaðáspe hta nįkšé?*
waa-ða-spe hta nįkšé
PREV-A2S-stay FUT 2S.CONT
'are you going to stay?'

(174a) *oðíhtą olį́į hta mįkšé*
oðíhtą o-lį́į hta mįkšé
car LOC-sit/dwell FUT 1S.CONT
'I'm going to ride in a car'

(174b) *oðíhtą oálįį hta mįkšé*
oðíhtą o-Wa-lįį hta mįkšé
car LOC-A1S-sit/dwell FUT 1S.CONT
'I'm going to ride in a car'

(175a) *nǫhpéhi mįkšé*
nǫhpé-hi mįkšé
PREV-hungry 1S.CONT
'I'm hungry'

(175b) *nǫhpéǫhi mįkšé*
nǫhpé-ǫ-hi mįkšé
PREV-P1S-hungry 1S.CONT
'I'm hungry'

(175c) *nǫhpéhi akxái*
nǫhpé-hi akxá-ðe
PREV-hungry 3.CONT-DECL
'he's hungry'

Many verbs, such as valence-reduced *wa_ðáawa* 'count stuff', normally inflect, as in (176a)–(176c), but occasionally, for unclear reasons, appear uninflected as in (177), accompanied by a continuative marker bearing person and number information.

(176a) *wabráawa atxǫhe*
wa-Wa-ðaawá atxǫhe
VAL-A1S-count 1S.CONT
'I count'

(176b) *waštáawa nįkše*
wa-Ya-ðaawá nįkše
VAL-A2S-count 2S.CONT
'you count'

(176c) *waðáawa akxai*
wa-Ø-ðaawá akxa-ðe
VAL-A3S-count 3.CONT-DECL
'he counts'

(177) *waðáawa ǫtxǫhé*
wa-ðaawá ǫtxǫhé
VAL-count 1S.CONT
'I count'

3.5.3 Doubly inflected verbs

There are quite a number of verbs that take inflection at two separate points in the stem, having two sets of agent inflectional markers, one at each of these two different places in the verb stem. In the case of a transitive verb, the patient inflection typically occurs along with the agent inflection, in the normal order, but at only the leftmost point. Many of these doubly inflecting stems are morphosemantically opaque. A few of the doubly inflected verbs are listed here, with indication of the type(s) of inflection they use in each case, since no uniformity of inflectional class prevails. That is, whether syncopating or regular inflection is used at a particular point of inflection depends solely on the segment that immediately follows that point of inflection; a doubly inflected verb may have regular inflection at one of its inflection points, syncopating at the other. The underscores show the two locations of the inflectional markers. All doubly inflected verbs have only one point of inflection for 1P agent, at the leftmost location.[24]

áa_lǫ_ði 'forget' (uses both regular *a-ða* inflection at the leftmost underscore and syncopating *ð*-stem inflection at the rightmost underscore): *ą́ąðalǫšcį* 'did you forget me?' (harmonized nasalization in first syllable *ą́ą* of 1S); *wáaðalǫšcį* 'you forget them'.

_hii_ðá 'bathe' (regular and *ð*-stem verb): *ðahįišce* 'did you bathe?'

_kǫ́_ða 'want' (fortisizing stop-stem and *ð*-stem verb)

_hpí_ǫ́ 'know, learn, know how to' (fortisizing stop-stem and nasal vowel stem)

The verb *waa__ðǫ́* 'sing' can on rare occasions appear doubly inflected, with regular inflection immediately preceding *ð*-stem inflection: for example, *awáabrǫ* (but more usually *waabrǫ́*) for 1S; *waaðáštǫ* (but more usually *waaštǫ́*) for 2S. For 1P, only *ąwáaðǫ* is used.

Another doubly inflecting verb, *_aža_į* 'think, believe' (e.g., A2S *ða-ažá-žį* 'you think', was mentioned in section 3.2.4. Its first point of inflection is for object pronominals and optional subject pronominal, and the second for obligatory subject pronominals. It is also special in that vowel contraction produces *ažį́* as its surface form.

Some of the verbs that are clearly doubly inflected are derived from singly inflecting verbs, such as the case of *o_hkí-ǫ_ðe* 'jump into trouble' (with regular and syncopating inflection), from *ǫ́_ðe* 'discard, toss', with the addition of reflexive *hkik*, and a preverb *o* (locative?), giving literally 'toss oneself'.

(178) *o_hkíǫ_ðe*
o-hkik-ǫ́-ðe
LOC-REFL-PREV-toss
'jump into trouble, jump into anything; fall in a hole'

[24] A few such optionally doubly inflected verbs have been encountered in the speech of one male; other verbs with this characteristic were *hiiða* 'bathe' (1S *ahíibra*), *xíða* 'stumble and fall'(1S *axíbra*); *aðée* 'go' (1S *abrée*). This may be symptomatic of language disuse.

Note that *ohkíǫðe* is a regular *ð*-stem verb and not a causative verb, although it closely resembles causatives. Double inflection of this verb is seen in the next three examples. (The *w* in (179) is epenthetic between the preverb *o* and the 1S inflection *a*.)

(179) *owáhkiǫbre*
o-Wa-hkik-ǫ́-Wa-ðe
LOC-A1S-REFL-PREV-A1S-toss
'I got into trouble'

(180) *oðáhkiǫ́šce nįkše*
o-Ya-hkik-ǫ́-Ya-ðe *nįkše*
LOC-A2S-REFL-PREV-A2S-toss 2S.CONT
'you sure got into trouble'

(181) *owáhkiǫ́bre hkǫ́bra įké*
o-Wa-hkik-ǫ́-ðe *Wa-kǫ́-Wa-ða* *ðįké*
LOC-A1S-REFL-PREV-toss A1S-PREV-A1S-want NEG
'I don't want to get in trouble'

Note that *_hkíǫ_ðe* means 'to divorce', from *ǫ́ðe* 'throw away', with reciprocal *hkik*, whereas the verb 'jump into' above used the (identical) reflexive *hkik*. In either case, A1P appears only at the leftmost point of inflection.

(182) *Jóhna éðǫǫpa ąhkiǫ́ðe*
Johna é-ðǫ́ǫpa ąk-hkik-ǫ́-ðe
John him-two A1P-REFL-PREV-toss
'I divorced John' (lit., 'John and I threw each other away')

The nonreciprocal simple transitive version in Osage would be *Jóhna ǫ́bre aðįhé* for 'I'm divorcing John', and *Jǫ́hna akxa ąwą́ðe* for 'John's divorcing me'.

4 Verb derivation

The agglutinative nature of Osage gives rise to a rich derivational morphology in the verbal complex. Chapter 3 covers the inflectional components and their interaction with some of the derivational elements. The present chapter examines the behavior of the most important of the derivational morphemes appearing in pre-root position, and the interaction among some of them. The simplified sketch of the basic organization of the verbal complex in table 4.1 will aid in elucidating which part of the grammar is being illustrated.

Most of the components in table 4.1 are discussed in this chapter, as indicated by the section numbers appearing in the table. Other parts of this chapter address the interaction of two or more derivational components. Section 4.3, on motion verbs, discusses compounding involving motion verbs and the interaction of vertitive *kik* with the root of simple motion verbs. Section 4.2.2 discusses interaction of valence reduction with the causative root. Interaction of causatives with the elements of object reference is discussed in sections 4.2.3 and 4.2.4. Along with the general topic of causation in Osage, nonderivational (syntactic and semantic) causatives are also discussed in section 4.2. Post-root phenomena (other than causatives) are dealt with separately, in chapter 5.[1]

4.1 Valence reduction

The valence reducer *wa* functions as a detransitivizer or tacit object, as it renders an object unnecessary. The *wa* itself can be thought of as a diffuse sort of object, approximately equivalent to 'stuff' or 'folks' as direct objects in English, or 'folks' as indirect object. As *wa* detransitivizes transitive verbs, obviating the need for a concrete object pronominal, the

[1] The motivation for the position of each class of elements in table 4.1 will not be covered here, as it is amply illustrated by the examples in this volume. However, it is perhaps worth mentioning a couple of forms that may not appear elsewhere, such as *taazíhiðe* 'make to brown by heat' showing juxtaposition of outer-instrumental, primary root, causative root; and *ístahkiðe* 'make oneself blessed by using' which shows the juxtaposition of locative, primary-root, reflexive, causative-root.

TABLE 4.1. BASIC ORGANIZATION OF THE VERBAL COMPLEX

DERIV	DERIV	INFL	DERIV	INFL	OBJ REF; INCEPTIVE; VERTITIVE	DERIV	**ROOT**	POST-ROOT MATERIAL
valence reducer *wa* (section 4.1)	primary root of causative (section 4.2.2) locative *i* (section 4.5) preverb *wį, é*	A1P *ąk*	outer instrumental (sections 4.4.7–4.4.9) locative *o, á* (section 4.5) preverb *ki, mą*	PAT AG (chap. 3)	suus *kik* vertitive *kik* reciprocal *hkik* reflexive *hkik* dative *ki* inceptive *ki* (section 4.6)	inner instrumental (section 4.4)	(includes causative *ðe*)	plurality negation iteration aspect posture declarative (chap. 5)

AG = agent pronominal; DERIV = derivation; INFL = inflection; OBJ REF = object reference; PAT = patient pronominal.

number of arguments of a verb is reduced from three to two or from two to one, reducing the valence of the verb.

The valence reducer *wa* should not be confused with P3P *wa*, which is a concrete third person theme or receiver 'them; to them'. The difference between this diffuse object (the valence reducer) and a true direct or indirect object is that the valence reducer is part of the derivational morphology of the verb. In some verbs valence reducer *wa* appears in a different location in the verb stem from the true object pronominal; compare (1a), (2a), and (3a) with (1b), (2b), and (3b). There is also an accentual difference (section 4.1.2).

(1a) *wašcéðe*
wa-šce-ðe
VAL-PREV-doctor
'doctor folks'

(1b) *šcéwáðe*
šce-wa-ðe
PREV-P3P-doctor
'doctor them'

(2a) *wacˀéðe*
wa-cˀe-ðe
VAL-die-CAU
'kill folks'

(2b) *cˀéwaðe*
cˀe-wa-ðe
die-P3P-CAU
'kill them'

(3a) *óðaaka!*
wa-o-ðaake-a
VAL-LOC-tell-IMPER
'tell [stuff]!'

(3b) *ówaðaaka!*
wa-o-wa-ðaake-a
VAL-LOC-P3P-tell-IMPER
'tell them!'

Additionally, since third person singular object pronominals are phonologically null (therefore undetectable in sentences), a sentence with a transitive verb in Osage will be taken to have a concrete P3S object pronominal ('him, her, it') if the diffuse valence reducer *wa* is not present; thus *bráahtą* 'I drink' will be interpreted as 'I drank it' and not 'I drank'.

To get the latter reading, the valence reducer *wa* must be present: *wabráahtą* 'I drank' ('I drank an unspecified something'; also used by extended meaning for 'I drank alcohol'). That is to say that the intransitive reading occurs by virtue of the valence reducer. If the valence reducer is not present, the sentence is assumed to have a phonologically null definite third person object.

4.1.1 Examples of valence-reduced verbs

The frequent occurrence of valence-reduced forms is noteworthy; they are preferred to plain transitive sentences when the agent is not being focused. The English glosses for sentences with valence-reduced verbs may contain passives and the literal meaning of the Osage sentence may be quite difficult to decipher based only on the English gloss (see examples with 'win' in section 4.1.4).

The semantic distance between corresponding forms with and without the valence reducer ranges from minimal to fairly significant. An example of the latter is *óðuucˀake* 'be lazy', from *wa* + *oðúucˀake* 'be tired'. Some valence-reduced verbs show additional peculiarities.

Some verbs with the valence reducer *wa* have been reanalyzed as transitive anew, and hence may take, in addition to the valence reducer, a noun object or even the 3P object inflection marker *wa*. Cases where reanalysis has taken place, so that the valence-reduced form with *wa* is used even when a concrete theme is present in the form of additional pronominal inflection, a noun, or both, tend to be sentences with plural noun objects if the valence reducer *wa* is still phonologically rather overtly detectable. Also, where *wa* is obscured, as in *o*-initial verbs where the addition of *wa* merely causes the *o* to become accented *ó* (and *wa* disappears), "extra" pronominals may cooccur with the reanalyzed valence-reduced verb. For example, consider *ówaðahi* 'you beat us' (with P1P *wa*), from *óhi* 'beat folks', itself from *wa* 'valence reducer' + *ohí* 'beat'. (See also sections 2.4.2.4 and 2.4.2.5).

As another example, the transitive verb *_ðaahtą́* 'drink' becomes intransitive *waðáahtą* with the addition of the valence reducer *wa*. The connotation of *waðáahtą* is 'drink alcohol' (reminiscent of English 'he drinks'), and this form has become lexicalized as transitive; even when the theme noun is present, *waðáahtą* may be used, especially when the object is an alcoholic beverage, as seen in (4):

(4) *hkáwacéženi toa wabráahtą brée hta mįkše*
hkáwa-céže-níi toa wa-Wa-ðaahtą́ Wa-ðée hta mįkše
horse-urinate-liquid some VAL-A1S-drink A1S-go FUT 1S.CONT
'I am going to drink some beer'

In (5), the 1P agent inflection *ąk* precedes the valence reducer *wa*. The valence reducer *wa*, usually accentless, receives second syllable accent when agent inflection *ąk* occurs to its left, making *wa* the second syllable.

(5) *ąwáðaahtą ną*
ąk-wa-ðaahtą́ ną
A1P-VAL-drink ITER
'we drink'

Corresponding to transitive *í_ðilą* 'think; think about doing something' (often taking a sentential complement representing the specific thing thought about) is a valence-reduced form *wa_ðílą*, approximately 'ponder things in general; think' (intransitive). The A1P *ąk* combines with the valence-reduced form, giving:

(6) *ąwáðilą įkše*
ąk-waðilą ąðįkše
A1P-think 1D.CONT
'we're thinking, pondering things'

The A1P *ąk* combines with transitive *íðilą* as follows:

(7) *ąną́ðilą ąðįkše*
ąk-n-íðilą ąðįkše
A1P-EP*n*-think 1D.CONT
'we're thinking about it [a specific thing]'

In some other minimal pairs with and without valence reducer *wa*, the meaning diverges to a greater degree between the two members of the pair. For example, corresponding to *_ðiihtą́* 'grasp; touch' is the valence-reduced verb *wa_ðíihtą* 'work'.

The verb *ðaašóe* 'smoke', derived from the intransitive 'smoke' with the addition of the instrumental prefix *ðaa* 'by mouth' (see section 4.4.1) may likewise be detransitivized with the addition of *wa*. The added connotation is 'smoking tobacco or cigarettes', much the same as *waðáahtą* above connotes 'drinking alcohol'.

(8) *wabráašoe*
wa-Wa-ðaa-šóe
VAL-A1S-by.mouth-smoke
'I'm smoking' (intransitive)

The valence reducer *wa* applies straightforwardly to the verb *_hpí_ǫ* 'know how to, learn how to, be skilled at'.

(9) *wa_hpí_ǫ*
wa-hpí-ǫ
VAL-PREV-learn
'learn how to do something/things/stuff'

Notice the use of valence reducer *wa* with *ii_táðe* 'give birth' in (10) and (11). The semantic link between valence reducer *wa* and plurality is weak; as evidence, note that the assumed product of birth is surely singular. If the non-valence-reduced verb is used, the phonologically null third singular object pronominal is assumed, as in (12), which is the usual expression for 'he was born'.

(10) *wéeðatái?*
wa-ii-Ya-táðe-ðe
VAL-PREV-A2S-birth-DECL
'did you give birth?'

(11) *wéetai ąðįkše*
wa-ii-taðe ąðįkše
VAL-PREV-birth 1D.CONT
'we [dual] gave birth'

(12) *iitáðe*
ii-Ø-Ø-táðe
PREV-P3S-A3S-birth
'she gave birth to him'

4.1.2 Contrasts with P3P *wa*

Although the position of the valence reducer *wa* and P3P *wa* do sometimes differ, as was noted above in section 4.1.1, they are often similarly situated, as seen in the examples below. Unaccented valence reducer *wa* contrasts with P3P *wá* 'them' object inflection in these pairs, especially (and perhaps only) in *ð* stems where the P3P inflection *wa* is generally accented. (Accent and *wa* are treated in section 2.4.2.5.) Accent alone distinguishes the members of the following pairs contrasting valence reducer *wa* and P3P *wá*.

(13a) *waðáaxtake*
wa-Ø-ðáaxtake
VAL-A3S-bite
'he bites'

(13b) *wáðaaxtáke*
wa-Ø-ðaaxtáke
P3P-A3S-bite
'he bites them'

(14a) *waðáawa*
wa-ðaawá-a
VAL-count-IMPER
'count'

(14b) *wáðaawa*
wa-ðaawa-a
P3P-count-IMPER
'count them!'

The next set of examples involves the verb *_mą_ðǫ́* 'steal' (in which the left inflectional slot is for object pronominals and the right slot for subject pronominals). The detransitivized (valence-reduced) version of this verb is *wa_mą́_ðǫ* 'steal something/stuff'. (See also section 2.4.2.5 for *mąðǫ́*). This verb exhibits unusual morphology in that it takes not only the valence reducer but also any object pronominal inflection left of the preverb *mą*, even though the subject inflection occurs in place just before the root *_ðǫ*. The P3P object pronominal *wá* thus precedes the preverb *mą*:

(15) *wámąbrǫ́ðe*
wa-mą-Wa-ðǫ́-ðe
P3P-PREV-A1S-steal-DECL
'I stole them'

The valence reducer *wa* (unaccented) also precedes the preverb *mą*.

(16) *wamą́ðǫe*
wa-mą-ðǫ́-ðe
VAL-PREV-steal-DECL
'steal'

(17) *wamą́štǫ́ ðįké ðáalį*
wa-mą-Ya-ðǫ́ ðįké ðáalį
VAL-PREV-A2S-steal NEG good
'you shouldn't steal'

(18) *wamáðǫ nąpe*
wa-mą-Ø-ðǫ́ ną-api-ðe
VAL-PREV-A3S-steal ITER-PL-DECL
'he steals all the time'

(19) *wamą́brǫ́ðe*
wa-mą-Wa-ðǫ́-ðe
VAL-PREV-A1S-steal-DECL
'I stole'

A1P *ąk* appears to the left of both preverb *mą* and valence reducer *wa*.

(20) *ą́mąðǫpe*
ąk-mą-ðǫ́-api-ðe
A1P-PREV-steal-PL-DECL
'we [plural] stole it'

(21) *ąwą́mąðǫpe*
ą-wa-mą-ðǫ́-api-ðe
A1P-VAL-PREV-steal-PL-DECL
'we [plural] stole things'

In (22) 'he stole things from you', a patient object *ði* 'from you' is present along with the valence reducer *wa* 'stuff'. The patient prefix occurs leftward of the preverb (*_mą*).[2]

(22) *waðímǫ́ akxai*
wa-ðí-mą-Ø-ðǫ́ *akxa-ðe*
VAL-P2S-PREV-A3S-steal 3.CONT-DECL
'he stole from you'

A sentence such as the following should be possible, although it was not found in the data gathered:

(23) *?wáwamąðǫ́pe*
wa-wa-mą-Ø-ðǫ-api-ðe
VAL-P1P-PREV-A1S-steal-PL-DECL
'he stole from us' (example not actually attested)

(P1P *wa...(api)* would be expected to deflect second syllable accent leftward; see section 2.4.2.7.) Again speculatively, it should be possible for this same sentence to mean 'he stole them from us' and 'he stole them from them'.

4.1.3 The verb 'give': valence-reduced recipient

The verb *_kʔú* 'give' is the basis for a set of derived forms of which several have initial *o* or *ó*. For the sake of brevity we will not treat here all

[2] The verb *mąðǫ́* can also mean 'rape'. Other readings of the following two sentences are 'he stole it from you' and 'he stole it from her/him' respectively.

(i) *ðímąðǫpe*
ði-mą-Ø-ðǫ-api-ðe
P2S-PREV-A3S-steal-PL-DECL
'you were raped' ('he stole you')

(ii) *mąðǫ́pe*
Ø-mą-Ø-ðǫ́-api-ðe
P3S-PREV-A3S-steal-PL-DECL
'she was raped' ('she was stolen')

the members of this group, focusing only on *k?ú* 'give' (a three-argument verb) and its valence-reduced form *wak?ú* 'give away, give to folks'[3] (a two-argument verb) where the valence reducer represents the recipients, i.e. 'to folks'. The *k?ú*-based verbs are special in that the most salient object (or "primary object") is the recipient; the valence reducer preferentially replaces the recipient.

Examples (24) and (25) show *k?ú* 'give' without valence reduction. In (24) both 'it' (the item given) as patient object and 'him/her/it' are zero, that is to say that the 3S receiver is also phonologically null P3S. There is a separate emphatic pronoun *ée* in the sentence exclusively referring to the person or organization receiving.

(24) *ée k?ú apáiðe*
ée *Ø-Ø-Ø-k?ú* *apa-ðe-ðe*
3.PRON P3S-P3S-A3P-give 3.CONT-DECL-DECL
'they gave it to him, to her, to a particular group or organization'

In (25), we see *wa* 'them' and *Ø* 'it'.

(25) *wak?ú apaiðe*
wa-Ø-Ø-k?ú *apa-ðe-ðe*
P3P-P3S-A3P-give 3.CONT-DECL-DECL
'they gave it to them'

In (26), the speakers' translation and explanation make it clear that *wa* is P3P 'them'.

(26) *mą́zeska huuhtą́ka waðák?upe*
mą́zeska huuhtą́ka wa-Ya-k?u-api-ðe
money much P3P-A2S-give-PL-DECL
'you gave them lots of money'

Example (27) and following examples show valence reduction. In (27) the unspecified receivers are represented by the valence reducer *wa*, with no certain object(s) or receivers in mind, and the emphatic pronoun *ée* refers to the givers. This is a context where we might imagine double valence reduction could occur, but in fact that does not seem to be the case, and we find only one *wa*. This sentences focuses on the event of the give-away. In (28), the objects given are named by the noun 'blanket' and valence reducer *wa* represents the unspecified recipients.

[3] The giveaway is an important ceremonial act in Osage culture.

(27) *ée wakʔú apai*
ée wa-Ø-kʔú apa-ðe
3.PRON VAL-A3P-give 3.CONT-DECL
'they are the ones that are giving away'

(28) *hakǫ́ta Jóhna haxį́ wakʔú ðe?*
haa-kǫ́ta Johna haxį́ wa-kʔú ðe
INDEF-way John-a blanket VAL-give QUES
'why did John-SYL give the blankets away?'

In (29), *tówa txą* 'those ones' represents the receivers (*kxą* is a variant of *txą* 'standing'). No certain items are in mind. This sentence is 'I'm giving stuff to those-ones', an unusual plural use of *tówa*.

(29) *tówa kxą áawakʔu mįkše*
tówa txą́ Wa-wa-kʔu mįkše
those-ones that.standing A1S-VAL-give 1S.CONT
'I'm giving stuff to that bunch of people'[4]

Example (30) exhibits vowel harmony, whereby the valence reducer *wa* has assimilated nasality from A1P *ąk* and accent shifts onto the second syllable valence reducer. It is likely that the valence reducer *wa* in this example again represents not 'stuff' but 'folks'—i.e., replaces the recipient, which is the indirect or oblique object in English.

(30) *ąwą́kʔu ąįkšé*
ąk-wa-Ø-kʔu ąðįkšé
A1P-VAL-P3S-give 1D.CONT
'we [dual] gave it to them' (i.e., to an indistinct someone: 'we gave it away')

As seen in (31) and (32), in certain contexts a sentence may be ambiguous as to whether it involves the valence reducer *wa* or *wa* P3P:

(31) *ðie waðákʔue*
ðie wa-Ya-kʔu-ðe
2S.PRON VAL-A2S-give-DECL
'you gave it to them; you gave stuff away'

[4] The reason for first syllable accent here is not clear. While second syllable accent is common, first syllable accent can sometimes be found, as in this verb, possibly due to the accent pattern at sentence level. Another, more likely, explanation for *áawakʔu* is that there are two underlying *wa* forms here (*a-wa-wa-kʔu*) and the first *a-wa* collapses to *áa*.

(32) *awák?u*
Wa-wa-k?u
A1S-VAL-give
'I'm giving it to them [to specific persons]; I am giving it to folks, to them [diffuse]'

Valence reducer *wa* preferentially replaces the recipient, the primary object. But in *wak?ú* 'give away', when the recipient is represented by pronominal inflection such as *ą* P1S 'me' as in (33), *wa* appears to represent the secondary object (the entity transferred, translated in the example below as 'it'). Passive English glosses are often found in such "give-away" sentences because the giver or actor is unnamed and presumably relatively unimportant ('someone gave me stuff; stuff was given to me').

(33) *ąwą́k?upe*
ą-wa-Ø-k?u-api-ðe
P1S-VAL-A3S-give-PL-DECL
'it was given to me'

4.1.4 *o* verbs

A special effect of valence reduction occurs in verbs with locative *o* prefix: *wa* + *o* becomes inherently accented *ó*. This arises directly from the merger of the two prefixes: that is, as *wa* is added to the verb, *o* becomes second syllable and thus receives accent, then *wa* and *o* merge, giving *ó*.

Thus, the valence-reduced form *wa* + *océ* 'look for' becomes *óce* 'look for things, search, hunt', which appears in (34), uninflected except for its 2S continuative auxiliary *ðaįšé*.

(34) *óce ðaįšé*
wa-o-ce *ðaįšé*
P3P-LOC-look.for 2S.CONT
'are you looking for things?'

Reanalysis of *óce* as transitive can take place. This has occurred in (35), where P3P *wa* 'them' also appears. (In this example, *óce* appears as *óta,* the imperative form exhibiting the effects of vowel collapse via the V1-V2 Rule; see section 2.3.3.2.) P3P *wa* 'them' in this example refers to, for instance, item(s) of clothing.

(35) *ówakita*
wa-o-wa-ki-cé-a
VAL-PREV-P3P-SUU-look.for-IMPER
'look for them yourself'

A final example of valence-reduced *óce* is (36), where it appears with *štą* 'incessantly'; *óceštą* is 'snoopy; a snoopy person, a snoop', describing people who like to get into other people's things.

(36) *ošpéžį nąlǫ́ǫha pai, šée apa ahú apai óceštąpe*
ošpé-žį nąlǫ́ǫha paðe, šée apa
bits-small hide IMPER.CONT those SUBJ
ahú apaðe óce-štą-api-ðe
arrive.here 3.CONT-DECL(?) search-incessantly-PL-DECL
'hide your change, because the people coming are *óceštą*'[5]

A two-argument verb *ðuucˀáke* 'be unable to; fail at' ('X is unable to Y') is related to a similar verb with unaccented *o* preceding the stem, *oðúucˀake* 'be tired of', which is also a two-argument verb. There is a third verb, composed of the same stem *oðúucˀake* but having an accented *ó* (presumably from the addition of *wa*), which is a one-argument verb: *óðuucˀake* 'be lazy'. All three verbs inflect in the active *ð*-stem syncopating pattern:

(37) *brúucˀake mįkšé*
Wa-ðuucˀáke mįkšé
A1S-unable 1S.CONT
'I am unable [to do X]'

(38) *obrúucˀake mįkšé*
o-Wa-ðuucˀáke mįkšé
PREV-A1S-unable 1S.CONT
'I am tired [of X]'

(39) *óbruucˀake mįkšé*
wa-o-Wa-ðuucˀáke mįkšé
VAL-PREV-A1S-unable 1S.CONT
'I am lazy'

Sometimes the usual shift of accent to second syllable can render the differences between valence-reduced and non-valence-reduced forms unobservable, especially in A1P sentences. The second syllable accent rule has applied to the non-valence-reduced A1P form in (40), obscuring the contrast between it and a valence-reduced form with stressed *ó*.

(40) *ąkóðuucˀake ąkátxai*
ąk-o-ðúucˀake ąkatxą́-ðe
A1P-PREV-unable 1P.CONT-DECL
'we're tired of it'

[5] *pai* (or *paðe*) in the first clause 'hide your change' is a special kind of imperative ending; see the imperatives with *pai* in section 5.1.6.3.

Sentence (41), with valence-reduced *óðuucˀake*, has no obvious subject inflection on the verb, perhaps because A1P inflection would have rendered this verb indistinguishable from the non-valence-reduced verb in (40).

(41) *óðuucˀake ąkátxai*
wa-o-ðúucˀake ąkatxą́-ðe
VAL-PREV-unable 1P.CONT-DECL
'we're lazy'

The interplay of derivational morphology and semantics as seen here is reminiscent of the set based on *oxpáðe* 'lose' in section 4.1.5.

Variously glossed as 'win [as a prize]', 'beat, best [someone in a game]', or 'be beaten' in English, the regular verb *o_hí* appears without valence reducer in (42)–(45). (In (42)–(43), A1P *ąk* precedes the preverb *o*, as is normal.)

(42) *ąkóhipe*
ąk-o-Ø-hi-api-ðe
A1P-PREV-P3S-beat-PL-DECL
'we beat him; we won'

(43) *ąkówahi*
ąk-o-wa-hí-e
A1P-PREV-P3P-beat-DECL
'we beat them; we won'

(44) *ąwáhipe*
o-ą-Ø-hí-api-ðe
PREV-P1S-A3P-beat-PL-DECL
'they beat me'

(45) *mą́zeska tóe owáhi*
mą́zeska tóe o-w-Wa-hí
money some PREV-EPw-A1S-beat/win
'I won some money'

This verb has a derived form with valence reducer *wa*: *óhi*, another instance of initial accent through addition of *wa*. Its gloss is 'beat or best folks, others' (intransitive) and by extension 'win' (intransitive). Valence-reduced *óhi* appears in (46)–(47). (Translations given by speakers can be misleading, as for (46), where the speaker's translation contains a passive 'be beaten'. More literally, this sentence is 'someone unnamed is about to win the game'; still more literally, 'almost they won'. The speaker's translation results from pragmatic extension.)

(46) *ðóha óhipe*
ðóha wa-ó-Ø-hi-api-ðe
almost VAL-PREV-A3P-beat-PL-DECL
'he's about to be beaten'

(47) *ée óhipe*
ée wa-ó-Ø-hi-api-ðe
3.PRON VAL-PREV-A3S-beat-PL-DECL
'he won; he beat folks'

Unaccented *o* in 'win' appears in (48) in the contrasting non-valence-reduced verb (contrast with (46)).

(48) *ðóha ohípe*
ðóha o-Ø-hí-api-ðe
almost PREV-A3S-win-PL-DECL
'he's about to win [it]'

Even though *óhi* is a valence-reduced verb, *wa* P1P may be added, as in (49), since *óhi* has been reanalyzed as transitive.[6] (Note the game-related translation 'broke' in this example. For the interlinear gloss from here on we occasionally use PREV for the *ó* deriving from *wa-o,* without splitting *wa* from *o* on the morpheme analysis line, for the sake of simplicity.)

(49) *ówaðahi*
ó-wa-Ya-hi
PREV-P1P-A2S-beat
'you broke us; you beat us'

Some *ó*-initial verbs will be affected by vowel harmony described in section 3.4.3.1. One such case of vowel harmony appears in (50). This example is more literally 'I beat folks'.

(50) *áwahi*
ó-w-Wa-hí-ðe
PREV-EP*w*-A1S-beat-DECL
'I won; I beat them'

At the beginning of this section, we saw that although the valence reducer *wa* in itself is not inherently accented, when it combines with verb-initial *o*, the result is accented *ó*. Transitive *oohǫ́* 'cook' is seen in the 1S form in (51). The second syllable accent rule has applied; this also happens in the 2S form *ooðáhą*. 1S and 2S forms often denasalize in utterances, as in this example (where the expected 1S form is *oo-a-hą*, with nasal *ą*).

[6] An alternative analysis is that this is another instance of P1P deflecting accent one syllable leftward. (See section 2.4.2.7.)

(51) *oowáha hta mįkšé*
oo-w-Wa-hǫ́ *hta* *mįkšé*
PREV-EPw-A1S-cook FUT 1S.CONT
'I'm going to cook [it]'

There is a valence-reduced form based on *oo_hǫ́* 'cook', namely *óohǫ* 'cook stuff', as seen in (52). This same form is also nominal: 'person who cooks' (53).

(52) *óohǫ ąwą́ąxta*
wa-óo-hǫ *ą-óxta*
VAL-PREV-cook P1S-love
'I like to cook'

(53) *óohǫ*
wa-oo-hǫ́
VAL-PREV-cook
'a cook [person by whom things get cooked]'

4.1.5 Stative with valence reducer: *oxpáðe* 'lose'

There are five similar forms in the *_oxpaðe* group, displayed in table 4.2.[7] A more abstract meaning for the root *xpáðe* should be 'separate, sever, deprive of' or perhaps more accurately 'become separated, severed from'. For ease of exposition the differing forms are numbered from one to five in the second column of the table.

Obviously, more is involved here than just valence reduction. So as not to split this analysis over several sections, other aspects of this set are mentioned here. The first three verbs in the table are homophonous: *oxpáðe*$_1$ 'fall'; *oxpáðe*$_2$ 'be/get lost'; and *oxpáðe*$_3$ 'lose' (transitive). The fourth form is a valence-reduced form with initial accent: *óxpaðe*$_4$ 'lose stuff' (intransitive), where the accented *ó* shows the incorporation of the valence reducer *wa*. This is a valence-reduced one-argument verb ('X loses stuff') in contrast with the unaccented *o* form, which is a one-argument verb with the meaning 'X gets lost' or 'X falls'; or, in the case of *oxpáðe*$_3$, a two-argument verb 'X loses Y [a specific item or specific items]'. The experiencer in all of the first four cases—the person who falls, gets lost, loses a specific thing, or loses stuff—appears in patient inflection; all four verbs are thus stative. Stress in the first three cases is readjusted to second syllable position after inflection is added to the verb.

[7] In passing, note again that this is a verb ending in *ðe* where inflection does not immediately precede the *ðe*. This is because it is not a causative, with *ðe* as its causative root, although at first glance it might seem so. Neither is it a *ð*-stem.

TABLE 4.2. *oxpaðe* STEMS

STATIVE			
intransitive	*oxpáðe*$_1$	'fall'	patient inflection for experiencer
	oxpáðe$_2$	'be/get lost'	patient inflection for person lost
transitive	*oxpáðe*$_3$	'lose [an item]'	patient inflection for experiencer (and for item lost?)
valence-reduced	*óxpaðe*$_4$	'lose stuff'	patient inflection for loser
ACTIVE			
transitive	*oxpáðe*$_5$	'lose a person'	agent inflection for loser, patient inflection for person lost

However, the valence-reduced form *óxpaðe*$_4$ 'lose stuff' keeps accent on the first syllable *ó*.

For *oxpáðe*$_3$ 'lose an item', the experiencer appears in patient inflection on the verb, and the item lost may appear as a noun within the sentence. Unfortunately, the sentence 'you lost them [inanimate]' is not in the data gathered and could not be elicited, but presumably would be *owáðixpaðe*. The item lost cannot be marked as the grammatical subject of the sentence by use of the subject-marking determiner *akxa* or *apa*. The noun experiencer (the loser) represented by the patient inflection on the verb, if overtly named by a noun, can be followed by such a subject marker (*akxa* or *apa*), as in (54)–(55).

(54) *wéleze Frances akxa oxpáði akxai*

wéleze	*Frances*	*akxa*	*o-Ø-xpáðe*	*akxa-ðe*
pencil	Frances	SUBJ	PREV-P3S-lose	3.CONT-DECL

'Frances has lost her pencil'

(55) *wéleze oxpáði akxai*

wéleze	*o-Ø-xpáðe*	*akxa-ðe*
pencil	PREV-P3S-lose	3.CONT-DECL

'she's lost her pencil'

Valence reduction applies to the verb *oxpáðe*$_3$ 'lose an item' to remove one argument (the item lost) from its argument structure, producing *óxpaðe*$_4$ 'lose stuff'. The valence-reduced form is still statively inflected; example (56) below shows P2S inflection *ði* for the semantic subject 'you'. This example also shows that if a continuative auxiliary (such as second person *nįkšé*) is present it will agree with the patient pronominal (the loser).

(56) *waléze oðíxpaðe nįkšé*
waléze o-ði-xpaðe nįkšé
book PREV-P2S-lose 2S.CONT
'you lost your book'

The valence-reduced form *óxpaðe*$_4$ 'lose stuff' in (57) contrasts with the stative-transitive *oxpáðe*$_3$ 'lose an item' in (58):

(57) *Frances akxa óxpaði akxai*
Frances akxa wa-o-Ø-xpáðe akxa-ðe
Frances SUBJ VAL-PREV-P3S-lose 3.CONT-DECL
'Frances lost something [some stuff]'

(58) *Frances akxa oxpáði akxai*
Frances akxa o-Ø-xpáðe akxa-ðe
Frances SUBJ PREV-P3S-lose 3.CONT-DECL
'Frances lost it'

In addition to these four stative forms, there is active-transitive *oxpáðe*$_5$ 'lose another person or persons'. In this instance agent inflection is used for the loser, and patient inflection for the person(s) lost. In the patient paradigm (for the persons lost), P3P *wa* 'them' is often omitted, for reasons that remain unclear. For *oxpáðe*$_5$, then, the loser takes agent form *ąk* for 1P, as in (59), and not patient 1P *wa...api*. The person lost in this example is 'you' (*ði* from the patient set).

(59) *ąkóðixpai*
ąk-o-ði-xpáðe
A1P-PREV-P2S-lose
'we lost you'

The first person plural form in (60) is more difficult to analyze. It may have two patient objects P1P *wa* and P3P *wa* (being, then, doubly stative in this instance) instead of valence reducer *wa*:

(60) *ówaxpáðape*
wa-o-wa-xpáðe-api-ðe
P1P-PREV-P3P-lose-PL-DECL
'we lost them'

Example (61), again with *oxpáðe*$_5$, shows agent inflection for the loser, A2S *ða*, and patient inflection for the person lost, P1S *ą*. The possibility of having humans lose humans (with this verb) may be a recent cultural borrowing from English, which may explain the variability in treatment of the loser.

(61) *ąwą́ðaxpai*
o-w-ą-Ya-xpáðe
PREV-EPw-P1S-A2S-lose
'you lost me'

In the valence-reduced *óxpaðe*$_4$ 'lose stuff' (from *wa* + *oxpáðe*, with valence reducer *wa* giving the initial accent), accent on the first syllable (*ó*) is not overridden by accent adjustment to second syllable.

(62) *óxpaðe*
wa-o-xpáðe
VAL-PREV-lose
'someone has lost something'

(63) *ówaxpaa ąkáðe*
wa-o-wa-xpáðe ąk-aðé
VAL-PREV-P1P-lose 1P.CONT
'we lost something'

(64) *ówaxpaði*
wa-o-wa-xpáðe
VAL-PREV-P1P-lose
'we lost something'

Vowel harmony and *w*-insertion have occurred in (65):

(65) *ą́waxpaði*
ó-ą-xpáðe
PREV-P1S-lose
'I lost something'

In both (66) and (67), 'they' is a regional variant of the singular 'he' or 'she', and the 'something' lost is defocused 'stuff'.

(66) *óxpaðape*
wa-o-xpáðe-api-ðe
VAL-PREV-lose-PL-DECL
'they lost something'

(67) *óxpaði apai*
wa-o-Ø-xpaðe apa-ðe
VAL-PREV-P3P-lose 3.CONT-DECL
'they've lost something'

4.1.6 Valence-reduced causative

From the regular verb *oðó_ðe* 'supervise, boss [as an event]' (transitive), a valence-reduced form *oðó(wa)_ðe* 'be boss; boss, direct, be in charge, oversee things' (intransitive) is produced, illustrating valence reduction just left of a secondary root *_ðe*. The plain transitive form appears in (68)–(70).

(68) *ónǫbre oðóaðe hta mįkšé*
ónǫbre oðó-Wa-ðe hta mįkše
food boss-A1S-CAU FUT 1S.CONT
'I'm going to be bossing, taking care of the food'

(69) *oðóðaðe*
oðó-Ya-ðe
boss-A2S-CAU
'you're bossing [it]'

(70) *oðóðe akxai*
oðó-Ø-ðe akxa-ðe
boss-A3S-CAU 3.CONT-DECL
'she's bossing [it]'

With the addition of the valence reducer *wa*, the verb becomes *oðówa_ðe*. The valence-reduced form also functions as a noun.

(71) *oðówai*
oðó-wa-ðe
boss-VAL-CAU
'boss things or people; a boss, a foreman'

The inflected 1S form is *oðóawaðe*, where *wa*-Metathesis has switched the order of valence reducer *wa* and A1S *(W)a*. In (72) the A2S form *Ya* appears.

(72) *waaðǫ́ hta apai, oðówaðaðe hta nįkšé?*
waaðǫ́ hta apa-ðe, oðó-wa-Ya-ðe hta nįkšé
A3P-sing FUT 3.CONT-DECL boss-VAL-A2S-CAU FUT 2S.CONT
'they're going to sing, are you going to see about it/things?'

4.1.7 Valence reducer in noun formation

We saw above in sections 4.1.4 and 4.1.6 that there is a set of nouns that are derived from valence-reduced forms of *o*-initial verbs, for example 'snoop' ('looks for stuff'), 'cook' ('cooks stuff') and 'boss' ('bosses things'), where *wa* has contracted with *o* to produce *ó*. In another productive set of nouns, the valence reducer precedes an *i* prefix. Informally speaking, *i* adds the idea of 'with; by means of'. In this sense many *wa* + *i* nouns name the tool used to effect the action of the verb, such as 'hammer' ('hammer stuff with'), 'broom' ('sweep stuff with'), and so on. (See section 2.3.3.1.)

In *wéapazo* 'index finger', the *i* prefix precedes the *á* locative prefix of the verb stem *ápazo* 'point', and the valence reducer *wa* precedes the *i*. Thus the etymological meaning of this noun is approximately 'point at things with', where 'things' is *wa*, and 'with' is *i*.[8]

(73) *wéapazo*
wa-i-apazo
VAL-with-point
'pointer, the index or first finger'

In the derivation of the noun *wéhkile* 'a visit' (a means to see folks) informally speaking we can say that *i* adds the semantics of 'with' or 'by means of'. The derivation starts from a bleached reciprocal *íi-hkik-ðe* 'see one another' (see section 4.6.3.2 for bleached reciprocals), with *hkik* 'each other' at the point of inflection in the verb *íi_ðe* 'see'. The valence reducer *wa* and the *i* prefix round out the derivation.[9]

(74) *wéehkile*
wa-i-íi-hkik-ðe
VAL-with-PREV-RECIP-see
'a visit'

4.2 Causative

In this section we will take a look at the several types of causatives found in Osage. The most coercive of the causatives, which involves the verb *káaɣe* 'make' occurring as the main verb with an embedded verb under it, is quite parallel to the English 'make' causative construction.

The morphological causative root *ðe* follows another verb root or stem (called here the primary root), producing a compound verb with inflection preceding the causative root: e.g. *cˀe_ðe* 'kill', with primary verb *cˀe* 'die'.

Various further constructions are based on the morphological causative. One is *waðe*, consisting of the valence reducer *wa* and the causative *ðe*. Interestingly, this has an impersonal sense: 'it makes one

[8] This ordering of *i* 'with' with respect to the valence reducer *wa* is the motivation for the leftmost column in table 4.1.

[9] The *i* prefix is assumed to be present by analogy with similar forms, but in fact cannot be detected since this verb itself is *i*-initial.

[verb]', or perhaps 'makes folks'. Additionally, the morphological causative *ðe* exhibits several forms involving object referent prefixes of various kinds. One of these is the dative (and homophonous suus) of the morphological causative, consisting of the primary root followed by *kiðe* (appearing commonly in speech as *kíe* or *kíape*). In addition, there are reflexive and reciprocal versions of the *ðe* causative, and a second type of dative causative, *kšíðe*, less common than *kíðe* above and with a slight difference in meaning.[10]

An inner instrumental prefix *ðuu* forms still other type of causative; it is treated in section 4.4, with the instrumentals. These *ðuu* forms typically function with middle verbs and with adjectivelike verbs, producing forms like 'make to ring', 'make to be clean', from the intransitive roots 'ring' and 'be clean'.[11]

A final type, which is grouped with causatives only semantically and not morphologically, and which is mentioned here briefly, is the semantically causative *hce* construction, which is a proposal construction or polite imperative, called here injunctive. This semantic causative is usually translated in English with a causative 'have', as in 'Have John call her', or alternatively and colloquially 'let, let's' as for example, 'Let's just you and me buy this', or with numerous other phrases of similar semantic intent.

The semantic realm of causation offers several degrees of intensity in the imposition of power over the causee by the first agent. From lesser intensity to greater, a continuum can be informally sketched for Osage as in table 4.3. The table also shows the section in which each type of causative is treated.

There are other semantically causative sentences that are outside the causative system sketched here. Since the English glosses can be identical to the English glosses of Osage true causatives, these are mentioned here and a couple of examples are given. Example (75) involves *íkˀuce* 'try', and (76) involves *kaaží* 'drive, herd; order, force, drive to, coerce, command'. These will not be discussed here.

[10] A deceptively similar dative form, *kšíɣe*, is also found with the meaning 'prepare/make something for someone'—not a causative at all, but sometimes glossed in English with the causative.

[11] In Lakota, according to Rood (p.c. 1995), the cognate of the Osage instrumental *ðuu* (mentioned above) is *yu*: e.g., *yuská* 'make white, by leaving in the sun to bleach'. And the Lakota cognate of the Osage morphological causative *ðe* is *yá*: *skayá* 'make white, by scrubbing or painting'. This pair contrasts similarly in both Lakota and Osage in that Lakota *ya* (corresponding to Osage *ðe*) implies more volition on the part of the agent than does *yu* (corresponding to Osage instrumental *ðuu*).

TABLE 4.3. CAUSATIVES

	+Volition of causee (less coercion by agent)	
'request, ask someone to do something, have or let someone do something' (proposal form, injunctive)	*hce*	4.2.5
'have someone engage volitionally; let, allow someone to do something'	*kiðe* (<*ki* + *ðe*) dative	4.2.4
'have someone do something for their own benefit'	*kšíðe* (<*ki-hi-ðe*?) dative	4.2.3
'make something be a certain way' (?) (instrumental)	*ðuu* + verb	4.4.2
'have/make someone do something; make something happen to someone'	primary root + *ðe* (e.g., *cˀéðe*)	4.2.2
'make/force someone to do something'	*káaɣe*	4.2.1
	–Volition of causee (more coercion by agent)	

(75) *ðe htóožu che Jóhna ąkˀú íkˀuca*
ðe *htóožu* *che* *Jóhna* *ą-kˀu* *íkˀuce-a*
those meat.pie STA John-a P1S-give try-IMPER
'try to make John-SYL give those meat pies to me'

(76) *Mary iihǫ akxa ákaažipe*[12]
Mary *iihǫ* *akxa* *á-Ø-kaaží-api-ðe*
Mary her-mother SUBJ her(?)-A3S-drive-PL-DECL
'Mary's mother made her do that'

4.2.1 *káaɣe* 'make'

The verb *káaɣe* 'make; do' (1S *hpáaɣe* ~ *ppáaɣe*, 2S *škáaɣe*, 3S *káaɣe*, 1P *ąkáaɣe*) is the simplest and most coercive form of causative in Osage. The verb *káaɣe* (and not the other, gentler forms such as *kíðe* and *kšiðe*), is the causative of choice for those sentences where (i) the action of the

[12] Use of *á* for P3S in *ákaažipe* in this example is rare or archaic.

embedded verb is nonvolitional or (ii) the action is not beneficial to the actor who is made to perform it; however, *káaɣe* is not limited to these circumstances.

In addition to its use in sentences meaning 'make someone do something' or 'make someone/something be a certain way', this causative also appears in constructions such as 'make X like/similar/equal to Y' and 'make X into Y':

(77) *wahkíla che káaɣi əpái*
wahkíla che káaɣe apa-ðe
law that A3P-make 3.CONT-DECL
'they're making it into law'

(78) *wahkǫ́ta ižį́ke iihǫ́ hpaxį́ įkše xǫ́ǫce íkǫce káaɣi apai*
wahkǫ́ta ižį́ke iihǫ́ hpaxį́ įkše xǫ́ǫce íkǫce
God son mother hair SIT cedar like
káaɣe apa-ðei
make 3.CONT-DECL
'they're making the cedar like Mary's hair'[13]

Káaɣe may govern either transitive or intransitive verbs, whether active or stative. In the two examples below we see forms of the verbs 'be hot' and 'be warm', which presumably would be stative but no longer seem to inflect in Osage. (A noncausative example is (81).)

(79) *táahkace káaɣa*
táahkace Ø-káaɣe-a
hot P3S-make-IMPER
'heat it up!'

(80) *táašcue káaɣa*
táašcue Ø-káaɣe-a
warm P3S-make-IMPER
'warm it up!'

(81) *táašcue akxái*
táašcue akxa-ðe
warm 3.CONT-DECL
'it's warm [e.g., an object, or food]'

In the causative construction with *káaɣe*, the semantic subject of the lower verb appears as object inflection on *káaɣe*, while object inflection alone appears on the lower verb (coding the lower verb's object). In the following two examples, the subject of the lower verb is understood as

[13] This refers to the ceremony of burning cedar in order to get a blessing from it. Mary is referred to as 'God's son's mother', forming a triple possessive with 'hair'.

A3P, which is phonologically null, so that it is impossible to establish whether the lower verb has subject inflection.

(82) *záani ɣaaké wakáaɣe akxai*
záani ɣaaké wa-Ø-káaɣe akxa-ðe
all cry P3P-A3S-make 3.CONT-DECL
'he made them all cry'

(83) *ɣaaké wahpáaɣe*
ɣaaké wa-Wa-káaɣe
cry P3P-A1S-make
'I made them cry'

But the absence of subject inflection on the lower verb is clear in (84) and (85), since an A1S subject *a* would be detectable in the lower verb (giving *iðáxa*).

(84) *íxa ąškáaɣe*
íxa ą-Ya-káaɣe
laugh P1S-A2S-make
'you make me laugh'

(85) *íxa ąkáaɣape*
íxa ą-Ø-káaɣe-api-ðe
laugh P1S-A3P-make-PL-DECL
'he/she/they made me laugh'

The embedded verb is transitive and inflected for object (*ąkˀú* 'give to me') in (86).

(86) *įįną́, ðe htóožu che ąkˀú wakáaɣa*
iiną́, ðe htóožu che ą-kˀu wa-káaɣe-a
my.mother, those meat.pie COLL.STA P1S-give P3P-make-IMPER
'make them give those meat pies to me, mother'

Other causatives are seen in (87), where the embedded verb is a dative in *ki*, in (88) where an unusual positional with locative prefix is embedded, and in (89).

(87) *ée kípą káaɣa*
ée ki-pą Ø-káaɣe-a
3.PRON DAT-invite P3S-make-IMPER
'make her invite him'

(88) *mǫ́šǫ íche káaɣa*
mǫšǫ́ í-che Ø-káaɣe-a
feather LOC-standing P3S-make-IMPER
'let the feather touch it' (lit., 'make the feather stand upright [and thereby touch something]')

(89) *oðíhtą̨ šką́a káaɣa*
oðíhtą̨ šką́ Ø-káaɣe-a
car move P3S-make-IMPER
'start the car' (lit., 'make the car move/function')

Although *káaɣe* is characteristically found in somewhat more coercive sentences, such as 'make her invite him' in (87), the noncoercive use is also found, as in (90).

(90) *wáazo žįkážį toa kíðalį wakáaɣape*
wa-kízo žįkážį toa Ø-kiðalį wa-káaɣe-api-ðe
P1P-fun children some P3P-enjoy P3P-make-PL-DECL
'it was fun to make the children happy'

The causee is represented by inflection on both causative verb and embedded verb, as in (91) and (92). The embedded verb *kaaskíke* 'tired' is a stative verb; although data is too scarce to be certain, it is probable that statives are more likely than actives to inflect when embedded under causatives.

(91) *škáace mąðį́pi, wáskike waškáaɣa pi*
škáce mąðį-a-api wa-kaaskike wa-Ya-káaɣe-api
play go-IMPER-PL P1P-tired P1P-A2S-make-PL
'you all go on and play, you make us tired'

(92) *škáace mąðį́pi, ą́ąskike ąškáaɣape*
škace mąðį-a-api, ą-kaaskike ą-Ya-káaɣe-api-ðe
play go-IMPER-PL, P1S-tired P1S-A2-make-PL-DECL
'you all go on and play, you [plural] make me tired'

4.2.2 Morphological causatives with *ðe*

The *ðe* causative stems take the *a-ða* (regular active) set of subject inflection markers just preceding *ðe*. The 1D/P subject inflection *ą* or *ąk* also appears at the same insertion point (but see section 4.2.2.3).[14] The primary root for *ðe* causatives may be active or stative, transitive or intransitive. Some of the primary roots are semantically opaque, others quite transparent. These morphological causatives appear with dative, suus, reciprocal, and reflexive object reference, and with valence reducers. Examples of each appear in this section. (For semantically opaque causatives, the primary root morpheme is glossed in examples as PREV, and the gloss of the entire causative verb appears under *ðe*.)

[14] These are not syncopating verbs as are most verbs in *ð* (such as *aðée* 'go', with organic *ð*: *brée*, *ščée*, in 1S and 2S), since the *ð* of the *ðe* causative historically was epenthetic.

As will be seen in many examples below, the *ð* of causative *ðe* elides just as other instances of *ð* in the language tend to do. The causative also undergoes the V1-V2 Rule in certain contexts, becoming *ða*, in identical fashion to noncausative stems in *ðe*.

One of the most transparent causatives is *cˀéðe* 'kill', made up of *cˀe* 'death, die' plus *ðe* 'cause'. The addition of *ðe* makes the intransitive verb 'die' into a transitive verb 'kill'.

Many *ðe* causatives involve making something be a certain way. Corn dries on its own (*púze* 'become dry; be dry'); if someone or something makes it dry or dries it, that is causative *púzeðe*.

(93) *hápa púzeða!*
hápa púze-Ø-ðe-a
corn dry-P3S-CAU-IMPER
'dry that corn!'

(94) *hápa ášihta púzeða!*
hápa ášihta púze-Ø-ðe-a
corn outside dry-P3S-CAU-IMPER
'dry the corn outside'

The motion verb *ahú* 'come [motion underway]', not surprisingly minus its initial *a* (see section 4.3), combines with causative *ðe*, producing *húðe* 'send, send over to here'; this extremely common form often elides the *ð*. A similar form *híðe* 'send there', based on *ahí* 'arrive there', also exists. (A form nearly synonymous to *húðe* uses *káaɣe: húukaaɣa* 'pass [it]!'.)

(95) *haxį che ąkˀú huðá*
haxį che ą-kˀú hú-ðe-a
blanket STA P1S-give come.here-CAU-IMPER
'give me those blankets [and make them come here]'

Another typical transparent pair is intransitive *híce* 'hurry' and the corresponding causative transitive *híceðe* 'make [someone] hurry; hurry [someone]'.

4.2.2.1 Causative with various object referents

It is convenient to use the verb *óxtaðe* to illustrate combinations of the causative with the object referents reflexive-reciprocal (*hkik-ðe*), dative, and suus (the last two with identical surface forms *ki-ðe*), both for the clarity of this verb's forms and for its cultural importance. The verb *óxta* is glossed here as 'cherished' and its causative *óxta_ðe* is variously 'make cherished', 'make dear', 'make precious', as in 'he made someone [to be as] something precious'. *óxta* is also variously 'blessed' or 'great'. These two verbs embody an important cultural concept, as is seen in the examples below, for which it is difficult to find an exact equivalent in English.

óxtaðe 'make dear' is the plain form of the causative—that is, without object reference prefixes. With suus *ki*, it means 'make one's own dear or special'. The suus is the most commonly occurring object reference form of this verb; it is seen in (96) and (97).

(96) *óxtakiə ąðé*
óxta-ki-ðe ąðé
cherished-Ø-DAT-CAU 1D.CONT
'we [two] cherish her'

(97) *žįkówahkihą óxtawakíe akxai*
žįkáowahkihą óxta-wa-Ø-ki-ðe akxa-ðe
grandchildren cherish-A3P-A3S-SUU-CAU 3.CONT-DECL
'he's making his grandchildren *óxta* [special, precious]'

The causative *óxtaðe* also occurs with reciprocal *hkik*, giving 'make each other dear' (98), and with reflexive *hkik* (identical in form to the reciprocal), with the gloss 'hold oneself dear' (99)–(102); a slightly different gloss of the reflexive is seen in (103).

(98) *óxtahkiapi*
óxta-hkik-ðe-a-api
cherished-RECIP-CAU-IMPER-PL
'cherish each other; regard each other as great'

(99) *óxtahkie*
óxta-hkik-ðe
cherished-REFL-CAU
'cherish oneself'

(100) *óxtaðahkie*
óxta-Ya-hkik-ðe
cherished-A2S-REFL-CAU
'you made yourself right and respectable'

(101) *óxtahkie*
óxta-Ø-hkik-ðe
cherished-A3S-REFL-CAU
'he's making himself important'

óxta can also be governed by *káaɣe* as in (102), although this is much less common than *óxtaðe*.

(102) *óxta káaɣe akxai*
óxta Ø-Ø-káaɣe akxa-ðe
cherished P3S-A3S-make 3.CONT-DECL
'somebody else is making him important'

Other examples of reflexive causatives (of different verbs) are seen in (103) and (104).

(103) *hkikˀą́ze hkíe*
hkikˀą́ze hkik-ðe
comfortable REFL-CAU
'make oneself comfortable'[15]

(104) *į́štáxi íkǫska hkíe apai*
į́štáxį íkǫska hkik-Ø-ðe apa-ðe
white.man equal REFL-A3S-CAU 3.CONT-DECL
'he's acting like, imitating, that white man; he's making himself equal to that white man'

(While 'pretend to be, emulate another' uses the cognate of *káaɣe* in Omaha-Ponca, in Osage a similar expression uses either *káaɣe* or the reflexive causative *hkik-ðe* 'make oneself', plus *íkǫska* 'equal', as in (104).)

4.2.2.2 Opaque morphological causatives

Among the less transparent *ðe* causatives is *šcé_ðe* 'doctor [administer care of a doctor]' in (105)–(109).

(105) *ąkóe šcéąðape*
ąkóe šcé-ąk-Ø-ðe-api-ðe
1P.PRON PREV-A1P-P3S-doctor-PL-DECL
'we doctored him'

(106) *šcéąða!*
šcé-ą-ðe-a
PREV-P1S-doctor-IMPER
'doctor me!'

(107) *šcéwiemąži*
šcé-wi-ðe-mąži
PREV-P2S<A1S-doctor-1S.NEG
'I won't doctor you'

[15] In this study, those *kíðe* and *kšíðe* causatives where the primary root is a common verb that appears independently, outside the causative construction, have been written with a space between the primary root and *kíðe* or *kšíðe*. This seems to coincide with speaker intuitions, accent patterns, intentional insertion of pauses, etc. In a few cases, such as the transparent *cˀéðe*, the primary root and causative affix are felt to form one word and concept. Such simple *ðe* causatives are written as one word. Nothing critical rests on this decision.

(108) *šcéawai hta mįkšé*
šce-Wa-wa-ðe hta mįkšé
PREV-A1S-P3P-doctor FUT 1S.CONT
'I'll doctor them'

(109) *tówa kše šcéða!*
tówa kše šcé-Ø-ðe-a
that.one LIE PREV-P3S-doctor-IMPER
'doctor him!'

Another semantically opaque causative verb is *ðakʔé_ðe*, very frequently used in Osage speeches and prayers. No meaning is obvious for the primary root or stem *ðakʔé*.

(110) *ðakʔéðe*
ðakʔé-ðe
PREV-be.kind
'be good or kind to; pity'

Another verb belonging to the category of semantically opaque *ðe* causatives is *mąxí_ðe* 'lie to; misrepresent oneself to; deceive'.

(111) *mąxíwapi akxai*
mąxí-wa-Ø-ðe-api akxa-ðe
PREV-P1P-A3P-deceive-PL 3.CONT-DECL
'they're lying to us now'

(112) *mąxíwaape*
mąxí-wa-Ø-ðe-api-ðe
PREV-P1P-A3P-deceive-PL-DECL
'they fooled us'

Another semantically opaque causative is *toníðe*, glossed by speakers as 'bawl out, almost kill; spare the life of someone; barely spare'. In this transitive form, *ni* or *oni* could be 'exist, live', but the rest is opaque at this point. The first syllable *to* (or perhaps underlyingly *ta*) would appear to have, or have had, a meaning something like 'barely', giving *toní* 'barely live, barely alive'.

Another popular semantically opaque *ðe* causative is *tašéðe* 'thump on the head'.

4.2.2.3 Collapse of *ðe* causative to single stem

Rarely but significantly, a speaker will treat a causative as a single-stem verb. The usual form for A1P with the verb *cʔé_ðe* 'kill' would be *cʔéąðape* 'we killed him', with A1P *ąk* appearing at the point of inflection. However, for at least one speaker, A1P *ąk* precedes the first stem:

ąc^ʔeðape 'we killed him'. The remainder of the paradigm for the same speaker is completely normal: *cʔewaðape* 'they killed us'; *cʔeąðape* 'they killed me'. It is not clear what her A1P valence-reduced form would be; she finds ***ąwácʔeðape*, ***ą́wacʔeðape*, and ***ącʔéwaðape* ungrammatical.

Normally, this causative verb *cʔé_ðe* 'kill' adds the valence reducer *wa* before *cʔé*, creating the detransitivized 'kill things/folks', as in (113).

(113) *wacʔéąðapaži nai*
wa-cʔé-ą-ðe-api-aži *na-ðe*
VAL-die-A1P-CAU-PL-NEG ITER-DECL
'we don't kill'

The homophonous concrete patient pronominal P3S *wa* appears (like any other patient inflection) at the usual point of inflection between the primary root and the causative, as in (114).

(114) *cʔéwaðape*
cʔe-wa-ðe-api-ðe
die-P3P-CAU-PL-DECL
'he killed them'

If the form in (113) were stripped of the valence reducer *wa*, it would be glossed with a concrete object: *cʔéąðapaži nai* 'we don't kill it/him/her'.

Similar behavior can be seen in a few other verbs, such as the valence-reduced form of the opaque causative *šcé_ðe* 'doctor', with the valence reducer similarly occurring leftward of the primary root.

(115) *wašcéðe*
wa-šcé-ðe
VAL-PREV-doctor
'doctor [folks]' (intransitive)

4.2.2.4 Impersonal valence-reduced causative

In contrast to the causatives just discussed in section 4.2.2.3, with valence reducer preceding the primary stem and acting as the diffuse object of that stem, the regular valence-reduced form of *ðe* causative is *waðe*, with valence reducer *wa* following the primary stem as the diffuse object of causative *ðe*. The valence reducer *wa* can be glossed 'folks', or impersonal 'one'; *waðe* can thus be glossed 'make folks, make one'; the usual translation is 'it makes one [verb]'. An examination of *kǫ́ða* 'want' and its corresponding valence-reduced causative *kǫ́ða_waðe* elucidates the reason for this. If valence reducer *wa* were to occur leftward of the primary stem *kǫ́ða*, giving *wakǫ́ða_ðe*, the meaning would be 'make to want stuff'—that is, the valency of the primary stem would be reduced. But with the configuration *kǫ́ða_waðe*, the *wa* is the object of the causative *ðe*, and the meaning is 'make folks want to X', as in (116).

(116) *óohǫ kǫ́ðawai*
wa-oohǫ́ kǫ́ða-wa-ðe
VAL-cook want-VAL-CAU
'it makes one want to cook'

I have also encountered the following form, with (pronominal?) *é* between *kǫ́ða* and *waðe*.

(117) *opáwįɣe kǫ́ða éewai*
opáwįɣe kǫ́ða ée-wa-ðe
ride want 3.PRON-VAL-CAU
'it makes one want to go riding'

Another example of a regular valence-reduced causative in *waðe* is (118).

(118) *tǫ́pewai akxa*
tǫ́pe-wa-ðe akxa
look-VAL-CAU 3.CONT
'it's worth looking at' (lit., 'it makes one look')

Closely related to this last example, but not an exact match semantically, is the following set of examples involving *tǫ́pe* 'look at, see' in which the subject of the causative makes one appear a certain way. This is an interesting causative because it seems to change the transitivity of *tǫ́pe* 'look at, see' (transitive) to *tǫ́pe* 'look, appear' (intransitive). Such an unusual change of transitivity leads one to suspect that this is a calque of English.

(119) *tǫ́pewai*
tǫ́pe-wa-ðe
look-VAL-CAU
'make one appear [a certain way, e.g., sloppy]'

(120) *ɣǫ́ǫce tǫ́pewai*
ɣǫǫce tǫ́pe-wa-ðe
sloppy look-VAL-CAU
'you look sloppy; it makes you look sloppy'

4.2.3 Benefactive dative stem of *ðe* causative: *kšíðe*

The dative stem of the morphological causative is *kšíðe*, where *ðe* is the causative root; the shortened surface form *kšie* also appears. The form *kšíðe* cannot be fully accounted for semantically or morphologically, due to scarcity of data. This form is much rarer in Osage than any of the other forms of the *ðe* causative. Its usual interpretation is 'have someone do something *for that person's own benefit*'; hence I have classed it as a benefactive dative. In some instances, it seems to involve the first agent in the activity that the second agent is made to engage in.

This form possibly derives from *ki-hi-ðe*, where *hi* is a relic of a causative root attested elsewhere in Siouan. Dakota has two causatives, *ye* and *khiye* (or *ya* and *khiya*), which would seem to be quite parallel to the *ðe* and *kšiðe* forms presented here.

(121) *haxį į kšie*
haxį į Ø-kšiðe
blanket wear P3S-CAU
'give him a blanket' (lit., 'let him wear a blanket; cover him with a blanket')

(122) *hiiðá ąðákšie*
hiiðá ą-Ya-kšiðe
bathe P1S-A2S-CAU
'you bathed me' (lit., 'you had me bathe')

(123) *hiiðá kšiape*
hiiðá Ø-Ø-kšiðe-api-ðe
bath P3S-A3P-CAU-PL-DECL
'she had him/them take a bath'

(124) *wáazoe ąkšie hta ąkái*
wa-kizó-ðe ąk-kšiðe hta ąkáðe
P3P-enjoy-DECL(?) A1P-CAU FUT 1P.CONT
'we're going to have a good time for them' (or 'we're going to show them a good time, e.g., hold a party for them')

(125) *wáazo wakšie*
wa-kizó wa-kšiðe-a
P3P-enjoy P3P-CAU-IMPER
'make them have a good time'

4.2.4 Dative or suus *kíðe* 'have'

The gloss for the dative and suus form of causative *ðe*, namely *kíðe*, is typically 'have [someone do something]' rather than 'make', reflecting less power or coercion exercised by the main subject. With the *ðe* causative, the dative *ki* and the suus *kik* are indistinguishable. If the sentence involves 'subject's own family or persons', then it will be a suus sentence, as in the following example.

(126) *žįkážį haxį į kíðape*
žįkážį haxį į ki-ðe-api-ðe
child blanket wear SUU-CAU-PL-DECL
'he had his children wear their blankets'

If the causee is merely an unrelated person (not family, not subject's own), then the *ki* in question must be dative. The following example is clearly dative:

(127) *ðóhta kiðe*
ðohta ki-ðe
friend DAT-CAU
'make friends of a person, hold a person dear'

The next example is ambiguous between suus and dative.

(128) *hiiðá kíape*
hiiða Ø-Ø-ki-ðe-api-ðe
bathe P3S-A3S-CAU-PL-DECL
'she bathed him' (lit., 'she had him bathe')

Sentence (129) is in principle ambiguous between dative and suus *ki*, but in the context where it was produced, the child in question was known to be the mother's own.

(129) *įįhǫ́ akxa šįtožį hiiðá kíape*
iihǫ́ akxa šįtožį hiiðá kik-ðe-api-ðe
mother SUBJ boy bathe SUU-CAU-PL-DECL
'the mother had the child take a bath'

4.2.5 Injunctive forms

The injunctive element *hce* is often followed by the verb *e[h]e* 'say, tell' (giving *hce-ée)*. (The verb 'say, tell' has the following forms: 1S *épše*, 2S *éše*, 3S *ée*.) The result is a construction with somewhat causativelike semantics, 'ask to; tell to; want (someone) to'.

The V1-V2 Rule applies, causing the final *e* of *ée* to disappear in favor of *a* in the usual contexts, that is, before imperative *a*, negative *aži*, or *api-ðe*. For the imperative, the surface form is Verb + *hce éa* 'tell him/her to [verb]', auditorily *hcéa*, from *hce ée a*. Imperative *hcéa* can be seen in examples (130)–(131).

(130) *wižįke líi ta, húu hcéa*
wižįke a-Ø-lí tą,
wižįke PREV-A3S-arrive.back.here when

a-Ø-hú *hce* *ée-a*
PREV-A3S-come.here INJ say-IMPER
'she wants you to send Wižįke [Sonny] to her when he gets here'

(131) *mąlį hcéa*
mą-kik-ðį hce-ée-a
PREV-VERT-go/walk INJ-say-IMPER
'tell him to go home; ask him to go home'

Other examples of *hce ée* appear below.

(132) *íiði hcée akxa*
ii-ðe *hce* *é-Ø-e* *akxa*
PREV-talk INJ PREV-A3S-say 3.CONT
'he asked me to talk about it' (or 'he's proposing that I talk about it')

(133) *Johna akxa Mogri Mary óhką hcée akxai*
Johna akxa Mogri Mary ó-Ø-Ø-hką
John SUBJ Mogri Mary PREV-P3S-A3S-help
hce *é-Ø-e* *akxa-ðe*
INJ PREV-A3S-say 3.CONT-DECL
'John told Mogri to help Mary' (or 'John is proposing that Mogri help Mary')

(134) *wižįke oðíhką hce épše*
wižįke o-ði-Ø-hką *hce* *é-Wa-e*
Sonny PREV-P2S-A3S-help INJ PREV-A1S-say
'I asked Sonny to help you'

See also section 7.3.2 for *hce* as a sentence-final element.

4.3 Motion verbs

The complex system of verbs of motion in Osage was very much alive with speakers, having at least eight forms distinguished in the 1990s, as illustrated in tables 4.4–4.7. We will look first at movement toward here (four verbs and their corresponding portatives). Then we will look at movement toward there (four verbs and their corresponding portatives). The motion verb matrix represents a crosscutting of the variables of direction (here vs. there), motion (accomplished vs. underway), and vertitivity (simple vs. returning). The intransitive motion verbs (e.g., 'go') are paralleled by transitive ones, the portatives ('go carrying, having'). The portatives are doubly conjugated, consisting of 'have' plus the eight plain verbs of motion.[16]

[16] Verbs indicating motion underway are given gerundial glosses ('going', 'coming') in discussion and in the tables belwo, but in examples are glossed 'go.there', 'come.here', etc., for simplicity.

The vertitive members of the motion verb matrix signify motion toward a place where the subject was previously—that is, return to the place from which the subject departed, or the subject's home. These include 'go back there', 'come back here', 'go home', 'come home'.

Tables 4.4–4.7 summarize this complex system. The following abbreviations are used in the tables and associated discussion:

Arr = arrival (verbs that indicate motion accomplished)

Mot = motion underway (verbs that indicate being en route)

Port = portative (carrying with)

vert = vertitive (returning to point of origin, or to home)

For example, "Port-Arr1" stands for "Arrival, portative version." Numbers code direction ('toward here' is marked with 1 and 2; 'toward there' is marked with 3 and 4) and vertitivity (vertitive forms are marked 2 and 4), allowing compact labeling of the examples in this section to relate them to the tables. In the tables, the verbs indicating motion still underway (coming, going, etc.) appear in the two righthand columns. The two lefthand columns of each table show the verbs indicating motion accomplished (arrival here or there, etc.). To each basic motion verb there corresponds a portative; these include "Port" in the mnemonic label. Thus, the four basic verbs of 'movement toward here' in table 4.4 form the four portatives in table 4.5, and the basic verbs of 'movement toward there' in table 4.6 form the portatives in table 4.7.

All portatives are compounds whose first member is *a_ðį́* 'have', a syncopating verb with the forms 1S *abrį́*, 2S *ašcį́* (Hominy dialect *aščį́*), 3S *aðį́*, 1P *ąkáðį*. The second member of the portative compound is the motion verb itself, which optionally drops its initial preverb *a*. In 'I'm bringing him something', for example, basically *abrį* 'I have' + *ali* 'I return here', the initial *a* of the second member may be lost (*abrį́li*) or may remain (*abrį́ali*). In *áðįku*, the *a* of *akú* seems not to surface at all.

The vertitive forms, indicating return, are made up of the suus prefix *kik* plus verb root. For example, the verb *a_ðée* 'go' with addition of *kik* gives the underlying form *a-kik-ðée*, which becomes surface *alée* 'go back/home'. (See section 4.6.4 for the reduction of *kik-ð* to *l*.) Since suus *kik* means 'subject's own', the original meaning of vertitive verbs would have been 'go to subject's own [place/home]', extended to mean also 'go back [to any location]'. Phonological processes affecting suus *kik*, such as the formation of *l* from *kik-ð* in the verb just discussed, apply also to the vertitive *kik* in these verbs of motion. Somewhat less regular phonological

TABLE 4.4. MOTION VERBS: MOVEMENT TOWARD HERE

ARRIVAL		MOTION UNDERWAY	
SIMPLE	VERTITIVE	SIMPLE	VERTITIVE
achí	*alí*	*ahú*	*akú*
'arrive here'	'return here; come home'	'coming here'	'returning here; coming home'
Arr1	Arr2	Mot1	Mot2

TABLE 4.5. PORTATIVE MOTION VERBS: MOVEMENT TOWARD HERE

ARRIVAL		MOTION UNDERWAY	
SIMPLE	VERTITIVE	SIMPLE	VERTITIVE
aðįachi	*aðįali*	*aðįahu*	*áðįku*
'bring here'	'bring back/home here'	'bringing here'	'bringing back/home here'
Port-Arr1	Port-Arr2	Port-Mot1	Port-Mot2

TABLE 4.6. MOTION VERBS: MOVEMENT TOWARD THERE

ARRIVAL		MOTION UNDERWAY	
SIMPLE	VERTITIVE	SIMPLE	VERTITIVE
ahí	*akši*	*aðée*	*alée*
'arrive there'	'arrive back/home there'	'going there'	'returning there; going home there'
Arr3	Arr4	Mot3	Mot4

TABLE 4.7. PORTATIVE MOTION VERBS: MOVEMENT TOWARD THERE

ARRIVAL		MOTION UNDERWAY	
SIMPLE	VERTITIVE	SIMPLE	VERTITIVE
aðįahi	*aðįakši*	*aðįaðe*	*aðįalee*
'take there'	'take back/home there'	'taking there'	'taking back/home there'
Port-Arr3	Port-Arr4	Port-Mot3	Port-Mot4

reduction is seen in *alí* 'return here', from *a-kik-chi*, and *aku* 'returning here', from *a-kik-hu*.

The verbs of motion group into conjugation classes as "syncopating" or "regular" by virtue of the inflectable initial segment. Therefore, it is only accidents of derivation that determine which class a motion verb will fall into. Three of the eight verbs in this section fall into the syncopating class. These syncopating motion verbs show initial *a* followed by an *h*-stem (*ahú*, *ahí*) or by a *ð*-stem (*aðée*). They will usually drop the initial *a* in 1S and 2S forms, but keep this *a* in simple third person unembedded, noninterrogative, nonimperative forms. 1S and 2S forms are as follows for these syncopating stems:

ahú 'coming here': *pšú*, *šú*

ahí 'arrive there': *pší*, *ší*

aðée 'going there': *brée*, *šcée*

Third person forms usually retain the initial *a* in all three of these verbs in unembedded, noninterrogative, nonimperative forms; e.g.:

(135) *aðée akxa*
a-Ø-ðée akxa
PREV-A3S-go 3.CONT
'he's going'

For the other five motion verbs, those that show the regular inflection pattern with A1S *a* and A2S *ða*, the preverb *a* is either present and obscured by the agent pronominals in 1S and 2S, or, more likely, absent.

achí 'arrive here': *achí*, *ðachí*

alí 'return here': *alí*, *ðalí*

akú 'returning here': *akú*, *ðakú*

akší 'arrive back there': *akší*, *ðakší*

alée 'returning there': *alée*, *ðalée*

For these regular motion verbs, the preverb *a* is usually present in third person forms, just as for *ahú*, *ahí*, and *aðée* above.

In all eight basic motion verbs, the preverb *a* is optionally dropped in four contexts: (i) when the motion verb is the second member of a compound construction, especially in third person compounds; (ii) when the motion verb is embedded syntactically under another verb or followed by causative *ðe* (e.g., *híðe* 'cause to arrive there'); (iii) in imperatives; and (iv) in questions, especially for *aðée* 'be going there' (*hoową́ki ðée?*

'where is he going?'). For example, with embedded *aðée*, the preverb drops, as in the following examples:

(136) *Mary ðée hce iiðáhǫ*
Mary (a)-Ø-ðée hce ii-ð-Wa-hǫ́
Mary (PREV)-A3S-go.there INJ PREV-EPð-A1S-ask
'I asked Mary to go'

(137) *Mary ðée hcáape*
Mary (a)-Ø-ðée hce-e-Ø-e-api-ðe
Mary (PREV)-A3S-go.there INJ-PREV-A3P-say-PL-DECL
'they asked Mary to go'

In (138), the preverb *a* is again dropped in the question, but it is present in the answer to the question (139).

(138) *ilǫ́ǫhpa hówai̥ki ðée?*
ilǫ́ǫhpa hówai̥ki (a)-Ø-ðée
firstborn.son where (PREV)-A3S-go.there
'where did Sonny go?'

(139) *ilǫ́ǫhpa akxa htą́wą ki aðáape*
ilǫ́ǫhpa akxa htą́wą ki a-Ø-ðée-api-ðe
firstborn.son SUBJ town to PREV-A3S-go.there-PL-DECL
'Sonny went to town'

The examples given in the rest of this section show an array of forms with and without the preverb *a*.

Below are a few examples of each of the eight motion verbs and their portatives, along with the inflectional paradigm for each. The paradigmatic forms given in each case are 1S, 2S, 3S, 1P.

4.3.1 Arrival here

Arr1 'arrive here' *a_chí*: *achí*, *ðachí*, *achí*, *ąkáchi*

(140) *achí*
'come, arrive here, get here, show up'

(141) *mąðí ðachíe?*
mąðí Ya-chí-ðe
walk A2S-arrive.here-DECL
'did you come afoot?'

(142) *hą́hkaži, oðíhta olį̥ achíe*
hą́hkaži, oðíhtą olį̥ a-Wa-chí-ðe
no, car sit.in PREV-A1S-arrive.here-DECL
'no, I came by car'

(143) *walézeaace achíe*
waléze-ðaacé a-Wa-chí-ðe
book-read PREV-A1S-arrive.here-DECL
'I came to class'

(144) *ðachí ée skə*
Ya-chí ée ska
A2S-arrive.here that SUPPOSE
'I assume you were here earlier'

Port-Arr1 'have + arrive here' = 'bring' *a_ðį-a_chí*: *abrįachi, aščįðachi, aðįachi, ąkáðįąkachi*

(145) *žąąnížį awíbrįachie*
žąąnížį a-wi-Wa-ðį-a-Wa-chí-ðe
candy PREV-P2S<A1S-A1S-have-PREV-A1S-arrive.here-DECL
'I brought you some candy'

Arr2-vert 'arrive back/home here' *a_lí*: *alí, ðalí, alí, ąkáli*

(146) *sitǫ́į alí*
sitǫ́į a-Wa-lí
yesterday PREV-A1S-arrive.back.here
'I got home yesterday'

(147) *ąkálipe*
ąk-a-li-api-ðe
A1P-arrive.back.here-PL-DECL
'we arrived home; we came back; we came home'

Port-Arr2-vert 'have + 'arrive back here' = 'bring back/home here' *a_ðį-a_lí*: *abrįali, aščįðali, aðįali, ąkáðįąkáli*

(148) *aðįali*
a-ðį-a-lí
PREV-have-PREV-arrive.back.here
'bring back'

(149) *awíbrįli*
a-wi-Wa-ðį-a-Wa-li
PREV-P2S<A1S-A1S-have-PREV-A1S-arrive.back.here
'I'm bringing you something'

(150) *aðįli*
aðį-alí-a
have-bring-IMPER
'bring me [something]' (lit., 'bring back something')

(151) *wižįke akxa haxį wį aðįalípe*
wižįke akxa haxį wį
my.son SUBJ blanket a
a-Ø-ðį-a-Ø-lí-api-ðe
PREV-A3S-have-PREV-A3S-arrive.back.here-PL-DECL
'my son brought back a blanket'

(152) *ecí pa ą́ąšcįðalie ðe*
ecí pa
those PLU
a-ą-Ya-ðį-a-Ya-lí-ðe *ðe*
PREV-P1S-A2S-have-PREV-A2S-arrive.back.here-DECL DECL(?)
'you brought me home to them'

(153) *ą́ąšcįðalíe ðe*
a-ą-Ya-ðį-a-Ya-lí-e *ðe*
PREV-P1S-A2S-have-PREV-A2S-arrive.back-DECL DECL(?)
'you brought it [things] home to me'

4.3.2 Arrival there

Arr3 'arrive there' *a_hí*: *pší*, *ši*, *ahí*, *ąkáhi*

(154) *ážą áažą pšíe*
ážą á-Wa-žą a-Wa-hi-ðe
bed PREV-A1S-lie PREV-A1S-arrive.there-DECL
'I went to bed'

(155) *kasįxci htáabre pšíe*
kasįta-xci htáabre a-Wa-hí-ðe
morning-early hunting PREV-A1S-arrive.there-DECL
'this morning I went hunting'

(156) *žóhpazi mǫnǫ́į océ pšíe*
žóhpazi mǫnǫ́į océ a-Wa-hí-ðe
quail prairie.chicken look.for PREV-A1S-arrive.there-DECL
'I went to look for quail and prairie chicken'

In the next sentence, the use of the continuative marker *akxa* with the motion-completed verb *ahí* gives the sense of 'right now it has arrived at'.

(157) *mį́įðohta ahí akxa*
mį́į-ðohta a-hi akxa
sun-half PREV-arrive.there 3.CONT
'it's straight up noon'

The *a* of *ahí* has elided in the imperative in the next example.

(158) *táatą šcíištą tą, hci ci hí ðį*
táatą Ya-ðiištą́ tą, hci ci a-hí-a ði
what A2S-finish when, house to PREV-arrive.there-IMPER 2S.PRON
'when you get through with what you're doing, come by the house'

In (159), a postposition *ci* 'to; at' is used with the destination of the motion verb, although usually *ahí* would occur without such postposition. By the translation 'go by', the speaker here meant 'stop in at'; the Osage expression is *pši* 'I arrive there'. Speakers often translate *a_hí* as 'get there', as well as 'go there' and other glosses.

(159) *wíe bríištą tą, waatáihci ci pší hta mįkšé*
wíe Wa-ðiištą́ tą, waatá-i-hci ci
1S.PRON A1S-finish when, prayer-with-house to
a-Wa-hí hta mįkšé
PREV-A1S-arrive.there FUT 1S.CONT
'when I get through, I'm going to go by the church'

(160) *pšíe*
a-Wa-hí-ðe
PREV-A1S-arrive.there-DECL
'I was [already] over there; I have been over there; I went there; I got there'

(161) *šíe*
a-Ya-hí-ðe
PREV-A2S-arrive.there-DECL
'did you go?; you went there'

(162) *ahípe*
a-Ø-hí-api-ðe
PREV-A3S-arrive.there-PL-DECL
'he got there'

(163) *ąkáhipe*
ąk-a-hí-api-ðe
A1P-PREV-arrive.there-PL-DECL
'we got there'

(164) *ecí pa žóąðale šíe ðe*
ecí pa žó-ą-Ya-le a-Ya-hie ðe
there PLU PREV-P1S-A2S-with PREV-A2S-arrive.there DECL
'you brought [i.e., took] me to them, you went with me to them'

Port-Arr3 'have + arrive there' = 'take' *a_ðį-a_hí*: *abrįpši*, *ašcįši*, *aðįahí*, *ąkáðįąkáhi*

(165) *wižįke akxa haxį wį aðįahípe*
wižįke akxa haxį wį
my.son SUBJ blanket a
a-Ø-Ø-ðį-a-Ø-hí-api-ðe
PREV-P3S-A3S-have-PREV-A3S-arrive.there-PL-DECL
'my son took a blanket over there'

The following two examples constitute a minimal pair for the 1S form, with and without elision of the preverb *a*.

(166) *haxį wį abrįpšie*
haxį wį a-Ø-Wa-ðį-a-Wa-hí-ðe
blanket a PREV-P3S-A1S-have-PREV-A1S-arrive.there-DECL
'I took a blanket [there]'

(167) *abrįapšie*
a-Wa-ðį-a-Wa-hí-ðe
PREV-A1S-have-PREV-A1S-arrive.there-DECL
'I took [it/something] there'

Arr4-vert 'arrive back there [returning]' *a_kší*: *akší*, *ðakší*, *akší*, *ąkáksį*

(168) *akšípe*
a-Ø-kší-api-ðe
PREV-A3P-arrive.back-PL-DECL
'they arrived home'

Port-Arr4-vert 'have + arrive back there' = 'take back' *a_ðį-a_kší*: *abrįakši*, *ašcįðakši*, *aðįakší*, *ąkáðįąkákši*
Logically, 'take back' extends to cover taking something home.

(169) *aðįakšipe*
a-Ø-Ø-ðį-a-Ø-kší-api-ðe
PREV-P3S-A3S-have-PREV-A3S-arrive.back.there-PL-DECL
'he took [something] home; he got [back] there with [something]'

(170) *wižįke akxa haxį wį aðįakšipe*
wižįke akxa haxį wį
my.son SUBJ blanket a
a-Ø-Ø-ðį-a-Ø-kší-api-ðe
PREV-P3S-A3S-have-PREV-A3S-arrive.back.there-PL-DECL
'my son took a blanket home [he got home with it]'

4.3.3 Motion underway to here

Mot1 'coming here' *a_hú*: *pšú, šú, ahú ~ hú, ąkáhu*

The *u* in *ahú* is extremely fronted. One speaker, when using this form, would always add (in English) "Here I would be speaking to someone already there [at the destination toward which I am moving]," thus establishing that the deictic center is 'here where you [the hearer] are'.

(171) *níhkašie toa ahú apái*

níhkašika toa a-Ø-hú apa-ðe
people some PREV-P3P-come.here 3.CONT-DECL
'there are some people coming'

(172) *pšú mįkšé*

a-Wa-hu mįkšé
PREV-A1S-come.here 1S.CONT
'I'm coming [this way]'

Whether or not the continuative marker appears in (172), it has the same meaning, and both versions, with and without *mįkšé*, could be glossed colloquially 'Here I come!'.

(173) *áhkita apa ahú əpai*

áhkita apa a-Ø-hú apa-ðe
police SUBJ PREV-A3S-come.here 3.CONT-DECL
'here comes the policeman'

Port-Mot1 'have + coming here' = 'bringing here' *a_ðį-ahú*: *abrįpšu, ašcįšu, aðįahu, ąkáðįąkáhu*

(174) *haxį wį abrįpšu mįkšé*

haxį wį a-Ø-Wa-ðį-a-Wa-hu mįkšé
blanket a PREV-P3S-A1S-have-PREV-A1S-come.here 1S.CONT
'I'm taking/bringing a blanket here'

(175) *wižįke akxa haxį wį aðįahu əkxái*

wižįke akxa haxį wį
my.son SUBJ blanket a
a-Ø-ðį-a-Ø-hú akxa-ðe
PREV-A3S-have-PREV-A3S-come.here 3.CONT-DECL
'my son is bringing a blanket [bringing it here]'

Mot2-vert 'coming back here' *a_kú*: *akú, ðakú, akú, ąkáku*

This verb, like *ahú,* has a very fronted *u*, so much so that attempts at writing by untrained learners result in *yu* (e.g., *akyu).*

(176) *akú apai*
a-Ø-kú *apa-ðe*
PREV-A3P-come.back 3.CONT-DECL
'they're coming back'

(177) *ąkáku ąkáðe*
ąk-a-kú *ąkáðe*
A1P-PREV-A3P-come.back 1P.CONT
'we're coming back'

(178) *htaacé hpíiži apa aakú apai*
htaacé hpíiži apa a-kú *apa-ðe*
wind bad SUBJ PREV-A3S-come.back 3.CONT-DECL
'a tornado is coming'

Port-Mot2-vert 'have + coming back here' = 'bringing back/home here' *a_ðį-akú*: *abrįaku, ašcįðaku, aðįaku, ąkáðįąkaku*

(179) *ówe che hcí hta áðįku!*
ówe *che hcí* *hta a-ðį-a-ku-a*
groceries STA house into PREV-have-PREV-returning.here-IMPER
'bring those groceries sitting there into the house'

4.3.4 Motion underway to there

Mot3 'going there [motion underway]' *a_ðée*: *brée, šcée, aðée, ąkáðe*
This is the only one of the eight motion verbs that has syncopating *ð*-stem inflection.

(180) *mįįðǫǫpá aðáape*
mįį-ðǫǫpá a-Ø-ðée-api-ðe
sun-two PREV-A3S-go.there-PL-DECL
'the moon went down'

An example of a misleading translation occurs in (181), which is more literally 'I'm going to go now', as if reassuring someone who is impatient for me to get there.

(181) *šo brée hta mįkšé*
šo *Wa-ðée hta mįkšé*
while A1S-go FUT 1S.CONT
'I'm coming'

Port-Mot3 'have + going there' = 'taking' *a_ðį-a_ðée*: *abrįbree, ašcįšcee, aðįaðee, ąkáðįąkáðe*

(182) *haxį wį abrįbree mįkšé*
haxį wį a-Wa-ðį-a-Wa-ðée mįkšé
blanket a PREV-A1S-have-PREV-A1S-go.there 1S.CONT
'I'm taking a blanket [there]'

Mot4-vert 'going back/home there' *a_lée*: *alée, ðalée, alée, ąkále*

(183) *aláape*
a-Ø-lée-api-ðee
PREV-A3P-go.back-PL-DECL
'they went home'

Sentence (183) implies that they left here with home as their destination.

Port-Mot4-vert 'have + going back/home there' = 'taking back' *a_ðį-a_lee*: *abrįalee, ašcįðalee, aðįalee, ąkáðįąkále*
The idea in the following example is that he left here with a blanket, headed for home, or that he headed back someplace. Note that *alée* does not shorten to *lée* here.

(184) *wižįke akxa haxį wį aðįalaape*
wižįke akxa haxį wį
my.son SUBJ blanket a
a-Ø-ðį-a-Ø-lée-api-ðe
PREV-A3S-have-PREV-A3S-return.there-PL-DECL
'my son took a blanket home/back with him'

4.3.5 Reflexive and suus forms

Reflexive and suus forms are attested for at least some portatives. For example, a reflexive version of the portative Mot4 ('going back/home there') is formed by adding reflexive *hkik* to *aðį* 'have', producing *ahkílį* 'have for oneself'. The reflexive 'have' is followed by *alée* 'go back there, go home' giving a new compound *ahkílįalee* 'take home for oneself'.

(185) *wižįke akxa haxį wį ahkílaaláape*
wižįke akxa haxį wį a-Ø-hkik-ðį-alée-api-ðe
my.son SUBJ blanket a PREV-A3S-REFL-have-go.home-PL-DECL
'my son took a blanket home as his own [to have for himself]'

In *ahkílaaláape* in the above example, the final *į* of the first verb *ahkílį* has become *a* by application of the V1-V2 Rule. Note that this form also occurs without such modification of *į*, as in the next example.

(186) *ahkílįaláape*
a-Ø-hkik-ðį́-alée-api-ðe
PREV-A3S-REFL-have-go.home-PL-DECL
'he took it home as his own [to have for himself]'

In addition to the reflexive version of the portative above, there is a suus version *aláðį* 'have as one's own'. This is formed by adding suus *kik* to the portative element *a_ðį́*, with an extra *ða*.[17] Suus *kik* combines with a following *ð* to form *l*, but disappears in the process, leaving no trace other than the *l*. (This is expected; see section 4.6.4.) The context for the example below is taking subject's own utensils on a fishing trip.

(187) *wióohǫži alábrį brée hta ąąhé*
wa-i-oohǫ́-žį *a-kik-ða-a-Wa-ðį*
VAL-with-cook-little PREV-SUUS-*ða/ðį*(?)-PREV-A1S-have
Wa-ðée hta ąðįhé
A1S-go FUT 1S.CONT
'I am going to take my little cooking utensils'

It would not be surprising to find *aláðį* 'have as one's own' combined with other motion verbs, although this is not attested.

4.3.6 Completed action vs. continuative

Arrival verbs can be used not only to report completed actions but also with continuative marker *apa* to describe arrivals that are happening, such as the following Arr2-vert sentence.

(188) *alí apai*
a-Ø-lí *apa-ðe*
PREV-A3P-come.back 3.CONT-DECL
'they're back' (i.e., they're coming through the door now)

The next example, with a Mot4-vert verb, involving the continuative plus future, expresses that departure is imminent: 'they're going to leave here for home'.

(189) *alée hta apai*
a-Ø-lée *hta apa-ðe*
PREV-A3P-go.home FUT 3.CONT-DECL
'they're going [to go] home'

In (190), *alée apa*, without the future *hta* seen just above, indicates action underway; the return journey is already underway.

[17] The same extra syllable *ða* (*ra in Proto-Siouan) occurs in this verb in related languages. Alternatively, this verb involves two instances of *aðį* 'have': *akikðį* + *aðį*, with application of the V1-V2 Rule..

(190) *alée apai*
a-Ø-lée *apa-ðe*
PREV-A3P-go.home 3.CONT-DECL
'they're on their way home; they're going home'

The Mot4 vertitive verb *alée* 'go back' is used upon leaving, when one says 'I'm going home'. It was customary to walk part way with the person departing, after which one would say 'I'm going back [not walking any further with you]'.

(191) *alée*
a-Wa-lée
PREV-A1S-go.home
'I am going back'

Motion verbs of arrival, in contrast to those of motion underway, convey past completed action when used without the continuative marker, like *achí* in the next example. (See section 5.6.6 for noncontinuatives.)

(192) *šįtožį akxa achípe ąži aláape, ší achíži hta akxai*
šįtožį *akxa* *a-Ø-chí-api-ðe* *ąži*
boy SUBJ PREV-A3S-arrive.here-PL-DECL but
a-Ø-lée-api-ðe
PREV-A3S-go.back-PL-DECL
ší *a-Ø-chí-aži* *hta* *akxa-ðe*
again PREV-A3S-arrive.here-NEG FUT 3.CONT-DECL
'the boy who came here left and he won't be back again' (lit., 'a boy came here but he [just] went back, [and] he won't come here again')

4.3.7 Other verbs in combination with motion verbs

Other verbs besides *aðį* 'have' occur preceding motion verbs in interesting sequences. We mention two examples here. The verb *žóle* 'accompany, be with' appears in (193) as a first member of the compound.[18]

(193) *ecí mįkšé ecí žówaðale ðalíe ðe*
e-ci *mįkšé* *e-ci* *žó-wa-Ya-le*
this-at 1S.CONT this-to PREV-P3P-A2S-with
Ya-lí-ðe *ðe*
A2S-return.here-DECL DECL
'you brought them (people) home to me' (lit., '[I'm here] [to-here them-with-you] [you-returned-here]')

[18] Another interesting but unrelated component in this sentence is the Osage *ecí mįkšé*, which is somewhat similar to the French *chez moi*. Likewise, *ecí pa* in (152) is similar to *chez eux*.

In (194) the doubly inflected *áa_lǫ_ðį* 'forget' combines with *alí* 'return here' (A2-vert).

(194) *tooská áðalǫǫšcį ðalíe*
tóoska áa-Ya-lǫ-Ya-ðį a-Ya-lí-ðe
potato PREV-A2S-PREV-A2S-forget PREV-A2S-return.here-DECL
'you forgot to bring back potatoes'

In addition, one finds *mąðį́* 'go, walk, begin movement, initiate action; function [e.g., as a machine functions or works]' interacting with other verbs in interesting ways. The similarity of *mąðį́* to the motion verbs in this section is threefold: *mąðį́* does denote motion; it has a vertitive form *mąlį́* (195); and it forms a portative with *aðį́* (196). It also appears in combination with motion verb *akú* 'return here, movement underway' (Mot2) in *akú mąðį́* (197).

(195) *mąlį́ hcéa*
mą-kik-ðį́ hce-ée-a
PREV-VERT-go/walk INJ-say-IMPER
'tell him to go home; ask him to go home'

(196) *káache aðį́mąðį*
kaa-che aðį́-mąðį-a
here-STANDING have-go/walk-IMPER
'take away this thing here'

(197) *nį́į tóe akú mąðį́*
níi tóe akú mąðį́-a
water some return.here go/walk-IMPER
'go get some water'

When the mode of movement is part of the semantics of the sentence, *mąðį́* means 'walk', as in the following Arr2-vert sentence.

(198) *mąðį́ alí apai*
mąðį a-Ø-lí apa-ðe
go/walk PREV-A3S-return.here 3.CONT
'she's walking home [as opposed to riding home]'

4.4 Instrumental prefixes

Like other Siouan languages, Osage has a series of instrumental prefixes which mark the means by which the action of the following verb is accomplished. These prefixes can be divided into two groups: an inner group (table 4.8) and an outer group (table 4.9). The inner group of prefixes occurs closer to the verb root, taking inflection to the left of the instrumental prefix: __Instr-Root. The outer group of prefixes occurs outside inflection: Instr__Root.

The inner instrumental prefixes generally transitivize an intransitive verb. Thus *ðaa* 'by mouth' transitivizes *xǫ* 'break' (intransitive) to form *_ðaaxǫ́* 'break by mouth [by biting]'.

(199) *štáaxǫ*
Ya-ðaa-xǫ́
A2S-by.mouth-break
'you break [it] by biting'

TABLE 4.8. INNER INSTRUMENTALS

INSTRUMENTAL PREFIX	TREATED IN SECTION
_ðaa 'by mouth'	4.4.1
_ðuu ~ *_ðii* 'by hand', causative	4.4.2
_kaa 'by striking'	4.4.3
_nąą 'by foot'	4.4.4
_paa 'by pushing'	4.4.6
_pu 'by pressing'; *_pi* 'by blowing'	4.4.5

The inner instrumentals are mostly quite productive. In contrast, for the outer instrumentals there is not much contemporary confirmation from speakers of Osage to support or explore their behavior. There are only three outer instrumentals claimed for related languages or by La Flesche for Osage. For one of these (*po* 'by shooting') no example sentences were readily available from speakers in the 1990s, perhaps because most of the remaining speakers at that time were women, who in their generation were less likely to be familiar with shooting vocabulary than men. One of the other two outer instrumentals, *pa_* 'by cutting', appears fully inflected as an outer instrumental, but may be merging with the nearly homophonous inner instrumental *_paa*. The final one, *taa* 'by heat', appears in the data without any inflection in the verb stem, and therefore provides no evidence of its "inner" or "outer" behavior.

TABLE 4.9. OUTER INSTRUMENTALS

INSTRUMENTAL PREFIX	TREATED IN SECTION
*pa_* 'by cutting'	4.4.7
*po_* 'by shooting' (no data)	4.4.8
*taa_* 'by heat' (not inflected?)	4.4.9

Below, the inner instrumentals are discussed first, in sections 4.4.1–4.4.6, followed by the outer instrumentals in sections 4.4.7–4.4.9. In the first group, extra attention is given to the complex case of *ðuu* ~ *ðii* 'by hand' and its overlap with causative *ðuu*; to *kaa* and its peculiar interaction with inflection; and to the semantics of inner *_paa* and its overlap with outer *pa_*.

4.4.1 *ðaa* 'by mouth'

The prefix *_ðaa* is quite a productive instrumental in Osage, meaning 'with the mouth, by mouth' and by extension, 'by speech' or 'with the teeth, by biting', all fairly transparent semantically. It takes syncopating *ð*-stem inflection; inflection precedes the *ðaa* prefix, making *ðaa* an inner instrumental. This instrumental interacts with suus, reflexive, and other elements quite productively. A few examples appear in this section, with a great many more found in the lexicon.

One of the most common of these *ðaa* instrumentals is based on the verb *šóce* 'smoke':

(200) *ðaašóe*
ðaa-šóce
by.mouth-smoke
'smoke; suck' (transitive)

Several *ðaa* forms have suus forms beginning with *l*. For example, *ðaacé* 'name' in (201) has a suus form, *láace* 'name subject's own', although the root *ce* is opaque.

(201) *žáže ðaatápe*
žáže ðaa-cé-api-ðe
name by.mouth-set(?)-PL-DECL
'they named him'

From *xǫ́* 'break' there is *ðaaxǫ́*:

(202) *ðaaxǫ́pe*
Ø-ðaaxǫ́-api-ðe
A3S-by.mouth.break-PL-DECL
'he [bit it and] broke it'

From *ðaaxǫ́* 'break with teeth, by mouth' we have the gloss 'chew on' in (203).[19]

(203) *ną́ɣe ðaaxǫ́ke šǫ akxái, híi ðiixǫ́kape*
ną́ɣe Ø-ðaaxǫ́-ke šǫ akxa-ðe
ice A3S-by.mouth.break-disperse while 3S.CONT-DECL

[19] Here *ke* is the 'plural disperse' marker usually seen following nouns.

híi Ø-ðii-xǫ́-ke-api-ðe
tooth A3S-CAU-break-disperse(?)-PL-DECL
'while he was chewing ice, he broke his tooth'

The suus form of *ðaaxǫ́* is *láaxǫ*. Besides meaning generally 'break something of one's own by mouth', as in (204), it may mean more specifically 'break one's [own] teeth', as in (205).

(204) *láaxǫ*
kik-ðaaxǫ́
SUU-by.mouth.break
'break something of subject's own [by mouth]'

(205) *híi láaxǫpe*
híi Ø-kik-ðaaxǫ́-api-ðe
tooth A3S-SUU-by.mouth.break-PL-DECL
'he broke a tooth'

In addition to the suus form *láaxǫ*, there is a reflexive form of *ðaaxǫ́* as seen in (206):

(206) *hkiláaxǫpe*
Ø-hkik-ðaaxǫ́-api-ðe
A3S-REFL-by.mouth.break-PL-DECL
'he bit himself [breaking the skin?]'

Perhaps based on *kį́į* 'fly' or *kˀį́* 'carry' is the verb *ðaakˀį́* 'spit'. Inflection such as singular patient *ą* occurs before the instrumental *ðaa*, as seen in (207).

(207) *ąðáakˀį įká ði*
ą-ðaakˀį́ ðįke-a ði
P1S-spit NEG-IMPER 2S.PRON
'don't spit on me'

The form *ðaanį́* 'consume; do away with [by mouth]', is often glossed simply as 'eat' or 'eat up'. The inflected forms of *ðaanį́* are *bráanį, štáanį, nį́ ~ ðaanį́, ąðáanį* for 1S, 2S, 3S, and 1P respectively.

(208) *ąðáanįįpe*
ą-ðaanį́į-api-ðe
A1P-consume-PL-DECL
'we ate'; 'we ate it up'; 'we consumed it'

(209) *nį́įpe*
Ø-nį́į-api-ðe
A3P-consume-PL-DECL
'they ate'; 'they ate it up'; 'they consumed it'

(210) *súhka záani ąðáanįįpe*
súhka záani ą-ðaanįį-api-ðe
chicken all A1P-consume-PL-DECL
'we ate all the chicken'

4.4.2 *ðii* ~ *ðuu* 'by hand', causative

Another inner instrumental taking syncopating inflection is *_ðii* ~ *_ðuu*, which seems to be by far the most common of the instrumental prefixes and which is especially interesting for several reasons. It forms clear pairs of intransitive and transitive verbs, converting intransitives to transitives. It applies to the so-called middle verbs like 'ring' as well as to adjectivelike verbs such as 'neat' (to produce 'neaten'). Its pronunciation varies between *ðuu* and *ðii*. Furthermore, it is indistinguishable in many contexts from *ðuu* ~ *ðii* 'cause, make', and indeed the two may well be only one. Suus and reflexive forms are well attested.

The overlap in pronunciation between the *ðuu* ~ *ðii* causative and the *ðuu* ~ *ðii* 'by hand' instrumental being examined here is not the only problem in sorting out these two forms. The semantics of causation coincide in some instances with the meaning of the 'by hand' prefix. For example, 'cause to ring' and 'ring by hand' are quite similar, and so are 'cause to break' and 'break by hand'. Whitman (1947), discussing Ioway-Otoe, gives *ri* 'by object toward', *ru* 'by hand toward', and *wa* 'by hand away', which would correspond to Osage *ðii*, *ðuu*, and *paa*, if any parallels do exist. Most likely, my separation of the prefixes *ðii* and *ðuu* is artificial, and they are in fact one and the same, meaning 'by hand'. However, in some applications, the meaning of the prefix is vague and extended. For example, the verb *ðuucˀáke* 'be unable' has no modern related form ***cˀáke*, nor can a meaning be assigned to *cˀáke* alone. We will examine both transparent and nontransparent cases here.

Very clear cases of derivation of transitives from intransitives occur. With intransitive *xǫ* 'break', the addition of *ðii* has the predictable effect: *_ðiixǫ́* ~ *_ðuuxǫ́* 'break; break by hand; break off [something long]'. (See also section 4.4.3 for *kaaxǫ́*.)

(211) *oðíhtą akxa xǫ́ akxai*
oðíhtą akxa xǫ́ akxa-ðe
car SUBJ break 3.CONT-DECL
'her car is broken'

(212) *áa ąðíixǫpe*
áa ą-ðii-xǫ́-api-ðe
arm P1S-by.hand-break-PL-DECL
'they broke my arm'

The patient pronominals, if present, precede the instrumental _*ðuu* or _*ðii* , as in (212) and (213). In most cases found, the meaning 'by hand' fits semantically. However, *ðuu* in *ðuuhpíižį* 'make bad' (213) seems to stray from the concrete meaning of 'by hand' or 'with the hands', as the agent making X bad is 'whiskey'; it may represent a slight extension of the same meaning. This sentence is more literally 'whiskey the-body to-you makes-bad FUTURE'; the second person possessor is treated as an argument of the verb.

(213) *hpéeceni akxa žúoka ðìðuuhpíiži hta akxái*
hpéece-níi akxa žúoka ði-ðuu-hpíiži hta akxa-ðe
fire-water SUBJ body P2S-CAU-bad FUT 3.CONT-DECL
'whiskey is bad for your health'

Below, the verb root *se* 'cut' appears with *ðuu* (see also examples of this root with *pa* 'by cutting' in section 4.4.6.2). (The root *se* 'cut' often surfaces with a particularly strident or long *s*, which might be represented by *ss*: *ðuussé* 'cut'.)

(214) *hpáxį ðuusá*
hpáxį ðuu-se-a
hair by.hand-cut-IMPER
'cut your hair!'

(215) *hpáxįðuusé*
hpáxį ðuu-sé
hair by.hand-cut
'a haircut'

Sentence (216) is more literally a third person sentence, 'he's cutting hair', but was offered with the 2S gloss. The raising of verb-final *e* to *i* is normal.

(216) *hpáxį ðuusí əkxái*
hpáxį Ø-ðuu-sé akxa-ðe
hair by.A3S-by.hand-cut 3.CONT-DECL
'you're getting a haircut'

A clear intransitive *hkaamą́* 'ring', as in 'the bell rings', is also transitivized by *ðuu*:

(217) *ðuuhkáamą*
ðuu-hkaamą́
by.hand-ring
'ring the bell, press the doorbell'

Another intransitive made transitive by *ðuu* is *léke* 'shatter, break as an egg or light bulb':

(218) *lékape*
Ø-léke-api-ðe
A3S-shatter-PL-DECL
'it broke'

(219) *ðuuléke*
ðuu-léke
by.hand-shatter
'break with the hands'

The following sentence is a clear example of the use of *ðuu* where either 'by hand' or 'cause' is a possible gloss.

(220) *hįįcéžį wíbruuleke*
hį́įce-žį wi-Wa-ðuu-léke
plate-small P2S<A1S-A1S-by.hand-shatter
'I broke your dish'

The verb *šką* 'start; change states, as weather; move', becomes transitive by adding *ðuu*:

(221) *oðíhtą šką́ ché ?*
oðíhtą šką́ ché
car move EVID
'is the car started?'

(222) *oðíhtą ðuušką́ ?*
oðíhtą ðuu-šką́
car Ø-CAU-move
'did he start the car?'

The fact that the stem *šką* takes *ðuu* does not preclude its use with the strict causative *káaɣe*, as in the following example.

(223) *oðíhtą šką́ škáaɣe?*
oðíhtą šką škáaɣe
car move A2S-make
'did you get the car started?'

Many *ðuu* ~ *ðii* forms have roots that are less transparent semantically, such as *ze* in *ðuuzé* 'take; choose' and *ha* in *ðíihą́* 'pick up; lift an object with the hand'.

(224) *ðuuzá*
ðuuzé-a
take-IMPER
'pick it up; get it; choose one!'

(225a) *bríiha*
Wa-ðiihá
A1S-pick.up
'I pick up'

(225b) *šcíiha*
Ya-ðíihá
A2S-pick.up
'you pick up'

(225c) *ąðíihai*
ąk-ðíihá-ðe
A1P-pick.up-DECL
'we pick up'

4.4.2.1 Variation between *ðuu* and *ðii*

As stated in the introduction to section 4.4.2, confusion is generated by the existence of the causative prefix *ðuu* and its overlap in pronunciation with 'by hand' *ðii* or *ðuu* (if indeed these two are distinct at all). Only in Quapaw, Omaha, and Ponca are *u* and *i* (and long *uu* and *ii*) regularly collapsed (always to *i* or *ii*). In Kansa and Osage, *u* has become fronted to *ü*, but occasionally unrounds, merging with *i*. It is perhaps the case that *ð* acts as a palatalizing consonant here, affecting *i* ~ *u* variation. This is especially likely since *y* does not exist as a consonant in Osage, or exists only rarely in surface forms as a variant of *ð*. The *ð* thus probably provides the context likely to affect high vowels *u* and *i*. When *w* follows, the tendency is for rounding to occur, as in *ðuwį* 'buy'.

Speakers show a great deal of tolerance in pronunciation of *ii* and *uu*, especially following *h* or *k*, where any *uu* or *u* is especially strongly fronted (*üü* or *ü*). In some verbs, *ii* and *uu* are interchangeable; for instance, *ðuwį́* 'buy', for which speakers consistently hear *ðiwį́* as identical. This is not however true for all *u* and *i* vowels in all verbs, as is mentioned in section 4.4.2.2.

Speakers do not detect any difference between *ðuuškí* 'wash [clothes]' and its variant *ðiiškí*. The same is true for its suus form *lúuški* ~ *líiški*, and for all such variation. That is, where variants exist, they are heard as identical, not as different but equally correct. The variants in (226) and (227) were both produced by the same speaker and heard as identical when repeated back.

(226) *ðiišúhpe* ~ *ðuušúhpe*
'open [as a door lock]'

(227) *ðiixǫ́ ~ ðuuxǫ́*
'break by hand'

The verb *ðiižóži* 'hurt' (transitive) varies freely with *ðuužóži* and speakers detect no differences between the two, nor do they distinguish them as two different forms on any level whatsoever. Likewise, *ðiixí* 'wake up' varies with *ðuuxí*.

(228) *wábriixi*
wa-Wa-ðiixí
P3P-A1S-wake
'I woke them up'

The verb 'bend [as a leg or arm]' also shows *ðii* ~ *ðuu* variation: *ðiišǫ́* ~ *ðuušǫ́*.

4.4.2.2 Invariant *ðuu* or *ðii*

Despite the tolerance for variation between *i* (*ii*) and *u* (*uu*) just discussed, there are some verbs where only one variant can be used.[20]

One such verb is *ðiihíce* 'play with, toy with, tease' in (229), which must not be not confused with *ðuuhúuce* 'pull, pull down, lower, take down as from a shelf or off the wall' in (230). Neither ***ðiihúuce* nor ***ðuuhíce* occurs in the data.

(229) *wíbriihice ąąhé*
wi-Wa-ðiihíce ąðįhé
P2S<A1S-A1S-tease 1S.CONT
'I was teasing you'

(230) *oðókinažį ðuuhúuce*
oðókinažį ðuuhúuce
pants pull
'pull your pants down'

The antonym of *ðuuhúce*, not surprisingly, is also a *ðuu* instrumental, *ðuumáši* 'raise'.

(231) *oðókinažį ðuumáši*
oðókinažį ðuumáši
pants pull.up
'pull your pants up'

[20] Rankin (p.c. 1995) suggests that it may be that as the use of Osage has declined, speakers have artificially separated *u* and *i* in some verbs, especially in unaccented position. Just which verbs show free variation between *u* and *i*, which consistently have *u*, and which consistently have *i* has not been fully established due to time limitations on the present project and speaker unavailability, but suggests itself strongly as a project for future research.

(232) *okáhapa ðuumáši*
okáhapa ðuu-máši-a
window CAU-up-IMPER
'raise the window'

4.4.2.3 Suus forms

Many suus forms with *ðuu* instrumentals are found. For instance, the suus form of *ðiiškí* ~ *ðuuškí* 'launder' is *líiški* ~ *lúuški* 'launder one's own', as in (233). (The process whereby *kik-ðuu* becomes *luu* is regular; see section 4.6.4.)

(233) *liiškí*
kik-ðíiški-a
SUU-launder-IMPER
'wash your own clothes yourself!'

Another verb of washing also has a suus form.

(234) *ðuužá*
'wash [body and other things, e.g., dishes]'

(235) *hkáące ðuużą́*
hkáące ðuużá-a
apple wash-IMPER
'wash the apples'

(236) *lúuža*
kik-ðuužá
SUU-wash
'wash part of body; wash subject's own'

4.4.2.4 *o* forms with *ðii*: causation vs. instrumentality

The locative prefix *o* 'location, final place, goal, culmination, fruition, event wherein' can precede various instrumentals, as in *okáaxpa* 'be thrown off' (*kaa* 'with sudden force' + *xpa* 'sever'). In some verbs its meaning is not transparent (see section 4.5). Thus, *ðíibrą* 'make something smell' (*ðii* 'by hand' + *brą* 'smell') contrasts with *oðíibrą* 'cedar-burning [the ceremony]'; the *o* seems to add the sense 'event', giving 'the event of making something smell', as in cedar-burning or cedar-smoking which is the act of causing cedar to smoke. In (237), the entire form is compounded with *xǫ́ǫce* 'cedar'.

(237) *xǫǫcóðiibra*
xǫ́ǫce-o-ðii-brą
cedar-LOC(?)-by.hand-smell
'smoke cedar'

The verb *oðíibrą* is so closely tied semantically with the ceremony of smoking cedar that even in sentences where 'cedar' is omitted, the English glosses are given with 'cedar'. The morpheme *brą* is itself 'odor, smell'. The verbs *ðíibrą* and *oðíibrą* may be semantically causative, or may imply 'waving the smoke with a feather [in the hand]', or 'applying cedar smoke to the body with the hands'.

Illustrative of the many instances in which speech or text data supplies misleading glosses is the following example, which we take to be 'I make [cedar] smell [therefore I smell it]'.

(238) *bríibra*
Wa-ðii-brą
A1S-by-hand-smell
'I smell cedar'

4.4.2.5 *ðuu* plus adjective or adjectival verb

While the instrumental *ðii* ~ *ðuu* combines, as we have seen, with semantically eventive intransitive verbs such as *xǫ* 'break', several of the more adjectival bases also combine with this prefix. From *stáko* 'neat' we have *ðuustáko* 'neaten'. 'Round' and 'clean' also combine with this instrumental, as seen in the next examples.

(239a) *ðuutáahpa*
ðuu-táahpa
by.hand-round
'made round'

(239b) *hpáxį ðuutáahpa*
hpáxį ðuu-táahpa
hair by.hand-round
'a bun [a hairdo]'

(239c) *wacúe ðuutáahpa*
wacúe ðuu-táahpa
bread by.hand-round
'bread made round, biscuits'

(240) *ðuuwásu*
ðuu-wásu
by.hand-clean
'make clean, cleanse [e.g., buffalo hide]'

ðuu is a productive affix even with borrowed words, such as 'kinky' in the following examples. (Fewer than half a dozen borrowed words of any kind have been found in Osage.)

(241) *hpaxį hkįhkįnį*
hpaxį hkįhkįnį
hair kinky
'curly hair; black (African) hair; tangled hair'

(242) *ðuuhkįhkį*
ðuu-hkįhkį
by.hand-kinky
'make curly'

(243) *hpaxį ðuuhkįhkį apai*
hpaxį ðuu-kįhkį apa-de
hair by.hand-kinky 3.CONT-DECL
'they're curling their hair'

4.4.3 *kaa* 'by striking'

Inner instrumental *kaa* 'by striking' or 'by sudden application of force' takes inflection to its left: _*kaa*. This instrumental, alone among the group of instrumentals, is itself suppressed in surface utterances where agent or patient inflection is overtly present—except for the A1P form where both agent inflection *ąk* and *kaa* appear. The contexts precluding emergence of *kaa* are, then, those where either first singular or second person agent pronominals occur, or where any person and number patient inflection is overtly present. *kaa* does surface when phonologically null third person agent inflection is present with no overt patient inflection. Agent inflection follows the regular pattern (1S *a*, 2S *ða*). Thus, for example, the forms of *kaaléke* 'shatter by striking' are: 1S *aaléke* 'I shatter'; 2S *ðaaléke* 'you shatter; 3S *kaaléke* 'she shatters'; 1P *ąkáaleke* 'we shatter'. In several *kaa* verbs, the 1S and 2S pronominals are accented, but no consistent rule emerges to govern such accent. The 1S and 2S pronominals often have a long vowel, but not always.

4.4.3.1 Agent inflection for *kaa* instrumental verbs

The agent inflection of *kaa* verbs is summarized in table 4.10.

No verbs have been found so far where *kaa* cooccurs with a syncopating stem, that is, a verb requiring other than the regular subject inflection (*a-ða*).

TABLE 4.10. AGENT INFLECTION OF *kaa* VERBS

	UNDERLYING FORM		SURFACE FORM
1S	*a* + *kaa* + stem	→	*a* + stem
2S	*ða* + *kaa* + stem	→	*ða* + stem
3S	*Ø* + *kaa* + stem	→	*kaa* + stem
1P	*ą(k)* + *kaa* + stem	→	*ąkaa* + stem
3P	*Ø* + *kaa* + stem	→	*kaa* + stem

From the root *xǫ́* 'break; be broken' are formed the transitives *ðiixǫ́* 'break; break off [usually something long]' (with instrumental *ðii*) and *kaaxǫ́* 'break a long object [by striking]' (with instrumental *kaa*). The paradigm of the latter is: 1S *áaxǫ*, 2S *ðáaxǫ*, 3S *káaxǫ* ~ *kaaxǫ́*, 1P *ąkáaxǫ*.

Similarly, the root *se* 'cut' preposes *kaa* 'by striking' to produce *kaasé* 'cut by striking; chop or cut with a long blade, as one chops or cuts long, rather thin sticks of wood for a fire'. Forms are 1S *áase*, 2S *ðáase*, 3S *káase* ~ *kaasé*, 1P *ąkáase*; but accent varies.

The verb *kaakšį́ce* 'shoot at and miss; miss a target with a projectile' contains *kaa* 'by striking [with guns, rocks thrown, etc.]', but its root is not otherwise attested. In this and other cases where the root to which *kaa* attaches is opaque semantically, *kaa* + root is glossed as a unit; thus the entire form *kaakšį́ce* appears on the morpheme line in examples below as 'miss'.[21]

(244a) *akšį́ce*
Wa-kaakšį́ce
A1S-miss
'I missed it'

(244b) *ðakšį́ce*
Ya-kaakšį́ce
A2S-miss
'you missed it'

(244c) *kaakšį́ce*
Ø-kaakšį́ce
A3S-miss
'he missed it'

(244d) *ąkáakšį́ce*
ą-kaakšį́ce
A1P-miss
'we missed it'

[21] One speaker sometimes pronounces this verb as *kaakšį́ze*.

(245) *kaakšįįtape*
Ø-kaakšįįce-api-ðe
A3S-miss-PL-DECL
'he missed'

In other verbs that seem to have less to do with 'striking' we find the same paradigm, as with *kaazą́* 'scold'.

(246a) *áazą*
'I scold'

(246b) *ðáazą*
'you scold'

(246c) *kaazą́*
'he scolds'

(247) *awáazą hta mįkše*
Wa-wa-kaazą́ hta mįkše
A1S-P3P-scold FUT 1S.CONT
'I going to bawl them out'

(248) *wakáazą štąpe*
wa-Ø-kaazą́ štą-api-ðe
VAL-A3S-scold ITER-PL-DECL
'he likes to bawl out people'

(249) *wáaząpe*
wá-Ø -kaazą́-api-ðe
P3P-A3S-scold-PL-DECL
'he bawled those two out'

Another *kaa* verb is *kaaléke* 'shatter; break by hitting', formed from the intransitive *léke* ~ *hléke* 'break, shatter' (both forms, *léke* and *hléke*, appear on the surface).

(250) *hlékape*
Ø-léke-api-ðe
A3S-shatter-PL-DECL
'it broke'

(251) *kaaléke*
kaa-léke
by.striking-shatter
'break by hitting [e.g., an egg or a dish]; fracture [e.g., head]'

For unclear reasons, perhaps having to do with the locative *á*, the verb 'close on' retains *kaa* plus the regular agent forms *a*, *ða*:

(252) *hcižé áðakasįce*
hcižé á-Ya-kaa-sįce
door LOC-A2S-by.striking-close
'you closed/slammed the door on it'

4.4.3.2 Patient inflection with *kaa*

Just as when *a* and *ða* agent inflection is present, *kaa* disappears when overt patient inflection occurs. The patient paradigm of *kaa* when there is no overt agent pronominal is summarized in table 4.11.

TABLE 4.11. PATIENT INFLECTION + *kaa* (IN A3S/P SUBJECT SENTENCES)

P1S	*ą + kaa*	→	*ą(ą)*
P2S	*ði + kaa*	→	*ði(i)*
P3S	*Ø + kaa*	→	*kaa*
P1P	*wa + kaa*	→	*wá(a)*
P3P	*Wa+ kaa*	→	*Wa(a)*

The disappearance of *kaa* after overt patient prefixes is shown in the following examples. (Note that none of these contain an overt agent prefix; either their agents are third person or the verb is imperative.)

(253) *ðíząpe?*
ðí-Ø-kaazą́-api-ðe
P2S-A3S-scold-PL-DECL
'did he scold you?'

(254) *wáazą apai*
wa-Ø-kaazą́ apa-ðe
P3P-A3P-scold-PL-DECL
'they're scolding them'

(255) *ą́zą įká*
ą́-kaazą́ ðįké-a
P1S-scold NEG-IMPER
'don't scold me'

(256) *wáli ą́ząpe*
wáli ą́-Ø-kaazą́-api-ðe
very P1S-A3S-scold-PL-DECL
'he's really bawled me out'

(257) *wáazą akxai*
wa-Ø-kaazą́ akxa-ðe
P3P-A3S-scold 3.CONT-DECL
'he's bawling them out'

When the patient 'them' is defocused, speakers occasionally produce sentences with no P3P *wa* representing 'them'. This has happened in (258), (259b), and (260b) below; in the absence of overt inflection, *kaa* has surfaced in these examples. In (259a) and (260a) are seen comparable examples where P3P *wa* is present, blocking *kaa*.

(258) *Johna akxa kaazą́pe*
Johna akxa Ø-Ø-kaazą́-api-ðe
John SUBJ P3P-A3S-scold-PL-DECL
'John is bawling them out [bawling out people]; John is scolding'

(259a) *žįkážį háachi wáazą akxai*
žįkážį háachi wa-Ø-kaazą́ akxa-ðe
children repeatedly P3P-A3S-scold 3.CONT-DECL
'he's always bawling the children out'

(259b) *žįkážį háachi kaazą́ akxai*
žįkážį háachi Ø-Ø-kaazą́ akxa-ðe
children repeatedly P3P-A3S-scold 3.CONT-DECL
'he's always bawling the children out'

(260a) *háachi žįką́žį wáazą apai*
háachi žįkážį wa-Ø-kaazą́ apa-ðe
repeatedly children P3S-A3S/P-scold 3.CONT-DECL
'he's/they're always bawling the children out'

(260b) *háachi žįką́žį kaazǫ́ apai*
háachi žįkážį Ø-Ø-kaazą́ apa-ðe
repeatedly children P3P-A3S/P-scold 3.CONT-DECL
'he's/they're always bawling the children out'

A few of the possible combinations of subject and object inflection with *kaazą́* 'scold' appear in table 4.12. In all forms in the table, *kaa* has been blocked by presence of overt inflection.

TABLE 4.12. AGENT AND PATIENT INFLECTION IN *kaa* VERBS

P3P + A1S	*awázą*	'I bawled them out'
P1S + A2S	*ąðáazą*	'you bawled me out'
P3P + A1P	*ąwáaząi*	'we bawled them out'
P2S + A1P	*ąðíizą*	'we bawled you out'
P1P + A2S	*waðáazą*	'you bawled us out'
P1P + imperative	*wazą́ą įkápi*	'don't scold us'
P3P + imperative	*wazą́ą įká*	'don't scold them'

Note that in the two examples in the table with A1P *ą(k)* 'we', the *kaa* is absent, even though A1P *ą(k)* alone does not block *kaa* (see table 4.10).

When P3P *wa* is omitted, too (as in the following examples), A1P *ą(k)* does not prevent *kaa* from appearing.

(261) *žįkážį háachi ąkǫ́ązą ąkai*
žįkážį háachi ąk-kaazą́ ąkáðe
children repeatedly A1P-scold 1P.CONT
'we bawl the children out every time'

(262) *háachi wižįke wisǫ́ka éðǫǫpa ąkǫ́ązą ąkai*
háachi wižįke wisǫ́ka éðǫǫpa ąk-kaazą́ ąkáðe
repeatedly Sonny my.brother both A1P-scold 1P.CONT
'we're always bawling out Sonny and wisǫ́ka [my brother]'

The verb *kaašúpe* 'pay' inflects following the active subject inflection pattern for *kaa* as seen above in table 4.10: *ášupe, ðášupe, kaašúpe, ąkáašupe.*[22] Patient pronominals block emergence of *kaa* in (265) and (266).

(263) *ąkáašupape*
ą-káašupe-api-ðe
A1P-pay-PL-DECL
'we pay'

(264) *kaašúpa ði*
kaašupe-a ði
pay-IMPER 2S.PRON
'you pay'

(265) *ą́ššupape*
ą́-Ø-kaašúpe-api-ðe
P1S-A3S-pay-PL-DECL
'he paid me for it'

(266) *ą́ššupa ðie*
ą-kaašúpe-a ðie
P1S-pay-IMPER 2S.PRON
'pay me for it'[23]

[22] At utterance level a double-long consonant [šš] is perceived. This often happens where the underlying form, but not the surface, includes *kaa*: *áššupe, ðáššupe.* Even when dative *ki* appears (see next section), the [šš] appears double: *ąðákiššupe hta nįkšé* 'are you going to pay me?; are you going to pay me for it?'. This tenseness or length is also characteristic of *s* in certain contexts.

[23] The same sentence in Osage can indifferently be glossed 'pay for it for me' and 'pay me for it'. Either translation seems to be possible regardless of whether dative *ki* is added to *kaašúpe*, as in (ii) and (iv) below, or not, as in (i) and (iii).

4.4.3.3 Blocking of *kaa* by inceptive *ki*

Besides the agent and patient pronominals, the inceptive *ki* also blocks *kaa*. (Inceptive *ki* adds the sense of 'back; in return; in turn', as in 'pay back; repay'.) Even where no overt agent or patient pronominal is present, *ki* blocks *kaa* from appearing in surface forms, as can be seen in (267)–(271) below. In a sense, inceptive *ki* is patterning here with inflection, although it is clearly a derivational element.

(267) *kíššupe*
ki-kaašupe
INCEP-pay
'pay back'

(268a) *ąkíššupa*
ą-ki-kaašupe-a
P1S-INCEP-pay-IMPER
'pay me [back] for it'

(268b) *ąkíššupe ði*
ą-ki-kaašupe-a *ði*
P1S-INCEP-pay-IMPER 2S.PRON
'pay me [back] for it'

(Note that ***ąkáašupa* for 'pay me for it' is ungrammatical.)

(i) *ąðášupe*
ą-ða-kaa-šupe
P1S-A2S-PREV-pay
'are you going to pay for it for me?; are you going to pay me for it?'

(ii) *ąkíšupa*
ą-ki-kaa-šupe-a
P1S-DAT-PREV-pay-IMPER
'pay for it for me; pay me for it; pay it for me'

(iii) *ą́šupa ðíe*
ą-kaa-šupe-a *ðíe*
P1S-PREV-pay PRON
'pay me for it'

(iv) *mą́zeska ožú áalǫbri, ąðákišupe hkǫ́bra*
mą́zeska-ožú *á-Wa-lǫ-Wa-ðį* *ą-ðá-ki-kaa-šupe*
money-put.inside PREV-A1S-PREV-A1S-forget P1S-A2S-DAT-PREV-pay
Wa-kǫ́-Wa-ða
A1S-PREV-A1S-want
'I left my purse at home, I want you to pay for it [the blanket]'

(269) *ðakíššupe?*
Ya-ki-kaašúpe
A2S-INCEP-pay
'did you pay [them] back?'

(270a) *kíššupe apai*
Ø-ki-kaašúpe apa-ðe
A3S-INCEP-pay 3.CONT-DECL
'he paid them back'

(270b) *kíššupe akxái*
Ø-ki-kaašúpe akxa-ðe
A3S-INCEP-pay 3.CONT-DECL
'he paid them back'

(271) *ąkíšupa*
ą-ki-kaašupe-a
P1S-INCEP-pay-IMPER
'you pay for me [treat me]!'

As can be seen in (268a)–(269) and (271)–(272), the inceptive *ki* in these *kaa* forms is not itself blocked by overt agent or patient inflection. By contrast, the *ki* that marks dative verbs is suppressed by overt agent or patient inflection (see section 4.6.5). Despite the dativelike meaning of the verb, *ki* in *kíšupe* cannot be the dative prefix, as unlike the dative prefix it is not suppressed by overt agent or patient inflection (271)-(272).

(272) *awánǫbre tą, ąkíšupa ði*
wa-Wa-nǫbre tą ą-ki-kaašúpe-a ði
PREV-A1S-dine if P1S-INCEP-pay-IMPER 2S.PRON
'if I eat, you pay for it!'

4.4.3.4 Stative *kaa* paradigm

The stative verb *káaskike* 'be tired' follows the paradigm in table 4.13. Presence of the patient pronominal precludes emergence of *kaa* , as it does in the case of *kaa* in active transitive verbs. The presence of *kaa* underlyingly is responsible for the accent on the patient pronominals.

TABLE 4.13. INFLECTION OF STATIVE *kaa* VERBS

1S	*ą́* + root
2S	*ðí* + root
3S	*káa* + root
1P	*wá* + root
3P	*káa* + root ~ *wá* + root

The stative verb *káaskike* 'be tired' follows this paradigm, showing variation *kaa* ~ *wa* in third person plural.[24]

(273) *ą́skike, ðískike nįkšé ?*
ą-kaaskíke, ði-kaaskíke nįkšé
P1S-tired P2S-tired 2S.CONT
'I'm tired, are you tired?'

(274) *káaskike akxái*
Ø-kaaskike akxá-ðe
P3S-tired 3.CONT-DECL
'he's tired'

(275) *kaaskíke ekxái*[25]
kaaskike akxá-ðe
tired 3.CONT-DECL
'they're tired'

(276) *waaskíke ekxái*
wa-kaaskike akxa-ðe
P3P-tired 3.CONT-DECL
'they're tired'

(277) *wáskike ąðikšé*
wa-kaaskike ąðikšé
P1P-tired 2P.CONT
'we're tired'

(278a) *ðiskíke káaɣe apai?*
ði-kaaskike Ø-káaɣé apa
P2S-tired A3P-make 3.CONT
'are they making you tired?'

(278b) *ąą, ą́ąskike káaɣi apai*
ąą, ą-kaaskike Ø-kaaɣé apa-ðe
yes.FEM P1S-tired A3P-make 3.CONT-DECL
'yes, they're making me tired'

[24] Another interesting behavior of this verb is the fact that its 2S form varies between *ði* (patient) and *ða* (agent) for at least one speaker:

žįkážį əpa ðáskike ðikáaɣé əpai
žįkážį apa Ya-kaskike ði-Ø-káaɣe apa-ðe
children SUBJ A2S-tired P2S-A3P-make 3.CONT-DECL
'the children are making you tired'

[25] We take the change in accent to be incidental in this and the following third person plural example.

This is the only stative *kaa* verb that emerged in this study. La Flesche (1932) lists two others; both seem to exhibit the same pattern as *káaskike*: *kahíða* 'blown by the wind' (1S *ą́hiða*, 2S *ðíhiða*) and *kacˀéha* 'be rendered unconscious', as in (279).

(279) *ąxíða[e]kǫ ąącˀeha*
ą-xiða éekǫ ą-kacˀéha
P1S-stumble.and.fall thus P1S-be.rendered.unconscious
'I was rendered unconscious by falling'

Examples (280)–(284) illustrate the stative *kaa* paradigm with 'tired' and the normal patient (object) paradigm with the causative *káaɣe* 'make' in 'make tired'. Example (284) reveals a nice contrast, where the expected P3P inflection *wa* does not appear on the *kaa* verb, but rather *kaa* only is seen.

(280) *škáace mąðį́pi, wáskike waškáaɣapi*
škáce mąðį́-a-api wa-kaaskike wa-Ya-káaɣe-api
play go-IMPER-PL P1P-tired P1P-A2S-make-PL
'you all go on and play, you make us tired'

(281) *škáace mąðį́pi, ą́skike ąškáaɣape*
škáce mąðį́-a-api ą-kaaskike ą-Ya-káaɣe-api-ðe
play go-IMPER-PL P1S-tired P1S-A2S-make-PL-DECL
'you all go on and play, you [plural] make me tired'

(282) *škáace mąðį́pi, wáskike waškáaɣe*
škáce mąðį́-a-api wa-kaaskike wa-Ya-káaɣe
play go-IMPER-PL P1P-tired P1P-A2S-make
'you all go on and play, you make us tired'

(283) *škáace mąðį́pi, ą́skike ąškáaɣe apai*
škáce mąðį́-a-api ą-kaaskike ą-Ya-káaɣe apa-ðe
play go-IMPER-PL P1S-tired P1S-A2S-make 3.CONT-DECL
'you all go on and play, you're making me tired'

(284) *škáace mąðį́pi, kaaskíke waškáaɣe*
škáce mąðį́-api kaaskíke wa-Ya-káaɣe
play go-IMPER-PL tired P3P-A2S-make
'you all go on and play, you're making them tired'

4.4.4 *nąą* 'by foot'

The inner instrumental *_nąą* 'by foot' occurs next to the verb root and takes regular inflection to its left. This instrumental does not show any of the paradigmatic irregularities seen in *kaa* in the preceding section.

(285) *nąąxǫ́*
nąą-xǫ
by.foot-break
'break by foot'

(286) *nąąléke*
nąą-léke
by.foot-shatter
'shatter with the foot'

The instrumental verb *nąąžį́* 'stand' becomes 'step on' with the addition of locative *á*: *á_nąąži*.

(287) *táatą hpíiži wį áðanąąžį́ skə táabrą ðąįše*
táatą hpíiži wį á-Ø-Ya-nąąžį́ ska táabrą ðąįše
thing bad a LOC-P3S-A2S-stand suppose smell 2S.CONT
'you must have stepped on something bad, because you're smelling bad'

4.4.5 *pu* 'by pressing'; *pi* 'by blowing'

The inner instrumental *_pu* conveys 'by pressing, smoothing, flattening, rubbing', as in *puštáha* ~ *púštaha* 'iron' (from *štáha* 'smooth; be smooth'). The only examples recorded either (i) had a prefixed *wa* valence reducer meaning 'stuff; things', in which cases regular inflection preceded the *wa*; (ii) optionally had *pu* replaced by the instrumental *ðuu* 'by hand'; or (iii) were not inflected other than by attaching a continuative auxiliary.

(288) *puštáhamąží*
pu-štáha-maží
by.pressing-smooth-1S.NEG
'I don't iron'

(289) *púštaha!*
pu-štáha-a
by.pressing-smooth-IMPER
'iron this!'

As an example of (ii), the two forms in (290)–(294), *púštaha* and *ðúuštaha*, can be used interchangeably. The latter is 'making flat' with the causative (or the 'by hand' instrumental) *ðuu* rather than the 'pressing' prefix *pu*. They are both used for 'ironing' activities, with no apparent difference in meaning. In (290) we see a doubly inflected form *_wa_ðuuštaha*, a valence-reduced form with a second point of inflection before the valence reducer *wa*; this may be an effect of obsolescence of the language. Doubly inflecting (290) contrasts with singly inflecting (291)—from the same speaker—where the first point of inflection is not present.

(290) *hǫ́pa ðé awábrúuštaha hta mįkšé*
hǫpa ðé Wa-wa-ðuu-štáha hta mįkšé
day this A1S-VAL-by.hand-smooth FUT 1S.CONT
'I'm going to iron all day'

(291) *hą́pa záani wabrúuštaha*
hą́pa záani wa-Wa-ðuu-štáha
day all VAL-A1S-by.hand-smooth
'I ironed all day'

The valence reducer *wa* precedes the instrumental *pu* 'by pressing', giving *wa-púštaha*, in (292) and (293).

(292) *wapúštaha*
wa-pu-štaha
VAL-by.pressing-smooth
'iron something'

(293) *hǫ́pa ðé awápúštaha hta mįkšé*
hą́pa ðé Wa-wa-pu-štáha hta mįkšé
day this A1S-VAL-by.pressing-smooth FUT 1S.CONT
'I'm going to iron all day'

The A1P of this valence-reduced instrumental is:

(294) *ąwą́púštaha ąkái*
ąk-wa-pu-štáha ąkáðe
A1P-VAL-by.pressing-smooth 1P.CONT
'we've been ironing'

The instrumental *pi* 'by blowing' is extremely rare in the data. Speakers were able to describe the motion of the verbs in the examples below and give equivalents in English—'by blowing' as on a fire to get it started, blowing dust off the tabletop, blowing dandelions away in the wind, blowing anything away on the palm of the hand—but were unable to use them in a sentence. Only two examples are in the data recorded from early years:

(295) *opíxa*
o-píxa
LOC-blow
'blow into or on something [e.g., horn, fire]'

(296) *píxą*
píxą-a
blow-IMPER
'blow it!'

4.4.6 *paa* 'by pushing'

paa historically and in related languages is 'by pushing'. In the speech of modern-day Osages in the 1980s and 1990s, this meaning of *paa* can be seen in a few clear examples, but in other instances the sense of 'pushing' is difficult to isolate. Of the forms gathered in this subsection, the only common semantic thread seems to be that the actions described involve movement downward or outward from the body, especially the arms, in reaching out, gathering, raising the hand or one's body, or by using outward motion with the arms as in hanging clothing. This recalls the Chiwere prefix and description (*wa* 'by hand away') mentioned in section 4.4.2. This Chiwere prefix *wa-* is the probable cognate of Osage *_paa*, and 'by hand away' will be added to the gloss of the latter here.

This *_paa* 'by pushing; by hand away' is an inner instrumental, that is, inflection appears to the left of *_paa*. Unfortunately, there is a tendency to confuse this *paa* or *pa* with the homophonous outer instrumental *pa_* 'by cutting'. The inner instrumental *_paa* 'by pushing, by hand away' inflects as a fortisizing stop stem (*hp, šp, p*). In contrast, the outer instrumental *pa_* 'by cutting' (see section 4.4.7) uses regular (*a-ða*) inflection (1S *pa-a,* 2S *pa-ða*), or else syncopating inflection, depending on the inflectable initial of the following root or stem. It appears that these two instrumentals may be in the process of merging in the last years of Osage as a viable spoken language. Both have a long vowel *paa* in many words, but show much variation in vowel length.

TABLE 4.14. INNER AND OUTER *pa*

INNER INSTRUMENTAL *_paa* (4.4.6)	OUTER INSTRUMENTAL *pa_* (4.4.7)
'by pushing, by hand away; by motion away with hands or with long tool with handle'	'by cutting; by using a cutting edge'
Fortisizing stop stem	Regular inflection or syncopating inflection following *pa*, depending on next segment
1S *hpaa*	*paa* or *pabr...*
2S *špaa*	*paða* or *pašt...*
3S *paa*	*pa*
1P *ąpaa*	*ąpa*
Variant: regularized as *pa_*	Variant: regularized by moving inflection leftward of *pa*? (*_pa*) (i.e., becoming an inner instrumental?)

La Flesche (1932) also shows varying patterns, using the expected syncopating inflection for some 'pushing' verbs in *_pa* (*hpa, špa, pa, ąpa*) but *a, ða* (regular) inflection following *pa_* for other 'pushing' verbs. Additional complexity stems from the fact that La Flesche does not actually draw a distinction between *_paa* 'by pushing, by hand away' and the outer instrumental *pa_* 'by cutting'. Anticipating the description of *pa_* 'by cutting' in section 4.4.7, we show some contrasts in table 4.14.

4.4.6.1 Typical verbs with *_paa*

paahí 'pick; pick up an item; pick from garden; pick flowers; pick up scattered things' shows the expected forms: 1S *hpaahí* 'I pick'; 2S *špáahi* 'you pick'; 1P *ąpáahipe* 'we pick'. Often the *i* is nasalized *į*. In first person, the accent would be expected to fall on the first syllable, but in (297) it seems to have shifted to second syllable.

(297) *wíe hápa hpaahíe*
wíe hápa Wa-paahí-ðe
1S.PRON corn A1S-pick-DECL
'I picked corn'

(298) *házu špáahi?*
házu Ya-paahí
grape A2S-pick
'did you pick grapes?'

(299) *hápa ąpáahi ąkái*
hápa ąk-paahí ąkáðe
corn A1P-pick 1P.CONT
'we are picking corn'

(300) *házu paahípe*
házu Ø-paahí-api-ðe
grape A3P-pick-PL-DECL
'they picked the grapes'

The verb *paaxcé* 'gather things up and tie in a bundle; to bundle' also involves reaching out the hands.

(301) *haxį haaskámį ški špáaxce hta nįkšé?*
haxį haaskámį ški Ya-paaxcé hta nįkšé?
blanket shawl also A2S-gather.and.tie FUT 2S.CONT
'these blankets and shawls, are you going to gather them up and tie them in a bundle?'

(302) *paaxcé apai*
paa-Ø-Ø-xcé *apa-ðe*
PREV-P3S-A3P-bundle 3.CONT-DECL
'they are gathering it up and tying it into a bundle'

The *c* of this verb appears as *t* when followed by *a* 'imperative' (303) or *aži* 'negative' (304). (This is expected; see section 2.3.3.4.)

(303) *paaxtá!*
Ø-paaxce-a
P3S-bundle-IMPER
'gather it up and tie it into a bundle!'

(304) *paaxtáži apai*
Ø-Ø-paaxce-aži *apa-ðe*
P3S-A3P-bundle-NEG 3.CONT-DECL
'they're not gathering it up and tying it into a bundle'

The verb *paaɣó* 'propel by pushing on, push on something to propel it' has a variant with final *(w)e* (which likely consists of a reduced *ðe* with an epenthetic *w*). Some speakers use *ɣ* and others clearly *x* for the medial consonant; these two consonants may be merging.

(305) *hpaaɣóe*
Wa-paaɣó-ðe
A1S-push-DECL
'I pushed'

(306) *wihpáaɣoe*
wi-Wa-paaɣóe
P2S<A1S-A1S-push
'I'm pushing you'

(307) *špaaɣó ðąįšé?*
Ya-paaɣó ðaįšé
A2S-push 2S.CONT
'are you pushing?'

(308) *ą́špaaɣo ðąįšé*
ą́-Ya-paaɣó ðąįšé
P1S-A2S-push-2S.CONT
'you're pushing me'

This verb, like many others in Osage, occasionally will appear uninflected followed by the continuative marker, as in (309) and (310).

(309) *ðe paaɣó hta ðą̨išé?*
ðe paaɣó hta ðai̜šé
that push FUT 2S.CONT
'are you going to push it?'

(310) *paaɣówe ðą̨išé?*
paaɣóe ðai̜šé
push 2S.CONT
'are you pushing?'

Another syncopating fortisizing stop-stem that also seems to involve *_paa* 'by pushing, by hand away' is *páacˀį* 'stoop over'. In this verb, it is difficult to discern what the 'by pushing' or 'by hand away' instrumental is contributing semantically: perhaps a movement of the upper body outward, a reaching with the upper body.

(311) *hpáacˀį̨e*
Wa-paacˀį́-ðe
A1S-stoop-DECL
'I stooped over'

(312) *špaacˀį*
Ya-paacˀí-ðe
A2S-stoop-DECL
'you stooped over'

(313) *ée paacˀį akxai*
ée Ø-paacˀį akxa-ðe
3.PRON A3S-stoop 3.CONT-DECL
'he is stooping over'

Another 'by pushing, by hand away' *_paa* verb is *paaɣáce* 'open out; open [e.g., an umbrella]; spread out'. No clearly inflected forms of this verb in 1S or 2S were found. It may also appear with prefix *o*, as in (315)–(316).

(314) *hlaaská əkxa paaɣáci akxái*
hlaaská akxa Ø-paaɣáce akxa-ðe
flower SUBJ A3P-open 3.CONT-DECL
'the flowers opened out'

(315) *hlaaská opáaɣa akxai*
hlaaská opáaɣa akxa-ðe
flower open 3.CONT-DECL
'the flowers are opening out'

(316) *opáaɣą káaɣa*
o-Ø-páaɣa káaɣe-a
PREV-P3S-open make-IMPER
'open it!'

4.4.6.2 *paasé* 'cut by pushing down on'

Still another syncopating fortisizing stop-stem using *_paa* 'by pushing [down on], by hand away' is *paasé* 'cut'. This verb deserves its own subsection because of the importance of distinguishing it from the nearly homophonous *pa_* which is also used in verbs of cutting. For *paasé*, the semantics of 'cutting' comes not from the prefix, but rather from the verb root *sé* 'cut' itself. The prefix *_paa* conveys only the meaning 'pushing down on'. This verb *_paasé* is used, e.g., for cutting meat, potatoes, etc. The vowel of the instrumental is often (but not always) long in the utterance (there is no discernable pattern), and the *s* is very tense. Accent also varies in the citation form.

(317) *paasé*
paa-sé
by.pushing-cut
'cut [a simple cut, by pushing down on]'

(318) *htáa hpáase mįkše*
htáa Wa-páa-sé mįkše
meat A1S-by.pushing-cut 1S.CONT
'I'm cutting meat'

(319) *htáa špáase nįkše*
htáa Ya-páa-sé nįkše
meant A2S-by.pushing-cut 2S.CONT
'you're cutting meat'

(320) *htáa páase akxai*
htáa Ø-páa-sé akxa-ðe
meat A3S-by.pushing-cut 3.CONT-DECL
'she's cutting meat'

(321) *hakxą́ta htáa paasé hta apai?*
haatxą́ta htáa Ø-páa-sé hta apa-ðe
when meat A3P-by.pushing-cut FUT 3.CONT-DECL
'when are they going to cut up the meat?'

In (322) the prefix *í* 'with; using' precedes *paa*:

(322) *mą́hį íhpaase*
mą́hį í-Ø-Wa-páa-sé
knife with-P3S-A1S-by.pushing-cut
'I cut it with a knife'

It is worth pointing out the interesting occurrence of 2S object inflection *ði* 'you' and 1S inflection *ą* 'me', respectively, on the main verb 'they want' in the next two examples. The semantic subject of the lower verb is raised to argument position in the main verb 'want'.

(323) *haakǫ́ta wacúe skúe špáase ðikǫ́ða apai?*
haakǫ́ta wacúe skúe Ya-páa-sé
why bread sweet A2S-by.pushing-cut
ði-Ø-kǫ́-Ø-ða apa-ðe
P2S-A3P-PREV-A3P-want 3.CONT-DECL
'why did they want you to cut the cake?'

(324) *haakǫ́ta wacúe skúe ppáase ąkǫ́ða apai?*
haakǫ́ta wacúe skúe Wa-páa-sé
why bread sweet A1S-by.pushing-cut
ą-Ø-kǫ́-Ø-ða apa-ðe
P1S-A3P-PREV-A3P-want 3.CONT-DECL
'why did they want me to cut the cake?'

4.4.6.3 False instrumental: *hpánąke* and *hpáhą*

A sort of false instrumental form emerges where words with a *hpa* sequence seem to be related to 'pushing'. Of course these do not contain the authentic *_paa* 'pushing' at all. The impostor sequence has an initial preaspirated *hp*. Still, the auditory distinction is slight, especially in initial position, and the semantics is quite similar. One example is *hpánąke* 'push someone causing them to run'. The root form *hpaną* actually involves the sense of 'being first' or 'arriving first'.

Elsewhere, *hpa* denotes a protuberance such as the nose or head or a mound of earth. Some of the examples of the "real" *_paa* 'by pushing, by hand away' (or even examples with *pa_* 'by cutting') at first glance seem to be related semantically to this notion of 'protuberance', but in fact are not. The clearest guide, however, is not the semantics but the presence of aspiration on the citation (third person) form *hpa* for the impostor, versus unaspirated *pa* or *paa* for the authentic instrumental.

Another false instrumental verb is *hpáhą* ~ *hpahą́* 'arise; get up from bed'. It is inflected in the regular pattern, with 1S, 2S, and 1P forms *ahpáhą, ðahpáhą, ąhpáhą*.

(325) *ąkóə ąhpáhą ąkái*
ąkóe ąk-hpáhą ąkáðe
1P.PRON A1P-arise 1P.CONT
'we're getting up'

There is an authentic instrumental verb *paahá* 'raise' (also rendered occasionally as *paahą́*, with nasal *ą*), a syncopating fortisizing stop-stem incorporating *_paa* 'by pushing, by hand away'. This verb contrasts with the impostor *hpáhą* ~ *hpahą́* 'arise' just mentioned.

(326) *šáake špáaha štą́*
šáake Ya-paahą́ štą́
hand A2S-raise ITER
'you're raising your hand all the time'

(327) *šáake hpaahá hta mįkšé*
šáake Wa-paahą́ hta mįkšé
hand A1S-raise FUT 1S.CONT
'I'm going to raise my hand'

The analysis here becomes even more complicated with the unexpected occasional use of the regular *a* and *ða* inflection on the instrumental *_paa*, as in (328) (instead of the more normal 1S *hp*, 2S *šp*, 3S/P *Ø*, as in (326) and (327)). This confusion may be owing to language obsolescence or to the prefix being in transition from fortisizing to regular inflection.

(328) *ðie šáake ðapáaha*
ðie šáake Ya-paahą́
2S.PRON hand A2S-raise
'hold up one's hand, lift something'

Raising one's hand is an important ceremonial act, and the commands in (329) and (330) were frequently used expressions.

(329) *šáake paahą́*
šáake paahą́-a
hand raise-IMPER
'hold up your hand'

(330) *šáake paahá pai*
šáake paahą́ paðe
hand raise-PL IMPER.CONT
'[you plural] raise your hand!'

4.4.6.4 Contrast of *pa_* vs. *_paa*: 'hatch'

A contrast between outer instrumental *pa_* and inner instrumental *_paa* can be seen in forms where each is attached to the same root. This situation arises with the root *léke* 'shatter'. Two verbs meaning 'hatch' are created, a regular verb using *pa_* 'by cutting' (followed by inflection) and a syncopating verb using *_paa* 'by pushing, by hand away' (preceded by inflection). The latter appears in (331), the former in (332).

(331) *haatkxą̨ta špáaleke hta nįkšé, súhka?*
haatxą̨ta Ya-paa-leke hta nįkšé, súhka
when A2S-by.pushing -shatter FUT 2S.CONT chicken
'when are you going to hatch, chicken?'

(332) *haatkxą̨ta páðaleke hta nįkšé, súhka?*
haatxą̨ta pa-Ya-leke hta nįkšé, súhka
when by.cutting-A2S-shatter FUT 2S.CONT chicken
'when are you going to hatch, chicken?'

If what one has in mind is the chicken using its beak to break out of the shell, then *páðaleke* for 2S is the version to be used. Interestingly, the speaker believed that the *špáaleke* version does not imply anything about how the chick broke the shell. Section 4.4.7 treats *pa_* 'by cutting'; other outer instrumentals appear in sections 4.4.8 and 4.4.9.

4.4.7 *pa_* 'by cutting'

*Pa_* 'by cutting' is an outer instrumental, mentioned above in section 4.4.6.4 as occurring in *pa_léke* 'hatch'.

As noted in section 4.4.6.2, *pa_* 'by cutting' can be used with the root that itself denotes cutting: *se* 'cut'. It also combines with *sce* ~ *šce* 'long' to give *_pascé* 'slice'.

The simple 'cut' (*_paasé*, with *_paa*; discussed in section 4.4.6.2) is treated as semantically interchangeable with *pa_scé* 'slice' (with *pa_*) in some situations. The regular inflection of *pa_scé* 'slice', following the instrumental, can be seen in (333)–(335). ('Cut up' is equivalent to 'slice' in these sentences.)

(333) *paašcé hta mįkšé*
pa-Wa-šce hta mįkšé
by.cutting-A1S-slice FUT 1S.CONT
'I'm gonna cut it up'

(334) *paðášce*
pa-Ya-šce
by.cutting-A2S-slice
'you cut it up [slice it]'

(335) *wacúə skúə paðášce hta ðąįšé ?*
wacúe skúðe pa-Ya-šce hta ðaįšé
bread sweet by.cutting-A2S-slice FUT 2S.CONT
'are you going to cut up the cake?'

Whereas in section 4.4.6.2 we saw *_paa* with *se* 'cut' (giving 2S *špaase*), in (336)–(337) below we see the outer instrumental *pa_* 'by cutting' with the same root.

(336) *paðáse*
pa-Ya-se
by.cutting-A2S-cut
'you cut'

(337) *wacúə skúə paðáse kǫ́ða apai*
wacúe skúðe pa-Ya-se Ø-kǫ-Ø-ða apa-ðe
bread sweet by.cutting-A2S-cut A3P-PREV-A3P-want 3.CONT-DECL
'they're wanting you to cut the cake'

Example (338) is ambiguous as to whether the *pa* prefix represents outer *pa_* 'by cutting' or inner *_paa* 'by pushing'.

(338) *wapáase*
wa-paa-se
means-by.pushing(?)-cut
'the butcher' (lit., 'one who cuts stuff')

The *paa* verb *_paasé* 'cut by pushing' rather than *pa_scé* 'slice' is used for cutting meat, unless cutting in thin strips, in which case *pa_scé* 'slice' can be used; *pa_scé* is also used for watermelon.

4.4.8 *po* 'by shooting'

Examples of *po* 'by shooting' are found in La Flesche (1932), such as (339), but only one emerged among the data collected for this study: *pólǫðį* 'startled; shocked' (as by suddenly emerging exciting news, the news being usually bad or negative, such as an impending divorce).

(339) *póbraska*
po-braska
by.shooting-flat
'flatten by shooting'

4.4.9 *taa* 'by heat'

A more precise gloss for *taa* is 'by extreme of temperature; by excess of or lack of heat', as witnessed by its use (as a root) in *ótaa* 'freeze, frozen'.[26] Hotness-related forms using *taa* are more common, however, than cold-related forms, so it will be handy to gloss *taa* as 'by heat' in most places.[27]

(340) *táahkace*
'hot; be hot'

(341) *taazíhi*
taa-zíhi
by.heat-brown
'fry, brown' (transitive or intransitive)

(342) *Mary akxa súhka taazihi akxa*
Mary akxa súhka taa-zihi akxa
Mary SUBJ chicken by.heat-brown 3.CONT
'Mary is frying/browning the chicken'

(343) *súhka taazíhi che?*
súhka taa-zíhi che
chicken by.heat-brown EVID
'is the chicken browning?'

The prefix *taa* also appears in *taazíhiðe* 'make brown [as by frying]', with causative *ðe*. Other verbs in *taa* are seen in (344)–(346).

(344) *táapuxe*
'boil over' (cf. *ápuxe* 'boil food')

(345) *táapuze*
táa-puze
by.heat-dry
'dry through heat; e.g., boil dry'[28]

[26] For the meaning 'by cold' associated with the instrumental prefix, see Kansa *odasčege* 'split from heat, *cold*, lightning' (where *da* corresponds to Osage *taa*; compare Kansa *onąsčege* 'split something with the foot').

[27] No examples have been found among speakers or even in La Flesche (1932) to date with the secondary meaning suggested by cognates in related languages: 'by spontaneous action' or 'by inner force', except perhaps *taabrą* 'emit an odor' (as from one's shoe after having stepped on something).

[28] The form *púze* 'dry' (including 'dry by wind') has another related form which is a near homophone of this example: *htáapuze* means 'dried food' (based on *htáa* 'deer; meat').

(346) *óhkilą táapuze əkxai*
óhkulą táa-puze akxa-ðe
clothing by.heat-dry 3.CONT-DECL
'the clothes are drying'

No clearly inflected verbs with *taa* were encountered or successfully elicited. Observe that *táapuze* 'dry' lacks 1S inflection in (347).

(347) *haxį táapuze mįkšé*
haxį táapuze mįkšé
blanket dry 1S.CONT
'I'm drying the blanket [anyone's blanket]'

The 'by hand' instrumental *ðuu* can also combine with *puze* 'dry' (intransitive) to form a transitive verb *ðuupúze* 'make dry', and this verb mixes with the *táapuze* paradigm. One speaker preferred *ščúupuze* for 2S (with instrumental *ðuu*). But this same speaker preferred *táapuze* for the 1S form; although 1S *brúupuze* was felt to be acceptable but not commonly used. The form *táapuze* connotes less direct involvement on the part of the agent than *ðuupúze*. In (347), uninflected *táapuze* is followed by the 1S continuative *mįkšé*.

In (348) likewise, 1S *mįkšé* appears. Use of the continuative auxiliary conveys that 'the corn is drying and I'm responsible for it'.

(348) *watáažoe táapuze mįkšé*
watáažoe táapuze mįkšé
hominy heat.dry 1S.CONT
'I'm drying corn for hominy'

Prefix *táa* combines with roots *brą* 'emanate an odor' to give *táabrą* 'emanate an odor, as in cooking or burning' (intransitive only):

(349) *óohǫ əkxa táabrą əkxai*
óohǫ akxa táabrą akxa-ðe
cook SUBJ smell 3.CONT-DECL
'the cooking is smelling'

(350) *táatą hpíiži wį áaðanąąžį skə táabrą ðąįše*
táatą hpíiži wį á-Ya-nąąžį ska táabrą ðąįše
thing bad a LOC-A2S-stand suppose smell 2S.CONT
'you must have stepped on something bad, because you're smelling bad'

In the following example, *táalį* 'burn' (intransitive) is based on an opaque root *lį*.

(351) *óohǫ əkxa táalį əkxa skə, táabrą əkxai*
óohǫ akxa Ø-táalį akxa ska, Ø-táabrą akxa-ðe
cooking SUBJ A3S-burn 3.CONT suppose, A3S-smell 3.CONT-DECL
'the cooking must be burning, because it's smelling'

4.5 Locative and benefactive prefixes *i*, *o*, and *á*

In Siouan languages the prefixes *i, o,* and *á* (and the long-voweled variants *ii* and *oo*) are called variously locatives, prepositional prefixes, inseparable prepositions, or adverbials. They pattern together morphologically; the term "locative" is a purely morphological classification with no semantic motivation. (Only *á* is locative in a semantic sense.) Here we continue to use the term "locative" for these prefixes to facilitate comparison with related languages.

The so-called locative verbs are merely verbs containing one of these prefixes. The point of inflection is right of the *o, i,* or *á* prefix (for example, *í_xa* 'smile', *oo_hǫ́* 'cook'). The A1P *ąk*, however, is placed left of the prefix *o* (*oo*) or *á* (for example, *ąk* + *oohǫ́* 'we cook') but rightward of *i* (*ii*).

4.5.1 *i* locatives

Called in related languages an "instrumental locative," the prefix *i* is neither a locative in a semantic sense, nor is it an instrumental similar to the instrumentals in the previous section (such as *nąą* 'by foot' and *ðaa* 'by mouth'). Semantically, though, the label "instrumental" makes some sense in that *i* carries the meaning of 'with' or 'a means to', as seen for example in (357)–(358) below. The *i* prefix increases the valence of the verb by adding another argument position; the normal verb 'eat' has two arguments ('X eats Y'), but with the addition of *i* we have three arguments: 'X eats Y with Z' (for example, 'you eat oatmeal with a spoon'). Thus *i* is a valence increaser as opposed to the valence reducer *wa*. Examples below include 'be sick with', 'eat with', 'drink with', 'bless with', 'hit with', 'buy with' and 'make with'.

The stative verb *íhpiiži* 'be sick with; feel ill owing to' can be used without mention of what is ailing the person, as 'be bad or ailing with [it]'. Contrasted to the adjectivelike *húheka* 'sick; be sick', *íhpiiži* means 'feel bad owing to something, be troubled by something' but is also glossed sometimes merely as 'be sick'.

(352) *íhpiiži*
i-Ø-hpiiži
with-P3S-be.troubled
'she's sick with it, in bad shape with it; she's distraught, troubled by it'

The cause of illness can be expressed by an overt constituent, such as the subordinate clause in (353).

(353) *brée brúucʔake ą̨hpíiži ą̨hé*
a-Wa-ðee Wa-ðuucʔáke i-ą̨-hpíiži ą̨ðį̨hé
PREV-A1S-go A1S-unable with-P1S-troubled 1S.CONT
'I'm sick about not being able to go'

When locative *i* is added to the intransitive stem *nǫ́hpe* 'afraid', the result is a stem meaning 'afraid of' (354a)–(354b).

(354a) *ínǫhpa*
í-nǫhpe-a
with-afraid-IMPER
'be careful of'

(354b) *ínohpaži*
í-nohpe-aži
with-afraid-NEG
'be not fearful of, be reckless around'

(To the last example, compare (355).)

(355) *nǫ́hpaži*
nǫ́hpe-aži
afraid-NEG
'not afraid'

The verbs 'eat with' and 'drink with', the latter forming a noun that names a utensil, appear in (356)–(358):

(356) *íðaache*
i-ðaaché
with-eat
'eat by means of, eat using; eat with [an implement, as a spoon]'

(357) *htaaníi hcúke íðaachapi*
htaa-nii hcúke i-ðaaché-a-api
meat-liquid spoon with-eat-IMPER-PL
'eat soup with a spoon'

(358) *níiðaahtą*
níi-i-ðaahtą́
water-with-drink
'dipper; ladle'

In the locative verb *ísta* 'bless with' in (359)–(361), the meaning of the stem *sta* is approximately 'peaceful, smooth, healed'. There is a reflexive causative form with *hkik-ðe*, seen in (361)–(362).

(359) *ísta*
i-sta
with-peaceful
'bless with'

(360) *mį́į íista*
mį́į íi-sta
sun with-peaceful
'bless oneself with the sun'

(361) *mį́į ístahkie*
mį́į i-sta-hkík-ðe
sun with-bless-REFL-CAU
'bless oneself with the sun'

(362) *Johna akxa žį̨káži̜ waatá apa, ístahkiepi*
Johna akxa žį̨káži̜ Ø-waatá apa i-sta-hkik-ðe-api
John SUBJ children A3S-pray 3.CONT with-bless-REFL-CAU-PL
'John is praying for the children and the children are asking God for a blessing' (lit., 'John is praying for the children, and they are blessing themselves with it')

The verb *ðakˀé_ðe* 'pity' has both the instrumental locative *i* and its usual causative secondary root *ðe* in the following example, taken from a prayer:

(363) *ónǫbre waatái ški íðakˀéwaðakíapí*
ónǫbre waatá-ðe ški i-ðakˀé-wa-Ya-kik-ðe-a-api
food prayer-this also with-pity-P1P-A2S-SUU-CAU-IMPER-PL
'pity us with this food and these prayers'

In 'hit with', the prefix *i* combines directly with the root *chį*. (The *o* locative form of the same root will be seen in section 4.5.2.)

(364) *ichį́*
i-chį́
with-hit
'hit with'

(365) *žą́ąxe aną́chįpe*
žą́ąxe ąk-i-Ø-chį́-api-ðe
stick A1P-with-P3S-hit-PL-DECL
'we hit him with a stick'

(366) *žą́ąxe aną́chipe*
žą́ąxe i-ą-Ø-chį́-api-ðe
stick with-P1S-A3S-hit-PL-DECL
'he hit me with a stick'

When valence reducer *wa* precedes the locative prefix, the *wa-i* sequence reduces to *we*, as in (367) and (368) (for the rule, see section 3.4.1.2).

(367) *šáake weáchįe*
šáake wa-i-Ø-Wa-chį́-ðe
hand VAL-with-P3S-A1S-hit-DECL
'I hit him with my hand'

Example (367) is approximately 'I used my hand to hit him with'. The valence reducer *wa* is often used in sentences where the tool (for example, hand) is named, that is, in sentences where the tool is the relevant item and not the patient (not the thing or person hit).

(368) *žą́ąxe wį weáchįe*
žą́ąxe wį wa-i-Ø-Wa-chį́-ðe
stick a VAL-with-P3S-A1S-hit-DECL
'I hit him with a stick'

The next two examples illustrate *ðuwį́* 'buy' with the prefix *i*.

(369) *haxį́ wébruwį*
haxį́ wa-i-Ø-Wa-ðuwį́
blanket VAL-with-P3S-A1S-buy
'I bought it [stuff] with a blanket'

(370) *mą́zeska íbruwį*
mą́zeska i-Ø-Wa-ðuwį́
money with-P3S-A1S-buy
'I bought it with money'

There is an interesting relationship between 'buy' and 'sell' involving the *i* prefix. 'Buy something with a blanket' is another way of expressing 'sell a blanket'; *wéðuwį* 'buy/acquire stuff with' (from *wa* + *íðuwį*) can be interpreted as 'sell'.

'Make out of' and 'make with' use the *i* prefix. The preceding argument may be either the material, such as wood, or the tool, such as a hammer. The valence reducer *wa* 'stuff' appears as a diffuse object (the patient of the base stem, not the argument added by *i*) in *wa* + *ikáaɣe*, 'make stuff with' (370)–(372).

(371) *íkaaɣe*
i-káaɣe
with-make
'make out of'

(372) *wékaaɣe*
wa-i-káaɣe
VAL-with-make
'make with'

(373) *kaalįįze wéškaaɣe nąe*
kaalįįze wa-i-Ya-káaɣe nąðe
flint VAL-with-A2S-make ITER-DECL
'you used to make them with flint'

(374) *žą́ąxe íkaaɣe akxai íiðaðe?*
žą́ąxe i-Ø-káaɣe akxai íi-Ø-ð-Wa-ðe
wood with-A3S-make 3.CONT PREV-P3S-EPð-A1S-see
'did you see the thing he made out of wood?' (lit., 'he was making it with wood, did you see it?')

4.5.2 *o* locatives

The prefix *o* (including long *oo*) signifies approximately 'location, final place, goal, culmination, fruition, event'. However, in many verbs its meaning is not at all apparent, such as *oohǫ́* 'cook'. The behavior of *o* with respect to inflection is quite consistent in all but a few unusual cases. Like *á* and *i* (the other members of the locative set), *o* precedes agent and patient inflectional markers: *oo_hǫ́* 'cook', *ó_hką* 'help'.

For a 1D/P agent, however, if patient inflection is also present, then normally *o* follows *ąk* while patient inflection remains at the point of inflection, after the *o*, as in (375).

(375) *ąkóðihką*
ąk-o-ði-hką
A1P-PREV-P2S-help
'we help you'

A typical member of the very large set of *o* verbs is:

(376) *ožú*
o-žú
LOC-pour
'put in or inside, pour into'

An example of an *o* locative with a reflexive *hkik* is:

(377) *ohkíǫðe*
o-hkik-ǫðe
LOC-REFL-toss
'throw oneself into a place'[29]

The verb 'hit' *o_chį́* is based on the same root seen in *i_chį́* 'hit with' (section 4.5.1).

(378) *žą́ąxe abrį́e awáchį*
žą́ąxe a-Wa-ðį́-ðe o-Ø-a-chį́
stick PREV-A1S-have-DECL LOC-P3S-A1S-hit
'I hit him with a stick' (lit., 'I had a stick and I hit him')

For contrast, the *i*-locative form of *ochį́* appears in sentence (379) 'I used them to hit him' (where 'him' = *Ø* and 'them' is represented by valence reducer *wa*).

(379) *weáchį́e*
wa-i-Ø-Wa-chį́-ðe
VAL-with-P3S-A1S-hit-DECL
'I hit him with them'

In (380) and (381), epenthesis of *w* between locative *o* and a following inflectional pronominal is seen, along with lowering of *o* to *a*. In (380), in addition, nasality has shifted from P1S *ą* to the locative prefix. (Lowering to *a* and nasality spreading are treated in section 3.4.2.)

(380) *Johna akxa ąwáchįpe*
Johna akxa o-ą-chį́-api-ðe
John SUBJ LOC-P1S-hit-PL-DECL
'John hit me'

(381) *Johna awáchį*
Johna o-Ø-Wa-chį́
John LOC-P3S-A1S-hit
'I hit John'

4.5.3 *á* locatives

Semantically, there are two groups of verbs with prefix *á*. First, I will examine *á* verbs with a somewhat benefactive sense, such as 'watch over' and 'dance for'. The second, more clearly position-related, use of *á* is as

[29] Note that *hkíǫðe* means 'divorce' ('throw each other away', reciprocal of *ǫ́ðe* 'throw away'). Other examples with this verb appear in section 3.5.3 where doubly-inflecting verbs are discussed, and below in section 4.6.2.3.

'on, upon' in expressions such as 'walk on', made up of *á* plus 'walk' as in *níi ámąðį* 'walk on water'.

The *á* locative prefix, when used in a benefactive sense, overlaps semantically with the dative prefix *ki*, which also forms semantic benefactives. (For dative *ki*, see section 4.6.5. Since *ki* becomes zero after overt inflectional prefixes, while locative *á* contracts with following P1S *ą* [see below], the two kinds of benefactive are homophonous in P1S forms.) Locative *á* (whether benefactive or positional) uses normal patient object inflection: *ą, ði, Ø, wa...api, wa,* rightward of *á*, as is shown in table 4.15.

TABLE 4.15. PATIENT INFLECTION WITH LOCATIVE *á*

UNDERLYING FORM		SURFACE FORM	PATIENT PERSON AND NUMBER
á + *ą* + verb	→	*áą* + verb	P1S
á + *ði* + verb	→	*áði* + verb	P2S
á + *Ø* + verb	→	*á* + verb	P3S
wa + *á* + verb	→	*áwa* + verb[a]	P1P
á + *wa* + verb	→	*áwa* + verb	P3P

[a] Occasionally an epenthetic *ð* appears instead: *wa* + *á* > *waðá*.

4.5.3.1 Benefactive locative *á*

The usual verb 'dance' is *waa_chí*, whose first person singular form is *awáachi*, and sometimes *áwaachį*. The plain second person form appears in (383).

(382) *awáachi* ~ *áwaachį*
Wa-waa-chí
A1S-PREV-dance
'I am dancing [not for anyone]'

(383) *waaðáchi hta nįkšé?*
waa-ða-chi hta nįkšé
PREV-A2S-dance FUT 2S.CONT
'are you going to dance?'

(384) *áwaachi*
á-Ø-waachí-a
LOC-P3S-dance-IMPER
'dance for him'

(385) *áwiwaachi*
á-wi-waachí
LOC-P2S<A1S-dance
'I danced for you'

(386) *áwiwaachi ąkxąhé*
á-wi-waachí ątxąhé
LOC-P2S<A1S-dance 1S.CONT
'I'll dance for you'[30]

When the locative *á* 'for' precedes the A1S *a*, a bimorphemic *á-a* sequence is formed, and provides context for insertion of an epenthetic *w*, as in (387).[31]

(387) *áwawaachi*
á-Ø-w-Wa-waachí
LOC-P3S-EP*w*-A1S-dance
'I danced for him'

No epenthetic *w* is inserted between locative *á* and P1S *ą*; this sequence merely becomes *ą́ą*.

(388) *ą́ąwaachi ðíe*
á-ą-waachi-a ðíe
LOC-P1S-dance-IMPER 2S.PRON
'dance for me'

The prefix *á* derives the locative-benefactive verb *á_ɣaake* 'cry for/about/because of someone; lament someone' from *ɣaaké* 'cry'. Patient inflection follows the *á* locative prefix.

(389) *áðiɣaaki apai*
á-ði-Ø-ɣaaké apa-ðe
LOC-P2S-A3P-cry 3.CONT-DECL
'they're crying for you'

(390) *áɣaake apai*
á-Ø-Ø-ɣaaké apa-ðe
LOC-P3S-A3P-cry 3.CONT-DECL
'they're crying for her'

[30] Even though this example is a future sentence semantically, no future marker is needed. This confirms the extended use of the standing auxiliary, as discussed in section 5.5.1.2, for the launch of an activity.

[31] This insertion takes place at the utterance level and is optional in some contexts, as in the following example:

áakaaspe
á-a-kaaspe
LOC-A1S-cover
'I cover it up'

4.5.3.2 Locative *á* 'upon'

Locative *á* forms a construction a bit reminiscent of the English *Clouds are spreading over the region* → *Clouds are overspreading the region*, where a preposition is compounded with a verb to form a transitive verb, with the object of the preposition becoming the object of the compound transitive verb. Osage verbs with locative *á* are transitive in this way too; thus, for instance, *ámąðį* 'walk upon' takes a direct object *níi* 'water' in *níi ámąðį* 'walk on water'.

Locative *á* plus the root *tǫ́pe* 'look; see' gives us *átǫpe* 'look out for, watch over, look after, keep watch on, look down on'. Glosses range from a warning of 'watch it' to a prayerful 'look down upon us'.

(391) *átǫpai*
á-Ø-tǫpe-ði
LOC-P3S-look-2S.PRON
'watch it [e.g., your purse or the baby]'

(392) *áwittǫ́pe mįkšé*
á-wi-Wa-tǫ́pe *mįkšé*
LOC-P2S<A1S-A1S-look 1S.CONT
'I'm looking down upon you'

Another set of *á* locatives have to do more directly with relative positions (pulling a window shut, crawling on, setting something on something else, going up, and so forth), most of which are expressed with prepositions in English.

(393) *okáhąpa áðiihtą, nížu akxai*
okáhąpa á-ðiihtą́-a, *nížu akxa-ðe*
window LOC-grasp-IMPER, rain 3.CONT-DECL
'close the window, it's raining'

In (394) and (395), the locative *á* here adds 'on [something]' to the plain verb *kaasįce* 'close' (which contains instrumental *kaa* in all inflected forms).

(394) *ákaasįce*
á-kaa-sįce
LOC-by.striking-close
'close or slam; close, slam on something or someone'

(395) *hcižé áðakasįce*
hcižé á-Ya-kaa-sįce
door LOC-A2S-by.striking-close
'you closed/slammed the door on it'

Sharing a base with *oolą́* 'put in, put on' is locative *álą*:

(396) *álą*
á-lą
LOC-put
'put upon'

There are a great many *á* locative verbs. In some cases the *á* clearly adds the meaning 'on; upon; over', as in *álą* 'put upon' in the preceding example. Other verbs with *á* fall into this 'upon' group, such as those in the following examples.

(397) *ále*
á-le
LOC-set
'set on' (e.g., set a kettle on the fire)[32]

(398a) *ážu*
á-žu
LOC-put
'put something on [top of] something else'

(398b) *áðažu?*
á-Ya-žu
LOC-A2S-put
'did you put [something] on top [of something else]?'

(398c) *áažu*
á-Wa-žu
LOC-A1S-put
'I put [it] on top'

Additional examples of such transparent *á* locatives are the following:

(399) *ánąąžį*
á-nąąžį
LOC-stand
'step on, stand on top of' (also used in comparisons)

(400a) *ðíe ški níi ámaščį áape*
ðíe ški níi á-mą-Ya-ðį áape
2S.PRON also water LOC-PREV-P2S-walk they.said
'they said you, too, walked on water'

(400b) *níi ámąði*
nii á-Ø-mąðį
water LOC-A3S-walk
'he walks on water'

[32] This verb forms a minimal pair, differentiated by accent and vowel length, with *alée* 'go'. Its antonym is *šíle* 'set off', e.g., 'set a kettle off the fire'.

(401) *áwisi*
á-wisi
LOC-jump
'jump over'

(402a) *ámįci*
á-mįcé
LOC-crawl
'crawl on'

(402b) *hpáažį akxa ánakoe ámįci akxai*
hpáažį akxa ánakoe á-Ø-mįcé akxa-ðe
baby SUBJ floor LOC-A3S-crawl 3.CONT-DECL
'the baby is crawling on the floor'

A second group of *á* locatives are less transparent semantically (that is, *á* does not clearly add the meaning 'upon'). For instance, from *kǫ́ze* 'teach, show how', *ákǫze* 'examine' (403) is formed.

(403) *hcéka ðiiníe che ákǫze hta akxa ska?*
hcéka ði-i-níe che á-Ø-kǫ́ze hta akxa ska
just P2S-with-hurt that LOC-P3S-examine FUT 3.CONT guess
'are you [i.e., is your malady] just now going to be examined, I guess?'

No *kaaspe* exists independently, but we find the form in (404).

(404) *ákaaspe*
á-kaaspe
LOC-even/level(?)
'cover something up; cover over [e.g., with a cloth or blanket, or with dirt]'

From *pázo* 'finger' is formed *ápazo* 'point at' (405); *pázo* is not known as a verb.

(405) *ápazo*
á-pazo
LOC-point
'point at'

In a third group of *á* locatives it is even less clear how the semantics of the *á* prefix relates to the following root. A good example is *á_nakʔǫ* 'listen' (406a)–(406b), formed by adding *á* to *nąkʔǫ́* 'hear; hear about' (407a)–(407c).

(406a) *ánąkʔǫ́*
ánąkʔą-a
listen-IMPER
'listen'

(406b) *áðanąk'ǫ hta nįkšé?*
á-Ya-nąk'ǫ hta nįkšé
LOC-A2S-listen FUT 2S.CONT
'are you going to listen to that?'

(407a) *nąk'ǫ́ kšíe ði*
nąk'ǫ́ kší-Ø-ðe-a ði
hear make-P3S-CAU-IMPER you
'be sure and let him hear about it'

(407b) *áhkaahtami ðanák'ǫ?*
áhkaahtami Ø-Ya-nąk'ǫ
bell P3S-A2S-hear
'did you hear the bell?'

(407c) *ðanák'ǫ?*
Ø-Ya-nąk'ǫ
P3S-A2S-hear
'did you hear about it [e.g., about the accident]?'

For *á* forms used in postpositions and other semantically locative forms, see section 6.6.2.

4.6 Object reference: dative *ki*, suus *kik*, reflexive *hkik*

4.6.1 General discussion

The prefixes *ki, kik*, and *hkik* correspond to three forms of object reference: the dative, suus, and reflexive forms, respectively. We speak of them as a group because these three principal kinds of auditorily somewhat similar elements in Osage appear in the same location in the verbal complex, that is, following patient and agent inflection. In the schema showing the order of placement in the verb of patient pronominals, agent pronominals and object referents, "PAT AG KI + root" (chapter 3), KI is an abbreviation for all three object reference prefixes *ki*, *kik*, and *hkik,* plus the vertitive *kik* and inceptive *ki*.

Recall that the segment (sound) immediately following the agent pronominal is referred to here as the inflectable initial of the verb (root or stem, as it is sometimes root and other times stem); thus, the verb *íi_ðe* 'see' is an *íi*-initial verb but its inflectable initial segment is *ð*. On this definition, KI prefixes (object reference, vertitive, and inceptive) have the effect of giving the verb a new inflectable initial. Thus, when a KI prefix is added to a syncopating verb, the resulting derived form takes the regular (nonsyncopating) type of agent inflection, as will be seen in the following sections.

Some of the object reference prefixes are homophonous with other prefixes. The dative form *ki* 'for another' is homophonous with the inceptive form (which refers to initiation of action), although unlike the dative, inceptive *ki* is not suppressed after pronominal prefixes (cf. section 4.6.5). The suus form *kik* 'one's own' is identical in form and conduct to the vertitive (which appears in motion verbs; see section 4.3). Additionally, the reciprocal 'each other' and reflexive 'oneself' are the same: *hkik*. The inceptive *ki* and vertitive *kik* are not object referents per se, but rather more strictly derivational morphemes. They are, however, grouped here since their point of occurrence and their phonology are the same as that of their homophones.

There are certain points of overlap in meaning and usage among the object reference forms. For instance, there is potential ambiguity between reflexive and suus: both can mean 'subject's own persons or things', and the two are ordinarily distinguished only by preaspiration in reflexive *hkik* vs. plain *k* in suus *kik*. Although it is much more common to use suus *kik* when speaking of one's own people, reflexive *hkik* does occur in the context of the supernatural (God, the Great Spirit, *Wahkǫta*) looking down upon us 'his own'. ('Look upon' in other contexts uses suus *kik*.)

The object reference forms (and vertitive and inceptive) constitute a paradigm: usually if one is present the others are not. Even if the meaning to be expressed in a given case might seem to require two object reference prefixes, only one is normally present. (Notably, where one might expect to find reflexive plus dative, or suus plus dative, typically only reflexive or suus appears.)

Notwithstanding these various complications, the morphology, semantics, and parameters of usage of the object reference elements can be accounted for in a fairly straightforward manner. All the object reference morphemes are productive in the language; moreover, the same classes of object reference are found in other Siouan languages as well. Table 4.16 summarizes important aspects of the usage of object reference and homophonous prefixes.

The form of the object reference prefixes is affected by various phonological processes. In the forms ending in *k* (reflexive *hkik* and suus *kik*), the final *k* disappears before regular verb stems. When *kik* (suus) or *hkik* (reflexive) precedes *p*, *t*, or *k* as the inflectable initial of the verb stem, final *k* of the object reference prefix again disappears, but preaspirates the following stop: *hp*, *ht*, or *hk*. Thus, for example, the suus form of *tǫpe* 'watch, look at' is *kihtǫpe* 'watch subject's own things'. (Such preaspi-

TABLE 4.16. OBJECT REFERENCE AND RELATED PREFIXES

	ki	*kik*	*hkik*
OBJECT REFERENCE	DATIVE *Semantics:* 'to someone'; benefactive 'for someone'; 'in someone's place'; 'someone else's, or with respect to someone else; with involvement of someone else' (e.g., 'for him', 'to his', 'on his', 'his'); includes malefactive *Grammar:* adds oblique object	SUUS (also called "reflexive possessive") *Semantics:* 'subject's own things or persons' *Grammar:* characterizes theme or recipient objects	REFLEXIVE *Semantics:* 'oneself'; 'subject's own' Also reflexive-benefactive 'for subject's own self; for subject's own' *Grammar:* characterizes theme or recipient objects RECIPROCAL *Semantics:* 'each other; for each other' *Grammar:* characterizes direct object In verbs of conversation, two reciprocal elements may be present.
DERIVATIONAL	INCEPTIVE 'again, anew' (as in 'redo', 'pay back')	VERTITIVE 'return' in motion verbs	

rated stops *hp ht hk* may also surface as geminates *pp tt kk*, especially preceding nasal vowels). When *hkik* or *kik* is added to a syncopating *ð* inflectable initial verb, *k* contracts with *ð* (informally speaking) to produce *l*. When *kik* (suus) precedes *ð*, then *kik* + *ð* → *l*, with the *kik* disappearing entirely.[33] This can be seen in many verbs: for example, from *ðiišk*í 'launder' is formed the suus verb *líiški* 'launder subject's own'.

Dative *ki* is not affected by the phonological processes just discussed, but has other peculiarities. Phonological aspects of the object reference prefixes are discussed in more detail in the following sections.

4.6.2 Reflexive

Reflexives take regular agent inflection, regardless of whether the stem to which the reflexive *hkik* is added is regular or syncopating. Reflexive inflection is shown in table 4.17.

[33] Elsewhere, *kil* is freely attested between vowels.

TABLE 4.17. AGENT INFLECTION WITH *hkik* REFLEXIVE

1S	*ahkik*
2S	*ðahkik*
3S	*hkik*
1P	*ą̨hkik*
3P	*hkik*

The following process takes place with stop stems:

hkik → *hkih* / __ *p,t,k*

That is to say, adding *hkik* will cause the inflectable initial *p*, *t*, or *k* (plain unaspirated stop) of the following stem to become preaspirated. Thus the reflexive of the *k* inflectable initial verb _*káaɣe* 'make' is _h*kihkáaɣe* 'make for oneself'. Other changes, discussed in section 4.6.2.1, occur when *hkik* is added to a *ð*-stem syncopating verb. With all other stems (stems with other consonants or a vowel as their inflectable initial), *hkik* loses its final *k*, appearing as *hki*, without affecting the stem.

Several grammatical types of reflexive are treated below: plain reflexive, benefactive reflexive, causative reflexive, and locative reflexive, both with basic reflexive semantics and with an extension of the reflexive meaning beyond 'oneself' to 'one's own.'

4.6.2.1 Phonology of the reflexive with *ð*-stems

Many reflexives are based on syncopating *ð* inflectable initial verbs. In these, the expected sequence *k* + *ð* is replaced by *l*, as in *hkilúwį* 'buy for oneself' (from *ðuwį́* 'buy'). As is amply illustrated by examples below, reflexives of *ð*-stem verbs are regular stems taking *a, ða, Ø* agent inflection before the reflexive prefix.

A more complete analysis of the *ð* inflectable initials with reflexive *hkik*, as suggested by Robert Rankin (p.c. 1995), would posit intermediate stages in the phonological derivation, and would be as follows:

ð → *l* / *k*__ (*hkik ð* → *hkik l*)

k → *g* / __*l* (*hkik l* → *hkig l*)

g → *d* (i.e., *hkig l* → *hkidl*; this accounts for the cluster *dl* that can sometimes appear on the surface utterance)

d → *Ø* (i.e., *hkidl* → *hkil*)

4.6.2.2 Plain reflexive 'oneself' with *ð*-stems

In this section are examples of reflexives with *hkik* with *ð*-stem verbs, where *l* has emerged based on the rule in section 4.6.2.1. The plain reflexive 'oneself' occurs quite frequently:

(408) *hkiláawa įkápi*
hkik-ðaawá ðįké-a-api
REFL-count NEG-IMPER-PL
'do not count yourself'

Reflexives of causatives with prefix *ðuu* are common.

(409a) *hkìluhpíiži*
hkik-ðuu-hpíiži
REFL-CAU-bad
'do oneself ill'

(409b) *wáli ąhkíluhpíiži, ąži óðąži ahkílabrį hta akxa*
wáli ą-hkik-ðuu-hpíiži ąži óðąži
really P1S-REFL-CAU-bad but anyway
Wa-hkik-ð-a-Wa-ðį hta akxa
A1S-REFL-EPð-PREV-A1S-carry FUT 3.CONT
'I did myself bad [I made a bad mistake] but I'll carry myself on anyway'[34]

(410) *hkìluhépe*
hkik-ðuu-hépe
REFL-CAU-small.amount
'lighten oneself' (euphemism for 'urinate')

Another reflexive of a *ð*-stem is *hkílaðį* 'have/hold oneself; carry oneself' (extended to mean 'conduct oneself in the proper manner, take care of oneself', an important concept in Osage society). This reflexive verb is either singly or doubly inflected in 1S (*_hkíla(_)ðį*), as *ahkílaðį* or *ahkílabrį* (with some preference for the singly inflected form); 2S is *ðahkílaðį*.

From *ðiizíðe* 'stretch' (transitive), the reflexive is:

(411) *hkilíiziə*
Ø-hkik-ðiizíðe
A3S-REFL-stretch
'he stretched [himself]'

[34] Notice *hta akxa* following a verb with 1S agent. This usage seems to mean 'it will be the case that [clause].'

The reflexive of *ðísǫ* 'turn around' (transitive) is seen in the following examples. The first is literal; in the second, the same reflexive verb is used metaphorically for 'changed his ways'.

(412) *níhka akxa hkílisǫpi áha, owíbrį tǫ wakˀǫ́ hta mįkšé*
níhka akxa hkik-ðísǫ-api i áha,
man SUBJ REFL-turn-PL IMM whenever
ǫ́-wi-Wa-ðe tǫ wakˀǫ́ hta mįkšé
PREV-P2S<A1S-A1S-toss when glad FUT 1S.CONT
aape
they.said
'the man turned around and said "I'll sure be glad when I get rid of you"'[35]

(413) *hkílisǫðe akxa*
Ø-hkik-ðísǫðe akxa
A3S-REFL-turn-3.CONT
'he turned around [he changed his ways]'

4.6.2.3 Plain reflexive with other inflectable initials

There are scores of examples of reflexive *hkik* added to stems other than *ð*-stems. The verb *ó_kˀǫhe* 'put oneself in' (with root *kˀǫ́he* 'lay into') has a reflexive form literally meaning 'lay oneself into' but metaphorically extended to mean 'interrupt'.

(414) *óhkikˀǫ́he*
ó-Ø-hkik-kˀǫ́he
PREV-A3S-REFL-lay.into
'he's interrupting'

Example (415) consists of a regularly inflected verb *o_hkíǫðe*,[36] based on *ǫ́ðe* 'throw away' plus the reflexive; its meaning is approximately 'toss oneself into a place'. There is also a reciprocal form *hkiǫ́ðe* 'separate, divorce' ('throw each other away').

(415) *ohkíǫðe*
o-hkík-ǫðe
LOC-REFL-toss
'fall in a hole, jump into anything, jump into trouble'

Based on the regular verb *opšé* 'obey, mind' is the reflexive *íe ohkípše* 'obey one's word, obey subject's own word, keep one's word'. (The gloss sounds very much like that of a suus verb, but the form is reflexive.)

[35] The verb for 'get rid of' is *ǫ́ðe*, literally 'toss'; it appears here with raising of *e* to *į*.

[36] Optionally doubly inflected *o_hkiǫ_ðe* (regular at the first point of inflection and syncopating at the second).

(416) *iə ohkípše*
ie o-hkik-pšé
word LOC-REFL-obey
'keep one's word'

'Freeze' as an intransitive verb is *ótaa*. (See section 4.4.9 for instrumental prefix *taa* 'by extreme of temperature'). In (417) we see *táa* functioning as a primary root in a reflexivized causative construction. The entire sequence *táa* + reflexive + causative (*táahkiðe*) means 'cause themselves to be frozen' or 'get frozen'.

(417) *síi táahkiðe*
sí taa-Ø-hkik-ðe
foot freeze-A3P-REFL-CAU
'I froze my feet' (lit., 'caused feet to freeze unto oneself', or '[my] feet caused themselves to freeze')

The reflexivized causative in (418) is transparently based on *cˀé* 'die'.

(418) *cˀéhkiðe*
cˀé-hkik-ðe
die-REFL-CAU
'kill oneself; commit suicide'

4.6.2.4 Reflexive benefactive

One of the meanings of the reflexive is 'for oneself'. To express this benefactive-reflexive meaning, one might have expected a sequence of reflexive plus benefactive prefixes (*hkik* + *ki*); but in fact only the reflexive prefix appears. The reflexive benefactive of the verb *káaɣe* 'make; do' appears in an imperative below:

(419) *ðie hkihkáaɣa*
ðie hkik-káaɣe-a
2S.PRON REFL-do-IMPER
'do it for yourself'

Similarly, semantically benefactive _*hkilúwį* 'buy for oneself' is morphologically clearly a simple reflexive based on *ðuwį́* 'buy'.

(420) *oðíhta wį ahkíluwį*
oðíhta wį Wa-hkik-ðuwį́
car a A1S-REFL-buy
'I bought a car for myself'

(421) *wie ahkíluwį əkxą́he*
wie Wa-hkik-ðuwį́ ąkxą́he
1S.PRON A1S-REFL-buy 1S.CONT
'I'm buying it for myself'

(422) *ðahkíluwį*
Ø-Ya-hkik-ðuwį́
P3S-A2S-REFL-buy
'you're buying it for yourself'

(423) *wahkíluwį əpái*
wa-Ø-hkik-ðuwį́ apa-ðe
VAL-A3S-REFL-buy 3.CONT-DECL
'he bought stuff for himself'

(424) *hkilúwį əkxai*
Ø-Ø-hkik-ðuwį́ akxa-ðe
P3S-A3S-REFL-buy 3.CONT-DECL
'he's buying it for himself'

(425) *ðée hkilúwį əpai*
ðee Ø-hkik-ðuwį́ apa-ðe
that A3S-REFL-buy 3.CONT-DECL
'she bought that for herself'

(426) *hkilúwį apai*
Ø-Ø-hkik-ðuwį́ apa-ðe
P3S-A3P-REFL-buy 3.CONT-DECL
'they bought it for themselves'

Another reflexive benefactive based on a *ð*-stem verb is *hkiláaxǫ* 'break something for oneself, with the mouth', based on *ðaaxǫ́* 'break with teeth' (*ðaa* 'by mouth', *xǫ́* 'break'):

(427) *ðaaxǫ́pe*
Ø-Ø-ðaa-xǫ́-api-ðe
P3S-A3S-by.mouth-break-PL-DECL
'he [bit it and] broke it'

(428) *hkiláaxǫpe*
Ø-Ø-hkik-ðáa-xǫ-api-ðe
P3S-A3S-REFL-by.mouth-break-PL-DECL
'he broke something for himself with his teeth'

4.6.2.5 Plain reflexive with *tǫ́pe* 'look'

Quite a bit of detail is given in this and the next two sections about *tǫ́pe* 'look', since this is a very productive and important verb in practical and ceremonial usage of the language. Another reason to take a close look at *tǫ́pe* is that this verb illustrates perhaps better than any other the complex interaction of pre-root morphemes in Osage, as we observe locative and reflexive elements and epenthesis of *ð* with this fortisizing stop-initial verb. Considering the sentences in detail gives the reader a feel for Osage morphology at work, through examination of sentences that are also especially relevant culturally.

The reflexive verb 'look at oneself' optionally has a second point of inflection to the right of the reflexive: *_hkih(_)tǫpe*; *a-ða* inflection occurs at the leftmost point, while 2S syncopating inflection optionally occurs at the rightmost point (as in (432) below). The tendency toward having two inflection points may be attributable to a reanalysis of the *ht* segment of *hkihtǫ́pe* as representing A1S inflection (see section 3.2.4.2 for inflection of *tǫ́pe* as a fortisizing stop stem). (Geminate *tt* and preaspirate *ht* are interchangeable here and are both surface reflexes of *ht*.)

(429) *hkihtǫ́pe*
hkik-tǫ́pe
REFL-look
'look at oneself'

(430) *hkihtǫ́pape*
Ø-hkik-tǫ́pe-api-ðe
A3S-REFL-look-PL-DECL
'he looked at himself'

(431) *hkihtǫ́pe ðiištą́*
hkik-tǫ́pe ðiištą́-a
REFL-look cease-IMPER
'quit looking at yourself'

(432) *ðahkíštǫpe*
Ya-hkik-Ya-tǫpe
A2S-REFL-A2S-look
'you're looking at yourself'

(433) *ahkíttǫpe*
Wa-hkik-Wa-tǫ́pe
A1S-REFL-A1S-look
'I'm looking at myself'

(434) *ąhkíttǫpe*
ąk-hkik-tǫ́pe
A1P-REFL-look
'we're looking at ourselves'

(435) *hkíttǫpa!*
hkik-tǫ́pe-a
REFL-look-IMPER
'look at yourself!'

4.6.2.6 Reflexive with locative *átǫpe* 'watch over'

The stem *áhkihtǫpe* includes the locative *á*, plus the reflexive, and is 'watch over one's own', a phrase used frequently in prayers in Osage. Often glossed instead as 'look down upon one's own', this verb refers to *Wahkǫ́ta* looking down upon his people, certainly an extended meaning of reflexive. This is an instance of reflexive referring rather unexpectedly to one's own people instead of oneself, a semantic role which suus *kik* generally fills in other verbs.

In (436) we see the portmanteau *wi* preceding the reflexive element, and the locative *á* preceding the inflection.

(436) *áwihkittǫpe mįkše*
á-wi-hkik-tǫpe *mįkše*
LOC-P2S<A1S-REFL-look 1S.CONT
'I will look down upon you [plural]; I'm looking after you'

Normally A1P *ąk* appears leftward of the entire stem, including prefixes *o* and *á*, but with this verb, the full form *ąk* does not occur left of the *á* prefix, for reasons that are unclear. This gives rise to the sequence *á-ąk* (simplified to *ą́-ą*) in (437). Normal patterns of inflection would give *ąkáðihkihtǫpe* instead of the form seen in this example.

(437) *ą́ąðihkihtǫpe hta ąðįkšé*
ąk-á-ði-hkik-tǫpe *hta* *ąðįkšé*
A1P-LOC-P2S-REFL-look FUT 1D.CONT
'we're going to look after you'

Epenthetic *ð* with *áhkihtǫpe*. Object pronominal 'us' P1P (*wa*) precedes the *á* prefix in this verb—surprisingly, since normally P1P *wa* would follow locative *á* (see table 4.1). The locative *á* does not undergo *wa*-Metathesis (for which, see section 3.4.1.1). The *wa-á* sequence thus formed supplies the context for optional *ð* epenthesis: *wa-á* → *wa-ðá* (discussed in section 2.3.2.4). The *ð* appearing in the context *wa*__*á* , then, is not A2S inflection *ða*; this is very clear in the imperative example (438) since the imperative is never inflected for subject.

(438) *waðáhkittǫpa*
wa-ð-á-hkik-tǫ́pe-a
P1D-EPð-LOC-REFL-look-IMPER
'look down on us'

The epenthetic nature of *ð* is also seen in (439), in an A3S form.

(439) *waðáhkihtǫpe apai*
wa-ð-á-hkik-tǫpe apa-ðe
P1P-EPð-LOC-REFL-look 3.CONT-DECL
'he is looking over us, watching over us'

In (440) and (441) the subordinated verb *á_hki_htǫpe* is inflected both at the first point of inflection (with regular A2S *ða*) and at the second point of inflection (with syncopating A2S *š*). The *ð* of A2S *ða*, however, is probably in fact elided in these examples; the *ð* that appears is probably the epenthetic *ð* called for in the context *wa__á*. That is, it is likely that the sequence *wa-á-ða-hkik* receives an epenthetic *ð* to become *waðáðahkik*, then one of the two *ða* syllables is deleted.

(440) *waðáhkištǫpapi hkǫ́bra*
wa-ð-á-Ya-hkik-Ya-tǫpe-api Wa-kǫ́-Wa-ða
P1P-EPð-LOC-A2S-REFL-A2S-look-PL A1S-PREV-A1S-want
'I want you to look down upon us'

(441) *waaðáhkištǫ́papi húðe hkǫ́bra*
wa-ð-á-Ya-hkik-Ya-tǫ́pe-api hú-ðe
P1P-EPð-LOC-A2S-REFL-A2S-look-PL come.here-CAU
Wa-kǫ-Wa-ða
A1S-PREV-A1S-want
'I want you to [come and] look down upon us'

Example (442) shows another version of the above sentences, this time with the subordinate verb perhaps uninflected for subject but inflected for object (*wa...api*). Again the epenthetic *ð* appears:

(442) *waðáhkihtǫpapi hkǫ́bra*
wa-ð-á-hkik-tǫpe-api Wa-kǫ́-Wa-ða
P1P-EPð-LOC-REFL-look-PL A1S-PREV-A1S-want
'I want you to watch over us; I want you to look down upon us'

Occasionally this *ð*-Epenthesis fails to apply, as in the next two examples. (Note also the change of *tǫ́pe* to *tǫ́pa*, via application of the V1-V2 Rule.)

(443) *waáhkittǫpapi húða*
wa-á-hkik-tǫ́pe-api húðe-a
P1P-LOC-REFL-look-PL come.here-IMPER
'come and look down upon us'

(444) *įhtáci wahkǫ́ta akxa waáhkittǫpe hta akxai*
įhtáci wahkǫ́ta akxa wa-á-Ø-hkik-tǫpe hta akxa-ðe
father god SUBJ P1P-LOC-A3S-REFL-look FUT 3.CONT-DECL
'God will look down upon us'

That *ð*-Epenthesis is optional is further confirmed by (445), which is an imperative (and thus cannot contain A2S *ða*); *ð*-Epenthesis has not occurred.

(445) *waáhkittǫpapi*
wa-á-hkik-tǫpe-a-api
P1P-LOC-REFL-look-IMPER-PL
'look down upon us'

4.6.2.7 Locative reflexive *áhkihtǫpe* 'watch out for oneself'

Moving away from the suuslike interpretation of reflexive *áhkihtǫpe* seen above ('watch over one's own'), in this section a semantically truer reflexive interpretation 'oneself' (corresponding to the object of the non-reflexive verb) is examined. This locative reflexive, *áhkihtǫpe* 'watch out for oneself' (with both locative *á* and the reflexive *hkik*), is a common Osage admonition.

(446) *áhkihtǫpe*
á-hkik-tǫ́pe
LOC-REFL-watch
'watch out for yourself/oneself'

(447) *taapóska ščée hta ðąišé tą áhkihtǫ́pa ði*
taapóska Ya-ðée hta ðąišé tą á-hkik-tǫ́pe-a ði
school A2S-go FUT 2S.CONT when LOC-REFL-look-IMPER 2S.PRON
'when you're going off to school, take care of yourself'

(448) *áhkihtǫ́papi!*
á-hkik-tǫ́pe-a-api
LOC-REFL-look-IMPER-PL
'you all take care of yourselves!'

4.6.3 Reciprocal *hkik*

The meaning of the *hkik* reciprocal includes 'each other, for each other'. Phonotactic behavior is identical to that of reflexive cases seen in section 4.6.2. The semantics of reciprocal *hkik* is straightforward in many instances.

(449) *haxį hkik?upe*[37]
haxį Ø-hkik-k?u-api-ðe
blanket A3P-RECIP-give-PL-DECL
'they gave each other blankets'

The next two examples are reciprocals based on *ǫ́ðe* 'toss, throw away'.

(450) *_hkíǫðe*
hkik-ǫ́-ðe
RECIP-PREV-toss
'throw each other away; separate, separation, divorce'

(451) *ąhkiǫ́ðe ąðe*
ą-hkik-ǫ́-ðe ąðe
A1P-RECIP-PREV-toss 1D.CONT
'we're separated; we're divorced'

A reciprocal based on *íiðe* 'see' appears in (452).

(452) *wéehkile*
wa-ii-hkik-ðe
VAL-PREV-RECIP-see
'a visit' (lit., 'a means to see each other')

(In this form, *kð* has become *l*. Not historically a *ð* stem, *íiðe* has been lexicalized as a reflexive *ð* stem by speakers in this example. On the other hand, in the case of the reciprocal verb *iihkiðe* 'see each other' without valence reducer *wa*, no such lexicalization has taken place and *l* does not appear.)

In addition to the normal reciprocals, there are super reciprocals, which employ two contiguous *hkik* prefixes; for example, *ohkíhkie* (*o-hkik-hkik-íe*) 'converse, talk to each other'. Also to be noted are bleached reciprocals, which have reciprocal morphology but are similar semantically to a simple dative; for example, *óhkíǫðe* means 'divorce a person' rather than 'divorce each other'. In the rest of this subsection we discuss these special cases, super and bleached.

4.6.3.1 Super reciprocals

Occasionally the reciprocal and plural nature of the object reference is emphasized in an iconic fashion by use of two *hkik* morphemes, giving the super reciprocal. The verb in (453) is *o_hkíe* 'converse with, talk to' with an extra *hkik* reciprocal. (The injunctive *htai* contributes the sense 'more than two persons', but is otherwise not significant here.)

[37] Before the ejective *k?*, the final *k* of *hkik* vanishes and has no effect on *k?*.

(453) *ąkóhkihkiə htái*
ąk-o-hkik-hkík-i-e *htái*
A1P-LOC-RECIP-RECIP-PREV-speak INJ.PL
'let's talk to each other [more than two persons]'

Another verb based on *íe* 'speak' is *í_hkie* 'speak in a certain language to each other', as in 'speak French to each other'. This verb appears in (454) in a super reciprocal sentence.

(454) *wažáže íe anáhkihkie hce*
wažáže í-e *ąk-í-hkik-hkík-ie* *hce*
Osage PREV-speak A1P-PREV-RECIP-RECIP-speak INJ.DUAL
'let's talk Osage to each other [two persons only]'

Compare the super reciprocal in (455), containing two *hkik* reciprocals, with the equivalent simple reciprocal in (456) with only one *hkik*. No difference of meaning is detected, other than an emphasis on reciprocity in the super reciprocal. (Geminate *tt* is equivalent to preaspirate *ht*.)

(455) *áhkíhkittǫpe*
á-hkik-hkik-tǫ́pe
LOC-RECIP-RECIP-watch
'watch out for each other'

(456) *áhkihtǫpa pai*
á-hkik-tǫpe *paðe*
LOC-RECIP-look IMPER.CONT
'you all [be] watch[ing] each other, take/taking care of each other'

4.6.3.2 Bleached reciprocals

The reciprocal *hkik* bleaches toward unidirectional transitivity as in 'X acts on Y', rather than true reciprocity where 'X acts on Y and Y acts on X'.

As originally suggested by Roger Higgins (p.c. 1983), the bleached reciprocal sense is similar to the case of English where the two sentences *he and she are talking to/with each other* and *he is talking with her* form a sort of analogical blend: *he is talking to each other with her*. This is reminiscent of the relation between *he and she are friends (with each other)* and *she is friends with him* (using plural *friends*). There are even closer parallels in German.

In (457) the reciprocal expression *hkíži* 'be angry with each other' is weakened to 'be angry with [another]'.

(457) *ókaaɣéįki akxa níhka hkíži kǫ́ða įkíape*
o-káaɣe-ðįké akxa níhka Ø-Ø-hkik-ži
LOC-make/do-NEG SUBJ man P3S-A3S-RECIP-angry.with
Ø-kǫ́-Ø-ða ðįké-api-ðe
A3S-PREV-A3S-want NEG-PL-DECL
'Useless didn't want the man to be mad at him'

Note that the subject in (457), the animal named 'Useless', appears as subject of the main (*kǫ́ða* 'want') clause, while the 'man' and the (bleached) reciprocal *hkíži* 'be angry with' appear in the embedded clause. A 2S form of this bleached reciprocal is:

(458) *ąðáhkiži*
i-ą-Ya-hkik-ži
PREV-P1S-A2S-REFL-angry
'you're mad at me'

o_hkíe 'converse', as in the following example, is also a bleached reciprocal. Semantic reciprocity is present to some extent ('converse with someone'), but the verb takes singular subjects: for instance, A1S is *o-a-hkie* or *owáhkie* (or *awáhkie*, with vowel harmony) 'I spoke/talked with her, I conversed with her'.

(459) *ohkíe šǫ́ akxai . . .*
o-Ø-hkik-íe šǫ akxa-ðe
LOC-A3S-RECIP-talk while 3.CONT-DECL
'while he was talking [to someone] . . .'

4.6.4 Suus

All verbs with the suus prefix *kik* 'subject's own [persons or things]' (added before the inflectable initial of the verb) take regular agent inflection to the left of *kik*, whether the verb without *kik* is regular or syncopating. By the Suus Rule given in this section, verbs with *ð* inflectable initial to which *kik* is added will now have a stem beginning with *l* (see center column of table 4.18). Other verbs will have the initial *k* of suus *kik* as their new inflectable initial (as in the left column of the table).

TABLE 4.18. AGENT INFLECTION WITH SUUS *KIK*

	BEFORE PLAIN STOP STEMS	INCORPORATING *ð* INFLECTABLE INITIAL	BEFORE ALL OTHER INFLECTABLE INITIALS
1S	*akih*	*al*	*aki*
2S/P	*ðakih*	*ðal*	*ðaki*
3S/P	*kih*	*l*	*ki*
1D/P	*ąkih*	*ąl*	*ąki*

The Suus Rule for the different stems can be summarized as follows:

Part A: When suus *kik* is added at the point of inflection preceding a verb with *ð* inflectable initial, the effect is that *kik* disappears and the *ð* inflectable initial is replaced with *l*:

kik ð → l

Part B: Preceding plain (that is, lenis) stop stems, the final *k* of *kik* has the same preaspirating or fortisizing effect on the following stop as seen in the reflexive:

kik → kih / _p,t,k

Part C: Otherwise, *kik* remains but the final *k* of *kik* elides:

kik → ki

The effects of parts B and C of the Suus Rule are examined in sections 4.6.4.1–4.6.4.2, and those of part A in section 4.6.4.3. Section 4.6.4.4 treats interaction of suus with locative prefixes, and section 4.6.4.5 a semantically more complex type of suus; section 4.6.4.6 briefly notes an instance of lexicalization of the suus prefix.

4.6.4.1 The Suus Rule with non-*ð*-stem verbs

Verbs with plain stops as inflectable initial convert those stops to preaspirated ones by part B of the Suus Rule. Pertinent examples can be seen in (461)–(462), showing suus forms of verb roots with plain stops as the inflectable initial (*t*, *k*, and *p*, respectively): *_kihtǫpe* 'look at subject's own'; *_kihkáaɣe* 'make up subject's own'; *í_kihpahǫ* 'recognize/know as subject's own'.

(460) *wacúa skúe akíhtoį hce*

wacúe skúðe Wa-kik-tǫ́pe hce
bread sweet A1S-SUU-look INJ
'let me look at my cake'

(461) *waðíla kihkáaɣe akxai*
waðíla Ø-kik-káaɣe akxa-ðe
mind A3P-SUU-make 3.CONT-DECL
'they made their own mind up'

(462) *íkihpahǫ akxai*
í-Ø-Ø-kik-pahǫ akxa-ðe
PREV-P3S-A3S-SUU-know 3.CONT-DECL
'he recognizes him as a relative [i.e., as his own]'

The next example shows the suus form of a nonsyncopating stem (where the base *kˀú* 'give' has neither a lenis stop like *p*, *t*, *k* nor a *ð* as its initial segment): *_kikˀu* 'give to subject's own'. By part C of the Suus Rule, the inflectable initial of the base is unaffected, while the final *k* of the suus prefix is deleted.

(463) *hpáaži įįhǫ́ akxa kíkˀupe*
hpáaži iihǫ́ akxa Ø-Ø-kik-kˀú-api-ðe
baby mother SUBJ P3S-A3S-SUU-PL-DECL
'the mother gave it to [her] baby'

With *kˀú* 'give', the suus element refers to the recipient (the primary object) in all examples in the corpus—'give to subject's own people'. (With other verbs, suus *kik* may refer to subject's own inanimate things, as in numerous examples above and below. Consequently, the preference or requirement that suus with *kˀú* refer to the recipient cannot be due to a ban on using suus for inanimate possessions.) Further examples of suus *kˀú* 'give' appear in (464)–(465). The recipient in these examples is also present in the sentence as a patient pronominal [*wa* 'them' and *ą* 'me'] , and the item given, the blanket, is also present as a noun.)

(464) *haxį waðákikˀu*
haxį́ P3P-Ya-ki-Ø-kˀú
blanket VAL-A2S-SUU-give
'you gave them [your own folks] blankets'

(465) *haxį ąðákíkˀu*
haxį́ ą-Ya-ki-kˀú
blanket P1S-A2S-SUU-give
'you gave me, your relative, a blanket'

4.6.4.2 Suus with *c* inflectable initial

Although the *c* of *océ* 'look for' is from underlying *t* (see chapter 2), part B of the Suus Rule does not affect the *c* as it would a *t* in the same configuration; this verb comes under Part C of the Suus Rule.

(466) *okíce*
o-ki-ce
PREV-SUU-look.for
'search for one's own'

A word of caution is in order when an attempt is made to identify suus sentences in Osage. In certain sets, there is ambiguity as to whether a surface *ki* is a suus *kik* 'subject's own', a dative *ki* 'for another' or an inceptive *ki* 'anew, again'. The form *okíce* in (466) is one of these where the three interpretations are possible: besides suus *o-_kik-ce* 'search for one's own', it could also be dative *o-_ki-ce* 'search for [something] for another', or inceptive *o-_ki-ce* 'search for [something] again'.

4.6.4.3 Suus *kik* with *ð*-stems

Examples in this section exhibit the common suus *l* formation that emerges with *ð* stems, where part A of the Suus Rule applies: *kð* becomes *l*, while *ki* disappears. The resulting verbs are given regular (*a-ða*) agent inflection, as can be seen in several of the examples below. In these examples, the suus element refers to the direct object (e.g., *įcé* 'face') and again identifies the object as subject's own.

(467) *įcé lúuža!*
įcé kik-ðuužá-a
face SUU-wash-IMPER
'wash your own face!'

(468) *įcé alúuža*
įcé Wa-kik-ðuužá
face A1S-SUU-wash
'I washed my face'

(469) *įcé alúužamąží*
įcé Wa-kik-ðuužá-maži
face A1S-SUU-wash-1S.NEG
'I didn't wash my face'

(470) *įcé ðalúuža?*
įcé Ya-kik-ðuužá
face A2S-SUU-wash
'did you wash your face?'

(471) *įcé lúužape*
įcé Ø-kik-ðuužá-api-ðe
face A3S-SUU-wash-PL-DECL
'he washed his face'

(472) *įcé ąlúužape*
įcé ąk-kik-ðuužá-api-ðe
face A1P-SUU-wash-PL-DECL
'we washed our faces'

Examples (473) and (474) illustrate the suus derivative of *ðiiški* 'launder'.

(473) *líiški*
kik-ðiiškí
SUU-launder
'launder subject's own'

(474) *wéhkilai ąlíškipe*
wéhkilai ą-kik-ðiiškí-api-ðe
clothes A1P-SUU-wash-PL-DECL
'we washed our clothes'

From the same stem are formed also a reflexive *hkilíiški* 'launder for oneself' (taking regular inflection); a valence-reduced form *waðíiški* 'do laundry'; a dative *kiðíiški* 'wash for another'; and an inceptive 'rewash', identical in form to the dative (see section 4.6.4.5).

Another suus verb, and one which is especially important culturally, is 'name subject's own', from *ðaacé* 'name', as in (476)–(477). In these suus forms, *kik* precedes *ðaa* 'by mouth', an inner instrumental.

(475) *táatą ðaatáape?*
táatą Ø-Ø-ðaacé-api-ðe
what P3S-A3P-name-PL-DECL
'what does one call it?' (lit., 'what did they name it?')

(476) *láace*
kik-ðaacé
SUU-name
'name subject's own'

(477) *táatą laatáape?*
táatą Ø-Ø-kik-ðaacé-api-ðe
what P3S-A3P-SUU-name-PL-DECL
'what did they name him [their relative]?'

Another suus verb where there is interaction of suus with instrumental *ðaa* 'by mouth' is found in (478):

(478) *híi láaxǫpe*
híi kik-ðaa-xǫ́-api-ðe
tooth SUU-by.mouth-break-PL-DECL
'he broke a tooth'

Example (479) shows the suus version of *ðiixǫ́* 'break' (formed from the same root, *xǫ́* 'break', combined with another inner instrumental *ðuu/ðii* 'by hand').

(479) *líixǫ*
kik-ðii-xǫ́
SUU-by.hand-break
'break [as parts of one's body]'

4.6.4.4 Suus with *á* locative

Suus *kik* also combines with other morphological elements such as the *á* locative. In (480), we see the suus form of *tǫ́pe* 'look'. In (481), locative *á* is added to *tǫ́pe*, creating *á_tǫpe* 'watch over; look out for', and the suus prefix is then added, giving *á_kihtǫpe* 'look out for subject's own'. ('That child' in (481) refers to the hearer's own child, a relative. The sentence is equivalent to 'watch your child'; the translation is the speaker's. The sentence is imperative, so its subject is understood rather than overtly marked by a second person prefix.)

(480) *kíttǫpa ði*
kik-tǫpe-a ði
SUU-look-IMPER 2S.PRON
'you look at your own things'

(481) *ákihtǫpe*
á-ki-tǫ́pe
LOC-SUU-look
'watch that child!' (lit., 'watch your own!')

The same suus verb is seen in the next example, with an epenthetic *ð* between the patient *wa* 'us' and the inherently accented locative *á* of the verb stem.

(482) *waaðákihtǫpapi*
wa-á-kik-tǫ́pe-a-api
P1P-LOC-SUUS-look-IMPER-PL
'look down upon us [your own]'[38]

[38] Confusion arises with this form, as a very similar (but nonpreaspirated) dative (*ki*) form also frequently occurs, with almost the same meaning as above (but minus 'your own'):

waaðákitǫpapi
wa-ð-á-ki-tǫpe-a-api
P1P-EPð-LOC-DAT-look-IMPER-PL
'look down upon us'

4.6.4.5 Interrupted suus and inceptive *ki* forms

The verb *ðuwį́* 'buy' has a plain suus version, *lúwį*, which is often loosely glossed as 'buy back'—that is, 'X buys something of X's own' that presumably X previously sold or had stolen or taken away, as in example (483).

(483) *áluwį*
Ø-a-kik-ðuwį́
P3S-A1S-SUU-buy
'I bought it back and it belonged to me' (lit., 'I bought my own')

Similarly, the suus form of *mą_ðǫ́* 'steal', *mąlǫ́*, can be translated 'steal subject's own, steal back'.

Besides the plain suus form *lúwį* 'buy one's own', *ðuwį́* 'buy' also forms an inceptive with a prefix *ki*, conveniently glossable as 'buy back'. (Speakers gloss suus and inceptive forms of this stem in very similar or identical ways, although as will be seen below their morphology differs.)

Yet another related form based on *ðuwį́* is what I will call the "interrupted suus" form. Interrupted suus verbs are those in which the suus element refers to an oblique benefactive argument of the verb, expressed in English as 'for subject's own people'.

Both interrupted suus verbs and the inceptive are particularly interesting because they have two points of inflection, one before and one after the prefix *ki(k)*. An overt agent prefix after *kik* prevents (interrupts) the change of *kð* to *l* (which is why I use the term "interrupted suus"). These categories are displayed in table 4.19.

TABLE 4.19. INTERRUPTED SUUS AND INCEPTIVE FORMS

CATEGORY	GLOSS	UNDERLYING FORM	SURFACE FORM
SUUS	'buy subject's own'	*_kik-ðuwį́*	*_lúwį*
INTERRUPTED SUUS (BENEFACTIVE)	'buy for subject's own'	*_kik_ðuwį́*	*_ki_ðuwį*
INCEPTIVE	'buy again' (i.e., 'buy back what one had or sold before'	*_ki_ðuwį́*	*_ki_ðuwį*

The examples below exemplify the categories mentioned in the table. The first two examples, (484) and (485), show the benefactive interrupted suus.

(484) *aakíbruwį*
Wa-kik-Wa-ðuwį́
A1S-SUU-A1S-buy
'I bought it for them [my relatives]'

(485) *ðakíšcuwį*
Ya-kik-Ya-ðuwį́
A2S-SUU-A2S-buy
'you bought it for them, your family'

The next two examples (homophonous with the first two) are inceptive:

(486) *aakíbruwį*
Wa-ki-Wa-ðuwį́
A1S-INC-A1S-buy
'I bought it back'

(487) *ðakíšcuwį*
Ya-ki-Ya-ðuwį́
A2S-INC-A2S-buy
'you bought it back'

The following example is neither suus nor inceptive, but merely a valence-reduced verison of the dative (with prefix *ki*) of *ðuuwį́*.

(488) *wakíðuwį*
wa-ki-ðuwį́-a
VAL-DAT-buy-IMPER
'buy something for them [not family]'

This example contrasts with the following one (489), which is the interrupted (benefactive) suus version ('buy for subject's own family'). Example (489), being imperative, has no overt agent prefix at the second point of inflection to prevent *kik-ð* from becoming *l* by the Suus Rule. This lack of an agent prefix on the stem *lúwį* makes the example appear to be merely suus, but it is in fact interrupted suus *_kik_ðúwį*.

(489) *wáluwį*
wa-kik-ðuwį
P3P-SUU-buy
'buy it for them [they are family]'

The plain suus form appears in (490), where the suus reference is to the direct object, what is bought (he bought his own item), and not to a family member recipient as is the case with the interrupted suus.

(490) *lúwįpe*
Ø-Ø-kik-ðuwį
P3S-P3S-SUU-buy
'he bought it back' (lit., 'he bought it, his own item')

4.6.4.6 Lexicalized suus

The verb *_ki_kaaɣe* 'make subject's own' has lexicalized the suus *ki* as part of the stem, retaining a subject inflection point rightward of *ki*.

(491) *žįkážį wíhta wáðohta níhkašika waðákiškaaɣe hkǫ́bra*
žįkážį *wíhta* *wáðohta* *níhkašika* *wa-Ya-ki-Ya-kaaɣe*
children mine straight person P3P-A2S-SUU-A2S-make
Wa-kǫ́-Wa-ða
A1S-PREV-A1S-want
'I want you to make my children [your relatives] proper people'

4.6.5 Dative

Dative *ki* connotes variously 'to another; for another; in another's place; affecting another's property or another's self; in presence of another; involving another' (or 'others'). It occurs in both active transitive and active intransitive verbs, and also in certain statives (see sections 4.6.5.1–4.6.5.2).

In terms of form, various types of *ki* verbs can be recognized. In a few verbs where *ki* signals 'in the presence of another', *ki* is placed within the preverb (that is, preceding agent and patient inflection), and is present throughout the paradigm. Examples include *éki_ǫ* 'do in the presence of others' and *éki_e* 'speak in the presence of others'; see section 4.6.5.6.

In some other verbs, *ki* has been incorporated into the stem (following agent and patient inflection), and again appears with all persons and numbers in the paradigm (section 4.6.5.6). Examples include *kíðe* 'let, allow another to do something' (section 4.2.4), *kšíðe* 'have someone do something for his/her own benefit (section 4.2.3), and *kšíɣe* 'make for another'.

The normal paradigm of dative *ki*, however, has the peculiarity that *ki* fails to appear in all persons and numbers. Whenever an overt (i.e., non-third-person-singular) agent or patient prefix appears, *ki* is suppressed. In these cases, because of the underlying presence of *ki*, accent generally falls on the agent or patient prefix. Agent and patient paradigms of normal *ki* verbs are shown in tables 4.20 and 4.21. Note that the regular (*a*, *ða*) forms of agent inflection appear.

When added to syncopating stems, dative *ki* has the peculiarity of inducing double 1S and 2S agent inflection: first a regular (but stressed) agent prefix, and then a contracted agent prefix of the appropriate sort for whatever type of syncopating stem it is. Examples that appear below include *kíðuwį* 'buy for another' (A1S *ábruwį* 'I bought it for him'), discussed in section 4.6.5.3, and *kípą* 'invite another' (P1S + A2S *ąðáašpą* 'you invite me'), discussed in section 4.6.5.4. When dative *ki* is overt (i.e., with third person agent and patient), it has no effect on the initial consonant of the following stem.

TABLE 4.20. AGENT INFLECTION WITH DATIVE *ki*

	UNDERLYING FORM		SURFACE FORM
1S	*a* + *ki* + verb	→	*á* + verb
2S/P	*ða* + *ki* + verb	→	*ðá* + verb
3S/P	*Ø* + *ki* + verb	→	*kí* + verb
1D/P	*ąk* + *ki* + verb	→	*ąk* + verb

TABLE 4.21. PATIENT INFLECTION WITH DATIVE *ki*

	UNDERLYING FORM		SURFACE FORM
1S	*ą* + *ki* + verb	→	*ą́* + verb
2S/P	*ði* + *ki* + verb	→	*ðí* + verb
3S	*Ø* + *ki* + verb	→	*kí* + verb
1D/P	*wa* + *ki* + verb	→	*wá* + verb
3P	*wa* ~ *Ø* + *ki* + verb	→	*wa* + verb ~ *ki* + verb

It is worth noting that inceptive *ki*, unlike dative *ki*, retains overt *ki* in all persons and numbers.

Semantically, dative *ki* verbs can be classified, informally and not exhaustively, into several types. These include:

- A benefactive sense, 'for another'. These can be compared with the benefactive use of locative *á* (section 4.6.5.3).

- Dative of interest or ownership; these are *ki* verbs (some active transitive, some stative intransitive) whose patient corresponds to the possessor of the same verb without *ki*. Examples include the stative *kixǫ́* 'have one's own break' and the active *kiðiixǫ* 'break another's' (section 4.6.5.2). "Super datives" such as *kíkǫða* 'want from another what is another's' (section 4.6.5.5) also belong here.

- Statives with experiencer arguments, namely the 'enjoy' type verbs discussed in section 4.6.5.1. These use the standard *ki* patient paradigm to express the experiencer. (It is not clear whether the experiencer-patient should be thought of as the subject or the object of these verbs; we will not try to debate this question here.)
- Looser involvement of another: 'in the presence of another, involving another', etc.

4.6.5.1 *ki* with stative verbs

Dative *ki* may be seen in an adjectivelike verb *kíwalį* 'be stingy; be excessively fond of to the point of not wanting to share with others; be attached to' in (492)–(494). (*walį* does not appear to occur on its own.)

(492) *ðíwalį nįkšé*
ði-kíwalį nįkšé
P2S-stingy 2S.CONT
'you're stingy with it'

(493) *kíwalį*
'he's stingy with it'

(494) *wáwalį*
wa-kíwalį
P3P-stingy
'they're stingy'

A general class of stative verbs with *ki* is that loosely referred to here as the 'enjoy' class; in addition to *kíwalį* 'stingy', it includes three verbs that are semantically similar to 'enjoy'. Dative semantics ('for another') is not present in these 'enjoy' verbs. To represent the activity, person, or thing, such as a food, that is enjoyed, all three verbs can take the citation (uninflected) form of a verb which describes an activity, an inflected form of such a verb, or a noun. Patient pronominals represent the experiencer of the emotion of enjoyment (thus these are stative verbs). It might seem tempting to label the thing enjoyed as subject (reminiscent of *gustar* in Spanish), but this is demonstrably not correct; the subject marker (*akxa* or *apa*) cannot be employed to mark that argument as subject, but where the noun experiencer appears in the sentence, it is often marked with a subject marker. These *ki* verbs are best classified as *ki* statives, with the thing enjoyed being the object, and the animate experiencer being the semantic subject, optionally marked with the subject marker if present as a noun. The meanings of these three verbs can be characterized in a very informal fashion, as in the examples below, where typical glosses in sentences are given, but no very clear semantic distinctions can be made based on the data at hand. (Perhaps cognates in related languages will help to draw a distinction.)

(495) *kíðalį*
'like, love to do something'

(496) *kíhǫǫ*
'really love to do something; be pleased'

(497) *kízo*
'have fun doing something; be fun; X is fun [where X may be an activity described by a verb]'

Examples of the three verbs follow, showing their inflection. (Pronominal prefixes are stressed, as is expected for *ki* verbs; see the introduction to section 4.6.5.) Of these verbs, *kíðalį* 'enjoy, like, love' has a completely normal paradigm of patient *ki* inflection. (Note that third person plural varies somewhat in a pattern not clearly understood at this point, and may have *ki* instead of the expected P3P prefix *wa*.)

(498) *žįkóhkihą apa waachí watǫ́į kíðalį apai*
žįkóhkihą apa waachí watǫ́pe Ø-ki-ðalį apa-ðe
grandchild SUBJ dances watching P3P-DAT-like 3.CONT-DECL
'your grandchildren are enjoying watching the dances'[39]

(499) *žąąnížį ðaaché ą́ðalį*
žąąnížį ðaaché ą-ki-ðalį
candy eat P1S-DAT-enjoy
'I enjoy eating candy'[40]

(500) *waðáahtą kíðalįpe*
wa-ðaahtą Ø-ki-ðalį-api-ðe
VAL-drink P3S-DAT-enjoy-PL-DECL
'he really likes to drink'

(501) *wižįke akxa waðáahtą kíðalįpe*
wižįke akxa wa-ðaahtą́ Ø-ki-ðalį-api-ðe
Sonny SUBJ VAL-drink P3S-DAT-enjoy-PL-DECL
'Sonny really likes to drink'[41]

The paradigm of *kíhǫǫ* 'like, enjoy, love' follows a stative *ki* pattern except for 2S, where the expected stative form *ðíhǫǫ* is occasionally

[39] This sentence was also offered without the subject marker *apa*.

[40] The embedded verb is optionally inflected, and the nominalizer *che* may be used as well: *žąąnížį bráache che ą́ðalį* [candy I.eat NOM I.enjoy].

[41] It is ungrammatical to use a subject marker on the thing liked: ***waðáahtą akxa kíðalįpe* ('he likes to drink').

replaced by active *ðáhǫǫ*. The 3P form in the *wa* variant (*wáhǫǫ*) has not emerged in the data, but rather *kíhǫǫ* is found.[42] The citation form of this verb is sometimes given as *hǫǫ*.[43]

(502) *wižįke akxa waðáahtą kíhǫǫ ape*
wižįke akxa wa-ðaahtą́ Ø-ki-hǫǫ-api-ðe
Sonny SUBJ VAL-drink P3S-DAT-like-PL-DECL
'Sonny really loves to drink'

(503) *waðáahtą kíhǫǫpe*
wa-ðaahtą́ Ø-ki-hǫǫ-api-ðe
VAL-drink P3S-DAT-love-PL-DECL
'he really loves to drink'

(504) *žįkážį watxą́ kíhǫǫ*
žįkážį watxą́ Ø-ki-hǫǫ
children squash P3P-DAT-enjoy
'those kids like squash'

(505) *žąąníe ą́hǫǫ*
žąąníe ą́-ki-hǫǫ
candy P1S-DAT-enjoy
'I like candy'

The paradigm of *kízo* 'enjoy, like, be happy' likewise follows the normal stative *ki* pattern. On the surface, this verb tends to have long vowels for the patient prefixes and *ki*: 1S *ą́ązo*, 2S *ðíizo*, 3S *kíizo*, 1P *wáazo*, 3P *kíizo*. For this verb, the 3P form may also be *wáazo*, as seen in (514) below.

(506) *ą́ązo*
ą-ki-zo
P1S-DAT-enjoy
'I enjoy [it]'

(507) *óohǫ ðíizo paašé?*
wa-oohǫ́ ði-ki-zo paašé
VAL-cook P2S-DAT-enjoy 2P.CONT
'are you enjoying the cooking?'

(508) *žįkóhkiha ðíizo paašé?*
žįkóhkiha ði-ki-zo paašé?
grandchildren P2S-DAT-enjoy 2P.CONT
'are you all enjoying your grandchildren?'

[42] The 1P form was first given by a speaker with active inflection *ąkáhǫǫ*, but later changed by the same speaker to *wáhǫǫ*.

[43] *hǫ́ǫži* 'bad', presumably from *hǫ́ǫ* plus *aži* 'negative', is likely a related form.

(509) *žąąníe kízo akxai*
žąąníe *Ø-ki-zo* *akxa-ðe*
sugar/candy P3S-DAT-enjoy 3.CONT-DECL
'he's enjoying the candy'

(510) *ą́ązomąžį́ mį́kšé*
ą-ki-zo-maží *mį́kšé*
P1S-DAT-enjoy-1S.NEG 1S.CONT
'I'm sad'

(511) *waðíhice kíizǫpe*
wa-ðiihíce *Ø-ki-zo-api-ðe*
VAL-tease P3S-DAT-enjoy-PL-DECL
'he likes to tease'

(512) *kíizo ðį́kí apai*
Ø-ki-zo *ðį́ké* *apa-ðe*
P3P-DAT-enjoy NEG 3.CONT-DECL
'they didn't enjoy it'

One does find *wa* as P3P, too, for this verb *kízo*, where as a rule *ki* signals proximate/present and *wa* signals obviative/absent. In informal terms, the proximate element is the one which is at hand, either in the pragmatic context or in the discourse, while the obviative element is more distant, either pragmatically or discursively. In (513) the 3P form uses *ki*, not *wa*, because the subject 'they' is dancing (which in the context of the Osage dances is rather like being on stage before an audience) and the speaker of the sentence is part of the audience. Additionally, the experiencer in (513) is also understood as the subject of the embedded verb 'dance'.

(513) *waachí kíizo apai*
waa-Ø-chí *Ø-ki-zo* *apa-ðe*
PREV-A3P-dance P3P-DAT-enjoy 3.CONT-DECL
'they're dancing and they're enjoying it; they are enjoying dancing'

However, when the subject 'they' is sitting (and therefore just a part of the audience and less a focal point than the dancers), the 3P form must be *wa*, as in (514). In this example, it should also be noted that the experiencer of *wáazo* is not understood as the subject of 'dance'.

(514) *waachí wáazo apai*
waachí *wa-ki-zo* *apa-ðe*
dance P3P-DAT-enjoy 3.CONT-DECL
'they're just watching the dance and they're enjoying it; they are enjoying the dance'

The P1P form does not vary, and is the expected *wa*, regardless of whether the subject is merely sitting and watching or is dancing when (515) is uttered.

(515) *waachí wáazo ąkakxai*
waachí wa-ki-zo ąkatxą́-ðe
dance P1P-DAT-enjoy 1P.CONT-DECL
'we're enjoying watching the dances'

The verb *kízo* appears in complex sentences with double embedding in (516) and (517), here as *wáazo* P1P 'fun for us'.

(516) *žįkážį toə kíðalį wakáaɣe wáazope*
žįkážį toa ki-ðálį wa-káaɣe wa-ki-zo-api-ðe
child some DAT-enjoy P3P-make P1P-DAT-enjoy-PL-DECL
'it was fun [for us] to make the children happy'

(517) *nǫ́ǫ pa íxažį iiðe wáazope*
nǫ́ǫ pa í-xa-žį ii-ðe wa-ki-zo-api-ðe
old.ones ART PREV-laugh-small PREV-see P1P-DAT-enjoy-PL-DECL
'it was fun [for us] to see the grownups smile'

4.6.5.2 Dative of interest

The verb *xǫ́* 'break' is intransitive. The dative version of *xǫ́* is also stative and intransitive. In (518), it appears with a noun 'arm' and a second argument seen in the verb as P1S *ą* 'me' in the sense 'unto me [the] arm broke'.

(518) *áa ą́xǫpe*
áa ą-Ø-ki-xǫ-api-ðe
arm P1S-A3S-DAT-break-PL-DECL
'my arm broke' (lit., 'arm broke unto me')

This structure is called the dative of interest, and denotes that the dative argument possesses the object (e.g., the body part) or has an interest in the item or action expressed in the object. Examples (519)–(524) illustrate further forms of this intransitive dative of interest verb *kixǫ́* 'break off'.

(519) *áa kiixǫ́pe*
áa Ø-Ø-ki-xǫ-api-ðe
arm P3S-A3S-DAT-break-PL-DECL
'his arm broke' (lit., 'arm broke unto him')

(520) *áa ðiixǫ́pe*
áa ði-Ø-ki-xǫ-api-ðe
arm P2S-A3S-DAT-break-PL-DECL
'your arm broke' (lit., 'arm broke unto you')

In the data available to me, it is the possessor (when an overt nominal) that receives a subject marker, like *John* in the following example.

(521) *John akxa áa kiixǫ́pe*
John akxa áa Ø-Ø-ki-xǫ́-api-ðe
John SUBJ arm P3S-A3S-DAT-break-PL-DECL
'John broke his arm; John's arm broke'

The stem *xǫ́* may be transitivized by adding the instrumental prefix *ðii* 'by hand; cause', giving *ðiixǫ́* 'break [it]' (transitive). From this, too, a dative of interest may be formed, *kíðiixǫ* 'break something belonging to another [such as an arm, leg, or other body part]'. Forms of this are seen in (520) and the following examples; the patient pronominals expressing the dative argument denote the possessor of the item broken.

(522) *áa ą́ąðiixǫpe*
áa ą-Ø-ki-ðii-xǫ-api-ðe
arm P1S-A3P-DAT-by.hand-break-PL-DECL
'they broke my arm'

(523) *áa ðíðiixǫpe*
áa ði-Ø-ki-ðii-xǫ-api-ðe
arm P2S-A3P-DAT-by.hand-break-PL-DECL
'they broke your arm'

(524) *áa kíðiixǫ*
áa Ø-Ø-ki-ðii-xǫ-api-ðe
arm P3S-A3P-DAT-by.hand-break-PL-DECL
'they broke his arm'

4.6.5.3 Dative benefactive vs. locative benefactive

In a nonmorphological, semantic sense, the concept of benefactive 'for someone' is expressed in the dative *kíðuwį* 'buy for another' with the standard *ki* paradigm: *ą́ðuwį* 'buy (it) for me', *ðíðuwį* 'buy (it) for you', *kíðuwį* 'buy (it) for him/her', *wáðuwį(api)* 'buy (it) for us' (the pluralizer *api* often appears as *pi* or is omitted from P1P forms), *wáðuwį* (occasionally *kíðuwį*) 'buy (it) for them'.

Double agent inflection is seen in this paradigm: the stressed *ki* agent forms (*a, ða, ki, ą*) are followed by the typical syncopating paradigm (*br, šc, ð, ą, ð*), as is seen in table 4.22.

For P2S with A1S, the portmanteau prefix *wi* 'I–you' is used (with *ki* omitted): *wíbruwį* 'I bought it for you'.

Dative *kíðuwį* may be contrasted with the locative benefactive *áðuuwį* 'buy for the benefit of', whose agent inflection is shown in table 4.23.

Semantically, *kíðuwį* differs from *áðuwį* in that *kíðuwį* implies that the persons benefitting from the action are present, whereas *áðuwį* implies that

TABLE 4.22. DATIVE BENEFACTIVE *(ki)ðuwį* 'BUY FOR ANOTHER'

ábruwį	'I bought it for him'
ðášcuwį	'you bought it for him'
kíðuwį	'she bought it for him'
ą́ðuwį	'we bought it for him'
kíðuwį	'they bought it for him'

TABLE 4.23. LOCATIVE BENEFACTIVE *áðuwį* 'BUY FOR THE BENEFIT OF'

ábruwį	'I bought it for him'
áščuwį	'you bought it for him'
áðuwį	'she bought it for him'
ą́ąðuwį	'we bought it for him'
áðuwį	'they bought it for him'

they are absent.[44] Thus dative *kíðuwį* is used if the intended recipient is present when the sentence is spoken. A native speaker commented of *kíðuwįpe* 'they bought it for them' that this form is "used if they [the recipients] are right there together with the speaker"; otherwise, the same speaker stated that *kíðuwį* and *áðuwį* are the identical in meaning.

Dative *kíðuwi* may also be used when the recipient is not present, but is somehow focused; in contrast, the locative *áðuwį* is never used when the recipient is present. Thus a more precise characterization of the difference between dative *kíðuwį* and locative *áðuwį* may turn out to be focus, rather than presence, and the opposition of proximateness vs. obviation may prove to be the best tool for describing the differences involved: focus or proximate status call the for *ki* version, and obviation or lack of focus call for the locative *á* version of this verb. A beneficiary is likely proximate if present, but may be proximate in the conversation when absent. The obviative beneficiary is always absent.

As a concrete example, Wižį́ke is not present when (523) is uttered; if Wižį́ke is present with the speaker, the *ki* form and not the *á* form must be used.

[44] Additionally, both *kíðuwį* and *áðuwį* may be used in the representative sense, as opposed to a benefactive sense: 'she bought it for him, or in his place'.

(525) *wižįke hkǫ́ǫce toe áðuwį*
wižįke hkǫ́ǫce toe á-Ø-ðuwį-a
Wižįke apple some LOC-P3S-buy-IMPER
'buy Wižįke some apples'

For (526), Wižįke may be either present or absent:

(526) *wižįke hkǫ́ǫce toe kíðuwį*
wižįke hkǫ́ǫce toe ki-Ø-ðuwį-a
Wižįke apple some DAT-P3S-buy-IMPER
'buy Wižįke some apples'

4.6.5.4 Contrast of dative with other forms: *pą* 'call'

An interesting case of a dative verb is *kípą* 'invite; call', based on the root *pą́*. This section examines the dative as well as other forms based on this root, as a means of portraying the similarity and complexity of linguistically related forms characteristic of the Osage language. The various forms of *pą́* are of great cultural interest, too, as they describe several important tribal traditions such as ceremonial calling up of a person, inviting one's own kin and others, calling a person's name out in public, and so forth.

Four verbs based on *pą́* are examined here: a dative verb *kípą* 'invite another, call another to appear'; a valence-reduced verb *wapą́* 'invite folks'; the plain verb *pą́* 'call to; holler for'; and the suus verb *kíhpą* 'invite one's own'. Of these four verbs, only the simple stem *pą́* is singly inflected; the others (the suus, the dative, and the valence-reduced verbs) are doubly inflected.

Dative excludes family, that is, the dative does not specify 'subject's own' or 'subject's relative' in an active sentence. Thus the 3S dative *ki* cannot appear as marking 'subject's own' in the sense of suus (section 4.6.4), but signals rather '[to/for] someone else'. The dative prefix is especially scarce in surface forms since the *ki* generally appears only in 3S forms and occasionally in 3P where no overt subject or object inflection precludes its surfacing, while suus forms (table 4.18) retain *ki* in all persons.

Dative _*kí*_*pą* 'invite another'. This verb is 'invite another [who is not a relative or one's own]' and is an active verb, a fortisizing stop stem with inflectable initial *p* on the root. The dative verb is doubly inflected with active subject inflection occurring at both the underscores indicated. On the surface in third person forms, there is often a long vowel in the first syllable *kí*. Regular *a-ða* inflection for subject appears at the left point of inflection, followed by underlying dative *ki* as a sort of preverb; then syncopating inflection occurs (1S *hpą*; 2S *špa*; 3S *pą*) at the second point of inflection on the fortisizing stop stem *pą́* (as seen in the examples below). As in other doubly-inflected verbs, the A1P form receives only one agent pronominal (at the leftmost point). Likewise patient pronominals representing the object occur only at the leftmost point.

Underlying *ki* as usual does not surface when an overt agent or patient prefix is present; it only appears when agent and patient are third person (and so phonologically null). Hence it is not very clear whether this doubly inflected verb stem has the first point of inflection preceding *ki* (*_kí_pą*) or following *ki* and immediately preceding the second point of inflection (*kí_ _pą*). The former representation has been chosen because the vowels of the leftmost (*a-ða*) subjects are often (though not always) long in this verb. Regular *a-ða* subjects left of *ki* in other verbs often occur with long vowels owing to underlying *ki*; so it seems reasonable to interpret the length heard in the 1S and 2S agent forms of *kípą* as evidence that the underlying structure is *_ki_pą*.

(527) *kípą*
Ø-Ø-ki-Ø-pą
P3S-A3S-DAT-A3S-invite
'she invites him'

(528) *áhpą*
Ø-Wa-ki-Wa-pą
P3S-A1S-DAT-A1S-invite
'I invite him'

(529) *ðášpą*
Ø-Ya-ki-Ya-pą
P3S-A2S-DAT-A2S-invite
'you invite him'

(530) *ąðáašpą?*
ą-Ya-ki-Ya-pą
P1S-A2S-DAT-A2S-invite
'did you invite me?'

(531) *wíhpą*
wi-ki-Wa-pą
P2S<A1S-DAT-A1S-invite
'I invite you'

(532) *ðípą*
ði-Ø-ki-Ø-pą
P2S-A3S-DAT-A3S-invite
'he/she invites you'

(533) *ðípą akxai*
ði-Ø-ki-Ø-pą *akxa-ðe*
P2S-A3S-DAT-A3S-invite 3.CONT-DECL
'he's calling you'

(534) *ðípąpe?*
ði-Ø-ki-Ø-pą-api-ðe
P2S-A3P-DAT-A3P-invite-PL-DECL
'did they invite you?'

(535) *péeški kípąpaží*
pée-éški *Ø-ki-Ø-pą-api-aží*
who-any A3S-DAT-A3S-invite-PL-NEG
'he didn't invite anybody'

(536) *ą́ąpą ąðį́kše*
ąk-Ø-ki-pą *ąðį́kše*
A1P-P3S-DAT-invite 1D.CONT
'we [dual] invited him'

Dative *_kí_pą* 'invite' combines with the coercive causative *káaɣe* in (537)–(538); these examples nicely contrast P3P *wá* and P3S *ki*.

(537) *ée wápą káaɣa*
ée *wa-ki-pą* *Ø-káaɣe-a*
3.PRON P3P-DAT-invite P3S-make-IMPER
'make her invite them'

(538) *ée kípą káaɣa*
ée *Ø-ki-pą* *Ø-káaɣe-a*
3.PRON P3S-DAT-invite P3S-make-IMPER
'make her invite him'

In all the examples of dative *_kí_pą* 'invite' above, the invitee is not a relative. If the invitee is a relative, not the dative but the suus form *_ki(k)_pą* 'invite one's own' is used: *ąkíppą htai* 'let's invite him [our relative]' (vs. *ą́ąpą htai* 'let's invite him [a nonrelative]'). The suus form is discussed at the end of this subsection.

Valence-reduced *wa_ _pą́* 'invite folks'. This is not a dative verb, so no *ki* will be present, as can be seen in the third person form (541) below. (Note also that valence reducer *wa* would be stressed in 1S, 2S, and citation forms if it were suppressing dative *ki*.) It is a valence-reduced version of *pą́*. Again, the root is doubly inflected, as shown by the two underscores, and the valence reducer *wa* precedes the two points of inflection. The first inflection point has regular inflection and the second has syncopating inflection. Presence of the valence reducer precludes appearance of patient inflection. The meaning here is 'issue invitations to folks' (i.e., to unfocused invitees).[45]

(539) *waðášpą nįkšé?*
wa-Ya-Ya-pą nįkšé
VAL-A2S-A2S-invite 2S.CONT
'are you inviting?'

(540) *wáahpą*
wa-Wa-Wa-pą
VAL-A1S-A1S-invite
'I invited'

(541) *wapą́*
wa-Ø-Ø-pą
VAL-A3S-A3S-invite
'he invited folks'

(542) *ąwápą*
ąk-wa-pą
A1P-VAL-invite
'we invited folks'

Plain form _pą 'call, holler for somebody'. 'Call to someone; holler for somebody' is distinct from 'call someone to appear before others'. It is important and illustrative to consider the semantics and the morphological differences between these two. The plain *pą́* is is not a dative verb, and the "plain" sense, 'holler for someone', cannot be expressed using *ki*.

If the subject calls the object to appear before others or invites the object to an event where others are involved, then the dative form with underlying *ki*, as above, is used. The distinction between 'call, invite to appear' and 'holler for/at' is illustrated by (543)–(544). The first has dative *kípą*; the second has the simpler nondative verb *_pą́* which uses normal patient inflection for object rather than the *ki* paradigm. Agent inflection with this plain form follows the syncopated pattern: 1S *ppą́* or *hpą́*, 2S *špą́*, 3S *pą́*, with no preceding regular (*a-ða*) agent inflection.

(543) *wižįke kípą*
wižįke Ø-Ø-ki-Ø-pą
Wižįke P3S-A3S-DAT-A3S-call
'she's calling Wižįke [not hollering, but calling for him to appear before others]'

[45] An alternative verb is available for invitations to feasts, with *kíkxo* 'feast, dinner', as in *wikíkxo mįkšé* 'I invite you to dinner'. It will not be discussed here.

(544) *wižįke pą́ akxái*
wižįke Ø-Ø-pą akxa-ðe
Wižįke P3S-A3S-call 3.CONT-DECL
'she's hollering Wižįke's name'

('Hollering for' is used here in the sense of 'yelling his name, calling to him', not with "representative" semantics ['hollering in his place as a substitute for him'].)

Another difference between plain *_pą* 'holler, call' and dative *_kí_pą* 'call to appear; invite another' (besides presence/absence of *ki*) is the double inflection of the dative verb.

The dative surface form *kípą* means 'invite, call to appear before others'. However, there is also a homophonous inceptive form. The two glosses are seen in the following examples.

(545a) *kíipą ðie*
Ø-ki-pą ðíe
P3S-DAT-invite 2S.PRON
'call him over here'

(545b) *kiipą ðie*
Ø-ki-pą ðie
P3S-INC-invite 2S.PRON
'call him back'

For the dative gloss 'call him over here' in (545a), dative *ki* emerges, as in other *ki* datives seen above, solely in instances where no first or second person agent or patient inflection is present. Under the inceptive interpretation 'call someone back', the paradigm has *ki* in all persons and numbers: 1S *ąkípą* 'call me back', 2S *ðikípą* 'call you back', 1P *wakípą-api* 'call us back', 3P *wapąpe* 'call them back' (544). That is to say, inceptive *ki* does not disappear as does its homophone dative *ki* when pronominal agents or patients are present.

(546) *ðikípąpe*
ði-Ø-ki-pą-api-ðe
P2S-A3P-INC-call-PL-DECL
'they called you back'

Suus *_ki_pą* 'invite subject's own'. 'Invite subject's own' is a doubly inflected suus stem *_ki(k)_pą*, similar to the dative form, but with *kik* 'suus' overtly present in all surface forms. Semantically, suus *_ki(k)_pą* contrasts with the dative *_ki_pą* in that the suus form of inviting applies only to inviting one's relatives (subject's own).

(547) *akíhpą hta mįkše*
Wa-kik-Wa-pą hta mįkše
A1S-SUU-A1S-invite FUT 1S.CONT
'I will invite [my people]'

(548) *wikíhpą*
wi-kik-Wa-pą
P2S<A1S-SUU-A1S-invite
'I'm inviting you [my relative]'

(549) *ðakíšpą hta nįkše?*
Ø-Ya-kik-Ya-pą hta nįkše
P3S-A2S-SUU-A2S-invite FUT 2S.CONT
'will you invite him [your relative]?'

(550) *waachípi tą akíhpą hta mįkšé*
waa-Ø-chí-api tą Ø-Wa-kik-Wa-pą hta mįkšé
PREV-A3P-dance-PL if P3S-A1S-SUU-A1S-invite FUT 1S.CONT
'if they dance I'm going to call him [invite him, my relative]'

4.6.5.5 Super dative

The form discussed here is *kíkǫða* 'want from another' or 'want what is another's, covet' (from *kǫ́ða* 'want'). The object of the verb is possessed by someone other than the subject, namely the dative argument.[46]

(551) *oðíhtą ðíhta kíkǫða akxai*
oðíhtą ðíhta Ø-ki-kǫ́-Ø-ða akxa-ðe
car 2S.POSS A3S-DAT-PREV-A3S-want 3.CONT-DECL
'he's wishing for your car' (i.e., he wishes he had a car like yours)

(552) *oðíhtą ðíhta ékǫ wį, kíkǫða akxai*
oðíhtą ðíhta é-kǫ wį Ø-ki-kǫ́-Ø-ða akxa-ðe
car 2S.POSS that-like a A3S-DAT-PREV-A3S-want 3.CONT-DECL
'he wants a car like yours'

Once again, dative *kí* is blocked when overt agent inflection appears, as it does in *hkǫ́bra* in (553):

[46] First, however, a caveat: There is a similar form which employs the reflexive *hkik* 'want for oneself':

hkihkǫ́ða apai
Ø-Ø-hkik-kǫ́-Ø-ða apa-ðe
P3S-A3S-REFL-PREV-A3S-want 3S-DECL
'he's wishing for what they have' (or 'he wants it as his own, for himself')

(553) *oðíhtą ðíhta ékǫ wį hkǫ́bra*
oðíhtą ðíhta é-kǫ wį Wa-ki-kǫ́-Wa-ða
car 2S.POSS that-like a A1S-DAT-PREV-A1S-want
'I want a car like yours'

4.6.5.6 Lexicalized dative

In several verbs, what was originally the dative prefix *ki* has been lexicalized as part of the stem. In such verbs, *ki* is no longer omitted in the presence of an overt agent or patient pronominal. In some of these verbs, *ki* now appears before agent inflection, as part of the preverb—a different position from that of the dative prefix.

***ki* in preverb: 'do'.** Related to the verb *é_ǫ* 'do' is a verb *éki_ǫ* (where *ki* appears in all person and number configurations) having the dative meaning 'do for another; do involving another, with regard to another or in the presence of another'. The verb without *ki* (*é_ǫ*), on the other hand, is used in contexts where the agent accomplishes the action of the verb without involvement of others, either as a party affected by his actions or as observers of his actions. The English gloss for *éki_ǫ* will often not include any overt reference to the "others" involved in the action, so that *éki_ǫ* and *é_ǫ* will frequently have identical glosses in English. Both verbs are nasal vowel initial syncopating verbs.

(554) *éekímą*
é-ki-Ø-Wa-ǫ
PREV-DAT-P3S-A1S-do
'I did it'

(555) *éemą*
é-m-ǫ
PREV-P3S-A1S-do
'I did it'

***Ki* lexicalized as *kši*.** Although it is not a widespread phenomenon in Osage, there are a few verbs where initial *kš-* represents *ki* in all inflected forms. Three of the verbs conditioning the formation of *kši* are: (i) the dative of *káaɣe* 'make', whose surface form is *kšíɣe* 'make for another' (discussed just below); (ii) the causative *kšíðe* 'make someone [do something]' (see section 4.2.3); and (iii) *kšíǫze* 'teach; show another' (cf. *kǫ́ze* 'teach'). The verbs with *kši* are ones in which *ki* is added to a *k*-initial root or stem, forming a new verb, or where *ki* has interacted with an historical ʔ-initial (now nasal-vowel-initial) root, as in 'teach'.

The verb *_kší_ǫze* 'teach another' may be based on 'cause to have knowledge'. Speakers routinely gloss *kšíǫze* in isolation as 'show someone how'.

(556) *hpímǫ akšímǫze*
Wa-hpí-Wa-ǫ *Ø-Wa-kší-m-ǫze*
A1S-PREV-A1S-know.how P3S-A1S-DAT-EP*m*-teach
'I know how, so I'm going to show [someone] how'[47]

A special historical change from *ki* + *káa* to *kši* is seen in *kšíɣe*, from the verb *káaɣe* 'make, do, prepare' with a preceding dative *ki* ('for another') incorporated in the stem. The gloss of *kšíɣe* is 'make, do, prepare for another'.[48] *kši*, reflecting the incorporated dative, appears even when overt agent or patient inflection is present, which is not the case with unincorporated *ki*: 1S *akšíɣe* 'I prepare for another'; 2S *ðakšíɣe* 'you prepare for another'. Typical uses are in sentences about preparing a bath for another (557), making a bed for someone (558), or cooking for someone (559).

(557) *hiiðá kšíɣape*
hiiðá Ø-Ø-kši-ɣe-api-ðe
bath P3S-A3S-DAT-prepare-PL-DECL
'she fixed a bath for him'

(558) *omíže kšíɣa*
omíže kši-ɣe-a
quilt DAT-prepare-IMPER
'put down a quilt [for someone]'

(559) *wisǫ́ka súhka wį óohǫ kšíɣape*
wisǫ́ka súhka wį oohǫ́ Ø-Ø-kši-ɣa-api-ðe
younger.brother chicken a cook P3S-A3P-DAT-prepare-PL-DECL
'they cooked a chicken for Sonny'

(560) *wíe na ąkšíɣapé*
wíe na ą-Ø-kši-ɣe-api-ðe
1S.PRON only P1S-A3P-DAT-prepare-PL-DECL
'they did it for me; they made that just for me'

For comparison, *káaɣe*, with no dative, can be used for 'make the bed' or 'arrange quilts to create a sleeping place', as in (561).

[47] The *-m-* appearing in 1S *akšímǫze* may be the reflex of A1S, although no reflex of A2S surfaces. Alternatively, it may be epenthetic (as I have marked it in this example).

[48] Although *káaɣe*, in addition to the meanings mentioned just above, is also used in coercive causative constructions where it is 'force, cause [someone to do something]', *kšíɣe* (derived from *ki* + *káaɣe*) cannot have a causative reading, *kšíɣe* being 'prepare for another' but not 'make another do something'.

(561) *omíže káaγa*
omíže káaγe-a
quilt make-IMPER
'make the bed'

When another person is mentioned ('make a bed for someone; fix a quilt for someone to sleep/sit on') one needs the dative form of *káaγe*, that is, *kšíγe,* as in (558).

To (559) one may contrast *kšíðe* in (562); this is a true causative form with incorporated dative, which is nearly homophonous in very relaxed pronunciation with *kšíγe*.

(562) *wisǫ́ka súhka wį̨ óohǫ kšiape*
wisǫ́ka súhka wį̨ oohǫ́ Ø-Ø-kší-ðe-api-ðe
younger.brother chicken a cook P3S-A3P-DAT-CAU-PL-DECL
'they made Sonny cook a chicken'

The English gloss of *kšíγe* can be somewhat misleading. As stated above, *kšíγe* does not carry the sense 'compel' or 'cause' another to do something, but rather merely 'prepare, make, construct something for another'. But occasionally by pragmatic extension the English translation produced by the Osage speaker uses a causative, as in (563) and (564).

(563) *hiiðá àwakšíγe*
hiiðá Wa-wa-kšíγe
bath A1S-P3P-prepare
'I had/made them take a bath' (lit., 'I prepared a bath for them')

(564) *šį́tožį hiiðá ðakšíγe*
šį́tožį hiiðá Ø-Ya-kšíγe
boy bath P3S-A2S-prepare
'you had the boy to take a bath' (lit., 'you prepared a bath for the boy')

The two following examples contrast simple noninceptive and nondative *káaγe* with dative *kšíγe*.

(565) *Mary əkxa haaská wį̨ káaγape*
Mary akxa haaská wį̨ Ø-káaγe-api-ðe
Mary SUBJ garment a A3S-make-PL-DECL
'Mary made a shirt'

(566) *Mary əkxa haaská wį̨ kšíγape*
Mary akxa haaská wį̨ Ø-Ø-kšíγa-api-ðe
Mary SUBJ garment a P3S-A3S-make.for-PL-DECL
'Mary made a shirt for him'

Example (566) contrasts as well with surface *kikáaγe*, as in (567), which has an inceptive reading. The dative of *káaγe*, although derived historically from *ki* + *káaɣe*, cannot surface as *ki* + *káaɣe* but instead only as *kšíɣe*. If a separate prefix *ki* is used with the verb 'make' (*káaɣe*), giving surface *kikáaɣe*, that form will be understood by speakers as inceptive, rather than dative, as seen in (567). Obviously, then, inceptive *ki* does not undergo the process whereby dative *ki* + *káaɣe* becomes *kšíɣe*. The inceptive *ki* has the approximate meaning of 'again; anew' or 're-[verb]'.

(567) *Mary əkxa haaská wį kikáaɣape*
Mary akxa haaská wį Ø-ki-káaɣe-api-ðe
Mary SUBJ garment a A3S-INCEP-make-PL-DECL
'Mary made over a shirt'

Examples already presented show that the *kši* of *kšíɣe*, unlike normal dative *ki*, remains even when overt agent or patient prefixes are present. Thus, for instance, the presence of P3P *wa* 'them; for them' does not prevent *kši* from appearing in the following example:

(568) *hcí che wakšíɣe hta apai*
hcí che wa-Ø-kšíɣe hta apa-ðe
house that P3P-A3P-make.for FUT 3.CONT-DECL
'they're going to fix that house up for them'

Compare a similar sentence without overt agent or patient prefix:

(569) *hcí wį kšiɣape*
hcí wį Ø-Ø-kšiɣe-api-ðe
house a P3S-A3P-make.for-PL-DECL
'they built a house for him'

Similarly, P2S inflection *ði* precedes *kšíɣe* in the following example (where ***ðikáaɣape* would be ungrammatical).

(570) *ðikšíɣape*
ði-Ø-Ø-kšíɣe api-ðe
P2S-P3S-A3S-make-PL-DECL
he made it for you

Other examples of patient inflection with *kšíɣe* are:

(571) *hiiðá ąkšíɣa*
hiiðá ą-kši-ɣe-a
bath P1S-DAT-prepare-IMPER
'make me a bath'

(572) *haaská wį ąkšíɣape*
haaská wį ą-Ø-kšíɣe-api-ðe
dress a P1S-A3P-make.for-PL-DECL
'they made a garment for me'

To the last example, compare (573), with no overt agent or patient prefix.

(573) *haaská wį kšíɣape*
haaská wį Ø-Ø-kšíɣe-api-ðe
garment a P3S-A3P-make.for-PL-DECL
'they made a shirt for him'

Lexicalized *ki*: 'live for', 'remember'. Dative *kiníe* 'live for another, for others' (from *ni* ~ *níe* 'live; be alive') shows the lexicalized dative *ki* in all persons and numbers, in a mixed paradigm: 1S *akínie*, 2S *ðikínie*, 3S *kiníe*.

In the verb *kisúðe* 'remember', dative *ki* has apparently been reanalyzed as part of the stem. (*súðe* is not attested outside this stem.) This permits overt inflection to occur with *ki*, as (574) with P3P *wa* and in (575) with P1S *ą*. (The latter was offered in a religious context, 'remember me [when you talk to God]', perhaps an appropriate closing to this chapter.)

(574) *wakísuežípe*
wa-Ø-ki-suðe-aži-api-ðe
P3P-A3-DAT-remember-NEG-PL-DECL
'he/they forgot them'[49]

(575) *ąkísue ði*
ą-ki-suðe-a ði
P1S-DAT-remember-IMPER IMPER.SG
'remember me'

[49] Here and in the next example the final *e* of the verb should collapse into the *a* of *aži* 'negative' and into the imperative a, respectively. This particular speaker sometimes refrains from application of the V1-V2 Rule.

5 Verb suffixes

In this chapter we will examine those elements which follow the verb root, paying particular attention to order of elements. These post-root elements are shown in table 5.1. (In the "Continuative" column of the table, *mįkšé* represents the entire set of continuative aspect markers given in sections 5.5 and 5.6, which are too numerous to include in this table.) The rest of this chapter considers these elements, more or less in their linear order. (The elements *hce* and *che*, from the "Declarative, complementizer, injunctive" column in the table, and *ska*, *che*, and *áape* from the "Epistemic" column, are discussed in sections 7.2 and 7.3.)

TABLE 5.1. VERB SUFFIXES (IN ORDER OF APPEARANCE AFTER THE ROOT)

	PLURAL	NEGATION	ITERATIVE, DURATIVE	FUTURE-POTENTIAL	CONTINUATIVE	DECLARATIVE, COMPLEMENTIZER, INJUNCTIVE	EPISTEMIC
	api	*aži*	*ną*	*hta*	*mįkšé*	*ðe*	*aape*
		ðįké	*štą*		etc.	*che*	*che*
			šǫ			*ną-ðe*(?)	*ska*
						hce	
Section where discussed	5.1	5.2	5.3	5.4	5.5, 5.6	5.7	5.1.5.2

5.1 Pluralizer *api*

Api is the pluralizing element par excellence in Osage. It can pluralize any one of a number of different arguments in the clause in which it appears. Typically the argument pluralized is the agent or patient pronominal to the left of the verb root. The pluralizer *api* occurs in a few other locations in addition to its common post-root position, and some of these will be discussed here. (For others, see sections 2.3.3, 7.2.3, and 7.2.6.)

Osage allows only one occurrence of *api* per verb, even if more than one argument of a given verb is plural. *api* can pluralize both agents and patients; consequently, there may be ambiguity as to which argument *api* is affecting.

When *api* is followed by the declarative ending *ðe*, the two contract as *ape* (see chapter 2). The initial *a* of *ape* (like that of *api* in other contexts) is frequently removed by the V1-V2 Rule, giving a surface declarative form *pe*.[1]

Most of the discussion in the present section centers on noncontinuative forms. In continuative clauses, distinctions of plurality, at least for agent (and experiencer in statives) in positive clauses, are most often marked not by *api* but rather by plural forms of the continuative aspect markers themselves; in such clauses, *api* typically only marks plurality of the patient.

api pluralizes any agent or patient pronominal except A1S *Wa* 'I', P1S *ą* 'me', and P3P *wa* 'them'. In combination with A1P *ąk*, *api* signals not simple plural, but rather three or more persons; *ąk* without *api* is dual, signalling only two persons (in noncontinuative sentences).

With second person inflection and in imperatives, *api* indicates two or more persons (simple plural). The same is true for possessives.

With third person subjects, *api* very frequently does not signal plurality. In that context, it instead usually signals completed, noncontinuative action, as discussed in section 5.1.5.

Uses of *api* with specific agent, patient, or other inflectional forms will now be examined in more detail.

5.1.1 A1P 'we'

In Osage, A1D 'we two' and A1P 'we [three or more]' use the same agent pronominal, *ąk*. The distinction between dual and plural agent in continuative aspect is shown by means of distinctive post-root continuative aspect markers, the most common being *ąkáðe* for plural and *ąðįkšé* for dual. In noncontinuative clauses, 1P agent is shown by prefix *ąk* with pluralizer *api* following the verb stem, while 1D agent is shown by *ąk* with no pluralizer. A minimal pair for A1P vs. A1D in noncontinuative aspect is *ąkáhipe* (from *ąkáhi api ðe*) 'we [three or more] arrived there' versus *ąkáhie* (from *ąkáhi ðe*) 'we two arrived there'.

The dual forms in Osage are not at all limited to being inclusive (i.e., speaker plus hearer), although this is the case in some related languages

[1] As mentioned in chapter 2, at least one speaker has been found to use *pie* where others use *pe* (<*apiðe*), but this same speaker says that *pie* is exactly equivalent to *pe*. For this speaker, although the ð of *api-ðe* has elided, the V1-V2 Rule has not applied to collapse *ie* to *e*.

such as Kaw; both A1D and A1P forms may be freely interpreted as either exclusive (speaker plus persons other than the hearer) or inclusive. Thus, the hearer of sentence (1) may either be included in or excluded from the group referred to by 'we'.

(1) *htóožu ąkóohǫ hta ąkái*
htóožu ąk-oohǫ́ hta ąkáðe
meat.pie A1P-cook FUT 1P.CONT
'we're going to cook some meat pies'

Merely pragmatic considerations will generally exclude the hearer in (2) and include the hearer in (3), but these are not grammatical considerations:

(2) *ąkálape*
ąk-alée-api-ðe
A1P-go.back-PL-DECL
'we left'

(3) *ąkále htai*
ąk-alée htai
A1P-go.back let's
'let's go'

The next two examples contain negated A1P verbs; the sequence of *api* plus the negator *aži* results in surface *(a)paži.*

(4a) *wacˀéąðapaží nae*[2]
wa-cˀé-ąk-ðe-api-aži nąa-ðe
VAL-death-A1P-CAU-PL-NEG ITER-DECL
'we don't kill'

(4b) *ąkóe ékiðapaži*
ąkóe é-ki-ðe-api-aži
1P.PRON PREV-PREV-think-PL-NEG
'we don't think so'

5.1.2 P1P 'us' (active), 'we' (stative)

The patient form for both 1P and 1D is *wa*. In stative verbs, this represents the subject 'we', often an experiencer; in active transitive verbs, it represents the object 'us'. Discontinuous from *wa*, and appearing at the right of the verb root, the pluralizer *api* distinguishes plural 'us' from dual 'us'. Dual forms (P1D) lack *api* and are simply *wa* + verb; plural forms (P1P) have *api* (*wa* + verb + *api*). Continuative clauses work somewhat differently (see below).

First person plural and first person dual forms, respectively, of the stative verb *o_xpáðe* 'fall' appear in (5) and (6) below.

[2] The *ð* of declarative *ðe* is deleted following the vowel of *nąa* 'iterative'.

(5) *owáxpaðape*
o-wa-xpáðe-api-ðe
PREV-P1P-fall-PL-DECL
'we [three or more] fell'

(6) *owáxpaðee*
o-wa-xpáðe-ðe
PREV-P1P-fall-DECL
'we [two] fell'[3]

When both agent and patient of a transitive verb are plural, a sequence of two *api*s might be expected, but only one *api* emerges. The result, from the English perspective, is ambiguity as to whether pluralization is to be interpreted as applying to the agent, the patient, or both, as can be seen in the following two examples. (Further ambiguity results from the homophony of P1P *wa* 'us' with P3P *wa* 'them'. Yet more ambiguity results from the fact that *api* with 3S subject often marks noncontinuative action rather than plurality [section 5.1.5].)

(7) *wáðixipee*
wa-Ø-ðixi-api-ðe
P1P-A3S-wake-PL-DECL
'they/he woke us/them up'

(8) *wakˀúpe*
wa-Ø-kˀú-api-ðe
P1P-A3P-give-PL-DECL
'they/he gave it to us/them'

Similar ambiguity is found in (9), where *api* can be understood as pluralizing P1P *wa*, A2S *Ya*, or both.

(9) *mąxíwaðáape*
mąxí-wa-Ya-ðe-api-ðe
deceive-P1P-A2S-CAU-PL-DECL
'you lied to us; you deceived us'

In examples (10)–(14), based on the stative verb *kízo* 'enjoy; like; have a good time' (with patient prefixes expressing the subject), *api* as pluralizer of the patient indicates completed action, as in (10).

(10) *wáazope*
wa-ki-zo-api-ðe
P1P-DAT-enjoy-PL-DECL
'we enjoyed it, we had a good time'

[3] Also correct, with no discernible change in meaning, are *ówaxpaðe* 'we [two] fell' and *ówaxpaðape* 'we [three or more] fell' with accent on the initial syllable.

Statives that are understood as continuative are optionally followed by continuative aspect markers, and plurality of the patient-subject is shown by use of a plural continuative marker, without *api*.

(11) *wáazo*
wa-ki-zo
P1P-DAT-enjoy
'we like it'

(12) *wáazo ąkáðe*
waa-ki-zo ąkáðe
P1P-DAT-enjoy 1P.CONT
'we like it'

(13) *wáazǫ ąkákxai*
waa-ki-zo ąkatxą́-ðe
P1P-DAT-enjoy 1P.CONT-DECL
'we're having a good time'

api marking plurality of the subject is in fact ungrammatical before a continuative marker; thus, ***wáazopi ąkákxai* is not an acceptable alternative to (13). *wáazo* can be followed by *api* in plural imperatives, like (14).

(14) *wáazoopi*
wa-ki-zo-a-api
VAL-DAT-enjoy-IMPER-PL
'you all, be glad'

When a continuative aspect marker occurs, *api* is allowed only as a pluralizer of an argument other than the active or stative subject. Examples may be seen in (15)–(19) below. (Examples (16) and (17) involve lexical causatives *mąxí_ðe* 'lie to, deceive' and *oðó_ðe* 'boss around'.)

(15) *Johna apa záani wéeðapi apai*
John-a apa záani wa-íi-Ø-ðe-api apa-ðe
John-SYL SUBJ all P1P-PREV-A3S-see-PL 3.CONT-DECL
'John saw every one of us'

(16) *mąxį́waapi akxái*
mąxį-wa-Ø-ðe-api akxa-ðe
deceive-P1P-A3P-CAU-PL 3.CONT-DECL
'they're lying to us now'

(17) *oðówaapi akxai*
oðó-wa-Ø-ðe-api akxa-ðe
boss-P1P-A3S-CAU-PL 3.CONT-DECL
'he's bossing us around'

(18) *ónǫbre wakʔúpi apai*
ónǫbre wa-Ø-kʔu-api apa-ðe
food P1P-A3S-give-PL 3.CONT-DECL
'we were fed, food was given to us' (lit., 'they/he gave food to us')

(19) *ée wakʔúpi apai*
ée wa-Ø-kʔú-api apa-ðe
that P1P-A3P-give-P1P 3.CONT-DECL
'they gave it to us'

P1P *wa...api* (for object of a transitive verb) may be seen in the embedded clause of (20). (No declarative *ðe* occurs in this context, so the pluralizer takes the surface form *api* rather than *ape*.)

(20) *waðáhkikhtǫpapi hkǫ́bra*
wa-ð-á-hkik-tǫ́pe-api Wa-kǫ́-Wa-ða
P1P-EPð-LOC-REFL-look-PL A1S-PREV-A1S-want
'I want you to look down upon us'[4]

5.1.3 A2P 'you [plural]'

Plurality (two or more) of second person is shown by the suffix *api* (followed in declarative contexts by *ðe*, with which it contracts to surface *(a)pe*). *api* pluralizes second person for both agent and patient inflection. It marks the plural nature of the experiencer in a stative verb, unambiguously pluralizing P2S *ði* with the doubly stative *óxta* in (21).

(21) *ðióxtape*
Ø-ði-óxta-api-ðe
P3S-P2S-love-PL-DECL
'you [plural] love him'

In general, if *api* occurs in a verb with 2S agent or patient subject inflection, it is interpreted as pluralizing that second person inflection, as in (22).

(22) *mǫ́zeska huuhtǫ́ka waðákʔupe*
mǫ́zeska huuhtǫ́ka wa-Ya-kʔu-api-ðe
money much P3P-A2S-give-PL-DECL
'you [plural] gave them lots of money'

Another reading for (22) would be 'you [plural] gave us lots of money' (with P1P *wa*). Even in this reading, the second person agent is obligatorily interpreted as plural; *waðákʔupe* cannot be interpreted as 'you [singular] gave it to us'. (A third reading for (22) is 'you [plural] gave away', with

[4] If the A2S subject is present at all in this sentence, it is obscured by the *á* locative with its preceding epenthetic *ð*. This sentence is reflexive, with suus semantics.

wa as the valence reducer; the second person agent is again obligatorily plural.)[5]

Contrasting singular and plural second person agent inflection is seen in an active verb in (23)–(24).

(23) *ąnǫ́ðai*
íi-n-ą-Ya-ðe
PREV-EP*n*-P1S-A2S-see
'you [singular] saw me'

(24) *ąnǫ́ðaape*
íi-n-ą-Ya-ðe-api-ðe
PREV-EP*n*-P1S-A2S-see-PL-DECL
'you all saw me'

Example (25) shows *api* on the verb of an embedded sentence (*škǫ́štapi tą* 'if you [plural] want'), as well as a second *api* on the plural imperative at the end of the sentence. (Declarative *ðe* is unlikely to occur in an embedded 'if' clause, so *(a)pi* appears on the surface, rather than contracting to *(a)pe*. Imperatives likewise lack the declarative marker. Note that there is no plural marking on the embedded verb *štaašóe* 'you smoke'.)

(25) *nąnióǫpa štaašóe škǫ́štapi tą, ékiǫpi*
nąnióǫpa Ya-ðaašóe Ya-kǫ́-Ya-ða-api tą, ékiǫ-a-api
pipe A2S-smoke A2S-PREV-A2S-want-PL if do-IMPER-PL
'if you [plural] want to smoke, go ahead'

The plural negative *paži* (from *api-aži*) marks second person plural in (26). Here again, there is no declarative *ðe* to contract with *(a)pi* to form *(a)pe*.

(26) *waachí ki štáapáži na*
waachí ki a-Ya-ðée-api-aži ną
dance to PREV-A2S-go-PL-NEG ITER
'you [plural] never go to dances'

In (27), *api* pluralizes the second person agent of the embedded verb 'learn'.

(27) *wažáže íe špížǫapi hkǫ́bra*
wažáže íe Ya-hpí-Ya-ǫ-api Wa-kǫ́-Wa-ða
Osage language A2S-PREV-A2S-learn/know-PL A1S-PREV-A1S-want
'I want you all to learn to talk Osage'

To pluralize the second person subject of a clause that has a continuative aspect marker, *api* does not occur. Instead, the 2S continu-

[5] The ditransitive verb *k?u* 'give' has the recipient as its primary object.

ative marker *ðaįšé* is replaced by *paašé*, the 2P continuative, as in the following sentence.

(28) *kasį hówaįke šcée hta paašé?*
kasį hówaįke Ya-ðée hta paašé
tomorrow where A2S-go FUT 2P.CONT
'where is everyone going tomorrow?' (lit., 'where are you [plural] going tomorrow?')

5.1.4 P2P 'you [plural]'

api also pluralizes the second person patient form, either as object of an active transitive clause, or as the experiencer (subject) of a stative clause. The following two examples neatly contrast P2S object in (29), without *api*, and P2P object in (30), with *api*.

(29) *wéeðiną ąkxái*
wée-ði-Ø-ną akxa-ðe
PREV-P2S-A3S-grateful 3.CONT-DECL
'he's grateful to you [singular], he's thanking you [singular]'

(30) *wéeðinąpi akxái*
wée-ði-Ø-ną-api akxa-ðe
PREV-P2S-A3S-grateful-PL 3.CONT-DECL
'he's grateful to you-all, he's thanking you-all'

5.1.4.1 P2P in portmanteau *wi*

As was discussed in section 3.1.5, there is a special portmanteau prefix *wi* for the combination of a 1S subject with a second person object. If a (noncontinuative) verb with *wi* is not followed by *api*, then the object is interpreted as singular.

(31) *íiwiðe*
íi-wi-ðe
PREV-P2S<A1S-see
'I see/saw you [singular]'

When a verb with *wi* is followed by *api*, then the second person object is interpreted as plural.

(32) *íiwiðaape*
íi-wi-ðe-api-ðe
PREV-P2S<A1S-see-PL-DECL
'I see/saw you-all'

(33) *záani íiwiðaape*
záani íi-wi-ðe-api-ðe
all PREV-P2S<A1S-see-PL-DECL
'I saw all of you'

Alternatively, P2S *ði* + A1S *Wa* may replace *wi*, as in (34). (Occasionally *ði* + *Wa* also replaces *wi* when the second person object is understood as singular.)

(34) *iiðiðáape*
íi-ði-ð-Wa-ðe-api-ðe
PREV-P2S-EPð-A1S-see-PL-DECL
'I saw you [plural]; I saw you all'

Variation between *wi...api* and *ði...api* for the plural second person patient (with first person agent) can be seen in (35) and the embedded clause of (36) below.

(35) *záani wawíhǫ́įpe* ~ *záani wawíhǫ́įpi*
záani wa-wi-hǫ́e-api-ðe
all PREV-P2S.A1S-address-PL-DECL
'I address you-all as friends and relatives'

(36) *záani waðíhǫ́ǫpi hkǫ́bra*
záani wa-ði-hǫ́e-api Wa-kǫ́-Wa-ða
all PREV-P2S-address-PL A1S-PREV-A1S-want
'I want to address you [plural] friends and relatives'

5.1.5 A3S and A3P 'he, she, they'

As we have already seen, *api* (with surface form *(a)pe*, when contracted with declarative *ðe*) appears in plural clauses for all three persons. Curiously, it can also appear in clauses containing only third person singular arguments in noncontinuative aspect. In fact, it is normal for *api* (in declarative clauses, *(a)pe*) to appear in 3S declarative clauses in Osage; declarative clauses without *api* in third person are hard to find. Although studies of related languages have suggested several conditions for appearance of *pe* with 3S, none of these earlier suggestions proves reliable for Osage. I will mention two of these suggestions briefly in section 5.1.5.1.

Without extensive samples of connected discourse, it is extremely difficult to determine what factors might be at work in the rare instances where noncontinuative clauses with 3S arguments lack *api*. Possibly absence of *api* could be explained by using the proximate/obviative distinction; absence of *api* might characterize obviative 3S sentences.[6] Since

[6] Roughly, a 3S subject is proximate when he, she, or it is somehow focused in the conversation, either by prior mention in the discourse or by contextual pragmatic considerations.

this distinction is potentially relevant to choice between the continuative *akxa* vs. *apa* in third person clauses (see section 5.6), it may also be important in determining which third person singular noncontinuative clauses contain *api* and which lack it. The handful of examples of completed action in 3S/3P sentences that appear without *api* may be sentences where the action is outside our present focus, or was outside the center of discourse when that action occurred. Ardis Eschenberg (1999) has discussed the proximate-obviative distinction for Omaha; however, this is purely speculation so far in Osage in the case of *api*. Examples of declarative clauses ending in *api* + *ðe* (surface *pe*) appear in (37)–(42):

(37) *ąkʔúpe*
ą-kʔú-api-ðe
P1S-give-PL-DECL
'they gave [it] to me'

(38) *ée záani ðaanįpe*
ée záani Ø-ðaanį-api-ðe
3S/P all A3S-consume-PL-DECL
'he ate it all up'

(39) *htáabre šǫðé mąščįka ðiksįįcape*
htáabre šǫ-ðe mąščįka Ø-ðii-kšįįce-api-ðe
hunting while-MOV rabbit A3S-CAU-miss-PL-DECL
'as he went hunting, he missed the rabbit'

(40) *hąkáaši ðáha achípe*
hąkáaši ðáha Ø-achí-api-ðe
late.night when A3P-arrive.here-PL-DECL
'they came late at night' (lit., 'when it was late night, they arrived here')

(41) *žą́ą íichįpe*
žą́ą í-Ø-Ø-chį-api-ðe
stick with-P3S-A3P-hit-PL-DECL
'they hit him with a stick'

(42) *ąwą́hkie ðiląpe*
o-ą-Ø-hkik-ie í-Ø-ðilą-api-ðe
PREV-P1S-P3S-RECIP-speak PREV-P3S-wish-PL-DECL
'he wanted to talk to me'

Use of *api* in negative clauses. In negative clauses with third person arguments, *api* is again a mark of noncontinuative aspect rather than a mark of plurality. The next three examples show negative sentences; the first is stative, and the two following it are active. (*api* plus the negator *aži* contract to become surface *(a)paži*.)

(43) *óxpaðapažie*
wa-o-Ø-xpáðe-api-aži-ðe
VAL-PREV-P3S-P3S-lose-PL-NEG-DECL
'he didn't lose it'

(44) *wawį́įkšapažie*
wa-wį́-Ø-kše-api-aži-ðe
VAL-PREV-A3S-tell.truth-PL-NEG-DECL
'he's/she's an untruthful person'

(45) *aðáapažie*
a-Ø-ðée-api-aži-ðe
PREV-A3S/P-PL-NEG-DECL
'he/they didn't go'[7]

Embedded third person. Statements made so far about the interpretation of *api* in clauses with third person arguments do not apply to embedded clauses. For example, in (46), one might have expected to see *api* after 3S *lee* 'he went back', since it is completive; but *api* does not appear, because that clause is embedded. (If *api* only were to appear in this clause, then the result would be *aláapi che*, where *pi che* is an evidential that would be semantically at odds with 'I saw him leave'; see section 7.2.3 for evidentials. We find instead the nominalizer *che* alone, corresponding roughly to 'that' in the English gloss.)

(46) *lée che iiðáðe íppahǫe*
a-Ø-lée *che* *íi-Wa-ðe* *í-Wa-pahǫ-ðe*
PREV-A3S-go.back NOM PREV-A1S-see PREV-A1S-know-DECL
'I knew that he left because I saw him leave'

One place where *api* with 3S does appear in an embedded clause is before the reportative element *aape* 'they say'; see section 5.1.5.2.

Use of *api* and continuative. In a third person nonembedded continuative clause, a continuative marker, either *apa* or *akxa*, is likely to follow the verb. In such clauses, *api* (between the verb and the continuative marker) usually signals plurality of nonsubject arguments. Examples may be seen in (15) and (16), repeated below as (47) and (48).

(47) *Johna apa záani wéeðapi apai*
John-a *apa* *záani* *wa-íi-Ø-ðe-api* *apa-ðe*
John-SYL SUBJ all P1P-PREV-A3S-see-PL 3.CONT-DECL
'John saw every one of us'

7 ***aðáažipe* is ungrammatical.

(48) *mąxįwaapi akxái*
mąxį-wa-Ø-ðe-api akxa-ðe
deceive-P1P-A3P-CAU-PL 3.CONT-DECL
'they're lying to us now'

However, in negative third person sentences with *aži*, a distinction between 3S and 3P can be made; see section 5.2.2.4.

5.1.5.1 Volition and previous mention as inadequate conditions for 3S *api*

For some related languages, it has been proposed that *api* is absent from third-person-only clauses if the action is nonvolitional or if the agent was not previously mentioned. In these languages, for example, the equivalent of Osage *cˀape* 'he died' (with *api*) is impossible because no volition is involved in dying (John Koontz, p.c. 1995). But in fact in Osage, singular *api* does occur with nonvolitional verbs, as in *cˀa pe* 'he died', *xíða pe* 'he [stumbled and] fell'; such examples are found regularly. Consequently, in Osage, volition cannot be a condition for the absence of *api*.

Another condition offered to explain the use of singular *api* in related languages is that if the 3S agent was previously mentioned, then *api* is employed, while if it is a new 3S agent, the verb will not have the pluralizer. This too is incorrect for Osage: even when the subject was not previously mentioned in the discourse, a sentence such as the following shows *api*:[8]

(49) *Mogri əkxa isǫka hcí íhta ci aðáape*
Mogri akxa isǫka hcí íhta ci a-Ø-ðée-api-ðe
Mogri SUBJ his.brother house 3S.POSS to PREV-A3S-go-PL-DECL
'Mogri went to his brother's house'

5.1.5.2 Reportative ending *apí áape* 'he/they said'

Another factor that in related languages is said to block the appearance of *api* (declarative *pe*) is the status of the information conveyed as reported rather than witnessed—perhaps the information is being circulated or rumored, and was only reported to the speaker who did not see the action take place and has no first-hand knowledge of it. While it is true for Osage that if the speaker saw the action taking place, the sentence will likely end in *pe*, it is also true that if the action was merely reported to the speaker, the sentence will again be likely to end in *pe*. In (50), for instance, the speaker of the sentence was present when the council meeting was adjourned, so no reporting of this information by others is encoded.

[8] If the subject marker *akxa* were replaced by *apa*, this sentence would still end in *pe*.

(50) *hkiistó panáape*
hkiistó Ø-panáa-api-ðe
meeting A3S-adjourn-PL-DECL
'he adjourned the council meeting'

The distinction between witnessed and reported events is grammatically relevant in Osage, but not to the occurrence of *api*. Rather, the grammatical feature in question is whether the sentence ends in declarative *ðe* (witnessed event, as in (50)) or in the reportative element *aape* 'they said' (as in (51) below; since in (51) *api* is not immediately followed by declarative *ðe*, it appears on the surface as *(a)pi*, not as *(a)pe*). Strictly speaking, *aape* is actually a higher verb (although I have treated it here rather informally as an epistemic marker at the end of a clause), and *hkiistó panáa-api* 'he adjourned the meeting' is embedded under this higher verb. (The reason declarative *ðe* does not surface after *panáa-api*, therefore, is that in embedded clauses *ðe* is generally precluded.) It is interesting that the speaker's English translation of (51) was passive, perhaps to emphasize the semantic distance of the speaker from direct knowledge of the event.

(51) *hkiistó panáapi áape*
hkiistó Ø-panáa-api áape
meeting A3S-adjourn-PL they.said
'the meeting was adjourned' (lit., 'he adjourned the meeting, they said')

In (51), the speaker reports knowledge gained from a third party.

Assuming that reportative *aape* is from the plural declarative of *é_e* 'say', its derivation is as follows:

*é_**e**-**a**pi-ðe*	(underlying)
***ea**-**a**pi-ðe*	(V1-V2 Rule)
***ea**-api-e*	(ð-Elision)
***aa**-api-e*	(V1-V2 Rule)
aape	(V1-V2 Rule)

api followed by reportative *aape* may drop its initial *a* in the usual way (52).

(52) *tówa akxa waachípi áape*
tówa akxa waa-Ø-chí-api é-Ø-e-api-ðe
those.ones SUBJ PREV-A3P-dance-PL PREV-A3P-say-PL-DECL
'they said those men danced'

Positionals *kše* 'lying' and *įkšé* 'sitting' as well as the continuative aspect markers may be followed by the reportative ending *áape*, as shown below. (The change of a final accented *é* to *í* seen in these forms is common before *áape*.)

(53a) *kší aape*
kše aape
3.CONT they.said
'it was/is said of one lying'

(53b) *nįkší aape*
nįkšé aape
2S.CONT they.said
'it was/is said of you sitting/lying'

(53c) *įkší aape*
įkšé aape
3.CONT they.said
'it was/is said of him/her sitting'

The next example illustrates the reportative following the continuative auxiliary *akxa*:

(54) *wižįke íe akxa áape*
wižįke í-Ø-e akxa e-Ø-e-api-ðe
Sonny PREV-A3S-speak CONT PREV-A3S-say-PL-DECL
'they said he talked' (lit., 'they said he was talking')

Likewise, the combination of the auxiliary *apá* followed by reportative *áape* 'they said' produces *apa áape*, auditorily *apáape* ('subject is/was doing so-and-so, they said').

The reportative element itself can be followed by a continuative marker. The usual gloss for this continuative reportative is 'that's what they say' or 'that's what they're saying' (or past continuative 'that's what they were saying'). This contrasts with the completed action reportative *áape* 'they said' mentioned above and is completely consistent with the use of aspect on other verbs. The continuative reportative *áapa* 'they're saying' appears often as *áapai*, that is, showing the (probably historically female) declarative *ðe* contracted to *e* and raised to *i*.

(55) *wižįke akxa wažáže íe ípahǫ áaapai*
wižįke akxa wažáže íe í-Ø-pahǫ
Sonny SUBJ Osage language PREV-he-knows
e-Ø-e-apa-ðe
PREV-they-say-CONT-DECL
'Sonny knows Osage, that's what they're saying'

(The embedded clause in (55), 'Sonny knows Osage', may also appear without the subject marker *akxa* on *wižįke*. There is no aspect marker on the embedded clause in (55)).

When a sentence describes some ongoing (continuative) action by someone not present, that sentence will likely end in the continuative marker *apa*, which in turn may be followed by *aapai* 'they are saying'; this would produce *apáapai* ('subject is/was doing so-and-so, they are/were saying').

The sense of *ðe* 'declarative' is that the speaker witnessed the act reported in the sentence; otherwise *áape* 'they said' may appear. It is unclear whether the *ðe* underlying *áape* also would signify that the speaker witnessed the reporting—that is, was present when the anonymous 'they' of *áape* 'they said' conveyed the information that the event had taken place. With little evidence available, we assume that it does.

5.1.6 *api* in imperatives

The pluralizer *api* is used frequently in imperatives. No distinction is made between dual or plural first person in imperative applications. Several informal rules for use of *api* in imperatives are given in this section.

5.1.6.1 Transitive noncontinuative imperative

An example of an active imperative with a patient pronominal is seen in (56); it has the ambiguity indicated in the glosses.

(56) *ówaðaaka*
wa-o-wa-ðaake-a
VAL-PREV-P1P/P3P-tell-IMPER
'tell us!; tell them!'

If in the command in (56), *ówaðaaka* was followed by *api* (*ówaðaakapi*), it would obligatorily refer to P2P 'us' ('you singular/plural tell us!'). That is, the only interpretation of *ówaðaakapi* is 'tell us', and not 'tell them' and the addressee is not specified for number. This observation is the basis for Rule 1:

RULE 1: In transitive imperatives of verbs with a patient prefix *wa*, if *api* appears, it is obligatorily interpreted as part of P1P *wa...api*. 'us'. In this case, the addressee is not specified as singular or plural.

If no *api* is present, then Rule 2 applies to imperatives with *wa*, producing the interpretations seen in the example above.

RULE 2: When a patient prefix *wa* alone appears without *api* in an imperative, the imperative has either a singular or plural addressee and *wa* refers to either 1P or 3P object.

It follows from Rule 2 that the command *wáatǫpa* in (57), offered as a plural-addressee command, may also be interpreted as having a singular addressee. However, if *api* is added as in (58), this command is interpreted only as involving P1P and not P3P, in accordance with Rule 1, and continues to have either a singular or plural addressee.

(57) *wáatǫpa*
wa-á-tǫ́pe-a
P3P-LOC-watch-IMPER
'you [plural], watch over them!'

(58) *wáatǫpapi*
wa-á-tǫ́pe-a-api
P1P-LOC-look-IMPER-PL
'look down on us'

Given Rule 1, a command to 'help them' cannot contain *api*, even when the speaker is addressing a group of people as in (59). So strong is the association of *api* with P1P *wa* that even when a noun or pronoun object is present in the sentence, such as *kóota pa* in (61), still the sentence will be interpreted as P1P and not P3P if it has a final *api* (*kóota pa ówahkąpi*) and the noun or pronoun will be ignored. In nonimperative contexts, the association of *api* with second person *ða* 'you' is quite strong, but in imperative contexts the association of *wa...api* to P1P is the strongest association, as stated in Rule 1.

(59) *ówahką*
ó-wa-hką-a
PREV-P3P-help-IMPER
'help them'

(60) *ówahką*
ó-wa-hką-a
PREV-P1P-help-IMPER
'help us'

(61) *kóota pa ówahką*
kóota *pa* *ó-wa-hką-a*
over.there those PREV-P3P-help-IMPER
'you-all help them'

Despite the strong association of *api* with P1P in imperatives, *api* is optional where P1P 'us' is the object, as in the interpretation *ówahką* 'help us' of (60) above (cf. Rule 2). Note that in (61), a command to a plural addressee, no *api* is used, which confirms the optionality of such use of *api* (Rule 2). In (62) below, contrasting with (61), the surface *pi* makes the object unambiguously P1P 'us' rather than P3P 'them'.

(62) *ówahkąpi*
ó-wa-hką-a-api
PREV-P1P-help-IMPER-PL
'help us!'

The fact that *api* applies to the P1P in such sentences (by Rule 1) results in ambiguity of addressee as to singularity or plurality; thus examples like (63) and others may have singular or plural addressee, as stated in the latter part of Rule 1.

(63) *wakˀúpi*
wa-kˀú-a-api
A1P-give-IMPER-PL
'[you (singular/plural)] give it to us'

In fact, transitive imperatives of all sorts never mark plurality of the addressee, as can be seen in (64).

(64) *ąwą́hką*
o-w-ą-hką-a
PREV-EP*w*-P1S-help-IMPER
'[you (plural)] help me!'

Consequently, we need a further rule for imperatives.

RULE 3: The pluralizer *api* will refer to the addressee of the command ('you') only if the verb is intransitive.

That is, in transitive imperatives, *api* only appears as part of the P1P marker *wa...api* 'us [plural]', and that only optionally.

5.1.6.2 Intransitive noncontinuative imperative

In intransitive imperatives, *api* is used to pluralize the addressee; a clear singular/plural contrast is seen in the following two examples. (Reflexives are considered intransitive for the purposes of this discussion.)

(65) *íihkiðapi*
íi-hkik-ðe-a-api
PREV-REFL-see-IMPER-PL
'[you (plural)] wake up!'

(66) *íihkiða*
íi-hkik-ðe-a
PREV-REFL-see-IMPER
'[you (singular)] wake up!'

More pairs of singular/plural intransitive commands appear in the next three examples. An optional particle *ði* (sometimes *ðį*), here analyzed as the second person pronoun, may appear at the end of an imperative with a singular addressee.

(67a) *waaškǫ́ ði*
waaškǫ́-a ði
do.best-IMPER 2S.PRON
'do your best! [singular]'

(67b) *waaškǫ́pi*
wáaškǫ-a-api
do.best-IMPER-PL
'do your best! [plural]'

(68a) *lį́į ði*
a-lį́į-a ði
PREV-sit-IMPER 2S.PRON
'[you (singular)] sit down'

(68b) *lį́įpi*
a-lį́į-a-api
PREV-lit-PL
'you all sit down'[9]

(69a) *tǫ́pa ði*
tǫ́pe-a ði
look-IMPER 2S.PRON
'[you (singular)] look!'

(69b) *tǫ́papi*
tǫ́pe-a-api
look-IMPER-PL
'[you (plural)] look!'

The following pair of examples shows presence of *api* on a plural reflexive imperative and its absence on a singular one.

[9] Also correct is:

lį́įðikaapi
lį́į-ði-ka-a-api
PREV-P2S-sit.down-IMPER-PL
'you all sit down'

The expected form is *lį́įkáapi* 'you all sit down'. These two forms are synonymous, according to one speaker who comments that for the *ka* form, one should be "close to the place where the seating will be." It is possible that the underlying form includes a 'plural, dispersed' marker *ke* and is *lį́į-ði-ke-a-api*. In this situation, each addressee is at a particular place and the places are scattered around.

(70) *áhkittǫpapi*
á-hkik-tǫ́pe-a-api
LOC-REFL-look-IMPER-PL
'you all take care of yourselves'

(71) *áhkihtǫpa*
á-hkik-tǫ́pe-a
LOC-REFL-look-IMPER
'look out for yourself'

5.1.6.3 Continuative imperative

Another ending found on plural imperatives (transitive or intransitive) is surface *pai*, rather than the expected surface *pi*. Use of *pai* implies continuation of the behavior being exhorted. It is glossed here as *páðe* 'imperative continuative' (IMPER.CONT).

(72) *áhkihtǫpa pai*
á-hkik-tǫ́pe-a paðe
LOC-REFL-look-IMPER IMPER.CONT
'you all watch each other, take care of each other; you all be taking care of each other'

(73) *haaská wasúhužike hpaahípai*
haaská wasúhu-aži ke hpaahí paðe
clothes clean-NEG DISP sort-IMPER IMPER.CONT
'be sorting the dirty clothes!'

Where *pi* alone appears, the mandate to continue is not present:

(74) *áhkihtǫpapi*
á-hkik-tǫ́pe-a-api
LOC-REFL-look-IMPER-PL
'you all take care of each other'

5.1.7 Use of *api* pluralizer in possessives

Possessives are pluralized with *api*. The rules involved are less strict than those for imperatives (section 5.1.6).

5.1.7.1 First person possessive

For first person dual, *api* appears optionally with the possessive pronoun: *ąkóhta* ~ *ąkóhtapi* 'our [dual]'. For first person plural, the *api* ending on the possessive is obligatory: *ąkóhtapi* 'our [plural]'. Thus, for *hci ąkóhta* 'our house' only two possessors are possible, while for *hci ąkóhtapi* 'our house', two may own the house, or more than two; if three own the house, then *hcí ąkóhta* alone is not the correct expression. The possessive pronoun follows the noun it modifies, as seen in the next example:

(75) *ówe che hcí ąkóhtapi aðįhį*
ówe che hcí ąkóhta-api aðį-ahi-a
groceries those house 1P.POSS-PL have-arrive.there-IMPER
'bring those groceries to our house'

5.1.7.2 Second person possessive

In the second person forms, it is simple singularity or plurality of the possessor that is signalled by absence or presence of *api*. Thus *hci ðíhta* 'the house belonging to you [one]' contrasts with *hci ðíhtaapi* 'the house belonging to you-plural [two or more].'

(76) *hcí ðíhta*
hcí ðíhta
house 2S.POSS
'your [singular] house'

(77) *hcí ðíhtaapi*
hcí ðíhta-api
house 2S.POSS-PL
'your [plural] house'

5.1.7.3 Third person possessive

Contrast between singular and plural third person possessors can be seen in the next two examples:

(78) *hcí íhta*
hcí íhta
house 3S.POSS
'his house'

(79) *hcí íhtaapi*
hcí íhta-api
house 3S.POSS-PL
'their house'

When the possessive form is at the end of a sentence where *api* + *ðe* may follow, the pluralizer of the possessive is omitted. Thus *hcí íhtaape* means either 'it's his house' or 'it's their house'; *api* in this sentence (in *ape*, from *api ðe*), should be interpreted as the *api* found on the predicate of a noncontinuative clause with third person arguments, rather than being interpreted as the pluralizer of the possessive. Two or more instances of *api* in contiguous sequence are not licensed: ***hcí íhtaapipe*. In non-sentence-final contexts, *api* applies clearly to the possessive, as in (80). The first *api* in (80) pluralizes the possessive *íhta* 'his, hers', making it 'theirs'. The second *api* (at the end of the sentence) is that used in noncontinuative declarative clauses with third person arguments.

(80) *hcí íhtaapi əkxa žúucape*
hcí íhta-api akxa žúuce-api-ðe
house 3S.POSS-PL SUBJ red-PL-DECL
'their house is red'

The pluralizer emerges freely in the phrase in (81) with the possessors' names in the normal sequence: possessors + possessed noun + possessive + pluralizer.

(81) *Máry Jóhna hcí íhtaapi*
Mary John-a hcí íhta-api
Mary John-SYL house 3S.POSS-PL
'Mary and John's house'

Now that we have covered the complex patterns of occurrence of *api*, we can continue with the slots following *api* in the verb suffixal complex, where things are simpler.

5.2 Negation

There are two negatives in Osage: *ðįké* and the less emphatic *aži*. Both are used in derivations of nouns and other forms, where they follow the item negated. The *ð* of *ðįké* is often elided, which is not surprising since *ð* elides in many words in Osage. As a verb *ðįké* is frequently heard in the form *ðįka!* or *įká!* in imperatives telling someone not to do something. The two negatives *aži* and *ðįké* are often interchangeable in a given expression. The concept 'not dirty, clean' can be expressed with either *aži*, as *ízizikaži*, or with *ðįké* as in:

(82) *ízizike įké ekxai*
ízizike ðįké akxa-ðe
dirty NEG 3.CONT-DECL
'it's not dirty'

5.2.1 Plain negative with *ðįké*

The negative slot in the verbal complex can contain either *ðįké* or *aži*. In (83) *ðįké* occurs, with a common raising of the final vowel (*ðįkí*) before a continuative ending.

(83) *ðáalį ąažį ðįkí apái*
ðáalį ą-Ø-ažį ðįké apa-ðe
good P1S-A3S-think NEG 3.CONT-DECL
'he doesn't think well of me; he doesn't like me'

In the imperative, the final *e* of *ðįké* is replaced by *a* as in (84), via the V1-V2 Rule. The final *e* of the verb *ohkíe* 'converse; speak to each other' that is negated in (84) does not undergo this change, since *ðįké* intervenes between it and the imperative marker *a*. Sentence (85) shows *ðįké* with the morphological causative 'kill' and (86) shows a valence-reduced stative verb negated with *ðįké*.

(84) *ąwą́hkie ðįka!*
o-ą-hkik-ie ðįké-a
PREV-P1S-RECIP-speak NEG-IMPER
'don't talk to me!'

(85) *wacˀéąðe ðįké*
wa-cˀé-ąk-ðe ðįké
VAL-die-A1P-CAU NEG
'we don't kill at all'

(86) *óxpaðe įké hta apái*
wa-o-Ø-Ø-xpáðe ðįké hta apa-ðe
VAL-PREV-P3S-P3S-lose NEG FUT 3.CONT-DECL
'he won't lose it'

5.2.2 Plain negative with *aži*

5.2.2.1 Singular, dual, and plural negatives with *aži*

The less emphatic negative *aži* takes the surface forms 1S *maží* (often heard as *mąží*), 2S *aži*, 3S *aži* or *(a)paži*; all plurals are *(a)paži* (from *api-aži*, via the V1-V2 Rule). When the pluralizer *api* is present, it will appear just before *aži*, and this results in the *paži* plural form of the negative.

The final *e* of the verb root disappears in favor of the *a* of *api-aži* (surface *(a)paži*, again by the V1-V2 Rule), as in *wacˀéąðapaží nae* 'we don't kill' (from the stem *cˀé_ðe* 'kill').

As in affirmative clauses, the pluralizer *api* appears in 1P forms (87), but is absent in 1D forms (88). Example (89) is the plural corresponding to (88).

(87) *ąkótapažie*
ąk-o-Ø-cé-api-aží-ðe
A1P-PREV-P3S-search.for-PL-NEG-DECL
'we [three or more] didn't look for it'

(88) *ąkóhkąaži áha, ékiǫ aží hta apai*
ąk-ó-Ø-hką-aži áha, éki-Ø-ǫ-aží hta apa-ðe
A1P-PREV-P3S-NEG whenever PREV-A3S-do-NEG FUT 3.CONT-DECL
'if we [two] don't help her, she won't do it'

(89) *ąkóhkąpaži áha, ékiǫ aží hta apai*
ąk-ó-Ø-hką-api-aži áha, éki-Ø-ǫ-aží hta apa-ðe
A1P-PREV-P3S-PL-NEG whenever PREV-A3S-do-NEG FUT 3.CONT-DECL
'if we [three or more] don't help her, she won't do it'

In negative statives, as well, *api* marks 1P but not 1D.

Second person plural negative is also marked with *api*:

(90) *waachí ki štáapáži na*
waachí ki Ya-ðe-api-aži nạ
dance to A2S-go-PL-NEG ITER
'you [plural] never go to dances'

api is also used in 3S negative clauses in the same (nonpluralizing) way it is used in declarative clauses.

(91) *óxpaðapažie*
wa-o-Ø-xpáðe-api-aži-ðe
VAL-PREV-P3S-P3S-lose-PL-NEG-DECL
'he didn't lose it'

Consequently, third person noncontinuative clauses where *paži* (from *api-aži*) appears are ambiguously singular or plural, as in (92) and (93).

(92) *wawį́įkšapažie*
wa-wį́-Ø-kše-api-aži-ðe
VAL-PREV-A3S-tell.truth-PL-NEG-DECL
'he's an untruthful person; they're untruthful'

(93) *aðáapažie*
a-Ø-ðée-api-aži-ðe
PREV-A3S/P-PL-NEG-DECL
'he/they didn't go'

The plural negative *paži* is often followed by the iterative *na* ~ *nạ*, as in the next two examples.

(94) *naníopa ạðáašoepáži nai*
naníopa ạk-ðáašoe-api-aži nạ-ðe
pipe A1P-smoke-PL-NEG ITER-DECL
'we don't smoke'

(95) *ạwą́lǫpaži nai*
ạk-walǫ-api-aži nạ-ðe
A1P-call.names-PL-NEG ITER-DECL
'we never call people names'

5.2.2.2 Negative *aži* and potential *hta*

In (96) and (97), we see negative *aži* followed by *hta* 'future, potential' plus a continuative auxiliary (singular without *api* in (96), plural with *api* in (97)).

(96) *aðáaži hta apai*
a-Ø-ðée-aži hta apa-ðe
PREV-A3S-go-NEG FUT 3.CONT-DECL
'he will not go'

(97) *aðáapaži hta apai*
a-Ø-ðée-api-aži hta apa-ðe
PREV-A3P-go-PL-NEG FUT 3.CONT-DECL
'they're not going to go'

5.2.2.3 Non-action verb and negative

Examples (98a)–(100) show positive and negative versions of the non-action verbs *nǫ́_hpe* 'be afraid' and *ínǫhpe* 'be fearful of', both active verbs.

(98a) *nǫ́hpe*
nǫ́hpe
afraid
'afraid'

(98b) *nǫ́hpaži*
nǫ́hpe-aži
afraid-NEG
'not afraid'

(99a) *íinǫhpa*
í-nǫhpe-a
PREV-afraid-IMPER
'be fearful, wary or careful of'

(99b) *íinohpaži*
í-nohpe-aži
PREV-afraid-NEG
'be not fearful of, be reckless around'

P1S *ą* inflection in the negative stative is seen in (100).

(100) *nǫ́ąhpaži*
nǫ́-a-hpe-aži
PREV-A1S-afraid-NEG
'I'm not afraid'

Alternatively, *nǫ́_hpe* takes the inflected 1S negative *maži*, either with (101a) or without (101b) the infixed inflectional element A1S *a*. This sort of variation between inflected and uninflected verb, and between inflected and uninflected negative, is common in Osage and for some two-verb constructions elsewhere in Siouan. The two versions below are synonymous and equally "correct," in addition to (100) just above.

(101a) *nǫ́ąhpamąži*
nǫ́-a-hpe-maži
PREV-A1S-afraid-1S.NEG
'I'm not afraid'

(101b) *nǫ́hpamąži*
nǫ́hpe-maži
afraid-1S.NEG
'I'm not afraid'

5.2.2.4 Negative with continuative

In negative continuative sentences, the negative *aži* immediately follows the verb root as in (102), without a preceding pluralizer *api*; the continuative marker follows the negative. However, pluralizer *api* may be present, as in (103) where it pluralizes the object inflection (here 'you').

(102) *íiðiðaži ekxai*
íi-ði-Ø-ðe-aži *akxa-ðe*
PREV-P2S-A3S-see-NEG 3S.CONT-DECL
'he doesn't see you'

(103) *íiðiðapaži ekxai*
íi-ði-Ø-ðe-api-aži *akxa-ðe*
PREV-P2S-A3S-see-PL-NEG 3S.CONT-DECL
'he doesn't see you [plural]'

Nonnegative third person continuatives (past, present, or future) are ambiguous as to number. Thus, both *aðee akxai* and *aðee apai* mean 'he/they are leaving'. But in negative clauses with *aži*, a distinction of number can be made. Thus *aðaapaži akxai* and *aðaapaži apai* are plural 'they are not leaving', while *aðáaži akxai* and *aðáaži apai* are singular 'he's not leaving'. (Examples in this paragraph were constructed by myself for ease of exposition, and need to be confirmed by actual Osage speakers.) The choice between *akxa* and *apa* as continuative is dictated by whether the subject is present at the speech event, as well as whether the verb involves movement through space (see section 5.6).[10]

5.2.2.5 Negative adverb

The negative *aži* normally used on verbs may appear on verb/adjectives as well (for example, *ízizikaži* 'not dirty', from *ízizike* 'dirty') or on adverbs.

In the next example, we find *olą-aži*, often glossed as 'missing the mark', 'not up to par', 'not quite right' (based on *oolą́* 'place into'); it functions here as an adverb, similar to 'poorly'.

[10] For *aðée akxai*, the subject must be still, perhaps still sitting, but have declared his (or their) intention to leave imminently.

(104) *hcéɣenii ochį oląązi káaɣape*
hcéɣenii ochį oolą-aži Ø-káaɣa-api-ðe
drum hit place.in-not A3S-do/make-PL-DECL
'he didn't hit the drum quite right (not up to par)'

5.2.2.6 Two negatives in one clause

Either *ðįké* or *aži* can combine with other words to derive new words. In (105) the verb is the lexicalized *_kisúaži*, made up of *kisúðe* 'remember' plus *aži*, with the meaning 'forget'.[11] In (106) *kisúaži* is itself negated by the other negative, *ðįké*, resulting in 'don't not remember':

(105) *ðakísuaži*
Ya-kisúðe-aži
A2S-remember-NEG
'you won't remember'

(106) *kisúaži ðįká!*
Ø-kisúðe-aži ðįké-a
P3S-remember-NEG NEG-IMPER
'don't forget it'

5.2.2.7 Negative modals 'not possible' and 'should not'

Affirmative clauses with the modal *ðąąché* 'possible' are seen in (107) and (108). (This modal may also receive the English gloss 'should' or 'could'.) Example (108) illustrates that the post-modal elements agree with the subject of the embedded verb; that is, *nįkšé*, the 2S continuative aspect marker, follows the impersonal *ðąąché*, rather than the embedded verb *ékižǫ* 'do' (which has a 2S subject).

(107) *nižúe ðąąchí ekxai*
nižúe ðąąché akxa-ðe
rain possible 3.CONT-DECL
'it might rain'

(108) *ékižǫ ðąąché nįkšé?*
é-ki-Ya-ǫ ðąąché nįkšé
PREV-PREV-A2S-do possible 2S.CONT
'is it possible for you to do that? could you do that?'

The modal *ðąąché* is seen negated by *aži* in the following example.

[11] This verb is offered by speakers when 'forget' is elicited, in spite of the existence of another verb for 'forget', the doubly inflecting *áa_lǫ_ðį*.

(109) *šcíihtą ðąącházie*
Ya-ðíihta ðąąché-aži-ðe
A2S-touch possible-NEG-DECL
'you shouldn't touch it' (lit., 'it is not possible that you touch it; you cannot touch it')

Sentence (110) has *ékižǫ* 'you do' embedded under a negated version of the modal *ðąąché* 'possible', which is itself embedded under the modal *ðáalį* 'should' (literally, 'good').

(110) *ékižǫ́ ðąąché įke ðáalįe*
é-ki-Ya-ǫ ðąąché ðįké ðáalį-ðe
PREV-PREV-A2S-do possible NEG good-DECL
'you shouldn't be thinking about doing that'

In (111)–(112), the main verb is the modal *ðáalį* 'should'. The negative is applied (semantically but not grammatically) to the higher verb 'should' in the English gloss, but in Osage, the meaning of 'should not' is expressed by negating the lower verb rather than negating *ðáalį*. Such negation may be via either *ðįké* as in (111) or *aži* as in (112); *ðįké* is probably more common in this context than *aži*. The same speaker offered both (111) and (112), with no semantic difference.

(111) *wamáštǫ́ ðįke ðáalį*
wa-ma-Ya-ðǫ́ ðįké ðáalį
VAL-PREV-A2S-steal NEG good
'you shouldn't steal'

(112) *wamáštǫ́ži ðáalį*
wa-ma-Ya-ðǫ́-aži ðáalį
VAL-PREV-A2S-steal-NEG good
'you shouldn't steal'

5.3 Iterative and durative: *štą, ną, šǫ*

In the ordered sequence of possible elements appearing after the verb root, the iterative *(štą* and *ną*) and the durative *(šǫ*) seem to occupy the same slot, and for this reason are treated here as a group. The durative *šǫ* is also discussed elsewhere (see section 7.2.7).

5.3.1 Iterative: *štą, ną*

The iterative markers, *štą* 'incessantly, so much, a lot, so often' and *ną* ~ *na* 'usually, habitually, once in a while; always', differ semantically only in degree of frequency of the verbal action, as follows: *ną* signals occasionally or customarily recurring action, 'generally', 'sometimes', 'frequently', while *štą* represents constantly repeated or recurring action, 'always; over and over, continually'. Both are used for present or past habitual action. They follow the pluralizer and negative marker, if these are present.

Other glosses, such as 'so much' or 'all the time', are possible for the iterative elements:

(113) *íxope štą akxai*
í-Ø-xope štą akxa-ðe
PREV-A3S-lie ITER 3.CONT-DECL
'he lies so much'

(114) *waðáašoe štą*
wa-Ø-ðaašóe štą
VAL-A3S-smoke ITER
'he smokes all the time'[12]

In (115) *ną* (in denasalized form) signifies 'habitually' ('we habitually drink alcohol').

(115) *ąwáðaahta na*
ąk-wa-ðaahtą ną
A1P-VAL-drink ITER
'we drink [alcohol]'

Other examples with *ną* are the following:

(116) *naniǫpažį huuwáli apa húheka ąkáaɣe nąpe*
naniǫpažį huuwáli apa húheka ą-Ø-káaɣe ną-api-ðe
cigarette many SUBJ ill P1S-A3P-make ITER-PL-DECL
'a lot of [too many] cigarettes make me sick'

(117) *žįkážį wíhta wažáže íe awákšuįze mąžį na*
žįkážį wíhta wažáže íe Wa-wa-kšuįze-mažį ną
child 1S.POSS Osage language A1S-P3P-teach-1S.NEG ITER
'I never taught my kids the Osage language'

(118) *oðíhtą kíwali ną*
oðíhtą Ø-kik-wáli ną
car A3S-REFL-stingy ITER
'he's stingy with his car'

[12] A semantic equivalent of the iterative, the adverb *íkiha* 'always, continually', provides another version of this sentence, with identical gloss:

íikiha waðáašoe
íkiha wa-Ø-ðaašóe
repeatedly VAL-A3S-smoke
'he smokes all the time'

(119) *kalíže wéškaaɣe nąe*
kalíže wa-i-Ya-káaɣe nǫ-ðe
flint P3P-with-A2S-make ITER-DECL
'you used to make them with flint'

Sentences which end in *nǫ* or *nǫ[ð]e*, as do (117)–(119) above, seem to be less common than those ending in *nǫpe* as in (116), but we do not explore here the reasons for this phenomenon. While an equivalent for *nǫ* or *nǫe* is not always offered in the English gloss by Osage speakers, the third person sequence *nǫpe* is quite often glossed 'usually', as in the next example:

(120) *oðíhtą kíwali nǫpe*
oðíhtą Ø-kik-wáli nǫ-api-ðe
car A3S-SUUS-stingy ITER-PL-DECL
'he's stingy with his car usually'

5.3.2 Durative *šǫ* 'while, still'

Also appearing in the same post-root slot as *štą* and *nǫ* is *šǫ*, approximately equivalent to 'while' when appearing in an embedded clause. It often appears in subordinate clauses dealing with an ongoing action or state. When appearing in a main clause, *šǫ* is equivalent to 'still'. (See section 7.2.7 for more discussion of *šǫ*.) In embedded clauses, *šǫ* 'while' is typically followed by continuative auxiliaries or positional articles (see section 6.3) such as *ðe* 'moving', *txą* 'standing [animate]', and others seen in examples below. When the exact position is not being emphasized, *akxa* is likely to be used, as in the fragment in (121).

(121) *óhkie šǫ akxái . . .*
wa-o-Ø-hkik-ie šǫ akxa-ðe . . .
VAL-PREV-A3S-RECIP-speak while 3.CONT-DECL
'while he was talking [to someone] . . .'

(122) *ohkíe šǫ akxái ihtáežį ąkxa mą́zeíeohkíe híðape*
o-Ø-hkik-ie šǫ akxa-ðe ihtáežį akxa
PREV-A3S-RECIP-speak while 3.CONT-DECL his.younger.sister SUBJ
mą́zeíeohkíe hí-Ø-ðe-api-ðe
phone.call arrive.there-A3S-CAU-PL-DECL
'he was talking [to someone] when his younger sister called' (lit., 'while he was talking, his younger sister made a phone call arrive there')

In variations on (122), when the position is uncommonly important, *šǫ* can be followed by *txą* 'standing, animate' or by *įkšé* 'sitting', depending on the position of the subject of the embedded clause. The sequence *šǫ txa* would indicate that 'he' was standing. If the subject 'he' in the embedded phrase in (122) above was sitting, then we have *įkšé* as in (123).

(123) *óhkie šǫ įkšé ihtéžį akxa mą́zeieohkie híðape*
o-Ø-hkik-ie šǫ įkšé ihtáežį akxa
PREV-A3S-RECIP-speak while 3.CONT his.younger.sister SUBJ
mą́zeieohkie hí-Ø-ðe-api-ðe
phone.call arrive.there-A3S-CAU-PL-DECL
'he was talking [to someone] when his younger sister called'

Other aspect markers such as *mįkšé* in (124) and other elements such as *ðe* 'moving' in (125) can follow *šǫ*:

(124) *ecí šǫ́ mįkšé waléze wį híðape*
é-ci šǫ mįkšé waléze wį hí-Ø-ðe-api-ðe
there-at while 1S.CONT letter a arrive.there-A3P-CAU-PL-DECL
'while I was there, they sent [me] a letter'

(125) *htáabre šǫ ðé mąščįka ðikšįįcape*
htáabre šǫ ðé mąščįka Ø-ðii-kšįįce-api-ðe
hunting while MOV rabbit A3S-CAU-miss-PL-DECL
'as he went hunting, he missed the rabbit'

5.4 Future/potential *hta*

The future is marked with *hta*, which is usually followed by a continuative auxiliary as in (126)–(128). The use of *hta* to mark future is quite straightforward and is amply illustrated throughout this volume in sentences with all persons and numbers of the verb.

(126) *ie wíhta šǫǫšǫ́ðe aðée hta akxai*
ie wíhta šǫǫšǫ́ðe Ø-aðée hta akxa-ðe
word 1S.POSS always A3S-go FUT 3.CONT-DECL
'my word will endure'

(127) *áðįkxa hta ðaįšé?*
a-ðįįkxa hta ðaįšé
PREV-recline FUT 2S.CONT
'are you going to lie down?'

(128) *šǫǫšǫ́e naníǫpa ðaašóe hta apai*
šǫǫšǫ́ðe naniǫpa Ø-ðaašóe hta apa-ðe
always pipe A3S-smoke FUT 3.CONT-DECL
'he will always smoke'

In a very few cases, *hta* is followed by some other element, for example, by *ðe* or *che*, or it occurs in sentence final position itself. Examples of each appear below.

5.4.1 First and second person *hta* plus third person continuative

One of the special applications of *hta* is for 'could' in an irrealis construction, as in (129).

(129) *kį̨į ékima hta akxai*
kį̨į é-ki-Wa-ǫ hta akxa-ðe
fly PREV-PREV-A1S-do FUT 3.CONT-DECL
'if I could fly'

The use of the third person *akxai* in (129) (rather than the expected 1S aspect marker, e.g. *mįkšé*, to agree with the subject) after *hta* is a device to convey the sense of 'could': 'if it were the case that I could fly'; that is, the combination of the first person inflected verb ('I do [fly]') with the third person *akxai* form gives this particular irrealis interpretation.

Another irrealis context appears in 'we will still be gossiping when the world ends' in (130), which shows one aspect marker, *ąðįkšé* (1D), embedded under another aspect marker, *akxa*. This refinement of the syntax creates an impersonal emphatic equivalent of the English future progressive: 'it will be the case that we are gossiping when the world ends'.

(130) *ątį́ðe ąðįkše hta akxái mǫ́žǫ įké etxa*
ąk-tį́ðe ąðįkšé hta akxa-ðe mǫ́žǫ́ ðįké etxą́
A1P-gossip 1D.CONT FUT 3.CONT-DECL world NEG that.time
'we will still be gossiping when the world ends'

The sentence-final position of the adverbial clause *mǫ́žǫ́ įké etxą* 'when the world ends' in this example is unusual but not unknown, and was possibly influenced by English word order.

Another structurally similar case, seen in (131) below, shows the third person ending *hta akxai* on a second person subject clause, with *hta akxai* being equivalent again to 'it will be the case that'. The clause boundary for the embedded clause immediately follows *ną*, which is within the lower clause. The structure is approximately 'It will be the case that [you're always going to dances]' (in Osage, [*waachíe watói šcée na*] *hta akxai*).

(131) *waachí watói šcée ną hta akxai*
waachí wa-tǫ́pe Ya-ðee ną hta akxa-ðe
dance VAL-look A2S-go ITER FUT 3.CONT
'you're always going to go to dances' (lit., 'it will be the case that you habitually go to dances')

5.4.2 Future/potential *hta* not followed by a continuative marker

Although the future/potential marker *hta* is normally followed by a continuative aspect marker such as *apa*, *hta* itself may be clause-final, or it may be followed by other elements, among them *ðe* or *che*.

5.4.2.1 Clause-final *hta*

Only in a handful of instances were sentences like (132) found, in which *hta* seemed to be a true future but occurred clause-finally. In this example, *hta* appears three times, first before an auxiliary *mįkšé*, and then twice clause-finally. At the end of this sentence, *mįkšé* may be present optionally.

(132) *hǫbrįke oowáhą hta mįkšé kasį, éhtaną hą́ðe brúuwasú hta nį owážu hta*
hǫbrįke oo-Wa-hǫ hta mįkšé kasį, éhtaną
beans PREV-A1S-cook FUT 1S.CONT tomorrow, therefore
hą́-ðe Wa-ðuuwasu hta níi o-Wa-žu hta
evening-this A1S-wash FUT water PREV-A1S-put.in FUT
'I'm going to cook beans tomorrow, therefore tonight I'll clean them and put them in water'

Sentence (133), translated into Osage from the English Bible (Matt. 25:35), shows *hta* at the end of the first clause after *ðįké* 'vanish; become nothing', where it is followed by the conjuction *ąži* 'but'.

(133) *mǫ́žǫ ðáalį ðékše mǫ́zǫ ðékše ðįké hta ąži íe wíhta šǫǫšǫ́ðe aðée hta akxai*
mǫ́žǫ ðáalį ðékše mǫ́zǫ ðékše ðįké hta ąži íe wíhta
world good that world this vanish FUT but word 1S.POSS
šǫǫšǫ́ðe Ø-aðée hta akxa-ðe
always A3S-go FUT 3.CONT-DECL
'heaven and earth shall pass away but my word will endure'

5.4.2.2 *hta ðe* and *hta che*

Occasionally *hta* is followed by *ðe*, as in the questions in the following two examples.

(134) *kší hta ðe?*
a-Ø-kší hta ðe
PREV-A3S-arrive.back.here FUT DECL
'is he coming back?'

(135) *ákahamį žúuce ðe, pée ðuuštáke hta ðe?*
ákaha-į žúuce ðe pée Ø-ðuuštake hta ðe
over-wear red that who A3S-undress FUT DECL
'who is going to undress that one with the red coat on?'

In these examples, ***hta akxái* would be ungrammatical, for reasons that are unclear. Perhaps the reasoning here (and above in (133)) for not using a continuative is that the action contemplated is of a noncontinuative nature—that is, it is limited to being a finite event. The cognate sequence in related languages has been called the future of certainty, but certainty does not seem to characterize *hta ðe* in Osage. Perhaps *ðe* gives (134) the interpretation 'will he arrive back there?'; the motion verb *akši* signals motion completed. This would contrast with a continuative interpretation 'is he now on his way back?', which would involve a verb of motion underway. The fact that deferred future *hta ðe* is felt to be obligatory in (135) may be due to the ceremonial nature of the context.

Future *hta* is sometimes followed by the evidential *che*. This sequence in (136) appears not to differ in meaning from *hta ąkái*, but could possibly be construed as an evidential. This example is in answer to an invitation to attend something.

(136) *ąkáhi hta chə*
ąk-a-hí *hta* *che*
A1P-PREV-arrive.there FUT EVID
'we will be there'

5.5 Continuative auxiliaries: first and second persons

One of the most unusual and interesting morphological features of Osage is that part of the verbal suffixal system which marks position of the subject of the sentence as 'sitting', 'standing', 'lying', or 'moving'. These forms are displayed in table 5.2. They occur towards the end of the verbal complex, often constituting its final element. (They may also follow a presumably nonverbal nominal, pronominal, or adjectival phrase.)

TABLE 5.2. ASPECT MARKERS (POSITIONAL AUXILIARIES) FOR FIRST AND SECOND PERSON SUBJECT

	'sitting'	'standing'	'lying'	'moving'
1S	*mįkšé*	*atxąhe*	*mįkšé*	*ąðįhé*
2S	*nįkšé*	*ðatxąše*	*žákšé*	*ðaįšé*
1D	*ąðįkšé*	*ątxą*	*ąðįkšé*	*ąðé*
1P	*ąkáðe*	*ąkatxą*	*ąkáðe*	*ąkáðe*
2P	*paašé* ~ *nąkxąše*	*paašé*	*paašé*	*paašé*

With two exceptions (1P *ąkáðe* 'we move/go' and 2S *žąkšé* 'you lie'), the positional markers differ from the true verbs 'sit' (*olįį*), 'stand' (*nąąží*), 'lie' (*ážą*), and 'move' (*aðée* 'go'). (As suggested by Koontz [p.c. 1995], *ðaįšé* 'moving (2S)' may derive from *ðaðįše* (*ðį* is 'moving' in Omaha-Ponca). The Osage continuative form is never heard as ***ðaðįšé*, however, but rather as *ðaįšé, ðąįšé, ðąąšé*, or *ðaašé*. For the 'moving (1S)' continuative, *ðį* does show up in emphatic pronunciation (*ąðįhé*), while only *ąąhé* or *ąhé* appears in nonemphatic contexts.

The exact interpretation of these markers beyond information concerning position and movement is complex; they do indicate shape but only in the sense of configuration expressed in the position (sitting, standing, lying, moving) of the semantic subject. They convey continuative aspect, and carry other semantic information as well, as discussed briefly below. Other Siouanists have referred to these aspect markers as "auxiliaries," and we use this term interchangeably with "(continuative) aspect marker." The aspect markers code number and person of the subject. Normally, the preceding verb is also inflected for subject by a pronominal marker; as noted in section 5.1, *api* is not used to mark plurality of a verb followed by an aspect marker.[13] Sometimes the preceding verb lacks any subject inflection, especially when it is of an adjectival nature.

Third person continuative markers are discussed in section 5.6, as they behave somewhat differently from the first and second person markers under discussion here.

When one of these aspect markers is present, it signals continuative aspect. Their absence signifies noncontinuative present or past, and most often calls for a past tense gloss for the sentence in English. The continuative auxiliaries are not always present where action of the verb is continuative; even if there is no auxiliary, the clause may be continuative if context implies continuativity strongly enough that the aspect marker can be omitted without introducing too much ambiguity. Contextual control is, of course, quite powerful in first and second person. When embedded under a higher verb, a clause will often (but not always) lack a continuative aspect marker, control of aspect coming from the higher clause.

Speakers interviewed used the aspect markers effortlessly and naturally in the final years of the twentieth century. Even though it is secondary to the semantics of the main verb, the aspect marker in an Osage clause occasionally is fully translated in the speakers' English glosses, as in the following case (in which the verb itself is not marked for 1S):

(137) *waðílą mįkšé*
waðílą mįkšé
think 1S.CONT[sitting]
'I am sitting here thinking'

[13] But see section 5.2.2.4 for negative 3P continuatives.

Certainly there are clear contrasts between continuative meaning of a clause with a continuative aspect marker, and noncontinuative meaning of the clause without aspect marker, as in the next two examples.

(138) *awáachi ąhé*
Wa-waa-chí ąðįhé
A1S-PREV-dance 1S.CONT[moving]
'I'm dancing'

(139) *awáachie*
Wa-waa-chí-ðe
A1S-PREV-dance-DECL
'I danced'

5.5.1 Special uses of aspect markers

5.5.1.1 'Moving' continuative aspect

In 1S and 2S, the 'moving' suffixes are rather consistently used to imply that the action has or had been ongoing for some time (the sense expressed in English by the perfect progressive tense, 'have/had been doing') as in the following five examples.[14]

(140a) *tíðe ąąhé*
tíðe ąðįhé
gossip 1S.CONT[moving]
'I have been gossiping'

(140b) *tíðe mįkšé*
tíðe mįkšé
gossip 1S.CONT[sitting]
'I'm gossiping'

[14] The following two examples also offer a contrast illustrating this principle.

(i) *íðixope ðąįšé*
í-ði-xope ðaįšé
PREV-P2S-lie 2S.CONT[moving]
'you have been lying'

(ii) *íðixope nįkšé*
i-ði-xope nįkše
PREV-P1S-lie 2S.CONT[sitting]
'you're telling a lie'

(141) *wiškí, hąpái ówǫ ąąhé*[15]
wi-ški, hą́pa-ðe ówǫ́ ąðįhé
1S-also day-this busy 1S.CONT[moving]
'I was/have been also busy today'

(142) *kóoci ašką́ ąąhé*
kóoci Wa-šką ąðįhé
long.time.ago A1S-move 1S.CONT[moving]
'I've been going on for a long time'

(143) *owíhkie ąąðįįhé*
o-wi-hkik-ie ąðįhé
PREV-P2S.A1S-RECIP-speak 1S.CONT[moving]
'I've been telling you'

(144) *wabríopxa ąąðįhé*
wa-Wa-ði-opxa ąðįhé
VAL-A1S-CAU-aware 1S.CONT[moving]
'I've been finding out; I am finding out'

Other examples are glossed by speakers using present or past progressive constructions, as in (145) and (146), or merely present habitual, as in (147).

(145) *owíhkie hkǫ́bra ąąhé*
o-wi-hkik-ie Wa-kǫ́-Wa-ða ąðįhé
PREV-P2S.A1S-RECIP-speak A1S-PREV-A1S-want 1S.CONT[moving]
'I wanted/was wanting to talk to you'

(146) *owíhkie ąąðįhé*
o-wi-hkik-ie ąðįhé
PREV-P2S.A1S-RECIP-speak 1S.CONT[moving]
'I'm telling you' ('I'm going as I'm talking to you')

(147) *íkiha táatą áwawakˀú ąhe*
íkiha táatą o-w-Wa-wa-kˀú ąðįhé
repeatedly thing PREV-EPw-A1S-VAL-lend 1S.CONT[moving]
'I loan them stuff all the time'

Another device that strengthens the perfect progressive nature of the sentence is the use of the iterative *štą* 'incessantly' following the verb root, as in the next example:

[15] *wiškí* in this example shows the first person singular inalienable possessive *wi-*. The inalienable possessive paradigm is also seen in the possessive pronouns 1S *wíhta*, 2S *ðíhta*, 3S *íhta*, in the kinship system (*wi-*, *ði-*, *i-*), and in other pronominal paradigms.

(148) *íkiha táatą áwawak?ú štą ąhe*
íkiha táatą o-w-Wa-wa-k?ú štą ąhe
repeatedly thing PREV-EPw-A1S-VAL-lend ITER 1S.CONT[moving]
'I've been loaning them stuff all the time'

Aspect markers are often optional and do not change the meaning of the sentence in any obvious way, as seen in the following two examples; possibly this is due to strong contextual effects. This optionality is seen both in statives (such as the examples here) and in actives.

(149) *wáazo*
waa-ki-zo
P1P-DAT-enjoy
'we like it'

(150) *wáazo ąkáðe*
waa-ki-zo ąkáðe
P1P-DAT-enjoy 1P.CONT
'we like it'

These two synonymous examples contrast with the completed-action clause ending in *pe* in the example below.

(151) *wáazope*
waa-ki-zo-api-ðe
P1P-DAT-enjoy-PL-DECL
'we enjoyed it, we had a good time'

5.5.1.2 'Standing' continuative aspect

There is an interesting semantic similarity between the use of the morpheme *txą* (sometimes denasalized to *txa*) in *etxą́* 'it's time' and its use in the 'standing' continuative paradigm. The 'standing' continuative is often used to convey imminence of action, the sense of launching into or being on the verge of undertaking an activity. (See modal *ðąąché etxą́* in section 7.3.3.) In (152) below, the 1P 'standing' marker *ąkatxą́* is used when the speaker is poised to begin action.

(152) *hpǫ́hka ąkítaake hta ąkatxái*
hpǫ́hka ąk-ki-taaké hta ąkatxą́-ðe
Ponca A1P-DAT-fight FUT 1P.CONT[standing]-DECL
'we're going to fight the Poncas'

When asked about the use of *ątxą́he* (or its variant *akxą́he*) '1S standing', one speaker replied that her sister "used to use this word often. She'd come in, stand there, and demand it." The implication is that the 'standing' marker implies that immediate action is contemplated. These are not absolute equivalencies, as the 'standing' marker can also be glossed in English using a simple present progressive tense, with no sense of launching into an activity; this is seen in (153) (where *kx* is a surface variant of *tx*):

(153) *wáazǫ ąkákxai*
waa-ki-zo ąkatxą́-ðe
P1P-DAT-enjoy 1P.CONT[standing]-DECL
'we're having a good time'

5.5.1.3 'Sitting' continuative aspect

The 2P aspect marker for 'sitting', *nakxą́še*, closely resembles the 2S aspect marker for 'standing', *ðatxą́še*, especially since *ð* varies with *n* in the language, and since *tx*, *kx*, and *tkx* vary with each other before *a* or *ą*. Whatever their similar or identical origins may have been, nowadays even speakers who do not replace *txą* with *kxą* or *tkxą* do use *nakxą́se* for '2P sitting' and *ðatxą́še* for '2S standing'. Moreover, use of *nakxą́še* is quite limited, and seems to be nearly restricted to addressing the crowd at the *ilǫ́ǫška* dances (Osage war dances held in June each year). Possibly it is archaic, and reserved for ceremonial situations. Used for addressing those present, *nakxą́še* refers to 'all of you, all you people [who are sitting]'. Otherwise the 2P aspect marker *paašé* is used for all positions.

(154) *ilǫ́ǫška zaanii xóhka ški nakxą́šé . . .*
ilǫ́ǫška záani xóhka ški nakxą́šé ...
war.dances all drummers also 2P.CONT[standing]
'all of you here at the *ilǫ́ǫška* dances, you drummers too...'

In 1S, *mįkšé* is a default aspect marker, used sometimes even when the speaker is standing; in the context of (155), *ątxąhé* '1S standing' would have been expected to appear instead of *mįkšé* '1S sitting/lying'.

(155) *ðachí nakxą́še weeą́na mįkšé*
Ya-chí nakxą́še wee-Wa-ną mįkšé
A2S-arrive.here 2P.CONT[standing] PREV-A1S-grateful 1S.CONT
'I'm grateful to you all for coming'

5.5.2 Aspect markers in questions

The fairly frequent absence of continuative aspect markers in nonfuture interrogative constructions may be due to the fact that most questions about what is happening 'now' are pragmatically controlled and therefore do not need additional indication of aspect. It may also be due to the fact that questions tend to be about completed past, inviting the use of noncontinuative aspect, which is manifested in Osage by the absence of a continuative aspect marker and presence of *ðe* 'declarative'. This is not an absolute. In future questions, especially, the continuative auxiliaries are used to distinguish second person plural from singular, as in the next two examples.

(156) *ščée hta paasé?*
Ya-ðée hta paašé
A2S-go FUT 2P.CONT
'are you [plural] going?'

(157) *ščée hta nįkšé?*
Ya-ðée hta nįkšé
A2S-go FUT 2S.CONT[sitting]
'are you [singular] going?'

The aspect markers are not customarily dropped when forming interrogative sentences with *tąhé* 'be well' or interrogative sentences of the type that are expressed in English with a copulative construction, or sentences with predicate adjectives in English ('Sonny is strong'). In almost all questions in the future, a continuative aspect marker follows the future *hta*, as in (158). (But see section 5.4.2.)

(158) *kasįe waachí watóə ščée hta paašé?*
kasįta waachí wa-tópe Ya-ðée hta paašé
tomorrow dance VAL-watch A2S-go FUT 2P.CONT
'are you all going to see the dance tomorrow?'

5.5.2.1 Continuative with stative verbs in questions

Example (159) has 2S patient inflection followed by the 2S aspect marker. It is not unusual to find clauses where the person and number marking of the post-root auxiliary agrees with a patient pronominal or with a nonsubject noun in the clause, choice of the aspect marker being based on the identification of the experiencer regardless of the experiencer's grammatical function in the sentence.

(159) *ðízo nįkšé?*
ði-zo nįkšé
P2S-enjoy 2S.CONT[sitting]
'are you enjoying it?'

5.5.2.2 Possessive pronouns in continuative aspect

The next two examples are clauses made up of a possessive pronoun plus a continuative aspect marker, involving no verb as such.[16]

[16] An alternative view would be to regard *hta* or *íhta* as a stative verb 'belong to', but under such an approach the inflection of the possessor would be highly irregular (1S *wi-*, 2S *ði-*, 3S *i-*, 1P *ąko-*). But *wíhta*, *ðíhta*, *íhta* exhibit the same prefixes of

(160) *wíhta mįkšé*
wihta *mįkšé*
1S.POSS 1S.CONT[sitting]
'it's mine'

(161) *ðíhta nįkšé*
ðihta *nįkšé*
2S.POSS 2S.CONT[sitting]
'it's yours'

A similar clause with the second person aspect marker *nįkšé* is seen in (162).

(162) *hcí ąkóhta ðiškíihta ðíihta nįkšé*
hcí *ąkóhta* *ði-škíhta* *ðíhta* *nįkšé*
house 1P.POSS 2S-also 2S.POSS 2S.CONT[sitting]
'our house is yours [too]'

5.5.3 Embedded aspect marker

An aspect marker can appear in an embedded clause, and in that position may be followed by a subordinating conjunction, such as *aha* in (163).

(163) *táatą ékižǫ ðaįšé aha wéeąna mįkšé*
táatą *é-ki-Ya-ǫ* *ðaįšé* *aha*
thing PREV-PREV-A2S-do 2S.CONT[moving] whenever
wée-Wa-na *mįkšé*
PREV-A1S-grateful 1S.CONT[sitting]
'whatever you're doing, I'm grateful'

This example is also correct with nominalizer *che* following the aspect marker in place of *aha,* as in (164).

(164) *táatą ékižǫ ðaįšé che wéeąna mįkšé*
táatą *é-ki-Ya-ǫ* *ðaįšé* *che*
thing PREV-PREV-A2S-do 2S.CONT[moving] NOM
wée-Wa-na *mįkšé*
PREV-A1S-grateful 1S.CONT[sitting]
'whatever you're doing, I'm grateful'

Sentence (163) paraphrased:' whenever you're doing something, I'm always grateful',; this contrasts with (164) which could be paraphrased: 'the thing that you're doing now, I'm grateful for it'.

---

inalienable possession as the kinship system (*wi-*, *ði-*, *i-*), and as other pronominal paradigms, implying that *-hta* is a nominal, not a verbal, root.

5.6 Continuative auxiliaries in third person: *akxa* and *apa*

Endings in Osage sentences, such as the continuative markers, are arrayed along axes of time (continuative vs. completed action); space (presence of the subject at the speech event vs. absence); motion (travel of the subject through space vs. lack of such movement); and, to a lesser extent, number (plural vs. singular). A learner of Osage can be exposed to hundreds of sentences without any clear generalization emerging with regard to uses of grammatical markers with respect to these parameters. The parameter of time is the most easily accounted for; it is marked by a clear 'completed action' marker and absence of a continuative auxiliary. Still, the question of what considerations dictate the selection of one of the endings over the others is a complex question, as can be seen in the discussion in this section.

On the whole, singular or plural status of the subject is irrelevant to the third person auxiliaries to be examined in this section (*akxa* and *apa*). Operative factors are whether the subject is present at the speech event, with the additional consideration of whether the subject is at rest (sitting or standing), in motion, or out of view. Additional conceptual complexity for the non-Osage speaker is introduced in understanding the selection of these aspect markers in sentences about the past.

Both *akxa* and *apa* mark continuative aspect and occur in minimal pairs contrasting with *pe* (past completed *pe* or iterative *nąpe*). For 1S and 2S, on the other hand, past completed action is indicated merely by the absence of a continuative auxiliary.

The third person auxiliaries *akxa* and *apa* are separate from the general positional articles (*txą, che, įkšé, kše, ke, ðe, pa*) treated in section 6.3. *akxa* and *apa* are also best thought of separately from the first and second person auxiliaries given in table 5.2 above and discussed in section 5.5. These third person forms relate to the paradigms for first and second persons in table 5.2 only in the sense that *akxa* marks 'nonmoving' (sitting, standing, and lying) positions, while *apa* marks 'moving'. But *akxa* and *apa* also encode information concerning presence vs. absence of the subject at the moment of the conversation.

An extended use of the auxiliaries *akxa* and *apa* incorporates a consideration of number, as follows: there are some sentences that are minimal pairs in which *akxa* signals singular subject and *apa* plural subject. However, this distinction is considered secondary here.

Throughout this discussion, it should be borne in mind that the continuative auxiliaries are often followed by declarative *ðe*, resulting in surface forms *akxai* (from *akxa-ðe*) and *apai* (from *apa-ðe*).

5.6.1 Choice between auxiliaries *akxa* and *apa*

The continuative aspect markers *akxa* and *apa*, also called "central" auxiliaries, are examined first. The term "central" separates *akxa* and *apa* from other auxiliaries, the positional auxiliaries of rare usage, *įkšé*, *kše*, etc. (discussed in section 5.6.8).

The uses of *akxa* and *apa* can be summed up as follows (see table 5.3): *akxa* is used if the subject is present at the speech event, in view, and at rest; *apa* is used otherwise (i.e., if the subject is absent, out of view, or in motion).

TABLE 5.3. CHOICE BETWEEN THIRD PERSON CONTINUATIVE *akxa* AND *apa*

SUBJECT PRESENT	
subject in the vicinity but in motion or out of view	*apa*
subject present with speaker and at rest	*akxa*
SUBJECT ABSENT	*apa*

As noted above, singularity or plurality of subject mostly plays no role in third person continuative auxiliary choice, nor does a difference between present continuative, past continuative, or future continuative. Whether the subject is human, nonhuman, or inanimate likewise makes no difference to selection of continuative auxiliary. Verbs of nonaction, denoting states, such as *hpíǫ* 'know', may take continuative auxiliaries if the subject is present (as discussed below in section 5.6.6).

This pattern can be contrasted with noncontinuatives exhibiting the endings *pe* and *nąpe*, discussed in section 5.6.6.

The following subsections examine the usages just outlined.

5.6.2 Subject absent: *apa*

As table 5.3 shows, *apa* is used as auxiliary in sentences with absent subjects, as in the following example (where the plural subject 'they' is not present at the speech act):

(165) *wacúe káaɣe apa*
wacúe Ø-káaɣe apa
bread A3P-make 3.CONT
'they were making some bread'

In both (166) and (167), the subject is not in the vicinity of the speaker; these sentences too correspond to the "subject absent" part of table 5.3.

(166) *žįkážį tą́hé apai?*
žįkážį tąhé apa-ðe
child well 3.CONT-DECL
'how are your children?' (lit., 'are the children all right?')

(167) *į́į ąpa skíke apai*
į́į apa skíke apa-ðe
rock SUBJ heavy 3.CONT-DECL
'the rock is heavy; the rocks are heavy'

If the speaker and the rock or rocks are present at the same location, a similar sentence is correct with final *akxa* signaling 'subject present':

(168) *į́į ekxa skíke akxa*
į́į akxa skíke akxa-ðe
rock SUBJ heavy 3.CONT-DECL
'the rock is heavy; the rocks are heavy'

In (169) the subject 'they' is either absent, or present and moving around:

(169) *ahí hta apai*
a-Ø-hí hta apa-ðe
PREV-A3P-arrive.there FUT 3.CONT-DECL
'they'll be there'

In the examples with *kǫ́ða* 'want' below, the subject is absent in the first, and present in the second. (Both sentences could have been interpreted as having plural subjects 'they' under the same 'absent' and 'present' parameters.)

(170) *kǫ́ða apa*
Ø-kǫ́-Ø-ða apa
A3S-PREV-A3S-want 3.CONT
'he is wanting'

(171) *kǫ́ða akxa*
Ø-kǫ́-Ø-ða akxa
A3S-PREV-A3S-want 3.CONT
'he is wanting'

In (172), the subject may be singular or plural, but must be present.

(172) *íxope akxai*
í-Ø-xope akxa-ðe
PREV-A3S/P-lie 3.CONT-DECL
'he's telling a lie; they're telling a lie'

In the following example, the subject 'he' must be present with the speaker of the sentence. If subject 'he' were absent, the sentence would end with *hta apai*, and would be identical to (169) just above.

(173) *ahí hta akxai*
a-Ø-hí *hta* *akxa-ðe*
PREV-A3S-arrive.there FUT 3.CONT-DECL
'he'll be there'

At any rate, with *akxa*, the subject 'they' must be present and at rest in the next example.

(174) *mą́zeíe ohkíe áha ohkíhkie akxái*
mą́zeíe *o-Ø-hkik-ie* *áha*
phone PREV-A3S-RECIP-speak whenever
o-hkik-hkik-ie *akxa-ðe*
PREV-RECIP-RECIP-speak 3.CONT-DECL
'they talked when he called' (lit., 'whenever he called, they talked')

In a past interpretation of a continuative sentence, one might ask if the 'absence' of the subject is based on the absence of the subject in the speaker's immediate surroundings at the time in the past that the action took place (which could be termed, rather, 'speaker's absence' when the action took place), or alternatively if this absence parameter requires that the subject of this action in the past be absent when the utterance occurs. Unfortunately speakers who could clarify these rather subtle distinctions were not available by the time this analysis was worked out in the early years of the twenty-first century; thus only data already collected was available for testing hypotheses. As far as I can tell, however, the presence of the subject at the time of the utterance takes precedence over presence/absence of the speaker at the event described by the sentence. If the subject is present at the time of utterance, *akxa* is used, whether the speaker was present at the past event or not; if the subject is absent at the time of utterance, *apa* is used. (The parameter of motion overrides that of subject presence; that is, *apa* appears if a subject is or was present but moving around in the vicinity.)

In the example just below, the subject 'they' is absent at the speech event.

(175) *mą́zeíe ohkíe áha ohkíhkie apái*
mą́zeíe *o-Ø-hkik-ie* *áha*
phone PREV-A3S-RECIP-speak whenever
o-Ø-hkik-hkik-ie *akxa-ðe*
PREV-A3P-RECIP-RECIP-speak 3.CONT-DECL
'they talked when they/he called' (lit., 'whenever he called they talked')

5.6.3 Subject present: *akxa*

Whether plural or singular, a verb with subject present (if it is not moving) will use *akxa*. (The first *akxa* in the example below, immediately after *šǫ́ke* 'dog', is a subject marker [section 6.1], not an auxiliary.)

(176) *šǫ́ke akxa wáli óhoo akxái*
šǫ́ke akxa wáli ó-Ø-hoo akxa-ðe
dog SUBJ really PREV-A3S-bark 3.CONT-DECL
'the dog is sure barking'

Although in elicited sentences it sometimes seems that *akxa* is used as singular and *apa* as plural, this is not a fixed rule. Example (177) is a typical sentence about a plural subject that is present; it contains *akxa*.[17]

(177) *tąhį akxai*
tąhé akxa-ðe
well 3.CONT-DECL
'they are well [and present]'

If the person whose feet are under discussion in (178) is present, we find *akxa*. Here and elsewhere in Osage, the possessor is considered the semantic subject of such a sentence and the entity whose presence dictates choice of auxiliary is the possessor. If the possessor is absent from the speech event, then *apa* will be used as auxiliary instead of *akxa*.

(178) *sí wáli ɣoį ekxai*
sí wáli ɣoį akxa-ðe
foot really stink 3.CONT-DECL
'his feet really stink'

In (179), *akxa* dictates that the subject is present when the sentence is uttered; otherwise, *apa* would replace *akxa*. Whether or not the speaker of the sentence will be present when the action takes place in the future makes no difference to the choice of auxiliary.

(179) *waníðe hta akxa*
wa-Ø-níðe hta akxa
VAL-A3S-give.away FUT 3.CONT
'he will be giving away'

[17] Another example contains the nonaction verb *ékiðe*:

ékiðe įkí ekxai
é-ki-Ø-ðe ðįké akxa-ðe
PREV-PREV-A3S/P-think NEG 3.CONT-DECL
'they aren't thinking about doing it'

Other factors interact with presence or absence of the subject to determine auxiliary choice. If the subject is present in the vicinity but is moving around, or nearby just out of sight, then *apa* will be used, just as it would be if the subject were completely absent (regardless of the subject's position or motion parameters). Thus, for instance, examples (180) and (181) in the next section, used of present but moving subjects, would also be used if the subject were absent and not moving.

5.6.4 Subject present but moving or out of sight: *apa*

In the following examples, with *apa*, the subject is moving; in (181), the speaker is looking out the window, seeing the subject go along. Movement, with respect to these markers, is considered travel in space, not merely hand movements, such as those involved in putting on a coat or cooking something if standing still.

(180) *aðée apa*
a-Ø-ðé *apa*
PREV-A3P-go 3.CONT
'they are on their way (moving)'

(181) *aðée apa*
a-Ø-ðé *apa*
PREV-A3S-go 3.CONT
'he is on his way (moving)'

If *apa* were replaced with *akxa* in sentence (181), the result (*aðée akxa*) could be translated 'he's in there going', implying that he is making preparations to leave but is still here with us. Alternatively, the speaker is looking at the subject who is a figure on the page of a book and who is going somewhere. If the figure is in the book, it is usually considered 'here' , that is, as being present with speaker, and the *akxa* ending is used, especially for nonmotion verbs. If in the same story another entity is considered to be farther away, this may be translated into 'not present', resulting in that entity having *apa* as auxiliary. If both are felt to be absent, both will use the same auxiliary (*apa*).[18]

The context for the next example is that the dogs are present in the vicinity but out of sight of the speaker, a situation that demands *apa* and disallows *akxa*.

[18] Obviously, the use of pictorial representations, whether stills or video, in elicitation of this part of Siouan grammar introduces ambiguity as to the presence/absence or movement/nonmovement of a subject portrayed in the example, and can produce misleading results. Related to this is the speaker's concept of characters in storytelling.

(182) *šǫ́ke apa mąšcį́ka ðuxí apái*
šǫ́ke apa mąšcį́ka Ø-ðuuxí apa-ðe
dog SUBJ rabbit A3P-chase 3.CONT
'the dogs are chasing the rabbit(s)'

However, replacing *apai* with *akxai* in this example is ungrammatical, as shown in example (183), because *akxa* does not allow motion while the verb *ðuxí* 'chase' obviously involves motion.

(183) ***šǫ́ke akxa mąšcį́ka ðuuxí akxai*
šǫ́ke akxa mąšcį́ka Ø-ðuxí akxa-ðe
dog SUBJ rabbit A3P-chase 3.CONT-DECL
('the dogs are chasing the rabbit(s)')

Although at the moment of the utterance in (184) below, the subject of the sentence (*šį́tožį* 'boy') is not present, the operative factor in the choice of the auxiliary is the fact that the boy was moving when seen (the speaker was there, and saw him moving); hence *apa* is used.

(184) *šį́tožį wį iiðáðe hkóopši apai*
šį́tožį wį ii-Ø-ð-Wa-ðe Ø-hkóopše apa-ðe
boy a PREV-P3S-EPð-A1S-see A3S-flee 3.CONT-DECL
'the boy that I saw was running away'

The subject 'he' in (185) is present and in motion around the vicinity (in the immediate area of the speech event) or out of view (but still in the vicinity) or, less likely in context, he is absent:

(185) *naniǫpaži kǫ́ða apai*
naniǫpaži Ø-kǫ́-Ø-ða apa-ðe
cigarette A3S-PREV-A3S-want 3.CONT-DECL
'he's wanting a cigarette'

In (186) the plural subject is present in the vicinity but moving and/or out of view, or is absent. Exactly the same is true of the singular subject in (187). (Again, there is no difference between singular and plural.)

(186) *tąhį́ apa*
tąhé apa
well 3.CONT
'they are well'

(187) *tąhį́ apa*
tąhé apa
well 3.CONT
'he is well'

In (177) (repeated below as (188)), the subject is present and at rest, in view, as evidenced by the use of *akxa* with a plural subject.

(188) *tąhį ekxái*
Ø-tąhé akxa-ðe
A3P-be.well 3.CONT-DECL
'they are well'

The context of dancing provides an interesting contrast. In both (189) and (190) the subject 'he' is present. Movement is considered to be travel across the floor (as 'travel' is used in dance), signalled by *apa* in (189); nonmovement (*akxa*) is lack of such travel, that is, dancing in place. The exact interpretation of movement in Dhegiha languages suggests itself as a topic for further study.

(189) *waachí apai*
waa-Ø-chí apa-ðe
PREV-Ø-dance 3.CONT-DECL
'he is dancing'

(190) *waachí akxai*
waachí akxa-ðe
PREV-Ø-dance 3.CONT-DECL
'he is dancing in place'

In (191), the subject must be present and sitting with the speaker as he or she utters the sentence. If, on the other hand, 'he' is moving around, or walking out of thę room, *apa* must be used, as in (192).

(191) *íxope štą akxai*
í-Ø-xope štą akxa-ðe
PREV-A3S-lie ITER 3.CONT-DECL
'he lies so much'

(192) *íxope štą apai*
í-Ø-xope štą apa-ðe
PREV-A3S-lie ITER 3.CONT-DECL
'he lies so much'

5.6.4.1 Plural vs. singular

Perhaps as an extension or recycling of the distinction between *akxa* and *apa*, one occasionally finds *akxa* used for singular subject and *apa* for plural, as in the two examples just below. Alternatively, perhaps it is only that Osage speakers, faced with finding a difference between the two following examples and having the presence vs. absence distinction unavailable to conscious articulation, reach for a parallel with English number distinctions. This, then, could be a recent and developing distinction in the language.

(193) *ahí hta akxa*
a-Ø-hí *hta* *akxa*
PREV-A3S-arrive.there FUT 3.CONT
'he'll be there'

(194) *ahí hta apa*
a-Ø-hí *hta* *apa*
PREV-A3P-arrive.there FUT 3.CONT
'they'll be there'

Possibly, too, this distinction of number could be predicated on the basis of the more diffuse or less focused nature of either a group of people or things (plural) or absent subjects, with the tendency being to regard imaginary plural subjects as being absent (therefore using auxiliary *apa*) and to regard imaginary singular subjects as being present and sitting or standing beside the speaker of the sentence and thus more focused and less diffuse (therefore, with auxiliary *akxa*). It seems likely that both plurality and absence lend diffuseness. It must be kept in mind that the plurality distinction via auxiliary selection is best thought of as but a tendency or an extension of the meaning, a secondary usage, and that the true meaning of *apa* is 'absent' or 'moving' and not 'plural'.

5.6.5 Tense and the continuative

Although *akxa* and *apa* carry information about aspect, they do not convey tense as it is thought of in English. It is informative to note the glosses given by the Osage speakers of the sentences below. The first English equivalent given by an Osage speaker for a simple Osage sentence that he or she has produced with the aspect marker *akxa* will likely be singular 'he' and in present habitual ('wants') or progressive ('is wanting') tense.

(195) *naniǫpažį wį kǫ́ða akxái*
naniǫpažį *wį* *Ø-kǫ́-Ø-ða* *akxa-ðe*
cigarette a A3S-PREV-A3S-want 3.CONT-DECL
'he wants (is wanting) a cigarette'

Most sentences with *apa* or *akxa* auxiliaries can be glossed optionally as present or past in English, as in (196).

(196) *naniópaži kǫ́ða apai*
naniópaži *Ø-kǫ́-Ø-ða* *apa-ðe*
cigarette A3P-PREV-A3P-want 3.CONT-DECL
'a whole bunch of them want cigarettes; a whole bunch of them wanted cigarettes'

In third person sentences, the future/irrealis marker *hta* is normally followed by a continuative; that is, we find *hta* plus either *akxa* or *apa*. (But see section 5.4.2.)

(197) *šǫǫšǫ́we naniǫ́pa ðaašóe hta apai*
šǫǫšǫ́we naniǫ́pa Ø-ðaašóe hta apa-ðe
always pipe A3S-smoke FUT 3.CONT-DECL
'he will always smoke'[19]

(198) *naniópaži ąkǫ́ða hta apai*
naniǫ́pažį ą-Ø-kǫ́-Ø-ða hta apa-ðe
cigarette P1S-A3P-PREV-A3P-want FUT 3.CONT-DECL
'a whole bunch of them will be wanting cigarettes from me'

(199) *ahí hta akxai*
a-Ø-hí hta akxa-ðe
PREV-A3S-arrive.there FUT 3.CONT-DECL
'he'll be there'

While in (197) and (198) the subject is absent from the speech event, sentence (199) was spoken with subject present; if the subject 'he' were not present, *hta apai* would have to have been used: *ahí hta apai* 'he'll be there'.

In (200), with *akxa* marking aspect on the verb, the main subject 'John' must be present and at rest. John has made a request of Mogri (that he help Mary), but the action (his helping Mary) has not been accomplished yet. If John were not present at the speech event, (200) would end in *hcée apai* instead of *hcée akxai.* (See also section 6.1 for subject marker *akxa*.)

(200) *Johna akxa Mogri Mary óhką hcée akxai*
John-a akxa Mogri Mary ó-Ø-Ø-hką
John-SYL SUBJ Mogri Mary PREV-P3S-A3S-help
hce-é-Ø-Ø-e akxa-ðe
INJ-PREV-P3S-A3S-say 3.CONT-DECL
'John told Mogri to help Mary'

Examples (201) and (202) will appear with (*apa* subject marker and) the aspect marker *apa* 'moving' (not the aspect marker *akxa*) even if the girls are present when the speaker is talking about it, because the verb is envisioned as involving movement. (Sentence (201), of course, could also be glossed as past.)

[19] Some speakers prefer *waðáašoe* to *ðaašóe,* even where a noun object is mentioned. See the discussion of valence reduction in section 4.1.

(201) *šímiži apa óhkạ apai*
šímiži apa ó-Ø-hkạ apa-ðe
girl SUBJ PREV-A3P-help 3.CONT-DECL
'the girls are helping'

(202) *sitúį šímiži apa óhkạ apai*
sitǫ́į šímiži apa ó-Ø-hkạ apa-ðe
yesterday girl SUBJ PREV-A3P-help 3.CONT-DECL
'yesterday, the girls were helping'

Sometimes the English gloss obscures the continuative nature of the sentence, as well as the semantics of the Osage verb used. In (203), *akxa* communicates the sense of 'right now it is arriving at being noon', or 'noon is arrived'. This example could also be interpreted as past/continuative: 'It was straight up noon'.

(203) *míðohta ahí akxa*
mį́įðohta a-Ø-hí akxa
noon PREV-A3S-arrive.there 3.CONT
'it's straight up noon'

Even when the English gloss appears to portray a completed action, the continuative may be called for in Osage. In (204), the use of the continuative marker *apa* in what would appear to be a completed action sentence may be explained by the following idea: 'John was going around seeing each of us, one at a time'; action was spread over a period of time (and involved movement on the part of the subject). Interestingly, forms ending in *pe* (completed action) are ungrammatical here: ***weðapipe* or ***weðapape* are impossible.

(204) *Jóhna apa záani wéeðapi apai*
John-a apa záani wa-íi-Ø-ðe-api apa-ðe
John-SYL SUBJ all P1P-PREV-A3S-see-PL 3.CONT-DECL
'John saw every one of us'

Note that (205) could initially be misleading, as one might expect *pe*, given the English gloss with simple past tense 'he cried'. However, the context, which implies a continuative reading, was 'the first time they roached his hair, he was crying while they did it' (speaker was not present and subject is not present at utterance).

(205) *ɣaaké apai*
Ø-ɣaaké apa-ðe
A3S-cry 3.CONT-DECL
'he cried'

The continuative is also glossed as past habitual, with 'used to', as seen in the following sentence, where 'he' is absent at utterance:

(206) *óhką apai*
ó-Ø-Ø-hką *apa-ðe*
PREV-P3S-A3S-HELP 3.CONT-DECL
'he used to help her'

5.6.6 Contrast with noncontinuative

The parameters for use of the continuative aspect markers given in section 5.6.1 can be contrasted with those for noncontinuative markers (see table 5.4 below). Choice of auxiliary was governed in past continuative sentences by presence vs. absence of the subject at the moment of the utterance, but this consideration does not apply to noncontinuative sentences. In noncontinuatives, the speaker's presence at the time the action took place is of greater importance than whether the subject is present or absent at the utterance. In a noncontinuative clause, if the speaker was not present and only received news of the information in the sentence by hearing it from another person, a reportative ending will appear. (See discussion of the reportative in section 7.3.1.)

Habitual or iterative ('always do something') is distinct from continuative ('be engaged in doing something'). Third person iterative usually occurs with endings *nąpe* or *štąpe*, while continuative takes the (continuative) aspect markers *apa* or *akxa*.

Equivalency or exact glosses between Osage and English are not possible without including a great deal of explanation. A few comments here will be helpful. In table 5.4, both reportative and generic sentences have been included for comparison and contrast. Generic statements also use the ending *pe*, and sometimes the iterative *nąpe*. Iterative completed action sentences such as 'he always dances' (with the idea of 'over and over again') will usually carry the iterative ending *nąpe*. A one-time event in the past will have *pe*. Nonaction verbs such as *hpíǫ* 'know' and *óxta* 'love' will often have *pe* in the present: *hpíǫpe* is either 'he knows it' or 'he knew it'; *ée ą́oxtapé* is 'he loves me'.

Some additional remarks may help to clarify the table.

Generic statements are, for example, 'Flowers are pretty', where 'flowers' is a generic category of things. These expressions end in *nąpe*. However, a statement about specific flowers such as 'The flowers here are looking pretty' is not generic, but rather is 'continuative with subject present', requiring *akxa*.

TABLE 5.4. NONCONTINUATIVE AND REPORTATIVE MARKERS FOR THIRD PERSON

TYPE OF SENTENCE	COMMENTS	ENDING USED
completed action	speaker was present when subject performed action of verb (subject may be present or absent when sentence is uttered)	*pe*
reportative		*aape* 'they said'
		aapa 'they are saying'
generic statement	subject present or absent	*nǫpe*
iterative (verbs of action)	action is recurring rather than ongoing (ongoing uses continuative marker)	
subject absent		*nǫpe*
subject present	choice between iterative *nǫpe* and continuative *apa/akxa* depends on focus: a sense of immediacy requires continuative	*nǫpe* or *apa/akxa*
iterative (verbs of nonaction)	a sense of inherent, unchanging condition	*nǫpe*
verbs of nonaction or state		
subject absent		*pe*
subject present	choice is optional	*pe* or *apa/akxa*

Third person singular sentences portraying finite events which do not carry the "plural" *api-ðe* (i.e., *pe*) are quite rare, and have been omitted for purposes of this discussion.

Certain verbs such as 'know' and 'lie around' group together as preferring *nǫpe* as an iterative ending more strongly than action verbs do, which are likely to use *apa* or *akxa*.

Verbs of nonaction are not necessarily grammatically stative verbs. (Recall that a "stative verb" for purposes of this grammar is one that marks subject by patient pronominals.)

5.6.6.1 Contrasting sentences: *pe* vs. continuative

The form *pe* (which is underlyingly *api-ðe*) signals on the one hand completed action or event, as in the three pairs of examples just below with *ísi* 'dislike', *aðée* 'go' and *kǫ́ða* 'want' respectively.

(207) *ísi akxa*
í-Ø-Ø-si *akxa*
PREV-P3S-A3S-dislike 3.CONT
'she doesn't like it'

(208) *ísipee*
í-Ø-Ø-si-api-ðe
PREV-P3S-A3S-dislike-PL-DECL
'she didn't like it'

(209) *aðée apa*
a-Ø-ðée *apa*
PREV-A3P/S-go 3.CONT
'he is going; they are going'

(210) *aðáape*
a-Ø-ðée-api-ðe
PREV-A3S/P-go-PL-DECL
'he/they went [left here, setting out on journey]'

(211) *kǫ́ða akxa*
Ø-kǫ́-Ø-ða *akxa*
A3S-PREV-A3S-want 3.CONT
'he is wanting'

(212) *kǫ́ðape*
Ø-kǫ́-Ø-ða-api-ðe
A3S-PREV-A3S-want-PL-DECL
'he [had] wanted'

The two examples below also contrast past continuative *akxa* with *pe*. An attempt is made in the translation of the second sentence, (214), to convey by using the past perfect 'they had talked' the sense of completed action or finite event marked by *pe*.

(213) *mą́zeíe ohkíe áha ohkíhkie akxái*
mą́zeíe *o-Ø-hkik-ie* *áha*
telephone PREV-A3S-RECIP-speak whenever
o-hkik-hkik-ie *akxa-ðe*
PREV-RECIP-RECIP-speak 3.CONT-DECL
'they talked when[ever] he called' (lit., 'whenever he called they talked/used to talk')

(214) *mą́zeíe ohkíe áha ohkíhkiape*
mą́zeíe *o-Ø-hkik-ie* *aha*
telephone PREV-P3S-RECIP-speak when

o-Ø-hkík-hkik-ie-api-ðe
PREV-A3S/P-RECIP-RECIP-converse-PL-DECL
'they had talked when he called' (lit., 'whenever he called they talked/held a talk')

The use of *štą* or *ną* to mark iterative present or past is seen in (215). Usually (but not always) the subject must be absent from the speech event when *štąpe* or *nąpe* is used. The subject of this sentence is not present while the speaker is talking and, according to the speaker, cannot be present if *štąpe* is used.[20]

(215) *íxope štąpe*
í-Ø-xope štą-api-ðe
PREV-A3S-lie-PL-DECL
'he lies so much'

In (216), since the verb *hpíǫ* 'know' is followed by *pe*, the subject is (probably) not present. Either if he is outside fixing his car, or if he is out of sight and mind, far away somewhere, *pe* is used. This is the case for both singular and plural subjects. A typical scenario is that a person asks the question, 'Who could I get to talk Osage?' and receives the answer *hpíǫ apai* 'he knows how', provided the subject 'he' is in the vicinity moving around. If the response is, rather, *hpíǫ akxai*, the subject 'he' must be present and at rest with the speaker. If the subject is not present, the most likely answer to the question is as in (216).

(216) *wažáže íe hpíǫpe*
wažáže íe Ø-hpíǫ-api-ðe
Osage language A3S-know.how-PL-DECL
'he's good at talking Osage; he knows Osage'

Especially for iteratives with *nąpe*, as in the next example, the distinction among the possible endings becomes so slight as to render them practically synonymous. In a sentence where the presence or absence of a human subject is not a consideration, any of the various endings discussed here can be appropriate. Sentence (217) was offered with three different versions of the second clause: first with *nąpe*, as shown; then with *apai* (*húheka ąkáaɣe apai*) rather than *nąpe*; and finally with *ną apai* (*húheka ąkáaɣe ną apai*); no difference in meaning among the three could be detected or described by the speaker.

[20] Example (215) is similar to a general statement 'he is a liar' (the noun 'liar' may be expressed as *íxopeštą*). The avoidance of *štąpe* if the subject is present may be due to the dictates of politeness (not using *štą* 'incessantly' in the subject's presence), rather than to grammatical considerations.

(217) *naniǫ́apažį huuwáli apa húheka ąkáaɣe nąpe*
naniǫ́apažį huuwáli apa húheka ą-Ø-káaɣe nąapi-ðe
cigarette many SUBJ ill P1S-A3P-make ITER-PL-DECL
'a lot of [too many] cigarettes make me sick'

In (218) and (219), *apai* and *pe* contrast. Example (218), with *apai*, indicates 'always, all the time'; (219), with *pe*, is the simple statement 'Meg is a pretty girl' (or 'Meg is a good girl', since *ðáalį* is 'pretty' or 'good').

(218) *Megə apa šímižį ðáalį apái*
Meg-a apa šímižį ðáalį apa-ðe
Meg-SYL SUBJ girl pretty/good 3.CONT-DECL
'Meg is a pretty girl'

(219) *Megə apa šímižį ðáalįpe*
Meg-a apa šímižį ðáalį-api-ðe
Meg-SYL SUBJ girl pretty/good-PL-DECL
'Meg is a pretty girl'

Some interesting English glosses emerge to capture the Osage semantics of the continuative versus completed action, as seen in the contrast of (220) and (221) with (222). The speaker went to considerable length to describe the context for (220) as 'they're just finishing up the food, they're still fixing it; they've been fixing it and they're still working on it'.

(220) *ónǫbre toə káaɣe apái*
ónǫbre toe Ø-káaɣe apa-ðe
food some A3P-make 3.CONT-DECL
'they're making some food'

(221) *káaɣe apai*
Ø-kaaɣe apa-ðe
A3P-make 3.CONT-DECL
'they're making it [the food] now'

(222) *káaɣape*
Ø-káaɣe-api-ðe
A3P-make-PL-DECL
'they made it [the food]'

In examples (223) and (224), a similar contrast of continuative state (of having lost something) versus completed action is seen with the stative verb *óxpaðe* 'lose stuff'.

(223) *óxpaði apai*
wa-o-Ø-xpaðe *apa-ðe*
VAL-PREV-P3P-lose 3.CONT-DECL
'they've lost something'

(224) *óxpaðape*
wa-o-xpáðe-api-ðe
VAL-PREV-lose-PL-DECL
'they lost something'

Example (225) below, glossed in past tense in English, is followed by a continuative sentence in (226) using the same verb. This second sentence uses a continuative version of the same verb *alée* 'go back there (motion underway)'. (See the discussion of motion verbs in section 4.3). The third example, (227), is more appropriate to express 'they're going to go home', that is, the intention of returning home.

(225) *aláape*
a-Ø-lée-api-ðe
PREV-A3P-return-PL-DECL
'they went home [they set out for home]'

(226) *alée apai*
a-Ø-lée *apa-ðe*
PREV-A3P-return 3.CONT-DECL
'they're on their way home'

(227) *alée hta apai*
a-Ø-lée *hta* *apa-ðe*
PREV-A3P-return FUT 3.CONT-DECL
'they're going home'

The following four examples involve the stative verb *ní_hce* 'be cold'. The first two examples are continuative and clearly contrast with *pe* in the third example (230). Note also the use of *akxai* in (231), as a past continuative, signaling that the subject of the sentence is present when the speaker utters the sentence ("utterance presence"). The secondary distinction between singular and plural subjects is seen in (228) and (229), where the singular subject 'he' is spoken of as if he were here (*akxai*), and the plural 'they' as if they were absent (*apai*).

(228) *níhci akxái*
ní-Ø-hce *akxa-ðe*
PREV-P3S-cold 3.CONT-DECL
'he's cold'

(229) *níhci apái*
ní-Ø-hce apa-ðe
PREV-P3P-cold 3.CONT-DECL
'they're cold'

(230) *níhcipe*
ní-Ø-hce-api-ðe
PREV-P3S-cold-PL-DECL
'he was cold'

(231) *níhci akxai*
ní-Ø-hce akxa-ðe
PREV-P3S-cold 3.CONT-DECL
'he was cold'

A similar contrast between continuative and noncontinuative appears in the next pair of examples:

(232) *wak?ó əkxa taakí ekxai*
wak?ó akxa Ø-taaké akxa-ðe
woman SUBJ A3S-fight 3.CONT-DECL
'that woman's fighting'

(233) *wak?ó əkxa táakape*
wak?ó akxa Ø-taaké-api-ðe
woman SUBJ A3S-fight-PL-DECL
'that woman has fought'

Example (234) has a singular subject although the verb is reciprocal (with *hkik*); it is a "bleached reciprocal" (treated in section 4.6.3.2). This example forms a minimal pair with (235) that illustrates the secondary distinction between singular and plural. Again, we have *pe* for past completed action in (236).

(234) *ohkíe akxai*
o-Ø-hkik-ie akxa-ðe
PREV-A3S-RECIP-speak 3.CONT-DECL
'he was/is talking (to someone)'

(235) *ohkíe apai*
o-Ø-hkik-ie apa-ðe
PREV-A3P-RECIP-speak 3.CONT-DECL
'they were/are talking to someone'

(236) *ohkíəpe*
o-Ø-hkik-ie-api-ðe
PREV-A3P-RECIP-speak-PL-DECL
'a whole bunch of them talked; he's talked to him'

To securely place the time in the past for past iterative sentences, time expressions such as *kóoci* 'a long time ago' are used. For such sentences *nąpe* is used rather than *apai*, as in (237).

(237) *kóoci óhką nąpe*

kóoci	*ó-Ø-Ø-hką*	*nąapi-ðe*
long.time.ago	PREV-P3S-A3S-help	ITER-PL-DECL

'a long time ago, he used to help her'

5.6.7 Dorsey's auxiliaries

Although my entire analysis was based on my own corpus of Osage sentences mostly in isolation, and many of them unfortunately but necessarily elicited, I find that my analysis, painstakingly arrived at through the years, happily coincides with Dorsey's (1883a) annotations, such as "*a apa* 'was saying as he moved'" (1883a: "The Devouring Mountain," line 13). Dorsey used auxiliary *akxa* (*akqá* in his orthography) throughout his Osage texts on verbs with nonmoving singular subjects which were themselves followed by subject marker *akxa* (glossed by Dorsey as "the subject"). Dorsey notes that *a apa* 'he says as he goes' is used because he (the crier), is in motion as he makes the proclamation: "Were he motionless, [*a akxa*] would be used" (1883a: "The Devouring Mountain," notes, p. 3). In fact, all the factors presented here in my analysis—moving/nonmoving and present/absent—seem to be borne out in Dorsey's Osage myths. The following retranscribed opening sentences from Dorsey show a contrast between *akxa* and *apa* after the verb *ecí* 'be there' in (238)–(239). In the second example, (239), Dorsey glosses *apa* as "moving," since the buffalo was moving. This exactly coincides with the analysis presented here, which was arrived at independently on the basis of a different corpus of data.

(238) *paxó wį waðášcuce ecí akxa ska*

paxó	*wį*	*waðášcuce*	*ecí*	*akxa*	*ska*
mountain	a	eat.stuff	there.was	CONT	SUPP

'there was once a devouring mountain' (Dorsey 1883a: "The Devouring Mountain," line 1)

(239) *hcé tóka wį ecí apa ska*

hcé	*tóka*	*wį*	*ecí*	*apa*	*ska*
buffalo	male	a	there.was	CONT	SUPP

'there was once a buffalo bull' (Dorsey 1883a: "The Wolf and the Buffalo," line 1)

Dorsey also uses the auxiliary *akxa* in a sentence with a plural subject that is not moving in (240), which likewise exactly coincides with my analysis.

(240) *oohǫ akxa ska*
oo-Ø-Ø-hǫ akxa ska
PREV-him-they-cook SUBJ SUPP
'they were boiling him perhaps' (Dorsey 1883a: "How Náqðe-cape Was Eaten by His Grandmother," p. 4, line 4)

5.6.8 Positional auxiliaries in third person: *įkšé* and others

The auxiliaries *akxa* and *apa* discussed up to this point should be considered "central" auxiliaries and separate from their cousins the "noncentral" positional auxiliaries *txą*, *che*, *įkšé*, *kše*, simply called positional auxiliaries here. The occurrence of the positional auxiliaries in clauses with third person subjects is extremely limited in the data seen in Osage so far; they are used only when the subject's position (standing, sitting, or lying) is uncommonly prominent in the speaker's mind. Otherwise, the central auxiliary *akxa* is appropriate for a present subject, whether sitting, standing, or lying, and the central auxiliary *apa* in sentences with an absent or moving subject. In the very rare instances where a noncentral positional auxiliary is used instead of *akxa* or *apa*, it usually also signals that the verb and its subject belong in the background of the discourse context and are not central to the conversation. Such positional auxiliaries were omitted from tables 5.3–5.4. The 'standing' positional *txą* has not appeared in post-root position in the data gathered. The positional *che* 'inanimate, standing' (or its homonym, nominalizer *che*) in complementizer position appears in embedded sentences, treated in section 7.2.4.

The most interesting cases are with *įkšé* 'sitting' and *kše* 'lying'. The positional *įkšé* shows up infrequently in the same slot as the aspect markers (the central auxiliaries *akxa* and *apa*) under certain circumstances. This does not necessarily mean that *įkšé* has the same status as *apa* and *akxa* (or *pe*). In general, and if generalizations can be drawn based on such rare examples as these are, *įkšé* is not likely to appear in a main clause; it appears following the verb root in three sorts of context.

(a) It may appear after a stative verb, as in (241).[21]

(241) *hįįce įkšé léke įkšé*
hįįce įkšé léke įkšé
dish SIT shatter SIT
'that dish sitting there, it's broken'

[21] *léke* in this example functions as 'be shattered', although it is related to intransitive *léke* 'shatter' and to transitive *kaaléke* 'shatter by sudden force.'

Example (242) shows another member of the positional auxiliary set, *kše* 'lying' in the same location, after an adjective/verb *húheka* 'sick'. Such examples of *kše* are rare indeed.

(242) *hkáwa kše húheka kše?*
hkáwa kše húheka kše
horse LIE sick LIE
'that horse lying there, is it sick?'

(b) It may appear in a question following an interrogative form with no true verb present, as in (243)–(245).

(243) *peehta įkšé?*
pée-hta įkšé
who-POSS SIT
'whose turn is it?'

(244) *háaðaskǫ įkše?*
háa-ðaskǫ įkše?
INDEF-size(?) SIT
'how big (small) is it?'

(245) *ðiihǫ́žį howaįkí įkšé?*
ði-iihǫ́žį howaįkí įkšé?
your-aunt where SIT
'where is your aunt?'

(c) It may appear in a backgrounded subordinate clause, as in (246).

(246) *óhkie šǫ́ įkšé ihtéžį akxa mázeie híðape*
wa-o-Ø-hkík-ie šǫ įkšé ihtaižį akxa
VAL-PREV-A3S-RECIP-speak while SIT younger.sister SUBJ
mą́zeie Ø-Ø-hi-ðe-api-ðe
phone.call P3S-A3S-arrive.there-CAU-PL-DECL
'he was talking [to someone] when his younger sister called' (lit., 'while he was [sitting] talking to someone his younger sister made a phone call arrive there')

In (247), an example almost identical to (246), the subject may be in any position (including sitting or standing or lying) when *akxa* is used in lieu of *įkšé*. Yet another version, with *óhkie šǫ́ apa* as the first clause, would signal by the *apa* that the speaker is not present where subject 'he' is located as the sentence is uttered. In contrast, in (247), with *óhkie šǫ́ akxa* (and also the subject marker *akxa* on the subject of the next clause *ihtéžį*), the speaker of the sentence is present where the subject 'he' and also the subject *ihtéžį* 'his younger sister' are located as the sentence is uttered (another instance of "utterance presence" of the subject).

(247) *óhkie šǫ́ akxai ihtéžį akxa mą́zeie híðape*
wa-o-Ø-hkík-ie *šǫ* *akxa-ðe* *ihtežį* *akxa*
VAL-PREV-A3S-RECIP-speak while 3.CONT-DECL younger.sister SUBJ

mą́zeie *Ø-Ø-híðe-api-ðe*
phone.call P3S-A3S-arrive.there-CAU-PL-DECL
'he was talking [to someone] when his younger sister called'

Use of *ðįkšé* (a form of *įkšé*) in a main clause where *akxa* is expected, as in (248), is likewise rare and characterizes a context in which 'she' is quite secondary in some sense; example (249) shows the more common version of this question.

(248) *áška olįį ðįikše?*
áška *o-Ø-lįį* *ðįkšé*
close PREV-A3S-sit EPð-SIT
'is she sitting close to you?'

(249) *áška olįį akxa?*
áška *o-Ø-lįį* *akxa*
close PREV-A3S-sit 3.CONT
'is she sitting close to you?'

For *įkše* as a modifier of a noun or pronoun signaling 'sitting', see section 6.3 (on positional articles).

5.7 Finite *che* vs. iterative *ną-ðe*

Another small set of expressions is found in a complementizer position at the right end of an embedded clause, occupying a different position from the iterative *štą* and *ną* discussed above and seen in table 5.1. These complementizer elements are *che* and *ną-ðe*. The data and the analysis are sketchy, but should be mentioned here, especially in view of the homophonous *ną* discussed in section 5.3.1.

The form *ną* 'habitually' may occur in this complementizer position and be preceded by a continuative aspect marker, such as *ðaįšé*, as in (250).

(250) *táatą háažǫ́ ðaašé nai wéeana mįkšé*
táatą *haa-Ya-ǫ́* *ðaįšé* *ną-ðe* *wée-Wa-na* *mįkšé*
thing INDEF-P2S-do 2S.CONT ITER-DECL PREV-A1S-grateful 1S.CONT
'whatever you do pleases me'[22]

According to Rood (p.c. 1995), the Lakota demonstrative cognate with Osage *ðe* can occur in this same position as a kind of resumptive

[22] In modifying this sentence, a second speaker used three different pronunciations of underlying *na-ðe*: *nai*, *nə* and *ną*.

pronoun for the preceeding sentence. In fact, the resumptive pronoun *ðe* does occur in Osage in a similar configuration but usually with a more prominent pronunciation than the *ðe* in (250). Pending further analysis we take *nąðe* and its shortened forms *nąe*, *nae,* and *nai* to be an iterative version of the resumptive pronoun *ðe*. In speech, the elements *che* and *nąe* discussed in this subsection are separated from the main clause by a pause; alternatively, they may even occur along with their entire phrase rightward of the higher verb.

Another element appearing in this complementizer position is *che*; the expression *wéena* 'grateful; be grateful' usually takes *che* on its complement clause. Contrast (250) above, where the iterative resumptive pronoun appears, with (251):

(251) *táatą škáaɣe che wéeana mįkšé*
táatą Ya-káaɣe che wée-Wa-na mįkšé
thing A2S-make/do NOM PREV-A1S-grateful 1S.CONT
'what you did pleased me'

See the discussion of nominalizer *che* in section 7.2.4, and the discussion of evidentials in section 7.2.3.

6 Nominal expressions and adjuncts

In this chapter we will give an overview of components of the clause other than the verb, with particular attention to modifiers of the noun or pronoun that are related to definiteness, position or configuration, and grammatical function in the sentence.

The previous chapter outlined postverbal continuative aspect markers. Those for first and second persons appear in a matrix governed by the parameters of position, i.e., whether sitting, standing, lying, moving, in addition to considerations of plurality; secondary usages based on initiation of action, or continuance or duration of action were also seen (section 5.5). The third person aspect markers (*akxa* and *apa*) form a separate set, for which other parameters such as presence/absence, motion/rest, and visibility of the subject were shown to operate (section 5.6). Some of the same morphemes recur in the nominal systems considered in the present chapter as subject markers and positional articles (see table 6.1).

TABLE 6.1. SUBJECT MARKERS AND POSITIONAL ARTICLES

SUBJECT MARKERS (ON THIRD PERSON SUBJECTS ONLY)	*akxa, apa*
POSITIONAL ARTICLES (ON THIRD PERSON NONSUBJECTS)	
sitting	*įkšé*[a]
standing (animate)	*txą*
standing (inanimate)	*che*
lying	*kše*
moving	*ðe*
plural	*pa*
multiple, scattered, dispersed	*ke*

[a] *įkšé* appears as *ðįkšé* in a few instances; the two are taken to be equivalent.

Subject markers are treated in section 6.1; the choice between *apa* and *akxa* in this function is governed by considerations almost, but not entirely, identical to the aspect marker parameters. Sections 6.2–6.5 examine briefly the nominal nonsubject system, and there a different set of parameters influences the choice of the modifier or pronoun. For the demonstratives in section 6.2, considerations of distance from the speaker (distinguishing three degrees) and proximity to the hearer are important. For the choice among the positional articles in section 6.3, the parameters are related to position or configuration, and have labels such as 'horizontal, long, lying', 'round, sitting', 'vertical, standing', 'scattered, dispersed' vs. 'gathered up', as well as 'animate' vs. 'inanimate'. Within this complex and interesting system of positional articles, plurality for inanimates is expressed by an overlay of the same system upon itself, in a sort of double-tiered analysis involving collocational configurations, discussed in section 6.4. The related configurational postpositions (*įkší, kši, ki, ci*) are discussed in section 6.5.

The rest of the chapter treats various other topics relevant to the nominal system or to other nonverbal components of the clause: further postpositions (section 6.6), equivalents of adjectives (section 6.7), numerals (section 6.8), adverbs (section 6.9), pronouns (section 6.10), noun derivation (section 6.11), and truncation (section 6.12). Nouns for kinship relations, which have distinctive inflectional properties, are discussed and listed in the Appendix.

6.1 Subject markers

I have elected to call subject markers those items one of which usually follows a noun or pronoun subject in Osage: *akxa* and *apa*. They are homophonous with the postverbal aspect markers *akxa* and *apa*,[1] and appear on both animate and inanimate subjects. The subject markers *akxa* and *apa*, like their postverbal auxiliary counterparts, signal nonmoving and moving respectively, but have the additional deictic significance 'here, close to the speaker' for *akxa* versus 'there farther from the speaker', or, importantly, 'unseen by the speaker' for *apa*, and extended use involves issues of singularity and plurality. Proximate/obviative status may eventually prove helpful in describing their usage in further detail. (See also section 5.6 for the postverbal aspect markers.) The subject markers discussed in this section never appear on objects of active transitive verbs. They may appear, however, on subjects of statives.

6.1.1 Articles and subject markers

The Osage equivalent of the English indefinite article 'a, an' is *wį*, which is also used for 'one'. (In counting, however, *wį́xce* 'one' is used instead of *wį*.) For indefinite plural, *tóa* (~ *tóe*) 'some' is used. Both follow the noun: *waléze wį* 'a book', *waléze tóa* 'some books'. However, unlike

[1] Of course, the aspect markers are often followed by *ðe* 'declarative', and so appear as *akxai* and *apai* on the surface. Subject markers do not take such forms.

English, the indefinite article is only optionally present, and the bare noun *waléze* may be 'a book', 'some books', and even 'the book(s)'; context will often dictate the exact choice of meaning.

Even though it is true that the appearance of the indefinite article *wį* 'a, an, one' on a noun usually blocks use of a subject marker, *akxa* and *apa* after nouns are best thought of as subject markers rather than as definite articles ('the'), since what they do most often and most prominently is to mark the subject of the sentence, regardless of its definiteness, and they do not appear on nonsubjects. Neither 'John's horse' nor 'Bill' is marked with *akxa* in (1), because these individuals are not subjects.

(1) *Johna hkáwa íhta Bill ąkˀúpe.*
John-a hkáwa íhta Bill ąk-Ø-kˀú-api-ðe
John-SYL horse 3S.POSS Bill A1P-P3S-give-PL-DECL
'we gave John's horse to Bill'

However, in (2) and (3) 'John' is a subject and *akxa* appears. 'John' in (2) is no more or less concrete or definite than the nouns in (1). Describing *akxa* as merely a definite article would not properly portray its use in the grammar. Claims that prominence is the factor shown by *akxa* and *apa* are simply unsustainable for the Osage data.

(2) *Johna akxa šǫ́žį Mary kˀú akxai*
John-a akxa šǫ́žį Mary Ø-Ø-kˀú akxa-ðe
John-SYL SUBJ puppy Mary P3S-A3S-give 3.CONT-DECL
'John is giving Mary the puppy'

(3) *Johna akxa ąwáchįpe*
John-a akxa o-ą-Ø-chį́-api-ðe
John-SYL SUBJ LOC-P1S-A3S-hit-PL-DECL
'John hit me'

Subject markers do not appear on objects, such as 'John' in (4).

(4) *Johna awáchį*
John-a o-Ø-Wa-chį́
John-SYL LOC-P3S-A1S-hit
'I hit John'

However, in addition to their principal function—marking subjects—the subject markers do in some minimal pairs add definiteness. The subject in (5) is indefinite, the subject of (6) more definite.

(5) *táatą ąkóhta wį xǫ́pe*
táatą ąkóhta wį Ø-xǫ́-api-ðe
thing 1P.POSS a A3S-break-PL-DECL
'something of ours broke'

(6) *táatą ąkóhta akxa xǫ́pe*
táatą ąkóhta akxa Ø-xǫ́-api-ðe
thing 1P.POSS SUBJ A3S-break-PL-DECL
'whatever it was that belonged to us broke; something of ours broke'

Likewise, in (7) no *akxa* appears, and the subject is interpreted as indefinite:

(7) *oðíhtą wį́ ípše*
oðíhtą wį́ í-Ø-pše
car a PREV-A3S-pass.by
'a car came by'

In (8), which contains a sequence of indefinite article *wį* plus *akxa*, the element *akxa* is acceptable only in a partitive sense, 'one from among a group'.

(8) *níhka wį akxa aðáape*
níhka wį akxa Ø-aðé-api-ðe
man a A3S-go SUBJ-PL-DECL
'one of these men went'

Discussing an indefinite three men, the subject marker is optional, and its presence adds specificity to the gloss, which would be approximately 'those three men went; a certain three men went'.[2]

(9) *níhka ðáabrį aðáape*
níhka ðáabrį Ø-aðé-api-ðe
man three A3S-go-PL-DECL
'three men went'

(10) *níhka ðáabrį akxa aðáape*
níhka ðáabrį akxa Ø-aðé-api-ðe
man three SUBJ A3S-go-PL-DECL
'a certain three men went'

[2] In negative sentences, the indefinite article *wį* 'a, one' or *tóe* 'some' or any sort of equivalent to 'the, that' is much less likely to appear. No equivalent of the English indefinite article appears in (i), nor does an equivalent of the English definite article appear in (ii):

(i) *htóožu níni hkǫ́bramąží mįkšé*
htóožu níni hkǫ́bra-maží mįkšé
meat.pie cold I-want-1S.NEG 1S.CONT
'I don't want a cold meat pie'

(ii) *htóožu ótaa ðįké*
htóožu ó-taa ðįké
meat.pie PREV-heat/cold NEG
'don't freeze the meat pie'

Still, it can at least be said that, in general, subject markers appear on common and proper nouns only when they are used as (definite or specific) subjects, whether of active or stative verbs.

(11) *Mary akxa htóožu toa káaɣape*
Mary akxa htóožu toa káaɣe-api-ðe
Mary SUBJ meat.pie some make-PL-DECL
'Mary made some meat pies'

(12) *hcí stáða*
hcí stáðe-a
house paint-IMPER
'paint the house'

(13) *hpáažį įįhǫ́ akxa kikˀúpe*
hpáažį iihǫ́ akxa Ø-Ø-ki-kˀu-api-ðe
baby mother SUBJ P3S-A3S-DAT-give-PL-DECL
'the mother gave it to her baby'

(14) *níi ekxa opˀą́ðe nąpé*
níi akxa opˀą́ðe ną-api-ðe
water SUBJ 3S.steam ITER-PL-DECL
'water steams'

(15) *waléze oxpáðe akxai*
waléze o-Ø-xpáðe akxa-ðe
book PREV-P3S-lose 3.CONT-DECL
'she's lost her book'

(16) *Frances akxa waléze oxpáðape*
Frances akxa waléze o-Ø-xpáðe-api-ðe
Frances SUBJ book PREV-P3S-lose-PL-DECL
'Frances lost her book'

Other stative sentences with a subject marker include 'ours is broken' (19), 'our house is warm' (20), 'coat is (coats are) warm' (21)–(23), 'car broke' (24), 'weather is bad' (27), 'dog is yellow' (35)–(36), 'tree is pretty' (62), 'apple is rotten' (63).

6.1.2 Pronominal expressions

These subject markers, *akxa* and *apa*, also mark as subjects various pronouns, as well as nouns modified by possessives.

(17) *tówa akxa waachípi áape*
tówa akxa waa-Ø-chí-api é-Ø-e-api-ðe
that.one SUBJ PREV-A3P-dance-PL PREV-A3P-say-PL-DECL
'they said those men danced'

(18) *tówa apa háachi hcí ohpéwį kǫ́ða apai*
tówa apa háachi hcí ohpéwį
that.one SUBJ continually house enter
Ø-kǫ́-Ø-ða apa-ðe
A3P-PREV-A3P-want 3.CONT-DECL
'those ones [dogs] keep wanting to come inside the house'

(19) *ąkóhta akxa xǫ́pe*
ąkóhta akxa Ø-xǫ́-api-ðe
1P.POSS SUBJ A3S-break-PL-DECL
'ours is broken'

(20) *hci ąkóhta akxa šcúuce akxai*
hci ąkóhta akxa šcúuce akxa-ðe
house 1P.POSS SUBJ warm 3.CONT-DECL
'our house is warm'

(21) *ákahamį ðíhta akxa šcúuce?*
ákahamį ðíhta akxa šcúuce
coat 2S.POSS SUBJ warm
'is your [singular] coat warm?'

(22) *ákahamį ðíhtapi akxa šcúuce?*
ákahamį ðíhta-api akxa šcúuce
coat 2S.POSS-PL SUBJ warm
'are your [plural] coats warm?'

(23) *ákahamį íhtapi apa šcúuce apai?*
ákahamį íhta-api apa šcúuce apa-ðe
coat 3.POSS-PL SUBJ warm 3.CONT-DECL
'are their coats warm?'

(24) *oðíhta ąkóhta akxa xǫ́pe*
oðíhtą ąkóhta akxa Ø-xǫ́-api-ðe
car 1P.POSS SUBJ A3S-break-PL-DECL
'our car broke'

In (25) and (26), the subject marker appears on the possessor of what is the grammatical subject in English ('car'). In these Osage sentences, however, the possessor is actually the grammatical subject of the clause. Sentence (25) is approximately 'Preston is always troubled with [lit., "bad on account of"] the car'. The same verb, *íhpiiži*, is elsewhere 'sick' or 'sick with'.

(25) *Preston apa oðíhta íikiiha íihpiiži apai*
Preston apa oðíhtą íkiha í-Ø-hpiiži apa-ðe
Preston SUBJ car always with-P3S-bad 3.CONT-DECL
'Preston's car is always going bad on him'

In (26), the possessor of the arm carries the subject marker but only optionally. Nearly parallel in English is 'John has a broken arm' (more literally, 'John is such that they broke his arm').

(26) *Johna akxa áa ðixǫ́pe*
John-a akxa áa Ø-ðixǫ́-api-ðe
John-SYL SUBJ arm P3S-break-PL-DECL
'John's arm is broken; John broke his arm'

Other sentences involving possessives, however, may treat the possessor as a constituent of the subject noun phrase (as in, e.g., example (35) below).

6.1.3 Inanimates

Subject markers are used not only on animate subjects but also on inanimate subjects, as seen in (14) and (20)–(24) above ('water', 'house', 'coat', 'car'). In (27) and (28) below, 'weather' is the subject, and in (29) and (30) respectively generic 'whiskey' (sitting or standing on the table in front of the speaker) and 'cigarettes'. As subject marker for inanimates, either *apa* (as in (23) and (30)) or *akxa* (as in the other examples) may be used.

(27) *situí mą́ąɣį akxa wálį hpíižiapé*
sitǫ́į mą́ąɣe akxa wálį hpíiži-api-ðe
yesterday weather SUBJ very bad-PL-DECL
'the weather was bad yesterday'

(28) *hǫpái mą́ąɣi akxa ðáalį ąkxái*
hǫ́pa-ðe mą́ąɣe akxa ðáalį akxa-ðe
day-this weather SUBJ good 3.CONT-DECL
'today the weather is good'

(29) *hpéceni akxa žúoka ðíðuuhpíiži hta akxái*
hpéece-níi akxa žúoka ði-Ø-ðuu-hpíiži hta akxa-ðe
fire-water SUBJ body P2S-A3S-CAU-bad FUT 3.CONT-DECL
'whiskey is bad for your health'

(30) *nąniǫpažį apa žúoka ðuhpíižipe*
nąniǫpažį apa žúoka Ø-ðuu-hpíiži-api-ðe
cigarette SUBJ body A3P-CAU-bad-PL-DECL
'cigarettes make your [i.e., one's] body bad'

6.1.4 Choice of subject marker

The choice of *apa* or *akxa* as subject marker is based in general on the same considerations as the choice of aspect marker, but some differences will be pointed out here. (See section 5.6 for aspect markers.) Subject marker choice is summarized in table 6.2.

TABLE 6.2. SUBJECT MARKER CHOICE

SUBJECT PRESENT IN VICINITY	
subject in motion and/or out of view	*apa*
subject at rest	*akxa*
SUBJECT ABSENT (REGARDLESS OF MOTION/REST)	*apa*

Briefly, *apa* is used unless the subject is present and at rest, in which case *akxa* is used. This applies to all subjects, regardless of their animacy or plurality. ("Present" here means "utterance presence"—i.e., that the subject is now present at the utterance of the sentence, not that the speaker was present at the event described by the clause.) From another perspective, we might say that moving (*apa*) vs. nonmoving (*akxa*) is the strongest consideration in choosing a subject marker, followed closely by absent (*apa*) vs. present (*akxa*), so that a subject who is present, if moving, will receive *apa* as subject marker. In the sections just below, examples appear illustrating each subcase.

6.1.4.1 Divergence from the auxiliary system: *akxa* for recently present subjects

A refinement of these parameters is needed. If the subject was just present but is now absent, that subject still receives the present marker *akxa*, while *apa* appears as continuative auxiliary on the verb. This, then, is a way in which the subject marker system diverges from the auxiliary system; that is, where a subject is now out of sight (or absent) but has just been with us, then that subject receives the *akxa* subject marker (as proximate—because the subject was just here) but the verb will have the *apa* aspect marker (for absent or moving). For example, if a boy has been here with us and leaves to go to church, we say:

(31) *šį̆tožį akxa wíkiehci ci aðée apai*
šį̆tožį akxa wíkie-hci ci aðée apa-ðe
boy SUBJ prayer-house to go 3.CONT-DECL
'the/that boy (now absent but just here) is on his way to church'

The same considerations apply to the past continuative aspect, as in (32).

(32) *šǫ́ke apa mąščįka ðuxí apai*
šǫ́ke apa mąščįka Ø-ðuuxi apa-ðe
dog SUBJ rabbit A3P-chase 3.CONT-DECL
'the dogs were chasing the rabbit(s)'

Sentence (32) would also be correct with *akxa* as subject marker (i.e., *šǫ́ke akxa mąščįka ðuxí apai*). This is a "retained" *akxa*, indicating that the subject 'dogs' was quite recently present with us (that is, where the speaker is located). If the subject had not been just recently present, then *akxa* as subject marker would be ungrammatical because the subject is in motion. Another possibility is that the subject marked with *akxa* is now with us but the event 'the dogs were chasing the rabbit(s)' occurred earlier. This sentence would be ungrammatical outside of these two situations—one in which the subject has just departed our company and "retains" the *akxa*, or the other where the subject is now present with us and at rest (not moving around) but earlier was in motion during the action reported by the verb (i.e., "utterance presence").

6.1.4.2 Divergence from the auxiliary system: motion is primary for auxiliaries

Another difference between continuative aspect markers and subject markers is that, for the aspect markers, motion is primary: if the verb implies movement through space, then *apa* is the continuative aspect marker of choice. (This is true despite whether the subject is present or absent at the time the sentence is uttered, but may be overridden under special circumstances.) Beyond this consideration, the use of continuative *akxa* or *apa* in chapter 5 generally parallels the use of subject markers *akxa* and *apa* on the subject of a given sentence.[3]

Eschenberg (1999) and others have viewed these properties of subject markers within a framework of obviation couched in terms of center stage and movement to offstage by the noun subject. Her analysis may prove to account for the few third person examples found in Osage where the expected subject marker *akxa* or *apa* does not appear. However, the analysis posited here for Osage quite adequately describes the choice between *akxa*, *apa*, and *pe* after the verb root, and between *akxa* and *apa* as subject marker, and perhaps will prove the better analysis of data from related languages as well, once examples from both free conversation and from discourse have been examined. (At any rate, Eschenberg's notion of "obviation" does not involve referent-tracking, in contrast to the traditional sense of that term.)

[3] Another axis along which sentences can be arrayed is auditory evidence. One speaker comments: "If you can hear it only, and not see it, [use *apa*]."

In the next example, the dog is proximate by virtue of having just been present or under discussion; hence the subject marker *akxa* is retained. But *apa* is used as aspect marker postverbally since motion is involved.

(33) *šǫ́ke akxa htą́wą kši aðée apai*
šǫ́ke akxa htą́wą kši a-Ø-ðée apa-ðe
dog SUBJ town to PREV-A3S-go 3.CONT-DECL
'the dog is on his way into town'

Neither subject marker *akxa* nor auxiliary *akxa* is acceptable in the ungrammatical sentence in (34). In the case of the subject marker, this is because the subject is out of sight (and was not just present), and also because *akxa* as subject marker does not reflect motion. Example (34) involves motion; the motion factor alone requires use of *apa* as subject marker and *apa* as aspect marker after the verb.

(34) ***šǫ́ke akxa mąščį́ka ðuxí akxai*
šǫ́ke akxa mąščį́ka Ø-ðuuxí akxa-ðe
dog SUBJ rabbit A3P-chase 3.CONT-DECL
('the dogs are chasing the rabbit(s)')

6.1.4.3 Divergence from the auxiliary system: iterative and completed action verb endings

Another circumstance in which the subject marker system and the auxiliary system diverge is in an iterative sentence. Here the subject markers are still used in accordance with the criteria already noted, but the verb will be followed by *nąpe* (or its more intensive version, *štąpe*) instead of a continuative marker. In a sentence which seems habitual or iterative, if there is a strong emphasis on the state being ongoing, then the continuative endings may be used, following the criteria sketched in section 5.6. Additionally, in a finite, completed action sentence, the subject markers again are used, but the verb will be followed by *pe*.

6.1.4.4 Inherent characteristics and generic statements

In sentences about inherent characteristics of the subject, the selection of subject marker is as described for nongeneric sentences. In the next example, the dog is out of range of vision or is moving around; hence *apa* is chosen as subject marker instead of *akxa*.

(35) *kšą́ka šǫ́ke íhta apa zípe*
kšą́ka šǫ́ke íhta apa zí-api-ðe
second.son dog 3S.POSS SUBJ yellow-PL-DECL
'second son's dog is yellow'

If either the possessor or possessed in (35) were currently or recently present, the sentence would have *akxa* as subject marker:

(36) *kšą́ka šǫ́ke íhta akxa zípe*
kšą́ka šǫ́ke íhta akxa zí-api-ðe
second.son dog his SUBJ yellow-PL-DECL
'second son's dog is yellow'

If the dog is present, then although we are discussing inherent characteristics of the dog, we may optionally use *akxa* as aspect marker as in (37), instead of *pe* as in the two preceding examples.

(37) *šǫ́ke akxa lézi akxai*
šǫ́ke akxa léze akxa-ðe
dog SUBJ spotted 3.CONT-DECL
'the dog is spotted [present]'

Or we may choose the *pe* ending if the dog is present, and must choose it if the dog is absent.

If the verb is not semantically one of action, then the subject marker *akxa* indicates 'present sitting or standing' (which is modified to 'present, lying' for dogs). Action or movement would demand *apa* as subject marker. The ending *pe* in (38) below is more common than *akxai* as in (37) above or (39) below. The aspect marker *akxa* conveys a sense of immediacy: 'the dog is good right now' or perhaps 'the dog is being good'.

(38) *šǫ́ke akxa ðáalįpe*
šǫ́ke akxa ðáalį-api-ðe
dog SUBJ good-PL-DECL
'the dog is good [present and lying or absent]'

(39) *šǫ́ke akxa ðáalį akxai*
šǫ́ke akxa ðáalį akxa-ðe
dog SUBJ good 3.CONT-DECL
'the dog is good [dog is present]'

6.1.4.5 Plurality in subject markers

The subject marker *akxa* is not limited to singular subjects and clearly can be applied to a plural subject which is present and at rest. However, in what seems to be a secondary (perhaps historically more recent) system, plural subject receives *apa* and singular subject receives *akxa* in contrasting sentences. When this secondary system (which could be termed a "plurality override") is imposed, the main system based on absence vs. presence and moving vs. nonmoving for selection of subject marker is overridden; *apa* is then used on a plural subject despite its presence with us as we speak (as well as *apa* being used as an auxiliary). The status of this singular/plural distinction is difficult to evaluate. Under our analysis, it is probable that Osage speakers are reaching for parallels with English and set up a secondary, extended usage of the markers *akxa* and *apa* to make a distinction between singular and plural, assigning *akxa* to singular and *apa* to plural. What they may be doing is assigning presence, correlating to clarity of focus, to a singular subject and absence or diffuseness to a plural subject.

Of course, this secondary usage on the axis of singularity vs. plurality may not be a recent development brought about by speakers seeking to differentiate the two, as I have suggested here, but rather a secondary usage which is historical and central to the language. Such a distinction appears in a very few places in the Dorsey texts (1883a, 1888), but its status there is difficult to evaluate as well. Until data from related languages with a more active speaking community helps clear up this issue, I regard the distinction of number merely as an extended or secondary usage of the subject markers *akxa* and *apa*. The intention here is to define the primary applications of *apa* and *akxa* as subject markers. Once the system governing their use is understood, innovations or secondary uses are easily tolerated within that basic comprehension.

6.1.4.6 *apa* 'present moving' vs. 'absent'

The subject marker *apa* can be singular or plural, but must be moving if singular. The speaker of (40) was emphatic that this example means either 'a person didn't go and he's walking', or 'they didn't go' and they are not here. (This example could be singular absent, also.)

(40) *tówa apa aðáapažie*
tówa apa a-Ø-ðée-api-aži-ðe
3.PRON SUBJ PREV-A3S/P-go-PL-NEG-DECL
'he didn't go [moving]; they didn't go [absent]'

6.1.4.7 *apa* 'moving present singular' vs. *akxa* 'nonmoving (sitting or standing) present singular'

Plural subject sitting or standing (or rather at rest, i.e., not traveling in space), is signalled by *akxa*. Plural subject moving is signalled by *apa*. If the subject is "up and around," *apa* is used, as in (36). The subject marker *akxa* can be used even if the subject is standing, as is the case in (41) below, also glossed 'that one standing there, he didn't go'.

(41) *tówa akxa aðáapažie*
tówa akxa a-Ø-ðée-api-aži-ðe
3.PRON SUBJ PREV-A3S-go-PL-NEG-DECL
'he didn't go'

(42) *į̨hǫ́ apa óohǫ apai*
iihǫ́ apa óo-Ø-hǫ apa-ðe
my-mother SUBJ PREV-A3S-cook 3.CONT-DECL
'mother is cooking'

If the subject is not moving around, one uses *akxa* 'sitting or standing', which signals sitting or standing still and present with the speaker and the hearer. In (42), the mother was said to be "up and around." This "up and around" *apa*, above, also connotes that the subject is at least partially out of range of vision. If the girls are present now as (43) is spoken, but the helping occurred yesterday, *akxa* is used as subject marker (marking "utterance presence") and the completed action *pe* follows the verb:

(43) *šímiži akxa óhkąpe*
šímiži akxa ó-Ø-hką-api-ðe
girl SUBJ PREV-A3P-help-PL-DECL
'the girls helped'

If the girls are not present now as the sentence is spoken, and the helping occurred yesterday, *apa* must be used as subject marker and the completed action *pe* follows the verb:[4]

(44) *šímiži apa óhkąpe*
šímiži apa ó-Ø-hką-api-ðe
girl SUBJ PREV-A3P-help-PL-DECL
'the girls helped'

If the subject is sitting or standing, but not moving in space, during the activity, *akxa* is used:

(45) *ðį̨hǫ́ akxa watáažoe oohǫ́ akxai*
ðiihǫ́ akxa watáažoe oo-Ø-hǫ́ akxa-ðe
your.mother SUBJ hominy PREV-A3S-cook 3.CONT-DECL
'your mother is cooking hominy (sitting or standing)'

The subject in (46) is shown as plural, but could have been interpreted as singular.

[4] In examples (43)–(44), one speaker preferred *ówahką* as the verb form, which is the valence-reduced form 'helped folks; helped out'.

(46) *šímiži apa óhkạ apai*
šímiži apa ó-Ø-hkạ apa-ðe
girl SUBJ PREV-A3P-help 3.CONT-DECL
'the girls are helping'

Of course, (46) can also mean 'the girls were helping'. This is expected, since the postverbal aspect marker *apa* signals either present continuative or past continuative.

A dog present with the speaker and moving around gets the *apa* subject marker:

(47) *haakǫ́ta šǫ́ke apa škạ́škạða?*
haakǫ́ta šǫ́ke apa škạ-škạ-ða
why dog SUBJ move-REDUP-CAU(?)
'why is this dog moving around so much?'

If a singular or plural subject is present in the vicinity but is nearby moving around or is out of the range of vision, then *apa* is used on the subject of an ongoing action, as in (48).

(48) *šǫ́ke apa mạšcį̣ka ðuxí apái*
šǫ́ke apa mạšcį̣ka Ø-ðuuxí apa-ðe
dog SUBJ rabbit A3P-chase 3.CONT
'the dogs are chasing the rabbit(s)'

As to the auxiliary, the same sentence as in (48) just above but with with ***ðuxí akxai* in the verb phrase is impossible, because the auxiliary *akxa* implies lack of motion. In (48), the dogs are present in the vicinity but out of sight of the speaker and are thought to be moving around, a situation that demands auxiliary *apa* and disallows auxiliary *akxa*.

As further evidence against the idea that *apa* is plural and *akxa* is singular, the sentence below, from one of Dorsey's texts, shows a singular subject 'grandmother' in motion with *apa* 'moving' subject marker:

(49) *ikó apá okíce achípe ska*
ikó apá o-Ø-Ø-ki-che
grandmother SUBJ PREV-him-she-SUU-seek
a-Ø-chí-api-ðe ska
PREV-she-arrive-PL-DECL SUPP
'his grandmother, seeking her own [grandson], came' (Dorsey 1883a: "How Náq¢e-cape Was Eaten by His Grandmother," line 4)

However, Dorsey does have a few subjects in one long myth ("The Raccoons and the Crawfish") which are followed by *apa* labeled "the plural subject." Presumably a sort of "plural override" is in effect, or, more likely, in each instance the *apa* is actually attributable to movement of the subject.

6.1.4.8 Distance in time: *apa*?

apa is used as subject marker (and also as continuative auxiliary) when the person doing the action is thought of as being far away; thus spatial distance or absence is an important parameter. If the subject is present it can have *apa* as subject marker, as in (50); or if the subject currently is or recently was right there with the speaker, *akxa* would be substituted. More importantly for this discussion, the aspect marker in postverbal position would be *akxa* if the children are sitting or standing and the situation is occurring right now, but is *apa* (as in (50)) if the children were dancing around at the moment the sentence is uttered (that is, they are now moving, but they have until a few moments ago been sitting or standing and watching television).

(50) *žįkóhkihą apa waachí watǫ́į kíiðálį apai*
žįkóhkihą apa waachí watǫ́į ki-ðálį apa-ðe
grandchild SUBJ dances watching DAT-like 3.CONT-DECL
'your grandchildren are enjoying watching the dances'

Likewise, the subject marker in (50) would be *apa* if it were a long time ago that this situation took place, according to one speaker, who indicated that if *apa* is used as both subject marker and auxiliary in the sentence, then the action is not happening now, but that the sentence is rather describing what the subject used to do. Obviously, this last comment is disproven by (50), as well as by many other examples. At this stage in the language, it is impossible to determine if this suggested 'past' usage or perceived inconsistency (that is, advocating a past reading for sentences where *apa* is subject marker and also auxiliary—a "past override") reflects language decay or if it is a secondary distinction, based on an opposition between a more focused here-and-now versus a less focused, more distant time—an opposition overriding the present/absent criterion for use of *akxa* vs. *apa*. This is another area for exploration in related languages with more active speech communities. (Of course, speakers of any language are likely to find it difficult to identify the pragmatics of usage of grammatical forms without some training; it is the researcher's job to portray the several variables mentioned here in order to stimulate production of the desired test sentences.)

6.1.5 Quantifier + subject marker

Quantity expressions such as *huuwáli* 'many' and *záani* 'all' may appear either preceding or following the subject marker, with a preference for the former placement, as in (51). It is interesting that the quantifier *záani* in (52) remains outside the noun subject, which is *níhkaši* 'man, person' and which is marked with the subject marker *apa*. The item owned was a horse.

(51) *naniǫpažį huuwáali apa húheka ąkáaɣe nąpee*
naniǫpažį huuwáli apa húheka ą-Ø-káaɣe ną‑api‑ðe
cigarette many SUBJ sick P1S-A3P-make ITER-PL-DECL
'a lot of cigarettes make me sick'

(52) *níhkaši apa záani aðį apai*
níhkaši apa záani a-Ø-ðį apa-ðe
man SUBJ all PREV-A3P-have 3.CONT-DECL
'all of them/the people own one; every man owns one'

6.1.6 Positional article *kše* 'lying'

The positional article *kše* is used on a noun when speaking of a person or thing in a lying position, such as a person confined to bed.[5]

(53) *įįhǫ́ kše tąhé įkše?*
iihǫ́ kše tąhé įkše
his/her/their.mother LIE well SIT
'is his/her [bedridden] mother all right?'

It is tempting to try to associate positional articles on subjects with stative verbs, as seen in the example just above. Example (54) below could also be construed as a nonactive with 'being a teacher' as the verb. Although (55), with the verb 'speak' would seem to show that *kše* can mark a subject in an active sentence, if we opt (more implausibly) for an interpretation of the verb of (55) as 'being a speaker', then it is nonactive.

(54) *ðįįhǫ́ kše wažáže íe wakǫ́ze šǫ ðįkše?*
ðiihǫ́ kše wažáže íe wakǫ́ze šǫ ð-įkše
your.mother LIE Osage language teach still EPð-LIE
'is your [bedridden] mother still teaching Osage?'

[5] The post-verbal aspect marker *įkšé* is used occasionally, especially in questions about persons not present, as in (53) and (54). Here *įkšé* 'sitting' marks the adjective/verb *tąhé*, possibly as the default positional. If the person under discussion is more central to the context or conversation, *akxa* is allowed as aspect marker, as in the example below, in which the mother was lying nearby:

ðįįhǫ́ kše tąhé akxai?
ðiihǫ́ kše tąhé akxa-ðe
your.mother LIE well 3.CONT-DECL
'is your [bedridden] mother all right?'

(55) *ðį̨hǫ́ kše wažáže ie šǫ́ ðįkše?*
ðiihǫ́ kše wažáže ie šǫ ð-įkše
your.mother LIE Osage language/speak still EPð-LIE
'is your [bedridden] mother still speaking Osage?'

At any rate, *kše* does modify nonsubject nouns regularly, whereas *akxa* and *apa* do not; moreover, *kše* does not seem to belong to the subject marker paradigm for active sentences. Thus *kše* lacks full status as a subject marker. Admittedly the difficulty in eliciting this type of sentence from speakers of a language in disuse hampers the analysis of *kše*. (See also section 6.3.4.)

6.1.7 Interrogative

Questions often lack a subject marker. (See section 7.6 for interrogative words and expressions.)

(56) *Johna záani wéeðapee?*
John-a záani wa-ii-Ø-ðe-api-ðe
John-SYL all P1P-PREV-A3S-see-PL-DECL
'did John see all of us?'

(57) *Johna haxį pée kˀúe?*
John-a haxį pée Ø-kˀú-ðe
John-SYL blanket who A3S-give-DECL
'who did John give the blanket(s) to?'

6.1.8 Conjoined subjects

The singular marker *akxa* goes on the first member of a conjoined subject, and the second noun is followed by *éeðǫǫpa* 'the two of them'. (Examples below contain both the subject marker *akxa* and the auxiliary *akxa*.)

(58) *ðihípe akxa wanáše eǫpa íiðe ðíla akxai*
ðihípe akxa wanáše ée-ðǫǫpa íi-Ø-ðe
Thihipe SUBJ Wanashe 3.PRON-two PREV-P3S-see
Ø-ðílą akxa-ðe
A3P-wish 3.CONT-DECL
'Thihipe and Wanashe want to see it'

(59) *mišecí akxa wanáše éeðǫǫpa alée hta akxa*
mišecí akxa wanáše ée-ðǫǫpá
Mišecí SUBJ Wanáše 3.PRON-two
a-Ø-lée hta akxa
PREV-A3P-go.back/home FUT 3.CONT
'Smokey and Mogri [English names of Mišecí and Wanáše] are going home'

In the two examples of conjoined first person subjects below, no first person singular pronoun ('I') is present, but the 1P/D verb *ąkále* 'we go home' and the aspect markers *ąðé* 'first person dual moving' and *ąkąðe* 'first person plural moving' semantically include the A1S subject. No subject marker *akxa* or *apa* is present in any A1D/P sentences found so far.

(60) *wanąše éǫpa ąkále hta ąðé*
wanąše ée-ðǫǫpá ąk-alée hta ąðé
Wanáše 3.PRON-two A1P-go.back/home FUT 1D.CONT
'Wanáše and I are going home'

(61) *Stephanie, David, éǫpa ąkále hta ąkąðe*
Stephanie David ée-ðǫǫpá ąk-alée hta ąkąðe
Stephanie David 3.PRON-two A1P-go.back/home FUT 1P.CONT
'Stephanie, David, and I are going home'

6.2 Demonstrative pronouns and modifiers

The complex system of demonstratives in Osage is made up of the pronouns listed in table 6.3, which can be used as either subjects or objects and which also function as demonstrative adjectives. They are used for both singular and plural in all cases except where noted. Interrogative demonstratives also exist, but will not be covered here. The slots in the table, representing positions within the noun phrase, will be used for reference as each form is discussed. Almost all of these lexical items defy simple definition, as they are used over a wide range of contexts with slightly different meanings and often have no exact parallel in English. The forms functioning as pronouns, in slot 2, seem to have longer vowels than their counterparts in other positions. The positional articles in slot 4 are treated in section 6.3.

More detailed remarks on individual demonstratives follow.

ðe: 'Here' or 'there', near speaker; 'this' or 'that' animate or inanimate (cf. *še* 'that' when nearer to hearer than to speaker). This demonstrative can have both temporal and spatial reference: 'this; here; now'. It can appear in slot 1 as a demonstrative adjective, in slot 2 (with long vowel, *ðée*) as a demonstrative pronoun, or in slot 3 as a demonstrative adjective. This *ðe* comes close to functioning like an article, but is more appropriately classified as a demonstrative adjective; e.g., *htóožu ðe* 'this/that/the/these/those meat pie(s)', i.e., 'the meat pie(s) previously mentioned or pragmatically controlled'. It is homophonous with the positional article *ðe* 'moving'.

ðée ðe (demonstrative pronoun combined with demonstrative adjective): 'Here' near speaker, within reach; 'this person or thing' next to speaker. Compare colloquial English 'this here one'.

TABLE 6.3. DEMONSTRATIVES AND POSITIONAL ARTICLES

1 (preceding a noun or pronoun)	2 (functioning as pronoun)	3 (following a noun or pronoun)	4
DEMONSTRATIVE ADJECTIVE	(NOUN OR) DEMONSTRATIVE PRONOUN	DEMONSTRATIVE ADJECTIVE	POSITIONAL ARTICLE
ðe	*ðee*	*ðe*	*txą*
še	*šee*	*še*	*che*
	ée	*ko*	*įkše*
	kaa	*ðo*	*kše*
	koota	*ka*	*ðe*
			pa
			ke

NOTE: Slot 2 items can be modified by a preceding or following demonstrative from slot 1 or 3, and/or by a following positional article. Nouns also appear in slot 2.

še: 'Here' or 'there', nearer hearer than speaker; animate or inanimate, slot 1, 2, or 3. This can be used in slot 2 as a pronoun (with long vowel, *šée*): 'that/those there' near hearer, or the location itself 'there' near hearer.

ka: This demonstrative is used in slot 3 as a demonstrative adjective, combined with slot 2 *ðee* (*ðéeka*) or with slot 2 *šee* (*šeeka*). It often occurs in the combination *káa įkšé*, with default positional *įkšé* from slot 4. Semantically it is related to the concept of precise place: 'right here' or 'right there'. Other meanings of this demonstrative include 'here', 'there', 'farther away and unseen', or 'present but invisible'. In slot 2 as pronoun, *kaa* refers to inanimates. The very concrete nature that 'here' or 'there' implies seems contradicted in some sense by the idea of invisibility. But *ka* ~ *kaa* may be thought of as abstract, representing entities as unseeable due either to their being out of sight or to their being intangible although present (such as a fact, an idea, an emotion, or an act committed). The vowel of this demonstrative is often long (*káa*). It may be related to or identical with the prefix *kaa* 'by sudden application of force'.

koo, kóota: 'Beyond speaker and hearer, and farther away (in space or time than some other item or marker)'. This demonstrative compares two items, persons, positions or times; it refers to inanimate entities. Possibly this term may derive from *ka-o*, where *o* adds the sense of 'towards'.

ée: This demonstrative refers to any 3S or 3P antecedent in discourse, animate or inanimate, or pragmatically controlled; it occurs in slot 2. Also attested is *e*ˀ*e* (where the two vowels are separated by a glottal stop), sometimes followed by *ðe*: *é*ˀ*e ðe* or *ée ðe* 'those are these ones here'.

ðǫ: This demonstrative is a slot 3 suffix only, often used with *še* (*šeðǫ*). It is sometimes denasalized to *ðo*. It may possibly be related to *kaðǫ́*, whose meaning may be 'immediately juxtaposed in space or time; right next to; and'. The element *ðǫ* is possibly derived from *ðe-o*, where *o* adds the sense of 'towards'.

Several examples below show combinations of two or more elements from those listed above. The examples are somewhat complex due to multiple deictic elements, but are quite representative of common patterns.

6.2.1 Combinations involving *še*

In the two examples below, *še* appears before the noun, singling out one individual from many. Both examples show a stative verb with continuative marker *akxa*.

(62) *še žą́ą žį ekxa ohtáza akxái*
še žą́ą žį akxa ohtáza akxa-ðe
that tree small SUBJ beautiful 3.CONT-DECL
'the little tree is pretty'

(63) *šé hką́ące akxa tožáðe akxái*
še hką́ące akxa tožáðe akxa-ðe
that apple SUBJ rotten 3.CONT-DECL
'that apple is rotten'

In (64) and (65), the element *ðǫ* (also denasalized *ðo*) appears, with an approximate meaning 'in close juxtaposition.' Extending the meaning suggested above for *ðǫ*, we can speculate that it is more exactly 'additional, up next to, contiguous to something else'. The expression *še ðo* is also used in an early recorded talk for 'and also', 'and then'.

(64) *šé ðo*
še ðǫ
there next.to
'there where you are'

(65) *še ðǫ méį*
še ðǫ mąðį-a
there next.to go-IMPER
'stay where you are'

The form *kaðǫ́* combines the same morpheme *ðǫ* with *ka* 'here', resulting in the meaning 'combined with or appearing in the same location with' or 'right next to', as in (66) (describing the U.S. flag).

(66) *žúuce, ská kaðǫ́ htóho*
žúuce, ská ka-ðǫ́ htóho
red white here-next.to blue
'red, white, and blue'

According to Koontz (p.c. 1995), *še* in (67) and (68) is used similarly to Omaha-Ponca *šu*, as in *šu bðe* 'I'm going in your direction'.

(67) *šé ðo brée*
še ðǫ Wa-ðée
there next.to A1S-go
'I'm coming over there thataway [where you are]'

(68) *šé ðo ha brée*
še ðǫ ha Wa-ðée
there next.to toward A1S-go
'I'm coming over there [toward where you are]'

(69) *še ðó hą ąkái htai*
še ðǫ ha ąk-aðée htai
there next.to toward A1P-go INJ.PL
'let's go that way [direction]'

The positional *txą* 'standing' follows *šée* or *še* + noun fairly commonly:

(70) *šée (ðo) nąąžį txa hú hcéa*
šée ðǫ nąąžį txą hú hce-ée-a
that/there next.to stand STA come.here INJ-say-IMPER
'tell the person standing there to come here'

If a man is standing in the vicinity, such as in the hallway just outside the room where the speaker is, the speaker may say to another:

(71) *šée txa hú hcéa*
šee txą hú hce-ée-a
that/there STA come.here INJ-say-IMPER
'tell him to come here'

(72) *šée txa kípą*
šee txą Ø-ki-pą-a
that/there STA P3S-DAT-call-IMPER
'call him [standing]'

In (70)–(73), *šee* in slot 2 is being used as a demonstrative pronoun representing a person marked with *txą* 'standing'; in (74), *še* as a modifier in slot 3 modifies a noun denoting an animal.

(73) *šée txa pée ðé?*
šee txą pée ðé
that/there STA who DECL
'who is that over there?'

(74) *hkáwa šé txa pée íhta?*
hkáwa še txą pée í-hta
horse that/there STA who 3S.POSS
'whose horse is that [standing] over there?'

A more adverbial application of *šee*, signalling place 'there', appears in (75), literally 'stand/stop there', or 'stand there near where you are'.

(75) *šée nąąžį!*
šee nąąžį-a
there stand/stop-IMPER
'wait!'

Combining *šée* with *ðe* 'moving', the expression in (76) is called out when someone is passing by, and is considered quite informal, even slang; it is approximately equivalent to 'Look who's going there!', spoken as if to a third party when no identifiable third party hearer is present. The irony of such a situation gives an informal, friendly tenor to the utterance.

(76) *šée ðe!*
šee ðe
that/there MOV
'that one there!'

(77) *šée ðe pée?*
šee ðe pée
that/there MOV who
'who is that?' (lit., 'that one over there, who is it?')

Combining *šée* with the 'sitting' positional produces 'that' (inanimate or animate), as in (78), which may be a bundle of items or a person. (Occasionally this combination is informally pronounced *šáa įkšé*, for unclear reasons.) The entity referred to by *šée įkše* 'that over there' may be close or far, seated anywhere within view but not extremely close to the speaker of the sentence, and, by the definition of *šee* ~ *še*, nearer to the hearer than to the speaker.

(78) *šée įkše*
šee įkše
that/there SIT
'over there, that'

(79) *ooląke sápe še įkše ðihta?*
ooląke sápe še įkše ðihta
hat black that/there SIT 2S.POSS
'is that black hat yours?'

6.2.2 *ka* and *ðéeka*

Slot 2 *káa* relates to the concept of place, and is used when the location is more precise than a location marked with *ðee* 'here/there' alone. *ðéeka* is 'right here'. *ka* or *kaa* alone is often used when handing over something or giving something to someone, as in (81). Also, *ka* or *kaa* is used as 'suddenly, immediately' in a temporal or spatial sense—possibly a semantic extension of instrumental *kaa* 'by striking', although seemingly random variations in length of the vowel make it difficult to identify the two (or more?) *ka* morphemes.

(80) *kaa!*
kaa
'here!'

(81) *ðéeka*
ðe-ka
these-here
'these'

Used pronominally, *ðéeka* may be followed by *wį* 'a; one', as in (82). There is also a classificatory or partitive sense to *ðéeka*; the approximate gloss in the following example is 'do you want one of this kind?' (e.g., 'one of this variety of peaches; one of these here').

(82) *ðéeka wį škǫ́ǫšta?*
ðee-ka wį Ya-kǫ́-Ya-ða
these-here one A2S-PREV-A2S-want
'do you want one of these?'

Also, *ðéeka* can refer to places, chairs, etc.:

(83) *ðéeka áðalįį škǫ́ǫšta?*
ðee-ka á-Ya-lįį Ya-kǫ́-Ya-ða
these-here LOC-A2S-sit.on A2S-PREV-A2S-want
'do you want to sit in one of these [chairs]?'

A strongly locative adverbial *ðéka* or *ðéeka* 'here' is seen also in (84)–(86); it functions as a modifier of the noun in (87).

(84) *ðéeka aðįku*
ðée-ka a-ðį-kú-a
this-here PREV-have-come.here-IMPER
'bring it here'

(85) *ðéeka*
ðée-ka
this-here
'here, this place, at this place'

(86) *ðéeka kú*
ðée-ka ku-a
this-here come.here IMPER
'come here'

(87) *kaahúuža mą́žą ðéka omą́ðįpe*
kaahúuža mą́žą ðé-ka o-Ø-mą-Ø-ðį-api-ðe
long.time earth this-here PREV-A3S-PREV-A3S-walk-PL-DECL
'he walked this earth a long time (he lived a long time)'

Adverbial *ðéeka* may also add *ha* for 'path' or 'direction', as in (88).

(88) *ðeekáha líi ði*
ðee-ka-ha a-líi ði
this-here-toward PREV-return.here 2S.PRON
'come back here; come back this way'

Note the semantic contrast between *ðeekáha* and *ðéeka*, with *ðeekáha* coinciding with 'this way; through here', as in (88)–(91), as opposed to *ðé(e)ka* 'here' in (84)–(86) above. (See also section 6.6 for more discussion of *ha*.)

(89) *ðeekáha kú*
ðée-ka-ha kú-a
this-here-toward come.back-IMPER
'come this way; come in this direction'

Example (89) implies movement 'in this direction towards speaker', without an indicated route. It contrasts with 'come right through this way' in (90) and (91) with *kšé* 'lying'; when these examples with *kšé* were uttered, the path (thought of as lying) was shown with the hand.

(90) *ðeekáha kše kú*
ðee-ka-ha kše ku-a
this-here-toward LIE come.back-IMPER
'come right through this way'

(91) *ðeekáha kše*
ðee-ka-ha kše
this-here-toward LIE
'this way' (path indicated by gesture)

6.2.3 *ée ðe* (anaphor + demonstrative pronoun)

The anaphoric element *ée* links to a referent from previous discourse: 'the aforementioned'. It combines with *ðe* 'this' to form *éeðe* 'the aforementioned; that', as in (92).

(92) *haxį ðeche éeðe níðape*
haxį ðe-che ée-ðe Ø-níðe-api-ðe
blanket this-STA aforementioned-this A3P-give.away-PL-DECL
'these are the blankets that they gave away'

In (92), *éeðe* is approximately 'these ones, these the aforementioned'. (For *ðeeche* 'this standing', see the discussion of collocations in section 6.4; collocations of sitting things [e.g., blankets] use the standing positional article *che*.)

The element *ée* functions as a pronoun for any 3S or 3P subject or object, such as 'they', 'her', etc.

(93) *ée hóxpape*
ée Ø-hóxpe-api-ðe
3.PRON A3P-cough-PL-DECL
'they coughed'

Example (94) has *ée* 'her' plus the patient pronominal prefix *wá* 'them', and (95) has *ée* 'her' as a pronoun but *Ø* 'him' as pronominal inflection.

(94) *ée wáapą káaɣa*
ée wá-ki-pą Ø-káaɣe-a
3.PRON P3P-DAT-invite P3S-make-IMPER
'make her invite them'

(95) *ée kipą káaɣa*
ée Ø-ki-pą Ø-káaɣe-a
3.PRON P3S-DAT-invite P3S-make-IMPER
'make her invite him'

6.2.4 *kóota*

As is seen in (96)–(97), the modifier *ðe* can occur on either side of the noun (*htóožu* 'meat pies' in these examples) without making a difference to the meaning. If *kóota* is used instead of *ðe* (98), the implication is that the meat pies are farther away, 'over there'.

(96) *htóožu ðé che ąkʔú*
htóožu ðe che ą-kʔu-a
meat.pie that STA P1S-give-IMPER
'give me those meat pies [plural]'

(97) *ðe htóožu che ąkʔú*
'give me those meat pies'

(98) *htóožu kóota che ąkʔú*
htóožu koota che ą-kʔu-a
meat.pie farther STA P1S-give-IMPER
'give me those meat pies'

Pronoun *kóota*, with the positional *kše* 'lying', signals a person lying in (99).

(99) *kootáa kše pée ée kše?*
koota kše pée ée kše
farther LIE who 3.PRON LIE
'that lying over there, who is it? [sic]'

Example (100) has both the pronoun *kóota* and a correferent noun *níhka*.

(100) *kóota ðe níhka tǫ́pa*
kóota ðe níhka Ø-tǫ́pe-a
farther that man P3S-look-IMPER
'look at that man farther over there'

The form with *ha* is also worth noting (*kootą́ha*, presumably cognate with Dakota *katą́* 'from over there' and *katą́hą* 'since then'). In Dakota, *hą* effects a semantic change from space to time. The syllable *tą* 'when' varies with *ta* in Osage. It may be in Osage that *kóta* is 'farther'; *kootą́ha* ~ *kootáha* 'farther back in time'; and *kootá į̨kšé* (*kootáį̨ke*) 'lying back there [in space or time]'; time periods use preferably the 'round or sitting' positional *į̨kšé*. But *ha* applies to space as well as time in Osage.

(101) *kóotaha*
koo-ta-ha
here-toward-toward(?)
'farther over, farther back in time; from farther'

See also the discussion in section 6.6.1 of *howaį̨kíha bree* 'which way do I go?', based on *howáį̨ke* 'where?' The related form *kootáį̨ke* 'there beyond; way over there', just mentioned, possibly derives historically from *ka-o-ta į̨kíe*, just as *howáį̨ki* possibly derives from *ha-o-wa-į̨kíe*.

(102) *koótaįke*
koo-ta-įkše-ci
farther-toward-SIT-to
'way over there, way back in time'

6.2.5 Other expressions with *ðe* and *txą*

I merely list here some other related expressions involving the combination of *ðe(e)* in slot 2 with *txą* in slot 4: *ðetxąche*, *ðetxąha*, *ðetxątą*. (Length of *e* in these forms varies.)

(103a) *ðetkxą́ąche*
ðe-txą́-che
this-time-STA
'from now on'

(103b) *ðetkxą́ąche etkxą ąkáðe hta ąkái*
ðe-txą́-che e-txą́ ąk-aðée hta ąkáðe
this-time-STA that-time A1P-go FUT 1P.CONT
'from now on (from this time on), we're going to go that way'

(103c) *ðetkxą́aha*
ðe-txą́-aha
this-time-whenever
'from here/now on'

(103d) *ðetkxą́atą*
ðe-txą́-tą
this-time-when
'from now on'

(104) *ðeetkxą*
ðe-e-txą́
this-the.aforementioned-time
'from now on' (as in "from right now we're gonna do it")

The expression *ðekǫ́ǫce* or *ðekǫ́ǫci* 'now' is another time expression involving *ðe*, and is very frequent. It may be a corruption of *ðetkxąci* (*t* → *tk* → *k*, plus lengthening of *ą* to *ąą*; recall that *ą(ą)* and *ǫ(ǫ)* are almost interchangeable [section 2.2.1.1]). The final *ce* or *ci* would be from the postposition 'at, to' (section 6.5).

(105) *ðekǫ́ǫci*
ðéka-ǫ-ce-i
this.place-(?)-in-from(?)
'from right now, right now'

6.3 Positional articles

Positional articles (slot 4 of table 6.3) are noun classifiers, with clearer definitions than those sketched for demonstrative pronouns and modifiers in section 6.2. Positional articles can appear after nouns that are not subjects of active verbs, such as the object in an active sentence, and the subject of a stative (see section 6.1.1). The counterparts of these positional articles are the subject markers *apa* and *akxa*, which are characteristically found on the subjects of active verbs but which may occur on subjects of stative verbs as well. Positional articles are not found on the subjects of active verbs; even if the subject is, e.g., standing, the positional article 'standing' is not normally used, but rather a subject marker *akxa* or *apa*.

Thus, use of the positional articles *che* 'standing [inanimate]' or *txą* 'standing [animate]' would be ungrammatical in (106)–(108) because positional articles do not mark subjects of active verbs.

(106) *hkáwa apa nǫ́ǫki apai*
hkáwa apa Ø-nǫ́ǫke apa-ðe
horse SUBJ A3S-run 3.CONT-DECL
'that horse is running'

(107) *hkáwa akxa wanǫ́bre akxa*
hkáwa akxa wa-Ø-nǫ́bre akxa
horse SUBJ PREV-A3S-dine 3.CONT
'that horse is eating [standing still]'

(108) *hkáwa akxa nąąží akxai*
hkáwa akxa Ø-nąąží akxa-ðe
horse SUBJ A3S-stand 3.CONT-DECL
'that horse is standing there'

Positional articles may also be used on subjects of statives (e.g., (122) below: *hkáwa kše húheka kše* 'that horse lying there, is it sick?'). Although positional articles are not normally found on subjects of active verbs, the subject markers *akxa* and *apa* may be used on the subjects of both stative and active verbs.

Note that while the principal criteria for the choice between the subject markers *akxa* and *apa* are the status of the subject as moving vs. at rest and as present vs. absent when the utterance is spoken, these considerations are not what determines which positional article is used on a given nonsubject noun. Each singular positional article specifies the inherent position or shape (configuration) of the noun or pronoun it modifies. (This may apply only to inanimates, however.) The choice of whether to use a positional article or to omit it in a given sentence it is much freer than is the use of a subject marker in an active sentence. Positional articles on nouns are usually quite optional, according to speakers, but subject markers must almost always be used.

These positional articles make up a rather remarkable system in Osage. Nouns, probably all inanimate nouns, are specified as taking one from among the set of positional articles, either standing, sitting, or lying. This could plausibly be considered a gender system based on position or configuration, although I have not worked out all the details, due to limitations of time and resources. When a positional article is used to modify the entity, the positional chosen must be the positional for which that noun is specified and no other positional article, especially for inanimates. For example, a picture 'sits' even when it is hanging on the wall. Certain other items 'stand', others 'lie', whatever their actual position at the moment. A wrong choice of positional article results in a distorted mental image. A dish 'lying' on the table would be a dish stretched or flattened into some unnatural shape because dishes inherently sit (as they do, in fact, in English). (Other considerations apply to plurals; see section 6.4.) Tentatively, it appears that some entities, such as 'tree', may be considered animate and have a different positional article if lying or standing, as will animate entities in general.

The demonstratives seen in the preceding section (slots 1, 2, 3) refer to distance from the speaker or hearer or both, in space or in time. The positional articles are used in combination with the demonstrative pronouns or in combination with nouns, but do not communicate distance from a deictic center based on the same parameters. They do indicate a certain mental distance or lack of focus, which in only some instances may be based on physical distance. The positional articles appear in the rightmost slot (slot 4).

Positional articles typically cooccur with backgrounded items, whether concrete, diffuse, or abstract. Such items are often persons or things whose identity is uncertain or whose location is only vaguely referenced. These vague persons or items cannot be grammatical active subjects with a subject marker. It is tempting to say in some cases that speakers use the positional articles when they wish purposefully to assign a secondary or out-of-focus status to an entity, to background that entity, marking it as outside their immediate discourse context or mental focus. I have noted only a few instances of a positional article appearing on a subject of an active verb, from among many thousands of collected sentences in Osage. In every instance, such a usage seems impressionistically to demote the subject to a secondary status. (I will use here expressions such as "backgrounded" and "out of focus," etc., quite informally to describe this usage, as the limited extent and type of data available in Osage at this point do not allow for a full analysis. I leave it to Dhegihanists with richer data from more actively spoken languages to identify the exact parameters to describe this phenomenon in those languages.)

Thus, the positional articles discussed in this subsection are not found on items that are central to the activities underway. Unless the modified noun is felt to be defocused, a positional article is not used. For example, no positional emerged in (109) and (110) even though the English gloss specifies position. This is likely because the items are too proximate or focused in the conversation.

(109) *hį́įce háažǫ hta nįkšé?*
hį́įce háa-Ya-ǫ hta nįkšé
plate INDEF-A2S-do FUT 2S.CONT
'what you going to do with those plates sitting over there?'

(110) *šį́tožį háažǫ hta nįkše?*
šį́tožį háa-Ya-ǫ hta nįkše
boy INDEF-A2S-do FUT 2S.CONT
'what are you going to do with that boy sitting there?'[6]

Speakers routinely reject positional articles (as opposed to subject markers) on subjects of active verbs except for a handful of examples. (They do however accept, and produce, either positional articles or subject markers on subjects of statives.)

Throughout this discussion, we will maintain the following order while listing the positional articles: 'sitting', 'standing', 'lying', 'moving', followed by plural. The positional articles are displayed in table 6.4.

The form *tówa* is used to refer to persons whose identity is uncertain or is unimportant to the conversation, and is often found modified with a positional article. *tówa* is also used for inanimates.

(111a) *tówa įkše*
'that one sitting'

(111b) *tówa txą*
'that one standing'

(111c) *tówa kše*
'that one lying'

[6] In this example, speakers will not accept insertion of *įkšé* after *šį́tožį*; in fact they cannot hear it as such but only as *kše*, which would give *šį́tožį kše* [boy LIE]. There may be some constraint on the use of the 'sitting' marker in this context. In some other contexts, *įkše* is used for 'sitting (singular)', but only if there is an intervening *ée* between the noun modified and the positional. Perhaps the demonstrative *ée* positions a preceding noun at a comfortably obviative distance to allow the positional article *įkšé* to be used, or some other cooccurence restriction such as *įkšé* for females and *kše* for males is at play here.

TABLE 6.4. POSITIONAL ARTICLES

	ANIMACY	POSITION AND SHAPE	ARTICLE
SINGULAR			
SITTING	animate and inanimate	sitting; round	*įkšé*
STANDING	animate	standing	*txą ~ txa*[a]
	inanimate	standing; upright; vertical	*che*
LYING	animate and inanimate	lying; horizontal; long; spread out	*kše*
MOVING	animate	moving	*ðe*[b]
PLURAL	animate	sitting; standing; moving	*pa*
	animate and inanimate	scattered, dispersed (any position or shape)	*ke*

[a] *txą ~ txa* is occasionally used for inanimate vertical.
[b] Homophonous with demonstrative *ðe* (animate/ inanimate, singular/plural, any position).

(111d) *tówa ðe*
'that one moving'

(111e) *tówa pa*
'those people (that group of people, sitting or standing, or moving)'

(111f) *tówa ke*
'those people (scattered)'

Sentences with *ðe* prove especially difficult to sort out. For example, *tówa ðe* is the best phrase to use for 'that one moving', but since *ðe* could also be interpreted as homophonous 'that' (demonstrative), this phrase can refer to (e.g.) that person either walking or merely standing.

6.3.1 *įkšé* 'sitting [animate/inanimate]'

Related to the continuative aspect marker *mįkšé* (1S), *nįkšé* (2S), the positional article *įkšé* signifies 'sitting'. (The continuative markers, however, are not used in the same manner as positional articles at all; see section 5.5.) Either *įkšé* is derived via *ð*-Elision from *ðįkšé*, or vice versa, with *ð*-Epenthesis, since this item occasionally shows up as *ðįkšé,* and both *ð*-Epenthesis and *ð*-Elision are common in the language.

The two examples below contain the indefinite pronoun *tówa* 'that one [unidentified]'. (The animate interpretation would also be possible for these examples.)

(112) *tówa įkšé tǫ́pa*
tówa įkšé Ø-tǫ́pe-a
that.one SIT P3S-look.at-IMPER
'look at that'

(113) *tǫ́ įkše, átǫpa*
tówa įkše, á-Ø-tǫpe-a
that.one SIT LOC-PREV-P3S-watch.over-IMPER
'watch this/that' ('look after the vaguely specified item over there by you')

įkšé 'sitting' appears with an animate interpretation in (114).

(114) *šée įkšé pée ðe?*
šée įkšé pée ðe
that.one SIT who QUES
'who is that guy sitting there?'

In the final clause of (115), *ée* 'that' refers to the preceding clause, the thing said. It is unclear why the positional article *įkšé* 'sitting' is used after the pronoun *ée*. *įkšé* does seem to be the default positional in Osage in nonconcrete cases such as this one and also whenever the position of a nonsubject person referred to is unknown because he or she is not present.

(115) *táatą ðéke hǫ́ǫžike éhtaha, ékiǫ ðįká, ée įkše áape*
táatą ðe-ke hǫ́ǫži-ke éhtaha, é-ki-ǫ ðįké-a,
thing that/this bad-DISP when(?), PREV-PREV-do NEG-IMPER
ée įkše e-Ø-e-api-ðe
the.aforementioned SIT PREV-A3P-say-PL-DECL
'they said you were not to do these bad things'

The positional *įkšé* cannot be used if the entity modified is in close proximity to the speaker. For example, to refer to a man sitting just across the table from the speaker, (116) is ungrammatical. In (117) a saddle blanket (not in close proximity) sits; a plate, likewise situated at some distance from the speaker, sits in (118). When a description of an item is requested as in (119), with *įkšé* (either article or auxiliary), it is implied that an innately sitting item not in close proximity is referred to.

(116) ***ðée įkše*
('this man here')

(117) *wákaštǫ įkše hkáwa áala*
wákaštǫ įkše hkáwa álą-a
saddle.blanket SIT horse LOC-put-IMPER
'put that saddle blanket on that horse'

(118) *hį́įce įkše húuðа*
hį́įce įkše hú-ðe-a
dish SIT come.here-CAU-IMPER
'hand me that plate'

(119) *háaðaską įkšé ?*
haa-ðaską įkšé
INDEF-size(?) SIT
'how big (small) is it?'

The third person continuative marker *įkšé* (parallel to *mįkšé* and *nįkšé* mentioned above) is seen after the (adjectival/stative) verb in (120):

(120) *hį́įce įkše léke įkšé*
hį́įce įkše Ø-léke įkšé
dish SIT A3S-shatter 3.CONT
'that dish is broken'

Items that sit must always sit, they do not lie, except for special cases such as a downed tree, which can also change from animate to inanimate when it is (to be) cut down. A dish or plate followed by *kše* 'lying', as in *???hį́įce kše*, is strange, as the dish would be pulled, stretched, or flattened into an unnatural configuration for a dish. We see that a picture 'sits' in (121); it does not 'stand', even when hanging on the wall.

(121) *icé waléze įkšé ą́ąhǫǫ*
icé waléze įkšé ą-hǫǫ
face graphic SIT P1S-like
'I like that picture [on the wall]'

Animals, on the other hand, may be lying, moving, standing, etc., as in (122).

(122) *hkáwa kše húheka kše?*
hkáwa kše húheka kše
horse LIE sick 3.CONT
'that horse lying there, is it sick?'

The subject of the verb *aðį* 'have' normally carries a subject marker *akxa* or *apa*, but below we see the semantic subject *wakˀó* 'woman' with a positional article, used in an obviative sense:

(123) *(tówa) wakˀó įkše táatą žáži aðįe?*
(tówa) wakˀó įkše táatą žáže a-Ø-ðį-ðe
(that.one) woman SIT what name PREV-A3S-have-DECL
'what is that woman's name?' (lit., '(that one) the woman sitting there, what's her name?')

The woman is sitting in (123). The use of *tówa* 'that one [unidentified]' reaffirms obviative status when using a noun such as *wak?ó* 'woman' or *níhka* 'man' with a positional article, as above in (123) or below in (124).

(124) *towa nį́hka įkšé táatą žáži aðįe?*
towa níhka įkšé táatą žáže a-Ø-ðį́-ðe
that.one man SIT what name PREV-A3S-have-DECL
'what is that man's name?' (lit., 'the unknown or unidentified man sitting over there, what does he have [for a] name?')

The form *į́kšé* is cognate with *įkhe* 'sitting' in other Dhegiha languages, just as Osage *txą* is cognate with *thą* 'standing animate' in related languages and Osage *che* with t^h*e* ''standing inanimate' in those same languages. There are some other forms in Osage which are probably related to *įkšé*. Although it implies a striking departure from conservation of the distinction between aspirates and nonaspirates, the endings *įki* or *įke* used in interrogative 'where' may be historically from *įkhe*, with the same origin as *įkšé* 'round [inanimate]'. The interrogative *howáįki* 'where' may be based on *howa* 'which of two or more', plus *įke* or *įki*. There is variation between *ki* and *ke* as the final syllable of *howáįki*, which is used for both 'where' as in (125) and 'where to' as in (126).[7]

(125) *howáįki ðalįįke nįkšé?*
howáįki Ya-lįįke nįkšé
where A2S-sit.down 2S.CONT
'where are you going to sit down?'

(126) *Johna howáįki ðée?*
John-a howáįki a-Ø-ðée
John-SYL where PREV-A3S-go
'where did John go?'

A remarkable application of *įkšé* (discussed more fully in section 6.4) is its use as a pluralizer when describing a group of items that characteristically lie but are now gathered into a bundle that sits.

(127) *káa įkšé*
these/those.here/there sitting
'these things gathered into a bundle'

Another usage (discussed in sections 5.3.2 and 5.6.8, and in section 7.2.7, on *šǫ* 'while') is seen in (128).

[7] Neither ***howaįkšé* nor ***howaįtxą* exist.

(128) *óhkie šǫ́ įkšé ihtežį akxa mą́zeie híðape*
óhkie šǫ įkšé ihtežį akxa mą́zeie hi-ðe-api-ðe
he-talk while SIT sister SUBJ phone.call arrive-CAU-PL-DECL
'he was talking [to someone on the telephone] when his younger sister called'

Although one might expect *txą* or *che* (both are 'standing') to be used with tall items such as trees, in fact *įkšé* 'round, sitting' is obligatory in some sentences, such as (129). The 'sitting' article *įkšé* would be used even for very tall trees. There may be a strong preference for use of *įkšé* with stative verbs. Or it may be that anything with a round base sits. In (130) as well, 'tree' appears with *įkšé*. But other articles may be used with *žą́ą* 'tree'—*che* as in (137), and *txą* as in (133).

(129) *žą́ą įkše ą́ąhǫǫ*
žą́ą įkšé ą-hǫǫ
tree SIT P1S-like
'I like that tree [tree is standing]'

(130) *žą́ą įkše ší tą hkilísąða*
žą́ą įkše a-Ya-hí tą hkilísąðe-a
tree SIT PREV-A2S-.arrive.there when turn-IMPER
'when you get to that particular tree, turn'

6.3.2 *txą* 'standing animate'

The underlying nasal vowel of *txą* is often denasalized, giving *txa*; in Hominy dialect, this article can have the form *kxą* (medially also *tkxą*).

(131) *šǫ́ke txa kǫ́ða akxai*
šǫ́ke txą Ø-kǫ́-Ø-ða akxa-ðe
dog STA A3S-PREV-A3S-want 3.CONT-DECL
'he wanted that dog'

In example (131), *txą* is used with an animate nonhuman; in (132), it is used on a human recipient (in this example, *į* is unidentified, perhaps a slip of the tongue). The morpheme *txą́* is also included in all first and second person forms of the 'standing' positional auxiliary (section 5.5).

(132) *tówa įkxą áawakˀu mįkše*[8]
tówa ðe(?)-txą́ Wa-wa-kˀu mįkše
PRON that(?)-STA A1S-VAL-give 1S.CONT
'I'm giving stuff to that person standing'[9]

[8] *wa-akˀu* becomes *awakˀu* by metathesis (chapter 2).

[9] The collocational formula for inanimate plurals (section 6.4) does not seem to apply at all to animates, although the gloss 'I'm giving stuff to that bunch of people (sitting or lying)' was offered as a possible gloss for this sentence; *tówa* can be plural.

One example was found with the article *txą* on the noun 'tree', understood to be standing (133).

(133) *žą́ą kxą ą́ąhǫǫ*
žą́ą txą ą-hǫǫ
tree STA P1S-like
'I like that tree'

Also worth noting is that *txą* in (133) belongs to the paradigm for animates, yet *žą́ą* 'tree' appears below in (137) with the article *che* 'inanimate standing' instead of *txą* 'animate standing'. This may be due to the fact that a tree is living but nonhuman, so that it may partake of either animate or inanimate paradigms, or the use of *che* in (137) may be due to the tree's imminent death.

6.3.3 *che* 'standing inanimate'

Although in English a coffee pot sits, the default positional for a coffee pot and several vertical objects in Osage is *che* 'standing inanimate'. Informal confirmation that positional articles imply 'backgrounded' status can be seen in the following contrast: *níi che* (134) refers only to water at some distance, while if the water were close by, *níi toa* 'some water' would be used. (But *níi che* must be used if the water is farther down the table.) In (135), although the deictics 'this' and 'here' are used in the English translation, *che* signals that the coffee is backgrounded, and presumably not in close proximity to the speaker.

(134) *níi che húukaaɣa*
níi che hú-káaɣe-a
water STA come.here-make-IMPER
'pass the water' (lit., 'water that-standing make-it-come-here')

(135) *mąhkásai ché*
mąhkásai ché
coffee STA
'this coffee sitting here'

Example (136) involves either plural or singular food item(s), and would not be acceptable with *įkšé* 'sitting' in lieu of *che*; we conclude that food stands (or at least some foods stand), or else *che* here refers to a collocation of sitting food items (see section 6.4).

Since no other examples of collocational plurality were found applying to animates, one should not construe *txą* in this example as treating an individual (who might otherwise carry the sitting marker *įkšé*) as a group with *txą́*, although it is tempting to do so. Perhaps the speaker was transferring the collocational plural mechanism erroneously to animates.

(136) *ónǫbre che kíicheðaa*
ónǫbre che ka-i-che-ðe-a
food STA here-by.means-STA-CAU-IMPER
'set the food down'

Positional articles are often optional; (137) would be correct with or without *che*.

(137) *žą́ą che aasé hta mįkšé*
žą́ą che a-sé hta mįkšé
tree that A1S-cut FUT 1S.CONT
'I'm going to cut that tree down'

Although the referent was not given, (138) could refer to a staff, an umbrella, or some other vertical inanimate object. Other possibilities are that the referent is a collocation of 'sitting' items (*įkšé*), which would require the 'standing' (*che*) positional; or that *che* may prove to be the default positional, imposed under circumstances that remain unclear. Interestingly, in (138), none of the other positional articles (e.g. *ke* 'scattered', *txą* 'standing animate', or *įkšé* 'sitting') could be used in place of *che*, no matter what the referent is.

(138) *wíhta che áalǫ́brį*
wihta che áa-Wa-lǫ-Wa-ðį
1S.POSS STA PREV-A1S-PREV-A1S-forget
'I forgot my own'

In another incarnation as default positional for inanimates, in (139) *che* appears in the common interrogative *howachéeški* '(inanimate) anything'. (Cf. *ðe* in *howaðéeški* 'anyone' in section 6.3.5.)

(139) *howachéeški íiðaðe?*
howa-ché-eški íi-ð-Wa-ðe
INDEF-STA-also/else PREV-EPð-A1S-see
'did you see anything?'

6.3.4 *kše* 'lying'

The positional article *kše* 'lying' is seen in (140)–(144). This positional is common with animates, where it can combine with the demonstrative *ée*, as in (140)–(144), and is also used for a fallen tree in (144). For 'that one lying' of unknown identity, *tówa kšé* is used. (See also section 6.1.6 for more examples of this article.)

(140) *šée ékše*
šée ée-kše
that/there 3.PRON-LIE
'that person there [lying]'

(141) *pée ékše?*
pée ée-kše
who 3.PRON-LIE
'who is that over there lying down?'

(142) *kootáa kše pée éekše?*[10]
kootá kše pée ée-kše
farther LIE who 3.PRON-LIE
'that lying over there, who is it? [sic]'

(143) *šǫ́ke ékše háažo?*
šǫ́ke ékše háa-Ya-ǫ
dog that-LIE INDEF-A2S-do
'what are you going to do with that dog lying there?'

(144) *žą́ą kše ą́ąhǫǫ*
žą́ą kše ą-hǫǫ
tree LIE P1S-like
'I like that tree' (tree is lying down)

6.3.5 *ðe* 'moving animate'

The case of the positional article *ðe* 'moving animate' is a complex one, seemingly in the process of transition. There is an overlap between the simple demonstrative (unspecified for movement) *ðe* 'this, that, these, those' and the positional article *ðe*. Since the demonstrative and the positional article are homophonous, and the former is singular or plural but the latter only singular, many sentences are several ways ambiguous. The ambiguity occurs not only with regard to plurality, but also in regard to the semantic component 'moving'. In (145), *ðe* may be interpreted as merely demonstrative without specifying 'moving'; i.e., the person indicated may possibly not be moving. Certainly *ðe* is frequently found for nonmoving entities, in phrases such as 'those meat pies'. The plural form (for moving entities) *pa* can even be combined with the demonstrative *ðe*, which gives *šée pa ðé* for 'those guys there (moving)'!

[10] See discussion of *kootá* in section 6.2.4.

(145) *šée éeðe!*
šée *ée-ðe*
that/there 3.PRON-MOV
'that person there!'[11]

This example is the phrase to use if one is referring to a fellow out there dancing (i.e., moving). The *ðe* in such an instance is the 'moving' positional article.

There may be a third *ðe*: a particle which intermittently appears at the end of interrogative clauses (glossed in the example below as QUES).

(146) *šée éeðe pee ðe?*[12]
šée *ée-ðe* *pée* *ðe*
that/there 3.PRON-MOV who QUES
'that guy, who is he?'

The plural of this sentence is *šée pa ðé pée ðe?* 'those guys [plural, moving], who are they?'.

A fourth homonym is the ubiquitous declarative *ðe*, seen on hundreds of examples in this volume. (The question particle in the example above and elsewhere may in fact be declarative *ðe*.)

Positional articles enter into the formation of certain pronouns. In (147), *ðe* 'moving animate' is used in *howaðéeški* 'anyone', while *che* (standing/vertical, inanimate) is used in *howachéeški* 'anything' (see section 6.3.3 above).

(147) *howaðéeški íiðaðe*
howa-ðe-eški *íi-Ya-ðe*
INDEF-MOV-also/else PREV-A2S-see
'did you see anyone?'

6.3.6 *pa* 'plural'

The positional article *pa* (glossed PLU in examples) signals plurality, but without communicating anything about movement or position. In (151), for instance, the receivers (*tówa pa* 'those ones') may be standing or sitting; in (150), *šée pa* can refer to people who are sitting.

(148) *šée pa*
šée *pa*
that/there PLU
'those folks standing over there'

[11] This example is an expression that can be indirectly addressed to the person walking by. It is quite informal, considered slang.

[12] The speaker would not accept ***šée ðe pee ekxai* for this sentence.

(149) *šée pa lį̨i hcéa*
šée pa lį̨i hce-ée-a
those PLU sit.down INJ-say-IMPER
'tell them to sit'

(150) *šée pa nąąžį hcéa*
šée pa Ø-nąąžį hce-ée-a
those PLU A3P-stand.up INJ-say-IMPER
'tell those people to stand up'

(151) *tówa pa áwawakˀú mįkše*
tówa pa Wa-wa-wa-kˀú mįkše
PRON PLU A1S-P3P- stuff-give 1S.CONT
'I'm giving stuff to that bunch of people (those ones)'

According to Koontz (p.c. 1995), in Omaha-Ponca *ma* (cognate with Osage *pa*) is used to signify 'the whole group [of animates]'. This resembles *ama*, the plural of *nį* 'move' in Quapaw. Osage *pa* seems to indicate a group regardless of whether it is sitting, standing, or moving. (If the members of a group of animates or inanimates were dispersed or scattered, however, *ke* would be used instead.)

It may be that an earlier distinction among *ðe* 'moving, singular', *pa* 'moving, plural' and the subject marker *apa* is weakening. If historically *pa* meant 'moving', as suggested by cognates in related languages, nowadays *pa* has lost, or is losing, the sense of 'moving' in Osage. This is explicable in terms of general weakening of use of the language; more specifically, it is explicable by the fact that within the subject marker paradigm, nearly homophonous *apa* may either signal 'present moving' or 'absent, unspecified for motion', and therefore could cause interference with the original meaning ('plural, moving') of positional *pa*. The quasi-homophone *apa* from the subject marker paradigm is not always plural, and may occur on singular nouns if they are moving, as in (152).

(152) *ðe wižįke apa waachí apai*
ðe wižįke apa waa-Ø-chí apa-ðe
that Wižįke SUBJ PREV-A3S-dance 3.CONT-DECL
'Wižįke there dances'

In (153), the positional article *pa* marks 'plural' as expected.

(153) *šée pa pée ðe?*
šée pa pée ðe
that/there PLU who DECL
'who are those guys?'

If (153) were singular, then the only alternative for 'subject moving' is *šée ðe pée ðe?* 'who is that guy [moving]?'. (However, *šée ðe pée ðe?* is also correct if the subject 'he' is sitting, possibly because the *ðe* of *šée ðe* in this case is taken as a demonstrative.)

An object marked with *pa* is seen also in (154) (with the not unexpected raising of *ee* to *ii* in *šée*). The object 'them' represents people who are present but at a distance from the speaker.

(154) *šíi pa iðási*
šée pa í-a-si
that/there PLU PREV-A1S-dislike
'I don't like them'

Example (154) was produced along with (155) as a minimal pair for 'moving, plural' vs. 'moving, singular'. However, no 'moving' connotation is necessarily present either in (154), since *pa* does not specify position or movement, or in (155), since *ðe* may be interpreted as simple demonstrative; these complications cloud the purity of the minimal pair.

(155) *šée ðe iðási*
šée ðe í-a-si
that/there MOV PREV-A1S-dislike
'I don't like him [moving]'

In modern Osage, *pa* on plural 'dogs' (156) does not specify position; this sentence can be used regardless of whether the dogs are sitting, standing, lying, or moving. The same is true of (157).

(156) *šǫ́ke tóowa pa, háažǫ hta nįkše?*
šǫ́ke tówa pa háa-Ya-ǫ hta nįkšé
dog that PLU INDEF-A2S-do FUT 2.CONT
'what are you going to do with those dogs there?'

(157) *níhkaši pa wátǫpa*
níhkaši pa wa-á-tǫpe-a
man PLU P3P-LOC-look-IMPER
'take care of those men [standing or sitting], look after them'

6.3.7 *ke* 'dispersed'

Sometimes *ke* modifies items which the speaker and hearer cannot see; it is abstract and plural. In others, it merely marks 'plural, scattered, diffuse', or is a simple pluralizer without much emphasis on dispersion. The form *ke* is possibly related to *ka* 'here'; *ka-i* might have become *ke*, since *a* + *i* becomes *e* elsewhere (for example, valence reducer *wa* + *i* becomes *we*;

see section 2.3.3.1).[13] (An alternative hypothesis is suggested immediately below in this section, however.)[14]

(158) *táatą éekǫ́ ke ąwáštaakaži ðáalį*
táatą é-ekǫ́ ke o-ą-Ya-ðaake-aži ðáalį
thing 3.PRON-like DISP P1S-PREV-A2S-recount-NEG good
'you shouldn't tell me things like that'

(159) *ðéke*
ðe-ke
that/this-DISP
'these [plural, scattered]'

(160) *táatą ðéke hǫ́ǫžike*
táatą ðe-ke hǫ́ǫži-ke
thing that/this-DISP bad-DISP
'these bad things'

ecí (or *eecí*) is a locative expression meaning '(it is) at/in that; there' and based on the third person pronoun *ée* and the postposition *ci*; the element *ci* itself is likely derived from *che* 'standing' plus *i* 'in, to'.

(161) *ecí tą*
ée-ci tą
3.PRON-at if
'if it's there'

The suffixation of *ke* to *ecí* 'it is there' adds plurality:

(162) *ecíke*
ee-cí-ke
3.PRON-at-DISP
'the things that are there, these here (things)'

The form *ecíkie* seems to have the same meaning as *ecíke*. This suggests that *ke* may not originate from *ka* + *i*, contrary to what was suggested at the beginning of this section.

(163) *ecíkie tą*
ée-ci-kie tą
there-at-DISP if
'if they're around there'

[13] The *i* of hypothetical *ka-i* might be the predecessor of the pluralizer *api*. This *i* occurs in La Flesche (1932) and in related languages as pluralizer.

[14] *ke* appears on a few verbs and singular nouns to indicate a single item divided, broken, or shattered into pieces. Thus, for example, from *ðixǫ́* 'break' (transitive) is formed *híi ðixǫ́ke* 'he broke his tooth (*híi*) in pieces'. Compare also *léke* 'shattered, in pieces'.

The 'dispersed, scattered' meaning attached to *ke* (or *kie*) is sometimes glossed informally as 'be around'. It is used either of abstractions such as 'bad things', or concretely, as in examples such as 'You could pick pecans if they're around.'

(164) *ecíke tą*
ee-cí-ke tą
there-at-DISP if
'if they're there' (i.e., if there are any around)

(165) *táatą hǫ́ǫžį ecíkie tą, ékiǫ ðįka pai*
táatą hǫ́ǫžį ee-cí-kie tą, ékiǫ ðįké-a paðe
thing bad there-at-DISP if do NEG-IMPER IMPER.CONT
'if there's anything bad around, don't do that' (lit., 'if bad things are around, don't be doing them')

ecí may also be followed by *pa* (166), in a usage reminiscent of the French *chez eux*.

(166) *ecí pa žóąðale šie ðe*
ee-cí pa žó-ą-Ya-le a-Ya-híe ðe
there-at PLU PREV-P1S-A2S-with PREV-A2S-arrive.there DECL
'you brought me to them' ('you went with me to them')

6.3.8 Other possible positional articles

There are other minor candidates for membership among the positional articles that are not examined in detail here. One is *pe*, as in *žą́ą pe* 'trees planted in a pattern', contrasting with *žą́ą ke* 'trees in random pattern as in the woods'. Another is *įke* in the rather mysterious *žą́ą įké* 'a group of trees; out in the trees; in the forest'. Both of these examples pertain to the same species and size of trees.

6.4 Inanimate collective plurals

Choice of positional article for inanimate collective plurals is determined by special principles. This remarkable system is quite alive and available to speakers, who do not falter in their choices of which article to use. They are remarkably decisive—especially given the stage of language disuse—in confirming all usages in this system. The use of a positional referring to a collocation or configuration made up of multiple members constitutes one of the few devices available in Osage for signalling plurality in a language with no overt plurals. The system can be sketched in three parts as follows.

(a) A group of round or sitting things, each of which if occurring alone could be followed by the article *įkšé*—e.g., grapes or meat pies—

uses *che* 'standing'. The imagery is that when round or sitting items are gathered into a group, they form a vertical object.

(b) A group of standing or vertical things (which individually would use *che* 'standing, inanimate') uses *kše* 'lying', as the items are considered to lie in a row. That is, a series of upright items form a row that lies horizontally; e.g., a line of upright fenceposts forms a fence which lies along a line in a certain configuration.

(c) A group of long objects or lying objects (each of which individually would use *kše* 'lying') is considered to make a round or sitting bundle, and takes *įkšé* 'sitting'. That is, long items may be tied into a bundle, and the bundle sits (e.g., as a shock of wheat or corn sits in a field).

6.4.1 'Sitting' > 'standing'

In the example below, *házu* 'grapes' takes the positional article *che* 'standing'. This is because grapes are individually round (a single grape cannot 'stand'), but here occur in bunches that are considered to stand. (The grapes are alive but soon to be picked; hence an inanimate plural occurs here.)

(167) *házu čóopažį che paahí*
házu čóopa-žį che pahí-a
grape small.amount-little STA pick-IMPER
'those few grapes, pick them'

If the grapes are scattered around individually, then *ke* 'scattered' must be used.

(168) *házu ke paahí*
házu ke paahí-a
grape DISP pick-IMPER
'pick the grapes; pick up the grapes'

Example (169) refers to meat pies piled on a porch step across the street. Thus it involves a collocation of round or sitting (*įkšé*) items, as did the grape example in (167), and again the 'standing inanimate' article *che* is used. One of the possible glosses refers to noncountable 'stuff'.

(169) *šée che*
šée che
that.there STA
'those things; that stuff'

If the items are nearby, *káa* replaces *šée*, as in (170). The expression *káa che* indicates a bundle, group, or stack, with *che* as a plural ending. A person sets the item(s) down and says *káa che* 'here!'.

(170) *káa che*
káa *che*
this.right.here STA
'these things here'

Example (171) is plural only, never singular, as in it the standing inanimate affix (*che* in *káa che*) is used for a collocation of things, the meat pies, that individually are round or sitting (*įkšé*). This, like the case of the grapes above, is a plural forced by configurational considerations.

(171) *htóožu káa che*
htóožu *káa* *che*
meat.pie here STA
'here's these meat pies for you'

Even if the speaker is holding a single rectangular meat pie upright and giving it to someone, the expression would be as in (172) (with no *che*). If plural meat pies are involved, the expression to use is (173), with *che*. As in (171), *che* in this context unambiguously means more than one meat pie.

(172) *htóožu wį káa*
htóožu *wį* *kaa*
meat.pie a this.right.here
'here's this meat pie for you'

(173) *htóožu tóe káa che*
htóožu *tóe* *kaa* *che*
meat.pie a this.right.here STA
'here's some meat pies for you'

This leads us to conclude that the usually 'sitting' item 'meat pie' cannot be referred to in singular with the 'standing' positional even though it is being held in a vertical or standing position. The 'standing' article will always indicate plurality for this item. An individual meat pie thus has a positional gender as 'sitting', although in space it can be held upright or can lie on a table horizontally. Any comments involving a singular meat pie will use either no positional article at all, or may use the 'sitting' article *įkšé*. Thus, both the simple expression *htóožu káa* 'here, here's a meat pie' as well as (174) involve a single meat pie only.

(174) *htóožu káa įkšé*
htóožú káa įkšé
meat.pie here SIT
'here's a meat pie'

If the meat pie is being held in the hand, no positional is used, as in (175), but if the meat pie is lying on the table, then the sitting positional is used, as in (176).

(175) *htóožu wíhta*
htóožu wíhta
meat.pie 1S.POSS
'this meat pie is mine'

(176) *htóožu įkšé wíhta*
htóožu įkšé wíhta
meat.pie SIT 1S.POSS
'this meat pie is mine '

In examples (177) and (178), the noun is again understood as plural. The meat pies (located on the table) are stacked, and take the article *che* 'standing inanimate'. (In (177), the possessive appears outside the positionally modified noun.)[15]

(177) *ðe htóožu che wíhta*
ðe htóožu che wihta
that meat.pie STA mine
'these meat pies are mine'

(178) *ðe htóožu che ąkˀu íkˀucapi*
ðe htóožu che ą-kˀu íkˀuce-a-api
that meat.pie STA P1S-give try-IMPER-PL
'try, you all, to give those meat pies to me'

Another item that 'sits' is a blanket. As expected within this system, if *che* 'standing' appears with 'blanket' (*haxį che*) its use forces a plural reading 'blankets'. Likewise *ðe che*, if used of blankets, is plural only—e.g., in (179) (where it happens to be discontinuous) and in (180). This accords with the finding that *che* 'standing, vertical' is used for collocations of 'sitting' (*įkšé*) items such as blankets. Example (181) is a clear plural without *ðe*.

[15] The obvious question is, What happens when you have plural, but not stacked, meat pies? This may be expressed as *htóožu ke* [meat.pie DISP] or *htóožu toe* [meat.pie some].

(179) *ðe haxį che tǫ́pa*
ðe haxį che tǫpe-a
this blanket STA look-IMPER
'look at these blankets'

(180) *haxį ðe che tǫ́pa*
haxį ðe che tǫpe-a
blanket this STA look-IMPER
'look at these blankets'

(181) *haxį che ąkʔú huða*
haxį che ą-kʔú hu-ðe-a
blanket STA P1S-give come.here-CAU-IMPER
'give me those blankets'

6.4.2 'Lying' > 'sitting'

In another manifestation of this device for signalling plurality, a configuration of multiple 'lying or long' entities is referred to with the 'sitting' positional article *įkšé*. That is, a collection or group of long or lying entities is treated as a sitting bundle (round) or as sitting in a bag or sack, for which *įkšé* is appropriate.

(182) *káa įkšé*
káa įkšé
these.here sitting
'these things tied into a bundle (or in a sack)'

6.4.3 'Standing' > 'lying'

One may deduce from examples with postpositions (example (213) in section 6.6.2 and example (191) in section 6.5.4) that a series of items that normally stand (*che*) take the *kšé* 'lying' article if lined up, although Osage speakers were unable to produce examples. The line is thought of as lying, as a fence made up of vertical objects lies along a line.

6.5 Configurational postpositions

Four configurational postpositions in Osage encode position of the noun object of the postposition and its number (plurality). These four postpositions, shown in table 6.5, all have the range of meanings 'toward, to', 'in, at' and possibly 'from'; in the table, 'to' is used for brevity. All of them derive from a positional article plus an element *-i* 'to'.

TABLE 6.5. CONFIGURATIONAL POSTPOSITIONS

POSTPOSITION	RELATED ARTICLE	WITH SINGULAR OBJECT OF POSTPOSITION	WITH COLLOCATIONAL OBJECT OF POSTPOSITION
įkši (sitting)	*įkšé*	'to a sitting animate or inanimate object'	'to a group of lying or long things'
ci (standing)	*che*	'to a standing object'	'to a group of sitting, round things'
kši (lying)	*kše*	'to a lying animate or inanimate object'	'to a group of vertical, standing things'
ki (dispersed)	*ke*	(plural only)	'to a group of dispersed things'

6.5.1 *įkši* 'in/to that (sitting or round)'

The 'sitting' or 'round' postposition *įkši* may be used, for example, with a pond in (183) and with the name of a town (Hominy, *Hą́mąðį* 'Nightwalker') when the town is conceived of as flat, round or sitting (184).

(183) *níitahpa įkší ąkáipe*
níi-táahpa įkšé-i ąk-aðée-api-ðe
water-round LIE-to A1P-go-PL-DECL
'we are going to that pond'

(184) *hą́mąðį įkši wétapee*
hą-mąðį įkšé-i wa-i-Ø-táða-api-ðe
night-walk SIT-in P1P-PREV-A3S-birth-PL-DECL
'we were born in Hominy'

6.5.2 *ci* 'in, at, to (standing)'

The common phrase *ecí* made up of the third person pronoun *ée* (shortened to *é*) plus the 'standing' postposition *ci* means 'at that place; at that time; be in that place.' Further examples of the 'standing' postposition can be seen below.

(185) *Johna táatą íiðe ðe, watǫ́ehci ce?*[16]
John-a táatą íi-Ø--ðe ðe watǫehci ci
John-SYL thing PREV-A3S-see DECL store STA-in
'what did John see in the store?'

(186) *hkąącólą lébra oðíhtą ci oolą́ akxa*
hką́ące-oolą́ lébrą oðíhtą ci oolą́ akxa
fruit-put.in ten car in put.in 3.CONT
'there are ten pies sitting in the car'

(187) *níhkašie lébra ecí apai, hkáwa tóopa ecí apai*
nihkašie lébrą e-cí apa-ðe hkáwa tóopa
man ten 3.PRON-in 3.CONT-DECL horse four
e-cí apa-ðe
3.PRON-in 3.CONT-DECL
'there are ten men there, there are four horses there'[17]

6.5.3 *kši* 'to (lying)'

Location at or motion towards a lying entity is marked by the postposition *kši* (cf. the positional article *kše*). The arbor is considered long or lying (188), and so uses *kše* 'lying' as its positional article. The town in (189) is also conceived of as 'lying'. A town may be an entity that takes different shapes in a speakers' minds, and one that also may change shapes as it grows, but at any rate may 'sit' or 'lie'.

(188) *áhcitą kší ąkái hce*
áhcitą kše-i ąk-aðée hce
arbor LIE-to A1P/D-go INJ
'let's go to the arbor'

(189) *hámąðį htą́wą kší ąkái hce*
hą́mąðį htą́wą kše-i ąk-aðée hce
Hominy town LIE-to A1P/D-go INJ
'let's go to Hominy'

In the next example, 'here' is thought of as a place that 'lies'.

[16] There is a tendency for dissimilation to occur in sequences of syllables with like vowels such as *hci ci*, which frequently becomes *hci ce*. This is likely a low-level phonetic phenomenon, although conceivably the lowered *ce* at least in this example may derive from an underlying sequence of *ci* followed by *ðe* 'declarative'. In addition, this example has unusual word order; *watǫehci ci* 'at the store' would be expected to occur at the beginning of the sentence, but has been added as an afterthought.

[17] This sentence is also correct with *akxa* as aspect marker on both phrases (giving *ecí akxái*), if the entities are present when the sentence is uttered.

(190) *ðekáaha kši, waaspé aha, ðáalį hta akxái*
ðe-kaa-ha kše-ci, wáaspe aha, ðáalį hta akxa-ðe
this-here-toward LIE-to wait when, good FUT 3.CONT-DECL
'it would be good if you stayed here'

6.5.4 *ki* 'to (multiple)'

To express multiple destinations, or a destination thought of in its multiplicity, or an event that is repeated and thus becomes several events, the multiple *ki* is used. (Positional *ke* indicates 'dispersed, multiple'.)

(191) *waachí ki štáapáži na*
waachí ke-i Ya-ðée-api-aži na
dance DISP-to A2S-go-PL-NEG ITER
'you [plural] never go to dances'

6.6 Other postpositions and locative expressions

A set of postpositions meaning 'to' (*įkší, kši, ci, ki*) that are clearly and directly related to configuration of the goal are discussed in section 6.5. Other postpositions, covering the concepts of 'toward', 'into', 'inside of', are not members of that configurational set and remain somewhat opaque. These forms contain one or another of the elements *ha* 'pathway toward, via' (section 6.6.1.1); *hta* 'inside; into' (section 6.6.1.2); and *á-* 'on; against; among' (section 6.6.2). (There is a form *žóle* 'accompany; with', which does not function as a postposition, though it is semantically similar.)

6.6.1 *hta* 'into' and *ha* 'toward'

In an attempt to elucidate the use of *hta* and *ha* it is helpful to distinguish as far as possible among the various Osage equivalents for English meanings such as 'to', 'into', 'toward', and 'in', 'inside', etc. in table 6.6.[18]

6.6.1.1 *ha* 'toward; along a path to; in direction of'

An interesting distinction is made in otherwise identical sentences, (192) and (193). Adding *ha*, as in (193), gives a connotation of more specifically directed action, perhaps with gestures, rather than action directed merely in a general way as in (192).

[18] Some related forms in Ponca are: *édi* 'in it'; *etta* 'to it'; *edíthą, ettáthą* 'from it' (with the difference between the latter two remaining obscure). Osage cognates are *ecí* and *ehtá* for the first two, and would be *ecítxą*(?) and *ehtátxą*(?) for the last two.

TABLE 6.6. POSTPOSITIONS 'TO', 'INTO', ETC.

ENGLISH EQUIVALENT	OSAGE
'to [a lying animate or inanimate object, or to a group of standing or vertical objects]'	*kši*
'into'	*kšíhta*[a]
'toward'	*kšíhtaha*[b]
'to [a standing object, or a group of round or sitting objects], in'	*ci*
'in that place'	*eci*[c]
'to the inside of that'	*ehtá*
'at that time or place'	*ecíhta*
'toward that way, toward that place'	*éhtaha*

[a] Incorporates *hta* 'into'.
[b] Incorporates *hta* 'into' + *ha* 'via a path toward'.
[c] See section 7.5.

(192) *še ðó aðáape*
še ðó a-Ø-ðée-api-ðe
there next.to PREV-A3S-go-PL-DECL
'he went that way'

(193) *še ðó ha aðáape*
še ðó ha a-Ø-ðée-api-ðea
there next.to toward PREV-A3S-go-PL-DECL
'he went that way [toward where they're sitting]'

The expression *howáįke* 'where' may also add *ha*, reflected in the English by 'through':

(194) *hòwaįkíha brée?*
howaįke-ha Wa-ðée
where-toward A1S-go
'through where should I go?; which way should I go?'

In (195), *ha* again refers to directed movement, this time as items are being moved into piles. The form *ha* also appears in the directed movement of sheathing or inserting in (196)–(197).

(195) *owé che ðáabrį ha káaɣa*
ówe che ðáabrį ha káaɣe-a
food STA three toward make-IMPER
'make three piles of groceries'

(196) *okˀǫ́ha*
okˀǫ-ha
hole-toward
'put inside, sheathe'

(197) *hpáažį okˀǫ́ha*
hpáažį okˀǫ́ha-a
baby sheathe-IMPER
'put the baby on the board'

Another use of *ha* is in expressions meaning 'after' or 'beyond' or 'over; above'.

(198) *álįįha*
álįį-ha
sit.upon-toward
'after, over and above'[19]

(199) *hpéðǫpa álįha akxai*
hpéðǫǫpa álįįha akxa-ðe
seven after 3.CONT-DECL
'it's after seven'

(200) *míoke lébra álįįha akxai*
mį́į-oðáake lébrą álįįha akxa-ðe
sun-tell ten after 3.CONT-DECL
'it's after ten o'clock'

Other expressions with a final *ha* are *óðeząha* 'among'; *óðizaha* 'to be a member, as of a club'; and *ákaha* 'on top of', shown in (201).

(201) *paaxó ákaha*
paxó ákaha
hill/mountain on.top
'the top of the hill'

6.6.1.2 *hta*

The expression *hta* indicates 'to the inside of' or 'into', as in (202)–(203).

(202) *ówe che hcí hta áðįku*
ówe che hcí hta aðį-kú-a
groceries those house into have-return.here-IMPER
'bring the groceries in the house'

[19] For 'after', another speaker preferred *álihai*, which she glossed as 'past, after; too long'.

(203) *hcí hta aðáape*
hcí hta a-Ø-ðée-api-ðe
house into PREV-A3S-go-PL-DECL
'he went into the house'

ha 'toward' may be added to *hta* 'into', as in (204)–(209). Example (204) contrasts nicely with (203) above. In (204), with *htaha*, we know that the subject went 'in the direction of the house', but whether or not he went inside remains unexpressed. (Elsewhere we have seen *kši* 'to' as in *hą́mąðį kši* 'to Hominy'.)

(204) *hcí htaha aðáape*
hcí htaha a-Ø-ðée-api-ðe
house toward PREV-A3S-do-PL-DECL
'he went directly to the house'

Adding *ha* to *ée htá* we get *ée htáha* 'toward that, along a path to that; in that direction', used in 'toward daylight' in (205). (Some demonstrative forms with *ha* are noted in section 6.2.2.)

(205) *hą́pa skáha ée htaha ahí akxai*
hą́pa ská-ha ée hta-ha
day clear/white-toward 3.PRON into-toward
a-Ø-hí akxa-ðe
PREV-A3S-arrive.there 3.CONT-DECL
'it's getting daylight'

Other phrases with *hta* + *ha* clearly as 'toward' include the following:

(206) *šée htáhą aðáape*
šée hta-ha a-Ø-ðée-api-ðe
there.by.you into-toward PREV-A3P-go-PL-DECL
'they went over that way [toward you]'

(207) *šée htáha okˀą́ hta apai*
šée htá-ha okˀą́ hta apa-ðe
there.by.you into-toward happening FUT 3.CONT-DECL
'they're having a doings over there toward you, in that direction'

'In the other direction' also, not surprisingly, is expressed by *htaha*, as in (208). In (209), we find the two forms in reverse order: *ha* + *hta*.

(208) *áma htaha*
áma hta-ha
other into-toward
'the other way, the other side'

(209) *ákaha hta*
ákaha hta
outside into
'outside of the area, on the other side [of a perimeter]'

Sometimes both *hta* and *ha* appear along with *kši*, as in (210), in a series of three postpositions. (Comparable series ***ki hta ha* and ***cí hta ha* have not been encountered, however.)

(210) *hą́mąðį kší hta ha*
hą́mąðį kše-i hta ha
Hominy LIE-to into toward
'toward Hominy'

6.6.2 Locative *á-*

Locative expressions involving initial *á-* are numerous. Some of the forms containing *ha* in the examples above also contain *á-*. The locative is well known in Siouan as a member of the set of locative prefixes *a, i, o* (see section 4.5).

(211) *ákiɣe*
'around edge [e.g., of a pond]'

(212) *ámaši*
'up; upstairs; at the top of [something]'

(213) *paaxó ámaši ki mąðí*
paxó ámaši kše-i mąðí-a
mountain up LIE-to go-IMPER
'go up into the mountains'

(214) *ámaši aðáape*
ámaši a-Ø-ðée-api-ðe
up PREV-A3S-go-PL-DECL
'she/he went upstairs'

To express 'around', as in 'around a tree, tepee, drum', *ápetxa* is used, which also means 'wrap'. For 'pass around, go around, walk around; around', there is *ápše*, seen in the next example.

(215) *níi ápše wák?u*
níi ápše wa-k?u
water around P3P-give
'pass the water around [to them]'

The form *áši*, seen in (216)–(217), also appears with *hta* as *áši hta* 'outside, outdoors; to outside', the opposite of *hcí hta* 'inside'.[20]

(216) *áši ðée*
áši a-ðée
outside PREV-go
'go outside'

(217) *ąnąhowa, áši ščée škǫ́šta tą*
i-ą-hoe-a, áši a-Ya-ðée
PREV-P1S-ask.permission-IMPER outside PREV-A2S-go
Ya-kǫ́-Ya-ða tą
A2S-PREV-A2S-want if
'ask me if you want to go outside'

The form *áška* 'near, close by; close to another thing or person' has a diminutive formed with *žį* 'small' (used as an intensifier):

(218) *áškažį líįka*
áškažį líįke-a
close-small sit.down-IMPER
'sit down [very] close to me'

Despite the translation, example (218) does not overtly code the meaning 'to me'. 'Close to you' is also expressed with *áška* 'close' (without overt expression of 'you'), seen in nondiminutive form in (219) and (220).

(219) *áška kú*
áška a-ku-a
close PREV-return.here-IMPER
'come close'

(220) *áška líįkáape?*
áška líįka-api-ðe
close she.sits-PL-DECL
'did she sit down close to you?'

Forms with *á-* include postpositions, adverbs, verbs, and even nouns. The following two nouns are typical: *ánašįle* 'steps; stairs'; *ápahta* 'fence'.

[20] The *a-* of the motion verb 'go' (which is not the *á* locative under discussion here) is dropped in (216) and (217).

6.7 Adjectives

All adjectives can function as verbs in Osage (or may be thought of as verbs), inasmuch as they appear as predicates in clause-final position, followed by *pe*. A clause of the form *Noun Adjective (pe)* will mean '(Noun) is (Adjective)' or 'he (she, it) is (Noun) (Adjective)' (e.g., 'he is a large man'). Some adjectives differ from verbs in that they can appear in noun phrase contexts such as *Noun Adjective Article*, whereas true nonadjectival verbs cannot. Thus, while the adjective *htą́ką* 'large' may be used as in Osage as a verb 'be large' and can appear in an Osage noun phrase *hcí htą́ką wį* [house large a] 'a large house', the Osage verb *ną́ąke* 'run' cannot appear in the adjective slot of such a noun phrase: the Osage equivalent to 'the running man' or 'the hearing mind' is ungrammatical, since 'run' and 'hear' are verbs that cannot function as adjectives. In this volume the more adjectival verbs are often identified as "adjective/verb" or "verb/adjective," but it should be remembered that any adjective in Osage, including numbers and quantifiers, can be used as an uninflected verb.

Many possible configurations which combine a noun with an adjective/verb (e.g., *hcí htą́ką* 'house large' for 'the house is large' or 'it's a large house') are attested. Unfortunately, the many examples of noun + adjective do not divide neatly into semantic categories that coincide with the syntax.[21]

Leaving aside arguments in support of or against verbal status of modifiers, what is needed is a characterization of each adjective based on its ability to carry either patient or agent inflection (that is, whether inflectional marking is obligatory, optional, or impossible, and which kind is used), noting any change in meaning encountered if it is inflected. Additionally, it is evidence of adjectival status if the form appears within a noun phrase; e.g., for 'be wonderful', 'be cold', and 'scare', can one find 'a wonderful woman', 'a cold man', 'a scary horse'? Other relevant properties of configurations in which an adjective/verb appears include whether or not its subject noun may have a subject marker or a positional article. Further, it must be ascertained whether the adjective/verb may be followed by a continuative or other ending. These properties are summarized in table 6.7.

[21] Nouns can also function as adjectives, just as they do in English. *wažáže* 'Osage, Osage tribe, Osage person' can modify a noun *íe* 'language': *wažáže íe* 'Osage language'. In fact, *wažáže* can function as a verb: *wažáže mįkše* 'I'm Osage'. Thus, clear separation of grammatical classes is not a characteristic of this language.

TABLE 6.7. PROPERTIES OF NOUN + ADJECTIVE/VERB CONFIGURATIONS

NOUN	ADJECTIVE/VERB	POST-ROOT
+/– subject marker	+/– inflection on stem	continuative *akxa* or *apa* permitted or not
+/– positional article	optional/obligatory inflection	*pe* permitted or not
		ną pe/štą pe permitted or not

Unfortunately, time constraints have not permitted such an analysis to be carried out for this volume, and in any case language disuse would probably make such study impossible. At this point, it can only be stated that most sentences found fit into multiple options in table 6.7, but do not fall into clear classes based on analysis done so far. In the subsequent sections some adjectivelike constructions are analyzed briefly with attention to whether they appear with a copular 'be' verb, whether they appear with a continuative auxiliary only, and whether they appear in a noun phrase. Also mentioned are deverbal adjectives, strings of adjectives, considerations of word order, and the use of intensifiers of adjectives. There is a good deal of overlap among the subsections that follow.

6.7.1 Copula verb *ðį* 'be'

While third person sentences of the type 'Sonny is tall' in Osage often consist of the bare noun 'Sonny' plus the bare adjective 'tall', for first and second person subject ('I'm tall, you're tall', etc.) we may find a verb *ðį* 'be; exist as'. (Most attestations to date have been in the second person form *nį*, or occasionally in 1S as *brį*. *ðį* itself has been attested only in 1P. The *ðį* forms are used both for temporary conditions and for permanent characteristics—'be Osage', 'be cold', 'be tall', 'be greasy' in (221)–(225). (See the discussion of active and stative verbs in section 3.1.1 for more.)

(221) *wažáže exci brįe*
wažáže excį Wa-ðį-ðe
Osage really A1S-be-DECL
'I'm a real Osage'

(222) *níhce brįe*
níhce Wa-ðį-ðe
cold A1S-be-DECL
'I'm cold'

In third person, a continuative marker is used instead of *ðį*, as in (223).

(223) *scéce akxa*
scéce akxa
tall 3.CONT
'he's tall'

Although a *ð*-stem verb, *ðį* has the 2S form *nį* rather than the expected ***šcį*.

(224) *ðóðo nį*
ðóðo Ya-ðį
greasy A2S-be
'you're greasy'

(225) *scéce nį*
scéce Ya-ðį
tall A2S-be
'you're tall'

The 1P inflection of *ðį* unexpectedly uses the 1P patient form *wa...api* instead of the syncopating 1P agent form *ąk*.

(226) *scéce waðįpe*
scéce wa-ðį-api-ðe
tall P1P-be-PL-DECL
'we're tall'

Example (227) can be either a question or a statement, and may refer to singular or plural 'you'.

(227) *wažáže nįe?*
wažáže nį-ðe
Osage you.are-DECL
'are you Osage?'

The second person form may pluralize as expected:

(228) *wažáže nįpe*
wažáže nį-api-ðe
Osage you.are-PL-DECL
'you [plural] are Osages'

For 1S and 2S, alternative configurations are available in which no verb is used. Instead, the aspect marker for 'moving', 'sitting', etc., is used to inflect the adjective/verb, as in (229)–(230). Example (231) shows that both the verb *nį* and the aspect marker may occur.

(229) *wažáže ðaįšé*
wažáže ðaįšé
Osage 2S.CONT
'you're Osage [walking]'

(230) *wažáže nįkšé*
wažáže nįkšé
Osage 2S.CONT
'you're Osage [sitting]'

(231) *wažáže nįe ðatxáše*
wažáže Ya-nį ðatxáše
Osage A2S-be 2S.CONT
'you're an Osage [standing]'

Likewise, although *ðį* is used in the second person singular expression for 'tall' in (225) above, a common 1S form is made up of just 'tall' plus the aspect marker, as in (232).

(232) *scéce akxą́he*
scéce atxą́he
tall 1S.CONT
'I'm standing here tall'

See section 6.7.2 for further discussion.

6.7.2 Inflection via aspect marker only

Some adjective/verbs, e.g. *tąhe* 'be well, in good shape', carry neither agent nor patient inflection, but instead use the aspect markers. In fact, almost all adjective/verbs which can be found with agent or patient inflection can also be used without such inflection and followed by the aspect markers. Adjectival *níhce* 'cold' is one of these.

(233) *níhce mįkšé*
níhce mįkšé
cold 1S.CONT
'I'm cold'

(Some examples of adjective/verbs inflected just by aspect markers were given in the preceding subsection: (229)–(230) and (232).)

The adjective *níni* 'cold' for inanimates is not the same word as the stative verbal form *níhce* 'be cold' for animates. The stative animate verb *níhce* 'be cold' cannot appear within the noun phrase, but the more adjectival *nini* 'cold [inanimate]' can, as in (234).

(234) *htóožu níni wį*
htóožu níni wį
meat.pie cold a
'a cold meat pie'

(235) *htóožu əkxa níni əkxai*
htóožu akxa níni akxa-ðe
meat.pie SUBJ cold 3.CONT-DECL
'the meat pie is cold'

táahkace 'hot' can be used within the noun phrase.

(236) *htóožu táahkace wį ąk?ú*
htóožu táahkace wį ą-k?ú-a
meat.pie hot a P1S-give-IMPER
'give me a hot meat pie'

When used as the predicate of a clause, *táahkace* cannot take inflection, but uses only aspect markers to show person and number. (When applied to people, *táahkace* refers to being hot as from weather, or as in the sweat house.)

(237) *táahkace mįkšé*
táahkace mįkšé
hot 1S.CONT
'I'm hot'

(238) *táahkace*
'it (object) is hot'

(239) *táahkace nįkšé?*
táahkace nįkšé
hot 2S.CONT
'are you hot?'

Interestingly, for the 1S negative of this stem, three different configurations are found: the negative element may be either *maži* (1S negator) or *aži* (negator without person marking), and the V1-V2 Rule may or may not apply to the final vowel of *táahkace*. (In addition, there is variation as to whether the continuative marker appears, as can be seen in the examples below.)

(240) *taahkataží mįkšé*
taahkace-aži mįkšé
hot-NEG 1S.CONT
'I'm not hot'

(241) *táahkatamąží mįkšé*
táahkace-maží mįkšé
hot-1S.NEG 1S.CONT
'I'm not hot'

(242) *táahkacemąžį*
táahkace-mąžį
hot-1S.NEG
'I'm not hot'

It is possible in a few instances to have a change of meaning when an adjective/verb form is used in the different configurations. Such is the case with the verb *tąhé* 'be healthy, well, in good health', which is in fact never (or almost never?) inflected with this meaning. The form ***ątąhe* for 'I am well' is ungrammatical or at best marginal. When *tąhé* appears with patient pronominals, it means 'wonderful' and not 'healthy'. The expression *tąhé ðaįšé* is ambiguous, meaning both 'you are a wonderful person' and 'you are well':

(243) *tąhé ðaįšé*
tąhé ðaįšé
well 2S.CONT
'you're wonderful; you're well'

Likewise for all the other persons and numbers:

(244) *tąhé ąąhé*
tąhé ąąhé
well 1S.CONT
'I'm wonderful; I'm well'

In summary, *tąhé* behaves semantically as follows:

uninflected + aspect marker:	'well'; 'wonderful'
uninflected, no aspect marker:	'well'; 'wonderful'
inflected + aspect marker:	'wonderful'
within noun phrase:	'wonderful'

To qualify for full adjectival status, a form should be capable of appearing also within a noun phrase constituent (as noted in the introduction to section 6.7). Whether or not *tąhé* does therefore qualify for adjectival status and is not merely a noninflecting verb depends on how we regard this change of meaning.

Koontz (p.c. 1995) suggests that there are two verbs *tąhé*, one being a stative verb taking patient inflection ('wonderful') and the other a noninflecting verb using the aspect markers only ('well'). The Lakota form *tąyą* is parallel in both syntax and semantics to the Osage, according to Rood (p.c. 1994).

6.7.3 Adjective within the noun phrase

As explained in section 6.7.2, when used within a noun phrase, *tą̨hé* means not 'well', but 'wonderful', as in (245). *tą̨hé* may also have this meaning as predicate of a clause, as in (246) (which would also be correct with subject marker *akxa* inserted after *níhkaši*). In 3S, inflection is zero, and thus cannot be detected.

(245) *níhkašiə tą̨hé wį achí hta akxai*
níhkašiə tą̨hé wį a-Ø-chí hta akxa-ðe
person wonderful a PREV-A3S-arrive.here FUT 3.CONT-DECL
a wonderful man is going to be here

(246) *nihkáši tą̨hápe*
nihkáši tą̨hé-api-ðe
person wonderful-PL-DECL
'he/she is wonderful; he/she is a wonderful person'

The form *ótaa* 'freeze [intransitive]; (to be) frozen' functions as an adjective within the noun phrase, as in (247), or as a verb, as in (248).

(247) *htóožu ótaa wį*
htóožu ótaa wį
meat.pie frozen a
'a frozen meat pie'

(248) *htóožu əkxa ótaa əkxai*
htóožu akxa ótaa akxa-ðe
meat.pie SUBJ frozen 3.CONT-DECL
'the meat pie is frozen'

Consider also the case of *ɣǫ́ǫce* 'sloppy-looking'. The verbal phrase 'you look sloppy; it makes you look sloppy' is *ɣǫ́ǫce tǫpewai*, and 'don't be sloppy' is *ɣǫ́ǫce ðįká*, made up of the adjectival *ɣǫ́ǫce* alone plus the negative *ðįké*. The form *ɣǫ́ǫce* can directly modify a noun:

(249) *žįkážį ɣǫ́ǫce hcí ci achipi wahkǫ́bra įké*
žįkážį ɣǫ́ǫce hci ci a-Ø-chi-api
child sloppy house to PREV-A3P-arrive.here-PL
wa-Wa-kǫ́-Wa-ða ðįké
P3P-A1S-PREV-A1S-want NEG
'I don't want sloppy children to come to my home'

Forms referring to size easily appear within the noun phrase:

(250) *táatą̨ lą́ðe wį hpáaɣe*
táatą̨ lą́ðe wį Wa-káaɣe
thing big a A1S-do
'I did a big thing'

The position of adjective/verbs and other modifiers (all of which are probably best thought of as verbs in Osage) within the noun phrase can be briefly sketched as follows.

- Adjective/verbs denoting size and color follow the noun they modify in Osage; e.g., 'thing big' in (250).
- Possessors precede the noun, but the possessive pronominal form itself follows: *Jóhna hci íhta* 'John house his'.
- Clearly deverbal adjectives (such as *taakéštą* 'quarrelsome', from *taaké* 'fight') usually follow the noun: *wakˀó taakéštą* 'a quarrelsome woman'.
- Nouns used as modifiers, such as *wažáže* 'Osage' in *wažáže íe* 'Osage language', precede the noun.
- Numbers (see section 6.8) follow the noun, as in *hkáwa ðǫǫpá* [horse two] 'two horses'.
- Quantifiers such as *záani* 'all' and *hépe* 'a little' follow the noun (251).

(251) *mąhkása hépe ąkˀú*
mąhkása hépe ą-kˀú-a
coffee little P1S-give-IMPER
'give me a little coffee!'

6.7.4 Other verbs as modifiers

Osage adjectivizes verbs by suffixation of *štą* 'repeatedly, always, incessantly'; these forms may appear within the noun phrase:

(252) *wažį́ka waaðǫ́štą wį hcí ce achípe*
wažį́ka waaðǫ́-štą wį hcí ce a-Ø-chí-api-ðe
bird sing-ITER a house to PREV-A3S-arrive.here-PL-DECL
'a singing bird came to our house'

(253) *wakˀo waðíhtąštą wį*
wakˀó waðíhtą-štą wį
woman work-ITER a
'a working woman'

As an example of a verb that takes agent inflection consider *nǫ́hpe* 'fear; be afraid'. This verb cannot be used within the noun phrase without further derivation. That is, ***šímįžį nǫ́hpe ðǫǫpá akxa ecí akxa* [girl fear two SUBJ be.here 3.CONT] 'two fearful/scared girls were here' or ***hkáwa nǫ́hpe* [horse fear] 'a scared horse' are syntactically impossible in Osage.

The verb *nǫ́hpe* can only be used within the noun phrase in the derived form *nǫhpéwai* (from *nǫhpe-wa-ðe*) 'make one fearful; be scary', as in (254).

(254) *hkáwa nǫhpéwai íiðaðe?*
hkáwa nǫhpé-wa-ðe íi-Ya-ðe
horse afraid-VAL-CAU PREV-A2S-see
'did you see a scary horse?'

The Osage counterparts of English deverbal adjectives will often retain their verbal status. As a case in point, consider 'sticky'. 'Stick to' is the simple transitive verb *ásta*. (This verb may be related to *stáðe* 'paint', which is approximately 'cause to have a smooth or an adhesive coat'.) The adjectival form 'sticky' is derived from the valence-reduced form *wástasta* 'stick to stuff', with detransitivizing prefix *wa*, plus reduplication to communicate either the plasticity or relentless nature of the event or state.

(255) *ónǫbre əkxa wástastai*
ónǫbre akxa wa-ásta-sta-ðe
food SUBJ VAL-stick-REDUP-CAU
'the food is sticky'

Although essentially a verb, *wásta* or *wástastaðe* can appear within a noun phrase, as in (256).

(256) *ónǫbre wástastai akxa ðáalį*
ónǫbre wa-ásta-sta-ðe akxa ðáalį
food VAL-stick-REDUP-CAU SUBJ good
'the sticky is food is good'

Full sentences in Osage may be made up of the bare noun plus an adjective/verb such as 'heavy' or 'large':

(257) *íį skíke*
íį skíke
rock heavy
'the rocks are heavy'

(258) *hcí wáli lą́ðee*
hcí wáli lą́ðe-ðe
house very big-DECL
'the house is [really] big'

The bare noun + adjective/verb is often is followed by *pe*, as in (259); a subject marker is optionally present (260) (cf. also (288)). In sentences (261) and (262), the verbs *wawį_kše* 'tell folks the truth' and *taaké* 'fight' are used as adjectives.

(259) *nihkaši lą́ðipe*
nihkaši lą́ðe-api-ðe
person big-PL-DECL
'he's a big man'

(260) *šímįžį apa ðáalįpe*
šímįžį apa ðáalį-api-ðe
girl SUBJ pretty-PL-DECL
'the girl is pretty' [not present]

(261) *níhkaši wawįkšape*
níhkaši wawįkše-api-ðe
person truthful-PL-DECL
'he's a truthful person'

(262) *wakˀó taakéštąpe*
wakˀó taaké-štą-api-ðe
woman fight-ITER-PL-DECL
'she's a quarrelsome woman'

Example (263) is essentially synonymous with (262) just above, but uses the more verbal form of 'fight' and contains a subject marker on *wakˀó*.

(263) *wakˀó akxa taaké štąpe*
wakˀó akxa Ø-taaké štą-api-ðe
woman SUBJ A3S-fight ITER-PL-DECL
'the woman quarrels a lot'

6.7.5 Multiple adjectives

When two adjectivelike forms occur in sequence, modifying the same noun, *ški* 'also' follows the second one optionally, as in (264). In (265), *ški* is absent. (See also the discussion of *ški* in section 7.4.1.)

(264) *hci ttąą ska ški*
hci ttąą ska ški
house big white also
'a/the big white house'

(265) *hci ska ttąą wį*
hci ska ttąą wį
house white big a
'a big white house'

6.7.6 Common adjectives and intensifiers

Standard syntactical diminutivization can be achieved by using *žį* 'small', and augmentation by using *ttąą* 'large' following the noun. The following adjectives apply to persons or to objects: *lą́ðe* 'big, large (size, not amount)'; *lą́ðe ttą ą* 'very large, chubby'; *huuscé* 'taller; too tall'; *čáahpa* 'short; short and round; rotund (person)'; *wahóšta* 'small'; *wahóšča* 'small' (diminutive of *wahóšta*); *čóopa* 'small amount; short'; *čóopa žį* 'very small amount; very short'; *huuttąą* 'large amount (of people, dishes, dollars, etc.)'; *wahókʔa* 'small; young'; *wahókʔa žį* 'very small; very young'. (Some examples of the interesting processes of affrication for diminutives can be seen in section 2.6, on sound symbolism.)

(Forms with *huu-* can be used to contrast: *šį́tožį apa záani čáahpažį apai, ąąžį wį huuscé* 'all those boys are short but one of them, he's tall', wherein *huuscé* is the semantic equivalent of 'be the tallest of all the boys'.)

6.8 Number system

The numbers from one through ten are as follows:

wį́xcį	'one'
ðǫǫpá	'two'
ðáabrį	'three'
tóopa	'four'
sáhta	'five'
šáhpe	'six'
hpéǫpa	'seven'
hkíetoopa	'eight'
lébrą hce wį́ke	'nine'
lébrą	'ten'

(*lébrą* 'ten' is most often heard with its final vowel denasalized: *lébra.*)

The numbers from eleven to nineteen have the form *lébrą* 'ten' + *álįį* 'sit on' + unit ('one', 'two', etc.); that is, 'one/two/three (etc.) sitting upon ten'. *álįį* normally appears in its shortened fast-speech form *ali* in numbers:

lébrą ali wį́xcį	'eleven'
lébrą ali ðǫ́ǫpa	'twelve'
lébrą ali ðáabrį	'thirteen'

Multiples of ten ('twenty' through 'ninety') are expressed by placing the multiplier after *lébrą* 'ten'; thus 'forty' is *lébrą tóopa*. Intermediate numbers ('twenty-one', 'thirty-four', etc.) are expressed by placing *ecí* 'be there' plus the unit expression after the decade expression; thus 'forty-three' is *lebra tóopa ecí ðáabrį* (lit., 'ten four are-there three').

'One hundred' is *lébrą huu(ttą́ą)* 'big tens; big number', or alternatively *waðáawa huu(ttą́ą)* (lit., 'number large'). Decades follow the 'hundred' expression with no special connector. Thus a three-digit whole number '143' is expressed in Osage as '100, 10, 4 + 3':

(266a) *waðáawa huuttą́ą lébra tóopa ecí ðáabrį*
waðáawa huuttą́ąka lébrą tóopa ecí ðáabrį
number many ten four be.there three
'one hundred forty-three'

(266b) *lebra huuttą́ą lébra tóopa ecí ðáabrį*
lébrą huuttą́ąka lébrą tóopa ecí ðáabrį
ten many ten four be.there three
'one hundred forty-three'

For multiples of 'hundred', the multiplier follows the 'hundred' expression, as in *lébrą huu ðǫ́ǫpa* 'two hundred'. (When there is a multiplier, abbreviated forms of 'hundred' are often used.)

'One thousand' is *žąąhkó(k)e* or *žą́ąhko(k)e* 'trunk; wooden box' (with accent on either the second syllable or the first).

6.9 Some common adverbs

Manner adverbs are formed by zero derivation from adjectives (or verb/adjectives); for example, *ðáalį* 'be good; good' also serves as the adverb 'well'.

The intensifier *wáli* (occasionally pronounced *wáhli* or even *wádli*) usually appears in the same place as 'very' in English—that is, immediately preceding the adjective it serves to intensify. However, it enjoys rather free order with respect to the items it modifies, sometimes appearing in initial position in the sentence and modifying the entire sentence, as in (267):

(267) *wáli íhaa lą́ðape*
wáli íhaa lą́ðe-api-ðe
very mouth big-PL-DECL
'she has a big mouth' (lit., 'really, [her] mouth is big')

Another form that acts as an intensifier is *excį* (~ *excí*) 'exactly, very, indeed, really', which follows the item modified.

(268) *lą́ðe excį*
lą́ðe excį
big exactly
'really big'

Expressions of quantity with initial *huu-* follow the noun they modify. Examples are *huuwáli* 'many, a lot; much' (for count and noncount nouns, though used mainly with count nouns); *huukǫ́ða* 'many' (for count nouns, often used for persons); *huuttą́ka* 'much' (for noncount nouns, used for 'money'). These expressions may also function as pronouns, as in (273). A shortened form *huu* also appears, as in (271).

(269) *huuwáli*
huu-wáli
large.amount-very
'a whole lot; many'

(270) *naniópažį huuwáli apa húheka ąkáaɣe nąpée*
naniópažį huu-wáli apa húheka
cigarette large.amount-very SUBJ ill
ą-Ø-káaɣe ną-api-ðe
P1S-A3P-make ITER-PL-DECL
'a lot of cigarettes make me sick'

(271) *naniópaži huu əkxa*
naniópaži huu akxa
cigarette large.amount 3.CONT
'there are a lot of cigarettes'

(272) *mą́ze huuwáli hpéece owále*
mą́ze huu-wáli hpéece o-Wa-le
iron/metal large.amount-very fire PREV-A1S-set.in
'I got too many irons in the fire'

(273) *ðáalį huukǫ́į ðalípe*
ðáalį huu-kǫ́ða Ya-lí-api-ðe
good large.amount-want A2S-return.here-PL-DECL
'it's good a lot of you are here'

(274) *mą́zeska huuttą́ka waðákʔupe*
mą́zeska huu-ttą́ka wa-Ya-kʔu-api-ðe
money large.amount-large P3P-A2S-give-PL-DECL
'you gave them lots of money'

The element *huu-* also appears in some other quantity expressions, such as *kaahúuža* 'long time, quite a while'.

The form *hépe* 'a bit' functions in a similar manner, appearing after the noun it modifies. It is also used pronominally, as in (275), and seems to modify or substitute for either count or noncount nouns. It also may modify verbs. The diminutive form is *hépežį*.

(275) *hépe ąkˀú*
hépe ą-kˀú-a
portion P1S-give-IMPER
'give me a piece/part'

The form *na* or *ną* 'only; just; exclusively' is quite common. It follows verbs, nouns, and pronouns; it is homophonous (or identical?) with the iterative 'repetitively', commonly found after the verb root (see section 5.3.1).

(276) *naniópaži ną kǫ́ða akxa*
naniópažį na Ø-kǫ́-Ø-ða akxa
cigarette only A3S-PREV-A3S-want 3.CONT
'he only wants a cigarette'

The form *šǫ* (also treated as 'while' in section 5.3.2) can sometimes be translated as 'still'; it comes just before the continuative marker and just after the verb.

(277) *wawépahǫ aní šǫ́ ąhé*
wawépahǫ a-Wa-ní šǫ́ ąðįhé
witness PREV-A1S-live still 1S.CONT
'I'm a witness and I'm still living' (or 'as a witness I live still')

The form *hóni* 'almost' modifies verbs in which the action almost occurred but did not take place; 'threaten to' is often a reasonable English translation for *hóni*.[22]

(278) *hǫpai hašíhta hóni ącˀé*
hǫpa-ðe hašíhta hóni Wa-cˀe
day-this previous almost A1S-die
some days back I almost died

(279) *hǫpai hašíhta hóni ącˀáapi*
hǫpa-ðe hašíhta hóni ąk-cˀe-api
day-this previous almost A1P-die-PL
'some days back we almost died'[23]

[22] Another adverb *ðǫ́ha* 'almost' is used where the action is or was expected to occur.

[23] The speaker who produced this example often uses *pi* in sentence final position instead of the *pe* which we have seen elsewhere. This represents either merely a difference in pronunciation, or the absence of the declarative *ðe*.

(280) *hóni axíbra*
hóni Wa-xí-Wa-ða
almost A1S-PREV-A1S-fall.stumbling
'I almost fell'

6.10 Pronominal system

In Osage the subject pronoun is not present except as encoded on the verb by inflection. Only for purposes of emphasis or contrast or in other marked discourse environments do independent pronouns appear. Demonstrative pronouns are discussed in section 6.2; interrogative and indefinite expressions are discussed in section 7.6.

There are a number of freestanding pronominal forms which appear in marked discourse environments; these are listed in table 6.8.

TABLE 6.8. INDEPENDENT PRONOMINAL FORMS

	EMPHASIS AND CONTRAST	EXCLUSIVITY ('only')	POSSESSION	INCLUSION ('also')
1S	*wíe*	*wína*	*wíhta*	*wiškíhta*
1P/D	*ąkóe*	*ąkóna*	*ąkóhta*	*ąkóhtaški*
2S	*ðíe*	*ðína*	*ðíhta*	*ðiškíhta*
2P	*ðíe*	*ðína*	*ðíhtapi*	*ðiškíhtapi*
3S	*ée*	*éena*	*íhta*	*eškíhta*
3P	*ée*	*éena*	*íhtapi*	*eškíhtapi*

These pronouns can represent subject, theme, receiver, object of postposition, or other grammatical functions. They are always contrastive, but the contrast may derive from either pragmatic controls or grammatical controls.

The pronouns in the first column in table 6.8 ("Emphasis and contrast") are used to emphasize subjects or objects of either active or stative verbs.

(281) *ðíe mąðį!*
ðíe mąðį-a
2.PRON go-IMPER
'*you* go [not someone else]!'

(282) *ąkóe ąhkíluwįpe*
ąkóe ąk-Ø-hkik-ðuwį-api-ðe
1P.PRON A1P-P3S-REFL-buy-PL-DECL
'we bought it for ourselves'

Likewise, the forms appearing in the second and fourth columns ("Exclusivity" and "Inclusion") can be used regardless of the function of the associated agent or patient, and with both active and stative verbs.

(283) *ðína ðikʔupe*
ði-na ði-Ø-kʔu-api-ðe
2S.PRON-only P2S-A3S-give-PL-DECL
'he gave it just to you'

(284) *hci ąkóhta ðiškíihta ðíihta nįkšé*
hci ąkóhta ði-škihta ði-hta nįkšé
house 1P.POSS 2S-also 2S-POSS 2S.CONT
'our house is yours'

(285) *wí[e], ąðą́hice*
wí[e] ąðą́hice
1S.PRON PREV-EPð-P1S-hurry
'as for me, I'm ready to go' (I hurried and am ready)

Pronouns of the third column ("Possession") function to modify nouns or pronouns, or as full pronouns, or even as verbs 'belong to X'.

(286) *wíihta*
wihta
1S.POSS
'it's mine'

(287) *táatą wíihta*
táatą wihta
thing 1S.POSS
'something of mine'

(288) *walézeáace ce žįkážį íhta apa škáci apai*
waléze-ðaacé ce žįkáži ihta apa Ø-škáce apa-ðe
book-name at child 3S.POSS SUBJ A3P-play 3.CONT-DECL
'her children are playing at the school'

(289) *ði ðíhta*
ði ðihta
2S.PRON 2S.POSS
'your own'

(290) *kšą́ka šǫ́ke íhta apa zípe*
kšą́ka šǫ́ke ihta apa zi-api-ðe
second.son dog 3S.POSS SUBJ yellow-PL-DECL
'Second Son's dog is yellow'

(291) *táatą ąkóhta wį*
táatą ąkóhta wį
thing 1P.POSS a
'something of ours'

(292) *ąkóhta akxa xǫ́pe*
ąkó.hta akxa Ø-xǫ́-api-ðe
1P.POSS SUBJ A3S-break-PL-DECL
'ours is broken'

The following examples are made up of the "emphasis and contrast" pronoun or an interrogative pronoun *pée* 'who' and the future marker *hta*, plus an aspect marker, and involve no verb as such. The pronoun itself can be thought of as functioning as a verb—'be I' (293), 'be you' (294), 'be he/she' (295)–(296), 'be who' (297).

(293) *wíe hta mįkšé*
wíe hta mįkšé
1S.PRON FUT 1S.CONT
'it's my turn'

(294) *ðíe hta nįkšé*
ðíe hta nįkšé
2S.PRON FUT 2S.CONT
'it's your turn'

(295) *ée htá įkšé*
ée hta įkšé
3.PRON FUT SIT
'it's his turn'

(296) *Maggie ée htá įkšé*
Maggie ée hta įkšé
Maggie 3.PRON FUT SIT
'it's Maggie's turn'

(297) *pée hta įkšé?*
pée hta įkšé
who FUT SIT
'whose turn is it?'

6.11 Derivation of nouns

6.11.1 Zero derivation

In this section, we look first at a few examples of cross-category derivation in which nouns derive from verbs. Usually no nominalizing morphology is involved, and the verb form is simply used as a noun, as indicated by the syntax of the sentence.

Below are examples of the considerable number of cases where a noun has the same form as a verb. In (298), the valence-reduced form (see section 4.1) 'teaches things' becomes 'teacher':

(298) *wakǫ́ze*
wa-kǫ́ze
VAL-teach
'teacher; teach'

The noun *oðówai* 'boss, foreman' is from a valence-reduced causative of *oðó* '[be] straight'.

(299) *oðówai*
oðóhta-wa-ðe
straight-VAL-CAU
'be in charge, be boss'

The noun *íe* 'one's word, language, words, prayer, speech' is zero-derived from the verb *í_e* 'speak, say'.

Another example is the noun *íhkihkawį* 'an exchange, a trade', as in (300)–(302), derived from the verb *íhkihkawį* 'trade'.

(300) *íhkihkawį ąkˀú pee*
íhkihkawį ą-Ø-kˀú-api-ðe
exchange P1S-A3P-give-PL-DECL
'they gave me back change (after a purchase)'

(301) *hkáwa íhkihkáwį ąkáaɣapee*
hkáwa íhkihkáwį ąk-káaɣe-api-ðe
horse exchange A1P-make-PL-DECL
'we traded horses'

(302) *íhkihkáwį hpáaɣe ą́ži mą́zeska brúuze*
íhkihkáwį Wa-káaɣe ą́ži mą́zeska Wa-ðuuzé
exchange A1S-make but money A1S-take
'I exchanged it but I took money' (lit., 'I made an exchange but I took money')

The verb *okˀą́* 'act; hold an act or event' is often used as a noun *ókˀą* 'a deed, an act, an event':

(303) *įįštáxį okˀą́ akxái*
įįštáxį o-Ø-kˀą́ akxa-ðe
white PREV-A3S-act 3.CONT-DECL
'he's acting like a white man; he's acting white'

The preverb *o* is quite common in Osage. Its meaning is often, but not always, 'place' or 'manifestation of' or 'concretization of' (see the discussion of locatives in section 4.5). The verb *íe* 'speak', for instance, adds *ó* to produce a verb *óie* 'argue', perhaps 'wherein there is speaking of things'; this verb is also used as a noun 'argument'.[24]

The verb *wį́kše* 'be truthful' (304) is also a noun 'truth' (305).

(304) *wį́ðakše*
wį-Ya-kše
PREV-A2S-be.truthful
'are you telling the truth?'

(305) *wį́kše owíbraake mįkšé*
wį́kše o-wí-Wa-ðáake mįkšé
truth PREV-P2S.A1S-recount 1S.CONT
'I'm telling you the truth'

And the expression *htaną́kʔa kʔǫ́* is both verbal ('play cards') (306) and nominal ('card game').

(306) *htaną́kʔa kʔǫ́ apái*
htaną́kʔa Ø-kʔǫ́ apa-ðe
paper A3P-play 3.CONT-DECL
'they're playing cards'

Other verbs identical to nouns are *waðílą* 'think; thought, mind, idea' and *waðáawa* 'count; numbers'.

6.11.2 Nouns derived by compounding

Although the distinction between nouns and verbs, and between verbs and adjectives, is not as clear in Osage as in English, nevertheless, these categories are used here, fairly loosely, to group types of derivational processes. This section illustrates several types of compound nouns: noun + noun, noun + adjective, noun object + verb, and verb + verb.

Most compounds in Osage are left-headed. As used here, "head" indicates the member of the compound that has the same syntactic category features as the compound word; the meaning of the compound is a subset of the meaning of the head.

6.11.2.1 Noun + noun

In Osage noun + noun (N + N) compounds, the rightmost member is the head, and the meaning of the compound is a subset of the meaning of the head. (These compounded words are written here with no spaces between

[24] Accented *ó* in this form is probably from *wa* 'valence reducer' + *o*, with the valence reducer interpreted as 'things, stuff'.

their members. This practice is not always followed in other parts of this book, merely for ease of visual perception.)

wažáže 'Osage(s)' + *íe* 'words, language' = *wažážeie* 'Osage language'

htaną́kʔa 'paper, document, legal paper' + *kʔó* 'game' = *htaną́kʔakʔó* 'cardgame'

htaną́kʔa 'paper, document, legal paper' + *mą́zeska* 'money' = *htaną́kʔamą́zeska* 'paper money'

hkiistó 'council' (noun) + *hci* 'house' = *hkiistohcí* 'council house'

įcé 'face' + *waléze* 'paper with writing' = *įcéwaleze* 'picture'

hpasú 'little point' + *koša* 'curves' = *hpasúkoša* 'paisley pattern cloth'[25]

6.11.2.2 Noun + adjective

In noun + adjective (N + A) compounds, the leftmost member (the N) is the head. The denotation of the compound is in a broad sense a subset of the denotation of the head. The order of elements is the same as that found in a clause, where noun subject is followed by adjective (or verb; recall that these categories overlap) as predicate.

mą́ze 'metal' + *ska* 'white' = *mą́zeska* 'money; silver'

hǫǫpé 'shoes' + *sce* 'tall, long' = *hǫǫpésce* 'boots'

hką́ącezi 'orange' + *cʔáðe* 'sour' = *hką́ącezicʔáðe* 'lemon'

hką́ące 'apple, fruit' + *zí* 'yellow' = *hką́ącezí* 'orange'

hpáata 'egg' + *žįka* 'little' = *hpáatažįka* 'baby'

níi 'water' + *skúðe* 'sweet' = *níiskuðe* 'salt'

žaaníe 'sugar' + *žį* 'small' = *žaaníežį* 'candy'

álįį 'chair' + *sce* 'long' = *álįisce* 'divan, couch'

waðílą 'mind' + *ttąą* 'big' = *waðíląttąą* 'smart person'

ną́ąɣe 'spirit, mind' + *ska* 'white,clear' = *ną́ąɣeska* 'sober person'

níi 'fluid' + *xoce* 'gray' = *niixóce* 'ash'

6.11.2.3 Noun + verb

Noun + verb (N + V) compounds are perhaps left-headed, inasmuch as the category (N) of the whole compound is the same as that of the left member; however, the meaning of the whole compound is not a subset of the meaning of the left member. These compounds are derived from verb phrases that in turn consist of a verb and its object noun.

[25] This is said to be the first cloth Osages saw.

hpéece 'fire' + *íska* 'use on oneself' = 'heatstove'

haaská 'cloth' + *mį* 'I wear' = 'shawl'[26]

súhka 'chicken' + *oðįįke* 'grab' = 'hawk'

hkiistó 'council' + *mąį* 'walk to' = 'councilmember'

hé 'lice' + *océ* 'look for' = *heóce* 'monkey'

įce 'face' + *oolą́* 'put in' = *įcólą* 'matter in eyes', colloquially 'sand/sleepy in eyes'

hci 'house' + *wažú* 'put something in' = *hcíwažu* 'headright'[27]

nąnúhu 'tobacco' + *okížu* 'put one's own in' (*kik* 'suus', *ožú* 'put in') = *naníǫkužu* '[fancy fringed beaded] tobacco bag'

htą́wą 'town' + *káaɣe* 'make' = 'townbuilder'

6.11.2.4 Verb + verb

Other nouns may derive from compounding of two verbs:

áhkihtǫpe 'watch out for each other' + *mąðí* 'walk, roam' = *áhkittǫmąi* 'armed man; police'[28]

6.11.3 Nouns derived by other means

6.11.3.1 Verb + aspect suffix

The iterative form *štą* 'incessantly' may attach to a verb to form a noun: *ohípe* 'win' + *štą* = 'a winner, a person who often wins'. Nouns thus formed may also be used as adjectives: *wakʔó taakéštąpé* 'she's a quarrelsome woman'. The iterative of less intensity, *ną*, is used in a similar fashion to *štą*. The nouns in this group are derived via zero derivation from the complex verb which is composed of the verb stem itself plus *ną/štą* 'iterative' and/or other suffixes such as *aži* 'negative'.

óhipe 'win' + *aži* 'not' + *ną* 'generally' + *ðe* 'declarative' = *óhipažinai* 'loser; [be] someone who never wins'

iitáðe 'give birth' + *ki* 'inceptive' + *etxą* 'the time comes' = *iitáekietxą* 'birthday; be the birthday of someone'

ókʔą 'act (verb)' + *štą* 'always' = *ókʔąštą* 'busybody, someone who is always into [involved in] everything; be into everything'

[26] This compound is unusual in that the verb has 1s inflection; or perhaps the *m* is epenthetic between 'cloth' and *į* 'wear'. *mį* 'robe' is found in La Flesche's data.

[27] Headrights are sums paid quarterly as royalties to tribal members holding mineral rights on land in Osage County, Oklahoma.

[28] The *pe* of *tǫ́pe* 'look' is omitted in this compound. This truncation commonly appears elsewhere as well.

6.11.3.2 Noun affix + verb

Besides the deverbal zero-affixed nouns mentioned above, there are numerous nouns derived from verbs by means of a noun affix—either the valence reducer *wa* or *o* 'culmination, place'.

wa + *íhkilai* 'put in' = *wéhkilai* 'payment'

o + *pazo* 'point at' = *ópazo* 'index finger'

o + *hiiðá* 'bathe' = *ohíiða* 'bathtub'

o + *lį̨į* 'sit; dwell' = *olį̨į* 'seat; a place to reside'

There are numerous names for tools with the meaning 'something to do something with' and the form noun affix + locative prefix + verb:

wa-i-kaaspá 'things, stuff' + 'with' + 'pound' = *wékaaspa* 'hammer'

wa-i-káapše 'things, stuff' + 'with' + 'brush, dress one's hair' = *wekáapše* 'hairbrush'

6.11.3.3 Other derivations of nouns

More than one process may be involved in the derivation of an expression, as in *owánǫbrehci* 'cafe, restaurant': *o* 'place' (noun affix) + *wanǫ́bre* 'dine' (verb) + *hci* 'house' (noun).

Some adjectival expressions are derived from nouns by a following element, and signify 'N-like': e.g., *pazó* 'pokeberry' (noun) + *ékǫ* 'like, similar to' (adverb) > *pazóekǫ* 'maroon'.

A few nouns come from compounds of adverb + verb: e.g., *wéhice* 'far away' + *anák*ˀ*ǫ* 'listen' = *wéhiceanak*ˀ*ǫ́* 'radio'; *ákaha* 'on top' + *mį* 'I wear' = 'coat'.

A few nouns are formed from related nouns by the addition of an instrumental prefix: *ðuu* 'by hand' + *hpéece* 'fire' = *ðuuhpéece* 'match; cigarette lighter'.

6.12 Word truncation

The entire final syllable *ka* is often dropped in the second or third member of compound words such as *hpáatažįka* 'baby' (*hpáata* 'egg' + *žįka* 'small'), and in other words ending in *ka*, e.g., *ttąka* ~ *ttǫ́ka* 'large'. (An example of the latter is *waðiląttą́ą* 'smart person, smart', from *waðilą* 'brain' + *ttǫ́ǫ* ~ *ttą*(*ka*) 'big'.) Retention of *ka* in *žįka* and *htąka* tends to sound archaic to at least one speaker.

waðilą 'brain' *ttǫ́ǫ* ~ *ttą*(*ka*) 'big' = 'smart person, smart'

In *sǫ́ke* 'dog', the *ke* is sometimes dropped: *šǫ́ke* 'dog' + *žįka* 'small' gives *šǫ́žį* 'puppy'.

The word *níhkašika* 'man' also means 'people' and 'person', and undergoes dropping of final *ka* plus accent shift, giving *nihkáši* or *níhkašíe* 'people'. Also found is *níhka* 'man', where the final two syllables have dropped.

(307) *níhka akxa kʔúpe*
níhka akxa Ø-Ø-kʔú-api-ðe
man SUBJ P3S-A3S-give-PL-DECL
'the man gave it to him'

(308) *nihkáši lą́ðipe*[29]
nihkáši lą́ðe-api-ðe
person big-PL-DECL
'he's a big/great man/person'

The truncated version *níhka* is most often used for 'the man', that man already mentioned in discourse, and seems to be predominately singular even though singular and plural are not directly distinguished morphologically in the language. In contexts of male-female contrast, *níhka* is the word used for 'male' as opposed to *wakʔó* 'woman'. The full form *níhkašika* may mean either 'people' or 'a person', whereas *nihkáši* (also *níhkašíe*) is often used in sentences to mean 'people' in general, or collectively: 'people don't like to spend that much money', 'a lot of people drive in from Cleveland', or more concretely, 'the people that were there'. *níhkašika* means 'the people' in a much less casual sense, 'the tribe' or 'the citizens'. *oníhkašika* means 'be/become a person; live'.[30]

(309) *níhkašíe achípe*
níhkašíe a-Ø-chí-api-ðe
person PREV-A3P-arrive.here-PL-DECL
'some people came'

(310) *níhkašíe tóe achípe*
níhkašíe tóe a-Ø-chí-api-ðe
person some PREV-A3P-arrive.here-PL-DECL
'some people came'

níhkašika would be ungrammatical in (310). But *níhka tóe* 'some people' would be identical in meaning to the original form used; therefore *níhka* is not exclusively singular. *níhkašika* would be ungrammatical in (311):

[29] The form for 'great' is usually *lą́ðe* (which also means 'large'). In this example, we see raising of *e* to *i*, giving *lą́ði*. Rankin (p.c. 1995) points out that *lą́ðe* may be derived from the Spanish word *grande*. The historical process would have been: Spanish *grande* > Southern Dhegiha *gðą́ðe* > Osage *lą́ðe*.

[30] In Kansa, *níhka* is 'man, person', *níhkašika* is 'tribe, people', *nihkaši* does not exist, and *ónihkašika* is 'clan, person, people, gens'.

(311) *níhka wį achípe*
níhka wį a-Ø-chí-api-ðe
man a PREV-A3S-arrive.here-PL-DECL
'a man came'

Note that *níhkašíe* is not always plural:

(312) *níhkašíe wį achípe*
níhkašíe wį a-Ø-chí-api-ðe
person a PREV-A3S-arrive.here-PL-DECL
'a person came'

(313) *níhka akxa k?úpe*
níhka akxa Ø-Ø-k?ú-api-ðe
man SUBJ P3S-A3S-give-PL-DECL
'that man gave it to him'

níhkašika would be ungrammatical in (314).

(314) *níhka wíhta*
níhka wihta
man 1S.POSS
'this is my man'

The final *pe* on several forms drops in compounds in a similar manner to *ka*. For example, *sápe* 'black' often becomes *sa*, as in *mąhkása* 'coffee' (*mą́hka* 'medicine'). Likewise *ce* can drop; thus *žúuce* 'red' becomes *žuu* in *hką́ące žúu* ~ *hką́ące žúe* 'tomato' (*hką́ące* 'fruit').

7 Clausal phenomena

Other than a handful of tapes made of speeches given at tribal events many years ago, long passages of Osage text are unavailable. The scarcity of text and the inability of Osage speakers from the early 1980s onward to produce any lengthy discourse diminishes the possibility of a complete analysis of phrasal and clausal phenomena. For the most part, the observations given in this chapter are based on isolated sentences. Fortunately, there are many conclusions that can be drawn from individual sentences.

7.1 Word order

7.1.1 General comments

In Osage, an SOV ("subject-object-verb") language, NPs usually precede the verb. The leftmost NP will be the subject, and will generally be followed by a subject marker (*akxa* or *apa*; these are also known as "articles" among Siouanists). Theme and recipient objects, if present, usually appear in that order but the inverse order is quite acceptable, too:

Subject Theme Recipient Verb

or

Subject Recipient Theme Verb

Time expressions as well as locative expressions such as postpositional phrases usually appear sentence-initially, and in that order if both are present. Adverbial subordinate clauses normally precede the main clause. However, the position of the adverbial subordinate clause may change if the main clause event precedes the subordinate clause event in time, in which case, the main clause often precedes.

Word order is so strongly verb-final that a sentence like the following is translated by speakers into English with 'and bread also' as an afterthought:

(1) *htáaliko che húukaaɣa wacúe škí*
htáaliko *che* *húu-káaɣe-a* *wacúe* *škí*
meat.gravy STA come.here-make-IMPER bread also
'pass that meat gravy, and bread also'

Notwithstanding the above, in a few stories collected by Dorsey (1883a), several NP subjects appear after the entire verb phrase, as in (2) (retranscribed here into modern Osage orthography):

(2) *kaðó, ilǫ́ɣe akxa ska iihkó akxa . . .*
kaðǫ́ *i-ki-ðǫ́ɣe* *akxa* *ska* *iihkó* *akxa . . .*
then PREV-her.own-ask 3.CONT suppose his.grandmother SUBJ
'right away his grandmother was asking about him . . .' (Dorsey 1883a: "How Na´q¢e-cape Was Eaten by His Grandmother," page 4, line 4)

I take this modified order to be storytelling style.

Yes-no questions exhibit identical word order to statements, with an obvious change of intonation. Wh-questions usually have the wh-word in sentence-initial position, although some variation is possible. (Interrogative sentences are discussed in section 7.6. Order of elements in the verbal complex is treated in chapters 3, 4, and 5.)

NPs involving a possessor generally have the form [possessor + possessed noun + possessive adjective], as in example (3) below. Other aspects of order within the NP, notably the fact that adjectives and numbers follow the noun they modify, are treated in section 6.7.

7.1.2 Theme and recipient

In standard word order, theme (loosely corresponding to "direct object") precedes receiver ("indirect object"). When both NPs are present, the theme usually precedes the receiver, as in (3) and (4). (None of the overt NPs in (3) is a subject, the subject being A1P *ąk*; hence no subject marker *akxa* or *apa* appears in the sentence.)

(3) *Jóhna hkáwa íhta Bill ąkʔúpe*
John-a *hkáwa* *ihta* *Bill* *ąk-Ø-kʔu-api-ðe*
John-SYL horse 3S.POSS Bill A1P-P3S-give-PL-DECL
'we gave John's horse to Bill'

(4) *Jóhn əkxa šǫ́žį Mary kʔú əkxai*
John *akxa* *šǫ́žį* *Mary* *Ø-Ø-kʔú* *akxa-ðe*
John-SYL SUBJ puppy Mary P3S-A3S-give 3.CONT-DECL
'John is giving Mary the puppy'

The order of theme and recipient can be reversed, as in (5) (same meaning as (4)), where recipient 'Mary' is followed by theme 'puppy':

(5) *John əkxa Mary šǫ́žį kʔú əkxai*
'John is giving Mary the puppy'

7.1.3 *ši* 'again' and *ški* 'also'

The form *ši* 'again' appears in immediately preverbal position. While time expressions normally appear as the first element in the sentence, this adverb immediately precedes the verb it modifies:

(6) *ókaaɣéįke akxa ší waachípe*
ókaaɣéįke akxa ši waa-Ø-chí-api-ðe
Useless SUBJ again PREV-A3S-dance-PL-DECL
'Useless danced again'

Likewise, *wáli* 'really' precedes the verb it modifies in (7). On the other hand, *ški* 'also' follows the element that it modifies, which can be as much as a clause. The entire phrase with *ški* will often, but not always, come after the entire body of the sentence, as it does in (7) (*sí ški* 'feet too').

(7) *šáake wáli ąhpíiži sí ški*
šáake wáli ą-hpíiži sí ški
hand really P1S-bad foot also
'my hands really hurt and my feet, too'

7.1.4 Embedded clauses

SOV word order holds within the embedded clause. In (8) the subject of the embedded clause is 'Mogri'. Embedded subjects do not usually carry a subject marker (*akxa, apa*).

(8) *John akxa Mogri Mary óhką kǫ́ða akxai*
John akxa Mogri Mary ó-Ø-Ø-hką
John SUBJ Mogri Mary PREV-P3S-A3S-help
Ø-kǫ-Ø-ða akxa-ðe
P3S-PREV-A3S-want 3.CONT-DECL
'John wants Mogri to help Mary'

7.1.5 Nouns as modifiers

Nouns used to modify other nouns generally precede the nouns they modify (see also section 6.7):

(9) *oðíhtą hci hcíže áðiitą*
oðíhtą hci hcíže áðiitą-a
car house door close-IMPER
'close the garage door'

7.1.6 Position of postpositional phrases

The order of postpositional phrases with respect to objects (such as themes) is somewhat free. Thus, for example, the following sentences show the postpositional phrase *hcí hta* 'into the house' both before and after the theme *ówe* 'groceries'.

(10) *ówe hcí hta aðį̨ku*

ówe	*hci*	*hta*	*aðį̨-kú-a*
foodstuff	house	into	have-return.here-IMPER

'bring the groceries in the house'

(11) *hcí hta ówe aðį̨ku*

hci	*hta*	*ówe*	*aðį̨-kú-a*
house	into	foodstuff	have-return.here-IMPER

'bring the groceries in the house'

7.2 Subordinating conjunctions

Subordinating conjunctions appear at the right end of the subordinate clause. (This will be referred to as "complementizer position.") The subordinate clause normally precedes the main clause, with some tolerance for the reverse order. All this is as expected in a postpositional (verb-final) language. Table 7.1 lists some subordinators, and indicates the section in which each is treated below.

TABLE 7.1. SUBORDINATORS

SUBORDINATOR	DESCRIPTION	APPROXIMATE GLOSS OR FUNCTION
aha (7.2.1)	indefinite sense	'whenever'
ðáha (7.2.2)	loose sequences (i.e., relative chronology of two events which are loosely related)	'when'
(pi) che (7.2.3)	evidential	backgrounding
che (7.2.4)	marking sentential complements of verbs such as 'know', 'think', 'request', 'grateful', 'wait', 'get enough'	nominalizer
piiaha (7.2.5)	tight sequences	'as soon as; whereupon; immediately'
tą̨ (7.2.6)	expected future action	'if; when'
šǫ (7.2.7)	durative	'while'

7.2.1 *aha* 'whenever'

The form *áha* marks a subordinate clause whose verb expresses continuative aspect reflecting present, past, or future actions or states. It has the meaning 'when, whenever, if'—that is, 'the indefinitely defined times that so-and-so occurred, occurs, or will occur'.

Given the ubiquitous *ð* elision occurring in Osage, one might suppose that *aha* (or *áha*) is merely a shortened form of *ðáha* 'when'. The two in fact have slightly different meanings. The indefinite sense in 'whenever' applies only to *áha* and not to *ðáha*. In contrast, *ðáha* has a more definite sense: 'when something happens', in those cases where the context includes a definite time of the event. Possibly the form *ðáha* is a combination of *ðe* 'that' + *aha* 'whenever', with the demonstrative *ðe* giving more definite sense. *aha* has no inherent accent and receives accent on the first or second syllable (or neither syllable) depending on the accent of surrounding forms: when immediately preceded by an accented syllable, it becomes *ahá*, or *aha* with equally unaccented syllables; when preceded by an unaccented syllable, it tends to be accented on its first syllable (*áha*).

Example (12) shows the more definite *ðáha*; example (13) shows the indefinite *aha*.

(12) *íiwiðe ðáha owíhkiemąží*
íi-wi-ðe *ðáha* *o-wi-hkik-íe-maží*
PREV-P2S<A1S-see when PREV-P2S<A1S-REFL-converse-1S.NEG
'when I saw you that time, I didn't talk to you'

(13) *íiwiðí aha owíhkiemąží hta mįkšé*
íi-wi-ðe *aha*
PREV-P2S<A1S-see whenever
o-wi-hkik-íe-maží *hta* *mįkšé*
PREV-P2S<A1S-REFL-converse-1S.NEG FUT 1S.CONT
'whenever I see you, I'm not going to talk to you'

Again, 'whenever' best captures the indefinite sense of *aha*, as in the following sentence:

(14) *iiðáði áha . . .*
ii-Ø-ð-Wa-ðe *áha* . . .
1PREV-P3S-EPð-A1S-see whenever
'if I see him/her . . .'

As further evidence that a definiteness distinction is at play here, although not conclusive evidence by any means, consider the English versions of prayers spoken by Osages. These contain many sentences of the type "Whenever we call on your name, Lord, you hear us"; "Whenever we need you, you will be there." The indefinite sense 'whenever' is reflected in the equally frequent occurrence of *aha* in the Osage versions of prayers, as in *owíbraacé aha* 'whenever I call your name' (lit., 'whenever I call on you').

So we see that *aha* is used in complementizer position in a clause where there is an indefinite sense, best expressed in English by 'whenever', 'whatever', or the colloquial 'any time' (as in 'any time that happened, he always . . .').

(15) *táatą škǫšta nįkší aha, oðípše hta akxái*[1]
táatą Ya-kǫ́-Ya-ða nįkšé aha,
thing A2S-PREV-A2S-want 2S.CONT whenever
o-ðí-Ø-pše hta akxa-ðe
PREV-P2S-A3S-obey FUT 3.CONT-DECL
'whatever you want will come true'

Another sentence with *aha* is (16), with subject change between the subordinate clause 'you' and the main clause 'I'. The continuative auxiliary *ðaįšé* precedes *aha* in (16), as did the auxiliary *nįkšé* in (15).

(16) *táatą ékižǫ ðaįšé aha wéeąna mįkšé*
táatą é-ki-Ya-ǫ ðaįšé aha
thing PREV-PREV-A2S-do 2S.CONT whenever
wée-Wa-na mįkšé
PREV-A1S-grateful 1S.CONT
'whatever you're doing, I'm grateful; anytime you do something, I'm grateful'

The inflected verb in the subordinate clause in (17) is *ahí* 'arrive there' in its A2S form *ši* 'you arrive there'. The verb *oðáha* 'follow', embedded under 'arrive', is uninflected, as is common for an embedded verb. The first clause of example (17) is more literally 'whenever you arrive at the place where you're following Jesus' teachings'.

(17) *wahkǫ́ta iižįke íe oðáha ší aha, ðáalį škaaɣé*
wahkǫ́ta ižį́ke íe oðáha a-Ya-hi aha,
god his.son speak follow PREV-A2S-arrive.there whenever
ðáalį Ya-káaɣe-ðe
good A2S-make-DECL
'whenever you follow Jesus' teachings, you will do good works'

[1] This sentence is also correct with *che* instead of *aha, che* being the more usual element to find preceding the expression of fulfillment. Osage speakers seem to find it difficult to formulate an exactly equivalent gloss for the main clause (that with *opšé*) of the sentence. Other glosses for this sentence are 'whatever you want will fit in there' and 'whatever you want it will be that way'.

7.2.1.1 Contrast with *tą* 'if; when'

The element *tą* 'if; when' (section 7.2.6) is more concrete in reference than *aha* 'whenever'. Sentence (19) with *tą* contrasts with the indefinite sense of *aha* 'whenever' in (18), although the English gloss is identical for the two.

(18) *íiwi[ð]e áha iiðáe hkǫ́bra*
íi-wi-ðe *áha* *ii-ð-Wa-e*
PREV-P2S<A1S-see whenever PREV-EPð-A1S-talk
Wa-kǫ́-Wa-ða
A1S-PREV-A1S-want
'when I see you I want to talk' (i.e., 'every time I see you, . . .')

(19) *íiwiðe tą iðáe hkǫ́bra*
íi-wi-ðe *tą* *i-ð-Wa-e* *Wa-kǫ́-Wa-ða*
PREV-P2S<A1S-see when PREV-EPð-A1S-speak A1S-PREV-A1S-want
'when I see you I want to talk' (i.e., 'if/when I see you, . . .')

Osage has at least two tools at its service for communicating the indefinite sense: *aha* 'whenever' as discussed in the previous section, and the indefinites beginning in *haa-* (see section 7.6; some examples of *haa-* also appear in sections 7.2.4 and 7.2.6). The burden of indefiniteness can be shifted from the subordinate conjunction onto an initial adverb. This can be seen in (20), with indefinite *haakǫ́*.

(20) *haakǫ́ škǫ́šta tą oðípše hta akxái*
haa-kǫ́ *Ya-kǫ́-Ya-ða* *tą*
INDEF-manner A2S-PREV-A2S-want if
o-ðí-Ø-pše *hta* *akxa-ðe*
PREV-P2S-A3P-obey FUT 3.CONT-DECL
'however way you want, it's going to be that way' (lit., 'if you want [it] to be some indefinite way, it will be so')

7.2.2 *ðáha* 'when' (loose sequence)

The form *ðáha* 'when' may be found in complementizer position of a clause expressing a completed past event; the following main clause also expresses completed action.

The use of *ðáha* in complementizer position signals a loose chronological relation between two events X and Y, approximately equivalent to 'at the time that X, then Y'.

(21) *hcíle wį achíe ðáha, ohkíhkiepe*
hcíle *wį* *a-Ø-hí-ðe* *ðáha,*
household a PREV-A3S-arrive.there-DECL when

o-Ø-hkik-hkik-ie-api-ðe
PREV-A3P-RECIP-RECIP-speak-PL-DECL
'a family came and they talked to one another' (lit., 'when a family arrived here, they talked')

The clause marked with *ðáha* may also follow the main clause:

(22) *záani ohkíəpe, hcíle wį hie ðáha*
záani o-Ø-hkik-ie-api-ðe, hcíle wį
all PREV-A3P-RECIP-speak-PL-DECL household a
a-Ø-hí-e ðáha
PREV-A3S-arrive.there-(?) when
'a whole bunch of them talked when the family came [went] over'

(23) *hcíle wį hie ðáha, záani ohkíhkiəpe*
hcíle wį a-Ø-hí-e ðáha,
household a PREV-A3S-arrive.there-(?) when
záani o-Ø-hkik-hkik-ie-api-ðe
all PREV-A3P-RECIP-RECIP-speak-PL-DECL
'a family came together and they talked together'

In (24), *hąkáaši* is 'late night'; the idea is: 'when it became late night, they came'.

(24) *hąkáaši ðáha achípe*
hą-káaši ðáha a-Ø-chí-api-ðe
night-late(?) when PREV-A3P-arrive.here-PL-DECL
'they came late at night'

A further illustrative example is the fragment in (25).

(25) *sitųį pšíe ðáha . . .*
sitǫį Wa-hí-e ðáha . . .
yesterday A1S-arrive.there-(?) when
'yesterday when I got there . . .'

In contrast to the sentences in this section, when describing a setting, Osage uses no complementizer; that is, *ðáha* is not used when a past continuative setting was holding as backdrop to a completed action that occurred ('they were talking when he arrived'). Example (26) is just such a case, with no adverb in the complementizer position, and no *ðáha* or other subordinator.

(26) *huuttą́ka ohkíhkie apai, hcíle apa hípe*
huu-ttą́ka o-Ø-hkik-hkik-íe-api-ðe,
amount-big PREV-A3P-RECIP-RECIP-speak-PL-DECL

hcíle *apa* *a-Ø-hí-api-ðe*
household SUBJ PREV-A3P-arrive.there-PL-DECL
'a whole bunch of them were talking when the family came over'

In (26), the subordinate clause (clause + no complementizer) is setting the stage ('a whole bunch of them were talking') for the foreground occurrence of an event ('the family came over').

7.2.3 *(pi) che* 'evidential'

The evidential *pi che* and its related form *che* appear at the end of a subordinate clause when that clause expresses an action or state that is more remote in the past than some other action or state under discussion, and, more importantly, when that clause has left sensory evidence of its truth value. The secondary distinction of plurality is drawn: singular *che* contrasts with plural *pi che*, composed of pluralizer *api* + *che*; but some special rules apply for their use in third person.

The pluralizer *api* causes the application of the V1-V2 Rule (discussed in section 2.3.3.2), affecting the final vowel of the preceding verb. Although in a sense *api* belongs with the preceding verb, in utterances *pi che* is a separate unit. The accent on *pi che* is often so weak as to be imperceptible. If an accent is discernible at all, it will be on the second syllable, and even in these cases such accent is most often much less prominent than accent in surrounding forms. Where we omit accent marking on *pi che* here, it is because of these circumstances; where accent was easily distinguishable auditorily, it is marked orthographically.

7.2.3.1 Evidential examples with *che* and *pi che*

The evidential semantics of *(pi) che* imply that the factuality of the event is deduced from some sort of sensory evidence, as opposed to the utterance being merely asserted (marked by *ðe* 'declarative'), or reported to the speaker by others (marked by *áape* 'they said' or another, similar, reportative form). *(pi) che* is glossed everywhere in this work as 'evidential' (EVID), though this term may apply only to a subset of the functional range of *(pi) che*. The parentheses around *pi* denote that both *che* and the full form *pi che* have the evidential function.

Typically, *(pi) che* appears at the end of an embedded clause. However, it can appear in sentence-final position:

(27) *hį́ce ðuléke che*
hį́ce *ðuu-léke* *che*
plate CAU-shatter EVID
'someone broke a dish, that's what they did'

The second part of the gloss of (27) 'that's what they did' is the speaker's attempt to portray the evidential nature of the sentence, although it is actually an explanatory comment for interpreting the sensory evidence shared by speaker and hearer, in this case probably auditory evidence such as a shattering noise coming from the kitchen. A typical use of *(pi) che* appears in (28); the verb is glossed as an active past perfect 'had prepared', representing the speaker's deduction based on visual evidence.

(28) *káaɣapi che bráache mįkšé*
Ø-Ø-káaɣe-api che Ø-Wa-ðaaché mįkšé
P3S-A3S-make-PL EVID P3S-A1S-eat 1S.CONT
'they had prepared it, I'm eating it'

Another fairly typical sentence with *che* is (29), where the evidence may be auditory:

(29) *oðíhtą šką́ ché?*
oðíhtą šką che-ðe
car move EVID-DECL
'is the car started?'[2]

Very frequently, the evidence is visual, as it clearly is in (30). Example (30) could also be glossed 'it appears that the children broke a dish [because I see it there]'. Contrast (30) with (31); the latter differs only in having *apa-ðe* rather than *pi che* as its final element, and the difference in translation clearly points up an evidential interpretation for *pi che*.

(30) *žįkážį ąpa hcéhežį ðuulékepi che*
žįkážį apa hcéhežį Ø-ðuu-léke-api che
child SUBJ dish A3P-CAU-shatter-PL EVID
'the children broke a dish' ("they've done it, and they've left it, and it's there")

(31) *žįkážį ąpa hcéhežį ðuuléke əpai*
žįkážį apa hcéhežį Ø-ðuu-léke apa-ðe
child SUBJ dish A3P-CAU-shatter 3.CONT-DECL
'the children broke a dish'

7.2.3.2 Glossing evidentials: English passive and perfect verbs

Although there is no grammatical passive in Osage, *pi che* has a semantic affinity with the English passive construction. Often a passive sentence emerges as the English gloss for an evidential sentence, as in 'that's what they did, the dish is broken' for (27).

pi che gives a sense of the impersonal forces at play, a shift away from identification of actors, as in (32) *ðáalį káaɣapi ché* 'it was well

[2] Stress on *ché* indicates the underlying presence of *ðe*.

prepared.' The turkey was thought to be well-prepared because it looked good or tasted good.

(32) *súhka ttą́ą oohǫ́ ðáalį káaɣapi ché*
súhka ttą́ą oohǫ́ ðáalį Ø-káaɣe-api che-ðe
chicken big cook good A3P-make-PL EVID-DECL
'the turkey was well prepared'

Another example of a passive English gloss is seen in (33), where the verb of the *pi che* clause is glossed in passive present perfect 'has been prepared'.

(33) *ónǫbre toa káaɣapi che, ðekǫǫci awánǫbre mįkšé*
ónǫbre tóe Ø-káaɣe-api che ðekǫǫci Wa-wa-nǫ́bre mįkšé
food some A3P-make-PL EVID now A1S-PREV-dine 1S.CONT
'some food has been prepared and I'm eating'

7.2.3.3 Overlap with positional article *che*

Evidential *che* is homophonous (or identical?) to the inanimate standing positional article *che*, also used for collocations of sitting items. Sentence (34) suggests an overlap of the positional article *che* with the evidential *che*, an interesting issue that is not examined in depth here.

(34) *házu čóopažį che*
házu čóopa-žį che
grape small.amount-little EVID
'there are very few grapes'

In this semantic territory we follow speakers' comments especially closely. If one omitted *che* from sentence (34), according to one speaker, "it would be a statement about the amount of grapes that exist, but with *che*, the grapes are sitting there." This *che* is used when talking about a bunch of grapes. (See the discussion of pluralization by means of positional articles in section 6.4.)

7.2.3.4 *che* vs. *pi che*

The appearance of the pluralizer *api* in *pi che* seems to diminish the importance of the actor in an evidential sentence. According to the speaker of sentence (35), it would be "even better with *pi che* [instead of *che*—that is, *okáhąpa kaalékepi ché*], meaning the window's *been broken*."

(35) *okáhąpa kaléke ché*
okáhąpa Ø-kaa-léke che-ðe
window A3P-by.striking-shatter EVID-DECL
'someone broke a window, that's the way it is'

With singular 'you' as subject, the singular version *che* is used, as in (36). Again, as in (35), the speaker employed an English past perfect to translate the example.

(36) *oðáhą che bráache mįkšé*
oo-Ø-Ya-hǫ́ *che* *Ø-Wa-ðaaché* *mįkšé*
PREV-P3S-A2S-cook EVID P3S-A1S-eat 1S.CONT
'you had cooked it and I'm eating it'

If *pi che* is used with a second person subject, that subject is considered pluralized by the *api* within *pi che*. For A1S sentences *pi che* cannot be used, but rather *che* alone, as in (37) below; first person singular cannot be pluralized with this device (nor with *api* anywhere).

(37) *owáhką bríištą che achípe*
ó-Wa-hką *Wa-ðiištą́* *che* *a-chí-api-ðe*
PREV-A1S-help A1S-finish EVID A3S-arrive.here-PL-DECL
'I had already finished helping her when they got there'

7.2.3.5 Backgrounding function of evidential *che* and *pi che*

In some examples, the role of *(pi) che* appears to be to signal that the clause it appears in is functioning as background in a rather loose sense—that is, represented as secondary, or preceding some other more important action or state which was or is the main topic of the conversation. This more important action or state may be found in the same sentence or another sentence. In (38), for example, the past perfect tense of the speaker's free translation ('he had wanted') reflects such a backgrounding of the information that someone wanted a cigarette; note, too, that the speaker's translation includes an additional clause 'she found out', representing an event later in time than the *pi che* clause.

(38) *naniópaži kǫ́ðapi che*
naniópaži *Ø-kǫ́-Ø-ða-api* *che*
cigarette A3S-PREV-A3S-want-PL EVID
'she found out that he had wanted a cigarette'

Even with nouns, this backgrounding effect of *che* can be seen: *toké* 'summer' becomes *toké che* 'last summer'.

Speakers attempt in translating sentences to portray the backgrounding effect of *pi che*. (All free translations are taken from speakers here, as elsewhere in this work.) In (39)–(41), it is interesting to compare the speaker's attempts in the English translations to express the differences between sentences with and without *pi che*. In (41), as in (38), *pi che*, although containing plural *api*, appears in a singular clause; this parallels the use of *pe* (from *api* + *ðe*) in (40).

(39) *wakʔó əkxa taakí ekxai*
wakʔó akxa Ø-taaké akxa-ðe
woman SUBJ A3S-fight 3.CONT-DECL
'that woman's fighting'

(40) *wakʔó əkxa táakape*
wakʔó akxa Ø-taaké-api-ðe
woman SUBJ A3S-fight-PL-DECL
'that woman has fought'

(41) *wakʔó əkxa táakapi che*
wakʔó akxa Ø-taaké-api che
woman SUBJ A3S-fight-PL EVID
'that woman's fought, that woman did fight'

Contrasting (42) and (43), which are identical except that one has *pe* and the other has *pi che*, it can be seen that there is more immediacy and prominence if the subordinate clause does not have *pi che*. For the clause ending in *káaɣa pe* in (42), the speaker clarified the sense, saying "they just finished preparing it"; that is, reference is made to the immediacy of food preparation in this nonbackgrounded clause. In contrast, the *pi che* clause in (43) is further in the past or more anonymous, secondary or backgrounded.

(42) *ónǫ́bre toa káaɣape, ðekǫǫci awánǫ́bre mįkšé*
ónǫbre tóe Ø-káaɣe-api-ðe, ðekǫǫci Wa-wa-Ø-nǫ́bre mįkšé
food some A3P-make-PL-DECL, now A1S-PREV-dine 1S.CONT
'they prepared some food and I'm eating it now'

(43) *ónǫbre toa káaɣapi che, ðekǫǫci awánǫbre mįkšé*
ónǫbre tóe Ø-káaɣe-api che ðekǫǫci Wa-wa-Ø-nǫ́bre mįkšé
food some A3P-make-PL EVID now A1S-PREV-dine 1S.CONT
'some food has been prepared and I'm eating it'

7.2.3.6 *pi che* vs. *iche*

A variant of *pi che* is *iche*. In sentence (44), *pi che* could be substituted for *iche* without altering the meaning.

(44) *oohǫ́ iche bráache mįkšé*
oo-Ø-Ø-hǫ́ i-che Ø-Wa-ðaaché mįkšé
PREV-P3S-A3P-cook-PL (?)-EVID P3S-A1S-eat 1S.CONT
'they've cooked it and I'm eating it (it was sitting there cooked)'

In (45), either *iche* or *pi che* would be correct, and the two are synonymous; *pi che* is slightly preferred, and certainly by far more frequent.

(45) *ónǫbre huuhtą́ka ážupi che*
ónǫbre huu-ttą́ka á-Ø-žu-api che
food amount-big LOC-A3P-put-PL EVID
'there is lots of food on the table'

Both *iche* and *pi che* can appear in clauses with either plural or singular subject. The following two examples are also equivalent. The *pi che* sentence shows the application of the V1-V2 Rule, with the final vowel of the verb becoming *a* (here long *aa*) when followed by *api*, but this does not happen in the *iche* sentence.

(46) *hkáwalį aðée iche*
hkáwa-alįi a-Ø-ðée i-che
horse-upon PREV-A3P-go-PL (?)-EVID
'they have gone on horseback'

(47) *hkáwalį aðáapi che*
hkáwa-alįi a-Ø-ðée-api che
horse-upon PREV-A3P-go-PL EVID
'they have gone on horseback'

7.2.3.7 *ðáha* and *pi che*

Often the clause occurring to the right of the *(pi) che* clause carries *ðáha* in complementizer position. Such sentences are used where two incidents occur close together in time. The clause marked with final *(pi) che* is thereby signaled as being the earlier of the two events, and is backgrounded. The English translation of a *(pi) che* clause that is followed by a *ðáha* clause is often in past perfect tense (e.g., 'I had left') and often contains 'already'. In (48), for example, the earlier of the events is the clause *aalée che* 'I went back, returned home', translated here as 'I had left'.

(48) *aalée che híe ðáha*
a-Wa-lée che a-Ø-hí-e ðáha
PREV-A1S-go.back EVID PREV-A3S-arrive.there-(?) when
'I had left when he got there'

Four other examples with *(pi) che* and *ðáha* appear in (49)–(52). (In examples (49) and (50), with second person subjects in their initial clauses, *che* marks singular subject and *pi che* marks plural subject.)

(49) *šcée che híe ðáha*
Ya-ðée che a-Ø-hí-e ðáha
PREV-A2S-go EVID PREV-A3S-arrive.there-(?) when
'you [singular] had already left when he got there'

(50) *štáapi ché híe ðáha*

Ya-ðée-api *che* *a-Ø-hí-e* *ðáha*
PREV-A2S-go-PL EVID PREV-A3S-arrive.there-(?) when
'you [plural] had already left when he got there'

(51) *aaðáapi che pšíə ðáha*

a-Ø-ðée-api *che* *Wa-hí-e* *ðáha*
PREV-A3P-go-PL EVID A3S-arrive.there-(?) when
'they had gone when I got there'

(52) *šímižį əpa óhką ðiištą́pi ché pšíe ðáha*

šímižį *apa* *wa-ó-Ø-hką* *Ø-ðiištą́-api* *che*
girl SUBJ PREV-A3P-help A3P-finish-PL EVID
Wa-hí-e *ðáha*
A1S-arrive.there when
'the girls had already helped her when I got there' (lit., 'the girls had finished helping when I arrived there')

Similarly, *(pi) che* is used in (53)–(55) to make a strong statement of chronology referring to something that was accomplished before the time of the event represented in the *ðáha* clause.

(53) *ówaðahką́ šcíištąpi che pšíe ðáha*

o-wa-Ya-hką́ *Ya-ðiištą́-api* *che* *Wa-hí-e* *ðáha*
PREV-VAL-A2S-help A2S-finish-PL EVID A1S-arrive.there-(?) when
'you all had already helped her when I got there'

(54) *ðįkápi che achíe ðáha*

ðįké-api *che* *a-Ø-chí-e* *ðáha*
be.lacking-PL EVID PREV-A3S-arrive.there-(?) when
'it was gone when he came in'[3]

(55) *Mary əpa ðįkápi che pšíe ðáha*

Mary *apa* *ðįké-api* *che* *Wa-hí-e* *ðáha*
Mary SUBJ be.lacking-PL EVID A1S-arrive.there-(?) when
'Mary was gone when I got there'

(56) *aalée che híe ðáha*

a-Wa-lée *che* *a-Ø-hí-e* *ðáha*
PREV-A1S-return.there EVID PREV-A3S-arrive.there-(?) when
'I had already left by the time he got there'

In (57), the first clause ends only in *pe*, and this event is represented as not preceding the event of the *ðáha* clause. In contrast, in (58), the first clause ends in *pi che*, and its event precedes that of the *ðáha* clause.

[3] Note that this sentence is ambiguous and can also be translated as 'they weren't there when he/I got there'.

(57) *aalápe híe ðáha*
a-Ø-lée-api-ðe *a-Ø-hí-e* *ðáha*
PREV-A3P-return.there-PL-DECL PREV-A3S-arrive.there-(?) when
'they left when he got there'

(58) *aláapi ché híe ðáha*
a-Ø-lée-api *che* *a-Ø-hí-e* *ðáha*
PREV-A3P-return.there-PL EVID PREV-A3S-arrive.there-(?) when
'they had already left when he got there'

Examples (59) and (60) are greetings offered by the host—upon arrival of one visitor for (59), of multiple visitors for (60).

(59) *ðáali ðachí che*
ðáalį *Ya-chí* *che*
good A2S-arrive.here EVID
'it is good that you [singular] came'

(60) *ðáalįę ðachípi che*
ðáalį *Ya-chí-api* *che*
good A2S-arrive-PL EVID
'it is good that you [plural] came'

Sentences (61) and (62) are often heard at Osage dances when an elder welcomes the public.

(61) *ðáalį huukǫ́į ðalípe*
ðáalį *huukǫ́ða* *Ø-ðalí-api-ðe*
good large.amount A3P-return.here-PL-DECL
'it's good a lot of you came back'

(62) *ðáalįe huukǫį ðalípi che*
ðáalį *huukǫ́ða* *Ø-ðalí-api* *che*
good large.amount A3P-return.here-PL EVID
'it's good that many of you all came back'

In the next section we contrast the evidential *che* with *che* in clauses of an irrealis or future type. In this latter type of clause, *che* is classed as a nominalizer rather than an evidential.

7.2.4 Nominalizer *che*

It must be emphasized that the nominalizer *che* treated in this subsection has a somewhat different role from that of the backgrounding or evidential *(pi) che* discussed above in section 7.2.3, although it too appears in complementizer position. The nominalizer *che* marks subordinate clauses under main verbs, somewhat parallel to *that* or *until* in English (for example, 'I will wait until he goes away').

(63) *lǫ́ aðée che iiðáahpe hta mįkšé*
lǫ a-Ø-ðée che i-ð-Wa-áahpe hta mįkšé
angry PREV-A3S-go NOM PREV-EPð-A1S-wait FUT 1S.CONT
'I will wait until he goes away mad'

(64) *íe owáhkipše che ée epše*
íe o-Wa-hkik-pše che ée é-Wa-he
word PREV-A1S-REFL-obey NOM the.foregoing PREV-A1S-say
'I said that I would keep my word'

This nominalizer *che* also can appear when the subordinate action is past, as in (65)–(66).

(65) *táatą haamáį ché lą́ði ekxai*
táatą haa-Wa-ǫ che lą́ðe akxa-ðe
thing INDEF-A1S-do NOM big 3.CONT-DECL
'what I did was important'

(66) *waaštǫ́ che íðibra?*
waa-Ya-ðǫ́ che í-ði-bra
PREV-A2S-sing NOM PREV-P2S-sate
'did you get enough [of you] singing?'

In clauses with second person subjects, the nominalizer *che* is preceded by *api* to mark plural. In (67) and (68) we see the contrast between singular *che* and plural *pi che* (from *api che*).

(67) *táatą záani škáaɣe che žáži?*
táatą záani Ya-káaɣe che aža-Ya-į
thing all A2S-make NOM PREV-A2S-believe
'do you think you can do all of it?'

(68) *táatą záani škáaɣepi che žáži?*
táatą záani Ya-káaɣe-api che aža-Ya-į
thing all A2S-make-PL NOM PREV-A2S-believe
'do you think you [plural] can do all of it?'

(69) *táatą záani škáaɣepi che žaamí*
táatą záani Ya-káaɣe-api che aža-Wa-į
thing all A2S-make-PL NOM PREV-A1S-believe
'I think you all can do it all'[4]

There is variation in the word order of *che* nominalized clauses with respect to the matrix clause. *wéena* 'be grateful' especially seems to appear rather frequently with inverted order, that is, with the *che* clause in second position, as in (70). In fact, this usage is so prevalent among the

[4] The sentence also could mean 'you all made it, I believe.' This speaker, as is not unusual, failed to apply the V1-V2 Rule before *api* in (68) and also in (69).

few Osage speakers of today that it seems unlikely that it is due to the influence of English word order. The formality involved in expressing gratitude may be a factor in this word order.

(70) *wéana mįkšé ąną́ðaahpe che*
wee-Wa-na *mįkšé* *i-ą-Ya-aahpe* *che*
PREV-A1S-grateful 1S.CONT PREV-P1S-A2S-wait NOM
'I am glad you [singular] waited for me'

The *che* clause may precede the *wéena* clause, however, as is seen in the following examples.

(71) *ąną́ðaahpe che wéeąna mįkšé*
i-ą-ð-áahpe *che* *wée-Wa-na* *mįkšé*
PREV-P1S-EPð-wait NOM PREV-A1S-grateful 1S.CONT
'I'm glad you [singular] waited for me'

(72) *ąną́ðapi che wéeąna mįkše*
íi-ą-Ø-ðe-api *che* *wée-Wa-na* *mįkše*
PREV-P1S-A3P-see-PL NOM PREV-A1S-grateful 1S.CONT
'I'm glad you all saw me'

(73) *tąąhé ąhé che wéeąna mįkšé*
tąhé *ąðįhé* *che* *wée-Wa-na* *mįkšé*
well 1S.CONT NOM PREV-A1S-grateful 1S.CONT
'I'm glad I'm well'

(74) *táatą háažǫ ðąįše che wéeąna mįkšé*
táatą *háa-Ya-ǫ* *ðaįše* *che* *wee-Wa-na* *mįkšé*
thing INDEF-A2S-do 2S.CONT NOM PREV-A1S-grateful 1S.CONT
'I like whatever you do' (lit., 'I'm grateful, I appreciate whatever you do')

Examples (75)–(78) again presumably involve the nominalizer *che*; it would be difficult to make the case for an evidential reading of *che* and *pi che* in these examples.

(75) *haxį́ háaną Jóhna wakʔú che, íhpahomąží mįkšé*
haxį́ *háa-ną* *John-a* *wa-Ø-kʔú* *che,*
blanket INDEF-only John-SYL VAL-A3S-give NOM
í-Wa-pahǫ-maží *mįkšé*
PREV-A1S-know-1S.NEG 1S.CONT
'I don't know how many blankets John gave away'

(76) *hǫ́pai táatą háamą che íhpahomąží*
hǫ́pa-ðe *táatą* *haa-Wa-ǫ́* *che* *í-Wa-pahǫ-maží*
day-this thing INDEF-A1S-do NOM PREV-A1S-know-1S.NEG
'I don't know what I did today'

(77) *táatą háažǫpi che íhpahǫmąží*[5]
táatą háa-Ya-ǫ-api che í-Wa-pahǫ-maží
thing INDEF-A2S-do-PL EVID PREV-A1S-know-1S.NEG
'I don't know what you [plural] did'

(78) *háažǫ ékišepi che íhpahǫmąží*
háa-Ya-ǫ éki-Ya-he-api che í-Wa-pahǫ-maží
INDEF-A2S-do PREV-A2S-say-PL EVID PREV-A1S-know-1S.NEG
'I don't know what you [plural] said you [plural] did'

In (77) and (78), *api* marks plurality of the second person subject. If the subject were 2S, *che* alone would appear instead of *pi che*.

7.2.5 Tight sequence: *piiaha*

piiaha is functionally equivalent to English 'as soon as', or to *apenas* in Spanish (*apenas llegó lo llamaron* 'no sooner had he arrived than they called him'); it emphasizes the tightness of the sequence of events, that is to say that one event immediately followed the other. The events may be related or not. Words explicitly meaning 'before' and 'after' are not heavily used in Osage, as the language relies more on iconic sequencing in syntax; in other words, text order and event order often match. It is possible that English sequencing patterns may be altering this iconicity in this late stage in the language.

The form *piiaha* is not a female declarative, as is its cognate in some related languages. In Osage, this form is found in both male and female speech, in Osage functioning much like 'whereupon' in English. As it turns out, in Lakota (Rood, p.c. 1995) there is an accented *í* prefix in place adverbs or thing adverbs that specifies a tight relation, as in, for example, Lakota *lazáta* 'behind' vs. *ílazata* 'right behind'. This tight relation is reminiscent of Osage *piiaha*.

I have chosen to segment *piiaha* in underlying representations as *api* 'plural' + *i* 'immediately' + *aha* 'when'. The element *api* in 3S is likely what contributes concreteness to *piiaha*, distinguishing it from *aha* 'whenever'. The prefix *i* 'with' is discussed in section 4.5.1. Alternative paraphrases for many of the sentences below are offered in parentheses.

(79) *šímižį əpa ówahką ðiištąpiiaha pšíe ðáha*
šímižį apa ó-wa-hką Ø-ðiištą-api-i-aha
girl SUBJ PREV-VAL-help A3P-finish-PL-IMM-when
Wa-hí-e ðáha
A1S-arrive.there-(?) when

[5] The first word, *táatą*, is optional in this sentence.

'the girls had just finished helping her when I got there' ('no sooner had the girls finished helping her than I arrived; the girls finished helping her whereupon I arrived')

(80) *šímižį əpa anǫ́ðapiiaha óhką apái*
šímižį apa íi-ą-ðe-api-i-aha
girl SUBJ PREV-P1S-A3P-see-PL-IMM-when
ó-Ø-Ø-hką apa-ðe
PREV-P3S-A3P-help 3.CONT-DECL
'the girls helped her when I got there' ('just as soon as the girls saw me, they helped her')

(81) *tąąké šǫǫpá, ąnǫ́ðapiiaha ðíištąpe*
Ø-taaké šǫ apa, íi-ą-Ø-ðe-api-i-aha
A3P-fight while 3.CONT PREV-P1S-A3P-see-PL-IMM-when
Ø-ðiištą́-api-ðe
A3P-finish-PL-DECL
'they were fighting but they stopped when they saw me' ('while they were fighting, they saw me and immediately they stopped')

(82) *ąnǫ́ðapiiáha taaké apai*
íi-ą-Ø-ðe-api-i-aha Ø-taaké apa-ðe
PREV-P1S-A3P-see-PL-IMM-when A3P-fight 3.CONT-DECL
'when they saw me they started fighting' ('upon seeing me, they fought')

(83) *níhka akxa hkíliisąpiiáha owíbre tą wakʔą́ hta mįkšé áape*
níhka akxa Ø-hkík-ðiisą́-api-i-aha,
man SUBJ A3S-REFL-turn(?)-PL-IMM-when
ǫ́-wi-Wa-ðe tą wakʔą́ hta mįkšé
PREV-P2S<A1S-A1S-toss if/when glad FUT 1S.CONT
é-Ø-e-api-ðe
PREV-A3S-say-PL-DECL
'the man turned around and said "I'll sure be glad when I get rid of you"'

(84) *ąnąðapiiáha awáhkie ðíląpe*
íi-ą-Ø-ðe-api-i-aha o-ą-Ø-hkík-ie
PREV-P1S-A3S-see-PL-IMM-when PREV-P1S-RECIP-A3S-speak
Ø-ðílą-api-ðe
A3S-wish-PL-DECL
'if/when he saw me he wanted to talk' (lit., 'as soon as he saw me, he wanted to talk' or 'he saw me, whereupon he wanted to talk')

In (85) *ną* 'only' precedes *piiaha*. The form *ną* here means 'just'. Its postverbal position is reminiscent of *šǫ* 'while', which is treated in section 7.2.7.

(85) *achi nąpiiáha, mą́zeohkíhkie akxa kaamą́ąpe*
a-Ø-chi ną-api-i-áha,
PREV-A3P-arrive.here only-PL-IMM-when

mą́ze-o-hkík-hkik-ie *akxa* *Ø-kaamą́-api-ðe*
metal-PREV-RECIP-RECIP-speak SUBJ A3S-ring-PL-DECL
'they were just arriving when the phone rang'

Order of the clauses may be reversed, with the *piiaha* clause appearing second:

(86) *owáhką bríišta ðachípiiáha*
ó-Ø-Wa-hką *Wa-ðiištą́* *Ya-achí-api-i-aha*
PREV-P3S-A1S-help A1S-finish A2Sarrive.here-PL-IMM-when
'I was through helping her when you all got there' ('no sooner had you arrived than I finished helping her')

Osage pragmatics allows *piiáha* to occur even without a subordinated clause, as in (87)–(88), although in the great majority of cases it is found in subordinated clauses. Both (87) and (88) are definitely felt to be complete sentences.[6]

(87) *hcéka alípiiáha*
hcéka *a-Ø-lí-api-i-áha*
newly PREV-A3P-return.here-PL-IMM-when
'they just got here'

(88) *alípiiáha*
a-Ø-lí-api-i-áha
PREV-A3P-return.here-PL-IMM-when
'they just got back'

[6] In the sentence below, a diminutive *žį* 'small' is added to *hcéka* 'new' as an intensifier; together they are the equivalent of expressing 'just' in 'just got back'.

(i) *hcékažį alípiiáha*
hcéka-žį *a-Ø-lí-api-i-áha*
newly-small PREV-A3S-return.here-PL-IMM-when
'she had just got back here'

Not all sentences which in English use 'just' will use *hcéka* in Osage. A different sentence construction entirely will also communicate the sense of 'just'. In the sentence below, the speaker used *šǫ* 'while', and the sentence was translated into English with 'just':

(ii) *mą́zeohkíhkie əkxa ðuuhkáamą šǫ́ akxa ahípe*
mą́zeohkíhkie *akxa* *Ø-ðuu-hkaamą́* *šǫ* *akxa*
telephone SUBJ A3S-CAU-ring while 3.CONT
a-Ø-hí-api-ðe
PREV-A3S-arrive.there-PL-DECL
'he was just arriving when the phone rang' (i.e., 'while the phone was ringing, he arrived')

7.2.6 *tą* 'if; when'

The word *tą*, discussed briefly in the section on *aha* (7.2.1.1), is often de-stressed to [tə̨]. Its approximate gloss is 'when, if, at the time of', typically in reference to future events. In the related Ponca language, the gloss for *tą* is 'during'. Often the semantic import in Osage is 'when' in the sense that the event or state of the clause is fully expected, as opposed to the conditional sense of 'if'.

(89) *ðalí tą hįįðá*
Ya-lí tą hiiðá-a
A2S-return.here when bathe-IMPER
'take a bath when you come back'

(90) *mį́įoðake tóopa tə̨ alée hta mįkšé*
mį́į-oðaake tóopa tą a-Wa-lée hta mįkšé
sun-tell four when PREV-A1S-return.there FUT 1S.CONT
'when it is four o'clock, I will be going home'

(91) *ókʔą hta ąkái tą háachi nužú ną apai*
ókʔą hta ąk-aðée tą háachi nížu ną apa-ðe
hold.event toward A1P-go when repeatedly rain ITER 3.CONT-DECL
'when we're going to have something it always rains'

(92) *háažǫ tą iiðáðe hkǫ́bra*
háa-Ya-ǫ tą íi-Wa-ðe Wa-kǫ́-Wa-ða
INDEF-A2S-do when PREV-A1S-see A1S-PREV-A1S-want
'I want to be seeing it as you do it' (lit., 'when you do whatever I want to see it')

One place where *tą* is commonly seen is in clauses whose verb is a numeral, representing times of the clock (93)–(94).

(93) *mį́įǫ́ke lébra tə̨ alí hta mįkšé*
mį́į-oðáake lébrą tą a-Wa-lí hta mįkšé
sun-tell ten when PREV-A1S-return.here FUT 1S.CONT
'I'll be back at ten o'clock' (lit., 'when it's ten o'clock, I will return here')

(94) *mį́įǫ́kə lébra hii tą alí hta mįkšé*
mį́į-oðáake lébrą a-hí tą
sun-tell ten arrive.there when
a-Wa-lí hta mįkšé
PREV-A1S-return.here FUT 1S.CONT
'I'll be back at ten o'clock' (lit., 'when ten o'clock arrives, I will return')

Occasionally, a *tą* clause will follow the main clause, as in (95):

(95) *ą́tǫpa iiðáe tą*
ą-tǫ́pe-a *i-Ya-e* *tą*
P1S-look-IMPER PREV-A2S-speak when
'look at me when you talk'

The form *tą* also expresses 'if', as in (96):

(96) *mą́ąɣe ðáalį tą, hóola ąkái hta ąkái*
mą́ąɣe ðáalį tą ho-oolą́ ąk-aðée hta ąkáðe
weather good if fish-put.in A1P-go FUT 1P.CONT
'if the weather is good, we are going fishing'

api may also precede *tą* as a plural marker, giving the surface form *pi tą*:

(97) *ąkóhkihkąpi tą . . .*
ąk-o-hkik-hką-api *tą*
A1P-PREV-RECIP-help-PL if
'if we help each other . . .'

Examples (98) and (99) contrast 2P and 2S.

(98) *háakǫ škǫ́štapi tą, oðípše hta akxai*
háa-kǫ *Ya-kǫ́-Ya-ða-api* *tą,*
INDEF-manner A2S-PREV-A2S-want-PL when
o-ði-Ø-pše *hta* *akxa-ðe*
PREV-P2S-A3P-obey 3.CONT-DECL
'however you all want it to be, they're going to listen to you'[7]

(99) *háakǫ škǫ́šta tą, oðípše hta akxai*
háa-kǫ *Ya-kǫ́-Ya-ða* *tą,*
INDEF-manner A2S-PREV-A2S-want when
o-ði-Ø-pše *hta* *akxa-ðe*
PREV-P2S-A3P-obey 3.CONT-DECL
'however you want it to be, they're going to listen to you'

A very relaxed version of *pi tą*, namely *pə tə*, is especially common in speeches of some Osage elders on old recordings, where it seems to function as a filler of sorts. This relaxed form is also seen in the sentence in (100):

(100) *šǫ́žį žįkážį kǫ́ða pə tə ðie ðuwį*
šǫ́ke-žįká *žįkážį* *Ø-kǫ́-Ø-ða-api* *tą*
dog-small child A3P-PREV-A3P-want-PL when
ðie *Ø-ðuwį́-a*
2S.PRON P3S-buy-IMPER
'if the children want a dog, you buy it'

[7] *pi che* would be ungrammatical here in lieu of *pi tą*.

7.2.7 *šǫ* 'while'

The durative element *šǫ* expresses the continuing aspect of some action or state, much like 'while' or 'meanwhile' in English. In contrast to the adverbial subordinators *tą*, *ðáha*, *aha*, *pi tą*, *pi che*, *piiaha*, all of which occur in clause-final position, *šǫ* is not in clause-final position, but follows the verb root and precedes the continuative auxiliaries. Thus, unlike the other expressions discussed in this section, *šǫ* is part of the verb phrase itself; it is nonetheless discussed here since it positions one clause in temporal relation to another. Surface representations are *šǫ* and *šǫwe*, often without any discernable accent. *šǫwe* is assumed here to be from *šǫ* + *ðe* 'this', with deletion of *ð* and epenthesis of *w*. Reduplication, with lengthening of the first syllable, enhances the perdurative sense in (102).

(101) *šǫwe*
šǫ-w-ðe
while-EP*w*-this
'while'

(102) *šǫǫšǫ́we*
šǫ́-šǫ́-w-ðe
REDUP-while-EP*w*-this
'always'

(103) *owíhką šǫwe achípe*
ó-wi-hką *šǫðe* *a-Ø-chí-api-ðe*
PREV-P2S<A1S-help while PREV-A3S-arrive.here-PL-DECL
'I was helping you when he came in' (lit., 'while I was helping you, he arrived here')

(104) *waatá šǫ mį̨kšé, záani ɣaaké wáhpaaɣe*
waa-Wa-tá *šǫ* *mįkšé,* *záani* *Ø-ɣaaké* *wa-Wa-káaɣe*
PREV-A1S-pray while 1S.CONT all A3P-cry P3P-A1S-make
'while I was praying, I made them all cry'

(105) *káakǫ šǫ́ ðaašé, ðálǫšči nənə*
kaa-kǫ́ *šǫ* *ðaįšé,* *Ya-lǫ-Ya-ðį* *nǫ-nǫ*
this-manner while 2S.CONT A2S-PREV-A2S-drunk ITER-ITER
'keep on until you get drunk'

Both *šǫ* and *piiaha* appear in (106).

(106) *taaké šǫǫ apaa, ąnąðapiiáha ðíištąpe*
Ø-taaké *šǫ* *apa,* *íi-ą-Ø-ðe-api-i-áha*
A3P-fight while 3.CONT PREV-P1S-A3P-see-PL-IMM-when

Ø-ðiištą́-api-ðe
A3P-finish-PL-DECL

'they were fighting but they stopped when they saw me' (lit., 'while they were fighting no sooner did they see me than they stopped')

As seen example (106), *šǫ* can be followed by a continuative auxiliary (*šǫ apa*). These continuative auxiliaries usually agree with the subject of the immediately preceding verb. They may, however, be "impersonal," as in (107), where third person *šǫ akxa* follows an A1S verb, with this mismatch of person forming a construction approximately equivalent to 'it was during that time that (I was talking to some people)'. (See section 5.4.1 for other first and second person sentences with third person continuative.)

(107) *áwahkie šǫ akxai wihtáeží ąkxa mą́zeíe híðape*
ó-Wa-hkik-ie *šǫ* *akxa-ðe* *wihtáeží* *akxa*
PREV-A1S-RECIP-speak during 3.CONT-DECL sister SUBJ
mą́zeíe *a-hí-ðe-api-ðe*
telephone.call PREV-arrive.there-CAU-PL-DECL

'I was talking to some people when my younger sister called' (lit., 'while I was having a conversation, younger sister made a phone call arrive there')

Similarly, (108) is more literally 'while he was talking to someone, his younger sister caused a phone-call to arrive there'. If the 'sitting' position of the subject in the first clause is uncommonly prominent in the speaker's mind, *įkšé* 'sitting' may be used as in (109).

(108) *óhkie šǫ akxai ihtáeží ąkxa mázeíe híðape*
wa-o-Ø-hkík-ie *šǫ* *akxa-ðe* *ihtáeží* *akxa*
VAL-PREV-A3S-RECIP-speak while 3.CONT-DECL younger.sister SUBJ
mą́zeíe *a-hí-ðe-api-ðe*
phone.call PREV-arrive-CAU-PL-DECL

'he was talking [to someone] when his younger sister called'

(109) *óhkie šǫ įkšé ihtáeží ąkxa mázeíe híðape*
wa-o-Ø-hkík-ie *šǫ* *įkšé* *ihtáeží* *akxa*
VAL-PREV-A3S-RECIP-speak while SIT younger.sister SUBJ
mą́zeíe *a-hí-ðe-api-ðe*
phone.call PREV-arrive-CAU-PL-DECL

'he was talking [to someone] when his younger sister called' (he is sitting)

The plural *api* does not appear with *šǫ*:

(110) *óhkie šǫ apa ihteží ąkxa mázeíe híðape*
wa-o-Ø-hkík-ie *šǫ* *apa* *ihtáeží* *akxa*
VAL-PREV-A3S-RECIP-speak while 3.CONT younger.sister SUBJ

mą́zeie *híðe-api-ðe*
phone.call arrive-CAU-PL-DECL
'they were talking [to someone] when younger sister called'

šǫ may appear in the only clause of a one-clause sentence, as in the next two examples, where *šǫ* has the meaning 'still':

(111) *owáhką šǫ ahé*
ó-Wa-hką *šǫ* *ąðį̨hé*
PREV-A1S-help while 1S.CONT
'I was still helping her'

(112) *wawépaho aní šǫ́ ąhé*
wawépahǫ *a-Wa-ní* *šǫ́* *ąðį̨hé*
witness PREV-A1S-live still 1S.CONT
'I'm a witness and I'm still living'

Interesting sequences can occur with *šǫ*, as in (113), where *óhką* 'help' is embedded under *ðiištą́* 'finish' in the first clause and *šǫ* follows the latter.

(113) *óhką briištą šǫ aðį̨hé ðachípe*
óhką *Wa-ðiištą́* *šǫ* *ąðį̨hé* *Ya-chí-api-ðe*
help Ø-A1S-finish while 1S.CONT A2S-arrive.here-PL-DECL
'I was through helping her when you [plural] came' (lit., 'while I was [still] finishing helping her, you [plural] arrived here')

7.3 Sentence-final elements

7.3.1 *áape* 'reportative'

Very common in Osage speech, and especially frequent in ceremonial speech, is the 'reportative' or 'they said' ending, which follows continuative auxiliaries and other post-root elements. This topic is discussed in section 5.1.5.2, and only sketched here. Based on the 3S/P form *ée* of the root *é_e* 'say, tell', the form *áape* and other forms emerge. Positing an underlying *h* in the verb root (*éhe*) serves to explain the otherwise irregular 1S and 2S forms (1S *épše*, 2S *éše*), but the *h* does not appear in the third person surface forms. The mechanics of the disappearance of *h* and the change of *e* to *a* in the reportative marker are likely the following. The verb *ée* 'say', followed by *api* 'plural', undergoes the application of the V1-V2 Rule (*ée* + *api* + *ðe* > *áapi* + *ðe*); then *áapi* + *ðe* becomes *áape*.

(114) *áape*
e-Ø-e-api-ðe
PREV-A3P-say-PL-DECL
'they said'

(115) *íe ohkípše nįkší aape*
íe o-hkik-pšé nįkšé e-Ø-e-api-ðe
word PREV-REFL-obey 2S.CONT PREV-A3P-say-PL-DECL
'they said you keep your word'

(116) *ahkóopše štą aapé*
Wa-hkóopše štą e-Ø-e-api-ðe
A1S-flee ITER PREV-A3S-say-PL-DECL
'she says I'm always sneaking off'

The reported speech *aape* is usually truncated by men in ceremonial speech, to *aap*, with a clearly long vowel. Interestingly, *aape* occurs rather frequently in translations to Osage of English sentences where the speaker imagines the information to have come from a third party, even when 'they said' is not given as part of the English gloss either by the elicitor or by the speaker in back translation.

7.3.1.1 *pi aape*

The ending *api* + *ðe* (>*pe*) commonly occurs on 3S sentences, as in (117). In this example, *pe* alerts us to the fact that the speaker was present when the council meeting was adjourned.

(117) *kiistó panáape*
kiistó Ø-paná-api-ðe
council A3S-adjourn-PL-DECL
'he adjourned the council meeting'

When *api* is not followed by the declarative *ðe*, but rather by the reported speech marker *aape* ending, the sequence *pi aape* emerges. (See section 5.1.5.2 for examples of this and similar items.)

In (118), *pi aape* tells us that the fact of the men dancing was reported to the speaker by others, that the speaker was not present when the men danced. (The men are present at a distance when the sentence is uttered; this is indicated by *akxa*.)

(118) *tówa akxa waachípi aape*
tówa akxa waa-Ø-chí-api é-Ø-e-api-ðe
those.ones SUBJ PREV-A3P-dance-PL PREV-A3P-say-PL-DECL
'they said those men danced'

7.3.2 *hce* and *htai* 'injunctive'

The impersonal injunctive *hce* is found in what can loosely be termed the "let's" or "proposal" construction; its plural counterpart is *htai*. (Both are identified as 'injunctive' [INJ] in interlinear glosses.) They follow the verb, and their meaning is approximately 'may it be that' or 'let it be that'; they function much like the exhortative *que* plus subjunctive verb in Spanish (*que hable* 'let him speak, have him speak').

It could be argued that the injunctives are really a special use of the future—that is, that in Osage, future is *hce* (with underlying form *hte* 'future'), which when followed by the continuative becomes *hta*. However, the future is *hta* everywhere in Osage no matter what follows, so we will continue to assume that the Osage injunctives (*hce* in singular and *htai* in plural) are not to be identified with the future marker *hta*.

We find *hce* often translated here as 'let' or 'have'. It appears in sentences with 1S, 1D, and 3S subjects.

(119) *brúwį hce*
Wa-ðuwį hce
A1S-buy INJ
'let me buy it'

(120) *ąkáe hce*
ąk-aðée hce
A1D-go.there INJ
'let's go, the two of us' (i.e., speaker and hearer)

(121) *waatá hce*
waa-Ø-tá hce
PREV-A3S-pray INJ
'let him pray'

The available data does not include any sentences where *hce* appears with a 2S subject, but such sentences should be possible: *?ščée hce* [you.go INJ] 'let's you go'.

The plural injunctive *htai* appears in the data in sentences with a 1P or 3P subject:

(122) *ąkáe htai*
ąk-aðée htai
A1P-go.there PL.INJ
'let's go, the three [or more] of us'

(123) *šáake lúuže htai*
šáake lúuža htai
hand wash PL.INJ
'let's have them wash their hands'

Again, *htai* is not attested with a 2P subject (*?šcée htai* [you.go PL.INJ]), and so we cannot state clearly that such sentences are possible, although they should be.

An imperative form made up of *hce* 'injunctive' and *ée* 'say' plus the imperative *a* appears commonly as *hcé ea*, as in (124). (No corresponding imperative form of plural *htai* occurs in the data.)

(124) *waatá hce éa*
waa-Ø-tá hce ée-a
PREV-A3S-pray INJ say-IMPER
'tell him to say the blessing; have him say the blessing' (lit., 'say that he pray; tell him to pray')

In (125) and (126), *hce* is followed by *ée* 'say, tell' and a continuative (*akxa*, *apa*). The form *hce aape* is also found in the configuration [noun + verb + *hce aape*] 'he/they told [noun] to [verb]', as in (127).

(125) *Jóhna akxa Mogri Mary óhką hce ée akxai*
John-a akxa Mogri Mary ó-Ø-Ø-hką hce
John-SYL SUBJ Mogri Mary PREV-P3S-A3S-help INJ
e-Ø-e akxa-ðe
PREV-A3S-say 3.CONT-DECL
'John told/was telling Mogri to help Mary'

(126) *tóowa apa Mogri isǫ́ka éðǫǫpa Mary óhką hce ée apai*
tówa apa Mogri isǫ́ka éðǫǫpa Mary ó-Ø-Ø-hką hce
those SUBJ Mogri his.brother both Mary PREV-A3P-help INJ
e-Ø-e apai
PREV-A3P-say 3.CONT-DECL
'those guys told/were telling Mogri and his brother to help Mary'

(127) *Mary ðée hce áape*
Mary a-Ø-ðée hce e-Ø-e-api-ðe
Mary PREV-A3S-go INJ PREV-A3P-say-PL-DECL
'they asked Mary to go'

In (128), *ée* 'tell; say' is replaced with *íihǫ* 'ask, request':

(128) *Mary ðée hce iiðáhǫǫ*
Mary a-Ø-ðée hce íi-ð-Wa-hǫ
Mary PREV-A3S-go INJ PREV-EPð-A1S-request
'I asked Mary to go'

'Let me' is a gloss for 1S sentences with *hce*, as in (129) and (130).

(129) *brúwį hce*
Wa-ðuwį hce
A1S-buy INJ
'let me buy it, just let me buy it'

(130) *katxá aðį́įkxa ažį́he hce*
katxą́ aðį́įkxa Wa-žį́he hce
awhile recline A1S-sleep INJ
'let me just lie down and sleep'

The injunctive *hce* cannot be preceded by a continuative, as seen in (131)–(132) (where ** indicates ungrammaticality):

(131) ***brúwį mįkšé hce*
Wa-ðuwį́ mįkšé hce
A1S-buy 1S.CONT INJ
('let me buy it')

(132) ***brúwį hta mįkšé hce*
Wa-ðuwį́ hta mįkšé hce
A1S-buy FUT 1S.CONT INJ
('just let me buy it')

The following examples show that this is true in clauses with an A1D subject; (134) (without continuative) is correct.

(133) ***ąkáðe ąðé hce?*
ąk-aðée ąðé hce
A1P-go 1D.CONT INJ
('let's go')

(134) *ąkái hce*
ąk-aðée hce
A1P-go INJ
'let's go [dual]'

Nor can *hce* be preceded by the future marker *hta*:

(135) ***ąkáðe hta hce*
ąk-aðée hta hce
A1P-go FUT INJ
('let's go')

Dual *hce*, as in (133)–(135), contrasts with plural *htai* (three or more, here labeled 'pl.INJ'), as in (136) and (137).

(136) *záani ąkái htai*
záani ąk-aðée htai
all A1P-go PL.INJ
'let's all go'

Although both *hce* and *htai* normally include the speaker, it is also possible that the speaker will not be included. In (131), for instance, the 3P subject is embedded under the plural injunctive *htai* 'let's' in the sense of 'let's have this happen'. No verb 'tell' is actually included. The sentence brings to mind a somewhat similar construction in English for some speakers: 'Let's have the children wash their hands now', a construction perhaps typical of elementary school settings. Similarly a photographer arranging people in their places for a group picture might say: 'Let's have the groom move just a bit more to the right, that's it.' The gentleness of this English injunctive seems quite parallel to the Osage sense in these *hce* /*htai* constructions.[8]

(137) *ónalį žįkážį šáake lúuža htai hpáxį ški káapše htai*
ónalį žįkážį šáake kik-ðuužá htai hpáxį ški Ø-káapše htai
hurry children hand SUU-wash PL.INJ hair also P3S-comb PL.INJ
'hurry up and tell the children to wash their hands and comb their hair'

7.3.3 Modal

The expressions treated here as modals do not inflect for person or number. They appear following the verb.

***ðąąché* 'possible'.** The first modal is *ðąąché*, translated variously as '(be) possible', 'seem like', 'may', 'might'. (See section 5.2.2.7 for more sentences with *ðąaché* and *ðáalį*.)

(138) *nižuu ðąąché etxá*
nižú ðąąché etxą́
rain possible be.the.time
'it seems like it might rain' (lit., 'it is the time that raining is possible')

(139) *nižúe ðąąchí ekxái*
nižú ðąąché akxá-ðe
rain possible 3.CONT-DECL
'it might rain'

Although *ðąąché* 'possible' is a modal, when it follows the clause it governs, it in turn may be followed (in rather typically Osage fashion) by a personal continuative auxiliary appropriate to the embedded clause. Thus in (140) the 2S continuative marker *nįkšé* appears in sentence-final position:

[8] Several alternatives (perhaps slightly more forceful) can be found among causative constructions for expressing a similar injunctive sense; for example, *kšíðe* 'have, let' (see section 4.2.3):

ée óhkąą kšíe
ée óhkąą Ø-kšíðe
3.PRON help P3S-DAT.CAU
'let her help'

(140) *ékižǫ ðąąché nįkšé?*
é-ki-Ya-ǫ ðąąché nįkšé
PREV-PREV-A2S-do possible 2S.CONT
'is it possible for you to do that?'

The form *ðąąché* undergoes the V1-V2 Rule when followed by negative *ažį*, as in (141).

(141) *brúwį ðąącháži*
Wa-ðuwį ðąąché-aži-ðe
A1S-buy possible-NEG-DECL
'I am unable to buy' (lit., 'it is impossible that I buy it')

An extension of the 'possible' sense includes the expression of obligation 'should'.

(142) *šcíihtą ðąąchážie*
Ya-ðiihtą́ ðąąché-aži-ðe
A2S-touch possible-NEG-DECL
'you shouldn't touch it' (lit., 'you mustn't touch it', 'touching it is an impossibility')

***etxą́* 'it is time'.** Another verb that functions similarly to the ones presented here is *etxą́* 'be (the) time' (see also (138) above, with both *ðąąché* and *etxą́*). In (143) and (144), *etxą́* appears in its denasalized version *etxa*.

(143) *etxá ðe*
etxą́ ðe
be.the.time-DECL
'it's the time'

(144) *ątįðe ąðįkše hta akxái mǫžǫ įké etxá*
ąk-tįðe ąðįkšé hta akxa-ðe mǫžǫ́ ðįké etxą́
A1P-gossip 1D.CONT FUT 3.CONT-DECL world NEG be.the.time
'we will still be gossiping when the world ends'

***ðáalį* 'should'.** Also appearing in final position is *ðáalį* 'good', used as a modal verb 'should':

(145) *žówaðále šcée ðáalį*
žó-wa-Ya-le Ya-ðee ðáalį
PREV-P1P-A2S-accompany A2S-go good
'you ought to go with us'

The following example shows an interesting combination of two modals with negation. Here too, 'good' has the semantics of 'should'.

(146) *ékižǫ́ ðą́ąché įke ðáalįe*
é-ki-Ya-ǫ ðą́ąché ðįké ðáalį-ðe
PREV-PREV-A2S-do possible NEG good-DECL
'you shouldn't be thinking about doing that'

***ska* 'suppose'.** This form is found with meanings such as 'I suppose', 'it must be that', or 'I guess'. It is here given the gloss 'suppositional' (SUPP). It is usually pronounced with a relaxed vowel, and is often found in storytelling style.

(147) *kʔǫ́su kʔǫ́ aðáape ska*
kʔǫ́su kʔǫ́ a-Ø-ðée-api-ðe ska
dice game PREV-A3P-go-PL-DECL SUPP
'I guess they went to play dice'

(148) *hcéka ðínie che ákǫze hta akxa ska?*
hcéka ði-nie che á-Ø-kǫze hta akxa ska
newly P2S-hurt STA PREV-A3S-examine FUT 3.CONT SUPP
'you just now going to be examined, I guess?'

This modal has the same status as *ðe* 'declarative', *áape* 'reportative', or *che* 'evidential'. These are epistemic modals communicating how the speaker came by the knowledge expressed: by supposing, by experiencing an event first hand, by having been told, or by seeing evidence.

7.4 Complex sentences

7.4.1 Connectors

In Osage, there are many connectors or fillers used in ceremonial speech. Some also appear as logical connectors in nonceremonial speech. It is difficult to determine the precise meaning of some of them. Several of these connectors or conjunctive adverbs are mentioned here. The first is *éna,* formed from *é* 'that; the aforesaid' + *na* (or *ną*) 'only', with additional meanings 'enough; that's enough; that's all'.[9]

(149) *éena*
é-na
that-only
'therefore; that's why; because'

[9] The form *éena* has varying pronunciations: *éna*, *eedna* with a very soft *d*, *eehna*, and also occasionally *éʔena*, with a very soft glottal stop. An approximate gloss is 'that only, just that', equivalent semantically to 'that is why'.

(150) *éena ǫ́skike*
é-na *ǫ-skike*
that-only P1S-tired
'that's why I'm tired'

(151) *opáwiɣe pšíe éena įįštáha ǫc?óka*
opáwiɣe *Wa-híe* *é-na* *įštáha* *ǫ-c?óka*
ride A1S-arrive.there that-only eyelids P1S-droop
'I went riding and that is why I'm sleepy'

An alternative to *éena* is *éetana* 'therefore' (also *éhtana*), used in the next example.

(152) *opáwįɣe pšíe éetana ǫ́škike*
opáwiɣe *Wa-híe* *étana* *ǫ́-škike*
ride A1S-arrive.there therefore P1S-heavy
'I went riding and that is why I'm tired'

Other connectors are *kaðó* 'and then right away; right next to; immediately following'; *kóe* 'and then'; *katxą* ~ *katxa* 'a while; after a while'.

In ceremonial style, talks given by several different orators exhibit as many individual variants of these linking expressions as there are orators. An important aspect of an individual's style or speech habits is his or her choice of connective elements inserted between clauses throughout a narrative. Seemingly little importance is placed on the logic of a connector's denotation in the specific syntactic or semantic context. Even if it is in other incarnations a logical subordinator of some kind (for example, *tą* 'if; when'), in the ceremonial speech style its main purpose appears to be to maintain the rhythmic flow of the utterance, linking clauses that are otherwise only tenuously or contextually related rather than related by the kind of logical sequencing of discourse that English speakers are accustomed to building into speech. The framework that applies for Osage public speaking is quite different from the one used for English. For Osage, the connectors join a series of clauses in a chain leading up to the place, every few phrases, where the speaker feels that a pause and a drop in intonation is called for. Then a new chain of conjoined phrases is begun.

One connector heard in speeches is *eekǫ́* 'like that, like the foregoing' (*ée* 'that' + *kǫ* 'like'). When this is used in speeches, in many instances its effect is similar to an English gerundial 'having [preceding clause situation]' or 'it being the case that [preceding clause situation]'.

The form *aha* 'whenever', treated above in section 7.2.1 as a subordinating conjunction, is also used as a connector in ceremonial speech.[10]

[10] *ché aha* is heard in speeches and prayers. One possible interpretion for this phrase is 'toward this', meaning approximately 'in this way'. This is an English expression heard often in speeches and prayers given in English by tribal members. This

Some other particles used as connectors, fillers or rhythmic elements in speech are *tą* 'if; when'; *pə tąha* (from *api* + *tą* + *ha*; historical declarative?); *pə tə* (from *api* + *tą*; see 7.2.6); *hį*, approximately equivalent to French *n'est-ce pas* 'isn't it so'; *hą́* or *há*, an exclamation also used in story-telling. Ceremonial speech style is a topic of interest to Osages and strongly suggests itself as a focus for future study, although the corpus is small.

Linkage similar to that expressed by the English conjunction 'and' is conveyed by *ški* 'also' in lists of smaller constituents such as nouns, prepositional phrases, and so forth, after the final constituent.

(153) *hpáata waší ški ąkʔú*
hpáata wašį ški ą-kʔú-a
egg bacon also P1S-give-IMPER
'give me bacon and eggs'

There is no Osage equivalent to the English use of *and* to conjoin sentences; rather, the elements are strung together with no intervening forms of any kind, as in examples (154)–(158).

(154) *mą́hkasa tóa ąwą́žu, wacúə skúe ški tóa ąkʔú*
mą́hkasa tóe o-ą-žú, wacúe skúðe ški tóe
coffee some PREV-P1S-put.inside, bread sweet also some
ą-kʔú-a
P1S-give-IMPER
'pour me some coffee and give me some cake, too'

(155) *wacúe káaɣį apai, šį́mižį ąpa óhką apái*
wacúe Ø-Ø-káaɣe apa-ðe, šį́mižį apa
bread P3S-A3S-make 3.CONT-DECL, girl SUBJ
ó-Ø-hką apa-ðe
PREV-A3P-help 3.CONT-DECL
'they're making bread and the girls are helping'

(156) *áðįįkxa ažį́he hta mįkšé*
a-Wa-ðįįkxa Wa-žį́he hta mįkšé
LOC-A1S-recline A1S-sleep FUT 1S.CONT
'I'm going to go lie down and sleep'

(157) *katxa aðįįkxa ažį́he hce*
katxa a-Wa-ðįįkxa Wa-žį́he hce
awhile LOC-A1S-recline A1S-sleep INJ
'let me just lie down and sleep'

English usage may reflect a literal interpretation 'whenever this' (*che* 'this [standing]' + *aha* 'whenever'), which is close in meaning to 'in this way'. Alternatively, this phrase may be historically *che* 'this [standing]' + *é* 'declarative-existential' + *ha* 'declarative'.

(158) *áðįįkxa žįhe mąðį*
a-ðįįkxa žįhe mąðį-a
LOC-recline sleep go-IMPER
'you better go lie down and sleep'

There is a rare form, *kaðǫ*, in expressions such as *žúuce ská kaðǫ́ htóho* 'red, white, and blue'. Perhaps *kaðǫ* differs from *ški* in that *ški* can be used to link bare verbs together, but *kaðǫ* links clauses. Also, *kaðǫ* seems to signal an abrupt or drastic change of quality or activity ('then immediately X'), either in a temporal or a spatial sense. In (159), *kaðǫ* is glossed as *ka* 'here' + *ðǫ* 'next to', reflecting its contrast with *šeðǫ́* 'there near you' (see section 6.2.1). But in (160) we return to 'immediately' as a reasonable and perhaps more conservative gloss for *kaðǫ*.

(159) *awą́hkie šǫ́ akxa kaðǫ ɣaaké ahípe*
o-ą-Ø-hkík-ie šǫ akxa ka-ðǫ Ø-ɣaaké
PREV-P1S-A3S-RECIP-speak while 3.CONT here-next.to A3S-cry
a-Ø-hí-api-ðe
PREV-A3S-arrive.there-PL-DECL
'he was talking to me, then suddenly he started to cry'

(160) * oą́hkie šǫ́ akxa kaðǫ waðíla ðúeži hįį nąąžíipe*
o-ą-Ø-hkí-ie šǫ́ akxa kaðǫ waðilá
PREV-P1S-A3S-RECIP-speak while 3.CONT immediately mind
ðuu-ée-aži a-Ø-hįį Ø-nąąží-api-ðe
CAU-that-NEG PREV-A3S-arrive.there A3S-stand-PL-DECL
'he was talking to me, then all of a sudden he changed his mind'

The form *ąži* is used for 'or' in (161), although usually it is glossed as 'but', as in (162). (The related form *éeži* means 'otherwise; other kind'). An unrelated form *ímą* is also used as 'or' (perhaps applicable to discussions of inanimate entities only), and equivalent to 'which'.

(161) *wáaspe hta nįkšé ąži ščée hta nįkšé?*
wáaspe hta nįkšé ąži Ya-ðée hta nįkšé
stay FUT 2S.CONT but A2S-go FUT 2S.CONT
'are you going to stay or are you going to go?'

(162) *iiðánahįmąži mįkšé ąži ą́ðanakˀǫžíe*
ii-ð-Wa-náhį-maži mįkšé ąži
PREV-EPð-A1S-agree-1S.NEG 1S.CONT but
a-ą-Ya-nakˀǫ́-aži-ðe
PREV-P1S-A2S-listen-NEG-DECL
'I objected to it but you didn't listen to me'

The form *ški* 'also' is used for 'even though':

(163) *íe ðíhta ąkóðaha ąkǫ́ða ąkái ški ąkǫ́laaži*

í-e	*ðihta*	*ąk-oðáha*	*ąk-kǫ́-ða*	*ąkáðe*	*ški*
PREV-speak	2S.POSS	A1P-follow	A1P-PREV-want	1P.CONT	also

ąk-ǫ́-la-aži
A1P-PREV-be.adequate-NEG

'even though we want to follow your word we fall short'

7.4.2 Inflection in subordinate clauses

In a complete treatment of the different types of embedded clauses in Osage, several variables should be considered, including (a) whether or not the subordinated verb has subject inflection or object inflection; (b) whether there is a subordinator/complementizer; (c) whether noncoreference of main and subordinate clause subjects is possible; (d) whether there is actual noncoreference of main and subordinate clause subjects.

Objects can occur on embedded verbs while not occurring simultaneously on the main verb, whether the subordinate inflects for subject or not. The subject of the lower verb can be raised to become the object of the matrix verb if the matrix verb is *kǫ́ða* 'want'.

Semantics of the verb will be of primary importance in categorizing the patterns. This section presents illustrative examples; a complete treatment of this topic has not been undertaken here, due to the limited scope of this volume. (Relative clauses are treated briefly in section 7.4.4.)

7.4.2.1 Coreferent subject: uninflected subordinate clause

When the subject of the embedded verb is coreferent with the matrix subject, the expected pattern would have the lower verb uninflected for subject, but more often than not, we find such inflection, as in section 7.4.2.2. First, some examples of uninflected lower verbs are presented in this section.

'Unable'. Verbs embedded under *ðuuc*ˀ*áke* 'be unable' can appear without inflection when subjects are coreferent, as in (164).

(164) *óohǫ brúuc*ˀ*ake*

óohǫ	*Wa-ðuuc*ˀ*áke*
cook	A1S-be.unable

'I cannot cook'

Verbs of motion: 'go/come in order to, for'. Uninflected subordinate verbs appear in the following three examples. When a motion verb, such as *achí* 'arrive here' or *ahí* 'arrive there' is the apparent matrix verb, as in (165)–(167), the most accurate analysis may in fact be that the preceding verb is compounded with the motion verb.

(165) *kasį̨xci htáabre pšíe*
kasį̨xci htáabre a-Wa-hí-ðe
morning hunting PREV-A1S-arrive.there-DECL
'this morning I went hunting'

(166) *žóhpazi mǫnóį océ pšíe*
žóhpazi mǫnóį océ a-Wa-hí-ðe
quail prairie.chicken look.for PREV-A1S-arrive.there-DECL
'I went to look for quail and prairie chicken'

(167) *Bob akxa ą́tǫį achípe*
Bob akxa ą-tǫ́pe a-Ø-chí-api-ðe
Bob SUBJ P1S-see PREV-A3S-arrive.here-PL-DECL
'Bob came to see me'

In the following two sentences, there is close cohesion between the lower verb and its object. That is, the lower verbs 'see' and 'speak' seem to compound with their objects in other contexts: *waachí-watǫ́e* 'dance spectator' and *wažáže-íe* 'Osage language'. Such cohesion between noun and verb intuitively feels tighter than the cohesion of 'see' and 'speak' with their matrix verbs 'arrive there' and 'arrive here'. An argument could be made for several different levels or degrees of cohesion between elements in Osage.

(168) *waachí watǫ́e ąkáhipe*
waachí wa-tǫpe ąk-a-hí-api-ðe
dance VAL-see A1P-PREV-arrive.there-PL-DECL
'we went to see the dance'

(169) *wažáže íe ąkáchipe*
wažáže í-e ąk-a-chí-api-ðe
Osage PREV-speak A1P-PREV-arrive.here-PL-DECL
'we came to speak Osage'

Sentence (166) above shows no subject inflection on the embedded verb *océ* 'look for'. Example (167) has P1S object inflection *ą* on *tǫ[p]e* 'see' and has phonologically null subject inflection, or no subject inflection.

With motion verbs in sentences like (166) and (167), noncoreference of subjects is theoretically possible—e.g., 'we went for Johnny to see the dance'; 'we came for Marsha to speak Osage'. Therefore, we might expect that both verbs in each sentence would carry subject inflection, but the embedded verbs in (168)–(169) do not.

Verb of motion: 'go doing'. In the 'in order to' sentences with 'come' and 'go' above, the apparently subordinate verb (uninflected for subject) may in fact be compounded with the motion verb. However, in another sort of combination of verb with motion verb, the lower verb is fully inflected (170). Perhaps the key to the contrast is the sense of 'go in order to V' earlier in (168)–(169) versus 'go while V-ing' in (170) below. That is, perhaps subject inflection is permitted in the lower clause when it expresses an action that is parallel and simultaneous with the main clause.

(170) *oáce brée ðe*
o-Ø-Wa-cé *Wa-ðée ðe*
PREV-P3S-A1S-look.for A1S-go DECL
'I went looking for it'

'Be finished' and 'not know how'. The two verbs 'finish; be finished doing' (*ðiištą́* and *ðaaštą́*, the latter applying to eating), are used with an uninflected lower verb in (171) and (172). The same is true of (173) and (174) with *kǫ́žįka* 'not know how'.

(171) *wanǫ́bre bráaštą*
wanǫ́bre Wa-ðaaštą́
dine A1S-finish
'I'm finished eating'

(172) *óohǫ bríištą*
óohǫ Wa-ðiištą́
cook A1S-finish
'I'm finished cooking'

(173) *óohǫ škǫ́žįka*
óohǫ Ya-kǫ́žįka
cook A2S-not.know
'you don't know how to cook'

(174) *waahǫ́ ppážįka*
wahǫ́ *Wa-kǫ́žįka*
address.folks A1S-not.know.how
'I don't know how to address folks'

7.4.2.2 Coreferent subject: inflected subordinate clause

The lower verb is often inflected for subject in clauses embedded under the matrix verbs *káaɣe* 'make', *kǫ́ða* 'want', *ík*ˀ*uce* 'try', and *ðuuc*ˀ*áke* 'be unable', even where the semantic subject of the matrix verb is coreferent with the subject of the embedded verb. Double marking like this might be expected where potential for noncoreferential subjects exists (such as with matrix verb 'make' or 'want'). It would not be expected where no potential seems to exist for different subjects in the matrix and lower clauses (for example, with matrix verb 'be unable' or 'try'). In Osage there are several counterexamples to these expectations, as we will see below in an example with 'try' with an inflected coreferent subordinate subject (183).

'Want'. The matrix verb in most desiderative constructions is *kǫ́ða* 'want'. Another desiderative verb is *íðilą* 'think of/about [doing]; contemplate [doing]; wish, want [to do]', as in (177a)–(177b). Noncoreference of main and lower clause subjects is possible with both *kǫ́ða* and *íðilą*. However, examples (175) and (176) have coreferent subjects in the two clauses, and both upper and lower verbs inflect for subject.

(175) *mą́zeska oowáta hkǫbrái*
mą́zeska oo-Wa-tá Wa-kǫ́-Wa-ða-ðe
money PREV-A1S-borrow A1S-PREV-A1S-want-DECL
'I want to borrow money'

(176) *ówena iðáe hkǫ́bra*
ówena í-ð-Wa-e Wa-kǫ́-Wa-ða
grateful PREV-EPð-speak A1S-PREV-A1S-want
'I want to say something in appreciation'

The pair of sentences in (177a)–(177b) again have coreferent subjects in upper and lower clauses. Both matrix and embedded verbs are inflected for subject, and object inflection appears on the embedded verb.

(177a) *ąwą́ðahkie íšciląi*
o-ą-Ya-hkík-ie i-Ya-ðílą-ðe
PREV-P1S-A2S-RECIP-speak PREV-A2S-wish-DECL
'you wanted to talk to me'

(177b) *owíhkie íbriląi*
o-wí-hkík-ie i-Wa-ðilą-ðe
PREV-P2S<A1S-RECIP-speak PREV-A1S-wish-DECL
'I wanted to talk to you'

Again, (178) and (179) show an inflected subordinate verb. In both sentences, the subordinate is inflected for subject and object; however, the object 'it' is zero in (179).[11]

(178) *owíhkie hkǫ́bra ąąhé*
ó-wi-hkik-ie Wa-kǫ́-Wa-ða ąðįhé
PREV-P2S<A1S-RECIP-speak A1S-PREV-A1S-want 1S.CONT
'I wanted to talk to you'

[11] Aspect in these constructions is fairly straightforward. It is tempting to try to insert a continuative auxiliary in the embedded sentences to force a continuative reading: ***iiðáðe mįkšé hkǫ́bra* 'I want to be seeing it [as it happens]'. Speakers consistently reject this sort of construction. For such a continuative, the speaker offered example (182), which incorporates the indefinite *háa-* prefix on the embedded verb 'do'.

(179) *iiðáðe hkǫ́bra*
ii-ð-Wa-ðe *Wa-kǫ́-Wa-ða*
PREV-EPð-A1S-see A1S-PREV-A1S-want
'I want to see it'

In (180), the embedded verb is inflected for subject and also for object:

(180) *žówaðalapi škǫ́ǫšta?*
žó-wa-Ya-le-api *Ya-kǫ́-Ya-ða*
PREV-P1P-A2S-accompany-PL A2S-PREV-A2S-want
'do you want to go with us?'

Examples of coreferent inflected subordinate verbs abound; more are seen in (181) and (182). The latter has two inflected subordinate verbs, the first under *tą* 'when'.

(181) *ðíe, haakǫ́ éše škǫ́šta tą ékiə*
ðíe, *haa-kǫ́* *é-Ya-e* *Ya-kǫ́-Ya-ða* *tą*
2S.PRON INDEF-manner PREV-A2S-say A2S-PREV-A2S-want if/when
é-ki-e-a
PREV-DAT-say-IMPER
'just say whatever you think!' (more literally, 'say whatever you want to say'; still more literally, 'if/when you want to say anything, say it')

(182) *háažǫ tą iiðáðe hkǫ́bra*
háa-Ya-ǫ *tą* *ii-Wa-ðe* *Wa-kǫ́-Wa-ða*
INDEF-A2S-do when PREV-A1S-see A1S-PREV-A1S-want
'I want to be seeing it as you do it'

'Try'. The subjects of all three clauses in example (183) are coreferent. (The verb *xíða* is 'fall stumbling', but is used euphemistically here for 'die'.)

(183) *mašcį íðakˀuce ąžį ðaxíða*
ma-Ya-ðį *í-Ya-kˀuce* *ąži* *Ya-xíða*
PREV-A2S-walk PREV-A2S-try but A2S-fall
'you tried to walk but you fell down'

7.4.2.3 Lower clause with object inflection only

'Try'. Only object inflection appears on the embedded verb, in both the plural command in (184) with intransitive 'you try', and the singular command in (185). There is no subject inflection on the embedded *ąkˀú* 'give me'.

(184) *ðe htóožu che ąkˀú íkˀucapi*
ðe *htóožu* *che* *ą-kˀu* *íkˀuce-a-api*
this/that meat.pie STA P1S-give try-IMPER-PL
'try, you all, to give those meat pies to me'

(185) *ðe htóožu che ąkˀú íkˀuca*
ðe *htóožu* *che* *ą-kˀu* *íkˀuce-a*
this/that meat.pie STA P1S-give try-IMPER
'try to give those meat pies to me'

7.4.2.4 Noncoreferent subject: inflection optional

'Want'. In both the next two examples, overt object inflection for 'us' appears in the lower clause, but the embedded verb can be either inflected or uninflected for subject. In the second example below, subject inflection *ða* 'you' does not occur in the embedded clause; noncoreference is possible, and yet the lower clause carries no subject inflection (while still carrying object inflection *wa* 'us'). Embedded verbs often lack subject inflection.

(186) *žówaðale škǫ́ǫšta?*
žó-wa-Ya-le *Ya-kǫ́-Ya-ða*
PREV-P1P-A2S-accompany A2S-PREV-A2S-want
'do you want to go with us?'

(187) *žówale škǫ́ǫšta?*
žó-wa-le *Ya-kǫ́-Ya-ða*
PREV-P1P-accompany A2S-PREV-A2S-want
'do you want to go with us?'

In the following two examples, the subject of the lower clause appears independently as object of the main clause: *ði* 'you' in (188) and *ą* 'me' in (189).

(188) *háakǫta wacúe skúe špáase ðikǫ́ða apai?*
háakǫta *wacúe* *skúe* *Ya-páa-se*
why bread sweet A2S-by.pushing-cut
ði-Ø-kǫ́-Ø-ða *apa-ðe*
P2S-A3P-PREV-A3P-want 3.CONT-DECL
'why did they want you to cut the cake?'

(189) *háakǫta wacúe skúe ppáase ąkǫ́ða apai?*
háakǫta *wacúe* *skúe* *Wa-páa-se*
why bread sweet A1S-by.pushing-cut
ą-Ø-kǫ́-Ø-ða *apa-ðe*
P1S-A3P-PREV-A3P-want 3.CONT-DECL
'why did they want me to cut the cake?'

'Unable'. In complex sentences with *ðuuc*ˀ*áke* 'be unable' as the matrix verb, it is common to find inflected lower verbs. Example (190) shows an inflected matrix verb 'you are unable', an inflected embedded 'you make me', and an uninflected secondarily embedded 'behave, go straight'. (For a fuller treatment of causatives, see section 4.2.)

(190) *óðohta ąškáaɣe ščúuc*ˀ*ake*
*óðohta ą-Ya-káaɣe Ya-ðuuc*ˀ*áke*
straight P1S-A2S-make A2S-be.unable
'you can't make me behave'

Example (191) below, from the same speaker on the same occasion, shows both the verbs 'make' and 'straight, behave' inflected under 'try' in imperative form. Additionally a fourth verb, *amąbrį* 'I go around; I walk among' (with A1S subject) appears in this example. Example (191) may be contrasted with example (185) 'try to give me', in which there is no subject inflection in the complement of 'try'.

(191) *oáðohta ąmąbrį ąškáaɣe ík*ˀ*uca*
*o-Wa-ðohta Wa-mą-Wa-ðį ą-Ya-káaɣe ík*ˀ*uce-a*
PREV-A1S-straight A1S-PREV-A1S-walk P1S-A2S-make try-IMPER
'try to make me behave'

7.4.2.5 Lower-clause object inflection not expressible on the matrix verb

It is not possible for the lower-clause object to appear on the matrix verb in desiderative constructions. This is seen in the ungrammaticality of (192). The prefix *wi* 'P2S<A1S' (informally 'I-to-you') must appear on the embedded verb only (*owíhkie* 'I talk to you'). Contrast with *owíhkie íbrilą* in (177b) above.

(192) ***ohkíe wibrílą*
o-hkík-ie wi-Wa-ðílą
PREV-RECIP-speak P2S<A1S-A1S-wish
('I wanted to talk to you')

7.4.3 Sentential subjects and objects

Verbs taking a sentential subject or object can be divided into those for which the subject or object is marked by an element in complementizer position such as *che* (see section 7.2.4) and those which do not have such an element. In the former, *che* typically appears at the end of the embedded clause, just before the main clause begins. Schematic examples are:

[sentence] *che ažamį* 'I think that [sentence]'

[sentence] *che wéeana* ‘I am grateful that [sentence]’

Sentential subjects or objects with no nominalizer (or other element in complementizer position) occur with other verbs, for example, with the *ki-* dative ‘enjoy’-type verbs. These matrix verbs take patient inflection *ą* and *ðį* (and surface *ki* in third person). (See section 4.6.5.1 for ‘enjoy’-type verbs, with syntactic examples: *kizo* ‘enjoy’; *kíhǫǫ* ‘like’, *kiðalį* ‘like; enjoy’, and so forth.)

In (193), both the main verb and the lower verb are inflected for subject and object, and the two verbs have different subjects.

(193) *į́į íiðachį íiwie ðe*
į́į ii-Ya-chį íi-wi-ðe ðe
rock PREV-A2S-hit.with PREV-P2S<A1S-see DECL
‘I saw you hit him with a rock’

(This sentence can alternatively be translated ‘I saw you hitting him with a rock’.) Sentence (194) contains the nominalizer *che*, contrasting nicely with (193). In (194), the main verb *iiðáðe* ‘I saw’ does not carry the portmanteau inflection *wi* ‘I-you’ seen in (193).

(194) *į́į wį íiðachį che iiðáðe*
į́į wį ii-Ya-chį che ii-ð-Wa-ðe
rock a PREV-A2S-hit.with STA PREV-EPð-A1S-see
‘I saw the rock that you hit him with’ (or ‘I saw [that] you hit him with a rock’)

In the following sentence too, the higher verb takes a sentential object, and the subjects of the upper and lower clauses are coreferent. Even so, both the upper and the lower clause verbs carry subject inflection.

(195) *táatą záani škáaɣe che [a]žážį?*
táatą záani Ya-káaɣe che aža-Ya-į
thing all A2S-make NOM PREV-A2S-believe
‘do you think you can do all of it?’ (lit., ‘do you think that you’ll do everything?’)

7.4.4 Relative clauses

Relative clauses in Osage are internally headed: that is, the noun referred to in the matrix clause and in the subordinate clause is actually contained within the subordinate and not in the matrix clause. Crosslinguistically, it is most common for the head noun to appear in modified or reduced form or to be omitted in either the matrix or the embedded clause. In an SOV language like Osage, relative clauses would be expected to be right-headed, that is, have the head noun (bolded) in the main clause and to the right of the subordinate clause:

[[__ blankets gave away] **man** I saw]
'I saw the man who gave the blankets away'

But in fact the head occurs within the subordinate clause in Osage. That is to say, whether the main clause grammatical function of the head is subject or object, the head is retained in situ in the subordinate clause, and is not reduced. However, the head is marked as indefinite (either lacking an article, or modified by an indefinite article *wį* 'a, one' or *tóe* 'some') even if it is clearly definite and known to the speaker in real life.

It is characteristic of Siouan languages for the shared noun of a relative construction to appear in the subordinate clause. The gap that appears in the matrix clause in Osage contrasts starkly with English, where the head noun remains in the main clause and is usually specific and definite, while the gap occurs in the subordinate clause. The examples below are grouped according to the function of the shared noun within the subordinate clause and the matrix clause, although this has no important consequences for relative clause form. Relative clauses in the examples below are enclosed in brackets.

Type A: object-object. The shared noun is object in the subordinate clause and object in the matrix clause.

The head in (196) is indefinite, 'some food'.

(196) [*ónǫbre tóa káaɣape*] *bráache mįkšé*
ónǫbre tóe Ø-káaɣe-api-ðe Ø-Wa-ðaaché mįkšé
food some A3P-make-PL-DECL P3S-A1S-eat 1S.CONT
'I'm eating the food that they fixed'

In (197), the deictic particle *ke* 'multiple, scattered, dispersed' appears at the end of the relative clause. This is an interesting location for *ke*, since its normal position is immediately following the noun it modifies.

(197) [*haxį́ hkǫ́bra*] *ke ðíe ðikˀú apai*
haxį́ Wa-kǫ́-Wa-ða ke ðíe ði-Ø-kˀu apa-ðe
blanket A1S-PREV-A1S-want DISP 2S.PRON P2S-A3S-give 3.CONT-DECL
'the blankets I want are the ones she gave you'

In sentence (198), *ée* (glossed '3.PRON') is equivalent to 'those' or 'the aforesaid'.

(198) [*haxį́ ðikˀu*] *ðe ée hkǫ́bra mįkšé*
haxį́ ði-Ø-kˀu ðe ée Wa-kǫ́-Wa-ða mįkšé
blanket P2S-A3S-give 3.DEM 3.PRON A1S-PREV-A1S-want 1S.CONT
'the blankets that she gave you are the ones I want'

In the following type A example, the relative clause ends in a nominalizer.

(199) [*ónǫbre waðákikˀupi*] *che ówina ąkátxa*
ónǫbre wa-Ya-ki-kˀu-api che ówena ąkátxa
food P1P-A2S-DAT-give-PL NOM grateful.for 1P.CONT
'we're thankful for this food you have given us'

Type B: subject-subject. The shared noun is subject in the subordinate clause and subject in the matrix clause.

(200) [*níhkaši wį́ sítui achípe*] *haxį́ wį́ ąkˀúpe*
níhkaši wį́ sitǫ́į a-Ø-chí-api-ðe haxį́ wį́
man a yesterday PREV-A3S-arrive.here-PL-DECL blanket a
ą-Ø-kˀú-api-ðe
P1S-A3S-give-PL-DECL
'the man that came yesterday gave me a blanket'[12]

The relative clause preceding the main clause can look very much like a phrase that has been moved leftward outside the main clause, and there may be a demonstrative pointing back to the preceding head (object) or phrase, such as *ðe* in (198) above. Sentences of this type are complex and merit closer examination within a larger corpus.

Type C: object-subject. The shared noun is object in the subordinate clause and subject in the matrix clause.

(201) [*waléze tóa ąwą́ðakˀú na*], *ðé ée ape*
waléze tóe o-ą-Ya-kˀu nąǫ
book some-PL-DECL PREV-P1S-A2S-lend ITER
ðé ée-api-ðe
3.DEM 3.PRON(?)-PL-DECL
'the books you loaned me are these'

This sentence was also offered without the final *pe*:

(202) [*waléze toa ąwą́ðakˀu na*], *ðée ðe*
waléze tóe o-ą-Ya-kˀu na ðée ðe
book some PREV-P1S-A2S-lend ITER 3.PRON DECL
'the books you loaned me are these'

(203) [*šį́tožį wį iiðáðe*] *hkóopši apai*
šį́tožį wį ii-ð-Wa-ðe Ø-hkóopše apa-ðe
boy a PREV-EPð-A1S-see A3S-flee 3.CONT-DECL
'the boy that I saw was running away'

[12] This same sentence is equally correct with *sitǫ́į* 'yesterday' in initial position, and in fact it is more common to find the temporal expression in first position in an Osage sentence. But perhaps the more internal placement of *sitǫ́į* assures that it modifies 'came' and not 'gave'.

In the pair of examples in (204)–(205), *na* 'only' appears in both singular and plural apparently meaning 'exactly' ('these are exactly they'). As is often the case, there is no quantifier or indefinite article on the head noun in (205), although *toe* 'some' for the English plural indefinite article appears in (204). (Replacement of the preverb vowel *o* of *ok^{ʔ}u* 'lend' by *ą* is due to vowel harmony with P1S *ą*.)

(204) *waléze toa ąwą́ðak^{ʔ}u na*
waléze tóe o-ą-Ya-k^{ʔ}u na
books some PREV-P1S-A2S-lend only
'these are the books that you loaned me'

(205) *waléze ąwą́ðak^{ʔ}u na*
waléze o-ą-Ya-k^{ʔ}u na
books PREV-P1S-A2S-lend only
'this is the book that you loaned me'

The English translation of (204) differs from that of (202) only in lacking emphasis. In Osage, however, the difference is that (204) lacks the final phrase *ðee ðe* 'these are they'. I assume that context supplied the sense 'these are' for (204), and that *na* 'only' helps to convey that sense. In this way, both (204) and (205) are each a sort of truncated relative clause, as the English translations provided by Osage speakers convey.

Type D: subject-object. The shared noun is subject in the subordinate clause and object in the matrix clause.

The continuative auxiliary *apa* appears in the embedded clause in (206).

(206) [*haxį žúuce apai*] *ée hkǫ́bra mįkšé*
haxį́ žúuce apa-ðe ée Wa-kǫ́-Wa-ða mįkšé
blanket red 3.CONT-DECL 3.PRON A1S-PREV-A1S-want 1S.CONT
'the blankets that are red are the ones I want'

In (207), the embedded indefinite 'a man' is the head of the relative clause.

(207) [*sitųį níhkaši wį achípe*] *John akxa íiðape*
sitǫ́į níhkaši wį a-Ø-chí-api-ðe John-a akxa
yesterday man a PREV-A3S-arrive.here-PL-DECL John-SYL SUBJ
íi-Ø-Ø-ðe-api-ðe
PREV-P3S-A3S-see
'John saw the man that came yesterday'

7.5 Expressions of existence

The semantic grouping labeled here "expressions of existence" includes the Osage counterparts of English 'be located there, be in a place'; 'live'; 'exist'; 'not exist'; 'be many'; 'be [a number]' (for example, '[be] three'). These are not necessarily existentials in Osage, but they are grouped here in order to facilitate the search for information on the part of the English speaker.

***ecí* 'be located there'**

(208) *eecí hta nįkše?*
ée-ci *hta* *nįkše*
3.PRON-at FUT 2S.CONT
'will you be there?'

See also the discussion of *eci* in section 6.3.7. The element *ke* in (209) is a pluralizing deictic element, marking 'plural, scattered, dispersed' (see section 6.3.7).

(209) *níhkašie ąnąsi ecíke*
níhkašie *i-ą-Ø-si* *ée-cí-ke*
person PREV-P1S-A3P-dislike 3.PRON-at-DISP
'there are people around that don't like me'

***aní* 'live' (regular verb)**

(210) *wawépahǫ aní šǫ́ ąhé*
wawépahǫ *a-Wa-ní* *šǫ́* *ąðįhé*
witness PREV-A1S-live still 1S.CONT
'I'm a witness and I'm still living'

***ðįké* 'not exist'**

(211) *hcí akxa ðįkí akxai*
hcí *akxa* *ðįké* *akxa-ðe*
house SUBJ nothing 3.CONT-DECL
'that house doesn't exist any more'

***ochí* 'be many, plentiful'.** The form *ochí* is quite productive. In addition to its function as a verb in (212), it appears as an element in several nouns and adjectives. For example, in the expression for 'smart' in (213) this same *ochí* occurs.

(212) *wécˀa ochie*
wécˀa *ochí-ðe*
snake be.plentiful-DECL
'there are lots of snakes'

(213) *waðíla ochí*
waðíla ochí
mind be.plentiful
'smart'

'Be a number'. There are several ways of expressing the equivalent of an English existential sentence in addition to those gathered together here. In general a bare noun or adjective is used either with or without a continuative aspect marker. Numbers may function in such a verblike manner, but do not accept personal markers. That is, the following sentences with personal marker *ði* are ungrammatical:

(214a) ***ðíðáabrį?*
ði-ðáabrį
P2S-three
('are there three of you?')

(214b) ***ðíðáabrįpi?*
ði-ðáabrį-api
P2S-three-PL
('are there three of you?')

Instead of (214a)–(214b), a sentence is used in which the uninflected number 'three' is followed by a continuative marker which may indicate person and number, as in (215). With a noun modified by 'three', the construction is similar. While the continuative marker if present, as in (216), can be thought of as a copula, it is also possible to find such sentences without the continuative marker. (See also section 6.7.)

(215) *ðáabrį paašé?*
ðáabrį paašé
three 2P.CONT
'are there three of you?'

(216) *hįįce ðáabrį akxa*
hįįce ðáabrį akxa
plate three 3.CONT
'there are three dishes'

7.6 Interrogatives and indefinites

There does not seem to be any question marker in Osage. It is true that some questions end in *ðe*, but there is no evidence to suggest that this is a different element from the declarative *ðe* or *-e* discussed elsewhere in this volume. At any rate, the *ðe* on questions appears to be optional. Before addressing the interrogative words themselves, it should be noted that yes-no questions such as 'Did you go to the dances?' have the same word order as the corresponding declaratives (e.g., 'You went to the dances'), with added question intonation. Often questions lack the subject markers *akxa* and *apa*, but there are many counterexamples. The continuative markers are often, but not always, dropped in questions. Continuatives are more frequently found following a bare noun or verb/adjective, as in (217) below, than in other interrogatives.

(217) *wažáže nįkšé?*
wažáže nįkšé?
Osage 2S.CONT
'are you Osage?'

There are a good many question words, grouping basically into words which use the indefinite prefix *háa*, those that use the related prefix *hówa*, and several isolates, such as *pée* 'who'. (In fact, *háa* is likely derived from *hówa* via vowel collapse.) This section will merely list the interrogative words in Osage, with a number of example sentences.

7.6.1 *pée* 'who'

The interrogative referring to humans is *pée*, which is singular or plural and can question any argument of the sentence: 'who, whom, to whom, whose' (for possessives, see section 5.1.7).

(218) *pée opénipé?*
pée o-Ø-péni-api-ðe
who PREV-A3P-find.out.about-PL-DECL
'who did they find out about?'

(219) *Jóhna haxį pée kˀúe?*
John-a haxį pée Ø-kˀú-ðe
John-SYL blanket who A3S-give-DECL
'who did John give the blanket(s) to?'

(220) *Jóhna pée haxį wakˀúe?*
John-a pée haxį wa-Ø-kˀú-ðe
John-SYL who blanket P3P-A3S-give-DECL
'who [plural] did John give the blanket(s) to?'

(221) *pée Jóhna haxį wakˀúe?*
pée John-a haxį wa-Ø-kˀú-ðe
who John-SYL blanket P3P-A3S-give-DECL
'who [plural] did John give the blanket(s) to?'

In questions, there is no movement of components, except for some fronting of the question word, as in (222). However, versions without fronting, as in (223), are equally correct.

(222) *pée Jóhna (akxa) íiðe?*
pée John-a (akxa) íi-Ø-ðe
who John-SYL (SUBJ) PREV-A3S-see
'who did John see?'

(223) *Jóhna akxa pée íiðe?*
John-a akxa pée íi-Ø-ðe
John-SYL SUBJ who PREV-A3S-see
'who did John see?'

The optional movement of a question word to the initial position in a sentence may be part of a general pattern of fronting of adverbs and certain objects. It may also reflect English patterns.

As evidenced in (224)–(226), sentences with *pée* can be ambiguous. *pée* may be interpreted as object or subject, no matter whether it precedes or follows other nominals. Word order is a rough guide, but not an absolute indicator of whether *pée* is subject or object.

(224) *pée John opéni (ðe)?*
pée John o-Ø-péni ðe
who John PREV-A3S-find.out.about DECL
'who found out about John?; who did John find out about?'

(225) *Jóhna pée íiðe?*
John-a pée íi-Ø-ðe
John-SYL who PREV-A3S-see
'who did John see?; who saw John?'

(226) *pée Jóhna íiðe?*
pée John-a íi-Ø-ðe?
who John-SYL PREV-A3S-see
'who did John see?; who saw John?'

Emphasis may be placed on the plurality of *pée* by following it with *háanǫ* 'which; how many', which incorporates the indefinite; this gives a form *pée háanǫ*, translatable as 'who all'.

(227) *Jóhna pée háanǫ wéeðe ðe?*
John-a pée haa-nǫ wa-íi-Ø-ðe ðe
John-SYL who INDEF-only P3P-PREV-A3S-see DECL
'who all did John see?'

In (228), 'grasp the feather, take up the quill' is the expression for 'vote', and *pée* asks 'for whom?'. Other sentences with *pée* follow, including one with *péeški* 'everybody' (230).

(228) *pée mǫšǫ́ oščįįke?*
pée mǫšǫ́ o-Ya-ðįįke
who feather PREV-A2S-grasp
'who did you vote for?'

(229) *pée íšpaho lée?*
pée i-Ø-Ya-pahǫ a-Ø-lée
who PREV-P3S-A2S-know PREV-A3S-return.there
'who that you know left?'

(230) *péeški ípahǫ́pe*
pée.eški í-Ø-Ø-pahǫ-api-ðe
everybody PREV-P3S-A3P-know-PL-DECL
'everybody knows him'

(231a) *pée ðąįšé?*
pée ðąįše
who 2S.CONT[moving]
'who are you?' (to someone knocking at the door)

(231b) *pée nįkšé?*
pée nįkšé
who 2S.CONT[sitting]
'who are you?' (sitting)

7.6.2 Other interrogatives: *táatą* and forms in *haa-*

Many of the question words are indefinites with initial *haa*. These include *háakǫta* 'why', *haakǫ́* 'what; which; how much', the indefinite verb *haaǫ́* 'do what' (related to *eǫ* 'do'), *haatxą́tą* 'when [in future]', and *haatxą́ci* 'when [in past]'.

7.6.2.1 'Why', 'how much/many', and 'what'

The word *haakǫ́ta* 'why' sounds almost equally accented on first and second syllables. The gloss for the final syllable *ta* is unclear.

(232) *haakǫ́ta*
haa-kǫ-ta
INDEF-manner-(?)
'why'

(233) *haakǫ́ta Jóhna lée?*
haakǫ́ta John-a a-Ø-lée
why John-SYL PREV-A3S-return.there
'why did John go home?'

(234) *haakǫ́ta Jóhna ðée?*
haakǫ́ta John-a a-Ø-ðée
why John-SYL PREV-A3S-go
'why did John leave?'

The question word corresponding to English 'what' is usually expressed by the indefinite *haakǫ́*. Obviously this is the base of *haakǫ́ta* above. The form *haakǫ́* appears in (236) to be a sort of default interrogative. Another use of *haakǫ́*, as 'how much', appears in (237), for which it was noted that it is not polite to ask to what degree someone is Osage.

(235) *haakǫ́?*
haa-kǫ
INDEF-manner
'what is it? what?'

(236) *haakǫ́ ðée?*
haa-kǫ a-Ø-ðée
INDEF-manner PREV-A3P-go
'which way did they go?; where did they go?'

(237) *haakǫ́ wažáže?*
haa-kǫ wažáže
INDEF-manner Osage
'how much Osage are you?'

The more common indefinite interrogative of quantity is *háanąą* 'how much; how many':

(238) *hą́ąną ašcį?*
háaną a-Ya-ðį
how.much/many PREV-A2S-have
'how much/many do you have?'

'What' can also be expressed by the form *táatą* 'thing'. This can be used as an interrogative verb:

(239) *táatą?*
thing
'what did you say?'

(240) *táatą ðaašé hǫpái?*
táatą ðaįšé hǫ́pa-ðe
thing 2S.CONT day-this
'what did you do today?'

The form *táatą* is used to ask for the Osage word for something, as in (241).

(241) *wažáže ie "dog" táatą ðaatápe?*
wažáže ie "dog" táatą Ø-ðaacé-api-ðe
Osage language "dog" thing A3P-name-PL-DECL
'what do Osages call "dog"?' (lit., 'what did the Osage language name "dog"?')

A related form is the equivalent of English "whatchamacallit" or "thingamajig," *táatą* 'what' + *ska* 'suppose'.

(242) *tą́ąska*
táatą-ska
thing-SUPP
'whatcha-call-it'

The verb *háaǫ* 'do [an indefinite thing]' is ubiquitous in Osage. First person forms are exemplified in (243)–(244).

(243) *haamǫ́ ~ háamą*
haa-Wa-ǫ
INDEF-A1S-do
'what I do; whatever I do; what did I do?'

(244) *ðée háama?*
ðée haa-Wa-ǫ
this INDEF-A1S-do
'what am I going to do with this?'

Both *táatą* and *háamą* can appear in a clause:

(245) *hǫ́pai táatą háamą che íhpahomąží*
hǫ́pa-ðe táatą haa-Wa-ǫ che í-Wa-pahǫ- maží
day-this thing INDEF-A1S-do NOM PREV-A1S-know-1S.NEG
'I don't know what I did today'

The second person form is exemplified in (246)–(250).

(246) *háažǫ*
háa-Ya-ǫ
INDEF-A2S-do
'what you do; whatever you do; what did you do? what did you do with it?'

(247) *háažǫ ðaašé hǫ́pái?*
háa-Ya-ǫ ðaįšé hǫ́pa-ðe
INDEF-A2S-do 2S.CONT day-this
'what did you do today?'

(248) *hcúka háažǫ?*
hcúka háa-Ya-ǫ
spoon INDEF-A2S-do
'what did you do with the spoons?'

(249) *háažǫ́ škǫ́šta tą éki*ą
háa-Ya-ǫ Ya-kǫ́-Ya-ða tą é-ki-ǫ-a
INDEF-A2S-do A2S-PREV-A2S-want when/if PREV-PREV-do-IMPER
'whenever you want to do something, go ahead' (lit., 'whatever you want to do, do it')

(250) *mǫ́šǫ oðįįke háažǫ hta nįkše?*
mǫ́šǫ oðįįke háa-Ya-ǫ hta nįkše
feather grasp INDEF-A2S-do FUT 2S.CONT
'how are you going to vote?' (or 'voting, what are you going to do?')

The third person form is *háaǫ*, sometimes shortened to *hǫ́ǫ* (251)–(253):

(251) *háaǫ ðe?*
haa-Ø-ǫ ðe
INDEF-A3S-do DECL
'what did he do?'

(252) *haxį hǫ́ǫ ðe?*
haxį haa-Ø-ǫ ðe
blanket INDEF-A3S-do DECL
'what did he do with the blanket?'

(253) *súhka hǫ́ǫ che?*
súhka haa-ǫ che
chicken INDEF-do EVID?
'how's the chicken doing [when it's cooking]?'

7.6.2.2 Future and past 'when'

The indefinite *haa-* combines with *txą́* or *etxą́* 'be the time' to form *haatxą́ta* 'when [in the future]'. The form for 'when [in the past]' is different: *haatxą́ci*. A possible derivation for the latter is *haatxą́* 'what time' + *ce* 'at' + *i* 'to(?)', while the future form may be *haatxą́* 'what time' + *ce* 'at' + *a* 'to(?)', where the difference between *i* and *a* is presumed to be associated with 'past' and 'future'. A variant of the future form is *haakxą́ta*, with the common replacement of *tx* by *kx*.

(254) *haakxą́ta ðalí hta ðaįše?*
haatxą́ta Ya-lí hta ðaįše
when A2S-return.here FUT 2S.CONT
'when are you coming back?'

haatxą́ci varies with *haatxą́ce* 'when [past]':

(255) *haatxą́ci hǫǫpé ðé šcúwį?*
haatxą́ce hǫǫpé ðe Ya-ðuwį́
when shoe this A2S-buy
'when did you buy these shoes?'

The interrogative 'when' may also appear noninitially in the sentence:

(256) *hǫǫpé ðé haatxą́ce šcúwį?*
hǫǫpé ðe haatxą́ce Ya-ðuwį́
shoe this when A2S-buy
'when did you buy these shoes?'

There are clear minimal pairs for the contrast between past and future 'when':

(257) *haatxą́ci ðalíe?*
haatxą́ce-i Ya-lí-ðe
when-at A2S-return.here-DECL
'when did you get back?'

(258) *haatxą́ta ðalíe?*
haatxą́ta Ya-lí-ðe
when A2S-return.here-DECL
'when will you be back?'

Although the 'when' form in (258) carries the semantic information 'future', a future marker *hta* may also appear on the sentence, as in (259).

(259) *haakxą́ta ðalí hta ðaiše?*
haatxą́ta Ya-lí hta ðaįšé
when A2S-return.here FUT 2S.CONT
'when are you coming back?'

7.6.2.3 Indefinites with *haa*

The *haa* question words also function as indefinites in noninterrogative sentences:

(260) *táatą háamą che lą́ði ekxai*
táatą haa-Wa-ǫ che lą́ðe akxa-ðe
thing INDEF-A1S-do NOM big 3.CONT-DECL
'what I did was important'

(261) *háamą hkǫ́bra ékimą hta mįkšé*
haa-Wa-ǫ Wa-kǫ́-Wa-ða é-ki-Wa-ǫ hta mįkšé
what-A1S-do A1S-PREV-A1S-want PREV-DAT-A1S-do FUT 1S.CONT
'I'll do whatever I want to'

éǫ 'do' and its derivative *ékiǫ* 'do' (dative; where *é* is deictic 'this, that') are the only verbs found so far with corresponding indefinite forms in *haa-* (such as *háaǫ* in (261)). For other verbs, there is no indefinite form; for example, in (262) there is no indefinite form of the verb 'think' to be used, in a sentence otherwise identical to (260) above.

(262) *táatą iiðilą che lą́ði ekxai*
táatą í-Ø-ðilą che lą́ðe akxa-ðe
thing PREV-A3S-think NOM big 3.CONT-DECL
'what he thinks is important'

Other lexical sets with an indefinite member include: *háaną* 'how much; however much', *éeną* 'that much', *káaną* 'that much'; and *haakǫ́* 'how; in whatever way', *eekǫ́* 'in this manner', *kaakǫ́* 'in exactly this way'.

7.6.3 'Where' and 'which': *hówa* and *íma*

The expressions *hówa* and *íma* are discussed in section 6.3 (on positional articles). The common forms in this group which are mentioned here, in order, are: 'where', 'anyone', 'anything', 'which' (all with *hówa*), and 'which' (with *íma*).[13]

'Where' may be stationary ('sit where?') or a goal ('go where?'). Both use the same Osage form: *howáįki* 'where'.

(263) *howáįki ðalįįke nįkšé?*
howáįki Ya-lįįke nįkšé
where A2S-sit.down 2S.CONT
'where are you sitting [down]?'

(264) *Jóhna howáįki ðée?*
John-a howáįki a-Ø-ðée
John-SYL where PREV-A3S-go
'where did John go?'

This form also may be followed by the 'standing' positional article *che*:

(265) *hcéhežį hówaįki che?*
hcéhežį hówaįki che
dishes where STA
'where are the dishes [sitting]?'

[13] 'Which' may refer to choice among many or between two only.

The two forms 'anything' and 'anyone' differ only in one syllable: 'anything' is *howachéeški*, 'anyone' is *howaðéeški*.

(266) *howachéeški íiðaðe?*
howa-che-eški *íi-Ya-ðe*
INDEF-STA-else/also PREV-A2S-see
'did you see anything?'

(267) *howaðéeški íiðaðe?*
howa-ðe-eški *íi-Ya-ðe*
INDEF-MOV-else/also PREV-A2S-see
'did you see anyone?'

Forms for 'everybody', seen in examples (268)–(269), are similar to that for 'anyone'. *háaški* in (268) is a shortened form of *howaðéeški*. (Indefinite *haa* appears to be merely a short form of *howa*, by vowel harmony and the V1-V2 Rule.)

(268) *háaški ípahǫ apai*
haa-ški *í-Ø-Ø-pahǫ-api-ðe*
INDEF-also PREV-P3S-A3P-know-PL-DECL
'everybody knows him'

Example (269) uses the form *péeški*.

(269) *péeški ípahǫpe*
pée-ški *í-Ø-Ø-pahǫ-api-ðe*
who-else/also PREV-P3S-A3P-know-PL-DECL
'everybody knows him'

As further illustration of the use of these terms, table 7.2 shows possible answers to the question, 'who should I call?'. The form *howaðéeški* undergoes vowel harmony or the V1-V2 rule, becoming *haaðéeški*. Subsequently *ð*-Elision occurs, producing *haaeški,* which further undergoes the V1-V2 Rule to produce *haaški.*[14]

The *háa-* and *hówa-* forms in the table, while approximately equivalent to 'everybody', are not interchangeable with *huukǫ́ða* 'many, everyone' in sentences such as (270), where neither *háaški* nor *péeški* can be used.

(270) *huukǫ́ða waachí apai*
huukǫ́ða *waa-Ø-chí* *apa-ðe*
many PREV-A3P-dance 3.CONT-DECL
'everybody is dancing'

[14] There is a homophonous form *háaški* 'in whatever direction'.

TABLE 7.2. 'ANYBODY' AND 'EVERYBODY'

ANSWER TO 'WHO SHOULD I CALL?'	INFORMAL ENGLISH TRANSLATION
péeški	'call just anybody, call everybody'
háaški *howáaški* *haaðéeški* *howaðéeški*	'call everybody, call whoever, call just anybody'
záani 'all'	'call all of them, call all of that group'

One form for 'which' consists of *hówa* plus *xcį* 'exactly'; this is followed by the 'standing animate' article *txą* (in denasalized form) in (271). The 'standing inanimate' article *che* appears instead in (272), forming a minimal pair with (271).

(271) *hówaxcį txá?*
hówa-xcį txą́
INDEF-exact STA[animate]
'exactly which one [person]?'

(272) *hówaxcį ché?*
hówa-xcį che
INDEF-exact STA[inanimate]
'exactly which one [inanimate]?'

The 'sitting animate' (or 'inanimate, round') element *įkšé* is part of the expression *hówaįkše* 'which' in (273), more precisely 'the one sitting where'.

(273) *hówaįkše škǫ́ǫšta?*
hówa-įkše Ya-kǫ́-Ya-ða
INDEF-SIT A2S-PREV-A2S-want
'which one do you want?'

The other common form for 'which' is *ímą*, which in Osage, unlike Lakota, is not restricted to dual, and can be 'which among many'. (The phrase 'of these' in the free translation of (274) stems from context only and is not present in the Osage.)

(274) *ímą Jóhna íiðe ðe?*
ímą John-a íi-Ø-ðe ðe
which John-SYL PREV-A3S-see DECL
'which of these did John see?'

Appendix: Osage kinship terms

Osage has a well-developed system of kinship terms, which has the following three characteristics.

(a) Possession of kinship terms is usually signaled by the inalienable prefix paradigm: 1S *wi-*, 2S *ði-*, 3S/P *i-*; there is no 1P form. Thus, 'my (a male's) younger brother' is *wisǫ́ka*, 'your (a male's) younger brother' is *ðisǫ́ka*, and 'his younger brother' is *isǫ́ka*. Kin terms in this paradigm do not occur unprefixed, except in some cases as an endearment (e.g., *hcíko* for *wihcíko* 'grandfather'). Some terms lack possessor marking: e.g., *iiną́* 'my mother' (vs. *iihǫ́* 'his mother'), *šíkxą* 'my/your/her husband's sister'. A very few terms may use possessive pronouns: e.g., *asíhpa (ðíhta)* 'your baby sister'.

(b) Gender of possessor (of "ego") is significant. The terms for a woman's relatives differ considerably from those for a man's relatives.

(c) Order of birth is significant. 'Son' and 'daughter' terms are specified according to order of birth, from first to fourth and beyond. Birth order (older and younger) also plays a role in the terms for 'aunt' and 'uncle', 'sister' and 'brother'.

Osage kinship terms with first person possessor ('my') are used both vocatively—that is, in speaking to that relative—and referentially—that is, in speaking about one's relative to someone else. If a 1S possessor kinship relationship exists between the speaker and the person referred to, the term for that relationship is used in preference to a term that would require a possessor form such as *wíhta*.

The kinship terms are widely used and quite common in both daily life (inserted into the English of daily speech) and in ceremonial events. When making a formal or informal speech, Osages begin by using a few of these terms to acknowledge their kinsfolk among the listeners or identify the listeners as kinsfolk or friends. Men might begin: *wihtą́ke, wižį́, wisǫ́ka, wawíhǫepi*; women might begin: *wižǫ́a, wihtéžį, wihcį́to, wisǫ́a, wawíhǫepi*, according to one speaker. The use of these kinship terms in casual or formal speech is more common than the use of the actual Osage name that has been given to a person.

The full set of kinship terms is presented in two tables in the remainder of this Appendix. Examining even part of these will give the reader an idea of the richness of the system. Terms for relatives of a male (to put it another way, terms used when the possessor or "ego" of the kinship term is male) are given in table A1; terms for relatives of a female are given in table A2. (Note that the two tables are virtually identical down through the 'mother's younger sister' terms.)

Some details of usage of specific kinship terms are provided in notes at the end of each table, signaled by raised letters in the table. Besides the glosses I report, there are extended uses, as has been pointed out by Mongrain Lookout (p.c. 1993). For example, the possessor (or "ego") will retain in certain cases the term for a certain relative throughout subsequent generations descended from that relative. These extended uses are not given in the present work.

TABLE A1. RELATIVE OF MALE

ENGLISH GLOSS	1S POSSESSOR ('my')	2S POSSESSOR ('your')	3S POSSESSOR ('his')
grandfather (paternal or maternal)	*wihcíko*; *hcíko*	*ðihcíko*	*ihcíko*
grandmother (paternal or maternal)	*iihkó*	*ðiihkó*	*iihkó*
father	*įhtáci*	*ðiðáce*	*iðáce*
father's brother	*įhtáci*; *įhtácižį*	*ðiðáce*; *ðiðácežį*	*iðáce*; *iðácežį*
father's sister (older or younger)	*wihcími*	*ðihcími*	*ihcími*
father's sister's husband	*wihtą́ha*	*ðihtą́ha*	*ihtą́ha*
father's sister's son	*hcióška*	*hcióška*	*hcióška*
father's sister's daughter	*wihcížo*	*ðihcížo*	*ihcížo*
mother	*iiną́*	*ðiihǫ́*	*iihǫ́*
mother's brother	*wįcéki*	*ðįcéki*	*įcéki*
mother's older sister	*iiną́*; *iiną́htą*	*ðiihǫ́htą*	*iihǫ́htą*
mother's younger sister	*iiną́žį*; *iiną́*	*ðiihǫ́žį*	*iihǫ́žį*
wife	*ilǫ́ǫhpa iihǫ́*[a,b]; name of son + *iihǫ́*; *wakˀó wíhta*	*ilǫ́ǫhpa iihǫ́*[a,b]; *ðiwákˀo*; *wakˀó ðíhta*	*íwakˀó*; *iwákˀo*; *wakˀó (íhta)*

TABLE A1. RELATIVE OF MALE (cont.)

ENGLISH GLOSS	1S POSSESSOR ('my')	2S POSSESSOR ('your')	3S POSSESSOR ('his')
wife's father	*wihcíko*; *hcíko*; *cˀáke*	*ðihcíko*	*ihcíko*
wife's mother	*wakˀóžį (wíhta)*[c]	*ðíwakˀóžį*; *wakˀóžį ðíhta*	*íwakˀóžį*
wife's brother	*wihtą́ha*	*ðihtą́ha*	*ihtą́ha*
wife's brother's son	*wihcóška*	*ðihcóška*	*ihcóška*
wife's sister	*wihą́ka*	*ðihą́ka*	*ihą́ka*
wife's sister's husband	—[d]		
brother (older)	*wižį́ðe*; *wižį́e*; *wižį́*	*ðižį́ðe*; *ðižį́*	*ižį́ðe*; *ižį́*
brother (younger)	*wisǫ́ka*	*ðisǫ́ka*	*isǫ́ka*
brother's wife	*wihą́ka*	*ðihą́ka*	*ihą́ka*
brother's son	*wižį́ke*	*ðižį́ke*	*ižį́ke*
brother's daughter	*wižǫ́ke*	*ðižǫ́ke*	*ižǫ́ke*
sister (older)[e]	*wihtą́ke*	*ðihtą́ke*	*ihtą́ke*
sister (younger)[f]	*wihtáižį*; *wihtéžį*	*ðihtáižį*; *ðihtéžį*	*ihtáižį*; *ihtéžį*
sister (baby)	*asíhpa*	*asíhpa (ðíhta)*	*asíhpa (íhta)*
sister's husband	*wihtą́ha*; *htą́ha*	*ðihtą́ha*	*ihtą́ha*
sister's son	*wihcóška*	*ðihcóška*	*ihcóška*
sister's daughter	*wihcížo*	*ðihcížo*	*ihcížo*
son (first)	*ilǫ́ǫhpa*; *ilǫ́htą*	*ilǫ́ǫhpa*; *ilǫ́htą*	*ilǫ́ǫhpa*; *ilǫ́htą*
son (second)	*kšą́ka*	*kšą́ka*	*kšą́ka*
son (third and beyond)	*kxážį*; *kxáke*	*kxážį*; *kxáke*	*kxážį*; *kxáke*
son (any)	*wižį́ke*	*ðižį́ke*	*ižį́ke*
son's wife	*wihcíni*; *míaɣe*	*ðihcíni*; *míaɣe*	*ihcíni*; *míaɣe*
daughter, first	*wakˀóhtą*; *wakˀóhpa*[b]; *míina* (Pawhuska)	*wakˀóhtą*; *wakˀóhpa (ðíhta)*[b]; *míina* (Pawhuska)	*wakˀóhtą*; *míina* (Pawhuska)

TABLE A1. RELATIVE OF MALE (cont.)

ENGLISH GLOSS	1S POSSESSOR ('my')	2S POSSESSOR ('your')	3S POSSESSOR ('his')
daughter (second)	*wihé*	*wihé (ðíhta)*	*wihé*
daughter (third)	*ašį́ka*	*ašį́ka*	*ašį́ka*
daughter (fourth and beyond)	*asížį*	*asížį*	*asížį*
daughter (any)	*wižǫ́ke*	*ðižǫ́ke*	*ižǫ́ke*
daughter (baby)	*asíhpa*	*asíhpa (ðíhta)*	*asíhpa (íhta)*
daughter's husband	*wihtǫ́ce*	*ðihtǫ́ce*	*ihtǫ́ce*
grandchild	*wihcóšpa*; *žįká owáhkihą*; *žįká ohkíhą*[g]	*ðihcóšpa*; *žįká ową́hkihą*; *žįká ohkíhą*[g]	*ihcóšpa*; *žįká owáhkihą*; *žįká ohkíhą*

[a] *ilǫ́ǫhpa iihǫ́* (lit., 'elder son's mother') can be used for 'wife' if the husband and wife have a son. All 1S possessor 'wife' terms can be used vocatively, or simply the wife's Indian name is used.

[b] Kinship terms with *hpa* may be baby names. At any rate, their use outside first and second person seems limited.

[c] *wakʔóžį* 'wife's mother' is also used to speak to or refer to any elderly woman.

[d] Rather than having a specific term for 'my wife's sister's husband', speakers use *ðišíkʔe* 'your sister's husband' when speaking to their wives, or *išíkʔe* 'her [i.e., wife's] sister's husband' when speaking to someone other than their wives.

[e] The 'older sister' terms designate the older of the sisters, not necessarily someone older than the person speaking. They are also used between any two female friends without regard to relative age.

[f] The sister designated by a 'younger sister' term need not be younger than the speaker, just younger than another sister.

[g] *hcošpá*, a shortened form of *wihcóšpa*, *ðihcóšpa*, is also used for 'my/your grandchild'. In addition to its original meaning, it is used to mean 'pal, friend, buddy'.

TABLE A2. RELATIVE OF FEMALE

ENGLISH GLOSS	1S POSSESSOR ('my')	2S POSSESSOR ('your')	3S POSSESSOR ('her')
grandfather (paternal or maternal)	*wihcíko*; *hcíko*	*ðihcíko*	*ihcíko*
grandmother (paternal or maternal)	*iihkó*	*ðiihkó*	*iihkó*
father	*įhtáci*	*ðiðáce*	*iðáce*

TABLE A2. RELATIVE OF FEMALE (cont.)

ENGLISH GLOSS	1S POSSESSOR ('my')	2S POSSESSOR ('your')	3S POSSESSOR ('her')
father's brother	*įhtáci*; *įhtácižį*	*ðiðáce*; *ðiðácežį*	*iðáce*; *iðácežį*
father's sister	*wihcími*	*ðihcími*	*ihcími*
father's sister's husband	*wihtą́ha*	*ðihtą́ha*	*ihtą́ha*
father's sister's son	*hcióška*; *hcioškạ́*	*hcióška*	*hcióška*
father's sister's daughter	*wihcížo*	*ðihcížo*	*ihcížo*
mother	*iiną́*	*ðiihǫ́*	*iihǫ́*
mother's brother	*wįcéki*	*ðįcéki*	*įcéki*
mother's older sister	*iiną́*; *iiną́htą*	*ðiihǫ́htą*	*iihǫ́*; *iihǫ́htą*
mother's younger sister	*iiną́žį*; *iiną́*	*ðiihǫ́žį*	*iihǫ́žį*
husband	*ilǫ́ǫhpa iðáci*; daughter's name + *iðáci*; *níhka wíhta*; *c*ʔ*áižį*[a]	*ilǫ́ǫhpa iðáce*; *ðiníhka*; *níhka ðíhta*	*iníhka*; *níhka íhta*
husband's father	*wihcíko*; *hcíko*	*ðihcíko*	*ihcíko*
husband's father's sister	—[b]		
husband's mother	*wak*ʔ*óžį (wíhta)*; *iihkó* 'grandmother'	*ðíwak*ʔ*óžį*; *wak*ʔ*óžį ðíhta*; *ðiihkó*	*íwak*ʔ*óžį*; *iihkó*
husband's brother	*wišík*ʔ*e*	*ðišík*ʔ*e*	*išík*ʔ*e*
husband's brother's son	—[c]		
husband's sister (older or younger)	*šíkxą*	*šíkxą*	*šíkxą*
brother (older)	*wihcįto*	*ðihcįto*	*ihcįto*
brother (younger)	*wisǫ́ežį*	*ðisǫ́ežį*	*isǫ́ežį*
brother (baby)	*kxahpái*	*kxahpái*	*kxahpái*
brother's wife	*wišíkxą*	*ðišíkxą*	*išíkxą*
brother's son	*wižįke*; *wihcóška*	*ðižįke*; *ðihcóška*	*ižįke*; *ihcóška*

TABLE A2. RELATIVE OF FEMALE (cont.)

ENGLISH GLOSS	1S POSSESSOR ('my')	2S POSSESSOR ('your')	3S POSSESSOR ('her')
brother's daughter	*wihcióžąke*; *wihcóžąke*	*ðihcióžąke*	*ihcióžąke*
sister (older)	*wižǫ́a*; *wihtą́ke*	*ðižǫ́a*; *ðihtą́ke*	*ižǫ́a*; *ihtą́ke*
sister (younger)	*wihtáežį*; *wihtéžį*	*ðihtáežį*; *ðihtéžį*	*ihtáežį*; *ihtéžį*
sister (baby)	*asíhpa*; *asíhpai*	*asíhpa (ðíhta)*; *asíhpai (ðíhta)*	*asíhpa (íhta)*; *asíhpai (íhta)*
sister's husband	*wišíkˀe*	*ðišíkˀe*	*išíkˀe*
sister's son	*wižį́ke*	*ðižį́ke*	*ižį́ke*
sister's daughter	*wižǫ́ke*	*ðižǫ́ke*	*ižǫ́ke*
son (first)	*ilǫ́ohpa*; *ilǫ́htą*	*ilǫ́ohpa*; *ilǫ́htą*	*ilǫ́ohpa*; *ilǫ́htą*
son (second)	*kšą́ka*	*kšą́ka*	*kšą́ka*
son (third and beyond)	*kxážį*; *kxáke*	*kxážį*; *kxáke*	*kxážį*; *kxáke*
son (any)	*wižį́ke*	*ðižį́ke*	*ižį́ke*
son (baby)	*kxahpái* ('baby brother')	*kxahpái* ('baby brother')	*kxahpái* ('baby brother')
son's wife	*wihcíni*; *míaɣe*	*ðihcíni*; *míaɣe*	*ihcíni*; *míaɣe*
daughter (first)	*wakˀóhtą*; *mína* (Pawhuska); *wakˀóhpa*[d]	*wakˀóhtą*; *mína* (Pawhuska); *wakˀóhpa (ðíhta)*[d]	*wakˀóhtą*; *mína* (Pawhuska)
daughter (second)	*wihé*	*wihé*	*wihé*
daughter (third)	*ašį́ka*	*ašį́ka*	*ašį́ka*
daughter (fourth and beyond)	*asížį*	*asížį*	*asížį*
daughter (any)	*wižǫ́ke*	*ðižǫ́ke*	*ižǫ́ke*
daughter (baby)	*asíhpa*; *asíhpai*	*asíhpa*; *asíhpai (ðíhta)*	*asíhpa*; *asíhpai (íhta)*

TABLE A2. RELATIVE OF FEMALE (cont.)

ENGLISH GLOSS	1S POSSESSOR ('my')	2S POSSESSOR ('your')	3S POSSESSOR ('her')
daughter's husband	*wihtǫ́ce*	*ðihtǫ́ce*	*ihtǫ́ce*
grandchild	*wihcóšpa*; *žį̨ká owáhkihą*; *žį̨ká ohkíhą*	*ðihcóšpa*; *žį̨ká owáhkihą*; *žį̨ká ohkíhą*	*ihcóšpa*; *žį̨ká owáhkihą*; *žį̨ká ohkíhą*

[a] *cˀáižį* 'husband' is also used for addressing or referring to any elderly man.
[b] Instead of a specific term for 'my husband's father's sister', speakers instead use *ðihcími* 'your father's sister' when speaking to their husbands, or *ihcími* 'his [i.e., my husband's] father's sister' when speaking to someone other than their husbands.
[c] Instead of a specific term for 'my husband's brother's son', speakers use *ðižį́ke* 'your brother's son' when addressing their husbands, or *ižį́ke* 'his [i.e., my husband's] brother's son' when speaking to someone other than their husbands.
[d] Kinship terms with *hpa* may be baby names. At any rate, their use outside first and second person seems limited.

References

Bailey, Garrick Alan. 1973. *Changes in Osage social organization 1673–1906.* University of Oregon Anthropological Papers 5. Eugene.

Baker, Mark. 1985. The mirror principle and morphosyntactic explanation. *Linguistic Inquiry* 16:373–415.

Boas, Franz, and Ella Deloria. 1941. *Dakota grammar*. Memoirs of the National Academy of Sciences 23(Pt. 2). Washington, D.C.

Bristow, Robert B. 1988. Wažáže íe waléze: Osage word list and sample sentences. Tulsa, Oklahoma. (MS. in Carolyn Quintero's possession.)

Dorsey, James Owen. n.d. Kansa and Osage dictionary slips. From vocabulary of Stubbs, Murray and others. [Collected ca. 1882.] Manuscript no. 4800/124. Dorsey Papers: National Anthropological Archives, Smithsonian Institution. Washington, D.C.

———. 1883a. Osage myths, letters, and phrases. Manuscript no. 4800/263. Dorsey Papers: National Anthropological Archives, Smithsonian Institution. Washington, D.C.

———. 1883b. Osage-English vocabulary. Manuscript no. 4800/268. Dorsey Papers: National Anthropological Archives, Smithsonian Institution. Washington, D.C.

———. 1888. *Osage traditions*. Sixth Annual Report of the Bureau of [American] Ethnology, 1884–85, 373–97. Washington, D.C.: Smithsonian Institution.

———. 1890. *The ȼegiha language.* Contributions to North American Ethnology 6. Washington, D.C.: U.S. Geographical and Geological Survey of the Territories.

Eschenberg, Ardis. 1999. Obviation in Omaha-Ponca. MS., State University of New York, Buffalo.

Greenberg, Joseph H. 1966. Some universals of grammar with particular reference to the order of meaningful elements. In *Universals of language*, edited by Joseph H. Greenberg, 73–113. Cambridge, Mass.: MIT Press.

Jesuit Archives. [ca. 1862.] Osage Mission papers. [Approximately one thousand pages in longhand, letters, word list, names, religious instruction, etc., written in Osage by Jesuits.] St. Louis, Missouri.

Koontz, John E. 1993. The contribution of Francis La Flesche to Dhegiha linguistics. MS., University of Colorado, Boulder.

La Flesche, Francis. 1921. *The Osage tribe: Rites of the chiefs; sayings of ancient men.* Thirty-Sixth Annual Report of the Bureau of American Ethnology, 1914–15, 37–604. Washington, D.C.: Smithsonian Institution.

———. 1925. *The Osage tribe: Rite of vigil.* Thirty-Ninth Annual Report of the Bureau of American Ethnology, 1917–18, 31–636. Washington, D.C.: Smithsonian Institution.

———. 1930. *The Osage tribe: Rite of the wa-xo'-be.* Forty-Fifth Annual Report of the Bureau of American Ethnology, 1927–28, 528–833. Washington, D.C.: Smithsonian Institution.

———. 1932. *A dictionary of the Osage language.* Bureau of American Ethnology Bulletin 109. Washington, D.C.: Smithsonian Institution.

———. 1939. *War ceremony and peace ceremony of the Osage Indians.* Bureau of American Ethnology Bulletin 101. Washington, D.C.: Smithsonian Institution.

Miner, Kenneth L. 1992. Winnebago field lexicon. Electronic MS.

Mithun, Marianne. 1991. Active/agentive case marking and its motivations. *Language* 67:510–46.

Quintero, Carolyn. 1983. Osage verbal morphology and phonology. Generals Paper in Linguistics, University of Massachusetts, Amherst.

———, ed. 1993. *Osage stories, as told by Jo Ann Shunkamolah.* Tulsa, Okla.: [self-published].

———. 1997. *Osage phonology and verbal morphology.* Ph.D. dissertation, University of Massachusetts, Amherst.

———. 1999. *First course in Osage.* Edited by Priscilla Hokiahse Iba. Tulsa, Okla.: [self-published].

———. 2002. Positional/configurational considerations in Osage. Paper presented at the Twenty-Second Conference on Siouan and Caddoan Languages, Spearfish, South Dakota, May 31–June 1.

Rankin, Robert L. 1999. A diachronic perspective on active/stative alignment in Siouan. MS., University of Kansas, Lawrence.

Rood, David S. and Allan R. Taylor. 1996. Sketch of Lakhota, a Siouan language. In *Handbook of North American Indians. Vol. 17: Languages,* edited by Ives Goddard, 440–82. Washington, D.C.: Smithsonian Institution.

Whitman, William. 1947. Descriptive grammar of Ioway-Otoe. *International Journal of American Linguistics* 13:233–48.

Wolff, Hans. 1952a. Osage I. *International Journal of American Linguistics* 18:63–68.

———. 1952b. Osage II. *International Journal of American Linguistics* 18:231–37.

———. 1958. An Osage graphemic experiment. *International Journal of American Linguistics* 24:30–35.

In *Studies in the Anthropology of North American Indians*

The Four Hills of Life: Northern Arapaho Life Movement, Knowledge, and Personhood
By Jeffrey D. Anderson

One Hundred Years of Old Man Sage: An Arapaho Life
By Jeffrey D. Anderson

The Semantics of Time: Aspectual Categorization in Koyukon Athabaskan.
By Melissa Axelrod

Lushootseed Texts: An Introduction to Puget Salish Narrative Aesthetics
Edited by Crisca Bierwert

People of The Dalles: The Indians of Wascopam Mission
By Robert Boyd

The Lakota Ritual of the Sweat Lodge: History and Contemporary Practice
By Raymond A. Bucko

From the Sands to the Mountain: Change and Persistence in a Southern Paiute Community
By Pamela A. Bunte and Robert J. Franklin

A Grammar of Comanche
By Jean Ormsbee Charney

Reserve Memories: The Power of the Past in a Chilcotin Community
By David W. Dinwoodie

Haida Syntax (2 vols.)
By John Enrico

Northern Haida Songs
By John Enrico and Wendy Bross Stuart

Powhatan's World and Colonial Virginia: A Conflict of Cultures
By Frederic W. Gleach

Native Languages and Language Families of North America (folded study map and wall display map)
Compiled by Ives Goddard

The Heiltsuks: Dialogues of Culture and History on the Northwest Coast
By Michael E. Harkin

Prophecy and Power among the Dogrib Indians
By June Helm

Corbett Mack: The Life of a Northern Paiute
As told by Michael Hittman

The Canadian Sioux
By James H. Howard

Yuchi Ceremonial Life: Performance, Meaning, and Tradition in a Contemporary American Indian Community
By Jason Baird Jackson

Printed in the United States
141808LV00003B/3/A

9 780803 23803